501 MOVIE STARS

CASSELL
ILLUSTRATED

A Quint**essence** Book

First published in Great Britain in 2007 by Cassell Illustrated
a division of Octopus Publishing Group Limited
2–4 Heron Quays, London E14 4JP
An Hachette Livre UK company

A CIP catalogue record for this book is available from the British Library.

ISBN-13: 978-1-84403-572-4
QSS.MVS

This book was designed and produced by
Quint**essence**
226 City Road
London EC1V 2TT

Project Editor	Victoria Wiggins
Editors	Rebecca Gee, Carol King,
	Fiona Plowman, Carey Scott
Editorial Assistant	Jenny Evans
Designer	Rod Teasdale
Editorial Director	Jane Laing
Publisher	Tristan de Lancey

Manufactured in Singapore by Pica Digital Pte Ltd.
Printed in China by SNP Leefung Printers Ltd.

CONTENTS

CONTENTS

CONTENTS

PREFACE

By Aubrey Day, Editor-in-Chief, *Total Film* and *Sky Movies*

Turn up at a dinner party and tell people you're a film journalist and one line of inquiry comes up again and again. And, no matter how many directors, producers, writers, or sundry other bright and beguiling studio folk you have ever interviewed, it won't concern any of them. No, the questions you'll face go something like this: 1. Who's the most famous actor you've met? 2. What were they like? 3. Did they look as good in real life? 4. Who's the nicest? 5. Who was the biggest pain to deal with?

The truth is, pretty much *everyone* shares a fascination with movie stars. Hollywood knows this, which is why film producers there pay such big bucks to have a Will Smith, a Jim Carrey, or a Tom Cruise in their movie. Got a questionable rom com script? Add Smith and suddenly it's a $200 million box-office success. Not sure whether a chick flick will draw them in? Reese Witherspoon's name above the title will probably make it a safe proposition.

It has always been this way. Paul Newman, Steve McQueen, Marilyn Monroe . . . names that still make you more likely to sit in front of the box and watch a movie when you might otherwise find something else to do.

Over the course of these pages, you'll find colorful details of some of the finest movie stars—from all over the world—ever to grace the silver screen. From the silent era shenanigans of Charlie Chaplin to the rebel yell of James Dean. Timeless legends (John Wayne, James Stewart, Humphrey Bogart) rub shoulders with method icons (Marlon Brando, Dustin Hoffman, Robert De Niro) and modern greats (Leonardo DiCaprio, Johnny Depp, Nicole Kidman).

Best of all, there are plenty of great actors who rarely get celebrated these days but should. Montgomery Clift, Jessica Lange, and Gene Hackman being just three of several dozen names I could mention.

Oh, and finally, in case we never meet at a dinner party, here are my answers: 1. Clint Eastwood or Jodie Foster. 2. Charming (both of them). 3. Um, yes. 4. George Clooney 5. I couldn't possibly say . . . .

Aubrey

London, England
April 2007

INTRODUCTION

By Steven Jay Schneider, General Editor

Oh, to be a movie star. Sure, some people say—and usually too loudly—that they'd *never* want to be one . . . but we all know what those people are full of. Come on, admit it! You and me, each and every one of us, would gladly take the downside—nasty rumors, vicious gossip, invasions of privacy (there must be other negatives, but I can't seem to think of any at the moment)—for that oh-so-glorious upside. Global adoration and adulation. Fame. Fortune. Friends. If not friends, then at least fans. Lots and lots and lots of fans. Constant catering. First-class travel all around the world . . . The list goes on and on.

Best of all, movie stars get to star in movies under the ultimate spotlight. To live out larger-than-life lives (not to mention overdramatic deaths) on the grandest of all stages, the cinematic one. Upon initial release, simultaneously appearing on thousands of movie screens in hundreds of cities across dozens of countries . . . and that's to say nothing of the eternal afterlife on TV, VHS, DVD . . . and don't forget all those sleazy-yummy tabloids.

Yep, let's face it, all of us in our heart of hearts want more than anything to be a movie star. (Quite a few of us would evidently settle quite happily for becoming a reality TV star instead.) And the delicious fact of the matter is that there's no formula for success here. Physical beauty helps, sure, but perfect symmetry is boring and an actor who looks flawless is more often than not destined to wind up on the daytime television soap opera circuit. Sex appeal's a definite plus, but not if you want to be taken seriously during awards season. Brains? Uh, sure . . . . Talent? Never hurts—but let's face it, we're talking about motion pictures here, not musical theater.

Ingredients for becoming a movie star surely include some (probably never all) of the above. Add a smidgeon of luck, a pinch of timing, a touch of *je ne sais quoi* . . . and a healthy dose of magic. Shake well and hire a good publicist. Now if, like most of us, you're unwilling to follow this admittedly asinine recipe, we hope and trust this rich book you're now holding will satisfy even the most ravenous star craving. *Bon appétit!*

Steven J. Schneider

Los Angeles, U.S.
April 2007

GEORGE ARLISS

Born: George Augustus Andrews, April 10, 1868 (London, England); died 1946 (London, England).

Star qualities: Decades of stagecraft and an aristocratic appearance; ideal for heavyweight roles as eccentrics, historical figures, and statesmen.

Top Takes...

Doctor Syn 1937
His Lordship 1936
Cardinal Richelieu 1935
The Iron Duke 1934
The House of Rothschild 1934
Voltaire 1933
The Working Man 1933
The King's Vacation 1933
The Man Who Played God 1932
Alexander Hamilton 1931
The Millionaire 1931
***The Green Goddess* 1930** ☆
***Disraeli* 1929** ★
The Green Goddess 1923
Disraeli 1921
The Devil 1921

A stately British stage actor of the (very) old school, George Arliss gave the impression of having been born with his monocle already in place, and once described himself in court as "the world's greatest living actor." The son of a printer and publisher, Arliss worked on the stage in Britain and the United States for decades before he appeared on the big screen. He was in his fifties when he made his first film in 1921. Hollywood in the 1920s and 1930s supported a large colony of actors who might be described as "incredibly British," and Arliss found plenty of work, acclaim, and popularity in both British and American films, tackling roles such as Voltaire, Cardinal Richelieu, Nathan Rothschild, and the Duke of Wellington.

Best known for playing British Prime Minister Benjamin Disraeli twice (in 1921 and 1929), he was the first British actor to win an Academy Award for Best Actor for his role in the talkie remake. Having successfully made the transition from silent movies to talkies—no mean feat—he also received a nomination for his role as the Raja of Rukh in *The Green Goddess* (1930). A surprising number of his roles involve duplicity and impersonation. He was a millionaire or aristocrat posing as poor in three separate films, and in another a tramp posing as a millionaire. In his last and most often revived film, the delightful barnstormer *Doctor Syn* (1937), he is a notorious smuggler disguised as a vicar, whereas *His Lordship* (1936) saw him as one twin pretending to be the other. Arliss appeared in a number of movies with his wife, Florence, including *Disraeli* (1929), *The Millionaire* (1931), and *The King's Vacation* (1933). He is also remembered for nurturing the career of Bette Davis at a time in the early 1930s when Hollywood was ready to discard her. **MC**

> "A man who never makes jokes is a standing joke to the world."
> —Benjamin Disraeli, *Disraeli*

EDMUND GWENN

Born: Edmund Kellaway, September 26, 1875 (Vale of Glamorgan, Wales); died 1959 (Los Angeles, California, U.S.).

Star qualities: Tiny, rotund, endearing character actor with comic timing; played whiskered old men with aplomb and a smile.

Edmund Gwenn started acting in the theater in 1895, having been thrown out of his Welsh family home at the age of seventeen for voicing his desire to become an actor. He soon found success, becoming a favorite of George Bernard Shaw, who cast him in the first production of *Man and Superman* in 1902 and then in five more of his plays. Yet he is best remembered as Kris Kringle, the department-store Santa who may be a real Father Christmas in *Miracle on 34th Street* (1947). Most actors would play for cherubic sentiment, but Gwenn holds back: twinkling and benevolent, but also allowing the possibility that Kris is just plain nuts. It was a performance that won him an Oscar for Best Supporting Actor, and on receiving his award he said, "Now I know there is a Santa Claus!"

In films from 1916, Gwenn was a favorite of Alfred Hitchcock, who used him as Johann Strauss the Elder in *Waltzes from Vienna* (1934), a genial assassin—"I'm quick"—in *Foreign Correspondent* (1940), and Captain Albert Wiles in *The Trouble with Harry* (1955). A fixture in British-set U.S. movies, he is often found as a butler, policeman, professor, priest, or headmaster. His roster of characters includes Katharine Hepburn's confidence-man father in *Sylvia Scarlett* (1935); a well-intentioned scientist who brings Boris Karloff back to life in *The Walking Dead* (1936); a feckless father in *Pride and Prejudice* (1940); a tinker befriended by a dog in *Lassie Come Home* (1943); and a deferential emissary of the afterlife in *Between Two Worlds* (1944). One of Gwenn's memorable later roles is as the insect expert consulted on the mutated ants in *Them!* (1954), a part parallel with the professor played by Gwenn's cousin Cecil Kellaway in *The Beast from 20,000 Fathoms* (1953). **KN**

Top Takes...

Calabuch 1956
The Trouble with Harry 1955
Them! 1954
Mister 880 1950 ☆
Life with Father 1947
Miracle on 34th Street 1947 ★
Lassie Come Home 1943
Foreign Correspondent 1940
Pride and Prejudice 1940
The Walking Dead 1936
Sylvia Scarlett 1935
Father and Son 1934
Waltzes from Vienna 1934
Smithy 1933
Channel Crossing 1933
The Real Thing at Last 1916

"Oh, Christmas isn't just a day, it's a frame of mind . . . ."

—Kris Kringle, *Miracle on 34th Street*

CHARLES COBURN

Born: Charles Douville Coburn, June 19, 1877 (Savannah, Georgia, U.S.); died 1961 (New York City, New York, U.S.).

Star qualities: Stage actor, producer, and director trained in Shakespeare; a Southern gentleman; monocled; able to do character parts and comedy roles.

Top Takes…

Charles Coburn came to films at the age of sixty, after the death of his first wife, with whom he had forged a successful stage career as the Coburn Players. He essentially treated the cinema as a lucrative retirement occupation, but it was a job that also brought him recognition. He was nominated three times for the Best Supporting Actor Academy Award, winning it for his part in the romantic comedy *The More the Merrier* (1943), in which he plays Benjamin Dingle, an older man who rents an apartment from a young woman, immediately sublets it to a young man, and then winds up playing Cupid.

His most lasting image is as a windily bogus gentleman on an ocean liner ("Colonel" Harrington), peering lecherously through his monocle and plotting swindles in partnership with Barbara Stanwyck in *The Lady Eve* (1941), yet he is equally happy on a later cruise as the prospective millionaire mark (Sir Francis "Piggy" Beekman) targeted by Marilyn Monroe in *Gentlemen Prefer Blondes* (1953). Otherwise, his stuffy, jowly, pot-bellied looks and croaking tones suited him to play hidebound establishment figures such as judges, politicians, academics, and fathers-in-law who temporarily stand in the way of virile young men in light drama or comedy such as *The Story of Alexander Graham Bell* (1939), *Edison, the Man* (1940), *Heaven Can Wait* (1943), *Monkey Business* (1952), and *How to Murder a Rich Uncle* (1957). Coburn is surprisingly disturbing in a rare, serious, dark role in *Kings Row* (1942), as the sadistic small-town surgeon who needlessly amputates Ronald Reagan's legs. A distinctive face, he often popped up in cameo roles in all-star efforts such as *Around the World in Eighty Days* (1956) and *The Story of Mankind* (1957). He died from a heart attack in 1961. **KN**

"No point having two window panes where one will do."

LIONEL BARRYMORE

Born: Lionel Herbert Blyth, April 28, 1878 (Philadelphia, Pennsylvania, U.S.); died 1954 (Van Nuys, California, U.S.).

Star qualities: Artist, novelist, composer, director, producer, and writer; member of an acting dynasty; prolific cinematic output; endurance; determination.

Lionel Barrymore chose to follow in the family tradition and acted on Broadway on and off for 25 years, but he was never the beneficiary—or victim—of the adulation poured upon his younger brother, John. He amassed numerous credits—19 films in 1912 alone—in the early days of cinema, and sensed the potential of the medium while the rest of his family remained fixated on the stage.

For two decades, he interspersed film acting with direction in movies such as *Just Boys* (1914) and *Madame X* (1929). But he eventually settled for character stardom as the lecherous preacher in *Sadie Thompson* (1928), and the benevolent leader and scientist in *The Mysterious Island* (1929). His career high came when he won an Academy Award for Best Actor for playing alcoholic defense attorney Stephen Ashe in *A Free Soul* (1931). His win was perhaps influenced by his mammoth turn in the longest take in a commercial movie, when he delivers a 14-minute uninterrupted monologue.

Like John, he loved roles played in disguise: posing as a little old lady in *The Devil-Doll* (1936). But after playing patriarch for Frank Capra in *You Can't Take It with You* (1938)—and in a series of *Dr. Kildare* films as crusty but wise Dr. Leonard Gillespie—he gravitated toward jovial or sinister old men, forever chuckling to himself at the errors of youth. Barrymore was married twice, despite his strict Roman Catholic upbringing. His siblings, Ethel and John, also endured the stigma of divorce. Although in a wheelchair from the late 1930s because of a hip injury and arthritis, Barrymore managed late career triumphs as the millionaire usurer Mr. Potter in Frank Capra's *It's a Wonderful Life* (1946), and a peppery old-timer in John Huston's *Key Largo* (1948). **KN**

Top Takes...

Key Largo 1948
It's a Wonderful Life 1946
Young Dr. Kildare 1938
You Can't Take It with You 1938
Captains Courageous 1937
Camille 1936
The Devil-Doll 1936
The Road to Glory 1936
David Copperfield 1935
Should Ladies Behave 1933
Dinner at Eight 1933
Rasputin and the Empress 1932
Grand Hotel 1932
A Free Soul 1931 ★
The Mysterious Island 1929
Sadie Thompson 1928

"I can remember when nobody believed an actor and didn't care what he believed."

WILL ROGERS

Born: William Penn Adair Rogers, November 4, 1879 (Oologah, Oklahoma, U.S.); died 1935 (Point Barrow, Alaska, U.S.).

Star qualities: Cowboy humorist; trick roper; horsemanship; warmhearted radio broadcaster, witty social commentator, and influential newspaper columnist.

Top Takes...

In Old Kentucky 1935
Doubting Thomas 1935
Life Begins at Forty 1935
Judge Priest 1934
State Fair 1933
Young as You Feel 1931
A Connecticut Yankee 1931
They Had to See Paris 1929
A Texas Steer 1927
Tiptoes 1927
Gee Whiz, Genevieve 1924
A Truthful Liar 1924
Fruits of Faith 1922
The Ropin' Fool 1922
Almost a Husband 1919
Laughing Bill Hyde 1918

"Even if you're on the right track, you'll get run over if you just sit there."

As a stage actor, radio personality, author, journalist, and movie star, Will Rogers enjoyed a diverse and prolific career. He graduated from military school in 1902, and went into the livestock business in Argentina. He was an expert horseman, and transported pack animals across the South Atlantic from Buenos Aires to South Africa for use in the Second Boer War (1899–1902). He stayed in Johannesburg, where he performed in Texas Jack's Wild West Circus, billed as "The Cherokee Kid." He used his skills with horse and lasso that he had learned working Texas Longhorn cattle on his family's ranch. On his return to the United States he went into vaudeville, where he found that audiences responded to his wry wit as much as his trick-rope skills, and by 1917 he was a star of the Ziegfeld Follies.

Rogers's first feature was *Laughing Bill Hyde* (1918), a successful movie that earned him a two-year contract with Samuel Goldwyn. Rogers made his Hollywood debut in *Almost a Husband* (1919). He made 12 films for Goldwyn, and a news series for Gaumont titled *The Illiterate Digest* (1920). Although he contributed to the scripts and titles, the silent screen didn't suit Rogers's conversational style. Rogers then produced three films in 1922: *Fruits of Faith, The Ropin' Fool,* and *One Day in 365* (which was not released), but the venture nearly ruined him financially. The coming of sound offered new opportunities. In 1930, Rogers signed a six-film contract with Fox Film Corporation for an unheralded $1,125,000. These roles were variations on his famous personality as the folksy U.S. citizen overflowing with homespun advice and witticisms. Popular titles from this period include *A Connecticut Yankee* (1931) and *Judge Priest* (1934). At the height of his popularity, Rogers was killed in a plane crash in 1935. **WW**

KING BAGGOT

Born: King Baggot, November 7, 1879 (St. Louis, Missouri, U.S.); died 1948 (Los Angeles, California, U.S.).

Star qualities: Tall; blue eyes; suave leading man of the silent era across a range of genres; handsome; prolific output; director; writer.

To contemporary movie audiences, the actor King Baggot is unknown, despite his appearances in a staggering number of films. Look closely, and he can be seen in some of Hollywood's classics ranging from *The Philadelphia Story* (1940) to *Bud Abbott and Lou Costello in Hollywood* (1945) and *The Postman Always Rings Twice* (1946). Yet most of his more than 300 movie appearances were in character roles, bit parts, or even uncredited, as his career arc nosedived while he made the transition from superstar of the silent screen to a forgotten extra when the talkies gradually took hold.

Born the son of a real estate investor in St. Louis, Missouri, Baggot headed for New York City and Broadway with the intention of making a career on the stage, which he did briefly, shining as the lead character in the play *More to Be Pitied Than Scorned*. But then Baggot was taken on at IMP Studios (what was the fledgling Universal Studios), making his film debut in *Love's Stratagem* (1909). He went on to appear in action movies and classics, such as the lead in *Ivanhoe* (1913). Unusual for the time, Baggot was also promoted by the studios, an early sign of what star vehicles were to become. He was noted for his ability to play multiple characters, such as the double act of *Dr. Jekyll and Mr. Hyde* (1913), and ten different characters in *Shadows* (1914). As he got older, he concentrated more on directing and codirected the Western *Tumbleweeds* (1925) together with William S. Hart. The secret of Baggot's staggering number of film appearances goes back to 1933, when he became one of several silent-movie veterans to be awarded a lifetime contract by the studio MGM. It was a symbolic gesture because he was rarely given more than a small role, and earned a weekly salary of $75. **CK**

Top Takes...

Good News 1947
The Postman Always Rings Twice 1946
Bud Abbott and Lou Costello in Hollywood 1945
The Clock 1945
Barbary Coast Gent 1944
Swing Fever 1943
Come Live with Me 1941
The Philadelphia Story 1940
Mississippi 1935
The Big Flash 1932
The Corsican Brothers 1915
Shadows 1914
Ivanhoe 1913
Dr. Jekyll and Mr. Hyde 1913
The Better Way 1911
Love's Stratagem 1909

> "[*The Better Way*] is so awful that they have turned it into a burlesque . . . ."—*New York Times*

SYDNEY GREENSTREET

Born: Sydney Hughes Greenstreet, December 27, 1879 (Sandwich, Kent, England); died 1954 (Hollywood, California, U.S.).

Star qualities: Physically imposing; versatile; Shakespearean and musical comedy stage performer; character actor able to play the ruthless and malevolent.

Top Takes…

Flamingo Road 1949
The Velvet Touch 1948
The Woman in White 1948
Ruthless 1948
The Hucksters 1947
That Way with Women 1947
The Verdict 1946
Devotion 1946
Three Strangers 1946
Christmas in Connecticut 1945
The Conspirators 1944
The Mask of Dimitrios 1944
Between Two Worlds 1944
Casablanca 1942
They Died with Their Boots On 1941
The Maltese Falcon 1941 ☆

"I am a man who likes talking
to a man who likes to talk."

—Kasper Gutman, *The Maltese Falcon*

Following a long career on the stage in England and the United States, Sydney Greenstreet was a late bloomer when at sixty-two he made his screen debut in John Huston's *The Maltese Falcon* (1941), achieving movie immortality as Kasper Gutman, "The Fat Man," a ruthless rogue whose eyes gleam while he recounts the history of the prized object he has spent his life pursuing. Warner Brothers snapped up Greenstreet and kept him busy for the rest of the decade, often teamed with his *Falcon* coconspirator Peter Lorre. They are especially good in *The Mask of Dimitrios* (1944) and *The Verdict* (1946), in which Greenstreet is a sacked Victorian Scotland Yard inspector who petulantly decides to commit a perfect murder.

Despite the brevity of his career on the big screen, he managed to cram in a number of memorable parts that saw him holding his own with Hollywood legends such as Humphrey Bogart, James Stewart, and Spencer Tracy. Greenstreet's specialty was shady characters, such as the proprietor of the Blue Parrot in *Casablanca* (1942) and Count Alessandro Fosco in *The Woman in White* (1948). But he could also slap on side-whiskers and play historical personages, such as Lieutenant General Winfield Scott in *They Died with Their Boots On* (1941) and William Makepeace Thackeray in *Devotion* (1946), or bluster as a bullying authority figure in comedy (*Christmas in Connecticut*, 1945) or melodrama (*Flamingo Road*, 1949). In *The Hucksters* (1947), an exposé of the advertising business, he spits at a business meeting to demonstrate that crassness can be memorable. Having retired from the movies in 1949 due to illness, Greenstreet worked on radio, aptly playing the fictional private detective Nero Wolfe. **KN**

W. C. FIELDS

Born: William Claude Dukinfield, January 29, 1880 (Philadelphia, Pennsylvania, U.S.); died 1946 (Pasadena, California, U.S.).

Star qualities: Virtuoso juggler; bulbous nose and muttering patter; played the misanthrope, the malcontent, and the egotist; writing and comic genius.

It is unsurprising that the comic genius William Claude Dukinfield reveled in renaming himself (as film character or as screenwriter) Otis Criblecoblis, Egbert Sousé, Eustace McGargle, or Cuthbert J. Twillie. It fit with the absurdist's vision of life as ludicrous torment to be found in films such as *The Old-Fashioned Way* (1934) and *Never Give a Sucker an Even Break* (1941)—a near-surreal fable set partly in a utopian Russian village in Mexico where the locals sup on alcoholic goats' milk.

Time and again, the eternally middle-aged W. C. Fields—well-meaning but boastful, secretive and irascible, his dreams damned to failure, his alcoholic thirst seldom sated—finds himself besieged by bawling brats, nagging wives, husband-hungry daughters, and belligerent neighbors. The bleary, blotchy-nosed response to the sheer nuisance that is other people is a double-take involving a shudder of the shoulders and a raising of the lower arms, followed by an arcane and near-blasphemous oath—"Godfrey Daniels!"—and drawled, nonsensical mumbling.

Over the years, although the films became technically more polished, the recipe changed little. *It's a Gift* (1934) is arguably Fields's masterpiece and one of the most evocatively dystopian movies made about the unending nightmare of family life. Two atypical gems, however, stand out: a memorably warm turn as Wilkins Micawber in *David Copperfield* (1935), and the finest of Fields's shorts, *The Fatal Glass of Beer* (1933). The quick patter and spontaneity to ad lib he learned in vaudeville stood him in good stead, and he was as famed for his comic one-liners offstage as well as on. This talent also helped him resurrect his career after his alcoholism took its toll in 1936 and he was admitted to a sanatorium. **GA**

Top Takes...

Never Give a Sucker an Even Break 1941
The Bank Dick 1940
My Little Chickadee 1940
You Can't Cheat an Honest Man 1939
Man on the Flying Trapeze 1935
David Copperfield 1935
It's a Gift 1934
The Old-Fashioned Way 1934
You're Telling Me! 1934
Alice in Wonderland 1933
The Fatal Glass of Beer 1933
Million Dollar Legs 1932
Fools for Luck 1928
The Potters 1927
Sally of the Sawdust 1925
His Lordship's Dilemma 1915

"Hollywood is the gold cap on a tooth that should have been pulled out years ago."

JOHN BARRYMORE

Born: John Sidney Blyth, February 14, 1882 (Philadelphia, Pennsylvania, U.S.); died 1942 (Los Angeles, California, U.S.).

Star qualities: Member of an acting dynasty; handsome; hell-raising; the perfect Hamlet; a matinee idol with a lust for life and women.

Top Takes...

Playmates 1941
The Great Profile 1940
Midnight 1939
Bulldog Drummond's Peril 1938
Bulldog Drummond's Revenge 1937
Bulldog Drummond Comes Back 1937
Twentieth Century 1934
Dinner at Eight 1933
Hamlet—Act I: Scene V 1933
Rasputin and the Empress 1932
A Bill of Divorcement 1932
Arsène Lupin 1932
Svengali 1931
Beau Brummel 1924
Dr. Jekyll and Mr. Hyde 1920
Raffles, the Amateur Cracksman 1917

"There are lots of methods. Mine involves a lot of talent, a glass, and some cracked ice."

John Barrymore comes from one of the United States's most famous acting dynasties. His father was stage actor Maurice Blyth; his mother, Georgie Drew, was the daughter of John Drew; and his siblings were Lionel and Ethel Barrymore. He was the father of Diana and John Drew Barrymore, and grandfather of Drew and John Blyth Barrymore. He flirted with a career as an artist before adopting the family stage name and turning to a full-time job as an actor, with significant success.

Lauded for his classical good looks, which earned him the nickname "The Great Profile," John was the Shakespearean matinee idol of his day, hailed for his stage role as Hamlet in both New York and London. A noted hell-raiser and drunkard, he is the role model for subsequent talent squanderers from his friend Errol Flynn onward. Without seeming to take the movies seriously, he managed much remarkable screen work between runs of inferior films accepted purely for the money.

As a heartthrob of the silent screen, John played amusing romantic adventurers in *Raffles, the Amateur Cracksman* (1917) and *Beau Brummel* (1924), but showed another side when cast as the spidery human monster in *Dr. Jekyll and Mr. Hyde* (1920). In the early 1930s, he could still stretch to heroic rogues such as the aristocratic thief in *Arsène Lupin* (1932), but preferred character villains such as the maestro in *Svengali* (1931). He clawed for his moments in all-star efforts such as *Grand Hotel* (1932), and—with siblings Lionel and Ethel—*Rasputin and the Empress* (1932). At his best as the manic, scheming producer in *Twentieth Century* (1934), he wound down with self-parody in *The Great Profile* (1940), and played the master-of-disguise Scotland Yard inspector Colonel Nielsen in the Bulldog Drummond series (1937–1938). **KN**

BÉLA LUGOSI

Born: Béla Ferenc Dezső Blaskó, October 20, 1882 (Lugos, Austria-Hungary); died 1956 (Los Angeles, California, U.S.).

Star qualities: Shakespearean stage actor; personified malevolence as the caped Count Dracula; heavy East European accent; eccentric; cult figure.

The son of a banker, Béla Lugosi took to the stage in his native Hungary in 1901 with some success, and made his film debut in the silent *Az Ezredes* (1917) (*The Colonel*). After serving in World War I he immigrated to the United States in 1920 to work as a character actor. It took only one film for Lugosi to be forever typecast. Universal Studios's *Dracula* (1931) marked him as the personification of Bram Stoker's undead count. To this day, impersonators of Dracula still invariably mimic Lugosi's strong accent when portraying the character.

Treated with some disregard by Universal, Lugosi was nevertheless able to craft another impressive role for the studio: the cunning and ugly Ygor first introduced in *Son of Frankenstein* (1939). After Universal nixed him as Dracula for two later films in its Frankenstein series, favoring John Carradine for the part, Lugosi was given the chance to don the cape once again in *Abbott and Costello Meet Frankenstein* (1948). But this luminescent performance was not enough to revive his career, and, after a publicized battle with morphine addiction, Lugosi spent his last years reduced to playing parts in the Grade Z films of Edward D. Wood Jr.—*Bride of the Monster* (1955), among others. Lugosi died of a heart attack and was buried wearing a Dracula cape, according to the wishes of his son and his fifth wife.

Reflecting the public's continual fascination with the actor, helped in part by Tim Burton's *Ed Wood* (1994), which garnered an Academy Award for Best Supporting Actor for Martin Landau's portrayal as Lugosi, and a favorable reevaluation of several of his non-Dracula roles, "Poor Béla" has in recent times overshadowed in popularity his chief horror rival from Universal Studios, Boris Karloff. **ML**

Top Takes...

Plan 9 from Outer Space 1959
Bride of the Monster 1955
Béla Lugosi Meets a Brooklyn Gorilla 1952
Abbott and Costello Meet Frankenstein 1948
The Body Snatcher 1945
Return of the Ape Man 1944
Voodoo Man 1944
The Return of the Vampire 1944
Frankenstein Meets the Wolf Man 1943
The Ape Man 1943
The Ghost of Frankenstein 1942
Ninotchka 1939
Son of Frankenstein 1939
Mark of the Vampire 1935
Dracula 1931
Az Ezredes 1917 (*The Colonel*)

> "I'll be truthful. The weekly paycheck is the most important thing to me."

LON CHANEY

Born: Leonidas Frank Chaney, April 1, 1883 (Colorado Springs, Colorado, U.S.); died 1930 (Hollywood, California, U.S.).

Star qualities: "The Man of a Thousand Faces"; talented as a makeup artist; capable of portraying a wide range of strange and frightening characters.

Top Takes...

The Unholy Three 1930
West of Zanzibar 1928
While the City Sleeps 1928
Laugh, Clown, Laugh 1928
The Big City 1928
London After Midnight 1927
Mockery 1927
The Unknown 1927
Mr. Wu 1927
Tell It to the Marines 1926
The Tower of Lies 1925
The Phantom of the Opera 1925
The Unholy Three 1925
The Monster 1925
He Who Gets Slapped 1924
The Hunchback of Notre Dame 1923
A Blind Bargain 1922
Shadows 1922
Oliver Twist 1922
The Light in the Dark 1922
The Penalty 1920
Treasure Island 1920
The Miracle Man 1919
The Mark of Cain 1916
The Ways of Fate 1913

The son of deaf-mute parents, Lon Chaney used sign language, pantomime, and facial expression to communicate with his family from an early age. At the height of his fame, he was dubbed "The Man of a Thousand Faces." Though retroactively incorporated into the roster of horror stars for his "monster" roles in *The Hunchback of Notre Dame* (1923) and *The Phantom of the Opera* (1925), he was less a forerunner of Boris Karloff or Béla Lugosi than a star chameleon, as fond of disguise as Alec Guinness or Peter Sellers. The typical Chaney screen character is a wretched, unlucky soul whose mind and/or body are warped by malign circumstance or the machinations of an outwardly handsome enemy. Aside from the famous unmasking scene in *Phantom*, he was rarely terrifying; his vile misdeeds are usually pushed aside in the finale as he dies to save a pure heroine with whom he is impossibly in love.

After directing six films, he concentrated on acting—though it was said that, outside his partnership with Tod Browning, he often worked with weaker directors like Wallace Worsley and Rupert Julian to gain influence over the way his scenes (mostly those depending on his self-applied makeup jobs) were shot.

RIGHT: Chaney performs alongside Lila Lee in his only talkie, 1930's *The Unholy Three.*

Chaney's first notable "gimmick" role was the bogus cripple who unbends at the direction of a fake faith healer in *The Miracle Man* (1919), which led to false noses, gruesome dentures, wigs, milky contact lenses, scars, and wrinkles as Blind Pew in *Treasure Island* (1920), Fagin in *Oliver Twist* (1922), and a Mongol peasant in *Mockery* (1927). His first star vehicle was as the legless mobster in *The Penalty* (1920), but his most memorably warped characters came in films directed by Tod Browning: a transvestite ventriloquist thief in *The Unholy Three* (1925) and an armless knife thrower in *The Unknown* (1927). Equally melodramatic, and as affecting, are Chaney's turns as pitiful clowns in *He Who Gets Slapped* (1924) and *Laugh, Clown, Laugh* (1928), but he showed he could appear convincingly with his own battered, homely face in tough-guy roles like the drill sergeant in *Tell It to the Marines* (1926). He made only one talkie, a 1930 remake of *The Unholy Three*. **KN**

ABOVE: Chaney seeks revenge as Phroso "Dead-Legs" in *West of Zanzibar.*

A Makeup *Artiste*

Chaney was skilled at realizing characters, from the peculiar to the grotesque:

- For *The Phantom of the Opera* (1925), Chaney put egg membrane on his eyeballs to make them appear cloudy. He glued his ears back and stretched his nose back with fish skin to make his overall appearance more eerily skull-like.

- He was prepared to suffer if it made his characters more credible. Playing a mad amputee in *The Penalty* (1920), Chaney strapped his legs behind him, forcing his knees into leather stumps, which acted as artificial legs. Ouch!

DOUGLAS FAIRBANKS

Born: Douglas Elton Thomas Ullman, May 23, 1883 (Denver, Colorado, U.S.); died 1939 (Santa Monica, California, U.S.).

Star qualities: Diminutive; trademark moustache; flair for wearing costumes and capes; athletic daredevil; swashbuckling superstar; director, producer, and writer.

Douglas Fairbanks was the laughing daredevil of the silent screen. He invented the slyly self-parodic action hero, setting the tone for a line of successors from Errol Flynn to Bruce Willis.

Initially a comedian, he played the drug-crazed detective Coke Ennyday in *The Mystery of the Leaping Fish* (1916). Fairbanks's athleticism—he loved doing his own stunts—trademark moustache, and cheerful air suited him to swashbuckling, with serious swordplay leavened by graceful slapstick. *The Mark of Zorro* (1920), in which he is both macho outlaw and comedy fop, was the first of the increasingly elaborate star vehicles, such as *The Three Musketeers* (1921), that he wrote and produced annually for a decade. In the talkies, Fairbanks's star shone less brightly after teaming with his second wife, Mary Pickford, for a creaky *The Taming of the Shrew* (1929), but his farewell role was wryly dignified as a middle-aged great lover in *The Private Life of Don Juan* (1934).

Fairbanks's legacy is not just confined to the screen. Ever financially savvy, he started his own production company, the Douglas Fairbanks Film Corporation, in 1917, which helped propel him to become one of Hollywood's top earners of the time. Such independence proved to be a thorn in the side of the studios, which attempted to monopolize film distribution. Undeterred, his business acumen led him to found the United Artists studio in 1919 together with Charles Chaplin, D. W. Griffith, and Pickford. They created their own distributorships, took artistic control over their output, and reaped a greater share of the profits. Fairbanks was also one of the founders of the Academy of Motion Picture Arts and Sciences, and cohosted (with director William C. de Mille) the first Academy Awards ceremony in 1929. **KN**

Top Takes...

The Private Life of Don Juan 1934
Mr. Robinson Crusoe 1932
The Taming of the Shrew 1929
The Iron Mask 1929
The Gaucho 1927
The Black Pirate 1926
Don Q Son of Zorro 1925
The Thief of Bagdad 1924
Robin Hood 1922
The Three Musketeers 1921
The Nut 1921
The Mark of Zorro 1920
The Mollycoddle 1920
A Modern Musketeer 1917
The Mystery of the Leaping Fish 1916
The Lamb 1915

"The man that's out to do something has to keep in high gear all the time."

WALTER HUSTON

Born: Walter Houghston, April 6, 1884 (Toronto, Ontario, Canada); died 1950 (Hollywood, California, U.S.).

Star qualities: Head of an acting dynasty; stagecraft; determination; versatile character actor who moved from Stetsons to suits; producer; singer.

Although trained as an engineer, Walter Huston was drawn to acting. After a brief period working in vaudeville, he returned to life as an engineer to support his first wife and only child, future director John Huston. He discovered that his engineering skills were lacking and returned to vaudeville in 1909, soon becoming a headlining act. Twenty years later he was a stage veteran when he went to Hollywood to appear in talking pictures. His long features suited him to playing the lead in D. W. Griffith's *Abraham Lincoln* (1930), but he was equally well cast in Westerns, as both baddies—Trampas in *The Virginian* (1929)—and goodies—the Wyatt Earp type in *Law and Order* (1932). He could also sport a modern suit as a crusading prison warden in *The Criminal Code* (1931), district attorney in *The Star Witness* (1931), or cop in *The Beast of the City* (1932).

Huston played more flawed authority figures, such as the corrupt U.S. president divinely inspired to pour the wrath of God on to bootleggers in the insane *Gabriel over the White House* (1933)—ironically, because offscreen Huston was a "wet," who celebrated with Jean Harlow at the Los Angeles Brewing Co. when Prohibition finally came to an end in April 1933. After title roles in *Rhodes of Africa* (1936) and *Dodsworth* (1936), he returned to the theater. As an older character actor, he got much juicier roles: the folksy devil Mr. Scratch in *The Devil and Daniel Webster* (1941); Doc Holliday in *The Outlaw* (1943); the drunken doctor in *And Then There Were None* (1945); the hellfire preacher in *Duel in the Sun* (1946); and unforgettably—with his false teeth out and working for his son—his role as the old-time prospector in *The Treasure of the Sierra Madre* (1948), which won him an Academy Award for Best Supporting Actor. **KN**

Top Takes...

The Furies 1950
The Treasure of the Sierra Madre 1948 ★
Duel in the Sun 1946
And Then There Were None 1945
The Outlaw 1943
Yankee Doodle Dandy 1942 ☆
The Devil and Daniel Webster 1941 ☆
Dodsworth 1936 ☆
Rhodes of Africa 1936
Gabriel over the White House 1933
Law and Order 1932
The Beast of the City 1932
The Star Witness 1931
The Criminal Code 1931
Abraham Lincoln 1930
The Virginian 1929

"Hell, I ain't paid to make good lines sound good. I'm paid to make bad lines sound good."

EMIL JANNINGS

Born: Theodor Friedrich Emil Janenz, July 23, 1884 (Rorschach, Switzerland); died 1950 (Strobl, Austria).

Star qualities: Stage actor; classic silent-screen star; versatile; massive size aided his screen presence; known for heavyweight, horror, character, and tragic roles.

Top Takes…

Der blaue Engel 1930 (The Blue Angel)
Betrayal 1929
Fighting the White Slave Traffic 1929
Sins of the Fathers 1928
The Patriot 1928
Street of Sin 1928
The Last Command 1928 ★
The Way of All Flesh 1927 ★
Faust 1926
Herr Tartüff 1926 (Tartuffe)
Varieté 1925 (Jealousy)
Der letzte Mann 1924 (The Last Laugh)
Das Leben ein Traum 1916
Nächte des Grauens 1916
Stein unter Steinen 1916
Arme Eva 1914 (Dear Eva)

"We can only realize the shadows of our dreams."

For a few years, Emil Jannings was rated the world's greatest movie actor. He was the first actor to win the Academy Award for Best Actor for both *The Way of All Flesh* (1927) and *The Last Command* (1928). His screen presence was impressive and he suited heavyweight roles—in every sense, given his corpulent physique—such as Danton, Henry VIII, Nero, and Peter the Great. He attained international fame in F. W. Murnau's silent *Der letzte Mann* (1924) (*The Last Laugh*) as the majestic hotel head porter humiliatingly reduced to bathroom attendant. This set the template for the classic "Jannings vehicle": a figure of pomp and dignity struck down by fate.

Murnau cast him again in the title role of *Herr Tartüff* (1926) (*Tartuffe*), and as Mephistopheles in *Faust* (1926), where his hammy devilry overbalanced the film. But these, and his lovelorn trapeze artist in Ewald André Dupont's *Varieté* (1925) (*Jealousy*), earned him an invitation to Hollywood, where Paramount Pictures fashioned several majesty-brought-low vehicles for him. The best of them, *The Last Command*, with Jannings as a former czarist general turned Hollywood extra, was directed by Josef von Sternberg. With the coming of sound, Jannings's thick German accent proved a disadvantage and he returned to Germany, where Sternberg gave him his last great role in *Der blaue Engel* (1930) (*The Blue Angel*) as the pompous schoolmaster Professor Immanuel Rath, ruined by lust for femme fatale and nightclub performer Lola Lola, played by the young Marlene Dietrich. An earnest pro-Nazi, Jannings was made head of the Universum Film AG studio under the Third Reich, where he made a number of Nazi propaganda movies. Blacklisted at the end of the war, he lived out his final years in bitter retirement. **PK**

GEORGE "GABBY" HAYES

Born: George Francis Hayes, May 7, 1885 (Wellsville, New York, U.S.); died 1969 (Burbank, California, U.S.).

Star qualities: Bearded, popular Westerns sidekick; star of his own comic-book series; played the crotchety, garrulous, tobacco-chewing old-timer.

In his youth George "Gabby" Hayes worked as a circus performer and semipro baseball player before moving to perform in vaudeville and burlesque. Such was his success that he retired in his forties, but he then lost a lot of his money in the stock market crash of 1929 and was forced back to work. When he became a regular fixture in the series Westerns of the 1930s, it was at first as a bad guy, in films such as *Riders of Destiny* (1933) and *West of the Divide* (1934), often starring opposite the young John Wayne. From 1936 he appeared regularly as Hopalong Cassidy's sidekick Windy Halliday; *Trail Dust* (1936) is a typical example. By then he was already past fifty, and the whiskery, garrulous, old-timer role suited him well.

At the end of the 1930s he began appearing regularly with Roy Rogers—his character usually named "Gabby"—in *The Arizona Kid* (1939), *Young Bill Hickok* (1940), and dozens of others. He occasionally made an appearance with Gene Autry, such as in *Melody Ranch* (1940), and with other Western stars. Toward the end of his career he played, as always, the grizzled old-timer in some Randolph Scott vehicles, including *Trail Street* (1947) and, his swan song, *The Cariboo Trail* (1950). From 1950 to 1954 he had his own TV Western series, *The Gabby Hayes Show*, aimed largely at children, after which he hung up his spurs. Offscreen he was a serious, well-dressed, and sophisticated man—the polar opposite of his film persona, whose preferred utterances were "yer durn tootin" and "young whipper snapper." He was married to Olive E. Ireland until her death in 1956. Despite his prolific screen appearances as a cowboy, Hayes didn't learn to ride a horse until he was past the age of forty. He even professed that he had never been a big fan of the Western genre. **EB**

Top Takes...

The Cariboo Trail 1950
Albuquerque 1948
Wyoming 1947
Trail Street 1947
Sunset in El Dorado 1945
Melody Ranch 1940
Young Bill Hickok 1940
The Arizona Kid 1939
Texas Trail 1937
Hopalong Rides Again 1937
Trail Dust 1936
The Plainsman 1936
Mr. Deeds Goes to Town 1936
Hop-Along Cassidy 1935
West of the Divide 1934
Riders of Destiny 1933

"Don't ever sneak into a camp like that, neighbor!"

—Oscar Winters, *The Cariboo Trail*

THEDA BARA

Born: Theodosia Burr Goodman, July 29, 1885 (Avondale, Ohio, U.S.); died 1955 (Los Angeles, California, U.S.).

Star qualities: Beautiful, seductive, sensual, sexy; haunting eyes; cinema's first vamp; the glamorous and exotic queen of the silent screen.

Top Takes…

The Prince of Silence 1921
La Belle Russe 1919
A Woman There Was 1919
When Men Desire 1919
The Lure of Ambition 1919
Salome 1918
The Soul of Buddha 1918
The Forbidden Path 1918
Madame Du Barry 1917
Cleopatra 1917
Camille 1917
The Darling of Paris 1917
Romeo and Juliet 1916
Under Two Flags 1916
Carmen 1915
A Fool There Was 1915

" … once on the streets of New York a woman called the police because her child spoke to me."

Although most of her films are lost, Theda Bara remains a potent image. In an era when female stars either were or pretended to be twelve-year-old innocents, Bara was the screen's first sexualized woman. Born the daughter of a Jewish tailor, her roots were reinvented by the Fox Film Corporation's studio publicity, which claimed she was the daughter of an artist and an Arabian princess born under the shadow of the Sphinx, and stressed that her stage name was an anagram of "Arab Death." She dyed her naturally blonde hair black to lend credence to this image. Her breakthrough came late, as the "vampire" in *A Fool There Was* (1915), derived from Rudyard Kipling's poem about a predatory woman. It had such a cultural impact that, as late as *Dracula's Daughter* (1936), films had to distinguish supernatural bloodsuckers from the metaphorical vampires, or "vamps," played by Bara.

Bara ran through the catalog of iconic fatal women of literature and history, sporting a variety of outrageous outfits: *Carmen* (1915), *Cleopatra* (1917), *Madame Du Barry* (1917), and *Salome* (1918). She essayed a few heroines: doomed but sympathetic harlots in *Under Two Flags* (1916) and *Camille* (1917), sensual innocents such as Juliet in *Romeo and Juliet* (1916), and as Esmeralda in *The Darling of Paris* (1917), a version of *The Hunchback of Notre Dame*. She was the first "camp" star, seeming to share the joke of her voluptuous villainy with audiences. Her career was over by the 1920s, as she suddenly seemed a relic of an already-forgotten era. In 1921 she married director Charles Brabin, who didn't want her to continue acting, so she never ventured into the talkies. With many prints of her films vanished, Theda Bara remains an iconic silent star. **KN**

ERICH VON STROHEIM

Born: Erich Oswald Stroheim, September 22, 1885 (Vienna, Austria-Hungary); died 1957 (Yvelines, Île-de-France, France).

Star qualities: Silent-movie director and producer; hot-tempered; obsessive perfectionism; played archvillains, Teutonic tyrants, the mad, and the bad.

The son of a Jewish hatmaker, Erich von Stroheim immigrated to the United States in 1909. By 1914 he was working in Hollywood, mostly in bit parts, and reinvented himself with an aristocratic background, claiming to be an Austrian noble, Count Erich Oswald Hans Carl Maria von Stroheim und Nordenwall. He moved into writing and directing, and became an important silent-film director—notably for *Foolish Wives* (1922) and *Greed* (1924)—but a reputation as a spendthrift genius cut short his career as a megaphone man. Not without resentment, he settled for resuming his former profession as a character actor. Shaven-headed, bull-necked, and glowering, he epitomized the enemy during World War I in *The Unbeliever* (1918) and *The Hun Within* (1918), and continued this characterization well into the talkies, gaining the nickname "The Man You Love to Hate."

Though a dignified, sympathetic German officer in Jean Renoir's *La Grande illusion* (1937), von Stroheim was back to Hunnish brutality as Field Marshal Erwin Rommel in *Five Graves to Cairo* (1943) and a blood-draining war criminal in *The North Star* (1943). He also caricatured himself: a movie director as mad genius in *The Lost Squadron* (1932) and, later, cruelly reduced to servitude in *Sunset Blvd.* (1950) as Max von Mayerling, for which he received an Academy Award nomination for Best Supporting Actor. Otherwise he had a B-picture vogue in Lon Chaney-style melodramas as twisted, pathetically lovelorn vaudeville acts such as the ventriloquist in *The Great Gabbo* (1929), or sundry mad scientists as in *The Lady and the Monster* (1944). After *Sunset Blvd.* he worked in Europe and was last seen as Ludwig van Beethoven in *Napoléon* (1955). **KN**

Top Takes...

Napoléon 1955
Alraune 1952
***Sunset Blvd.* 1950** ☆
The Mask of Dijon 1946
The Great Flamarion 1945
The Lady and the Monster 1944
The North Star 1943
Five Graves to Cairo 1943
La Grande illusion 1937 (*The Grand Illusion*)
The Crime of Dr. Crespi 1935
The Lost Squadron 1932
The Great Gabbo 1929
Foolish Wives 1922
Blind Husbands 1919
The Hun Within 1918
The Unbeliever 1918

> "In Hollywood—in Hollywood, you're as good as your last picture."

AL JOLSON

Born: Asa Yoelson, May 26, 1886 (Srednik, Russian Empire); died 1950 (San Francisco, California, U.S.).

Star qualities: Singer; composer; whistler; electrifying entertainer; sang tearjerkers with an operatic twist and dramatic gestures; string of hit songs.

Top Takes...

Swanee River 1939
Rose of Washington Square 1939
The Singing Kid 1936
Go Into Your Dance 1935
Wonder Bar 1934
Hallelujah I'm a Bum 1933
Big Boy 1930
Mammy 1930
Say It with Songs 1929
The Singing Fool 1928
The Jazz Singer 1927
Mammy's Boy 1923

Known for adopting the theater convention of blackface makeup, a "belting" singing technique, hits such as "My Mammy" and "Sonny Boy," and influencing a generation of crooners such as Bing Crosby, Al Jolson had a career that closely parallels the role he played in the very first talkie, Warner Brothers's musical biopic *The Jazz Singer* (1927). He was the son of a rabbi who immigrated to Washington, D.C., fascinated by ragtime; he got his start by entertaining the troops during the Spanish-American War. By his early teens, Jolson had graduated to Broadway and for almost 30 years was a featured headliner, earning him the sobriquet "The World's Greatest Entertainer." Jolson's records, despite the absence of concrete charts for this period, were frequently hits. Songs Jolson sung were also best sellers in sheet music, and helped launch the careers of George and Ira Gershwin with "Swanee."

Despite the high profile of *The Jazz Singer*, Jolson's subsequent films, *The Singing Fool* (1928), *Mammy* (1930), and *Hallelujah I'm a Bum* (1933) were less successful. Having moved on from Broadway, yet never finding tremendous favor in Hollywood, Jolson moved to radio with three fruitful incarnations of *The Al Jolson Show* throughout the 1930s and 1940s. It was with *The Jolson Story* (1946) and *Jolson Sings Again* (1949), although starring Larry Parks, that the great entertainer had a comeback, providing the singing voice for Parks's performance. Jolson's popularity was such that in 1948, when fellow singers Crosby, Frank Sinatra, and Perry Como were at their peak, he was voted the "Most Popular Male Vocalist" by a *Variety* poll. He died of a heart attack on October 23, 1950, and on that day Broadway lowered its lights for ten minutes in his honor. **MK**

"Wait a minute, wait a minute, you ain't heard nothin' yet!"

—Jakie Rabinowitz, *The Jazz Singer*

ROSCOE "FATTY" ARBUCKLE

Born: Roscoe Conkling Arbuckle, March 24, 1887 (Smith Center, Kansas, U.S.); died 1933 (New York City, New York, U.S.).

Star qualities: Brains more than blubber; contract-bound to weigh more than 250 pounds; used his size to comic effect; surprisingly acrobatic.

Roscoe Arbuckle hated the nickname "Fatty." It reduced him to a mere attribute, ignoring his extraordinary physical grace and acrobatic agility, his absurdist comic imagination, his cinematic proficiency, his Midwestern hardworking ethic, his loyalty. But that handle, cruel or no, made him a top-tier movie star. In his day, Arbuckle was one of Hollywood's greatest comedians, the top-drawing male star of Mack Sennett's legendary Keystone Studio. He appeared with Charlie Chaplin, costarred with Mabel Normand, and discovered Buster Keaton.

If history were just, Arbuckle would be celebrated alongside Chaplin, Keaton, and Harold Lloyd, remembered for such classics as *When Love Took Wings* (1915) and *The Garage* (1919). Yet Arbuckle is beloved by a coterie of insiders but unknown to the public at large, many of his films have been lost forever, and no one mentions his name without discussing the scandal that halted his career and forced him into blacklisted exile. A party on Labor Day 1921 in San Francisco ended with the death of actress Virginia Rappe—three rape and manslaughter trials ensued, but Arbuckle was acquitted on all counts.

Arbuckle started out in vaudeville, and soon rocketed to stardom. His gag-happy approach was too expensive for Keystone's tight budgets, so he set up his own studio, Comique, in 1917. Arbuckle's ingenious features *Leap Year* (1921) and *The Fast Freight* (1921) were distributed only in Europe. Years after the scandal faded, a petition by friends in the industry won him a run of talkie shorts produced by Warner Brothers in 1932 to 1933. From these he was to rebound into starring roles in comedy shorts, but a heart attack struck him the night after he signed a feature contract, ending the turbulent life of one of comedy's true geniuses. **DK**

Top Takes...

Tomalio 1933
Close Relations 1933
How've You Bean? 1933
Buzzin' Around 1933
In the Dough 1932
Hey, Pop! 1932
The Back Page 1931
Crazy to Marry 1921
Traveling Salesman 1921
The Dollar-a-Year Man 1921
Brewster's Millions 1921
The Fast Freight 1921
Leap Year 1921
The Bell Boy 1918
The Butcher Boy 1917
When Love Took Wings 1915

"I don't weigh a pound over one hundred and eighty and, what's more, I never did."

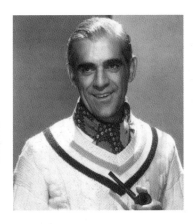

BORIS KARLOFF

Born: William Henry Pratt, November 23, 1887 (Camberwell, London, England); died 1969 (Midhurst, Sussex, England).

Star qualities: Master of horror with a forte for playing the exotic; created the consummate Monster character; larger than life with makeup.

Top Takes...

Boris Karloff was in his early forties when James Whale cast him as The Monster in *Frankenstein* (1931). An Anglo-Indian from a family prominent in diplomatic and social circles, young Billy Pratt chose a life on the stage and emigrated from England to Canada in 1909, reinventing himself as the foreign-sounding "Boris Karloff." He toured Canada and the United States in stock companies for ten years, arriving in California to spend the 1920s as a busy film actor, mostly in bit part ethnic roles, with a specialty in fur trappers of the northern woods.

Karloff's Caligari-like mesmerist in *The Bells* (1926) is an early indication of an aptitude for the macabre. After a showcase part as a murdering convict in *The Criminal Code* (1931), his British lisp and brutal face often featured in gangster pictures— he is memorably gunned down in a bowling alley in *Scarface* (1932). In *Frankenstein*, sporting the classic Jack P. Pierce makeup and bereft of dialogue, he gives a remarkable, affecting performance, eclipsing Béla Lugosi as the movies' leading horror man. Whale retained Karloff as another grunting brute in *The Old Dark House* (1932), but Karloff soon showed (*The Mask of Fu Manchu*, 1932; *The Ghoul*, 1933) he could talk as

RIGHT: Karloff aptly plays a retired horror movie actor in Peter Bogdanovich's *Targets*.

well as emote through makeup, and his distinctive, often-imitated tones became as essential to the horror film as the flat-headed and big-booted look of The Monster.

He reunited with Whale for *Bride of Frankenstein* (1935), in which he resisted the idea that The Monster talk ("Alone: bad. Friend: good!"), yet delivered another heartbreaking performance. When horror was out of fashion, he found work as exotics or genial comedy menaces. But he was central to successive waves of horror—outstanding for Val Lewton (*The Body Snatcher*, 1945), amusing for Roger Corman (*The Raven*, 1963) and, in his last years, melancholy for Michael Reeves (*The Sorcerers*, 1967) and Peter Bogdanovich (*Targets*, 1968).

Although remembered by the public for his penchant for the gruesome, among family, friends, and the industry he was known for his kindness and compassion, notably for his work as a founding member of the Screen Actors Guild. **KN**

ABOVE: Boris Karloff in his archetypal role as The Monster in *Frankenstein*.

Creating The Monster

Karloff was not first choice to play The Monster, but he made the role his own:

- Not a big man in real life, clever makeup, shoe supports, and padding added to Karloff's screen presence. Unfortunately, the heavy brace that was integral to his costume led to back problems, and he underwent several operations as a result. In later years, he was often offered parts in a wheelchair to help ease the pain.
- Karloff's Monster does not look like Mary Shelley's character. Makeup artist Jack P. Pierce invented the flat head, heavy eyelids, and bolts through the neck.

LOUIS JOUVET

Born: Jules Eugène Louis Jouvet, December 24, 1887 (Crozon, France); died 1951 (Paris, France).

Star qualities: Icon of French cinema; sharp features; sad eyes; versatile leading man of dramas; gravitas; giant of French theater; writer; director.

Top Takes...

Knock 1951 (*Dr. Knock*)
Une histoire d'amour 1951 (*Love Story*)
Retour à la vie 1949 (*Return to Life*)
Un revenant 1946 (*A Lover's Return*)
Volpone 1941
Sérénade 1940 (*Schubert's Serenade*)
L'école des femmes 1940
La Fin du jour 1939 (*The End of the Day*)
Hôtel du Nord 1938
L'alibi 1937
Forfaiture 1937
La kermesse héroïque 1935
    (*Carnival in Flanders*)
Knock, ou le triomphe de la médecine 1933
    (*Knock*)
Shylock 1910

"Nothing is more futile ... but nothing is more necessary than the theater."

Louis Jouvet's first love was the theater, and he took on many of his movie roles to enable him to keep his theater company afloat. And that was to the benefit of French cinema, given his meticulous acting style and high standards.

Although rejected three times by the Conservatoire de Paris, Jouvet was undeterred in his determination to become an actor. He decided to make his way by the back door, and in 1908 he joined a stage company as an administrator, and then debuted on stage two years later. In 1913 he was appointed director of the Théâtre du Vieux-Colombier in Paris, but his stage career was interrupted by World War I, and he served in combat at the front.

After the war, he headed to the United States and New York, where he appeared with his theater troupe in a repertory of acclaimed productions from 1919 to 1921. On his return to France, he became the director of the Théâtre des Champs-Élysées. By the early 1930s he was recognized as one of the best stage performers in France. His productions of works by the French playwright Jean Giraudoux won particular acclaim during this period, both for the acting and Jouvet's scenic decor and lighting. He made his film debut early in *Shylock* (1910). Among his most notable performances were in Marcel Carné's love-triangle melodrama *Hôtel du Nord* (1938), and as an aging actor in Julien Duvivier's drama *La Fin du jour* (1939) (*The End of the Day*). War interrupted his career once more, and during World War II he left France and toured South America with his theater company. He returned to Paris after the war was over and became director of Paris' L'Athénée theater. He continued to appear on stage and screen until his death. **CK**

BARRY FITZGERALD

Born: William Joseph Shields, March 10, 1888 (Dublin, Ireland); died 1961 (Dublin, Ireland).

Star qualities: Diminutive; Irish brogue; soft-spoken blarney; comic appearance; jolly, character actor; well-suited to nostalgic roles.

Barry Fitzgerald started out in banking but had a desire to try out acting and joined Dublin's Abbey Theatre. There he appeared in Sean O'Casey's play *Juno and the Paycock*. He was later to star in the screen version of *Juno and the Paycock* (1930), adapted and directed by Alfred Hitchcock. He made his Hollywood debut in another screen version of an O'Casey play, John Ford's *The Plough and the Stars* (1936), and stayed there until his death in 1961, specializing in soft-spoken blarney as the United States's most popular Irish character actor. Short of stature and comic in appearance, he was usually given sentimental or whimsical roles, and was a particular favorite of Ford's, who used him on several occasions, most famously in *The Quiet Man* (1952). The diminutive Fitzgerald was often cast alongside strapping actors such as John Wayne to exaggerate the fearlessness of his characters. Other notable appearances include as a drunkard, who really can see a leopard sitting next to him in *Bringing Up Baby* (1938); a rare dramatic lead in *The Naked City* (1948), and his Oscar-winning Best Supporting Actor role as the elder priest in *Going My Way* (1944). He was nominated for both the Academy Award for Best Actor and Best Supporting Actor for that same performance, a feat never repeated since then because the Academy changed the rules regarding nominations.

Hollywood rarely felt the need to give its supporting players challenging or untypical roles, and sadly Fitzgerald was seldom stretched. Only once was his good-natured twinkle used to brilliantly disruptive effect: in René Clair's masterly screen version of Agatha Christie's *And Then There Were None* (1945), where his jolly Irishman act is revealed as a mask behind which lurks a cold-blooded murderer. **MC**

Top Takes...

Broth of a Boy 1959
Happy Ever After 1954
The Quiet Man 1952
Silver City 1951
Union Station 1950
The Story of Seabiscuit 1949
Top o' the Morning 1949
The Naked City 1948
And Then There Were None 1945
Going My Way 1944 ★
How Green Was My Valley 1941
The Dawn Patrol 1938
Four Men and a Prayer 1938
Bringing Up Baby 1938
The Plough and the Stars 1936
Juno and the Paycock 1930

"No patty-fingers, if you please. The proprieties at all times."

—Michaleen Flynn, *The Quiet Man*

MAURICE CHEVALIER

Born: Maurice Auguste Chevalier, September 12, 1888 (Paris, France); died 1972 (Paris, France).

Star qualities: Gallic charm and sophistication; the French *monsieur*; sexy; singer and dancer; melodic voice; comic timing; straw boater hat, cane, and tuxedo.

Maurice Chevalier is the dapper old Frenchman with the straw hat and harmless twinkle in his eye from *Gigi* (1958). But by that time, he had been a star for three decades.

Chevalier started his career as an acrobat, until he had an accident that forced him to turn instead to singing and acting. His film debut was in the silent *Trop crédules* (1908). He served in the French army in World War I, but was captured and imprisoned. While in prison, he learned English from fellow prisoners, not realizing this would later prove useful. After the war he came to prominence in the Paris cabaret scene in the 1920s, writing well-known songs such as "Valentine."

He moved to Hollywood at the height of the pre-Code era, and had the good fortune to end up at Paramount Pictures, the most stylishly European of the main studios. Here Chevalier worked with the likes of Ernst Lubitsch, George Cukor, and Rouben Mamoulian in a series of vehicles combining music, witty dialogue, and cultural sophistication of a kind unthinkable in a Hollywood movie today. He received Oscar nominations for Best Actor for *The Love Parade* (1929) and *The Big Pond* (1930). For U.S. viewers, the feeling of confidentiality and familiarity he established with his audience—what he once termed a "mysterious, uninterrupted conversation"—was made even more agreeable for its being conducted in a heavy French accent. In a sense, Chevalier was the first truly modern sex symbol, a charming but latently dangerous figure with a real and pronounced sexuality, who exerted a bewitching influence over viewers. His charm is always evident; for a sense of his danger, look at the "I'm an Apache" number inserted into the otherwise genteel Ruritanian fantasy of Mamoulian's *Love Me Tonight* (1932). **MC**

Top Takes...

Monkeys, Go Home! 1967
I'd Rather Be Rich 1964
Panic Button 1964
Can-Can 1960
Count Your Blessings 1959
Gigi 1958
Love in the Afternoon 1957
Ma pomme 1950 (*Just Me*)
The Merry Widow 1934
Love Me Tonight 1932
Une heure près de toi 1932 (*One Hour with You*)
The Big Pond 1930 ☆
The Love Parade 1929 ☆
Innocents of Paris 1929
Gonzague 1922
Trop crédules 1908

"The cinema is rather like a beautiful woman whom you would court only by telephone."

CHARLES CHAPLIN

Born: Charles Spencer Chaplin, April 16, 1889 (Walworth, London, England); died 1977 (Vevey, Switzerland).

Star qualities: Iconic depiction of the slapstick Tramp; multitalented as a comic actor and filmmaker; unafraid to tackle the world's conscience; moustache.

Sir Charles Spencer Chaplin's contribution to the art of cinema cannot be overestimated. As the biggest ever silent-movie star, and as director, studio head (he cofounded United Artists), and composer, he excelled in virtually all areas of filmmaking. Above all, he gave the world The Tramp (aka Charlot), one of the most popular icons of the twentieth century: a bowler-hatted and cane-wielding clown who wore oversize shoes and trousers and sported a moustache.

Chaplin achieved fame and independence early in his movie career. After arriving in the United States from London, he toured in vaudeville before he moved to Hollywood, where, in his second role, in Keystone Studio's *Kid Auto Races at Venice* (1914), he introduced the character of a tramp upsetting social norms and values. After he started directing his own films (fittingly, his first efforts in 1915 were called *His New Job* and *The Tramp*), Chaplin balanced his tramp's slapstick routines with pathos, making his character at once funny and touching, rebellious and pitiful. By 1917, The Tramp had become the most popular movie character in the world.

Top Takes...

A Countess from Hong Kong 1967
Limelight 1952
Monsieur Verdoux 1947
***The Great Dictator* 1940** ☆
Modern Times 1936
City Lights 1931
The Circus 1928
The Gold Rush 1925
The Idle Class 1921
The Kid 1921
A Dog's Life 1918
The Immigrant 1917
The Rink 1916
Behind the Screen 1916
The Count 1916
The Vagabond 1916
The Fireman 1916
Burlesque on Carmen 1915
Shanghaied 1915
The Tramp 1915
In the Park 1915
A Night Out 1915
His New Job 1915
His Favorite Pastime 1914
Kid Auto Races at Venice 1914

LEFT: Chaplin hunts for gold in his role as The Lone Prospector in *The Gold Rush*.

The Great Dictator

"I am not a communist, neither have I ever joined any political party or organization in my life," was Chaplin's response to the House Un-American Activities Committee when he was investigated in 1947. His political tendencies and social conscience were known to be leftist, but around World War II, in an era of suspicion and name-calling, Chaplin often found himself in trouble:

- In 1942 Chaplin was vocal in his support for the opening of a second European front to aid the Soviet Union. He allegedly inferred that the spread of communism would be no bad thing, likening it to "human progress."
- His screen persona shared characteristics with Adolf Hitler. Although Hitler despised Chaplin (who he believed to have Jewish ancestry), he modeled his moustache on Chaplin's Tramp because he thought this would boost his popularity. The Tramp's original moustache was made from crepe paper.
- *The Great Dictator* (1940) was banned across Nazi-occupied Europe, but Hitler apparently watched the film twice. It was Chaplin's biggest box-office hit.
- Chaplin's relationships with women were also controversial. Nabokov's *Lolita* is said to be based on Chaplin's marriage to sixteen-year-old Lita Grey, who was 19 years his junior.

Gradually, Chaplin attuned his films to the mood of the times, broaching sensitive issues. *The Immigrant* (1917), for instance, is frank in its criticism of the treatment of immigrants by U.S. customs. The Tramp's kick to an officer's butt was not received well by conservatives in the United States, but audiences loved it. Chaplin consolidated the popularity of The Tramp through masterpieces such as *A Dog's Life* (1918), *The Kid* (1921), and the underrated *The Idle Class* (1921). He also became a free agent, able to spend several years on each movie. While this slowed down production, it guaranteed perfection. *The Gold Rush* (1925) and *City Lights* (1931) are filled with carefully choreographed gags while maintaining an emotional tactfulness.

The advent of the talkie

With his next two films, *Modern Times* (1936) and *The Great Dictator* (1940), Chaplin reached his zenith. Their comedic timing, original humor, evocation of emotions through the tiniest of movements, and cinematographic skill—especially in toying with the edges of the camera frame—push the boundaries of comedy to the limit, while their depiction of class disparity and message of tolerance gave them a topical relevance. *The Great Dictator* was Chaplin's first talkie, and he exploited this by making The Tramp speak out loud to deliver his antifascist message. Sadly, the world did not listen, and after World War II Chaplin seemed to stop caring. The Tramp disappeared, and the few films he made afterward, such as *Limelight* (1952), are reflective and acquiescent in tone.

His offscreen life was as colorful as his films were black and white. His early years were troubled: his mother suffered from schizophrenia and was committed to an asylum in 1903, and Chaplin lived a life moving between the poorhouse and various charity homes. He married four times, had eleven children and many high-profile and stormy romantic liaisons, one of which led to a paternity suit in 1944. The controversy and scandal that surrounded him were not only confined to his love life. He was branded a coward during World War I by many

ABOVE: The Tramp precariously makes his way across a tightrope in *The Circus*.

British, and was accused of communist sympathies by the U.S. government in 1947. In 1952, following a tour to promote *Limelight*, he was refused reentry to the United States and so moved to Switzerland. He did not return to the United States until 1971, when he attended the Oscars to collect an honorary lifetime achievement award. Even in death scandal haunted him. In 1978 his body was stolen from his grave by a group hoping to extort money from his family. His body was eventually recovered and reburied under concrete to ensure he could rest in peace.

Yet because his films enjoyed regular rereleases, and he received numerous awards—not to mention a knighthood—Chaplin never left the public stage or consciousness. So when he died in 1977, age eighty-eight, the world knew it had lost one of the geniuses of cinema. **EM**

"All I need to make a comedy is a park, a policeman, and a pretty girl."

SESSUE HAYAKAWA

Born: Kintaro Hayakawa, June 10, 1889 (Nanaura, Chiba, Japan); died 1973 (Tokyo, Japan).

Star qualities: Dashingly handsome matinee idol of silent era; Hollywood's first Asian movie icon; portrayed exotic villains or lovers; producer, writer, and director.

Top Takes…

The Geisha Boy 1958
The Bridge on the River Kwai 1957 ☆
Tokyo Joe 1949
Forfaiture 1937 (The Cheat)
Yoshiwara 1937
Daughter of the Dragon 1931
The Great Prince Shan 1924
Sen Yan's Devotion 1924
La Bataille 1923
The Dragon Painter 1919
The Bottle Imp 1917
The Honorable Friend 1916
Alien Souls 1916
The Cheat 1915
The Typhoon 1914
The Wrath of the Gods 1914

Sessue Hayakawa was destined for a career in the navy, but a swimming accident caused him to rupture an eardrum, and he failed the required physical test. He turned to the stage, and founded the Japanese Imperial Company theater troupe, which toured the United States in 1913. There, he was discovered by producer Thomas H. Ince and was offered a film contract. He then appeared in several silent features, including *The Typhoon* (1914) and Cecil B. DeMille's *The Cheat* (1915), which made Hayakawa Hollywood's first Asian-American star.

Despite his popularity, Hayakawa was frequently typecast as the exotic villain or lover, so he decided to form his own production company. He borrowed $1 million from a former classmate at the University of Chicago, and set up Hayworth Films in 1918. Over the next three years he produced—and sometimes starred in, alongside his wife, Tsuru Aoki—23 films. The company also found financial success, making $2 million a year, and Hayakawa adopted a lavish lifestyle, even having a castle built as his home. When his work in the United States slowed, he relocated to Europe, where he worked as an actor, playwright, and novelist. He remained there through World War II, and made the transition to talkies in projects such as *Tokyo Joe* (1949) with Humphrey Bogart. It was the World War II-set *The Bridge on the River Kwai* (1957) that won Hayakawa his greatest success. Playing Colonel Saito, the honor-bound Japanese prison camp officer counterpart to Alec Guinness in the movie, Hayakawa was nominated for the Best Supporting Actor Oscar, and often considered that role and performance his pinnacle achievement in a long career. Indeed, Hayakawa retired from acting soon after in 1966, and lived as a Zen Buddhist priest until his death. **JK**

> "You endure but you have no courage. I hate the British!"
>
> —Col. Saito, *The Bridge on the River Kwai*

RIGHT: Hayakawa as the inscrutable colonel in the war film, *The Bridge on the River Kwai*.

CLAUDE RAINS

Born: William Claude Rains, November 10, 1889 (Camberwell, London, England); died 1967 (Laconia, New Hampshire, U.S.).

Star qualities: Small in stature but large in talent; an ability to smile warmly, scowl menacingly, and cackle loudly; landed a diversity of roles.

Top Takes…

Lawrence of Arabia 1962
The Lost World 1960
The Man Who Watched the Trains Go By 1952
The Passionate Friends 1949
Notorious 1946 ☆
Mr. Skeffington 1944 ☆
Phantom of the Opera 1943
Casablanca 1942 ☆
Now, Voyager 1942
Here Comes Mr. Jordan 1941
Mr. Smith Goes to Washington 1939 ☆
Four Daughters 1938
The Adventures of Robin Hood 1938
They Won't Forget 1937
The Invisible Man 1933
Build Thy House 1920

"What in heaven's name brought you to Casablanca?"

—Captain Louis Renault, *Casablanca*

The son of the British stage actor Frederick Rains, Claude Rains chose to follow in the family tradition and first appeared onstage at the age of eleven in *Nell of Old Drury*. He first went to the United States in 1913, but returned to England to serve as a soldier in World War I, where he almost lost the sight in one eye following a gas attack. His first movie part was in the British silent *Build Thy House* (1920). He worked as a stage actor and teacher at London's Royal Academy of Dramatic Art—where he had refined his own acting talents—his most famous pupils being Sir Laurence Olivier and Sir John Gielgud.

Rains returned to the United States and Broadway in 1927, later making his talkie debut as *The Invisible Man* (1933). His face emerged only in the finale, but his abrasive voice and demented laugh gave The Invisible Man a chillingly solid presence. Rains stuck around Hollywood as a character actor who could carry a film by himself if needed, but was most often outstanding amid strong ensemble casts. He became a naturalized citizen of the United States in 1939.

A sampling of Rains's witty, wicked, or genial roles includes a corrupt senator in *Mr. Smith Goes to Washington* (1939), Bette Davis's shrink in *Now, Voyager* (1942), a Jewish banker in *Mr. Skeffington* (1944), and a subtly sympathetic Nazi in *Notorious* (1946). But he is perhaps best known for his role as the French policeman Captain Louis Renault in *Casablanca* (1942). His line, "Round up the usual suspects" has gone down in movie history, as has his memorable exit at the end of the film with Humphrey Bogart's Rick Blaine. Rains received four Academy Award nominations for Best Supporting Actor—including one for *Casablanca*—but remarkably never won an Oscar. **KN**

EDWARD ARNOLD

Born: Gunther Edward Arnold Schneider, February 18, 1890 (New York City, New York, U.S.); died 1956 (Encino, California, U.S.).

Star qualities: Larger-than-life frame; rich baritone voice; early penchant for roles as a cowboy and later the corrupt man seduced by power.

The features of certain character actors almost automatically conjure up the kinds of personalities they habitually portrayed onscreen. The son of German immigrants to the United States, Edward Arnold had an imposing, full-framed figure that seemed tailor-made for the captains of industry with which he has come to be associated. The fact that he was a star in cowboy movies for Essanay from 1915 to 1919 seems almost unfathomable, because Arnold comes across as altogether urban and was habitually dressed in a well-tailored suit.

Arnold had gained extensive stage experience by the time he returned to the screen in 1932. He could admittedly be charming as well as commanding, evidenced by his appearance as the nineteenth-century mogul in *Diamond Jim* (1935), French monarch Louis XIII in *Cardinal Richelieu* (1935), the house-bound shamus in *Meet Nero Wolfe* (1936), and a wistful timber tycoon in *Come and Get It* (1936). He effortlessly sent up his persona in the screwball comedy *Easy Living* (1937), and displayed the appropriate rectitude as the famous orator in *The Devil and Daniel Webster* (1941).

Frank Capra employed Arnold as part of his stock company and clinched his impression as the corrupt power broker on three occasions: *You Can't Take It with You* (1938), *Mr. Smith Goes to Washington* (1939), and *Meet John Doe* (1941). In these appearances, Arnold effortlessly effused arrogance and disdain, all the better to act as counterpoint to Capra's saintly protagonists. Arnold spent the 1940s at MGM, although in less revealing roles, and one wonders how he would have added to the universe of film noir had he been invited. He was president of the Screen Actors Guild from 1940 to 1942, and continued to serve there until his death. **DS**

Top Takes...

Miami Expose 1956
The Ambassador's Daughter 1956
Man of Conflict 1953
Annie Get Your Gun 1950
Command Decision 1948
The Devil and Daniel Webster 1941
Meet John Doe 1941
Mr. Smith Goes to Washington 1939
You Can't Take It with You 1938
Easy Living 1937
Come and Get It 1936
Meet Nero Wolfe 1936
Cardinal Richelieu 1935
Whistling in the Dark 1933
A Broadway Saint 1919
Be My Best Man 1917

"From now on, I think you'd better work directly with me."

—D. B. Norton, *Meet John Doe*

STAN LAUREL AND OLIVER HARDY

Laurel: Born Arthur Stanley Jefferson, June 16, 1890 (Ulverston, Cumbria, England); died 1965 (Santa Monica, California, U.S.).

Hardy: Born Oliver Norvell Hardy, January 8, 1892 (Harlem, Georgia, U.S.); died 1957 (North Hollywood, California, U.S.).

Star qualities: One stout, one lean; Laurel's "whiny face" and childlike innocence; Hardy's assumed worldliness, small moustache, and exasperation with his partner.

Stan Laurel and Oliver Hardy stand as one of the most beloved comedy duos of all time. They began their careers as solo players until Leo McCarey, supervising producer at Hal Roach Studios, decided to make them a team in 1927. Soon, they were silent-movie stars. The advent of sound later allowed audiences to hear their distinctive voices, thus their transition from silent shorts to sound features was more successful than most.

Like many successful comedy teams, their characters (particularly during the Hal Roach era) could easily be seen as overgrown children. Even when they played married men, as in the popular *Sons of the Desert* (1933), they always exuded a desire to play hooky from the responsibilities of life—only to make a mess of things later.

Hardy usually played the idea man, an aggressive braggart who refused to believe he was as dim-witted as his friend. Meanwhile, Laurel would be far more passive, though always supportive of his pal. Inevitably disaster and physical harm would befall them both, but their friendship always survived. Laurel's devotion to Hardy was constant, and Hardy was smart

Top Takes...

Atoll K 1951
Nothing but Trouble 1944
The Big Noise 1944
The Dancing Masters 1943
Air Raid Wardens 1943
A-Haunting We Will Go 1942
The Flying Deuces 1939
Block-Heads 1938
Swiss Miss 1938
Way Out West 1937
Pick a Star 1937
The Bohemian Girl 1936
Thicker than Water 1935
The Live Ghost 1934
Sons of the Desert 1933
Me and My Pal 1933
Towed in a Hole 1932
Their First Mistake 1932
Pack Up Your Troubles 1932
Scram! 1932
The Music Box 1932
Another Fine Mess 1930
Early to Bed 1928
Hats Off 1927
Duck Soup 1927

RIGHT: The team demonstrates the motto "See no evil, hear no evil, and speak no evil."

ABOVE: Laurel kindly fixes Hardy's trousers where they have torn in *Hollywood Party*.

enough to know that a friend that rare was a friend worth keeping. Hence, despite the brutal slapstick that populated some of their most amusing scenes, it is the charm of their friendship that is their greatest comedic strength—epitomized by the "At the Ball, That's All" dance number in *Way Out West* (1937). Laurel and Hardy perform a sweet and amusing dance that serves little purpose in the story except to illustrate their affection for life and for each other. The joy they exhibit is infectious with the other characters in the scene, as well as the audience. For many fans it is a scene that stands as their finest.

By 1940—after starring in nearly 100 shorts and features—they opted to leave the Hal Roach Studios and sign up with Twentieth Century Fox and MGM. Deprived of the opportunity to improvise and inject their own ideas, these later films failed to emulate the success of their earlier works. Their last film, *Atoll K*, was released in 1951. **DW**

The Gags

The details of the team's appeal are many: Hardy's tie fiddling, Laurel's head scratching and high-pitched whimpering, and many well-executed sight gags. The gags often started small and escalated in destructive force. In *Big Business* (1929), Stan and Oliver are Christmas tree salesmen. A minor argument results in the duo's destroying an entire home, bit by bit, while the homeowner, a prospective customer, retaliates by consigning Stan and Oliver's car to the scrap heap. Most often such disastrous outcomes were the result of Laurel following through on Hardy's ideas.

CLARA KIMBALL YOUNG

Born: Clarisa Kimball, September 6, 1890 (Chicago, Illinois, U.S.); died 1960 (Los Angeles, California, U.S.).

Star qualities: Tall, dark-haired, natural beauty; curvaceous leading lady and vamp of silent-screen era; comedienne; dramatic gestures style of acting.

Top Takes…

Women Go on Forever 1931
A Wife's Romance 1923
The Worldly Madonna 1922
What No Man Knows 1921
Hush 1921
Eyes of Youth 1919
Cheating Cheaters 1919
The Easiest Way 1917
The Price She Paid 1917
The Common Law 1916
The Foolish Virgin 1916
Camille 1915
Lola 1914
My Official Wife 1914
Beau Brummel 1913

"Miss Young does good work as Daisy Bowman in most of her scenes."—*New York Times*

An early example of the headstrong star taking on the system, Clara Kimball Young had been a performer since early childhood, signing with Vitagraph Studios in her late teens. Here she appeared in dozens of one-reelers and a few features, including her major success, directed by her husband James Young, *My Official Wife* (1914), in which she plays a young revolutionary who plots to kill the Russian czar. Allegedly the film featured a cameo by Bolshevik revolutionary and Marxist theorist Leon Trotsky; in fact it was a look-alike extra.

Shortly thereafter, Young was snapped up (both privately, causing problems in her marriage, and professionally) by producer Lewis Selznick, who set about changing her image. She was remodeled as a sexy vamp in films such as *Lola* (1914). While the behind-the-scenes complications slowly resolved themselves in divorce court, Young became increasingly dissatisfied with the salacious direction of her screen work. Signed exclusively to Selznick, she had no say in the kinds of roles she was given, and no freedom to work elsewhere.

She took Selznick to court and announced the formation of a new company with her latest mentor, Harry Garson, but the legal proceedings dragged on, and her work with Garson was often disappointing. She seemed tired and bored in these movies, and the audiences began to drift away. The 1920s arrived along with the svelte flapper look; Young's matronly curves were no longer fashionable and she became a has-been. She wandered into vaudeville, Westerns, and dead-end work, announcing her retirement in 1941. Young had a late career renaissance in the 1950s, when she was sought by TV chat show hosts, and she became the Hollywood correspondent for *The Johnny Carson Show* (1956–1957). **MC**

RIGHT: Young, in full bridal attire, reclines pensively in this image from 1916.

Top Takes...

THE MARX BROTHERS

Groucho: Born Julius Henry Marx, October 2, 1890 (New York City, New York, U.S.); died 1977 (Los Angeles, California, U.S.).

Star qualities: Vaudeville act turned comic brotherhood; unique onstage names, appearances, and personalities; satire; impromptu quips.

Comedy does not always age well. Usually constructed around the subversion or satire of social norms, the success of comedy often declines over time as that norm shifts and changes; some comedic movies are timeless (those of Harold Lloyd, Buster Keaton, Jacques Tati), but it is unlikely that anyone who is not a committed fan would randomly enjoy anything from 1950s sitcoms to Andy Hardy romps, Keystone Kops silents to *Pillow Talk* (1959). It is a testament to the genius of the Marx Brothers—Groucho, Chico (1887–1961), Harpo (1888–1964), and occasionally Zeppo (1901–1979)—that their best movies are just as funny now as they were upon release.

The brothers began their careers in vaudeville under the management of their mother, Minnie, and their first two films were stage adaptations, *The Cocoanuts* (1929) and *Animal Crackers* (1930). They would do three more films for Paramount Pictures: *Monkey Business* (1931), *Horse Feathers* (1932), and *Duck Soup* (1933). Incredibly, *Duck Soup*—a comedic masterpiece of barely controlled anarchy and surrealism, as well as a sharp antiwar satire—was their one box-office failure for Paramount, and they were dropped from the studio's roster of talent.

RIGHT: The Marx siblings come to blows in one of their earliest movies, *The Cocoanuts.*

The Marx Brothers were rescued by the gifted young producer Irving Thalberg, who took them to MGM in 1935 and restructured their movies to create plot-driven features with romances and musical numbers, as opposed to the somewhat random collection of individual skits represented by their Paramount Pictures quintet. The first two films—*A Night at the Opera* (1935) and *A Day at the Races* (1937)—found the brothers back at the top. Their relationship with MGM soon soured, however, and upon Thalberg's sudden death in 1936, they found they had lost their principal ally at the studio.

Though they have their moments, most of the post-*Night* and *Day* work is largely forgettable filler, unworthy of the Marx Brothers' brilliance. As the 1950s arrived, the brothers went their separate ways, with only Groucho sustaining an individual career of interest, as the long-time host of radio and TV's *You Bet Your Life* game show. **TC**

ABOVE: Groucho, Harpo, and Chico sport typical comic attire in *Go West*.

Snappy Stage Names

Each brother had a unique onscreen persona, trademark, and stage name:

- Wisecracking ringleader Groucho may have been named for his less-than-cheerful temperament, or because he was somewhat stingy, carrying his money in a grouch bag around his neck.
- Fast-talking faux-Italian Chico was named after his love of "chicks" (ladies).
- Wild mute Harpo played the harp.
- Handsome romantic lead Zeppo's stage name may have derived from another vaudevillian's chimpanzee, Mr. Zippo.

WALLACE REID

Born: William Wallace Reid, April 15, 1891 (St. Louis, Missouri, U.S.); died 1923 (Los Angeles, California, U.S.).

Star qualities: Tall, blue-eyed, clean-cut looks; "The Screen's Most Perfect Lover"; part of an acting family; famed for car-racing movies; writer and director.

Top Takes...

Thirty Days 1922
The Ghost Breaker 1922
The Dictator 1922
The World's Champion 1922
Don't Tell Everything 1921
Forever 1921
The Affairs of Anatol 1921
Excuse My Dust 1920
Double Speed 1920
The Roaring Road 1919
Less Than Kin 1918
The House of Silence 1918
Rimrock Jones 1918
The Squaw Man's Son 1917
The Chorus Lady 1915
The Birth of a Nation 1915

"Let's not kiss any more, dear, until after breakfast."

—Anatol Spencer, *The Affairs of Anatol*

Wallace Reid was a major silent star whose death from morphine addiction shocked audiences, who had instinctively associated him with the clean-cut persona he had established in more than 200 film appearances. Although the drug had originally been administered for relief from the pain of an on-set injury on *The Valley of the Giants* (1919), Reid had soon become addicted, and this, coupled with the heavy drinking customary in Hollywood at the time, killed him at the age of thirty-one. His death led to widespread calls for Hollywood to be held accountable for its excesses; among the many measures for which it was partly responsible was the eventual implementation of the Hays Code in the 1930s.

The son of actor, writer, and director Hal Reid and actress Bertha Westbrook, the young Reid first hit the stage in his parents' act at age four. His first ambition was to be a cameraman, but given that he was tall, handsome, and well built, he often ended up in front of the camera, earning the nickname "The Screen's Most Perfect Lover." Also a writer and director, he abandoned that side of his career reluctantly when his acting stardom took off. Reid's star vehicles included several built around the theme of daredevil car racing that play like straight-faced Harold Lloyd movies (*The Roaring Road*, 1919; *Double Speed*, 1920). Today, Reid is remembered chiefly for a supporting role in *The Birth of a Nation* (1915) and costarring with Gloria Swanson in Cecil B. DeMille's *The Affairs of Anatol* (1921). After his death, his wife, Dorothy Davenport (billed as Mrs. Wallace Reid), coproduced and appeared in a movie exposing drug trafficking called *Human Wreckage* (1923). She toured the United States to promote the film and warn of the dangers of drug addiction. **MC**

EDDIE CANTOR

Born: Edward Israel Iskowitz, January 31, 1892 (New York City, New York, U.S.); died 1964 (Los Angeles, California, U.S.).

Star qualities: "Banjo Eyes"; singer, composer, comedian, writer, and producer; resilient; politically and civic minded; outspoken; defiant; quick-witted; generous.

1890s

Born to Russian Jewish immigrants, Eddie Cantor was orphaned at the age of three. His early years were spent in poverty in the care of his grandmother and he entered—and won—talent contests for the cash. He went on to become one of the foremost vaudevillian performers on stage and screen. From his early days in the Ziegfeld Follies, Cantor began writing his own songs and comedy material, and was a major early recording star, affectionately known as "Banjo Eyes" because of his blackface makeup, until the late 1920s.

Despite his early Broadway successes, *Kid Boots* (1923) and *Whoopee!* (1928), Cantor went bankrupt in the stock market crash of 1929. Hollywood and radio resurrected Cantor, who had just made a movie version of *Whoopee!* (1930)—a film noteworthy as an early experiment in the Technicolor process. He also had his own hour-long Sunday night variety radio program *The Eddie Cantor Radio Show* (1931–1934), which was immensely popular, as Cantor won his audience over with tales about his wife, Ida Tobias, and the couple's five children.

Cantor was a highly political and philanthropic individual: he was the first president of the Screen Actor's Guild (1933–1935), founded the March of Dimes charity to combat polio, and was heavily outspoken against the Nazis during the 1930s. In his early days with Florenz Ziegfeld, Cantor was part of a double act with early African-American comedian Bert Williams (the two performed in blackface together), and defied NBC in the 1950s by performing with Sammy Davis Jr. on *The Colgate Comedy Hour*. By the mid-1950s, Cantor had retired from show business due to failing health, but he lived to see the musical biopic *The Eddie Cantor Story* (1953), in which he is played by Keefe Brasselle. **MK**

Top Takes...

If You Knew Susie 1948
American Creed 1946
Show Business 1944
Forty Little Mothers 1940
Ali Baba Goes to Town 1937
Strike Me Pink 1936
Kid Millions 1934
Roman Scandals 1933
The Kid from Spain 1932
Palmy Days 1931
Whoopee! 1930
Insurance 1930
A Ziegfeld Midnight Frolic 1929
Special Delivery 1927
Kid Boots 1926

"... they're not calling it the stock market any more. They're calling it the stuck market."

MARY PICKFORD

Born: Gladys Marie Smith, April 8, 1892 (Toronto, Ontario, Canada); died 1979 (Santa Monica, California, U.S.).

Star qualities: "Little Mary"; radiant, blonde-ringletted purity; innocent beauty; the perpetual child; best-known female star of the silent era; early retirement.

Top Takes...

Secrets 1933
Kiki 1931
The Taming of the Shrew 1929
Coquette 1929 ★
My Best Girl 1927
Little Annie Rooney 1925
Rosita 1923
Pollyanna 1920
Heart o' the Hills 1919
Daddy-Long-Legs 1919
Stella Maris 1918
The Little Princess 1917
Rebecca of Sunnybrook Farm 1917
The Little American 1917
The Poor Little Rich Girl 1917
Less Than the Dust 1916
Hulda from Holland 1916
The Eternal Grind 1916
Tess of the Storm Country 1914
The New York Hat 1912
My Baby 1912
The One She Loved 1912
A Gold Necklace 1910
Wilful Peggy 1910
An Arcadian Maid 1910

The name Mary Pickford occupies as sure a place in the pantheon of silent screen icons as those of Charlie Chaplin or Rudolph Valentino. The big difference is that most film fans can name at least a half-dozen Chaplin movies. Pickford survives by virtue of her physical beauty, her nickname ("America's Sweetheart"), and her reputation as both high-ranking Hollywood royalty and shrewd businesswoman (she was one of the key founders of United Artists). Her movies seem almost incidental, are rarely revived, and not widely available to the home collector. Not that she would have minded: she once expressed the odd wish that they all be destroyed at her death.

This may be because of the fact that her career ended rather unspectacularly in the early years of sound. She had tired of it, and of the peculiar restrictions her screen image imposed upon her, choosing to retire quietly in 1933. Though it is unfair to claim that she never took adult roles, by far her greatest successes were those in which she played children: *The Poor Little Rich Girl* (1917), *Rebecca of Sunnybrook Farm* (1917), *Daddy-Long-Legs* (1919). She played the twelve-year-old title character in *Little Annie Rooney* (1925) at the age of thirty-two.

RIGHT: With braided hair and girlish looks, Pickford is convincing as *Little Annie Rooney*.

Pickford made four talkies, all of them provocative departures from formula, as if she was intent upon forcing a new, more modern screen image on her public against their will. The first, *Coquette* (1929), is a pre-Code women's picture ending in tragedy, with Pickford not only speaking for the first time but also sporting a modern, short hairstyle. The movie was praised critically—Pickford won a Best Actress Oscar for this performance—but audiences did not want Mary without her curls. Neither did they want to see her as the title character in *Kiki* (1931), a feisty, sexy, shrill, and often very irritating French chorus girl causing romantic strife. It is a boisterous, exhausting performance, wrongly pitched for farce or romantic comedy, and the movie flopped badly. *Secrets* (1933) fared a little better, but reaction to the story of a pioneer couple, in which Pickford progresses impressively from youth to old age, was still lukewarm. She never appeared onscreen again. **MC**

ABOVE: Pickford plays against type as a street singer in Ernst Lubitsch's *Rosita*.

America's Sweetheart

Despite her Canadian origins, Mary Pickford was the original "America's Sweetheart," a title that has since been awarded to the likes of Julia Roberts. The nickname was coined by B. P. Schulberg of Famous Players, and he used it to promote Pickford's movies. Schulberg claimed that it was derived from a conversation he overheard in the street— "She's not just your little sweetheart, she's everybody's sweetheart"—but in wartime there may have been patriotic reasons behind the nickname. Posters for *The Little American* (1917) included images of Pickford wrapped in a U.S. flag.

BASIL RATHBONE

Born: Philip St. John Basil Rathbone, June 13, 1892 (Johannesburg, South Africa); died 1967 (New York City, New York, U.S.).

Star qualities: Tall and lean; pencil-line moustache; a gentle gentleman; athletic; swashbuckling villain; deft swordplay duelist; Sherlock Holmes incarnate.

Top Takes...

The Great Mouse Detective 1986
The Comedy of Terrors 1964
Tales of Terror 1962
Casanova's Big Night 1954
Sherlock Holmes and the House of Fear 1945
Sherlock Holmes Faces Death 1943
Sherlock Holmes and the Voice of Terror 1942
The Mark of Zorro 1940
The Adventures of Sherlock Holmes 1939
The Hound of the Baskervilles 1939
***If I Were King* 1938** ☆
The Adventures of Robin Hood 1938
Make a Wish 1937
***Romeo and Juliet* 1936** ☆
Captain Blood 1935
Innocent 1921

Born in South Africa, Basil Rathbone moved to England with his family when he was a child. On the insistence of his father, who disapproved of acting as a profession, Rathbone spent a year working for an insurance company before heading for the stage. He honed his skills as a Shakespearean actor before serving in military intelligence during World War I, for which he was awarded the Military Cross. He returned to the theater after the war before going to the United States and Broadway. He made his film debut in the silent *Innocent* (1921).

Rathbone was on his way to becoming cinema's favorite villain, with roles in *Captain Blood* (1935) and *The Adventures of Robin Hood* (1938), when he was chosen to star as Sherlock Holmes in Twentieth Century Fox's *The Hound of the Baskervilles* (1939). Nigel Bruce played his Dr. Watson. The movie's success impelled a sequel, *The Adventures of Sherlock Holmes* (1939), and a Holmes radio show, which also starred Rathbone and Bruce. Universal Studios took over the series with *Sherlock Holmes and the Voice of Terror* (1942). Eleven more movies followed, all with Rathbone as Holmes and Bruce as Watson. The popular Holmes radio show also continued, with the duo acting in more than 200 episodes. Despondent over his identification with the character and the fact that he was offered no other roles, Rathbone elected not to sign up for more Holmes radio shows and movies after 1946. When success became elusive, he returned to Holmes in a failed play in 1953, and in a series of audio recordings of the original Sir Arthur Conan Doyle stories. Even after death, Rathbone could not escape Holmes. His last film credit is the use of his voice for Sherlock Holmes in the animated *The Great Mouse Detective* (1986), 19 years after he died. **ML**

"When you become the character you portray, it's the end of your career as an actor."

WILLIAM POWELL

Born: William Horatio Powell, July 29, 1892 (Pittsburgh, Pennsylvania, U.S.); died 1984 (Palm Springs, California, U.S.).

Star qualities: Slim, suave, smooth, and sophisticated; debonair screen super sleuth and romantic lead; deft comic timing.

Following drama school and a stint in vaudeville and on Broadway, William Powell made his screen debut in *Sherlock Holmes* (1922). Employed by Paramount Pictures in 1924, he was kept busy throughout the 1920s, often in period pictures as nobles, rogues, and supporting rotters. Given his later suave image, it is a surprise that in *The Great Gatsby* (1926), he played the gas station owner rather than one of the preppy leads. With clipped moustache, smooth manner, fine voice, and cynical eyewink, he was well suited to drawing rooms and cocktail cabinets in the talkies. In *The Canary Murder Case* (1929), he was Philo Vance, annoying know-it-all society sleuth—a role he reprised several times.

Powell soon grew tired of his Paramount roles, so in 1931 he defected to Warner Brothers. In *The Thin Man* (1934), he played another detective, Nick Charles, who works his cases while in a perpetual alcoholic stupor and has a cute relationship with witty wife Nora, played by Myrna Loy. It won him the first of three Oscar nominations for Best Actor. Powell and Loy teamed up again in a series that stretched to *Song of the Thin Man* (1947), and Nick slowly matured from drunken sot to fatherly buffoon. Powell had two other Academy Award–nominated roles as the butler in *My Man Godfrey* (1936) and the father in *Life with Father* (1947). But he is perhaps at his best in still-underrated quick-fire comedies such as *Libeled Lady* (1936) and *I Love You Again* (1940). In his personal life, he was famed for his penchant for romancing his costars: Eileen Wilson (his first wife), Carole Lombard (his second wife), Jean Harlow, and Diana Lewis. Powell quit acting at age sixty-three and refused many comeback role offers, spending the rest of his life in retirement with his third wife, Lewis. **KN**

Top Takes...

Fernes Jamaica 1969
Mister Roberts 1955
How to Marry a Millionaire 1953
Song of the Thin Man 1947
Life with Father 1947 ☆
I Love You Again 1940
Libeled Lady 1936
My Man Godfrey 1936 ☆
The Great Ziegfeld 1936
Reckless 1935
The Thin Man 1934 ☆
The Benson Murder Case 1930
The Canary Murder Case 1929
The Last Command 1928
The Great Gatsby 1926
Sherlock Holmes 1922

"There is more money in being liked by an audience than in being disliked by it."

HAROLD LLOYD

Born: Harold Clayton Lloyd, April 20, 1893 (Burchard, Nebraska, U.S.); died 1971 (Los Angeles, California, U.S.).

Star qualities: Industrious optimist; signature round glasses; daredevil stunts; prolific and inventive performer, producer, and director; progressive techniques.

Top Takes...

The Sin of Harold Diddlebock 1947
Professor Beware 1938
The Milky Way 1936
The Cat's-Paw 1934
Movie Crazy 1932
Feet First 1930
Welcome Danger 1929
Speedy 1928
The Freshman 1925
Girl Shy 1924
Why Worry? 1923
Safety Last! 1923
Dr. Jack 1922
Grandma's Boy 1922
A Sailor-Made Man 1921
Never Weaken 1921
Haunted Spooks 1920
Two Scrambled 1918
Bride and Gloom 1918
That's Him 1918
Are Crooks Dishonest? 1918
Over the Fence 1917
Spit-Ball Sadie 1915
Just Nuts 1915
Samson 1914

Even if you've never seen his films, you've seen him—dangling from a clock face a dozen stories high. This image, from the climax of *Safety Last!* (1923), is an enduring icon of classic slapstick. Harold Lloyd did not like to be remembered as a "thrill comedian," which was only one facet of a long and illustrious career. He was that, true, but was also a striver, an optimist, a winner who sometimes stumbled haphazardly into unexpected success—in short, much like his screen persona.

Lloyd's original ambition was to become a serious actor. Lurking about studio lots, taking jobs as an extra, Lloyd met fellow aspirant Hal Roach. Together they would make movies—once Roach had learned directing at Essanay Studios and Lloyd had been seasoned at Keystone Studio's factory.

In his earliest work for Roach, Lloyd played a Charlie Chaplin knockoff called Lonesome Luke. Few of these movies survive today but they were very popular at the time. Disaster struck on the set of his 1920 short *Haunted Spooks*, when a "prop" bomb mangled his right hand. Lloyd was thenceforth obliged to wear a prosthetic hand, lest his audience become aware of the dangers faced by such a daredevil. In films like *Never Weaken*

RIGHT: Lloyd as the gullible Ezekiel Cobb in the political comedy *The Cat's-Paw*.

(1921) and *Speedy* (1928), he crafted elaborate, stunt-filled spectaculars that were as breathtaking as they were funny.

Lloyd took funny business seriously. Following an amicable split with Roach, he established his own studio and maintained ownership of his films, which were plentiful: he was more prolific than Chaplin and Buster Keaton combined. Lloyd is credited with inventing the preview system, recutting and reshooting films based on audience reactions to test screenings. He also embraced the coming of talkies, remaking 1925's *Welcome Danger* in 1929 to retrofit it for sound.

Lloyd's sound comedies were less popular. Unlike his peers, he could not blame the bumpy transition on studio interference or problems with his speaking voice—it was simply that his role as an earnest go-getter was out of step with Depression-era attitudes. His last movie, *The Sin of Harold Diddlebock* (1947), remains more a curio than a satisfying feature. **DK**

ABOVE: The enduring image of Lloyd dangling from a clock face in *Safety Last!*

The "Glasses" Character

In 1917, Lloyd began experimenting with an alternate character built around a pair of wide-rimmed glasses. Exactly who came up with the glasses, and when, is the subject of enduring controversy— everybody wants a piece of success. And success it was—even in faraway Imperial Japan, Lloyd fandom took hold and "Roido"-style glasses became the height of fashion. In his "Glasses" character, Lloyd was a handsome and charming everyman. He was a generous performer whose costars Snub Pollard and Sunshine Sammy Morrison ended up starring in their own series of one-reel movies.

MAE WEST

Born: Mary Jane West, August 17, 1893 (Brooklyn, New York, U.S.); died 1980 (Hollywood, California, U.S.).

Star qualities: Iconic, racy, blonde bombshell; risqué; voluptuous; pioneering feminist and gay-rights activist; mistress of the double entendre; prolific writer.

Top Takes…

Sextette 1978
Myra Breckinridge 1970
The Heat's On 1943
My Little Chickadee 1940
Every Day's a Holiday 1937
Go West Young Man 1936
Klondike Annie 1936
Goin' to Town 1935
Belle of the Nineties 1934
I'm No Angel 1933
She Done Him Wrong 1933
Night After Night 1932

Despite being famous for her risqué films of the early 1930s, Mae West should more properly be known as an early feminist and gay-rights activist. She began in vaudeville in 1905 at the age of twelve, and is reputed to have invented the "shimmy" dance in 1913 to accompany the song "Everybody Shimmies Now." By the mid-1920s, West had emerged as a writer as well as performer, and fostered controversy with her sexually explicit plays. *Sex* (1926) brought her up on obscenity charges (she was sentenced to ten days in jail), while *The Drag* (1927), a play about homosexuality, was banned outright from Broadway. But it was the play *Diamond Lil* (1928) that really catapulted her to fame, inventing the iconic persona of the racy, blonde bombshell whose every line is a double entendre.

In 1932 West signed with Paramount Pictures and filmed *Diamond Lil* as *She Done Him Wrong* (1933), costarring with the then-unknown Cary Grant. Despite almost single-handedly saving Paramount Pictures from bankruptcy, West was too racy for Middle America, and her movies became another victim of the Hays Code. West continued making films for Paramount until 1938. She did a one-off movie for Universal Studios, *My Little Chickadee* (1940), starring opposite W. C. Fields. She decided that because of the repressive censorship, she would have more freedom of self-expression back on the stage, and she returned to successfully work in the theater. West became more of an icon than a performer; during World War II, inflatable life jackets were referred to as "Mae Wests." West reappeared on film in the 1970s in *Myra Breckinridge* (1970), and her last film was *Sextette* (1978). Both are considered classic cult movies. West died from complications after a stroke in 1980. **MK**

"When caught between two evils I generally pick the one I've never tried before."

RIGHT: Fur-clad Mae West stands voluptuous in *Every Day's a Holiday*.

LILLIAN GISH

Born: Lillian Diana de Guiche, October 14, 1893 (Springfield, Ohio, U.S.); died 1993 (New York City, New York, U.S.).

Star qualities: Star of the silent screen; talented but restrained performer; perfect for Victorian melodrama; virginal; levelheaded.

Top Takes...

The Whales of August 1987
A Wedding 1978
The Unforgiven 1960
The Night of the Hunter 1955
The Cobweb 1955
Duel in the Sun 1946 ☆
His Double Life 1933
The Wind 1928
The Scarlet Letter 1926
La Bohème 1926
The White Sister 1923
Orphans of the Storm 1921
Way Down East 1920
The Greatest Question 1919
True Heart Susie 1919
Broken Blossoms 1919
Hearts of the World 1918
Intolerance: Love's Struggle Throughout the Ages 1916
The Birth of a Nation 1915
Judith of Bethulia 1914
The House of Darkness 1913
The Musketeers of Pig Alley 1912
Two Daughters of Eve 1912
An Unseen Enemy 1912

RIGHT: Gish, as Mimi, is seduced by John Gilbert's Rodolphe in *La Bohème.*

If anyone can be said to have been the first truly great actor in the cinema, it is surely Lillian Gish. Together with her sister Dorothy, she acted in traveling theater before going into the movies at the behest of D. W. Griffith, whom they met while visiting their old friend Gladys Smith—later better known as Mary Pickford—at the Biograph Studios. Griffith immediately put the sisters into the short he was then shooting (*An Unseen Enemy*, 1912), thus beginning an association that, in the case of Lillian, would lead to such classics as *Judith of Bethulia* (1914), *The Birth of a Nation* (1915), *Intolerance: Love's Struggle Throughout the Ages* (1916)—in which she plays the girl rocking humanity in its cradle—*True Heart Susie* (1919), *Way Down East* (1920), and *Orphans of the Storm* (1921). Like Griffith, she came out of Victorian melodrama, but what distinguished Gish from most of her contemporaries was the comparative restraint of her acting; filmed in the director's trademark close-ups in movies as early as *The Musketeers of Pig Alley* (1912), she had learned early on that less could be more. That said, when called on to emote—as when she is locked in a closet in *Broken Blossoms* (1919)—she could do so with ferocious energy.

By the 1920s Gish had established her reputation as an actress of great skill and dedication; though her somewhat virginal image was at odds with the flappers then fashionable, she wielded considerable power, choosing directors and movies carefully. King Vidor's *La Bohème* (1926) and two films for Victor Sjöström (*The Scarlet Letter*, 1926; *The Wind*, 1928) saw her at the peak of her powers. But with the advent of the talkies, in a world where (onscreen, at least) modern women were often seen as seductresses or fighters in pursuit of men's power, the Gish persona seemed slightly old-fashioned, and she effectively retired from film to work in theater. Occasionally, she would return to deliver a characteristically subtle performance, as in *The Night of the Hunter* (1955), in which her maiden godmother character is invested—without a drop of maudlin sentiment—with all the pure, sturdily down-to-earth goodness one suspects could be found in Gish in real life. **GA**

ABOVE: Gish looks prim and uncomfortable as Letty Mason Hightower in *The Wind*.

Griffith and Gish

Lillian Gish had an intimate working relationship with director D. W. Griffith and went on to star in many of his movies. It has also been alleged that the pair were romantically involved for a time. Despite Griffith's clear infatuation with young Lillian, he initially found it hard to distinguish between the Gish sisters, assuming they were twins. In Lillian and Dorothy's first movie for Biograph Studios, *An Unseen Enemy* (1912), Griffith apparently made the girls sport different colored hair ribbons—one red, one blue—so that he could easily tell one sister from the other and direct accordingly.

EDWARD G. ROBINSON

Born: Emanuel Goldenberg, December 12, 1893 (Bucharest, Romania); died 1973 (Hollywood, California, U.S.).

Star qualities: In the right place at the right time; his looks and voice made him ideal in gangster roles; versatile with a comic talent.

Edward G. Robinson emigrated from Romania to the United States when he was ten, having grown up in a Yiddish community. He first appeared on the New York stage in 1913 and had a successful theatrical career until 1931, when he became an overnight hit in movies with his portrayal of the gangster Rico Bandello in *Little Caesar*. Robinson's diminutive frame, dynamic movement, and rasping voice created a movie icon, his performance so mesmerizing that his mannerisms soon became a stereotype for screen gangsters. His rapid-fire verbal delivery was ideal for the new medium of talking pictures. A series of roles as gangsters and other low-life characters followed. In some of these, Robinson parodies his screen personality. Thus, in *The Little Giant* (1933) he is a gangster put out of work by the repeal of Prohibition who tries to break into polite society. In *The Whole Town's Talking* (1935) Robinson has a dual role as a tough gangster on the run and as a respectable citizen who is his double. *A Slight Case of Murder* (1938), *Brother Orchid* (1940)—in which Robinson is a gangster hiding out in a monastery—and *Larceny, Inc.* (1942) also show Robinson playing a crook for laughs.

Top Takes...

Soylent Green 1973
Song of Norway 1970
Mackenna's Gold 1969
Never a Dull Moment 1968
All About People 1967
The Cincinnati Kid 1965
The Outrage 1964
Two Weeks in Another Town 1962
The Ten Commandments 1956
Key Largo 1948
The Stranger 1946
Scarlet Street 1945
The Woman in the Window 1944
Double Indemnity 1944
Flesh and Fantasy 1943
Larceny, Inc. 1942
The Sea Wolf 1941
A Dispatch from Reuter's 1940
Brother Orchid 1940
Dr. Ehrlich's Magic Bullet 1940
A Slight Case of Murder 1938
The Whole Town's Talking 1935
The Little Giant 1933
Little Caesar 1931
The Bright Shawl 1923

RIGHT: Robinson and Steve McQueen battle it out for poker glory in *The Cincinnati Kid*.

A pair of biopics in 1940 (*Dr. Ehrlich's Magic Bullet*; *A Dispatch from Reuter's*) showed that Robinson could do serious drama too. But his best work was still to come. In Billy Wilder's film noir, *Double Indemnity* (1944), he plays Barton Keyes, a wily insurance investigator on the track of temptress Barbara Stanwyck. A brace of films for Fritz Lang followed. In *The Woman in the Window* (1944) he plays a mild-mannered professor who dreams he has fallen into the clutches of another femme fatale, this time Joan Bennett. *Scarlet Street* (1945) has a similar plot, with Robinson as a hen-pecked clerk who is milked by fraudsters. In these later roles, Robinson was able to draw on his sensitive offscreen self, as he was a cultured man with an impressive art collection. Robinson reprised his gangster role in *Key Largo* (1948), in which he spars with Humphrey Bogart. After that his most memorable appearances came in cameo roles, before his death in 1973. **EB**

ABOVE: Robinson found stardom as the gun-wielding title character in *Little Caesar*.

An Avid Collector

Cultured offscreen, Robinson had a huge passion for collecting art—as well as cigar bands and cigarette cards:

- "No cigar anywhere was safe from me. My father and uncles and all their friends turned their lungs black trying to satisfy my collector's zeal."

- He was devastated in 1956 when he had to sell his art collection to help settle his divorce from first wife, Gladys Lloyd.

- "I have not collected art. Art collected me. I never found paintings. They found me. I have never even owned a work of art. They owned me."

JACK BENNY

Born: Benjamin Kubelsky, February 14, 1894 (Chicago, Illinois, U.S.); died 1974 (Los Angeles, California, U.S.).

Star qualities: Stand-up comedian with superb comic timing; self-effacing humor; mocking manner; master of the running gag; violinist; producer.

Top Takes…

A Guide for the Married Man 1967
The Horn Blows at Midnight 1945
The Meanest Man in the World 1943
To Be or Not to Be 1942
Charley's Aunt 1941
Love Thy Neighbor 1940
Buck Benny Rides Again 1940
Man About Town 1939
Artists and Models Abroad 1938
Artists & Models 1937
College Holiday 1936
The Big Broadcast of 1937 1936
It's in the Air 1935
Broadway Melody of 1936 1935
The Medicine Man 1930
Chasing Rainbows 1930

The perennial thirty-nine-year-old, Jack Benny was a radio, TV, and movie star known for his self-effacing humor, mocking manner, and unparalleled ability to mangle a violin. By the time of his screen debut, as the master of ceremonies in *The Hollywood Review of 1929* (1929), Benny had spent years performing in vaudeville and nightclubs. He started learning the violin at the age of six. Despite his painful but comic attempts to master the instrument onstage, he was in reality an accomplished player. His screen persona possessed inverse traits to the real Jack Benny, who was a modest individual. In 1932, Benny made his radio debut with NBC's weekly show *The Jack Benny Program,* which ran for 16 years. A deal with Paramount Pictures brought the musical comedies *College Holiday* (1936), *Artists & Models* (1937), and *Man About Town* (1939). Later films such as *Buck Benny Rides Again* (1940) capitalized on his radio persona with Benny playing himself.

Benny's best and most praised onscreen role was as a vain actor pitted against Nazis in Ernst Lubitsch's satire *To Be or Not to Be* (1942). Following the disappointment of *The Horn Blows at Midnight* (1945), Benny focused on radio and TV work. His radio show transferred to CBS in 1948 and ran for seven years. He also started a TV version of *The Jack Benny Program* in 1950; it ran until 1965. Benny continued to do cameo parts in film, and even lent his voice to cartoons. He was preparing to star in the adaptation of *The Sunshine Boys* (1975) before his death in 1974. His role was filled by his good friend George Burns. In his will, Benny stipulated that flowers be delivered to his widow, Mary Livingstone, every day for the rest of her life, and she duly received a rose daily until she passed away six years later. **WW**

"I don't care *who* gets the laughs on my show, as long as the *show* is funny."

WALTER BRENNAN

Born: Walter Andrew Brennan, July 25, 1894 (Swampscott, Massachusetts, U.S.); died 1974 (Oxnard, California, U.S.).

Star qualities: Singer; king of character parts; sidekick extraordinaire; stuntman; slight build; grunting voice; toothless; the old-timer cowboy in Westerns.

If Walter Brennan's real estate business had been successful, the big screen may have been deprived of his talent. He made a fortune in Los Angeles real estate after World War I, then lost it when the stock market took a sudden plunge; he moved into doing stints as a movie extra, stuntman, and in bit-part roles to raise money. He claimed to have two styles of acting: "Teeth in and teeth out." After the age of thirty-eight, when he lost most of his teeth in an accident, he specialized in coots whose character names tended to include "Old," "Old Man," "Pa," or "Grandpa," memorably as Old Atrocity in *Barbary Coast* (1935).

Dental misfortune elevated Brennan from unbilled bit roles such as a neighbor in *Bride of Frankenstein* (1935) to character superstardom as a three-time winner of the Oscar for Best Supporting Actor, the first as Swedish logger Swan Bostrom in *Come and Get It* (1936). He remains the only person to have won the Best Supporting Actor Academy Award three times. For Howard Hawks, he was an ideal eccentric sidekick: to Humphrey Bogart in *To Have and Have Not* (1944), in which his signature line was "Wuz you ever stung by a dead bee?" and to John Wayne in *Red River* (1948) and *Rio Bravo* (1959). Most happily cast in Westerns, he varied his run of comical tagalongs with the occasional villain, roguish as Judge Roy Bean—"And that's m'rulin'!"— in *The Westerner* (1940), or cold-eyed as Old Man Clanton in *My Darling Clementine* (1946). In later life, he had four top 100 singles, including "Old Rivers" (1962). He also made appearances in TV series such as *Alias Smith and Jones*, and was a genial presence in old-timer reunion efforts such as the *Over-the-Hill Gang* TV movies. Walter Brennan died in 1974, leaving a wife of 54 years, three children, and the legacy of five decades of screen performances. **KN**

Top Takes...

Smoke in the Wind 1975
Support Your Local Sheriff! 1969
Rio Bravo 1959
Bad Day at Black Rock 1955
Red River 1948
My Darling Clementine 1946
To Have and Have Not 1944
The Pride of the Yankees 1942
Sergeant York 1941 ☆
The Westerner 1940 ★
Kentucky 1938 ★
Come and Get It 1936 ★
Fury 1936
These Three 1936
Barbary Coast 1935
Bride of Frankenstein 1935

"Don't spill none of that liquor, son. It eats right into the bar."
—Judge Roy W. Bean, *The Westerner*

POLA NEGRI

Born: Barbara Apolonia Chalupiec, December 31, 1894 (Lipno, Poland); died 1987 (San Antonio, Texas, U.S.).

Star qualities: Petite, dark-haired sex symbol; silent-screen vamp; glamorous; trained in ballet; singer; comic timing; famed for femme fatale roles in melodramas.

Top Takes…

The Moon-Spinners 1964
Hi Diddle Diddle 1943
Madame Bovary 1937
Mazurka 1935
The Way of Lost Souls 1929
The Woman from Moscow 1928
Loves of an Actress 1928
The Secret Hour 1928
The Woman on Trial 1927
Barbed Wire 1927
The Cheat 1923
Bella Donna 1923
The Spanish Dancer 1923
Madame DuBarry 1919 (Passion)
Studenci 1916 (Students)
Bestia 1915 (Beast)

"I don't care whether I am beautiful or not. I want a chance to act."

The ongoing tradition of bringing European stars to Hollywood began with Pola Negri. Born in Poland, she became a star in German films shortly before the end of World War I. Her international reputation was consolidated by a number of movies for director Ernst Lubitsch, most notably *Madame DuBarry* (1919), which had stormed Britain and the United States under the new title *Passion*. As a result, both Negri and Lubitsch were offered, and accepted, Hollywood contracts.

But from the first, Negri's work was overshadowed by her tabloid celebrity, and indulgent behavior: she announced her engagement to Charlie Chaplin apparently without consulting him first (they never wed); collapsed with grief at the funeral of her lover Rudolph Valentino; and on the rebound from the latter, married her second husband, Serge Mdivani, in 1927. Through an accident of timing she had arrived in Hollywood when the vamp was giving way to the flapper, and was ill-equipped to play the latter. Soon Greta Garbo, a much more successful attempt at the same experiment, would establish the enigmatic goddess as a Hollywood archetype, but Negri was stately and grandiose without being terribly mysterious. The final blow, as for so many, was the arrival of sound, which limited her range still further given that she had a thick Polish accent. She worked briefly in Britain and France before returning to Germany in the early 1930s to renewed success. She made movies under the Nazi-managed Universum Film AG, but decided to flee the regime in 1938 and returned to the United States three years later. She made *Hi Diddle Diddle* (1943) before going into retirement for 20 years. Walt Disney persuaded her back on to the big screen for her last film, *The Moon-Spinners* (1964). **MC**

RUDOLPH VALENTINO

Born: Rodolfo di Valentina d'Antonguolla, May 6, 1895 (Castellaneta, Italy); died 1926 (New York City, New York, U.S.).

Star qualities: "The Great Latin Lover"; exotic good looks; excelled at playing stylish villains and reluctant heroes; turbulent private life; poet; cinema's first real celebrity.

The story of the life, career, and death of Rudolph Valentino, the first real male sex symbol in movie history, is filled with legends, anecdotes, and mysteries. Some of these are merely trivial (like the rumor about his supposed relationship with screenwriter June Mathis, in whose tomb he lies buried between her and her husband), some are revealing (like the story of his spoiled youth, or the suggestion that he was gay), some puzzling (like the tale of the woman dressed in black who came to lay flowers on his grave every year), but together they show exactly what an impact Valentino had—and still has—on the public imagination.

With his smoldering, brooding, Mediterranean looks and his piercing stare and seductive posture, he was the first male star to acquire a true legion of fans. That following, and the fact that he got married (and divorced) twice within a few years, was convicted of bigamy, and had an on-off affair with Pola Negri, fueled a continuous stream of speculation about his tempestuous private life, including accusations that he was too "effeminate," a devotee of the occult, and a drug addict.

Top Takes...

The Son of the Sheik 1926
Cobra 1925
The Eagle 1925
A Sainted Devil 1924
Monsieur Beaucaire 1924
The Hooded Falcon 1924
The Young Rajah 1922
Blood and Sand 1922
Beyond the Rocks 1922
The Sheik 1921
Camille 1921
The Conquering Power 1921
Uncharted Seas 1921
The Four Horsemen of the Apocalypse 1921
Stolen Moments 1920
Once to Every Woman 1920
Passion's Playground 1920
An Adventuress 1920
Eyes of Youth 1919
Nobody Home 1919
A Rogue's Romance 1919
Virtuous Sinners 1919
The Homebreaker 1919
The Married Virgin 1918
A Society Sensation 1918

LEFT: Valentino is the epitome of Latin lothario in this profile shot from 1923.

Tributes to The Sheik

Since his death in 1926, Rudolph Valentino has remained something of an enigma. Rumors abound, and several versions of his life story have been filmed—most famously, Ken Russell's *Valentino* (1977). Here are a few examples of his intriguing (and sometimes amusing) legacy:

- For several years, his grave was visited on the anniversary of his death by a mysterious woman dressed in black, who laid flowers on his grave. After much speculation, the woman was revealed as someone Valentino had visited when she was ill as a girl. The pair had made a pact that whoever lived longer would pay tribute to the other. Since then, there have been several Women in Black.

- It has been said that the body in the open casket at Valentino's funeral was really a wax imitation of the star. His family was apparently concerned that his body would be mauled by the adoring public.

- Valentino was an aspiring poet, and published the sentimental volume *Day Dreams* in 1923. It was immensely popular among his admirers and sold thousands of copies.

- "Sheik" condoms were introduced in the 1930s, in homage to his most famous role. Valentino's silhouette was featured on the packaging for years.

1890s

But Valentino's offscreen reputation should not overshadow his professional achievements. The son of a traveling circus performer turned veterinarian, Valentino was thrown out of several schools and a prominent military academy before completing a course in the science of farming at agricultural college. After a yearlong stint in Paris, at the age of eighteen he moved to the United States, where he had a wide range of jobs, including those of tango dancer, gigolo, and petty thief. Valentino gradually moved into acting, first with small bits, then bigger parts, usually portraying the villain. His appearance in *Stolen Moments* (1920) shows that he played such parts with verve; in fact, he made villains stylish. He married Jean Acker, another aspiring actor, around this time. Although the couple were not divorced until 1923 (by which time Valentino had already lined up his second wife, Natacha Rambova), the marriage reportedly lasted no more than six hours.

From scoundrel to sheik

Rudolph Valentino got his big break with *The Four Horsemen of the Apocalypse* (1921), an antiwar movie by Rex Ingram and June Mathis, who insisted Valentino be offered the lead role. The movie was so successful that it is still considered the best-grossing silent film ever. It made Valentino a huge star and worldwide heartthrob overnight. But Valentino's accomplishment in this picture lies not just in his magnetic sex appeal. It also lies in his smooth, flawless transition from an initially hedonistic, lazy character (who dances a devilish tango) to a responsible, somewhat reluctant hero.

Reluctance and moral ambiguity (and indeed sexual ambivalence) became trademarks for Valentino's further career. Both men and women fell for his seductive charms, and swooning in public became commonplace—in line with sexual liberation and the newly established flapper movement of the 1920s. *The Sheik* (1921), which started a fad for Arabic fashion, *Camille* (1921), *Blood and Sand* (1922), *The Young Rajah* (1922), *The Eagle* (1925), and *The Son of the Sheik* (1926) were films flavored with exotic tones in which he could relish playing a

(usually foreign) seducer. *Blood and Sand*, another June Mathis screenplay, was the first of four onscreen partnerships with Nita Naldi, along with *A Sainted Devil* (1924), *The Hooded Falcon* (1924) (unfinished), and *Cobra* (1925). In 1926, a writer from *The Chicago Tribune* labeled Valentino a "pink powder puff." Valentino responded in manly fashion, challenging the author of the piece to a boxing match. The match never took place.

ABOVE: Valentino and Vilma Bankey sport Arabic fashion with flair in *The Son of the Sheik.*

Valentino did not get much chance to enjoy his fame. He died suddenly, at the age of thirty-one, because of complications from a perforated ulcer (perhaps the result of drugs). It is a testimony to his popularity that, after his death was announced, several fans committed suicide and riots broke out at his funeral, which was attended by almost 100,000 fans and mourners—cinema's first celebrity death. **EM**

"To generalize on women is dangerous. To specialize in them is infinitely worse."

HATTIE McDANIEL

Born: Hattie McDaniel, June 10, 1895 (Wichita, Kansas, U.S.); died 1952 (Los Angeles, California, U.S.).

Star qualities: "Hi-Hat Hattie"; plump big-band vocalist; songwriter; radio performer; pioneering black actress; comic timing; famed for mammy-maid roles.

1890s

Top Takes…

Between her uncredited debut in 1932 and her final role in 1949, Hattie McDaniel made a total of 94 screen appearances, the overwhelming majority of them as cooks or maids. Her father was born into slavery and later became a Baptist preacher; her mother was a singer. The youngest of 13 children, McDaniel abandoned her schooling and started her career touring with the family's minstrel group. She got her big break when she joined George Morrison's band, Melody Hounds, and went on to become a radio singer. She later headed for Hollywood and started to get bit parts in movies.

She became the first black actress to win an Oscar—for Best Supporting Actress—in perhaps the most famous maid role of all time: Mammy in *Gone with the Wind* (1939). She was the first African-American to attend the Academy Awards as a guest, not a servant. Sadly, the honor, which she accepted with poignant gratitude, did not lead to the widening of opportunities that it should have done, and she continued in bit parts for the rest of her film career.

In response to criticism from the black community, McDaniel justified these subordinate roles by explaining that the choice was either to play a servant or be one. Yet her maids do have their own style, often displaying sharp-tongued familiarity with their employers. This characteristic is seen to best effect in *Alice Adams* (1935), in which she serves dinner while keeping up a running commentary of observations and grumbles. Her final years were spent successfully in radio and TV as the eponymous Beulah (1950–1953); another maid but, surprisingly, the lead role, and a big hit with audiences. It was during the run of these shows that she was diagnosed with the cancer that claimed her in 1952. **MC**

> "Why should I complain about making $700 a week playing a maid?"

GEORGE RAFT

Born: George Ranft, September 26, 1895 (New York City, New York, U.S.); died 1980 (Los Angeles, California, U.S.).

Star qualities: Deft dancer; ladies' man; sharp dresser; played the tough guy and the hood; gangster lifestyle; turned down some golden opportunities.

George Raft was a boxer and a dancer with a few gangster friends, and made a credible hood in *Scarface* (1932), where he perfected that coin-tossing trick. He grew up poor in New York's "Hell's Kitchen" neighborhood, and his association with mobsters added credibility to the villains, convicts, and private eyes he frequently played. Such were his criminal connections that he was prohibited from entering the United Kingdom in 1966, and is said to have used his influence to stop a Mafia plan to murder the then president of the Screen Actors Guild, James Cagney. If he now seems foolish for turning down *The Maltese Falcon* (1941) and *Double Indemnity* (1944), consider that he was big enough to be offered the roles Humphrey Bogart and Fred MacMurray made their own. He played himself in *Broadway* (1942) and lived to see the sharper-faced Ray Danton star in *The George Raft Story* (1961)—he sold the rights to his life story because he had financial problems.

Raft appears, often as a second lead, in some excellent Warner Brothers crime films, such as *The Glass Key* (1935) and *Johnny Allegro* (1949). But he was rarely more than a sleek, dead-eyed presence, unhappy playing hoods but unconvincing as a straight-arrow hero in the likes of *Background to Danger* (1943) or *Nocturne* (1946). The caliber and box-office success of these films were not consistent with the celebrity status Raft enjoyed in Hollywood, alongside the likes of Cagney and Edward G. Robinson. He spoofs his old movies as Spats Colombo in *Some Like It Hot* (1959), snatching a tossed coin from a minion and snarling, "Where did you get that cheap trick?" After that, he was in hits such as *Ocean's Eleven* (1960) and *Casino Royale* (1967) as characters hurried offscreen before audiences put a name to the face. **KN**

Top Takes...

The Man with Bogart's Face 1980
Skidoo 1968
Silent Treatment 1968
Casino Royale 1967
Ocean's Eleven 1960
Some Like It Hot 1959
Johnny Allegro 1949
Nocturne 1946
Background to Danger 1943
Manpower 1941
They Drive by Night 1940
Each Dawn I Die 1939
The Glass Key 1935
Bolero 1934
If I Had a Million 1932
Scarface 1932

"Part of it went on gambling, and part of it went on women. The rest I spent foolishly."

BUD ABBOTT AND LOU COSTELLO

Abbott: Born October 2, 1895; died 1974 (Los Angeles, California, U.S.).
Costello: Born March 6, 1906; died 1959 (Los Angeles, California, U.S.).

Star qualities: "Who's on First?" routine; burlesque entertainers; one straight man, one clown; one short and dumpy, one tall and slender.

Top Takes...

Abbott and Costello Meet the Mummy 1955
Abbott and Costello Meet the Invisible Man 1951
Bud Abbott Lou Costello Meet Frankenstein 1948
The Noose Hangs High 1948
Buck Privates Come Home 1947
The Time of Their Lives 1946
Bud Abbott and Lou Costello in Hollywood 1945
Here Come the Co-Eds 1945
Lost in a Harem 1944
In Society 1944
Ride 'Em Cowboy 1942
Keep 'Em Flying 1941
Hold That Ghost 1941
In the Navy 1941
Buck Privates 1941
One Night in the Tropics 1940

"Comics are a dime a dozen. Good straight men are hard to find."—Lou Costello

"Who's on First?" is one of the immortal comedy sketches, not least because it depends on a straight man with all the answers and a dumbfounded hinge, the doofus who can't see through the semantics built right into the question. For "What" is on second, "I Don't Know" is on third, "Today" is catching, and "Tomorrow" is pitching. When performed with particular attention to delivery, the scene is magic. Such is the case with Bud Abbott and Lou Costello, two comedians from New Jersey who teamed up and made movie history with one of the most successful vaudeville-to-cineplex transitions ever.

William Alexander Abbott, the straight man and the taller of the two, worked his way around the country managing various theaters from the end of his teens until 1931. In that year, he first partnered with Costello (born Louis Francis Cristillo), the pudgy clown who had spent the 1920s trying to break into movies. Together they worked any venue they could schedule. The Abbott and Costello partnership became official in 1936, and two years later they were featured on the *Kate Smith Hour* radio show, entertaining a national audience. Following this success, the pair signed with Universal Studios, making their debut in *One Night in the Tropics* (1940). Unexpectedly popular, they costarred the next year in *Buck Privates*, a box-office record breaker, and began broadcasting a radio show. Throughout the war years their jovial mix of physical humor, pratfalls, jokes, and situational bits exactly fit the national appetite. After the war, their films began featuring the stock-in-trade of studio monsters in a series of ever more inventive horror comedies and far-flung adventures. By 1957 the partnership was over and both men were struggling with debts. The Abbott and Costello magic had gone. **GCQ**

BUSTER KEATON

Born: Joseph Frank Keaton VI, October 4, 1895 (Piqua, Kansas, U.S.); died 1966 (Los Angeles, California, U.S.).

Star qualities: "The Great Stone Face"; specialized in vaudeville and physical comedy; performed his own stunts; poker face; flat hat and slapshoes.

Buster Keaton is a giant of the cinema. An odd description, perhaps, for a fairly short man renowned for a minimalist acting style—he used to be known as "The Great Stone Face"—and for his attention to details of authenticity; a man, moreover, who "only" worked in comedy. But Keaton knew comedy was a serious business, and applied himself to it with such dedication, imagination, and expertise that he became one of the greatest artists in the history of film.

Keaton's parents were in vaudeville, and he joined their act as a three-year-old, quickly acquiring the strength and skills of an acrobat that would later stand him in good stead when he performed his own stunts in his movies. Ever the daredevil, he even fractured his neck during one filming session, but the damage was not discovered until a routine physical examination years later. In 1917 Keaton began acting in shorts starring Roscoe "Fatty" Arbuckle. Soon, he was devising many of the gags, and in 1919 he took to directing his own two-reelers. The comic invention was extraordinary, not only for the speed and frequency of gags but for its cinematic

Top Takes...

It's a Mad Mad Mad Mad World 1963
The Triumph of Lester Snapwell 1963
The Adventures of Huckleberry Finn 1960
Around the World in Eighty Days 1956
Limelight 1952
Paradise for Buster 1952
The Misadventures of Buster Keaton 1950
Grand Slam Opera 1936
Spite Marriage 1929
The Cameraman 1928
Steamboat Bill, Jr. 1928
College 1927
The General 1927
Battling Butler 1926
Go West 1925
Seven Chances 1925
The Navigator 1924
Sherlock Jr. 1924
Our Hospitality 1923
Three Ages 1923
Cops 1922
The Boat 1921
One Week 1920
The Garage 1919
The Butcher Boy 1917

LEFT: Keaton is poker-faced for good reason as he suffers on board *The Love Nest*.

Becoming Buster

How did Joseph Frank Keaton VI become "Buster"? The true origins of the nickname are unknown, but here are a few theories:

- Renowned magician Harry Houdini performed in a number of shows with the Keaton family act, which was reputed to be one of the riskiest in vaudeville. Joe Keaton, Buster's father, would demonstate how to discipline a troublesome child by throwing Buster all over the stage, into the orchestra pit, and even into the audience. Buster proved to be a resilient little fellow. One day, before a show, Houdini watched in astonishment as 18-month-old Joseph tripped and tumbled down an entire flight of stairs, rising at the bottom, unharmed. Houdini remarked to the boy's mother, "Some Buster!" and the nickname stuck. There is no recorded evidence that Houdini was the culprit; it is not even known whether he was touring with the Keatons at the time. But nothing disproves the story either.

- Joe Keaton witnessed the same incident and christened his son "Buster" in honor of his remarkable robustness.

- Buster's father made the whole thing up as a good story to tell onstage.

- It seems that everyone wanted to take responsibility for coming up with the moniker. Even the Kansas midwife who delivered Buster claimed to have named him thus on the day he was born!

sophistication. Keaton was not a director simply to record slapstick pratfalls with a static camera; rather, the comedy derived from character, place, situation, and story, and he used composition, camera movement, and cutting not merely to capture meaning and humor but to explore and enhance them. Hence, even a short as early as *One Week* (1920) is a small masterpiece, and typifies Keaton's fascination with the ordinary man confronted by seemingly hostile forces beyond his control: in this case, a build-it-yourself house he tries to assemble notwithstanding raging winds, his own architectural failings, and the "help" offered by his wife.

Poker-faced but endlessly expressive

Even before he began making his own shorts, Keaton had stopped smiling onscreen. The stoic stare displayed his awareness that life was absurd, treacherous, perilous, and therefore no laughing matter; the only dignified and useful response was determined pragmatism. Not that Keaton's beautiful face wasn't expressive; on the contrary, his watchful eyes, like the graceful gestures and athletic movements of his wiry, supremely functional body, spoke volumes about his characters' inner lives. As he moved into features, the extra screen time allowed Keaton to add great depth and detail to the characters he played. Though *Three Ages* (1923) was merely a brilliant spoof of historical epics like D. W. Griffith's *Intolerance* (1916), the eleven features made over the next six years arguably represent the most fully sustained outpouring of creative genius the cinema has known: *Our Hospitality* (1923); *Sherlock Jr.* (1924); *Go West*; *Seven Chances* (both 1925); *Battling Butler* (1926); *College*; *The General* (both 1927); *Steamboat Bill, Jr.*; *The Cameraman* (both 1928); and *Spite Marriage* (1929).

Such was Keaton's directorial skill that the films succeed both as hilarious comedies and as tense dramas, superbly staged, lit, shot, and acted, and often emotionally and even philosophically profound. *Sherlock Jr.* reflects on its own status as a movie, with Buster menaced by the very editing; in *Steamboat Bill, Jr.*, a scene (played straight to camera with the

audience taking the place of a mirror) where he is made to try on various hats alludes to his own manufactured persona when he is horrified at seeing his familiar flat boater suddenly placed on his head. Modernist before the term was even coined, such moments never detract from the overall drama but confirm Keaton's intuitive fecundity.

ABOVE: Keaton uses the back projection technique to add drama to *The Cameraman*.

His career was ruined not by the arrival of sound but by bad management, marital troubles, and a drinking problem; the opportunities afforded him by the studios in the talkie era failed to allow for his haphazard but inspired methods of comic creation. Keaton's performances in talkies are saddening reminders of talent unrecognized and wasted; but the glorious treasure trove of silent masterpieces from the 1920s shines on, undimmed. **GA**

"The first thing I did in the studio was to want to tear that camera to pieces."

GEORGE BURNS

Born: Nathan Birnbaum, January 20, 1896 (New York City, New York, U.S.); died 1996 (Los Angeles, California, U.S.).

Star qualities: Radio star; stand-up comedian, singer, and dancer; comic prop cigar; deadpan delivery; the straight man in husband-and-wife double act.

Top Takes...

Radioland Murders 1994
18 Again! 1988
Oh, God! You Devil 1984
Going in Style 1979
Just You and Me, Kid 1979
Sgt. Pepper's Lonely Hearts Club Band 1978
Oh, God! 1977
The Sunshine Boys 1975 ★
College Swing 1938
A Damsel in Distress 1937
The Big Broadcast of 1937 1936
The Big Broadcast of 1936 1935
Six of a Kind 1934
International House 1933
The Big Broadcast 1932
Lambchops 1929

George Burns was an accomplished vaudevillian before moving to radio with his soon-to-be second wife, Gracie Allen, in one of the most successful radio situation comedies of all time, *The Burns and Allen Show*. Originally Burns played the comic part of the duo before he realized that his wife got more laughs and switched to become the straight man. The couple was seduced away from NBC to CBS in the late 1940s. CBS chairman William Paley saw the opportunity to adapt the show to television in 1950, and it ran until Allen's retirement in 1958 because of failing health. The marriage was believed to be one of the happiest in show business, and when Allen died in 1964, Burns was heartbroken. He visited her grave at the Forest Lawn Cemetery in Glendale, California, every month for the rest of his life. Burns spent the intervening ten years producing for television and performing in nightclubs with a variety of stars.

In 1974, Burns's best friend, Jack Benny, was slated to star in a film version of Neil Simon's *The Sunshine Boys* but was forced to pull out due to his own poor health. Burns reluctantly stepped into the role as vaudevillian Al Lewis. Although Burns had made several low-key film appearances in the 1930s, *The Sunshine Boys* marked a new epoch in his career, and he won an Oscar for Best Supporting Actor—age eighty at the time, he was the award's oldest recipient. This movie was followed by *Oh, God!* (1977), its two sequels in 1980 and 1984, and *Just You and Me, Kid* (1979), among others. Burns continued to work well into his nineties, arguing that, "The happiest people I know are the ones that are still working." His final film was *Radioland Murders* (1994). Despite booking himself to play the London Palladium for his one-hundredth birthday, ill health prevented him from performing. **MK**

> "We were the only couple on radio who got married because we had to."

BLANCHE SWEET

Born: Sarah Blanche Sweet, June 18, 1896 (Chicago, Illinois, U.S.); died 1986 (New York City, New York, U.S.).

Star qualities: Fair-haired beauty; oval face; petite; doe-eyed; popular leading lady of the silent era; "The Biograph Blonde"; known for her energetic roles.

Blanche Sweet came from a vaudeville and stock theater family, and was carried on to the stage to make her first appearance when she was just eighteen months old. She was a dancer by the time she was four, and went on to dance with the Gertrude Hoffman troupe, appearing with Chauncey Olcott on Broadway. She made her film debut for the pioneering Edison Studio in the silent, *A Man with Three Wives* (1909). At age fifteen, Sweet made a huge impression in D. W. Griffith's *The Lonedale Operator* (1911), single-handedly operating a remote railroad station and fending off bandits attempting to rob a money train, all in the space of 15 minutes. The film, a real milestone for Griffith in terms of formal innovation, established her as his first major star, and a rival to Mary Pickford. Pickford left Biograph Studios soon after as a result. Sweet remained hugely popular in such movies as *The Massacre* (1913) as a feisty frontier gal, and in the title role of the first U.S. feature, *Judith of Bethulia* (1914), her best-known picture and Griffith's finale at Biograph.

Lured to Famous Players-Lasky (later to be known as Paramount Pictures) by a large salary increase, Sweet worked for Cecil B. DeMille in *The Warrens of Virginia* (1915) and *The Captive* (1915), but the two did not get along, and her performances were considered inferior to her work for Griffith. Reappraisal is impeded by the fact that most of her Famous Players-Lasky films have been lost, but it is certainly true that her popularity began to decline at around this time. After more than 150 film appearances, she made three talkies before retiring from the screen in 1930. Most notable among the latter was Mervyn Le Roy's excellent *Show Girl in Hollywood* (1930), in which she gave a superb performance as a washed-up silent star. **MC**

Top Takes...

The Silver Horde 1930
Show Girl in Hollywood 1930
The Woman in White 1929
The Far Cry 1926
Bluebeard's Seven Wives 1925
Tess of the D'Urbervilles 1924
Anna Christie 1923
The Unpardonable Sin 1919
The Thousand-Dollar Husband 1916
Stolen Goods 1915
The Captive 1915
The Warrens of Virginia 1915
Judith of Bethulia 1914
A Woman Scorned 1911
The Lonedale Operator 1911
A Man with Three Wives 1909

"Miss Sweet is not only an attractive person, but possesses talent . . . ."—*New York Times*

RUTH GORDON

Born: Ruth Gordon Jones, October 30, 1896 (Quincy, Massachusetts, U.S.); died 1985 (Edgartown, Massachusetts, U.S.).

Star qualities: Petite; distinguished stage actress; prize-winning writer; prolific playwright; aptitude for portraying the eccentric, awkward, and zestful old lady.

The daughter of a sea captain, Ruth Gordon trained at the American Academy of Dramatic Arts in New York. After a brief foray as an extra in silent movies in 1915, she headed for Broadway and for the next 20 years performed on the stage in the United States and England. Gordon returned to the big screen in the 1940s, in roles such as Mrs. Lincoln in *Abe Lincoln in Illinois* (1940) and Mrs. Ehrlich in *Dr. Ehrlich's Magic Bullet* (1940). But she quit acting soon after to concentrate on writing in collaboration with her second husband, Garson Kanin. They worked with George Cukor, crafting scripts for *A Double Life* (1947), *Adam's Rib* (1949), *The Marrying Kind* (1952), *Pat and Mike* (1952), and *The Actress* (1953)—an autobiographical film based on Gordon's own life story. The couple won three Academy Award nominations for their screenplays, and the Spencer Tracy–Katharine Hepburn onscreen pairings were said to be inspired by their own marriage.

In later life, Gordon returned to acting, usually playing eccentric free spirits. It was then that she became a true movie star. After kooky cameos such as in *Inside Daisy Clover* (1965), she won an Oscar as the clucking Satanist neighbor in *Rosemary's Baby* (1968)—a role she reprised in a TV movie sequel, *Look What's Happened to Rosemary's Baby* (1976). She tangled testily with Geraldine Page in *What Ever Happened to Aunt Alice?* (1969), and had an iconic role in *Harold and Maude* (1971) as a young Bud Cort's eighty-year-old love interest. She worked steadily thereafter, as the most amiable murderer ever to bandy alibis with Peter Falk on *Columbo* (1977), winning an Emmy for a guest spot on the TV series *Taxi* (1979), and as a flapper to the last in *Maxie* (1985). Ruth Gordon died of a stroke in the same year. **KN**

Top Takes…

"All I wanted out of a career was to look like Hazel Dawn and wear pink feathers."

GLORIA SWANSON

Born: Gloria May Josephine Svensson, March 27, 1897 (Chicago, Illinois, U.S.); died 1983 (New York City, New York, U.S.).

Star qualities: Legendary petite beauty; the epitome of Hollywood glamour; silent-movie comedienne; dramatic lead of talkies dramas; sizzling screen presence.

Then was the silent era, and Gloria Swanson's face was one of Paramount Pictures' most valuable in the days when she and Cecil B. DeMille turned out such delicacies as *Don't Change Your Husband* (1919) and *Male and Female* (1919). She was an instinctive silent performer; her style has not dated, still seeming fresh and astonishingly naturalistic. And, of course, she was beautiful.

Neither onscreen, where she specialized in sophisticated modern comedies, nor in her life was there anything remotely tragic or unfulfilled about her. It is true that *Queen Kelly* (1929), that legendary, unfinished collaboration between Swanson and Erich von Stroheim—and byword for hubris and excess— made Hollywood wary, but her early sound films were not box-office disasters. Swanson anticipated, rather than acted upon, the public mood, and retired in the early 1930s a wealthy and independent woman.

Then there is Norma Desmond, the faded silent-movie star out to make a comeback. The tendency to confuse (or knowingly conflate) the two has slipped into orthodoxy, and in fairness *Sunset Blvd.* (1950) does everything it can to encourage it by casting DeMille and von Stroheim as her mentors and utilizing clips from *Queen Kelly*. It is a great performance in a great film, but the only thing Swanson and her screen character Desmond have in common is their triumphs. Swanson's later work was mostly on TV, but she returned to the big screen in the 1970s. Her swan song was *Airport 1975* (1974), in which she played herself. Offscreen, she was married six times; her name was also romantically linked with numerous men, including Rudolph Valentino, Cecil B. DeMille, and Kennedy clan patriarch Joseph P. Kennedy Sr. **MC**

Top Takes...

Airport 1975 1974
Three for Bedroom C 1952
Sunset Blvd. 1950 ☆
Father Takes a Wife 1941
Music in the Air 1934
The Trespasser 1929 ☆
Queen Kelly 1929
Sadie Thompson 1928 ☆
Manhandled 1924
Don't Tell Everything 1921
The Affairs of Anatol 1921
Male and Female 1919
Don't Change Your Husband 1919
The Pullman Bride 1917
Teddy at the Throttle 1917
Sweedie Goes to College 1915

"I have decided that when I am a star, I will be every inch and every moment a star."

THE THREE STOOGES

Moe Howard: Born Moses Horwitz, June 19, 1897 (Brooklyn, New York, U.S.); died 1975 (Los Angeles, California, U.S.).

Larry Fine: Born Louis Feinberg, October 5, 1902 (Philadelphia, Pennsylvania, U.S.); died 1975 (Woodland Hills, Los Angeles, California, U.S.).

Star qualities: Distinctive hairstyles; provocative slapstick; punching; eye poking; elaborate routines involving saws and explosives; interchangeable third Stooge.

Top Takes...

Spread out! From the moment they first trod the vaudeville boards in 1922 until the retirement of the last member in the early 1970s, The Three Stooges reigned as one of America's most popular and enduring comedy brand names. Theirs was an aggressive slapstick of punches, slaps, and jabs to the eye.

Over 50 years, the boys ridiculed all conceivable occupations: The Three Stooges as doctors! Cooks! Exterminators! Underneath this broad farce hid a subtler satire on employment, embedded in their personas. Stern taskmaster Moe, always delegating to his bumbling subordinates, was the CEO of the group (both onscreen and off); Larry was middle management, incapable of independent thought; the third Stooge was the worker and the comic focal point. It was this role that proved volatile, filled by many comedians over the years.

The story begins with Ted Healy (1896–1937), a top-billed vaudeville star given to exasperated reactions at the tomfoolery of others. Enter Moe Howard, his brother Shemp (Samuel Horwitz, 1895–1955), and Larry Fine, the original Stooges. Together they made one movie (*Soup to Nuts*, 1930) before

RIGHT: The Three Stooges sport typically bemused expressions and daft attire.

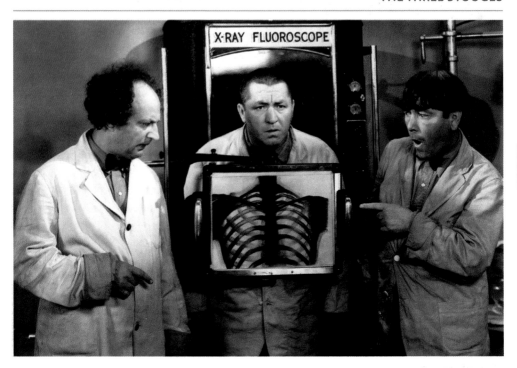

Shemp ceded his role to younger brother Curly (Jerome Horwitz, 1903–1952). Contract disputes separated the Stooges from Healy, and Moe, Larry, and Curly landed at Columbia Pictures, making short comedies at the pace of nine a year for a record-breaking 24 consecutive years. Curly had to retire in 1947 and Joe Besser (1907–1988) later filled in, but Columbia eventually stopped production on Stooge comedies in 1957.

The resurgent popularity of the Stooges shorts on TV opened up new opportunities for features, live appearances, and even a cartoon series. Portly comic Joe DeRita (1909–1993) replaced Besser, and continued the act after Larry's stroke and Moe's retirement in 1970. Few would argue that late-period work like *The Three Stooges Meet Hercules* (1962) holds a candle to early pioneering classics like the 1934 Oscar-nominated *Men in Black*, but one has to admire their perspicacious survival in the cutthroat world of show business. **DK**

ABOVE: Larry, Curly, and Moe look puzzled as fugitives in a hospital in *Dizzy Doctors*.

Slap Happy

The Stooges loved to hurt each other. Here are some of their favorite moves:

- Double Cheek Slap: Both cheeks were cracked simultaneously with two hands.
- Forehead Slap: Larry's receding hairline was the usual target—Moe would pat him affectionately before smacking him.
- Eye Poke: Moe perfected this trademark trick by landing his fingers just above the eyes, on the forehead.
- Nose Tweak: Moe's specialty, he would rapidly tweak the end of one of his fellow Stooges' noses. Looks painful!

FREDRIC MARCH

Born: Ernest Frederick McIntyre Bickel, August 30, 1897 (Racine, Wisconsin, U.S.); died 1975 (Los Angeles, California, U.S.).

Star qualities: Tall and handsome; revered star of stage and screen by contemporaries; career spanned vast range from leading man to character actor.

Top Takes...

The Iceman Cometh 1973
Hombre 1967
Seven Days in May 1964
The Desperate Hours 1955
Death of a Salesman 1951 ☆
The Best Years of Our Lives 1946 ★
The Buccaneer 1938
Nothing Sacred 1937
A Star Is Born 1937 ☆
The Barretts of Wimpole Street 1934
Death Takes a Holiday 1934
Dr. Jekyll and Mr. Hyde 1931 ★
The Royal Family of Broadway 1930 ☆
The Marriage Playground 1929
The Studio Murder Mystery 1929
The Wild Party 1929

Fredric March started out as a bank teller, but after a stint as an extra in silent movies set in New York City he turned to acting and Broadway. He would shift between the stage and the screen for most of his life. He first appeared in Hollywood movies in evening-suit roles such as in *The Wild Party* (1929); these were followed by a wicked John Barrymore impersonation in *The Studio Murder Mystery* (1929)—in which March's second wife, Florence Eldridge, costarred—and *The Royal Family of Broadway* (1930). He succeeded Barrymore in a remake of *Dr. Jekyll and Mr. Hyde* (1931), impossibly handsome as Henry Jekyll but showing range as the puckish brute Hyde, terrifying in intimate scenes with Miriam Hopkins. He won the first of two Academy Awards for Best Actor for this role.

March became no stranger to plaudits from contemporaries. Altogether he received five Oscar nominations, putting him alongside names such as Gary Cooper, Gregory Peck, and James Stewart. In 1946 he tied with José Ferrer for the very first Best Actor Tony Award for his role in *Years Ago*, becoming the only actor ever to win the highest honors of stage and screen in a single year. Established as a leading man, March could ably play the romantic as Robert Browning in *The Barretts of Wimpole Street* (1934); the swashbuckling adventurer in *The Buccaneer* (1938); or the drunken actor as in *A Star Is Born* (1937). He matured into an impressive character actor: the returning sergeant in *The Best Years of Our Lives* (1946), Willy Loman in *Death of a Salesman* (1951), and the householder threatened by Humphrey Bogart in *The Desperate Hours* (1955). Following surgery for the prostate cancer that later killed him, March returned to film his swan song as a Eugene O'Neill barfly in *The Iceman Cometh* (1973). **KN**

"An actor has no more right to be temperamental than a bank clerk."

WALTER PIDGEON

Born: Walter Davis Pigeon, September 23, 1897 (Saint John, New Brunswick, Canada); died 1984 (Santa Monica, California, U.S.).

Star qualities: Singer; handsome; rich baritone voice; snappy dresser; a gentle gentleman; leading man in romantic dramas in his youth; character parts when old.

Walter Pidgeon was a long-serving leading man. Classically trained as a baritone singer at the New England Conservatory of Music in Boston, he opted for a career on the stage in plays and musicals before he went to Hollywood in 1926 to act in silent films, although he drifted back to New York to appear on the stage throughout his career. He worked steadily (he is in the 1927 and 1930 versions of *The Gorilla*); and was typically third-billed under the romantic leads, as in *Too Hot to Handle* (1938). He got to be a sleuth in two *Nick Carter* movies and might have settled for B-stardom, but playing the pastor Mr. Gruffydd in John Ford's *How Green Was My Valley* (1941) installed him as a leading man in important films in which he was usually overshadowed by a divalike costar. His films with Greer Garson—with whom he was almost a box-office team—brought him the most recognition, being nominated for the Academy Award for Best Actor for his performances in *Mrs. Miniver* (1942) and *Madame Curie* (1943). Nevertheless, the titles of their successful pairing emphasizing her role say it all.

After the flop of *The Miniver Story* (1950), Pidgeon was back to sleuthing in *Calling Bulldog Drummond* (1951) and had a run of good support roles in films such as *Funny Girl* (1968). A venture into science fiction found him unloosing "monsters from the id" as Dr. Edward Morbius in *Forbidden Planet* (1956) and as Admiral Harriman Nelson in *Voyage to the Bottom of the Sea* (1961). He never retired and, in the latter part of his career, was a frequent actor in TV dramas.

Offscreen, Pidgeon was influential as president of the Screen Actors Guild (1952–1956). His first wife died in childbirth in 1926, and he married his secretary, Ruth Walker, five years later. The couple were together until his death in 1984. **KN**

Top Takes…

Funny Girl 1968
Voyage to the Bottom of the Sea 1961
Forbidden Planet 1956
Executive Suite 1954
The Bad and the Beautiful 1952
Calling Bulldog Drummond 1951
That Forsyte Woman 1949
Mrs. Parkington 1944
Madame Curie 1943 ☆
Mrs. Miniver 1942 ☆
How Green Was My Valley 1941
Too Hot to Handle 1938
The Shopworn Angel 1938
The Girl of the Golden West 1938
Saratoga 1937
Mannequin 1926

"You didn't need to carry money. Your face was your credit card—all over the world."

RANDOLPH SCOTT

Born: George Randolph Scott, January 23, 1898 (Orange County, Virginia, U.S.); died 1987 (Los Angeles, California, U.S.).

Star qualities: Southern charm; soft-spoken; smart; handsome, with rugged cowboy looks; played the heroic good guy; producer.

Top Takes...

Ride the High Country 1962
Comanche Station 1960
Ride Lonesome 1959
Buchanan Rides Alone 1958
The Tall T 1957
Seven Men from Now 1956
The Bounty Hunter 1954
Pittsburgh 1942
The Spoilers 1942
My Favorite Wife 1940
Virginia City 1940
Rebecca of Sunnybrook Farm 1938
Follow the Fleet 1936
Roberta 1935
The Virginian 1929
The Far Call 1929

Randolph Scott always retained his well-mannered Southern charm, even though almost his entire screen career took place in the rugged world of the Western, together with his famous palomino horse, Stardust. Despite having a degree in textile engineering and manufacturing from the University of North Carolina, Scott chose to head for Hollywood and was hired as Gary Cooper's dialogue coach for *The Virginian* (1929), in which he also played a bit part. In the 1930s he acted in a series of routine Zane Grey adaptations, and then briefly and implausibly escaped into the world of Fred Astaire and Ginger Rogers musicals with *Roberta* (1935) and *Follow the Fleet* (1936).

After playing opposite his close friend—and, some even suggested, lover—Cary Grant in the comedy *My Favorite Wife* (1940) and in a couple of war movies, it was pretty much Westerns all the way until his last and perhaps best film, Sam Peckinpah's *Ride the High Country* (1962). In these later Westerns, Scott matures. Though still soft spoken and with impeccable manners, he projects a stoicism that often hides an inner grief. Nowhere is this seen to better effect than in the series of Westerns he made with director Budd Boetticher: *Seven Men from Now* (1956), *The Tall T* (1957), *Ride Lonesome* (1959), and *Comanche Station* (1960). In these films Scott is a loner, pitting his wits and values against a series of charming but unscrupulous villains, sadness etched on his handsome face. His popularity was such that he was billed above names such as John Wayne in *Pittsburgh* (1942) and Joel McCrea in *Ride the High Country*. Scott retired while on a high to enjoy the million-dollar proceeds of both his fame and some savvy investments. Religious in later life, he was a close friend of the Reverend Billy Graham. **EB**

"She stays here . . . we're packin' gold not petticoats."

—Gil Westrum, *Ride the High Country*

RIGHT: The gun-wielding, rugged Scott plays the role of cowboy to perfection.

TOTÒ

Born: Antonio Clemente, February 15, 1898 (Naples, Campania, Italy); died 1967 (Rome, Italy).

Star qualities: Crumpled face of a clown; superb comic timing; master of physical gesture; prolific output; poet and songwriter; the Italian everyman.

Top Takes...

Capriccio all'italiana 1968 (Caprice Italian Style)
Uccellacci e uccellini 1966
  (The Hawks and the Sparrows)
Totò d'Arabia 1964 (Totò of Arabia)
Totò e Cleopatra 1963 (Totò and Cleopatra)
Totò diabolicus 1962
Totò, Peppino e la dolce vita 1961
  (Totò, Peppino and La Dolce Vita)
Tototruffa '62 1961
I Tartassati 1959
Miseria e nobiltà 1954 (Poverty and Nobility)
Totò all'inferno 1954
Totò e le donne 1952 (Totò and the Women)
Totò Tarzan 1950
Totò le Moko 1949
Totò al giro d'Italia 1948

Although he was born the illegitimate son of an impoverished noble, it was not until 1946 that Totò was eventually given a title that recognized his noble birth, Antonio Griffo Focas Flavio Ducas Comneno Porfirogenito Gagliardi De Curtis di Bisanzio. He grew up poor in Naples and learned his craft performing *guitti*, in the tradition of the *commedia dell'arte*, before he moved to Rome to perform in the *avanspettacolo* musical revues. It was not until the late 1930s, after refining his comic talents, that Totò found fame through the medium of film.

His heavy-lidded eyes and melancholic face were suited to his own form of *commedia all'italiana*, playing as it did on his down-at-heel everyman persona. His iconic status and box-office draw was such that *Totò al giro d'Italia* (1948) was the first of more than 36 movies that bore his name in the title, most of which relied on his modern embodiment of the classic *Pulcinello* (Punch) and *Arlecchino* (Harlequin) characters that would typically see him use a combination of guile and wit to triumph over his bureaucratic and bullying adversaries.

Much of Totò's prolific output often played with conventions of classical literature or parodied hits of the day, such as *Totò all'inferno* (1954), *Totò Tarzan* (1950), and *Totò d'Arabia* (1964), (*Totò of Arabia*) and frequently saw him starring alongside Peppino De Filippo and Aldo Fabrizi. An accomplished poet and songwriter, he is as famous for writing the song "Malafemmena" ("The Bad Girl") about his love/hate relationship with his first wife, as for his acting. Totò was rather more enamored with his second wife, Franca Faldini, whom he married in 1954. Posthumously, Totò's reputation with Italian critics has grown to match the appeal garnered during his lifetime that earned him the name *Il Principe* (The Prince). **RH**

" Totò especially is beguiling, a lovely caricature of the Italian everyman . . . ."—*New York Times*

DOROTHY GISH

Born: Dorothy Elizabeth de Guiche, March 11, 1898 (Massillon, Ohio, U.S.); died 1968 (Rapallo, Liguria, Italy).

Star qualities: Petite, graceful comedienne with a lighthearted touch and a talent for pantomime; warmhearted charm and innocent good looks.

Had Dorothy Gish not been the sister of the finest actress in silent movies, her reputation would stand far higher. But she seems never to have resented Lillian's greater fame and dramatic status, and in her own right she was a superb natural comedienne. Lillian herself paid tribute to her sister's bubbly sense of fun—with a wry side-glance at her own serious image—when she observed, "When Dorothy arrives, the party begins. When I arrive it usually ends."

Like Lillian, Dorothy joined their mother's stage act, and started performing and modeling young to help support the family, given that their father had deserted them. Both started out in films following an introduction by actress Mary Pickford to Biograph Studios director D. W. Griffith (in Dorothy's case at age fourteen), and the sisters made several of their early movies together, although their adult teamings were rarer: in Griffith's *Hearts of the World* (1918), his *Orphans of the Storm* (1921), in which they touchingly played long-separated sisters, and in Henry King's *Romola* (1924).

Dorothy also starred in Lillian's sole movie as director, the comedy *Remodeling Her Husband* (1920). Once filming ended, she married her costar, James Rennie. The couple divorced in 1935. She played light comedy deftly and often, and could also carry period roles with elegance, as in the title role of *Nell Gwynne* (1926), the first of a run of films in England with Herbert Wilcox. Her last silent movie was as the title character in *Madame Pompadour* (1927). When sound arrived Gish found herself written off as a has-been; despite finding small parts in films, her movie stardom was essentially over, and she spent the rest of her career chiefly devoted to the stage. She died in 1968 at the age of seventy. **PK**

Top Takes...

The Cardinal 1963
Madame Pompadour 1927
Nell Gwynne 1926
Romola 1924
Orphans of the Storm 1921
Remodeling Her Husband 1920
The Hope Chest 1918
Battling Jane 1918
Hearts of the World 1918
Stage Struck 1917
The Little Yank 1917
Old Heidelberg 1915
The Saving Grace 1914
Judith of Bethulia 1914
The Musketeers of Pig Alley 1912
An Unseen Enemy 1912

"I thought comedians had to have black on their faces or red beards."

PAUL ROBESON

Born: Paul Bustill Robeson, April 9, 1898 (Princeton, New Jersey, U.S.); died 1976 (Philadelphia, Pennsylvania, U.S.).

Star qualities: Tall, handsome, charismatic, and extremely intelligent; multilingual; professional athlete; powerful bass-baritone voice; outspoken civil rights activist.

Top Takes...

Born to the Reverend William D. Robeson (an escaped slave) and Maria Louisa Bustill, Paul Robeson possessed seemingly infinite talents. He excelled as a scholar and athlete, graduating first from Rutgers University, and then later from Columbia University School of Law. After a stint as a professional football player, Robeson briefly embarked upon a career as an attorney.

But performing was Robeson's true passion, and he distinguished himself as a concert singer and as a Broadway star in productions of *The Emperor Jones* (1924) and *All God's Chillun Got Wings* (1924). In 1943, he starred in the first integrated presentation of Shakespeare's *Othello*. Robeson starred in 12 feature films, including a memorable turn in a dual role as fraudulent Reverend Isaiah T. Jenkins and his brother Sylvester in *Body and Soul* (1925). However, it is for his role as Joe in *Show Boat* (1936) that Robeson will forever be remembered. His rendition of "Ol' Man River" stands as one of the most famous musical performances in Hollywood history.

Robeson's warm persona won him numerous admirers, including Eleanor Roosevelt, Pablo Neruda, and Harry S. Truman. Increasingly active in politics, Robeson openly supported the fledgling Soviet Union, which awarded him the 1953 Stalin Peace Prize. As a Black Nationalist, he angrily chastised the U.S. government for its perpetuation of racism nationally, and its imperialist activities around the globe. This stance eventually found Robeson the target of anticommunists such as Senator Joseph McCarthy, who considered him a threat to national security and revoked his passport in 1950. The travel ban ended in 1958, but Robeson continued to be surrounded by controversy. He died revered as a hero by millions. **JM**

> "My weapons are peaceful, for it is only by peace that peace can be attained."

IRENE DUNNE

Born: Irene Marie Dunne, December 20, 1898 (Louisville, Kentucky, U.S.); died 1990 (Los Angeles, California, U.S.).

Star qualities: The "First Lady of Hollywood"; a Southern belle; singer; comic timing; shone in musicals; dramatic depth; inventive; glamorous; civic-minded.

One of the most luminous stars of the 1930s and 1940s, Irene Dunne emanated a sense of moral rectitude but never hesitated to draw upon a flair for the ridiculous. Both spheres of her personality are revealed in the delightful recital scene in *The Awful Truth* (1937), where she concludes an operatic solo with high-spirited laughter as she observes her partner, Cary Grant, fall to the floor from his chair.

She studied as well as taught music, failed an audition for the Metropolitan Opera Company, and then secured her reputation in the musical theater, specifically in the role of Magnolia Hawks in the touring company of *Show Boat*. Signed to RKO Pictures in 1930, she emoted vividly in some of the most tear-drenched women's movies of the day, including two classic loan-outs to Universal Studios: *Back Street* (1932) and *Magnificent Obsession* (1935). Dunne returned to her theatrical roots alongside Fred Astaire and Ginger Rogers in *Roberta* (1935), and in the second screen version of *Show Boat* (1936).

Her antic side took over in several successful screwball farces: *Theodora Goes Wild* (1936), *The Awful Truth* (1937), and *My Favorite Wife* (1940), once again alongside Cary Grant. The two tugged at the audience's heartstrings in *Penny Serenade* (1941), as she did with Charles Boyer in *Love Affair* (1939). In the 1940s, Dunne took on more maternal roles, and the air of rectitude increased in kind: *Anna and the King of Siam* (1946), *Life with Father* (1947), and *I Remember Mama* (1948), for which she received her fifth and final Academy Award nomination. Her last memorable role was as Queen Victoria in *The Mudlark* (1950). Two years later, she retired from movies and gave much of her time to political causes, notably as a U.S. delegate to the United Nations. **DS**

Top Takes...

The Mudlark 1950
***I Remember Mama* 1948** ☆
Life with Father 1947
Anna and the King of Siam 1946
Together Again 1944
Penny Serenade 1941
My Favorite Wife 1940
***Love Affair* 1939** ☆
***The Awful Truth* 1937** ☆
***Theodora Goes Wild* 1936** ☆
Show Boat 1936
Magnificent Obsession 1935
Roberta 1935
No Other Woman 1933
Back Street 1932
***Cimarron* 1931** ☆

"I don't know why the public took a liking to me so fast. Popularity is a curious thing."

FRED ASTAIRE

Born: Frederic Austerlitz Jr., May 10, 1899 (Omaha, Nebraska, U.S.); died 1987 (Los Angeles, California, U.S.).

Star qualities: Multitalented actor, singer, choreographer, and expert dancer; top hat and tails; legs insured for $1 million; a loyal, kind, and modest perfectionist.

Fred Astaire lived a long life in the movies dating back to the 1930s. Sure, he was a great hoofer and snappy dresser. Yes, he was suave, and it is clear that he could sing. Yet one small biographical fact of note usually escapes any summary attempt to shower accolades on his many song and dance routines and acting performances: he was made a widower in 1954, after 21 years of marriage to Phyllis Livingston Potter. Eventually he married Robyn Smith in 1980, but died seven years later.

Somehow this double tragedy—outliving one wife and dying in the care of another—suggests a man of unusual tendencies. Perhaps the point is too easily put, but Astaire seems to have been a loyal person in an industry that is anything but. In fact, polyamorous and cutthroat seem closer to the mark in Hollywood, so it is with a pause for decency that Astaire can be remembered—ever the kindly gentleman.

Astaire entered showbiz as a boy dancer. Partnered with his sister, Adele, until she retired in 1932, he moved to Hollywood, where he signed with RKO Pictures. The next year he was loaned to MGM for *Dancing Lady*, but returned to RKO for *Flying Down to Rio* (1933), his first movie with Ginger Rogers.

Top Takes...

Ghost Story 1981
The Towering Inferno 1974 ☆
Silk Stockings 1957
Funny Face 1957
The Band Wagon 1953
The Belle of New York 1952
Let's Dance 1950
Three Little Words 1950
The Barkleys of Broadway 1949
Easter Parade 1948
Blue Skies 1946
Yolanda and the Thief 1945
The Sky's the Limit 1943
Holiday Inn 1942
You'll Never Get Rich 1941
The Story of Vernon and Irene Castle 1939
Carefree 1938
A Damsel in Distress 1937
Shall We Dance 1937
Swing Time 1936
Follow the Fleet 1936
Top Hat 1935
Roberta 1935
The Gay Divorcee 1934
Flying Down to Rio 1933

RIGHT: Astaire has the ladies enthralled in his role as Steve Canfield in *Silk Stockings*.

1890s

ABOVE: Astaire and Ginger Rogers at the peak of their powers in *Swing Time*.

Reputed for his perfectionism and ability to choreograph dance for the camera, Astaire saw his career move into high gear in the mid-1930s with *Top Hat* (1935) and *Shall We Dance* (1937). The war years featured *Holiday Inn* (1942) and *The Sky's the Limit* (1943), but Astaire enjoyed a career resurgence in the postwar years due to new onscreen pairings: first with Judy Garland (*Easter Parade*, 1948), then Cyd Charisse (*The Band Wagon*, 1953), and finally Audrey Hepburn (*Funny Face*, 1957).

Astaire seemed to retire in the mid-1960s, making rare TV appearances (*Dr. Kildare*). By 1970 he was playing bittersweet characters aware of their age, as in *The Towering Inferno* (1974), earning an Oscar nomination, and *Ghost Story* (1981). In these final years, the little screen seemed somehow more suitable, and so it was that Generation X first discovered the old song-and-dance machine when Astaire appeared as Chameleon on the science fiction series *Battlestar Galactica* in 1979. **GCQ**

Fred and Ginger

Astaire made ten musicals with Ginger Rogers. Theirs was a popular and memorable partnership, and they are credited with revolutionizing the genre. Katharine Hepburn once quipped, "He gives her class and she gives him sex." Here are some of their best bits:

- "The Carioca" (*Flying Down to Rio*)—their first critically acclaimed performance.
- "Let's Call the Whole Thing Off" (*Shall We Dance*)—dancing on roller skates!
- "Cheek to Cheek" (*Top Hat*)—Ginger wore a gown coated in ostrich feathers for this number, which exasperated Fred.

CHARLES LAUGHTON

Born: July 1, 1899 (Scarborough, Yorkshire, England); died 1962 (Hollywood, California, U.S.).

Star qualities: Director, producer, teacher, and writer; innovative; tortured; flamboyant; antireligious; played offbeat, literary, and historical characters.

Top Takes...

Advise & Consent 1962
Spartacus 1960
Witness for the Prosecution 1957 ☆
The Strange Door 1951
The Suspect 1944
This Land Is Mine 1943
The Hunchback of Notre Dame 1939
Jamaica Inn 1939
I, Claudius 1937
Rembrandt 1936
Mutiny on the Bounty 1935 ☆
Ruggles of Red Gap 1935
The Private Life of Henry VIII 1933 ★
Island of Lost Souls 1933
The Sign of the Cross 1932
The Old Dark House 1932

"Hollywood is a goofy place ... If one weren't a little mad one wouldn't be there."

Charles Laughton had a very British education and officer training at the Jesuit school Stonyhurst College before serving in World War I. After the war, he trained as an actor at London's Royal Academy of Dramatic Art. He worked on the stage before making his film debut in 1932. He remains best known for his larger-than-life historical and literary characters: Nero in *The Sign of the Cross* (1932); the title character in *The Private Life of Henry VIII* (1933), which won him an Oscar; Captain Bligh in *Mutiny on the Bounty* (1935); *Rembrandt* (1936); Quasimodo in *The Hunchback of Notre Dame* (1939); and Sempronius Gracchus in *Spartacus* (1960). That said, while the flamboyance that marks these films may also be enjoyed in *Island of Lost Souls* (1933), *Jamaica Inn* (1939), which he also produced, and *Witness for the Prosecution* (1957), his more understated playing of ordinary mortals is often more satisfying: *Ruggles of Red Gap* (1935), *The Suspect* (1944), and *Advise & Consent* (1962) are arguably the finest performances of an actor who was tormented by his appearance and his secret homosexuality.

Despite his two Academy Award nominations for Best Actor and one Oscar win, Laughton's most enduring achievement is surely the single movie he is credited with directing, *The Night of the Hunter* (1955), a brilliant blend of dark Depression-era drama, lyrical fairy tale, and expressionist horror that remains unique in Hollywood history. He didn't act in it himself, but the performances he elicited from Robert Mitchum, Lillian Gish, Shelley Winters, and others are extraordinary. Laughton was able to capitalize on his experience as a stage director with a track record in Broadway productions such as George Bernard Shaw's *Don Juan in Hell* and Herman Wouk's *The Caine Mutiny Court-Martial.* **GA**

JAMES CAGNEY

Born: James Francis Cagney, July 17, 1899 (New York City, New York, U.S.); died 1986 (Stanfordville, New York, U.S.).

Star qualities: Versatile song and dance man; electrifying presence; staccato delivery; raspy voice; the diminutive king of gangster movies.

Notwithstanding countless impersonators sneering "You dirty rat!"—which he never said in a movie—James Cagney remains inimitable. No actor has ever seemed so electrifyingly energetic, be it in the jaunty, surprisingly delicate movements (he had been a vaudeville hoofer before being signed up by Warner Brothers); the snappy, rat-a-tat delivery of dialogue; or the mercurial intelligence evident in his clear, fiery, watchful Irish eyes. Liberal in his politics and happily married for 64 years, Cagney led a private life that was the antithesis of the hard-talking heavies he often portrayed.

Cagney's angular, amazingly kinetic expression of an insatiable lust for life brought a forceful amorality to the otherwise tepid *The Public Enemy* (1931), effectively helping to kick-start the gangster genre. Sadly, despite excellent performances in movies such as *The Crowd Roars* (1932) and *Ceiling Zero* (1935), this meant that he tended too often to be typecast in crime fare. While his work in *"G" Men* (1935), *Angels with Dirty Faces* (1938), *The Roaring Twenties* (1939), and especially *White Heat* (1949)—where his psychotic Cody Jarrett is like a force of nature—was supremely convincing throughout, it has overshadowed likewise superb performances in films as diverse as the musical dramas *Footlight Parade* (1933) and *Yankee Doodle Dandy* (1942)—for which he won an Oscar for Best Actor—the magical Shakespeare adaptation *A Midsummer Night's Dream* (1935)—where he was a wonderful Bottom—and the Cold War comedy *One, Two, Three* (1961). Far too lively an actor ever to mellow, he then retired to concentrate on painting and to live on his farm, appearing in only one more movie, *Ragtime* (1981), as a memorable, elderly but ruthless police chief. **GA**

Top Takes…

Ragtime 1981
One, Two, Three 1961
Man of a Thousand Faces 1957
***Love Me or Leave Me* 1955** ☆
White Heat 1949
***Yankee Doodle Dandy* 1942** ★
The Roaring Twenties 1939
***Angels with Dirty Faces* 1938** ☆
A Midsummer Night's Dream 1935
"G" Men 1935
Footlight Parade 1933
Hard to Handle 1933
The Crowd Roars 1932
The Millionaire 1931
The Public Enemy 1931
Sinners' Holiday 1930

"Never relax. If you relax, the audience relaxes. And always mean everything you say."

HUMPHREY BOGART

Born: Humphrey DeForest Bogart, December 25, 1899 (New York City, New York, U.S.); died 1957 (Hollywood, California, U.S.).

Star qualities: Legendary—the ultimate tough guy, the ultimate movie star who delivers the ultimate lines, the ultimate man; "Bogie"; trademark lisp.

Top Takes…

The Harder They Fall 1956
The Desperate Hours 1955
We're No Angels 1955
The Barefoot Contessa 1954
Sabrina 1954
The Caine Mutiny 1954 ☆
Beat the Devil 1953
The African Queen 1951 ★
Sirocco 1951
In a Lonely Place 1950
Knock on Any Door 1949
Key Largo 1948
The Treasure of the Sierra Madre 1948
The Big Sleep 1946
To Have and Have Not 1944
Passage to Marseille 1944
Sahara 1943
Casablanca 1942 ☆
The Maltese Falcon 1941
High Sierra 1941
They Drive by Night 1940
Dark Victory 1939
Angels with Dirty Faces 1938
Dead End 1937
The Petrified Forest 1936

RIGHT: Bogart and Peter Lorre look
mournful as captives in *Passage to Marseille*.

Humphrey Bogart is a legend. Several polls have named him the greatest movie star of all time, including the American Film Institute in 1999. It is a testament to Bogart's talents to note that, even by his own admission, most of his performances are unremarkable, yet he has endured.

Bogart made a handful of classic movies that will always be appreciated. If there is much mediocrity to sit through—and even if, as has been suggested by people such as director John Huston, the actor's career suffered from his own self-involved appropriation of the sharp-tongued, hell-raising, womanizing Bogart persona—there is undeniable magic onscreen. As satirized in numerous films and television programs, "Bogie"— the nickname given to him by his friend and fellow actor Spencer Tracy—is the man all other men aspire to be.

Born the son of a surgeon and a commercial illustrator, Bogart was nearly forty by the time he made an impact as an actor. Not a natural student, he was expelled from the prestigious Phillips Academy in 1918. He spent time in the Naval Reserve before straying into acting, attracted by

the nocturnal, glamorous lifestyle. After playing minor parts on Broadway, he moved to the big screen. His career throughout the 1930s was undistinguished, filled with more than 30 B-list features in which Bogart appeared as a variety of tough guys, gangsters, and stock roles in which he was not capable of excelling. Bogart complained that Warners was handing him the second-tier parts passed on by big stars like James Cagney.

ABOVE: Bogart looks suave as club owner Rick Blaine in the classic film, *Casablanca*.

There are exceptions during this period. *Dead End* (1937), *Angels with Dirty Faces* (1938), and *They Drive by Night* (1940) are memorable, but Bogart became a star with *High Sierra* (1941). The film's cowriter, John Huston, would again use Bogart well in *The Maltese Falcon* (1941). But the best was yet to come. *Casablanca* (1942) teamed Bogart with Ingrid Bergman in this beloved and iconic wartime romantic drama.

"Acting is like sex: you either do it and don't talk about it, or you talk about it and don't do it."

Bogart the Hell-raiser

"I never should have switched from scotch to martinis," were Humphrey Bogart's last words. Never one to turn down a drink, "Bogie" was a boisterous presence in Hollywood. Here are just a few examples of his troublemaking antics:

- After dining one night at the exclusive Beverly Hills restaurant Chasen's, Bogart and fellow diner Peter Lorre seized the restaurant's huge safe, rolled it on to the street, and left it there for all to see.

- He was often at Romanoff's in Beverly Hills, sporting inappropriately casual attire and poking fun at the owner.

- Bogart was candid about the movie industry, and was quick to criticize his fellow actors and directors. "If he isn't any good, why can't you say so?"

- A keen sailor, he named a boat "Sluggy" after his third wife, the hot-tempered Mayo Methot. The couple were dubbed "The Battling Bogarts" in the press.

- In 1950, Bogart paid a late-night visit to the El Morocco Club in New York with his friend Bill Seeman and two giant stuffed pandas. Bogart demanded a table for four, and introduced the pandas as their "dates." They were later thrown out after a fight. When asked, "Were you drunk?" Bogart replied, "Isn't everybody at three in the morning?"

- Bogart was the founder of the original "Rat Pack"—a Hollywood drinking club.

Bogart's charismatic performance as exiled American club owner Rick Blaine affirmed his place in movie history and gave him the opportunity to shine in a romantic lead role. His portrayal of a hardened, cynical man who still found room for love and a conscience showed that Bogart had depth as an actor and could play a tough guy struggling with a soft heart. The movie captured the mood of the moment and the emotional dilemmas faced by the public at the time. It also gave Bogart the opportunity to deliver some of the most famous lines ever written and that have been parodied ever since, including "Here's looking at you." Bogart himself is thought to have had a hand in this; it is not in the draft screenplays, and has been said to have risen out of the poker lessons Bogart gave Bergman between takes.

Life and love after *Casablanca*

But the two subsequent movies that brought Bogart together with director Howard Hawks and Bogart's real-life love Lauren Bacall, *To Have and Have Not* (1944) and the iconic film noir *The Big Sleep* (1946), may be even better. Bogart and Bacall's offscreen romance transferred to explosive chemistry onscreen, and Hawks capitalized on it by adding extra scenes.

There would be other outstanding roles to follow. Bogart worked with Huston again in *The Treasure of the Sierra Madre* (1948), *Key Largo* (1948), *The African Queen* (1951), for which he won an Academy Award for Best Actor, and *Beat the Devil* (1953). But Bogart's best performance is in an underrated thriller produced by his own company, *In a Lonely Place* (1950). It reunited Bogart with his *Knock on Any Door* (1949) director Nicholas Ray, and the film is a haunting, powerful study of rage, self-loathing, and masculine identity in violent crisis, with Bogart as an unstable screenwriter incapable of controlling his temper. It disproves the belief that he was unable to fully immerse himself in a character and shed the "Bogie" image for a role. Other than the Huston collaborations, his 1950s work is unremarkable. He was happily married to his fourth wife, Bacall, until he died of cancer in 1957. **TC**

RIGHT: Bogart and Katharine Hepburn take a break during filming of *The African Queen*.

SPENCER TRACY

Born: Spencer Bonaventure Tracy, April 5, 1900 (Milwaukee, Wisconsin, U.S.); died 1967 (Los Angeles, California, U.S.).

Star qualities: A highly versatile and talented actor; understated; rugged face; macho; troubled; long-term lover of Katharine Hepburn.

Top Takes…

Guess Who's Coming to Dinner 1967 ☆
It's a Mad Mad Mad Mad World 1963
Judgment at Nuremberg 1961 ☆
Inherit the Wind 1960 ☆
The Last Hurrah 1958
The Old Man and the Sea 1958 ☆
Bad Day at Black Rock 1955 ☆
Broken Lance 1954
The Actress 1953
Pat and Mike 1952
Father of the Bride 1950 ☆
Adam's Rib 1949
State of the Union 1948
The Sea of Grass 1947
The Seventh Cross 1944
Woman of the Year 1942
Stanley and Livingstone 1939
Boys Town 1938 ★
Captains Courageous 1937 ★
San Francisco 1936 ☆
Fury 1936
20,000 Years in Sing Sing 1932
Quick Millions 1931
Up the River 1930

Spencer Tracy joined the U.S. navy at age seventeen, but at the end of World War I, he took to the stage. After a decade of solid work he was spotted by John Ford, who took him to Hollywood to star in *Up the River* (1930), a comedy about two jailbirds. His craggy face, burly figure, and forceful presence suited him to tough-guy roles, and he appeared in a series of gangster and prison dramas, such as *Quick Millions* (1931) and *20,000 Years in Sing Sing* (1932), before being signed by MGM in 1935. Tracy's realistic, understated style of acting soon made him a major star, and he won back-to-back Oscars for *Captains Courageous* (1937) and *Boys Town* (1938). In 1942 Tracy was teamed with another MGM star, Katharine Hepburn, in *Woman of the Year*. Tracy is the gruff, macho newspaperman who marries a star reporter (Hepburn). The two struck sparks off each other, and the onscreen relationship was to be deepened and refined in several further movies, including *Keeper of the Flame* (1942), *State of the Union* (1948), *Adam's Rib* (1949), in which the pair are lawyers appearing on opposite sides in a case involving a marital dispute, and *Pat and Mike* (1952), in which Hepburn is a sports star and Tracy her manager.

RIGHT: The chemistry between Tracy and Hepburn is palpable in *The Sea of Grass*.

ABOVE: Tracy on set with the author of

Their relationship was developing offscreen too. Tracy, a Catholic, would not divorce his wife, but he lived separately from her for years while his and Hepburn's romance was an open secret in Hollywood. As he matured, Tracy graduated to roles as the occasionally irascible but loving paterfamilias, as in the comedy *Father of the Bride* (1950), in which his daughter is Elizabeth Taylor, and *The Actress* (1953), a movie based on an autobiographical play by Ruth Gordon, who had written the scripts for a couple of Tracy's movies.

Tracy had a wholly unsympathetic role in *Edward, My Son* (1949), and was a notable presence as a patriarchal rancher in *Broken Lance* (1954) and as a one-armed avenger in *Bad Day at Black Rock* (1955). In 1967 came Tracy and Hepburn's final collaboration, *Guess Who's Coming to Dinner*, in which they play the parents of a daughter intent on marrying a black man. Tracy died a few weeks after completing work on the film. **EB**

ABOVE: Tracy on set with the author of *The Old Man and the Sea*, Ernest Hemingway.

Kate and Spence

"I saw Spence and Kate's friendship developing right under my eyes," was director George Stevens's assessment of the budding Tracy–Hepburn relationship on the set of *Woman of the Year* (1942). This was the beginning of a 25-year on and offscreen love affair. Married man Tracy was happy to stay that way—"I can get a divorce whenever I want to. But my wife and Kate like things just as they are." Hepburn, married once before, felt that actors were not suited to the institution. Tracy died soon after filming *Guess Who's Coming to Dinner* (1967), leaving Hepburn heartbroken. She never watched the film.

1900s

HELEN HAYES

Born: Helen Hayes Brown, October 10, 1900 (Washington, D.C., U.S.); died 1993 (Nyack, New York, U.S.).

Star qualities: "The First Lady of the U.S. Theater"; child star of stage; leading lady of drama; exceptionally long career; demure; writer.

To Broadway audiences of the 1920s and 1930s, Helen Hayes was the most important actress in the United States, and throughout the twentieth century she remained a U.S. institution whose death seemed as frankly impossible as Bob Hope's. She began acting at the age of five when her mother, an aspiring actress, had her try out for a part, and continued until she was eighty-five. She was one of only nine people to receive all four U.S. entertainment awards: a Tony, Oscar, Emmy, and Grammy. Yet movie audiences never fully embraced her, perhaps because her name very quickly became associated with fatalistic weepies—to which her soulful face was well-suited—perhaps because she didn't look like Joan Crawford.

Her role as a prostitute in her first talkie, *The Sin of Madelon Claudet* (1931), earned her an Oscar for Best Actress and set her on a course of nuns, nurses, and suffering housewives. She was an ideal Catherine Barkley, dying in Gary Cooper's embrace in *A Farewell to Arms* (1932), still the best film version of an Ernest Hemingway novel. *The White Sister* (1933) and *What Every Woman Knows* (1934) followed. But despite her stage triumphs, too many of her films failed at the box office, and in 1935 she retired from the screen for nearly 20 years. She returned in the 1950s as a grande dame, notably as Ingrid Bergman's grandmother, the Dowager Empress Maria Feodorovna, in *Anastasia* (1956), and then again in the 1970s as a little old lady for Disney and TV. The 1980s saw Hayes in some TV movies as Agatha Christie's sleuth Miss Jane Marple. But her career was still on a high in later years, when she won her second Oscar, this time for Best Supporting Actress, for her role as a stowaway in *Airport* (1970). Broadway dimmed its lights when she died at the age of ninety-two. **MC**

"I must refrain from talking too much about retirement. It's beginning to sound absurd."

1900s

JEAN ARTHUR

Born: Gladys Georgianna Greene, October 17, 1900 (Plattsburgh, New York, U.S.); died 1991 (Carmel, California, U.S.).

Star qualities: Petite; husky and sexy voice; comedienne; played the innocent and ingénue; reclusive, shy, and sophisticated.

Blondes were rife in Hollywood in the 1930s, but Jean Arthur bleached her brunette hair regardless. However, her other distinctive asset, her husky, sexy voice, was uniquely hers. A model early on, she made her film debut in the silent *Cameo Kirby* (1923), but it was when talkies arrived that she became a star. She played comedy and drama equally well, coming to prominence opposite Edward G. Robinson in John Ford's gangster comedy *The Whole Town's Talking* (1935) before giving outstanding performances in two Frank Capra films: *Mr. Deeds Goes to Town* (1936) and *Mr. Smith Goes to Washington* (1939). In each scenario she befriends the naive hero, and defends him against the crooks and cynics seeking to destroy him. Director Capra once described her as "my favorite actress."

In between these films, Arthur starred in Howard Hawks's melodrama about airmail pilots, *Only Angels Have Wings* (1939); Arthur more than held her own against Rita Hayworth as her rival for the affections of Cary Grant. Arthur's fundamental wholesomeness is also to the fore in George Stevens's wartime comedy *The More the Merrier* (1943), for which she was nominated for an Academy Award for Best Actress. Arthur had been an appealing Calamity Jane in Cecil B. DeMille's *The Plainsman* (1936); in her last major role, another Western, she played a farmer's wife in George Stevens's *Shane* (1953), attracted by the glamour of the buckskin-clad Shane played by Alan Ladd. Notoriously publicity shy, she was tired of movies by the end of her career. She briefly had a TV series, *The Jean Arthur Show* (1966), but it ran for only 11 weeks. She then retired from the screen world and turned her talents to teaching at Vassar College and North Carolina School of the Arts. **EB**

Top Takes...

Shane 1953
A Foreign Affair 1948
The More the Merrier 1943 ☆
The Talk of the Town 1942
The Devil and Miss Jones 1941
Too Many Husbands 1940
Mr. Smith Goes to Washington 1939
Only Angels Have Wings 1939
You Can't Take It with You 1938
Easy Living 1937
History Is Made at Night 1937
More than a Secretary 1936
The Plainsman 1936
Mr. Deeds Goes to Town 1936
The Whole Town's Talking 1935
Cameo Kirby 1923

"I guess I became an actress because I didn't want to be myself."

AGNES MOOREHEAD

Born: Agnes Robertson Moorehead, December 6, 1900 (Clinton, Massachusetts, U.S.); died 1974 (Rochester, Minnesota, U.S.).

Star qualities: Stagecraft; adept comic timing; character actress; superb in roles as the scheming, jealous, and manipulative woman.

Top Takes...

Charlotte's Web 1973

Dear Dead Delilah 1972

The Singing Nun 1966

Hush . . . Hush, Sweet Charlotte 1964 ☆

Who's Minding the Store? 1963

How the West Was Won 1962

Jessica 1962

Bachelor in Paradise 1961

Pollyanna

Johnny Belinda 1948 ☆

The Opposite Sex 1956

Mrs. Parkington 1944 ☆

Jane Eyre 1944

Journey Into Fear 1943

The Magnificent Ambersons 1942 ☆

Citizen Kane 1941

"I guess I'll remain a bridesmaid for the rest of my life."

—On failing to win an Oscar

"It's not hot; it's cold!" Aunt Fanny's withering response to her nephew's telling her not to lean against the boiler during the famously lengthy kitchen scene in *The Magnificent Ambersons* (1942) is a pinnacle of screen acting: with these few words, wailed in ridicule before she reminds him that they cannot pay the bills, actress Agnes Moorehead manages to convey self-pity, panic, dread, regret, love, embitterment, frustration, and an awareness of both the ludicrous absurdity and the tragic transience of life.

The daughter of a Presbyterian minister, Moorehead studied at New York's Academy of Dramatic Arts at the same time as Rosalind Russell. She is seldom mentioned in lists of great performers, yet here and in her even less conspicuous first movie role in *Citizen Kane* (1941), she demonstrates a talent so remarkable it explains why Orson Welles would have brought a far from beautiful or charismatic woman from his Mercury Players radio troupe to the big screen. Sadly, few directors later made imaginative use of her skills; often she was typecast as a gossip, harridan, or outright bitch. Still, besides working again with Welles on *Journey Into Fear* (1943) and *Jane Eyre* (1944), she turned in solid performances in *Mrs. Parkington* (1944), *Johnny Belinda* (1948), and *Hush . . . Hush, Sweet Charlotte* (1964), all of which won her Oscar nominations for Best Supporting Actress. Fame, however, came from playing the witch Endora in the TV series *Bewitched* from 1964 to 1971. Her role as the scheming mother, who uses her magic powers to befuddle and outfox her well-meaning but gauche mortal son-in-law, showed off her comic timing, her flowing outfits, and her liking for purple—she was so fond of the color, friends nicknamed her "The Lavender Lady." **GA**

RIGHT: Moorehead in her Oscar-nominated role as Fanny in *The Magnificent Ambersons*.

CLARK GABLE

Born: William Clark Gable, February 1, 1901 (Cadiz, Ohio, U.S.); died 1960 (Los Angeles, California, U.S.).

Star qualities: The quintessential lothario; macho and charismatic icon; powerful voice and trademark thin moustache; romantic appeal eclipsed that of his peers.

Top Takes...

The Misfits 1961
Run Silent Run Deep 1958
The Tall Men 1955
Lone Star 1952
Command Decision 1948
Gone with the Wind 1939 ☆
San Francisco 1936
Mutiny on the Bounty 1935 ☆
The Call of the Wild 1935
Manhattan Melodrama 1934
It Happened One Night 1934 ★
Dancing Lady 1933
Hold Your Man 1933
No Man of Her Own 1932
Red Dust 1932
The Secret Six 1931
The Finger Points 1931

Clark Gable was nicknamed "The King of Hollywood." In the 1930s, he reigned as the epitome of onscreen masculinity—roughly wooing women, but not with the psychotic edge of a James Cagney, and setting female hearts aflutter without the Rudolph Valentino sissiness that alienated regular guys. Legions of fans of Margaret Mitchell's *Gone with the Wind* (1939) would allow no one but Gable to play the role of Rhett Butler, though Mitchell herself voted for Basil Rathbone (!).

Gable did bit parts and extra work in silent movies, but his manly growl was suited for the talkies: after a few gangland parts (*The Secret Six*, 1931; *The Finger Points*, 1931), he found himself ideally cast as the apparently cynical adventurer in *Red Dust* (1932), making love to Jean Harlow and Mary Astor and finding excuses to rip his shirt in the tropical heat. MGM kept him working with Joan Crawford (*Dancing Lady*, 1933) and Harlow (*Hold Your Man*, 1933), but his next breakout role came as a punishment. The studio passed him on to Frank Capra and Columbia Pictures to costar with Claudette Colbert in the screwball comedy romance road movie *It Happened One Night* (1934). Here was the Gable audiences loved—a man's man out

RIGHT: Gable with Claudette Colbert and Roscoe Karns in *It Happened One Night.*

to tame a hoity-toity skirt, crunching carrots and not wearing an undershirt. Gable won the Best Actor Oscar, and was confirmed as a major star in big roles in big pictures: the good-guy gangster in *Manhattan Melodrama* (1934), leader of the mutineers in *Mutiny on the Bounty* (1935), and the gambler who learns a lesson during the earthquake in *San Francisco* (1936). Gable had a famous flop as the Irish politician in *Parnell* (1937), but bounced back in the all-time classic *Gone with the Wind* (1939). In the late 1930s, he was married to Carole Lombard—his costar only in *No Man of Her Own* (1932).

After Lombard's premature death in a plane crash in 1942, Gable quit Hollywood to serve in the U.S. air force. He returned to the screen as an older man, often in officer roles (*Command Decision*, 1948) or solid Westerns (*Lone Star*, 1952). In *The Misfits* (1961), his last film, he is an aging modern-day cowboy, but still virile enough to rope and land Marilyn Monroe. **KN**

ABOVE: Gable still manages to charm Marilyn Monroe in his last film, *The Misfits*.

Hollywood Romeo

Clark Gable was the epitome of a Hollywood leading man—ruggedly good looking, he got the girl on and offscreen. Early on in his career he was involved with a string of older women: some believe he was searching for a maternal substitute (his mother died during his infancy); others said that he was advancing his career. He married five times but the great love of his life was Carole Lombard; he was devastated by her death in 1942. On his womanizing Gable himself commented: "Hell, if I'd jumped on all the dames I'm supposed to have jumped on, I'd have had no time to go fishing."

MELVYN DOUGLAS

Born: Melvyn Edouard Hesselberg, April 5, 1901 (Macon, Georgia, U.S.); died 1981 (New York City, New York, U.S.).

Star qualities: Stagecraft; suave; politically liberal; sophisticated leading man in romantic comedy and drama and in later years a character actor.

Top Takes...

The Changeling 1980
***Being There* 1979** ★
The Seduction of Joe Tynan 1979
Twilight's Last Gleaming 1977
The Candidate 1972
One Is a Lonely Number 1972
***I Never Sang for My Father* 1970** ☆
Hotel 1967
Rapture 1965
The Americanization of Emily 1964
***Hud* 1963** ★
Billy Budd 1962
They All Kissed the Bride 1942
Ninotchka 1939
The Vampire Bat 1933
Tonight or Never 1931

The son of a Russian-Jewish immigrant concert pianist and teacher, Melvyn Douglas dropped out of high school to make a career on the stage. After a mix of flops and successes on Broadway, culminating in *Tonight or Never*, Hollywood beckoned, and in 1931 Douglas starred in the movie version of the hit play. The same year he married his costar in the Broadway version, Helen Gahagan. His wife's life as an actress was short-lived because she entered politics in the 1940s and was elected to the United States House of Representatives from California for three terms. In 1950, she ran for the United States Senate, but was defeated by Richard Nixon.

Douglas steadily played pleasant, intelligent, romantic leads throughout the 1930s: a stalwart in minor efforts such as *The Vampire Bat* (1933), as well as in classics such as *Ninotchka* (1939), where he played opposite Greta Garbo. Like his wife, Douglas was a liberal Democrat, and he suffered the consequences of that, being "gray-listed" in Hollywood from the late 1940s to the early 1950s. This meant that although not officially blacklisted, he wasn't offered any film work. Instead he acted on TV and on Broadway, with distinction, winning both Tony and Emmy awards. He returned to the movies as an older character actor in *Billy Budd* (1962), and then won an Oscar for Best Supporting Actor for the dignified, disappointed cattleman in *Hud* (1963). Douglas's exile from the movie world seemed to have given him a greater depth and maturity as a performer. He continued to demonstrate his versatility with a succession of plum senior roles—often as sharp minds suffering the onset of senility—including *I Never Sang for My Father* (1970) and *Being There* (1979), for which he won his second Academy Award. **KN**

"The Hollywood roles I did were boring: I was soon fed up with them."

GARY COOPER

Born: Frank James Cooper, May 7, 1901 (Helena, Montana, U.S.); died 1961 (Los Angeles, California, U.S.).

Star qualities: Made for Westerns; tall, dark, and handsome ladies' man; soft-spoken; aloof but intense screen presence.

Although born in Montana, and a real-life Westerner, Gary Cooper went to school in England for several years before attending college in Iowa, where he gained stage experience. Working as an extra in Hollywood for a year or two, he got his break in *The Winning of Barbara Worth* (1926), playing with Ronald Colman. More than six feet tall, with a winning smile and a slow, diffident way of speaking, Cooper was a natural for Westerns and other action films. In 1929 he had the title role in *The Virginian*, based on Owen Wister's classic Western novel. In *Morocco* (1930), Josef von Sternberg's romance of the Foreign Legion, Cooper was the perfect foil for Marlene Dietrich.

"Laconic" is the term often used to describe Cooper's screen persona; his slightly gauche, unsophisticated charm made him an ideal casting for *Mr. Deeds Goes to Town* (1936), Frank Capra's tale of an innocent taking on the city slickers. Indeed Cooper proved to have quite a gift for comedy, as shown in the Ernst Lubitsch classic *Bluebeard's Eighth Wife* (1938) and in Howard Hawks's *Ball of Fire* (1941). Hawks also directed one of Cooper's biggest hits, *Sergeant York* (1941), the true story of a reluctant World War I hero, for which Cooper received his first Academy Award. Westerns and other action films came at regular intervals, including *The Plainsman* (1936), *Beau Geste* (1939), and *Unconquered* (1947).

In 1952 came the film for which Cooper is probably best remembered. In *High Noon* he played a sheriff deserted by the townspeople when faced with a dangerous gang of outlaws. He won a second Best Actor Oscar for this role. Perhaps Cooper's last great film was *Man of the West* (1958). By this time he was suffering from cancer, his lined face lending emphasis to the tragic implications of his role. He died in 1961. **EB**

Top Takes...

Man of the West 1958
High Noon 1952 ★
Distant Drums 1951
The Fountainhead 1949
Unconquered 1947
The Pride of the Yankees 1942 ☆
For Whom the Bell Tolls 1943 ☆
Ball of Fire 1941
Sergeant York 1941 ★
Beau Geste 1939
Bluebeard's Eighth Wife 1938
The Plainsman 1936
Mr. Deeds Goes to Town 1936 ☆
Morocco 1930
The Virginian 1929
The Winning of Barbara Worth 1926

> "I say he's a crack comedian, and isn't competition for me at all."
> —On Cary Grant

MARLENE DIETRICH

Born: Maria Magdalena Dietrich, December 27, 1901 (Berlin-Schöneberg, Germany); died 1992 (Paris, France).

Star qualities: Long-legged sex bomb; cabaret singer with a seductive voice; highest-paid actress of the day; fashion icon; often had affairs with her costars.

Top Takes…

Just a Gigolo 1979
Judgment at Nuremberg 1961
Touch of Evil 1958
Monte Carlo 1957
Witness for the Prosecution 1957
Around the World in Eighty Days 1956
Rancho Notorious 1952
Stage Fright 1950
A Foreign Affair 1948
Seven Sinners 1940
Kismet 1944
Golden Earrings 1947
Destry Rides Again 1939
Knight Without Armour 1937
The Garden of Allah 1936
Desire 1936
I Loved a Soldier 1936
The Devil Is a Woman 1935
The Scarlet Empress 1934
The Song of Songs 1933
Blonde Venus 1932
Shanghai Express 1932
Morocco 1930 ☆
Der Blaue Engel 1930 (*The Blue Angel*)

RIGHT: Dietrich on location in the Arizona desert for *The Garden of Allah* in 1936.

Marlene Dietrich was blonde eye candy in lumpen German movies of the 1920s, but she didn't become a real star until the talkies introduced her distinctive, heavy accent. The American director Josef von Sternberg cast her as the trampily glamorous singer Lola Lola in *Der Blaue Engel* (1930) (*The Blue Angel*) and established her screen persona as a devastating woman who ensnares and ruins an older man. Exuding earthy sexuality, she sprawls casually *en déshabillé* and delivers songs in her imitable, but trademarked, husky voice.

Von Sternberg put Dietrich under contract, took her to Hollywood, then crafted exquisite, bizarre vehicles for her, often stressing her ambiguous sexuality. In male evening dress as another cabaret performer, she kisses a woman on the lips in *Morocco* (1930)—for which she received her only Academy Award nomination. The Dietrich of von Sternberg's American films is more fantastical than Lola Lola: the tawdry sparkle of the Blue Angel club gives way to exotic imaginings of the Far East (*Shanghai Express*, 1932) or Old Russia (*The Scarlet Empress*, 1934). Lasting cult movies, these films were too sophisticated for an America falling for Shirley Temple and tended to flop.

1900s

After *The Devil Is a Woman* (1935), Dietrich broke with von Sternberg. *Destry Rides Again* (1939), her canny comeback, successfully reinvented Lola Lola for U.S. consumption and modified her image—now, she tended to play a brawling showgirl/harlot who sins (and sings) in style but is redeemed (often taking a bullet for the hero so he can marry the "good girl") at the end. Sadly, the humor of *Destry* was too often left out of the mix, and most of Dietrich's 1940s films are unremarkable. Thereafter, she worked rarely—stiff for Alfred Hitchcock (*Stage Fright*, 1950) but with some of the old sparkle for Billy Wilder (*A Foreign Affair*, 1948; *Witness for the Prosecution*, 1957) and Fritz Lang (*Rancho Notorious*, 1952). Her best cameo was as the gypsy clairvoyant ("You don't have a future—it's all used up") in Orson Welles's *Touch of Evil* (1958). Dietrich's career ended when she broke her leg onstage in 1975; she spent her last years bedridden in her Paris apartment. **KN**

ABOVE: Dietrich in her breakthrough role as the alluring Lola Lola in *The Blue Angel*.

Screen Siren

Marlene Dietrich had great personal magnetism and attracted moviegoers and her costars alike. She was renowned for her love affairs, with both men and women, and was romantically linked to costars, such as Yul Brynner, as well as some high-profile names, including Frank Sinatra and John F. Kennedy. The great love of her life was said to be French actor Jean Gabin. Rather than damaging her career, the romances seemed to fuel the androgynous star's popularity. She was married to Rudolf Sieber from 1924 to 1976; the couple lived apart for all but five years of their marriage but stayed friends.

TALLULAH BANKHEAD

Born: Tallulah Brockman Bankhead, January 31, 1902 (Huntsville, Alabama, U.S.); died 1968 (New York City, New York, U.S.).

Star qualities: Legendary stage actress; bonne viveuse; party girl; outspoken, racy, flamboyant, witty, outrageous; famed for her affairs with both sexes; charismatic.

Top Takes...

The Daydreamer 1966
Fanatic 1965
A Royal Scandal 1945
Lifeboat 1944
Stage Door Canteen 1943
Faithless 1932
Devil and the Deep 1932
Thunder Below 1932
The Cheat 1931
My Sin 1931
Tarnished Lady 1931
His House in Order 1928
The Trap 1919
Who Loved Him Best? 1918

Tallulah Bankhead was a Broadway legend, although her stage roles tended to be taken by Bette Davis when the plays came to be filmed, and *All About Eve* (1950)—in which Davis plays a character based on Bankhead—is better known than the few films Bankhead did make. She went to great lengths to send up her career with an enthusiastic embrace of vice and witty, pithy comments upon her own degradation: "My father warned me about men and booze, but he never mentioned a word about women and cocaine." Frequently impersonated—her signature expression was a drawled "Hello, dahling"—she became a caricature of herself, aptly ending her career as a cartoon villain on the *Batman* TV show.

The daughter of a U.S. Democrat politician, Bankhead won a beauty contest at age sixteen. This encouraged her to head for Broadway, and so she went to live with an aunt in New York. Finding no luck, she decided to move to England in 1923, where her fortune changed and she became a West End success on the stage. This drew the attention of Paramount Pictures and she returned to the United States to make *Woman's Law* (1927), followed by *His House in Order* (1928). Neither film was well received so she returned to the stage. The swing between stage and screen continued for the rest of her career, and she only ever dabbled in movies, where the roles she landed did not do justice to her abilities. After minor work in the early 1930s, such as in *Devil and the Deep* (1932), she graced the screen with amusing self-portraits, as the lady journalist in Alfred Hitchcock's *Lifeboat* (1944), and Catherine the Great in Ernst Lubitsch and Otto Preminger's *A Royal Scandal* (1945). She returned once more to screen, interestingly as a dowdy, religious maniac in *Fanatic* (1965). **KN**

"It's the good girls who keep diaries; the bad girls never have the time."

STEPIN FETCHIT

Born: Lincoln Theodore Monroe Andrew Perry, May 30, 1902 (Key West, Florida, U.S.); died 1985 (Los Angeles, California, U.S.).

Star qualities: The first black superstar; intelligent, trailblazing, defiant, controversial; comic supporting actor; character actor; writer; played a stereotype 1930s black man.

Stepin Fetchit is slowly coming to be recognized as the great comic supporting actor he was widely hailed as in his 1930s heyday. The problem is that his persona was that of the slow-witted, servile black man. That this limited and restricting stereotype represented about the sum total of options available to a young black comic at the time is undeniable; what is less clear is what those who have denigrated him would have had him do instead. When the only choice is not to appear at all, or to do the job so well that you steal every scene you are in, it's lucky Fetchit went for the second option.

It is an ironic fact, often forgotten, that players such as Fetchit and Mantan Moreland were often cast so as to attract black audiences, not alienate them. Successful comedians on the black circuit, their fans viewed an appearance in a mainstream Hollywood movie as an empowering achievement. Fetchit became a superstar and a millionaire, at one time owning 12 cars and employing 16 servants.

Born to West Indian immigrant parents, Fetchit became a journalist and comic entertainer in vaudeville before making his film debut in *The Mysterious Stranger* (1925). He went on to make many films, reaching his peak in the 1930s when he costarred with Will Rogers in several movies, including John Ford's *Steamboat Round the Bend* (1935). After being declared bankrupt in 1947 he kept working, albeit sporadically. He became a friend of boxing champion Muhammad Ali and converted to Islam in the 1960s. He received the Special Image Award from the U.S. National Association for the Advancement of Colored People in 1976. He made his last appearance in Michael Winner's Hollywood satire *Won Ton Ton, the Dog Who Saved Hollywood* (1976). **MC**

Top Takes...

Won Ton Ton, the Dog Who Saved Hollywood 1976

Amazing Grace 1974

The Sun Shines Bright 1953

Harlem Follies of 1949 1950

I Ain't Gonna Open That Door 1949

Zenobia 1949

Steamboat Round the Bend 1935

Charlie Chan in Egypt 1935

Judge Priest 1934

Swing High 1930

Show Boat 1929

The Tragedy of Youth 1928

In Old Kentucky 1927

The Mysterious Stranger 1925

"When people saw me and Will Rogers like brothers, that said something to them."

NORMA SHEARER

Born: Edith Norma Shearer, August 10, 1902 (Montréal, Québec, Canada.); died 1983 (Los Angeles, California, U.S.).

Star qualities: Fashion-model looks; slender, poised, seductive, ever chic, and stylish; glamorously well dressed; obsessive about her appearance and image.

Top Takes...

Her Cardboard Lover 1942
We Were Dancing 1942
Escape 1940
The Women 1939
Idiot's Delight 1939
Marie Antoinette 1938 ☆
Romeo and Juliet 1936 ☆
The Barretts of Wimpole Street 1934 ☆
Riptide 1934
Smilin' Through 1932
Private Lives 1931
A Free Soul 1931 ☆
The Divorcee 1930 ★
Their Own Desire 1930 ☆
The Trial of Mary Dugan 1929
The Student Prince in Old Heidelberg 1927

"Never let them see you in public after you've turned thirty-five. You're finished if you do!"

As wife of legendary producer Irving Thalberg, it is often said, perhaps unfairly, that Norma Shearer enjoyed a privileged status at MGM that had not been earned by talent alone. Supposedly she was always given first pick of the best roles; so it is ironic that so few of her films can be easily recalled today.

The daughter of a Canadian Mountie and an actress, Shearer moved to New York with her family when she was young. She won a beauty contest at age fourteen, and initially worked as a fashion model. Her career in films began as an extra in 1919, graduating to featured roles in 1922, the year before Thalberg arrived at MGM and put her under contract. They married in 1927, though it is alleged that Louis B. Mayer had little regard for Shearer and would have dropped her were it not for Thalberg. Instead she rose swiftly, working for Ernst Lubitsch in *The Student Prince in Old Heidelberg* (1927), starring in MGM's first talkie, *The Trial of Mary Dugan* (1929), and collecting an Oscar for Best Actress for *The Divorcee* (1930). There followed a strange run of vanity projects, insulated from commercial reality by Thalberg's protective reputation: *Strange Interlude* (1932), *The Barretts of Wimpole Street* (1934), and *Romeo and Juliet* (1936), for which she got her fifth Oscar nomination.

After Thalberg's premature death in 1936, Shearer played the title role in *Marie Antoinette* (1938), tried hard in *Idiot's Delight* (1939), and triumphed amid the stiffest competition in George Cukor's *The Women* (1939), her best and most often revived film, and by far her finest performance. After turning down the lead role in *Mrs. Miniver* (1942), she finally stepped out of the spotlight. She married a ski instructor 20 years her junior, Martin Arrouge, with whom she remained until she died. **MC**

JOHN HOUSEMAN

Born: Jacques Haussmann, September 22, 1902 (Bucharest, Romania); died 1988 (Malibu, California, U.S.).

Star qualities: Director; producer; teacher extraordinaire; writer; innovator; one-time mentor and friend of Orson Welles.

Romanian-born of a French father and English mother, John Houseman was educated at one of England's most prestigious schools, Clifton College, before heading to the United States in 1924, where he would have a career as a major stage and movie producer. He founded the Mercury Theater company in New York together with Orson Welles. Following some successful stage productions, the company took to the radio in 1938 as *The Mercury Theater on the Air*, a series that included one of the most famous radio broadcasts ever heard, *The War of the Worlds*. So realistic was the adaptation of H. G. Wells's science-fiction novel that many listeners believed the Martians had landed, and chaos ensued.

Houseman then went to Hollywood with Welles and the Mercury Theater to make *Citizen Kane* (1941). After an acrimonious breakup with Welles, he worked for the Office of War Information during World War II, and was involved in radio programs for *Voice of America*. Between 1945 and 1962 he produced 18 films, including George Marshall's *The Blue Dahlia* (1946) and Fritz Lang's *Moonfleet* (1955).

Houseman made his acting debut as an admiral refusing to join the coup in *Seven Days in May* (1964). A decade later he turned in an Academy Award-winning performance as Professor Charles W. Kingsfield Jr.—the demanding mentor to law students in *The Paper Chase* (1973)—a role he reprised in the TV series (1983–1986). After Kingsfield, he continued to work on both TV and the big screen, including spoofing Sydney Greenstreet in *The Cheap Detective* (1978). His contribution to acting was also as a teacher, notably at New York's Juilliard School, where he nurtured future stars such as Kevin Kline and Robin Williams. **KN**

Top Takes...

Another Woman 1988
Bright Lights, Big City 1988
Murder by Phone 1982
Rose for Emily 1982
Ghost Story 1981
My Bodyguard 1980
Wholly Moses! 1980
The Fog 1980
Old Boyfriends 1979
The Cheap Detective 1978
St. Ives 1976
Three Days of the Condor 1975
Rollerball 1975
The Paper Chase 1973 ★
Seven Days in May 1964
Too Much Johnson 1938

"You come in here with a skull full of mush and you leave thinking like a lawyer."

RALPH RICHARDSON

Born: Ralph David Richardson, December 19, 1902 (Cheltenham, Gloucestershire, England); died 1983 (Marylebone, London, England).

Star qualities: Director; stage actor; stellar Shakespearean performer; knighted; played anything from the serious to the lighthearted.

Sir Ralph Richardson did such a sterling impression of absentminded dottiness, from his mild-mannered but murderous curate in his first film, *The Ghoul* (1933), with Boris Karloff, to the childish but moving old earl in *Greystoke: The Legend of Tarzan, Lord of the Apes* (1984), that he was often underrated. He understood the movies far better than his fellow theatrical knights, John Gielgud and Laurence Olivier, and delivered at least one all-time top-ten performance as the butler in *The Fallen Idol* (1948).

Richardson was brought up by his Roman Catholic and teacher mother, who left his Quaker father when Richardson was a baby. Despite her hope that he would enter the priesthood, Richardson headed for the stage and made his debut in 1926, moving to the West End in 1930. He achieved great acclaim in the theater, both for his work in Shakespearean and more modern plays, such as Somerset Maugham's *Sheppey* (1933) and J. B. Priestley's *Cornelius* (1935). After serving in World War II, he returned to London's Old Vic to become a codirector along with Laurence Olivier, hoping to revive the fortunes of the bombed-out theater. A tour of the United States followed. Richardson's versatile career moved continually between stage, radio, TV, and movies. It includes the expected classical roles as well as the important historical parts: Alexei Karenin in *Anna Karenina* (1948), the Duke of Buckingham in *Richard III* (1955), and William Gladstone in *Khartoum* (1966). However, he was able to play almost any role—even the comic and whimsical—such as a cameo part as the computer librarian in *Rollerball* (1975), and God in *Time Bandits* (1981). He was the deserving recipient of a knighthood in 1947. **KN**

"I don't like my face at all. It's always been a great drawback to me."

EDGAR BERGEN

Born: Edgar John Bergen, February 16, 1903 (Chicago, Illinois, U.S.); died 1978 (Las Vegas, Nevada, U.S.).

Star qualities: Ventriloquist with an irreverent aristocratic wooden sidekick; radio performer; master of double entendre and quick-witted dialogue.

Still the most famous ventriloquist in entertainment history, Edgar Bergen and his top-hatted, monocled dummy Charlie McCarthy were the stars of one of radio's most enduring variety shows, running from 1937 to 1956. The show joined the Radio Hall of Fame in 1990. Bergen's luck was to have created in Charlie an amusing, wisecracking comic persona that was funny in its own right, regardless of the fact that he was never the most technically accomplished ventriloquist. Bergen had taught himself ventriloquism at the age of eleven.

Starting out in vaudeville and some movie shorts, such as the partnership with the Ritz Brothers in *The Goldwyn Follies* (1938), Bergen and his puppet pal ironically found real success in radio. It is said that Bergen was seen doing his act at a Hollywood party by Noel Coward, who then recommended him to appear on Rudy Vallee's show. The popularity of Bergen and Charlie's radio appearances with W. C. Fields and their banter peppered by double entendre, led to a film, *You Can't Cheat an Honest Man* (1939). This led to a vehicle of their own: *Charlie McCarthy, Detective* (1939). Bergen also made several solo appearances as a supporting actor, most notably in *I Remember Mama* (1948). His last appearances were in Michael Winner's acidic salute to old Hollywood, *Won Ton Ton, the Dog Who Saved Hollywood* (1976), and in *The Muppet Movie* (1979), released after his death and dedicated to his memory. *The Muppet Show* creator Jim Henson said that Bergen and Charlie McCarthy were the reason he became interested in puppetry. Bergen is the father of actress Candice Bergen, and remains the only ventriloquist to have been awarded an honorary Oscar (in 1938). Aptly, the statuette was made of wood. **MC**

Top Takes...

The Muppet Movie 1979
Won Ton Ton, the Dog Who Saved Hollywood 1976
Rogues' Gallery 1968
Don't Make Waves 1967
One Way Wahini 1965
Mystery Lake 1953
Captain China 1950
I Remember Mama 1948
Mickey and the Beanstalk 1947
Here We Go Again 1942
Look Who's Laughing 1941
Charlie McCarthy, Detective 1939
You Can't Cheat an Honest Man 1939
Letter of Introduction 1938
The Goldwyn Follies 1938

"Hard work never killed anybody, but why take a chance?"—Charlie McCarthy

BING CROSBY

Born: Harry Lillis Crosby, May 2, 1903 (Tacoma, Washington, U.S.); died 1977 (Madrid, Spain).

Star qualities: Comedian; producer; iconic musician; innovator; phenomenal radio and recording success; relaxed vocal style; casually dressed crooner; golden voice.

Nicknamed "Bing" after a comic-book character, Bing Crosby breezed through many lightweight movies with the same casual air that made him a successful crooner. He didn't have to work as hard at anything as Frank Sinatra, and yet took the time to win a Best Actor Oscar for his role as a priest in *Going My Way* (1944), and show real acting chops as a haggard drunk opposite Grace Kelly in *The Country Girl* (1954).

Crosby studied law but was keener on playing in a band and headed to Los Angeles in 1925 to make it as a musician. CBS heard his voice and gave him a live radio show. His radio success led Paramount Pictures to seek him out for movies in the early 1930s, and so he sang his way pleasantly through the likes of *The Big Broadcast* (1932) and *Pennies from Heaven* (1936). His luck came when he was teamed with Bob Hope and Dorothy Lamour in *Road to Singapore* (1940), which spun off a successful series of globe-trotting, increasingly surreal comedies in which genial, jovial Bing more than once demonstrates a streak of utter ruthlessness, as he not only steals girls from his best friend but surprisingly often plots Hope's painful death. He sang "White Christmas" in *Holiday Inn* (1942), and then delivered an extended reprise in *White Christmas* (1954). Four of the songs Crosby sang in movies—"Sweet Leilani" (1937), "White Christmas" (1942), "Swinging on a Star" (1944), and "In the Cool, Cool, Cool of the Evening" (1951)—won Oscars. In later years, he took it easy on the golf course alongside his pal Hope, aside from the occasional cameo, in such films as *Robin and the 7 Hoods* (1964). Despite his easygoing public persona, his private life had its share of tragedy: widowed at forty-nine, he remarried five years later; and two of his seven children committed suicide. **KN**

> "He was an average guy who could carry a tune."
>
> —His own epitaph

FERNANDEL

Born: Fernand Joseph Désiré Contandin, May 8, 1903 (Marseille, Bouches-du-Rhône, France); died 1971 (Paris, France).

Star qualities: Comedian; singer; director; less than handsome; large build, horsey teeth, doe-eyed; often played the naive, the silly, and the clown.

At the age of five, Fernandel assisted his father on stage, where he subsequently started out as a singer and a comedian. Like fellow countryman Jean Gabin, with whom he would later form a production company, he made his debut on the big screen in 1930, but continued his successful career on stage and never stopped singing.

Fernandel played likable, naïve, sometimes silly, sometimes resourceful characters in comedies such as *François Premier* (1937) (*Francis the First*) and *Fric-Frac* (1939), and quickly became a star. Marcel Pagnol used his Southern personality on different occasions, notably for dramatic purposes in *La Fille du puisatier* (1940) (*The Well-Digger's Daughter*). After World War II, he sometimes ventured into darker productions, such as *L'Armoire volante* (1948) (*The Cupboard Was Bare*); satirical farces like *L'Auberge rouge* (1951) (*The Red Inn*); or detective films such as *L'Homme à l'imperméable* (1956) (*The Man in the Raincoat*). But he managed to do so without changing his persona, or losing sight of the popular audience that appreciated him.

If Fernandel's career marked time during the 1940s, the next decade saw him at his commercial peak with hits such as *La vache et le prisonnier* (1959) (*The Cow and I*). He also ventured into U.S. and Italian films. His first Hollywood movie was *Around the World in Eighty Days* (1956), in which he played David Niven's French coachman. His performance led to his costarring with Bob Hope in *Paris Holiday* (1958) as two men stuck on an ocean liner. From 1951 to 1965, Fernandel played an anticommunist, quick-tempered, pugilistic but bighearted parish priest in the five installments of the Italian series *Don Camillo*, a part for which he is still widely known today. **FL**

Top Takes...

La vache et le prisonnier 1959 (*The Cow and I*)
Paris Holiday 1958
L'Homme à l'imperméable 1957
  (*The Man in the Raincoat*)
Around the World in Eighty Days 1956
Don Juan 1956
L'Auberge rouge 1951 (*The Red Inn*)
L'Armoire volante 1948
  (*The Cupboard Was Bare*)
La Fille du puisatier 1940
  (*The Well-Digger's Daughter*)
Fric-Frac 1939
François Premier 1937 (*Francis the First*)

1900s

"If I have created a style, a kind of cinema, I did not do it on purpose."

BOB HOPE

Born: Leslie Townes Hope, May 29, 1903 (Eltham, London, England); died 2003 (Toluca Lake, California, U.S.).

Star qualities: Comedian; producer; writer; dancer; singer and crooner of the sentimental and lighthearted; fast-talking king of ad-libbing; patriotic.

Top Takes...

Sir Bob Hope was among the screen's greatest star comedians and an acknowledged model for everyone from Woody Allen to Eddie Murphy. He emigrated from England to the United States in 1908, and after years as a dancer and singer in vaudeville, he made a few shorts such as the *The Old Grey Mayor* (1935) before a featured spot in *The Big Broadcast of 1938* (1938) elevated him to stardom. *Thanks for the Memory* (1938) takes its title from the song he performed in the earlier film, which became his signature tune and set the tone for his subsequent star vehicles.

Paramount Pictures partnered Hope happily with Bing Crosby and Dorothy Lamour in the *"Road to . . . "* series from 1940 in *Road to Singapore*, but Hope was as funny without Crosby in *The Cat and the Canary* (1939), *My Favorite Blonde* (1942), *The Paleface* (1948), and others. His screen character is a fast-talking coward, braggart, and lecher who blunders blithely into tight spots: pursued by a zombie in *The Ghost Breakers* (1940) and swashbuckling villains in *Casanova's Big Night* (1954). His vehicles became more strained in the 1950s and 1960s, and a semiserious political biopic, *Beau James* (1957), didn't click, but he remained a presence in U.S. entertainment throughout his life on radio, TV, and the stage, always receiving awards and plaudits. Hope hosted the Academy Awards ceremony 18 times. Famous for entertaining the troops during World War II and the Korean and Vietnam wars, in 1997 Congress made him an honorary U.S. veteran—the only person to receive that distinction. He was given an honorary knighthood by Queen Elizabeth II in 1998, and by the end of his life had received five special Academy Awards for contributions to the industry. **KN**

"Welcome to the Academy Awards—or as it's known at my house, Passover."

JEANETTE MacDONALD

Born: Jeanette Anna MacDonald, June 18, 1903 (Philadelphia, Pennsylvania, U.S.); died 1965 (Houston, Texas, U.S.).

Star qualities: "The Iron Butterfly"—beautiful but tough; distinctive red hair and blue-green eyes; talented soprano; excelled in flirtatious, comic roles.

An accomplished soprano and deft practitioner of high comedy, Jeanette MacDonald is best remembered for her appearances in MGM operettas, often partnered with baritone Nelson Eddy. The pairing was as famous for singing as the Fred Astaire and Ginger Rogers partnership was for dancing. But MacDonald's career began under Ernst Lubitsch at Paramount Pictures, in his European-style musical comedies—all smart technique, sophistication, and drawing room innuendo.

In *The Love Parade* (1929), her breakthrough hit, *One Hour With You* (1932), and *Love Me Tonight* (1932, as "Princess Jeanette") she is partnered with Maurice Chevalier and is kittenish and very funny. But problems with Paramount led to a defection to MGM, where she found one excellent dramatic role alongside Clark Gable and Spencer Tracy in *San Francisco* (1936), and eight musicals costarring with Eddy. They were "America's Singing Sweethearts" and—with their hit album—retain an enormous following, but the buttoned-up MacDonald of these years is no match for the one in a 1932 *Hollywood on Parade* short who sings in her underwear, reclining in an ornate bed before a live orchestra; it captures perfectly the coquettish image she projected in her Paramount work.

In later years, MacDonald moved into serious opera, taking lessons from grande dame Lotte Lehmann and performing several times with the Chicago Lyric Opera. She also worked in theater and radio. She married actor Gene Raymond in 1937. Raymond bore a striking resemblance to Eddy, fueling speculation that MacDonald and Eddy were romantically involved for a time. Both Eddy and her husband were devastated when MacDonald died from a heart attack at the age of sixty-one. **MC**

Top Takes...

Three Daring Daughters 1948
Cairo 1942
I Married an Angel 1942
Smilin' Through 1941
Bitter Sweet 1940
New Moon 1940
Broadway Serenade 1939
Sweethearts 1938
The Girl of the Golden West 1938
Maytime 1937
San Francisco 1936
Naughty Marietta 1935
The Merry Widow 1934
Love Me Tonight 1932
One Hour with You 1932
The Love Parade 1929

"I have an Irish temper, I know I have Scottish thrift, and, like the English, I love a good show."

NIKOLAI CHERKASOV

Born: Nikolai Konstantinovich Cherkasov, July 27, 1903 (St. Petersburg, Russia); died 1966 (Moscow, Russia).

Star qualities: Tall, imposing screen presence; stage actor; character actor of heavyweight historical roles; mime artist; Stalin favorite.

Top Takes...

Ivan Groznyy II: Boyarsky zagovor 1958
  (*Ivan the Terrible, Part Two*)
Don Kikhot 1957 (*Don Quixote*)
Stalingradskaya Bitva I 1949
  (*The Battle of Stalingrad Part I*)
Akademik Ivan Pavlov 1949 (*Ivan Pavlov*)
Ivan Groznyy I 1944 (*Ivan the Terrible, Part One*)
Lenin v 1918 godu 1939 (*Lenin in 1918*)
Aleksandr Nevskiy 1938 (*Alexander Nevsky*)
Pyotr pervyy I 1937 (*Peter the First*)

It's unusual to find that Nikolai Cherkasov, an actor so connected with grand and serious roles, had his roots in stage comedy; a career that began in the almost playful and relaxed manner of experimental Russian theater was soon transformed into stiffness and pretentiousness. Cherkasov's trajectory was from movement to gesture, from outburst of physical energy to pose. This was inevitable when Cherkasov, after the Soviet dictator Joseph Stalin took notice of him, became his favorite actor: someone who could transpose to the screen historical personifications and anticipations of the Great Leader of World Revolution. So, Cherkasov, Deputy of the Supreme Soviet, was destined to play only larger-than-life characters: Prince Alexei in *Pyotr pervyy I* (1937) (*Peter the First*), twice Maxim Gorky in *Lenin v 1918 godu* (1939) (*Lenin in 1918*) and *Akademik Ivan Pavlov* (1949) (*Ivan Pavlov*), Franklin D. Roosevelt in *Stalingradskaya Bitva I* (1949) (*The Battle of Stalingrad*), and *Don Kikhot* (1957) (*Don Quixote*) in Grigori Kozintsev's adaptation of Miguel de Cervantes's masterpiece.

This tendency reached glorious affirmation and subtle parody in Sergei Eisenstein's films *Aleksandr Nevskiy* (1938) (*Alexander Nevsky*) and *Ivan Groznyy I* and *II* (1944 and 1958) (*Ivan the Terrible, Parts One and Two*). Although these pictures aimed to show the strength of leaders with the will to change history, Cherkasov was only a puppet in the director's mise-en-scène, and it is easy to sense the discomfort he must have felt as a result of Eisenstein's use of framing. He was more a signifier than a person: his value was more iconographic than performative. Ultimately, however, this is an example of Cherkasov's craft: he learned that in life, and in cinema, you must obey your master. **AB**

> "Stalin liked my father. He was the only one he was prepared to speak to."

1900s

CLAUDETTE COLBERT

Born: Lily Claudette Chauchoin, September 13, 1903 (Paris, France); died 1996 (Speightstown, Barbados).

Star qualities: Gallic screen siren; petite, doe-eyed, amusing, sexy, and elegant; comic timing; often played the endearing romantic heroine in comedies and dramas.

One of the most charming and vivacious stars of Hollywood's golden age, Claudette Colbert was born in Paris in 1903, but her family immigrated to the United States when she was three years old. Stardom arrived in the pre–Hays Code era, in racy women's pictures such as *The Lady Lies* (1929) as a shopgirl who falls for an older man, and *Honor Among Lovers* (1931) as a secretary in love with her boss. The Colbert of these years, with black, sometimes bobbed, hair and vampish makeup, is much sexier than in her later star vehicles. This is especially the case in her work for director Cecil B. DeMille: as Empress Poppaea, she bathes nude in asses' milk in *The Sign of the Cross* (1932); she wears some very fetishistic costumes as the Egyptian siren in *Cleopatra* (1934); and in the jungle adventure comedy, *Four Frightened People* (1934), she plays a liberated teacher who seems to lose another layer of clothing with each scene.

After 1934 Hollywood softened her image, permed and lightened her hair, and cast her as the ideal wife and hostess. Her talent for comedy was well exploited by the likes of Preston Sturges, Ernst Lubitsch, and Sam Wood, and she consistently drew audiences into movie theaters. But her finest performance remains her best known: the spoiled heiress Ellie Andrews on the run in Frank Capra's joyous comedy *It Happened One Night* (1934), in which she famously stops traffic by adjusting her stockings at the roadside, and for which she won an Oscar for Best Actress. She felt so sure she would lose out to Bette Davis that she didn't even attend the ceremony.

Colbert spent her later years working on the stage in the United States and England, as well as doing a number of guest spots in TV shows before she retired to Barbados. She was last seen in *Parrish* in 1961. **MC**

Top Takes...

Parrish 1961
The Planter's Wife 1952
The Secret Fury 1950
Bride for Sale 1949
Sleep, My Love 1948
Guest Wife 1945
Since You Went Away 1944 ☆
It's a Wonderful World 1939
Private Worlds 1935 ☆
Cleopatra 1934
It Happened One Night 1934 ★
Four Frightened People 1934
The Sign of the Cross 1932
Honor Among Lovers 1931
The Lady Lies 1929

"Audiences always sound like they're glad to see me, and I'm damned glad to see them."

CARY GRANT

Born: Archibald Alexander Leach, January 18, 1904 (Horfield, Bristol, England); died 1986 (Davenport, Iowa, U.S.).

Star qualities: Tall, dark, and handsome; tanned; suave with a brilliant smile; smart dresser; inspiration for Ian Fleming's James Bond.

Top Takes...

Walk Don't Run 1966
Charade 1963
Operation Petticoat 1959
North by Northwest 1959
The Pride and the Passion 1957
An Affair to Remember 1957
To Catch a Thief 1955
I Was a Male War Bride 1949
Notorious 1946
None but the Lonely Heart 1944 ☆
Arsenic and Old Lace 1944
Penny Serenade 1941 ☆
The Philadelphia Story 1940
His Girl Friday 1940
Bringing Up Baby 1938
The Awful Truth 1937
She Done Him Wrong 1933
Madame Butterfly 1932
Blonde Venus 1932

Upon his death on November 29, 1986, Cary Grant was survived by four ex-wives (Dyan Cannon, Betsy Drake, Barbara Hutton, and Virginia Cherrill), one widow (Barbara Harris), and one daughter (Jennifer). Having expired in, of all places, Davenport, Iowa, while on a career retrospective tour, Grant lived through most of the twentieth century, across which he helped define a genteel Hollywood sophistication, even though he was born and brought up in England.

His early life was unremarkable, neither impoverished nor rich, neither unusual nor eventful, save for his mother's institutionalization when he was nine, about which Grant knew nothing until he reached adulthood. The eventual revelation of this family secret would prove remarkably influential, leaving Grant constantly troubled by issues of trust—especially with intimate relations—largely because he felt so totally cheated of honesty within the mysteries of his birth family. He left school at fourteen, lying about his age and forging his father's signature on a letter in order to join a group of comedians, the Bob Pender stage troupe. He learned pantomime and

RIGHT: Grant plays the paleontologist to perfection in the comedy *Bringing Up Baby*.

1900s

acrobatics while touring the English provinces. In 1920 he was sent to Broadway for the show *Good Times* and stayed to pursue his preferred career.

ABOVE: Grant as an advertising executive turned fugitive in *North by Northwest*.

For a number of years Grant supported himself with odd jobs until his performances in Broadway comedies earned him some notice. He made his move to Hollywood in 1931. A few credits soon filled his résumé (*Blonde Venus*, 1932; *Madame Butterfly*, 1932), but then Mae West intervened, including him in her popular vehicle *She Done Him Wrong* (1933) with the famous line, "Why don't you come up some time and see me?" She had recognized the appealing combination of verve, sexual allure, sophistication, and gentlemanly bearing that would make Grant a star. Soon afterward established as a handsome leading man and wordly

"Everybody wants to be Cary Grant. Even I want to be Cary Grant."

No to James Bond

James Bond's creator Ian Fleming said that he had partly based the character of his debonair spy on Cary Grant. This seems perfectly natural when one looks at the cool, suave, man of the world persona the actor had so successfully established in movies such as *To Catch a Thief* (1955) and *North by Northwest* (1959). However, when Grant was approached for the role in the first Bond movie *Dr. No* (1962), he turned it down saying that at fifty-eight, he felt he was too old to do the part justice.

- Eventual Bond players, Sean Connery and Roger Moore, were both chosen supposedly for their likenesses to Cary Grant—Connery for his looks and Moore for his sense of humor.

- During the filming of *Dr. No*, Fleming initially found Connery's portrayal "unrefined" but he changed his mind when the movie was completed.

- Writer Ian Fleming also had other actors in mind when visualizing his James Bond—these included David Niven and Rex Harrison.

- The actual Bond character was based on a real-life spy, Merlin Menshall, who worked for Fleming during World War II.

- Cary Grant passed on a number of other high-profile roles, including Humbert Humbert in *Lolita* (1962) and Henry Higgins in *My Fair Lady* (1964).

RIGHT: Grant with costar and offscreen lover Sophia Loren in *The Pride and the Passion*.

comedian, he eventually costarred in some of the classic screwball comedies, including *The Awful Truth* (1937), *Bringing Up Baby* (1938), and *His Girl Friday* (1940), before he turned in a signature performance in *The Philadelphia Story* (1940).

Always a capable physical performer for both comic and dramatic ends, Grant set an important precedent for the worldly man, the irresistible lover, and the unreliable but still appealing urban sophisticate. His accent, posture, attitude, comportment, and overall mythos suggested superiority—of judgment, of training, of ability, of breeding. There was the tanned face, parted hair, and gleaming smile. There was also the tall, athletic build, able to embrace risk and constantly suggesting virility with every turn. Altogether, these traits made Grant malleable for various directors, perhaps most famously, Alfred Hitchcock.

Later roles and fatherhood

Grant's mature roles include *Notorious* (1946), *I Was a Male War Bride* (1949), *To Catch a Thief* (1955), *An Affair to Remember* (1957), *North by Northwest* (1959), *Operation Petticoat* (1959), and *Charade* (1963). Then, dramatically, he retired from the actor's life at the age of sixty-two and became a father in 1966. His last 20 years seem to have been devoted to his legacy and his daughter, which is a remarkable feat for one of Hollywood's all-time biggest leading men—all the more so when considering that age has been notoriously, even ridiculously, kind to men who have continued to work long after their bodies have clearly betrayed the passing of years.

Bestowing him with an honorary Oscar and two nominations—for *Penny Serenade* (1941) and *None but the Lonely Heart* (1944)—along with four Golden Globe nominations, the critical establishment was never unkind to Grant; nor did it fawn over him. It seems that his unique talents, indeed his persona, were a bit too far beyond the mold to be fully respected during his career's active period. But his influence lives on, coloring characters like James Bond and claiming new fans with each retrospective of his body of work. **GCQ**

JOHN GIELGUD

Born: Arthur John Gielgud, April 14, 1904 (London, England); died 2000 (Wotton Underwood, Buckinghamshire, England).

Star qualities: Eminent Shakespearean actor; the Hamlet of his generation; witty, hardworking, and charming; captivating voice; self-deprecating; writer; director.

Sir John Gielgud was a major star of the British stage for seven decades. There is a sense that he felt obliged to appear in films, but never wholly gave of his talent—he was certainly never a movie star on a level with Laurence Olivier or a screen actor as subtle as Ralph Richardson (the other "knights of the stage").

Born to a family with an acting tradition, Gielgud made his professional stage debut in Shakespeare's *Henry V* at the age of seventeen. After some early movie appearances (*The Clue of the New Pin*, 1929; *Insult*, 1932; *The Good Companions*, 1933), he worked with Alfred Hitchcock as W. Somerset Maugham's spy Ashenden in *Secret Agent* (1936). Nobody was happy with the results and he never played a romantic lead onscreen again.

Gielgud quit movies for nearly two decades, returning only when Shakespeare was screenwriter, as a thin, backstabbing Cassius in *Julius Caesar* (1953), the Chorus in *Romeo and Juliet* (1954), and the Duke of Clarence in Olivier's *Richard III* (1955). He also played Henry IV in Orson Welles's *Campanadas a medianoche* (1965) (*Chimes at Midnight*), and (interestingly and unconventionally) an ailing, clear-minded Prospero in Peter Greenaway's *Tempest*-derived *Prospero's Books* (1991).

Top Takes...

Elizabeth 1998
Hamlet 1996
Shine 1996
Prospero's Books 1991
Plenty 1985
Gandhi 1982
Arthur 1981 ★
Chariots of Fire 1981
The Elephant Man 1980
Providence 1977
Galileo 1975
Murder on the Orient Express 1974
Julius Caesar 1970
The Charge of the Light Brigade 1968
Campanadas a medianoche 1965
  (*Chimes at Midnight*)
The Loved One 1965
Hamlet 1964
Becket 1964 ☆
Richard III 1955
Romeo and Juliet 1954
Julius Caesar 1953
The Good Companions 1933
Insult 1932
The Clue of the New Pin 1929

RIGHT: Gielgud's wily Cassius plots with James Mason's Brutus in *Julius Caesar*.

1900s

Gielgud is one of only nine actors to win an Oscar (as the sniping butler in *Arthur*, 1981), a Grammy, an Emmy, and a Tony. His screen work loosened up from the mid-1960s, and he showed a gift for stuffy, arch comedy (*The Loved One*, 1965; *The Charge of the Light Brigade*, 1968; *Murder on the Orient Express*, 1974). He specialized in cameos as fussy, obstreperous historical kings, cardinals, ministers, popes, academics, and doctors (*Becket*, 1964; *Galileo*, 1975; *The Elephant Man*, 1980; *Chariots of Fire*, 1981; *Shine*, 1996; *Elizabeth*, 1998). But his best performance came as the aged novelist, struggling with memory, fantasy, deteriorating health, and a werewolf story in Alain Resnais's *Providence* (1977).

Offscreen, Gielgud succeeded Olivier as director of London's National Theatre and wrote a number of books about his life and career. Having outlived his long-term partner, Martin Hensler, Gielgud died of natural causes, aged ninety-six. **KN**

ABOVE: Gielgud as the bitter, dying writer in *Providence* with Ellen Burstyn.

Hamlet of a Generation

Although John Gielgud was hailed as the finest Hamlet of the twentieth century, his own Danish prince was never preserved on celluloid. When he first played Hamlet in 1929, it was the first time that an English actor under the age of forty had played the role in London's West End. Gielgud made the part his own with the unique speed of his delivery and exquisite vocals. Over the years he would develop and refine his interpretation of Hamlet, and it became his definitive role. He turned down an offer to film his Hamlet in the 1930s, but later took parts in various filmed or televised versions of the play.

JEAN GABIN

Born: Jean-Alexis Moncorgé, May 17, 1904 (Paris, France); died 1976 (Île-de-France, France).

Star qualities: A French institution; handsome, demanding, often a cigarette dangling from his lips; played the classic antihero, ill-fated victims, and losers.

Top Takes…

Holed up on the top floor of a Paris tenement building, the police closing in, Jean Gabin furiously harangues the rubbernecking crowd below: "Yes, I'm a killer! But the streets are running with killers! Everybody kills!" Even as a murderer in Marcel Carné's *Le Jour se lève* (1939) (*Daybreak*), Gabin identifies with the common man.

The son of cabaret entertainers, Gabin started out on the stage at age fifteen before making his debut in the silent *Ohé! Les Valises* (1928). He worked for many years on the stage and in music halls, including the Folies Bergères and the Moulin Rouge. Down-to-earth glamour and antiromantic romanticism were his stock-in-trade during the 1930s. Stoic, gentle beneath a truculent exterior, the doomed proletarian hero at odds with the law, he met his fate without complaining in Julien Duvivier's *La Belle équipe* (1936) (*They Were Five*), Carné's *Quai des brumes* (1938) (*Port of Shadows*), and Jean Renoir's *Les Bas-bonds* (1936) (*The Lower Depths*), *La Grande illusion* (1937) (*The Grand Illusion*), and *La Bête humaine* (1938) (*The Human Beast*).

He moved to Hollywood during the German occupation of France. After World War II, with his style of hero out of fashion, Gabin lost his way a little. Jacques Becker put him back on track as the aging crime boss in *Touchez pas au Grisbi* (1954) (*Grisbi*). Gray-haired, thicker set, and exuding wry experience, Gabin settled into a series of authority-figure roles, sometimes even on the right side of the law; he played Inspector Maigret several times. Increasingly stubborn, he took to working only with directors he could dominate, and the quality of his later films declined, but to the last he remained hugely popular with the public and an institution in French cinema. **PK**

"I don't like watching love stories. Same old eternal triangle."

ROBERT MONTGOMERY

Born: Henry Montgomery Jr., May 21, 1904 (Beacon, New York, U.S.); died 1981 (New York City, New York, U.S.).

Star qualities: Tall, suave, and dashingly handsome; stylish dresser; stagecraft; versatile; played the romantic lead and private eye of film noirs; director; producer.

Robert Montgomery passed much of his career as the male half of the kind of luminous couples that populated the sumptuous fare produced by MGM, his studio for the course of the 1930s. He was attractive, well-spoken, wore clothes with style, and emanated the requisite panache required to squire Greta Garbo, Joan Crawford, and other luminaries.

He worked on the New York stage before signing with MGM in 1929. With Garbo, he costarred in *Inspiration* (1931); with Crawford in *Untamed* (1929), *Letty Lynton* (1932), *No More Ladies* (1935), and *The Last of Mrs. Cheyney* (1937). He broke with this pattern when he played the serial killer in *Night Must Fall* (1937), although equally challenging parts did not follow, and he left MGM in 1940.

As a freelancer, diversity came his way. He appeared in Alfred Hitchcock's underrated farce *Mr. & Mrs. Smith* (1941), with Carole Lombard, and the hugely successful *Here Comes Mr. Jordan* (1941). Military service in World War II interrupted this trend, as he joined the navy, and he relived the experience onscreen in John Ford's stirring *They Were Expendable* (1945).

Subsequently, Montgomery stepped behind the camera, with mixed success. His two most notable releases fell in the realm of film noir: the moody south-of-the-border yarn *Ride the Pink Horse* (1947), and the Raymond Chandler adaptation *Lady in the Lake* (1947), in which the camera wholly took over the perspective of the physically absent Philip Marlowe. Montgomery starred in the former, and voiced the dialogue of the shamus in the latter. Television thereafter occupied his attention, although he directed one last movie, a biopic of Admiral Halsey starring James Cagney, *The Gallant Hours* (1960). **DS**

Top Takes…

The Gallant Hours 1960
Your Witness 1950
June Bride 1948
Ride the Pink Horse 1947
Lady in the Lake 1947
They Were Expendable 1945
Unfinished Business 1941
Here Comes Mr. Jordan 1941
Mr. & Mrs. Smith 1941
Yellow Jack 1938
Night Must Fall 1937
The Last of Mrs. Cheyney 1937
No More Ladies 1935
Letty Lynton 1932
Inspiration 1931
Untamed 1929

"Enjoy the applause and the adulation of the public. But never, never believe it."

JOHNNY WEISSMULLER

Born: Janos Weissmuller, June 2, 1904 (Freidorf, Banat, Romania); died 1984 (Acapulco, Mexico).

Star qualities: Adonis good looks; world-class athlete; tall, muscular bodybuilder, lithe in a loincloth; yodeling yell; the ultimate Tarzan; action-movie hero.

Top Takes…

Won Ton Ton, the Dog Who Saved Hollywood 1976
Jungle Moon Men 1955
Cannibal Attack 1954
Killer Ape 1953
Valley of Head Hunters 1953
Voodoo Tiger 1952
Fury of the Congo 1951
The Lost Tribe 1949
Jungle Jim 1948
Tarzan and the Mermaids 1948
Tarzan Triumphs 1943
Tarzan's New York Adventure 1942
Tarzan and His Mate 1934
Tarzan the Ape Man 1932
Glorifying the American Girl 1929

The son of Romanian immigrants, Johnny Weissmuller was a sickly child who took up swimming to build his strength. He later became a world-class swimming champion and star of the U.S. Olympic Squad, winning five gold medals. In 1929 he quit professional swimming and worked for the BVD bathing-suit company before MGM showed an interest. He first appeared as Adonis in a fig leaf in *Glorifying the American Girl* (1929), and then landed the role that defined his career in *Tarzan the Ape Man* (1932). Lithe, long-haired, nearly-naked, and inarticulate, Weissmuller's Tarzan is intriguingly partnered with Maureen O'Sullivan's sophisticated but melting Jane. Famed for the line, "Me Tarzan, you Jane," Weissmuller claimed he never said it; it was "Tarzan, Jane." Their jungle idyll is expanded, with Tarzan picking up a few more words, in *Tarzan and His Mate* (1934).

Although O'Sullivan eventually got free of the series, Weissmuller stayed on for ten more sequels at two different studios, MGM and RKO Pictures. The sex was sifted out of the formula but the adventure remained, and Weissmuller's Tarzan has any number of iconic moments: ripping through jackets as he prepares for *Tarzan's New York Adventure* (1942), and snarling "Die Nazi" as he enters the war effort in *Tarzan Triumphs* (1943). When Weissmuller left the series after *Tarzan and the Mermaids* (1948), the distinctive yodeling yell he invented remained on the soundtrack. Paunchier and in tropical shorts rather than a loincloth, Weissmuller continued adventuring in a run of "Jungle Jim" films, including *Jungle Jim* (1948) and *Voodoo Tiger* (1952). From *Cannibal Attack* (1954) onward, the "Jungle Jim" name was dropped and the hero became simply "Johnny Weissmuller." **KN**

"The public forgives my acting because they know I was an athlete."

RALPH BELLAMY

Born: Ralph Rexford Bellamy, June 17, 1904 (Chicago, Illinois, U.S.); died 1991 (Santa Monica, California, U.S.).

Star qualities: Shakespearean stage performer; second lead; strong character actor; famous for parts as the charming but dull man; champion of actors' rights.

Ralph Bellamy was such a fresh-faced, openhearted likable fellow with a measured but charming style of dialogue delivery that he was usually cast as the nice-but-dim guy who doesn't get the girl: immortally as Cary Grant's victim in *The Awful Truth* (1937) and *His Girl Friday* (1940), or the above-suspicion witness who turns out to be the killer, as in *Lady on a Train* (1945).

After a period as a stage actor with his own traveling troupe, Bellamy hit Broadway in 1929. He made his film debut as a snarling gangster in *The Secret Six* (1931), but gravitated to more civilized roles such as the pipe-smoking, earnest psychiatrist in *Blind Alley* (1939) and "regular Joe" sleuth Ellery Queen in a mystery series that began with *Ellery Queen, Master Detective* (1940). Underused at Universal Studios in the 1940s, where he met the Wolf Man and the Frankenstein Monster (both played by Lon Chaney Jr.), he temporarily abandoned movies for TV and Broadway.

In the 1960s Bellamy returned to the cinema by recreating his great stage success as Franklin D. Roosevelt in *Sunrise at Campobello* (1960). Thereafter, he was seen to advantage as a humorless cattle baron in *The Professionals* (1966), a twinkling Satanist obstetrician in *Rosemary's Baby* (1968), and a tyrannical tycoon in *Trading Places* (1983). Offscreen, Bellamy was ever a champion of actors' rights and was one of the founders of the Screen Actors Guild. He served with distinction as president of Actors' Equity from 1952 to 1964 (he resisted the blacklisting of the McCarthy era), helping set up the first pension fund for actors. The veteran actor's peers acknowledged his efforts with an honorary Academy Award in 1987 for his services to the acting profession. Bellamy gave his final film performance in *Pretty Woman* (1990). **KN**

Top Takes...

Pretty Woman 1990
The Good Mother 1988
Trading Places 1983
Rosemary's Baby 1968
The Professionals 1966
Sunrise at Campobello 1960
Lady on a Train 1945
Delightfully Dangerous 1945
Guest in the House 1944
The Great Impersonation 1942
The Ghost of Frankenstein 1942
The Wolf Man 1941
Ellery Queen, Master Detective 1940
His Girl Friday 1940
Blind Alley 1939
The Secret Six 1931

"I always [say] if I can't get the girl at the end of the picture, at least give me more money."

PETER LORRE

Born: László Löwenstein, June 26, 1904 (Rózsahegy, Austria-Hungary); died 1964 (Los Angeles, California, U.S.).

Star qualities: Distinctive accent, piercing voice, and unique mannerisms; rotund; first-ever James Bond screen villain; creator of cinema's definitive psychopath.

With his bulging eyes, hunched posture, and high-pitched whine, Peter Lorre was the screen's ultimate "weak man." Most of his characters are cowards, unable to contain fits of outrage and prepared to sell their soul. Yet he always portrayed them as cultured, intelligent, and with an alluring smile. Given that, it is no surprise that Lorre invented the psychopath for cinema. In his first movie, Fritz Lang's chilling *M* (1931), Lorre plays a whistling child molester with such haunting conviction and eerie realism that his performance became the model for every screen serial killer since. The part made him instantly famous.

After he fled Germany when Hitler came to power, it took Lorre a few years to find his feet on the international scene. But after two successful collaborations with Alfred Hitchcock, *The Man Who Knew Too Much* (1934) and *Secret Agent* (1936), he became well entrenched in Hollywood. It was inevitable that he would play mostly crooked or feeble foreigners for the rest of his career, but there were exceptions: in the *Mr. Moto* serials (1937–1939) he proved he could be righteous and straight, and the lovely comedy *I Was an Adventuress* (1940) revealed that he was funny, too. Still, it is when Lorre portrayed people

RIGHT: Peter Lorre at his most memorable, as the creepy child killer Hans Eckert in *M*.

1900s

cornered or ready to jump ship, unpredictable and sweaty, that he was at his best. Three movies demonstrate that beyond any doubt: in *The Maltese Falcon* (1941), Lorre is the epitome of greed as Joel Cairo, ready to backstab anyone who comes in his way. In *Casablanca* (1942), he adds a tragic, romantic ring to a part that in the hands of any other actor would have been a merely functional role. Lorre's ambiguity is one of the main reasons for the movie's everlasting cult reputation. And in *Arsenic and Old Lace* (1944), Lorre's Dr. Einstein added a unique mix of lunacy and desperation to an already zany story.

After World War II, Lorre focused on TV appearances and independent horror features, such as *The Beast with Five Fingers* (1946) and *The Raven* (1963). He died a naturalized U.S. citizen, having directed one film, *Der Verlorene* (1951) (*The Lost One*), about a Nazi scientist who kills his wife, a dark, ironic comment on the psychopath psyche that had made his fame. **EM**

ABOVE: Lorre with Humphrey Bogart, his frequent costar, in *The Maltese Falcon*.

Impersonating Lorre

Peter Lorre's silken voice and distinctive accent was instantly recognizable and became much imitated. It also led to a successful career in radio, where he had his own shows. Lorre's unforgettable qualities engendered many impersonations in cartoons, such as the character Ren from *Ren and Stimpy*, Morocco Mole from *Secret Squirrel*, and Mr. Gruesome from *The Flintstones*. In the 1940s Spike Jones's hit record cover version of "My Old Flame" featured voice actor Paul Frees doing a Lorre impression. Lorre once quipped: "All that anyone needs to imitate me is two soft-boiled eggs and a bedroom voice."

GREER GARSON

Born: Eileen Evelyn Greer Garson, September 29, 1904 (London, England); died 1996 (Dallas, Texas, U.S.).

Star qualities: "The Duchess"; flaming-red hair; leading lady of serious dramas; intelligent, elegant, and refined acting style; often played the noble woman.

Top Takes...

The Happiest Millionaire 1967
The Singing Nun 1966
Sunrise at Campobello 1960 ☆
Her Twelve Men 1954
Julius Caesar 1953
The Miniver Story 1950
Julia Misbehaves 1948
Desire Me 1947
The Valley of Decision 1945 ☆
Mrs. Parkington 1944 ☆
Madame Curie 1943 ☆
Random Harvest 1942
Mrs. Miniver 1942 ★
Blossoms in the Dust 1941 ☆
Pride and Prejudice 1940
Goodbye, Mr. Chips 1939 ☆

"If you're going to be typed, there are worse molds in which you can be cast."

World War II produced three enduring female images: Rosie the Riveter (the woman excellent at a man's work); Betty "Legs" Grable (queen of the pinups); and Greer "The Duchess" Garson's Mrs. Miniver (Hollywood's image of middle-class respectability and the quiet virtues of endurance, self-possession, good-heartedness, and humility).

The moguls did not know at first to what use Garson's considerable charisma could be put. She first received acclaim for her part as the lively Katherine Chipping, wife to a teacher, in *Goodbye, Mr. Chips* (1939), which won her the first of seven Oscar nominations for Best Actress. Playing opposite the stolid, ruggedly handsome yet unthreatening Walter Pidgeon in *Mrs. Miniver* (1942), Garson achieved a phenomenal popularity in this idealized version of contemporary Britain. Equally capable of disarming with her charm a frightened German pilot and winning the annual village rose contest, her lead character mediated between classes and exemplified the emotional strength that wartime required the good bourgeoise to possess.

Garson was equally good as the scientist's wife who quietly refuses to take a backseat to her husband in *Madame Curie* (1943). Her postwar film career was a disappointment, however, including *The Miniver Story* (1950), a misguided attempt to rekindle a then-bygone era of shared sacrifice and sentimentality. Although her stage career offered steady work, her later screen roles were mostly minor, though she did play a convincing Calpurnia in *Julius Caesar* (1953). Her only affecting portrayal was a nostalgic resurrection of "Miniverness," and the war years: as a young, dutiful, yet strong Eleanor Roosevelt in *Sunrise at Campobello* (1960). **BP**

DICK POWELL

Born: Richard Ewing Powell, November 14, 1904 (Mountain View, Arkansas, U.S.); died 1963 (Los Angeles, California, U.S.).

Star qualities: Director; producer; dancer; baby-faced tenor; the consummate private eye; versatile, with roles in musicals, comedies, and dramas.

Dick Powell started out as a vocalist in his band, the Charlie Davies Orchestra, before he was signed by Warner Brothers in 1932, and made his movie debut as a singing bandleader in *Blessed Event* (1932).

He had two distinctive, separate film careers as an actor. In the 1930s he was the ever-cheery juvenile in musicals, wooden in romantic scenes and warbling ditties as massed ranks participated in Busby Berkeley's choreographed kaleidoscopes: *42nd Street* (1933), *Footlight Parade* (1933), and *Gold Diggers of 1933* (1933). It was during this period that he married his first wife, Joan Blondell, with whom he costarred in 12 films. He coasted on geniality until the mid-1940s, when—after playing the movies' best-ever Philip Marlowe in *Murder, My Sweet* (1944)—he reinvented himself as a tough guy with a heart, a film noir lead qualified to discern the comical streak in Raymond Chandler's narration.

Powell thereafter alternated hardboiled trench coats, as in *Pitfall* (1948), with urban whimsy, reading the next day's paper in *It Happened Tomorrow* (1944), and a dog reincarnated as a private eye in *You Never Can Tell* (1951). He also took on occasional historical action roles as a U.S. cavalry spy in *Station West* (1948) and a presidential bodyguard in *The Tall Target* (1951). In the 1950s, Powell concentrated on producing and directing—mostly B-movies such as *Split Second* (1953), but his film *The Enemy Below* (1957) won an Academy Award for Special Effects. He also moved into acting on television, resurrecting his Philip Marlowe in Climax's *The Long Goodbye* (1954), and is sterling as the pipe-smoking screenwriter married to flirt Gloria Grahame on the big screen in *The Bad and the Beautiful* (1952). **KN**

Top Takes...

The Bad and the Beautiful 1952
You Never Can Tell 1951
The Tall Target 1951
Right Cross 1950
The Reformer and the Redhead 1950
Station West 1948
Pitfall 1948
To the Ends of the Earth 1948
Johnny O'Clock 1947
Cornered 1945
Murder, My Sweet 1944
It Happened Tomorrow 1944
Footlight Parade 1933
Gold Diggers of 1933 1933
42nd Street 1933
Blessed Event 1932

"The best thing about [being a director] is that you don't have to hold your stomach in."

RAY MILLAND

Born: Reginald Alfred John Truscott-Jones, January 3, 1905 (Neath, Glamorgan, Wales); died 1986 (Torrance, California, U.S.).

Star qualities: Suave, charming, and athletic; the archetypal British gentleman; prolific output; went from romantic and comedy lead to character actor.

Top Takes…

The Last Tycoon 1976

Frogs 1972

Love Story 1970

Panic in Year Zero! 1962

A Man Alone 1955

The Girl in the Red Velvet Swing 1955

Dial M for Murder 1954

The Lost Weekend 1945 ★

Ministry of Fear 1944

Reap the Wild Wind 1942

Arise, My Love 1940

French Without Tears 1940

Beau Geste 1939

Bulldog Drummond Escapes 1937

Charlie Chan in London 1934

The Flying Scotsman 1929

Ray Milland was for most of his career an accomplished, pleasant leading man. His one great role was opposite Jane Wyman as the alcoholic writer in Billy Wilder's *The Lost Weekend* (1945), for which he won a Best Actor Oscar. Ever known as a man who avoided the Hollywood limelight, he didn't say a word on accepting his Academy Award, and instead chose to bow gracefully before exiting the stage.

Born in Wales, he served as a guardsman with the Royal Household Cavalry in London before he entered British films with *The Flying Scotsman* (1929). It was at this point that he changed his name, and is known for telling his agent: "I really don't care what you call me. But I must keep the initial 'R' because my mother had it engraved on my suitcases." A few more movies followed before he headed for Hollywood in 1930. There he played evening-clothes roles in the likes of *Charlie Chan in London* (1934), rising to B-leads as the sleuth in *Bulldog Drummond Escapes* (1937), while cultivating A-films as one of the Geste brothers in *Beau Geste* (1939). His home studio was Paramount Pictures, which landed him in sophisticated romances such as *Arise, My Love* (1940), a Cecil B. DeMille adventure *Reap the Wild Wind* (1942), and interesting film noirs such as *Ministry of Fear* (1944). In the 1950s Milland proved an icy murderer in Alfred Hitchcock's *Dial M for Murder* (1954). From 1955 onward he started directing himself in a number of movies, including a good Western, *A Man Alone* (1955), and the grim nuke quickie *Panic in Year Zero!* (1962).

Doffing his toupee (he blamed his premature baldness on having his hair curled for *Reap the Wild Wind* (1942)), Milland retired to play bullying older-generation figures in films such as *Love Story* (1970) and *Frogs* (1972). **KN**

> "The greatest drawback in making pictures is the fact that filmmakers have to eat."

ANNA MAY WONG

Born: Wong Liu Tsong, January 3, 1905 (Los Angeles, California, U.S.); died 1961 (Santa Monica, California, U.S.).

Star qualities: Beautiful; graceful; languid; sexy; coiffured; famed for her skin and beautiful hands; trailblazing, determined pioneer.

Anna May Wong was the first Chinese-American movie star, although Hollywood tended to consign her to exotic set-dressing roles. The daughter of the owners of a Chinese laundry, she worked as a photographer's model while in her teens. She benefited from a 1920s fashion for "oriental" stories such as *Shame* (1921), *Bits of Life* (1921), and *Drifting* (1923), and was sexy as a Mongol slave in the fantasy epic *The Thief of Bagdad* (1924). This high-profile role led to her casting as Tiger Lily in *Peter Pan* (1924) and more elaborate Asian-themed films such as *Mr. Wu* (1927), with Lon Chaney.

At the end of the 1920s Wong was too often sidelined in small roles, given the racial prejudice and stereotypical typecasting she faced as a Chinese-American. She fought against it for much of her life, saying of her "Dragon Lady" roles: "Why is it that the screen Chinese is always the villain?" She often played a dancer or some other euphemism, as in *The Chinese Parrot* (1927) and *The Crimson City* (1928), when all she ever wanted was to play a contemporary American woman.

Seeking work, Wong left the United States in 1928. She became popular in Britain, where she landed a star role in the comparatively lavish British movie *Piccadilly* (1929). She also ventured to mainland Europe and took on roles in German films such as *Schmutziges Geld* (1928) (*Show Life*). Back in the United States, she played Fu Manchu's heiress in *Daughter of the Dragon* (1931), Marlene Dietrich's sidekick in *Shanghai Express* (1932), a Holmesian femme fatale in *A Study in Scarlet* (1933), and a rare Chinese female sleuth in *Daughter of Shanghai* (1937). Her later career was scanty, although she had a minor role in *Portrait in Black* (1960). Wong died of a heart attack at the age of fifty-six. **KN**

Top Takes...

Portrait in Black 1960
Daughter of Shanghai 1937
A Study in Scarlet 1933
Shanghai Express 1932
Daughter of the Dragon 1931
Piccadilly 1929
Schmutziges Geld 1928 (*Show Life*)
The Crimson City 1928
The Chinese Parrot 1927
Mr. Wu 1927
Peter Pan 1924
The Thief of Bagdad 1924
Drifting 1923
Bits of Life 1921
Shame 1921

"I see no reason why Chinese and English people should not kiss onscreen."

JOAN CRAWFORD

Born: Lucille Fay LeSueur, March 23, 1905 (San Antonio, Texas, U.S.); died 1977 (New York City, New York, U.S.).

Star qualities: Passionate, ambitious actress; hardworking; talented dancer, strong voice, and striking good looks; her seductive charm won her international acclaim.

1900s

Top Takes...

Berserk! 1967
I Saw What You Did 1965
Strait-Jacket 1964
What Ever Happened to Baby Jane? 1962
Autumn Leaves 1956
Queen Bee 1955
Johnny Guitar 1954
Sudden Fear 1952 ☆
Possessed 1947 ☆
Humoresque 1946
Mildred Pierce 1945 ★
A Woman's Face 1941
Susan and God 1940
Strange Cargo 1940
The Women 1939
Mannequin 1937
The Last of Mrs. Cheyney 1937
Love on the Run 1936
The Gorgeous Hussy 1936
Sadie McKee 1934
Rain 1932
Letty Lynton 1932
Grand Hotel 1932
Possessed 1931
Our Dancing Daughters 1928

RIGHT: Crawford demonstrates the extent of her appeal in this publicity shot from 1932.

Joan Crawford won a dance contest in 1923 and was awarded her professional name after a contest held by *Photoplay* magazine. She survived decades in the business as a top-ranking star, projecting an innate toughness and terrifying style that masked the fact that she wasn't as talented as Bette Davis, as beautiful as Greta Garbo, as sexy as Barbara Stanwyck, or as mysterious as Marlene Dietrich.

In the mid-1920s she was the incarnation of the jazz age—notably in *Our Dancing Daughters* (1928)—and married into the nearest thing Hollywood had to royalty by becoming Mrs. Douglas Fairbanks Jr. (it didn't last). Unlike such sensations of the roaring twenties as Clara Bow, Crawford survived into the talkie era, although she soon sought standout roles (surprisingly often as whores) amid strong casts: as the ambitious stenographer out to snare a wealthy patron in *Grand Hotel* (1932) and Somerset Maugham's island temptress Sadie Thompson in *Rain* (1932). She also started indiscriminately taking title roles, such as *Letty Lynton* (1932), *Sadie McKee* (1934), *The Gorgeous Hussy* (1936), and *The Last of Mrs. Cheyney* (1937). She suffered from being unable to hold her own—

1900s

unlike Katharine Hepburn or Myrna Loy—in an equal onscreen relationship with a male movie star, seeming forced and shrill next to Clark Gable in *Love on the Run* (1936) and Spencer Tracy in *Mannequin* (1937). Crawford's transformation from pinup to diva was sealed by *The Women* (1939), in which she relishes queening it over the all-female cast ("There is a name for you ladies, but it isn't used in high society . . . outside of a kennel"), and tipped over into kitsch with *Strange Cargo* (1940) and *A Woman's Face* (1941). After another Anita Loos comedy (*Susan and God*, 1940), MGM ran out of things for Crawford to do, and she transferred to Warner Brothers. The studio gave her a signature role in *Mildred Pierce* (1945), for which she won her Best Actress Oscar (she was to be nominated twice more after this success). As Mildred, a career

ABOVE: Crawford with rival Bette Davis on the set of *Whatever Happened to Baby Jane?*

"Send me flowers while I'm alive. They won't do me a damn bit of good after I'm dead."

Joan vs. Bette

One possessed movie looks and glamour while the other had the acting credentials and chalked up ten Oscar nominations. By the time Joan Crawford and Bette Davis teamed up as the warring sisters in *What Ever Happened to Baby Jane?* (1962), the jealousy between the two Hollywood stalwarts was legendary. But Davis said that there was no feud and that they weren't competitors, because they played different types. The crew on *Baby Jane* testified to their polite professionalism on set. Crawford claimed that the idea of a feud was exploited for publicity purposes. Yet neither actress was ever at a loss for words when it came to the other, and the pair kept the public entertained with their sniping remarks:

- Bette of Joan: "She's slept with every male star at MGM except Lassie."
- Joan of Bette: "I don't hate [Davis]. I resent her. I don't see how she built a career out of a set of mannerisms . . . Take away the pop eyes, the cigarette, and those funny clipped words and what have you got? She's phony. But I guess the public likes that."
- Bette of Joan: "I admire her, and yet I feel uncomfortable with her. To me, she is the personification of the Movie Star. I have always felt her greatest performance is Crawford being Crawford."
- Joan of Bette: "She can be such a bitch, but she's so talented and dedicated."

woman who goes from housewife to tycoon, Crawford plays an insanely devoted mother (to a worthless slut), is bewitching to a range of middle-aged men, and shows off her striking eyes and cheekbones in a succession of noirish portrait shots. She made other high-class melodramas, toying with violinist John Garfield in the romance *Humoresque* (1946) and cracking up in the thriller *Possessed* (1947).

Tough lady of melodrama

By the time Crawford assumed her roles as a pants-wearing Western saloonkeeper in *Johnny Guitar* (1954) and the archly named *Queen Bee* (1955), her image was so fixed that her films had to partake of camp to get by. Robert Aldrich cast her as an older woman miserably in love with a younger man in *Autumn Leaves* (1956), and later revived her career (and Bette Davis's) by persuading her to play the wheelchair-bound, creepily reasonable, tight-faced victim in *What Ever Happened to Baby Jane?* (1962). Although she refused to return for Aldrich in *Hush . . . Hush, Sweet Charlotte* (1964), Crawford found a late-career niche in psychohorror, as an axe murderess in *Strait-Jacket* (1964), a victim of a reverse shower murder in *I Saw What You Did* (1965), and a ringmistress in *Berserk!* (1967). Since her death, her own screen image has been commingled in the public mind with the strange portrait of her delivered by Faye Dunaway ("No wire hangers!") in *Mommie Dearest* (1981). **KN**

ABOVE: Joan with Fred MacMurray in the Nazi-era spy movie *Above Suspicion*.

JOSEPH COTTEN

Born: Joseph Cheshire Cotten, May 15, 1905 (Petersburg, Virginia, U.S.); died 1994 (Westwood, California, U.S.).

Star qualities: Good looks and poise; charming, versatile leading man of almost every movie genre; famed for film noir roles; writer.

Joseph Cotten studied acting at the Hickman School of Expression in Washington, D.C., before heading to New York in 1924. He had no success in pursuing his acting career and so worked in advertising before entering the theater world as a stage manager and a critic. In 1930 Cotten finally made his Broadway debut, which led to work as an actor on stage and radio shows. He got an opportunity at the movies because of his friendship with director Orson Welles. The pair met while working on Broadway, and Cotten was soon persuaded to join Welles's Mercury Theater Company. Cotten was alone among the Mercury Theater players introduced in *Citizen Kane* (1941). He went on to became a proper movie star, with a career spanning 40 years and 70 films, in roles as character actor, leading man, and action and romantic hero.

He signed with David O. Selznick, who stuck him with the wet-blanket role in *Duel in the Sun* (1946) but gave him a shot at ethereal romance in the delirious *Portrait of Jennie* (1948). Despite their volatile friendship, Welles stood by Cotten, making him the heart of *The Magnificent Ambersons* (1942) and joining him in scripting *Journey into Fear* (1943), before turning up in a virtual cameo, as the late Harry Lime, that revived the wonders and the heartbreaks of the pairing in *The Third Man* (1949). Hollywood tended to see Cotten as staid and dreary, but Alfred Hitchcock drew extraordinary work out of him as the serial murderer in *Shadow of a Doubt* (1943), charming until he gets to the subject of rich widows. He then went international, playing Southern colonels in spaghetti Westerns such as *I Crudeli* (1967) (*The Cruel Ones*) and taking on roles in the occasional offbeat horror movie such as Mario Bava's *Orrori del castello di Norimberga* (1972) (*Baron Blood*). **KN**

Top Takes...

The Survivor 1981
Heaven's Gate 1980
Gli Orrori del castello di Norimberga 1972 (*Baron Blood*)
The Abominable Dr. Phibes 1971
I Crudeli 1967 (*The Cruel Ones*)
Hush ... Hush, Sweet Charlotte 1964
A Blueprint for Murder 1953
Niagara 1953
The Third Man 1949
Portrait of Jennie 1948
Duel in the Sun 1946
Journey into Fear 1943
Shadow of a Doubt 1943
The Magnificent Ambersons 1942
Citizen Kane 1941

> "I didn't care about the movies really. I was tall. I could talk. It was easy to do."

HENRY FONDA

Born: Henry Jaynes Fonda, May 16, 1905 (Grand Island, Nebraska, U.S.); died 1982 (Los Angeles, California, U.S.).

Star qualities: Distinctive prowl; intense blue eyes; natural acting style; ladies' man; rugged; hotheaded.

Top Takes...

On Golden Pond 1981 ★
Fedora 1978
Midway 1976
C'era una volta il West 1968
  (*Once Upon a Time in the West*)
Battle of the Bulge 1965
Fail-Safe 1964
How the West Was Won 1962
The Longest Day 1962
12 Angry Men 1957 ☆
The Wrong Man 1956
War and Peace 1956
Mister Roberts 1955
Fort Apache 1948
The Fugitive 1947
My Darling Clementine 1946
The Grapes of Wrath 1940 ☆
Drums Along the Mohawk 1939
Young Mr. Lincoln 1939
Jezebel 1938
You Only Live Once 1937
The Trail of the Lonesome Pine 1936
I Dream Too Much 1935
Way Down East 1935
The Farmer Takes a Wife 1935

RIGHT: Fonda won his only Best Actor Oscar for his performance in *On Golden Pond*.

Having made his acting debut in amateur theater in Omaha, Nebraska, Henry Fonda gained experience on Broadway before appearing in the movie version of *The Farmer Takes a Wife* (1935), a play in which he scored a big success. His Hollywood career took off spectacularly, with performances in the backwoods drama *The Trail of the Lonesome Pine* (1936), Fritz Lang's *You Only Live Once* (1937), and the period saga *Jezebel* (1938), in which he costarred with Bette Davis. In 1939 he made his first film with director John Ford, *Young Mr. Lincoln*, quickly followed by two more Ford projects, *Drums Along the Mohawk* (1939) and *The Grapes of Wrath* (1940), for which Fonda received an Academy Award nomination.

Fonda's lean frame, soft voice, and air of moral integrity made him much in demand. In Preston Sturges's *The Lady Eve* (1941), Fonda showed that he could play comedy too, appearing as an unworldly innocent duped by a confidence trickster. After war service, Fonda resumed his partnership with Ford as Wyatt Earp in *My Darling Clementine* (1946), as a Mexican priest in *The Fugitive* (1947), and in *Fort Apache* (1948), in a rare unsympathetic role as a martinet army colonel.

1900s

At this point Fonda took an extended leave from Hollywood, returning to Broadway to play his most popular (and Tony Award–winning) role in *Mister Roberts*, a comedy set on a U.S. navy ship in World War II. He was later lured back to star in the movie version in 1955. It was a troubled production. John Ford had been assigned to direct, but he wanted many changes; Fonda, who had invested so much in the project, argued with him, and at one point they came to blows. Ford was replaced as director and the pair never worked together again. Fonda went on to give a series of great performances in Alfred Hitchcock's *The Wrong Man* (1956), *12 Angry Men* (1957), and *Fail-Safe* (1964). In Sergio Leone's *C'era una volta il West* (1968) (*Once Upon a Time in the West*), against type, he played a coldhearted killer. A notorious womanizer, Fonda was married five times. The Fonda dynasty lives on in children Peter and Jane, who both have had highly successful movie careers. **EB**

ABOVE: Fonda as Tom Joad in the movie version of Steinbeck's *The Grapes of Wrath*.

An Acting Dynasty

Peter and Jane Fonda both followed Henry into acting and have written about the emotionally strained relationships they had with their famous father. (Their mother committed suicide in 1950.) As onscreen father and daughter in *On Golden Pond* (1981), Henry cries genuine tears on camera when Jane's character unexpectedly grabs his hand and says she wants to be his friend. Her brother Peter's performance as a tough, reserved man in *Ulee's Gold* (1997) is said to be based on his father. Henry confessed that he tried to stay out of their careers so that they'd know they had made it on their own.

CLARA BOW

Born: Clara Gordon Bow, July 29, 1905 (Brooklyn, New York, U.S.); died 1965 (Los Angeles, California, U.S.).

Star qualities: The first screen sex symbol; iconic 1920s flapper; famed for her "Clara Bow" red lips; free spirit; the original "It" Girl.

Top Takes…

Hoop-La 1933
Love Among the Millionaires 1930
The Saturday Night Kid 1929
The Wild Party 1929
Three Weekends 1928
Ladies of the Mob 1928
Red Hair 1928
Hula 1927
It 1927
The Runaway 1926
Free to Love 1925
The Adventurous Sex 1925
Capital Punishment 1925
Enemies of Women 1923
Down to the Sea in Ships 1922
Beyond the Rainbow 1922

One of the most iconic stars of the silent screen, Clara Bow is remembered less for her movies than for her nickname, The "It" Girl, and a number of unfounded rumors and scandals. She was born into grinding poverty in Brooklyn, enduring regular beatings from her father and dependent upon a violent, mentally unstable mother, who once tried to kill her while sleeping. By the age of ten Bow had watched her grandfather collapse and die while pushing her in a swing and her best friend burn to death in a domestic accident. Her salvation came when she won a part in the film *Beyond the Rainbow* (1922) in a magazine competition. Stardom followed swiftly in a series of high-spirited flapper roles.

Nervous, untutored, and insecure, Bow was adored by the public (at her peak, receiving more than 45,000 fan letters a month) but openly shunned by the Hollywood community, who considered her uncouth and stupid. When the talkies arrived, her success waned because of her thick accent. Crippled by bouts of depression, she came to loathe her career. She married the cowboy actor Rex Bell in 1933, then chose to retire at the young age of twenty-six. She never returned to show business and was diagnosed as a schizophrenic in 1949.

Despite this, she was an enormously gifted actress, with an instinctive flair for comedy and a naturalism fully the equal of that of Louise Brooks, who was one of her few consistent champions. Bow was perhaps the first movie actress to exude sexuality, applying her red lipstick in a heart shape to erotic effect. This was imitated by her legions of female fans, who were said to be putting a "Clara Bow" on their lips. All of her films are enjoyable, especially the silents *Hula* (1927) and *It* (1927) and her first talkie, *The Wild Party* (1929). **MC**

> "A sex symbol is a heavy load to carry when one is tired, hurt, and bewildered."

MYRNA LOY

Born: Myrna Adele Williams, August 2, 1905 (Radersburg, Montana, U.S.); died 1993 (New York City, New York, U.S.).

Star qualities: Played the femme fatale on the silent screen before developing into the perfect screen wife; beautiful, svelte, graceful, elegant, and sophisticated.

Myrna Loy's family moved to Los Angeles when she was in her teens. She was drawn to acting and was first spotted by Rudolph Valentino's second wife, Natacha Rambova. Mrs. Valentino was in the audience one evening at a local theater, recognized Loy's talent, and arranged for her to have a screen test, which Loy failed. Undeterred, Loy finally entered films in the mid-1920s, her first movie being *What Price Beauty?* (1925). She was often cast as slinky, exotic vamps in the Theda Bara mold in films such as *Exquisite Sinner* (1926) and *Don Juan* (1926). In the early talkies, these parts continued: camp follower in *The Black Watch* (1929), Morgan Le Fay in *A Connecticut Yankee* (1931), Eurasian hypnotist-murderer in *Thirteen Women* (1932), and nymphomaniac daughter of Fu Manchu in *The Mask of Fu Manchu* (1932).

In the mid-1930s, Loy broke out of this typecasting and established a lasting image as a smart, capable, modern wife— usually with William Powell or Clark Gable—in tart thrillers, comedies, dramas, and musicals: Nora Charles in *The Thin Man* (1934), and sequels such as *Manhattan Melodrama* (1934), *The Great Ziegfeld* (1936), and *Too Hot to Handle* (1938). She made six *Thin Man* movies altogether. By 1938 Loy's career had reached its zenith and she was voted "Queen of Hollywood" in a poll that voted Clark Gable as the "King." She became more matronly over the years, but still glowed as the wife Fredric March comes home to in *The Best Years of Our Lives* (1946), Cary Grant's long-suffering helpmate in *Mr. Blandings Builds His Dream House* (1948), and Clifton Webb's brood mare in *Cheaper by the Dozen* (1950). Later, she was in *Airport 1975* (1974). By the time of her death, she had made 129 movies in total. **KN**

Top Takes...

The End 1978
Airport 1975 1974
Cheaper by the Dozen 1950
Mr. Blandings Builds His Dream House 1948
The Best Years of Our Lives 1946
Too Hot to Handle 1938
The Great Ziegfeld 1936
The Thin Man 1934
Manhattan Melodrama 1934
The Mask of Fu Manchu 1932
Thirteen Women 1932
A Connecticut Yankee 1931
The Black Watch 1929
Don Juan 1926
Exquisite Sinner 1926
What Price Beauty? 1925

"Labels . . . limit your possibilities. But that's how they think in Hollywood."

GRETA GARBO

Born: Greta Lovisa Gustafsson, September 18, 1905 (Stockholm, Stockholms län, Sweden); died 1990 (New York City, New York, U.S.).

Star qualities: "The Face"; legendary beauty; low voice; iconic mystique; elegant, sophisticated screen goddess; reclusive; mistress of the ultimate early exit.

1900s

Top Takes…

Two-Faced Woman 1941
***Ninotchka* 1939** ☆
Camille 1936
Anna Karenina 1935
Queen Christina 1933
As You Desire Me 1932
Grand Hotel 1932
Anna Christie 1931
***Romance* 1930** ☆
***Anna Christie* 1930** ☆
A Woman of Affairs 1928
The Temptress 1926
Gösta Berlings saga 1924
   (*The Atonement of Gosta Berling*)
Herr och fru Stockholm 1920
   (*Mr. and Mrs. Stockholm Out Shopping*)

> "If only those who dream about Hollywood knew how difficult it all is."

A model in her teens, Greta Garbo secured her first part in the advertising short *Herr och fru Stockholm* (1920) (*Mr. and Mrs. Stockholm Out Shopping*). Small roles followed, and Garbo went on to drama school. Mauritz Stiller gave her the lead in *Gösta Berlings saga* (1924) (*The Atonement of Gosta Berling*), and soon she and Stiller were offered contracts with MGM. So it was as a silent sex symbol that Garbo came to the United States and as a silent sex symbol that U.S. audiences first saw her. Her swift transformation into enigmatic goddess—and the most iconic star in talking cinema—was an act of necessity: Garbo was simply different from the rest. Her body was large, her voice almost masculine, her personality inscrutable and remote. Meticulous care was lavished on her star vehicles because that was what they needed, and sensitive crafting made each mask seem an extension of Garbo herself: the character who wants to be alone in *Grand Hotel* (1932), *Queen Christina* (1933), *Anna Karenina* (1935), and *Camille* (1936).

The effort paid off, although moody historical dramas were never an easy sell in the United States. It was Garbo herself: her mystery, her elusiveness, and her distaste for celebrity that transfixed the fan magazines and kept the public intrigued. European audiences put the actual films into profit—an important reason her career ended at the beginning of World War II. She was already itching to break the mold, and her last two movies, the comedies *Ninotchka* (1939)—for which she received her third Academy Award nomination for Best Actress—and *Two-Faced Woman* (1941), worked only in parts. She retired in 1941 and moved to New York City, becoming more or less a recluse. Her fans would have expected nothing less. **MC**

JOEL McCREA

Born: Joel Albert McCrea, November 5, 1905 (Pasadena, California, U.S.); died 1990 (Los Angeles, California, U.S.).

Star qualities: Tall, good looks, and sexual magnetism; steely blue eyes; amiable leading man in romantic dramas and comedies; veteran cowboy in Westerns.

Born on Hollywood's doorstep, Joel McCrea was drawn to the movie world around him. He studied acting at Pomona College, then got into films as an extra and by working as a stuntman before getting his first major role in *The Jazz Age* (1929). It is said that he drove women crazy, and writer Anita Loos is reported as saying that she fainted when she saw McCrea on the beach. After playing some bit parts, McCrea made a good impression on silent-screen comedienne Marion Davies and her lover, newspaper tycoon William Randolph Hearst, who helped him out with studio contracts.

Top Takes...

Mustang Country 1976
Cry Blood, Apache 1970
Sioux Nation 1970
The Young Rounders 1966
Ride the High Country 1962
Wichita 1955
Stranger on Horseback 1955
Stars in My Crown 1950
Ramrod 1947
The Virginian 1946
The Palm Beach Story 1942
Sullivan's Travels 1941
Foreign Correspondent 1940
Union Pacific 1939
Barbary Coast 1935
The Jazz Age 1929

He was one of the most gifted actors of all those who made their mark in the Western. Although appearing in a few examples of the genre in the 1930s, such as Cecil B. DeMille's *Union Pacific* (1939), McCrea first distinguished himself in Alfred Hitchcock's *Foreign Correspondent* (1940), in which he was both agreeable and resourceful as the feckless reporter Johnny Jones, and in a brace of classic Preston Sturges comedies, including *Sullivan's Travels* (1941) and *The Palm Beach Story* (1942), in which he played opposite Veronica Lake and Claudette Colbert, respectively. Lake was also to star with him when he returned to the Western in the later 1940s, in *Ramrod* (1947). Dependable, likeable, charming, and possessing unquestionable moral integrity, McCrea's was the ideal persona for the Western, which he graced throughout the 1950s, in such excellent films as *Stars in My Crown* (1950), *Wichita* (1955), and *Stranger on Horseback* (1955).

> "I have no regrets, except perhaps . . . I should have tried harder to be a better actor."

He gave one of his best performances when he costarred with Randolph Scott in Sam Peckinpah's *Ride the High Country* (1962), playing an aging gunfighter down on his luck, looking to complete one last mission before settling down. **EB**

GILBERT ROLAND

Born: Luis Antonio Dámaso de Alonso, December 11, 1905 (Juárez, Chihuahua, Mexico); died 1994 (Beverly Hills, Los Angeles, U.S.).

Star qualities: Tall, debonair, and dashingly handsome; leading man of silent films; mature character actor of talkies; often played "Latin lover" roles; writer.

Top Takes...

Barbarosa 1982
Cheyenne Autumn 1964
The Bad and the Beautiful 1952
The Miracle of Our Lady of Fatima 1952
We Were Strangers 1949
Angels with Broken Wings 1941
Una Viuda romántica 1933
  (*The Romantic Widow*)
She Done Him Wrong 1933
Resurrección 1931
Camille 1926
The Plastic Age 1925

Dark, moustached, and debonair Mexican actor Gilbert Roland was a popular presence in Hollywood movies for 50 years without ever becoming a major star. He moved with his family to the United States with the onset of the Mexican Revolution between 1910 and 1911. Roland trained as a bullfighter before entering movies at the age of twenty; he was noticed by a Hollywood scout and asked to appear as an extra. He decided he wanted a career on the big screen and changed his name in homage to movie stars John Gilbert and Ruth Roland. Cast opposite Clara Bow in *The Plastic Age* (1925), he had a dashing allure that made an instant impression both on audiences and on Bow, who became his lover. He was also teamed on four occasions with Norma Talmadge; their affair led to Talmadge's divorce from movie producer husband Joseph Schenck. But after the divorce, Talmadge changed her mind about marriage with Gilbert and wed performer George Jessel instead.

While many actors suffered from the transition to sound, Roland's ability to speak Spanish proved an advantage. Early talkies were often shot in various languages for different markets and Roland made several Spanish-language U.S. movies, including *Resurrección* (1931) with fellow Mexican star Lupe Velez. In Hollywood, Roland's accent seemed to make him simultaneously attractive to audiences and difficult to cast, and he often appeared as a Frenchman. Through the later 1930s and 1940s, he alternated minor roles in major films with B-movie leads. He then appeared in a series of Westerns as the popular character "The Cisco Kid." In 1954 he was still considered dashing enough to put Jane Russell over his shoulder and carry her away in *The French Line* (1954). **MC**

"Death comes soon enough so why kill yourself crying about it?"

JOHN CARRADINE

Born: Richmond Reed Carradine, April 5, 1906 (New York City, New York, U.S.); died 1988 (Milan, Italy).

Star qualities: Tall and gaunt; thin face; distinctive deep voice; Shakespearean stage actor; prolific output; played villain roles in Westerns and horror movies.

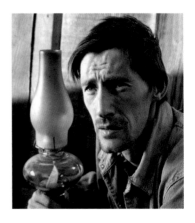

John Carradine's first credited screen role was in a remake of the silent-film classic *Tol'able David* (1930), under the name of Peter Richmond. The son of an artist and a surgeon, Carradine went to art school to study sculpture before he made his debut in the theater in 1925. He moved to Los Angeles in 1927, where he sought work as a sketch artist and scenic designer. Cecil B. DeMille rejected Carradine's designs but gave him voice work in several movies. Not until 1935 did he rename himself John Carradine. He became one of the most sought-after character actors in Hollywood. Tall, gaunt, with a deeply sonorous voice—earning him the nickname "The Voice"—he soon became a favorite of director John Ford in *The Prisoner of Shark Island* (1936), *Mary of Scotland* (1936), and *The Hurricane* (1937), before two memorable roles in Ford classics, as the gambler Hatfield in *Stagecoach* (1939) and as the preacher Casy in *The Grapes of Wrath* (1940).

Carradine acted frequently in stage plays while continuing his movie career, Shakespeare being a favorite. Occasionally he graduated to leading roles in minor films, such as Count Dracula in the B-feature horror movie *House of Dracula* (1945), and he was a frequent performer in TV in the 1950s, especially in Western series such as *The Rifleman* and *The Life and Legend of Wyatt Earp.* Married four times, divorced twice, and widowed once, Carradine had four sons. Three of them, David, Keith, and Robert, appeared together as the Younger brothers, members of Jesse James's gang, in *The Long Riders* (1980). Carradine took guest spots in his son David's Western-with-martial-arts show, *Kung Fu* (1972–1975). He died during a trip to Milan at the age of eighty-two, with the last words, "Milan. What a beautiful place to die." **EB**

Top Takes...

Peggy Sue Got Married 1986
Billy the Kid versus Dracula 1966
The Unearthly 1957
The Ten Commandments 1956
The Black Sleep 1956
House of Dracula 1945
Bluebeard 1944
The Grapes of Wrath 1940
Stagecoach 1939
Alexander's Ragtime Band 1938
Of Human Hearts 1938
The Hurricane 1937
Mary of Scotland 1936
The Prisoner of Shark Island 1936
Les Misérables 1935
Tol'able David 1930

"I've made some of the greatest films ever made—and a lot of crap, too."

LON CHANEY Jr.

Born: Creighton Tull Chaney, February 10, 1906 (Oklahoma City, Oklahoma, U.S.); died 1973 (San Clemente, California, U.S.).

Star qualities: Singer; part of showbiz family; tall character actor; master horror monster; iconic "Wolf Man".

Top Takes…

Dracula vs. Frankenstein 1971
Spider Baby, or The Maddest Story Ever Told 1968
Hillbillys in a Haunted House 1967
Springfield Rifle 1952
High Noon 1952
Abbott and Costello Meet Frankenstein 1948
My Favorite Brunette 1947
House of Dracula 1945
The Mummy's Curse 1944
House of Frankenstein 1944
Son of Dracula 1943
The Mummy's Tomb 1942
The Ghost of Frankenstein 1942
The Wolf Man 1941
One Million B.C. 1940
Of Mice and Men 1939

Lon Chaney Jr. lived in the shadow of his famous father, silent-screen star Lon Chaney. He often grumbled that he was "starved" into changing his name to capitalize on his father's stardom, and dropped the "Junior" from 1942 onward. But he was always keen to become an actor; he spent his childhood traveling with his parents while they did vaudeville shows and learned monster-makeup tips from his father, a master of disguise. Yet it was only after his father died in 1930 that young Chaney followed in his footsteps onto the big screen, mainly doing bit parts and working as a stuntman.

After a bustle of 1930s poverty-row efforts, typically as glowering thugs, Chaney was outstanding as the unsophisticated Lennie in the film version of John Steinbeck's *Of Mice and Men* (1939). Universal Studios signed him as a horror star, casting him as The Monster in *The Ghost of Frankenstein* (1942), The Mummy in four quickies, including *The Mummy's Tomb* (1942), and Dracula in *Son of Dracula* (1943), while giving him his own iconic role in *The Wolf Man* (1941). Reprising the werewolf Larry Talbot through sequels climaxing with *Abbott and Costello Meet Frankenstein* (1948), Chaney was also busy as Lennie-parody morons, as in *My Favorite Brunette* (1947), and Western varmints, as in *Springfield Rifle* (1952). After a good role as the veteran lawman in *High Noon* (1952), he spent the rest of his career in horrors or Westerns, sliding from studio product to makeshift exploitation such as *Hillbillys in a Haunted House* (1967) and *Dracula vs. Frankenstein* (1971). Despite his ongoing battle with alcoholism, Chaney had a late career highlight in Jack Hill's extraordinary black comedy *Spider Baby, or The Maddest Story Ever Told* (1968), for which he also sings the title song. **KN**

> "I tried for three years to make a go of things without capitalizing upon dad's name."

MARY ASTOR

Born: Lucile Vasconcellos Langhanke, May 3, 1906 (Quincy, Illinois, U.S.); died 1987 (Los Angeles, California, U.S.).

Star qualities: Beautiful, rusty redhead; novelist; pianist; resilient, although dogged by scandal; young starlet who became a feature player, usually in matriarchal roles.

The daughter of ambitious German immigrants, Mary Astor took acting lessons and entered beauty contests as a child. The latter brought her to the attention of Hollywood talent scouts, and she was signed at age fourteen. She was in movies from 1921 onward and a star in the 1930s and 1940s, but is best remembered for her role as the duplicitous Brigid O'Shaughnessy in *The Maltese Falcon* (1941). In her career-defining turn, Astor was cast against type as a femme fatale: with her upswept hair and classy mendacity, she is almost matronly beside the sexpots who would dominate film noir.

Astor came to *Falcon* as a Best Supporting Actress Oscar winner for the forgotten soap *The Great Lie* (1941). Three years after Brigid, she became the matriarch in *Meet Me in St. Louis* (1944), which led to Marmee March in *Little Women* (1949). From the 1950s on, she worked mostly in TV—giving her Norma Desmond in a 1956 *Robert Montgomery Presents* version of *Sunset Blvd.* Her last screen role was a minor grotesque in *Hush . . . Hush, Sweet Charlotte* (1964).

Her offscreen life was as up and down as her career; married four times, she was dogged by scandal. She suffered a breakdown following the tragic death of her first husband, director Kenneth Hawks, in a plane crash in 1930. In 1934, Astor was sued by her parents for support and the feud was thrust into the public eye. Her court battles continued through the mid-1930s when her divorce from her second husband, Dr. Franklin Thorpe, made the headlines with a custody battle over their daughter and accusations of adultery. Her ensuing alcoholism led her to a stint in rehab, after which she converted to Roman Catholicism and wrote five novels and a best-selling autobiography, *My Story*. **KN**

Top Takes...

Hush . . . Hush, Sweet Charlotte 1964
Little Women 1949
Meet Me in St. Louis 1944
The Palm Beach Story 1942
The Maltese Falcon 1941
The Great Lie 1941 ★
Brigham Young 1940
Midnight 1939
The Prisoner of Zenda 1937
Man of Iron 1935
Convention City 1933
Red Dust 1932
Dressed to Kill 1928
Don Juan 1926
Beau Brummel 1924
The Beggar Maid 1921

"I was never totally involved in movies. I was just making my father's dream come true."

GEORGE SANDERS

Born: George Sanders, July 3, 1906 (St. Petersburg, Russia); died 1972 (Castelldefels, Barcelona, Spain).

Star qualities: Tall; singer with baritone voice; urbane; upper-class English accent; suave; screen super sleuth; specialized in playing cads and villains.

Top Takes...

Psychomania 1971

The Jungle Book 1967

The Rebel 1961

Village of the Damned 1960

Viaggio in Italia 1954 (*Journey to Italy*)

King Richard and the Crusaders 1954

***All About Eve* 1950 ★**

The Ghost and Mrs. Muir 1947

The Private Affairs of Bel Ami 1947

The Picture of Dorian Gray 1945

Quiet Please: Murder 1942

The Moon and Sixpence 1942

Man Hunt 1941

Rebecca 1940

The Man Who Could Work Miracles 1936

Find the Lady 1936

Born in Russia to British parents, George Sanders returned to England with his family on the eve of the Russian Revolution. Educated at a private school in Brighton, Sanders worked in the textile and tobacco industries before becoming an advertising copywriter. He had a beautiful baritone voice and took up a colleague's suggestion to switch careers to acting, starting out as a chorus boy in London's West End. He went on to cabaret, radio, and theatrical understudy, finally making an impact in the film *Find the Lady* (1936). After a quick succession of roles in British films, Sanders went to Hollywood and turned his cultivated tones to series sleuths The Saint and The Falcon.

Sanders had one of the movies' best voices, suited to Wildean epigrams such as *The Picture of Dorian Gray* (1945), and languid tiger growls as Shere Khan in *The Jungle Book* (1967). A sought-after support player, he specialized in cads such as Jack Favell in *Rebecca* (1940). His career high came as the acidic critic Addison DeWitt in *All About Eve* (1950), for which he won an Academy Award for Best Supporting Actor.

Director Albert Lewin, who cast Sanders as Lord Henry Wotton in *Dorian Gray*, combed literature to find him perfect roles such as the caddish journalist in *The Private Affairs of Bel Ami* (1947). He is creepily good as a bibliophile in the tiny *Quiet Please: Murder* (1942), a rare Sanders star vehicle. In decline, he still managed fascinating work: Roberto Rossellini's *Viaggio in Italia* (1954) (*Journey to Italy*), and Mr. Freeze on the *Batman* TV series (1966–1968). Offscreen, Sanders also liked to cultivate a caddish image and was married four times. He committed suicide in 1972 by taking an overdose of barbiturates, leaving a note saying he was bored. Apparently, this had always been his intention. **KN**

> "Dear World, I am leaving because I am bored. I feel I have lived long enough."

JOHN HUSTON

Born: John Marcellus Huston, August 5, 1906 (Nevada, Missouri, U.S.); died 1987 (Middletown, Rhode Island, U.S.).

Star qualities: Top director, tour de force writer, and producer; sculptor and painter; boxer; tall character actor; part of an Oscar-winning acting dynasty.

The son of legendary screen actor Walter Huston, John Huston grew up in showbiz and started performing onstage in vaudeville with his father when he was only three years old. His parents divorced when he was seven and he spent his childhood on tour with his father or with his newspaper reporter mother. He started his professional acting career on Broadway when he was eighteen. For Huston, being a movie star was an afterthought to directing and writing. He entered movies as a fix-it scenarist, and rose from touching up scripts such as *Murders in the Rue Morgue* (1932) to writing important films such as *High Sierra* (1941). His debut as a writer-director was with *The Maltese Falcon* (1941), and he worked steadily for the rest of his life on commercial and personal projects.

Huston took a few onscreen bit parts in his own movies, notably the white-suited tourist hassled for handouts in *The Treasure of the Sierra Madre* (1948), but didn't act for anyone else until Otto Preminger cast him as a church dignitary in *The Cardinal* (1963). After that, he played a string of wily, craggy, often malevolent, sometimes genial authority figures: the medical money-man in *Candy* (1968), M in *Casino Royale* (1967), the marquis's degenerate churchman uncle in *De Sade* (1969), an instantly recognizable chimp in *Battle for the Planet of the Apes* (1973), the monumentally corrupt Noah Cross in *Chinatown* (1974), the voice of TV's Gandalf in *The Hobbit* (1977), and the Joe Kennedy figure in *Winter Kills* (1979). Married five times, he was the father of actress Anjelica Huston, actor and director Tony Huston, and director Danny Huston. Huston became a citizen of Ireland in 1964 and lived there for many years. He was filming a cameo role in his son Danny's *Mr. North* (1988) when he died from emphysema. **KN**

Top Takes...

Momo 1986
Wise Blood 1979
Winter Kills 1979
The Visitor 1979
The Wind and the Lion 1975
Breakout 1975
Chinatown 1974
Battle for the Planet of the Apes 1973
The Other Side of the Wind 1972
Man in the Wilderness 1971
Myra Breckinridge 1970
De Sade 1969
Candy 1968
Casino Royale 1967
The Cardinal 1963 ☆
The Treasure of the Sierra Madre 1948

"Hollywood has always been a cage . . . a cage to catch our dreams."

LOUISE BROOKS

Born: Mary Louise Brooks, November 14, 1906 (Cherryvale, Kansas, U.S.); died 1985 (Rochester, New York, U.S.).

Star qualities: Beautiful, sexy, and famous for her bobbed hairstyle; sleek and elegantly dressed; icon of the jazz era; dancer; flapper; vamp; outspoken; author.

An icon of the twentieth century, Louise Brooks moved to New York at age fifteen, joining the Denishawn Dance Company. Two years later, she appeared as a chorus dancer in George White's Scandals, and soon afterward in the Ziegfeld Follies. Her star began to rise when, in 1925, she was signed by Paramount Pictures.

Between 1925 and 1938 Brooks appeared in 24 movies. Yet it was a European picture that featured her most famous role. In the silent *Die Büchse der Pandora* (1929) (*Pandora's Box*), under the direction of G. W. Pabst, Brooks gave a sparkling and erotically charged performance as the nymphomaniac Lulu, the role responsible for her enduring fame. Her dark hair cut into a bob was copied by flapper female fans, both emulating her sleek style and the free-spirited, almost brazen, image of the modern woman it embodied.

She made two other films in Europe, *Tagebuch einer Verlorenen* (1929) (*Diary of a Lost Girl*), again with Pabst, and *Prix de beauté* (1930) (*Miss Europe*). However, famed for obstinacy and ill temper, Brooks refused to return to Hollywood to film sound retakes for her silent *The Canary Murder Case* (1929) and, when she returned to the United States, she found herself blacklisted and an industry outcast. After the John Wayne Western *Overland Stage Raiders* (1938), Brooks retired from acting, residing briefly in Wichita, Kansas, near her family, but then moving to New York, where she worked for a while as a salesgirl. After years removed from the public eye, she reappeared in the 1950s, writing witty, well-researched articles for film periodicals for the next two decades. Many of these pieces were collected in her best-selling autobiography, *Lulu in Hollywood* (1982). **SU**

Top Takes...

Overland Stage Raiders 1938
Empty Saddles 1936
God's Gift to Women 1931
It Pays to Advertise 1931
Prix de beauté 1930 (*Miss Europe*)
Tagebuch einer Verlorenen 1929
   (*Diary of a Lost Girl*)
The Canary Murder Case 1929
Die Büchse der Pandora 1929 (*Pandora's Box*)
Beggars of Life 1928
A Girl in Every Port 1928
The City Gone Wild 1927
Evening Clothes 1927
Ten Years Old 1927
Just Another Blonde 1926
The American Venus 1926

"A well-dressed woman, even though her purse is painfully empty, can conquer the world."

RIGHT: Brooks in her definitive role as the tragic Lulu in *Pandora's Box*.

CESAR ROMERO

Born: Cesar Julio Romero Jr., February 15, 1907 (New York City, New York, U.S.); died 1994 (Santa Monica, California, U.S.).

Star qualities: Tall, debonair, and sophisticated; moustache; dancer; comedian; cackling laugh; played suave, Latin lovers and Mexican cowboys.

Top Takes...

Born of Cuban parents in New York City, Cesar Romero started out as a ballroom dancer before he appeared in the 1927 production of *Lady Do* on Broadway. His screen debut was in *The Shadow Laughs* (1933), and he played various Latin hoods and gigolos in movies such as *The Thin Man* (1934) and *Hold 'Em Yale* (1935). After playing sidekick in *Return of the Cisco Kid* (1939), he took over the lead role of the Mexican cowboy hero in a series beginning with *The Cisco Kid and the Lady* (1939), and was a suavely sinister magician in *Charlie Chan at Treasure Island* (1939). In the 1940s he was more often found in Twentieth Century Fox A-features, polished up as a Latin lover, occasional dancer, and all-around charmer in films such as *Dance Hall* (1941) and *Week-End in Havana* (1941).

Romero performed well in a rare heavyweight role as the Spanish explorer Hernán Cortés in the Tyrone Power vehicle *Captain from Castile* (1947), but slipped back to supporting actor in the comedy *Julia Misbehaves* (1948), although he put in good work. In 1953 he starred in the 39-part espionage TV series *Passport to Danger* (1954–1955). A regular TV guest star, he appeared in series such as *77 Sunset Strip* (1963). But his late career signature role was as The Joker in the TV series *Batman* (1966–1968). He refused to shave off his beloved trademark moustache for the part and instead had makeup slathered on top of it. He reprised the cackling clown prince of crime in the 1966 movie, and then turned up as a white-haired buffoon villain in Disney comedies such as *The Computer Wore Tennis Shoes* (1969), and as Jane Wyman's mature swain on the TV soap opera *Falcon Crest* (1981–1990). Despite his screen image as the Latin Romeo, Cesar Romero never married, and was homosexual. **KN**

> "We Latins make splendid lovers and splendid older men."

BUSTER CRABBE

Born: Clarence Linden Crabbe, February 17, 1907 (Oakland, California, U.S.);
died 1983 (Scottsdale, Arizona, U.S.).

Star qualities: Tall, chiseled good looks; Olympic-winning athlete; muscular;
specialized in playing boys' comic-book action heroes and cowboys; author.

Raised in Hawaii, Larry Crabbe—nicknamed "Buster" by his family—found he had a talent for swimming that led him to become an Olympic team swimmer for the United States, winning both gold and bronze medals. Crabbe followed his teammate Johnny Weissmuller into movies, playing a Tarzan imitation in *King of the Jungle* (1933) and Edgar Rice Burroughs's hero in *Tarzan the Fearless* (1933), and went on to star in more than 100 films. He toiled as a square-shooting, square-jawed cowboy, relieved by the occasional college athlete as in *Hold 'Em Yale* (1935), before having his brown hair dyed blond to star in his most famous role, Universal Studios' serial *Flash Gordon* (1936) and its sequels.

Along with *Buck Rogers* (1939), Flash made Crabbe a hero to boys of all ages: he exposes his chest when bound in chains, escapes death traps between chapters, selflessly rescues Dale Arden (and the world) from Ming the Merciless, and espouses all manner of clean-living virtues. In the 1940s, he starred as Billy the Kid with a saddle sidekick played by Al "Fuzzy" St. John in a series of Saturday matinee Westerns in which the Kid is a straight-up, misunderstood hero. Historical carping about depicting the real-life, low-down killer as a good guy eventually prompted a change of character name to "Billy Carson" without any alteration to the format. Crabbe took his heroism to TV in the 1950s' *Captain Gallant of the Foreign Legion* (1955–1957), and appeared as dignified, retired fighter pilot Brigadier Gordon in *Buck Rogers in the 25th Century* (1979). In later years he ran his own swimming pool business, and wrote *Energetics*, a book on physical fitness for the over-fifties. He continued to appear in minor movies, and filmed *The Comeback Trail* (1982) the year before he died. **KN**

Top Takes...

The Comeback Trail 1982
Buck Rogers 1977
Jungle Siren 1942
Billy the Kid's Smoking Guns 1942
Billy the Kid Trapped 1942
Billy the Kid's Round-up 1941
Billy the Kid Wanted 1941
Jungle Man 1941
Flash Gordon Conquers the Universe 1940
Buck Rogers 1939
Flash Gordon 1936
Hold 'Em Yale 1935
Tarzan the Fearless 1933
King of the Jungle 1933

"Some say my acting rose to the level of incompetence and then leveled off."

KATHARINE HEPBURN

Born: Katharine Houghton Hepburn, May 12, 1907 (Hartford, Connecticut, U.S.); died 2003 (Old Saybrook, Connecticut, U.S.).

Star qualities: A Hollywood superstar; tall, athletic actress who did her own stunts; highly intelligent, natural redhead with an alluring yet feisty charm.

Top Takes...

Love Affair 1994
On Golden Pond 1981 ★
Rooster Cogburn 1975
The Trojan Women 1971
The Lion in Winter 1968 ★
Guess Who's Coming to Dinner 1967 ★
Long Day's Journey Into Night 1962 ☆
Suddenly, Last Summer 1959 ☆
Summertime 1955 ☆
Pat and Mike 1952
The African Queen 1951 ☆
Adam's Rib 1949
State of the Union 1948
Keeper of the Flame 1942
Woman of the Year 1942 ☆
The Philadelphia Story 1940 ☆
Holiday 1938
Bringing Up Baby 1938
Stage Door 1937
Quality Street 1937
Sylvia Scarlett 1935
Alice Adams 1935 ☆
Little Women 1933
Morning Glory 1933 ★
A Bill of Divorcement 1932

RIGHT: Hepburn as the determined Jo March in George Cukor's Little Women.

Katharine Hepburn was not only one of the very finest actresses to work in Hollywood, but one of the most unlikely Hollywood stars. She was not, for one thing, conventionally beautiful—although she could, of course, appear quite ravishing, not only as the elegantly attired social aristocrat in *The Philadelphia Story* (1940), but even in drag in *Sylvia Scarlett* (1935). Those two films by George Cukor—undoubtedly the director most sympathetic to her talents and crucial to her career—demonstrate the other qualities that make Hepburn so unusual among U.S. movie stars: the slim, sporty, tomboyish androgyny, the almost masculine air of strong-willed independence, the self-confidence and intelligence born of a well-heeled, well-educated, upper-crust New England upbringing.

The daughter of a surgeon and a suffragette, she began acting as a teenager even before going to study at Bryn Mawr College. A year after graduation, she was playing bit parts on Broadway, although her career proceeded in fits and starts due to an outspokenness that provoked arguments with various directors and producers. She made her screen debut playing

1900s

John Barrymore's daughter in Cukor's *A Bill of Divorcement* (1932); besides the two aforementioned titles, she would go on to work with him on *Little Women* (1933), *Holiday* (1938), *Keeper of the Flame* (1942), *Adam's Rib* (1949), *Pat and Mike* (1952)—these last two costarring her offscreen partner Spencer Tracy—and *Love Among the Ruins* (1975) for TV. (Her onscreen chemistry with Tracy was to endure across nine movies.) For some years she was regarded as "box-office poison" by the movie moguls, who didn't really know how to respond to her intellectual superiority, no-nonsense honesty, and thoroughbred sense of dignity. Nevertheless, after a spate of uneven films—of which *Alice Adams* (1935) and *Sylvia Scarlett* were by far the best—she hit her stride with *Quality Street* (1937), *Stage Door* (1937), *Bringing Up Baby*

ABOVE: Hepburn in *Guess Who's Coming to Dinner*, her lover Spencer Tracy's last film.

"I always wanted to be a movie actress. I thought it was very romantic. And it was."

Unconventional Kate

Tall, feisty, and redheaded, Katharine Hepburn refused to conform to the Hollywood rules of glamour. She often appeared without makeup and in trousers at a time when it was not fashionable for women to do so, and declined to give interviews or pose for photographers. The daughter of a suffragette, Hepburn never regarded women as inferior to men, always made her own decisions, and was outspoken about her opinions. Her refusal to play the Hollywood game sometimes left her out in the cold. But she never pretended to be anyone other than her true self, for better or worse, as illustrated by the quotations below:

- "I never realized until lately that women were supposed to be inferior."
- "Enemies are so stimulating."
- "I often wonder whether men and women really suit each other. Perhaps they should live next door and just visit now and then."
- "I wear my sort of clothes to save me the trouble of deciding which clothes to wear."
- "Only when a woman decides not to have children, can a woman live like a man. That's what I've done."
- "Plain women know more about men than beautiful ones do."
- "If you always do what interests you, at least one person is pleased."

RIGHT: Hepburn makes convincing royalty as Eleanor of Aquitaine in *The Lion in Winter*.

(1938), and *Holiday*. Starring opposite Cary Grant in the last two, Hepburn revealed a brilliant, brittle talent for both comedy and darker, more serious drama; her deft timing, her nuanced subtlety, and her mercurial intelligence remain undimmed to this day.

Wooing back Hollywood

Still, however, Hollywood remained wary and unsure of her commercial potential; passed over for Scarlett O'Hara, Hepburn herself commissioned Philip Barry, author of *Holiday*, to write *The Philadelphia Story*. When she played the Tracy Lord part on Broadway it was a smash hit. She next took the property to MGM and, after being rewarded with box-office success and a third Academy Award nomination, she was back in business. Her next project was *Woman of the Year* (1942), the first of her comedies with Tracy, which also saw a slight softening of Hepburn's persona. This was probably crucial to the growing affection for her on the part of studios and audiences alike; although films like *State of the Union* (1948), *The African Queen* (1951), and *Summertime* (1955) proved her enduring popularity, she had lost some of the sharp, sparky, sexy fire that had made many earlier roles so memorable. She also began to work less frequently, mainly because of her famous but very private affair with Tracy.

Many of Hepburn's movies were theatrical or literary in origin (or, indeed, tone)—*Suddenly, Last Summer* (1959), *Long Day's Journey Into Night* (1962), *Guess Who's Coming to Dinner* (1967), *The Lion in Winter* (1968), *The Trojan Women* (1971)—but they became increasingly imbued with a sentimentality quite at odds with her best work, culminating in *Rooster Cogburn* (1975) and a cameo in *Love Affair* (1994), where, despite failing health, she emerged from retirement for Warren Beatty. Of her few later roles, only *On Golden Pond* (1981)—where she sparred with the likewise lovable curmudgeon Henry Fonda—was properly worthy of her talents. She should undoubtedly be remembered primarily for her achievements prior to 1950, which remain, quite simply, magnificent. **GA**

LAURENCE OLIVIER

Born: Laurence Kerr Olivier, May 22, 1907 (Dorking, Surrey, England); died 1989 (Steyning, West Sussex, England).

Star qualities: Hugely talented Shakespearean actor; legendary onstage presence; natural fury; romances with costars; career-oriented; gifted director.

Top Takes...

Clash of the Titans 1981
The Boys from Brazil 1978 ☆
A Bridge Too Far 1977
Marathon Man 1976 ☆
Sleuth 1972 ☆
Battle of Britain 1969
Oh! What a Lovely War 1969
Othello 1965 ☆
Uncle Vanya 1963
Spartacus 1960
The Entertainer 1960 ☆
The Devil's Disciple 1959
The Prince and the Showgirl 1957
Richard III 1955 ☆
Carrie 1952
Hamlet 1948 ★
The Chronicle History of King Henry the Fift with His Battell Fought at Agincourt in France 1944 (Henry V) ☆
That Hamilton Woman **1941**
Pride and Prejudice 1940
Rebecca 1940 ☆
Wuthering Heights 1939 ☆
Fire Over England 1937

Master Shakespeare translator, teller of tales, and actor of actors, Sir Laurence Olivier is, for many, the epitome of stagecraft and brilliance in dramatic performance. Olivier had a strict religious upbringing in the household of his father, an Anglican priest. His mother died when he was twelve, but Olivier was encouraged by his father to pursue an acting career. He had his primary education at St. Edward's School, Oxford, where he participated in school plays, and subsequently attended The Central School of Speech and Drama in London before joining The Birmingham Repertory Company.

In 1930 he married his first wife, the actress Jill Esmond, herself a rising star of the theater, and by the mid-1930s he had forged a reputation for performing the Bard's work with gusto and flair, especially when paired onstage with other great actors such as John Gielgud, with whom he worked on *Romeo and Juliet* in London in 1935. Olivier had also begun working in films, although the stage remained his central passion, thereby demonstrating a sound commercial motive at the heart of his craft—movies may pay well, but the stage is

RIGHT: In the 1948 film *Hamlet*, Olivier plays the Prince of Denmark and directs himself.

ABOVE: Olivier with his wife Vivien Leigh.
The couple made three movies together.

where the living art is conducted, connecting performers with live audiences, show after show.

During this same period he met Vivien Leigh, his second wife (1940–1960), and the pair began a conquest of Hollywood, inasmuch as Hollywood regularly mined English talent for a sense of sophistication, craft, and pedigree sorely lacking in product written solely in Southern California. Leigh's crossover hit of 1939 was *Gone with the Wind*, earning her the first of her two Oscars for Best Actress, and his was *Wuthering Heights*, which established him as a big-screen lead. The pair were onscreen lovers in several films, including *Fire Over England* (1937) and *That Hamilton Woman* (1941), but the truth of their union was better expressed live, onstage, where they both worked frequently throughout their lives.

"Acting is illusion, as much illusion as magic is, and not so much a matter of being real."

Larry and the Bard

The English playwright Charles Bennett said of Laurence Olivier: "He could speak Shakespeare's lines as naturally as if he were actually thinking them." After wowing London theater audiences alternating the parts of Romeo and Mercutio in *Romeo and Juliet* in 1935, Olivier's first foray into Shakespeare on the big screen came in 1936 when he played Orlando in *As You Like It*. It was an inauspicious debut and Olivier vowed that if he were ever to repeat the experience, he would need creative control. Olivier went on to direct himself in *Henry V* (1944), *Hamlet* (1948), and *Richard III* (1955). With *Hamlet*, Olivier became the first actor ever to direct himself in an Oscar-winning performance.

- Olivier desperately wanted to play Macbeth on the big screen. Elizabeth Taylor's then-husband, Michael Todd, planned to produce it in 1958 with Olivier and Vivien Leigh as his Lady, but Todd was killed in a plane crash.

- He worked with his close friend Ralph Richardson on the movie version of *Richard III* in 1955. The film was not successful and Olivier never directed another Shakespearean film again.

- *Henry V* provided the opportunity for some good British propaganda during World War II. Winston Churchill arranged for Olivier to take the cast and crew to Ireland to film away from the bombing.

RIGHT: Olivier in a chilling performance as the ex-Nazi criminal in *Marathon Man*.

Rebecca (1940), *Pride and Prejudice* (1940), and *The Chronicle History of King Henry the Fift with His Battell Fought at Agincourt in France* (1944) followed in the 1940s, mixed in with Olivier's wartime service in the air force. Then, following the end of the war, came *Hamlet* (1948), one of his greatest accomplishments, which he starred in, adapted, and directed himself to win two Academy Awards for Best Actor and Best Picture, and an Oscar nomination for Best Director.

From leading man to supporting player

Credits in the 1950s included *Carrie* (1952), *Richard III* (1955), and *The Devil's Disciple* (1959); the 1960s began with Olivier's divorce from the manic depressive Leigh and new marriage to Joan Plowright, his costar in *The Entertainer* (1960), a play he had first done in London and followed across the Atlantic to Hollywood. His work in *Spartacus* (1960), *Uncle Vanya* (1963), *Othello* (1965), and *Battle of Britain* (1969) gradually saw him fade from leading man to frequent support actor, although some of his more memorable movie roles still lay ahead: in *Sleuth* (1972), *Marathon Man* (1976), *A Bridge Too Far* (1977), and *The Boys from Brazil* (1978).

For the younger generation, though, Olivier is Zeus from *Clash of the Titans* (1981), his robed frame seeking purchase above the concerns of the lesser gods and mortal men. That this odd memory stakes its claim in the wake of all that came before is a sore spot, especially when considering Olivier's celebrated careers in television and onstage. But the point is that our greatest artists sometimes work for the sake of a paycheck or the simple pleasures of entertaining children. So one may still recall Olivier's Zeus saying, "If we, the gods, are abandoned or forgotten, the stars will never fade."

After eleven Academy Award nominations, with two wins and two honorary statues, after eight Emmy Award nominations with four wins, after three Golden Globe Award nominations and two wins with one honorary award, the least that can be said for Laurence Olivier is that he is a star. As such, he is immortal and will never be forgotten. **GCQ**

JOHN WAYNE

Born: Marion Robert Morrison, May 26, 1907 (Winterset, Iowa, U.S.); died 1979 (Los Angeles, California, U.S.).

Star qualities: Prolific Hollywood leading man; an enduring icon of the Western genre; world famous for his slow delivery and deep voice.

Top Takes…

The Shootist 1976

Brannigan 1975

McQ 1974

True Grit 1969 ★

The Green Berets 1968

The Sons of Katie Elder 1965

How the West Was Won 1962

The Longest Day 1962

The Man Who Shot Liberty Valance 1962

The Alamo 1960

The Searchers 1956

Big Jim McLain 1952

The Quiet Man 1952

Rio Grande 1950

Sands of Iwo Jima 1949 ☆

She Wore a Yellow Ribbon 1949

Red River 1948

Fort Apache 1948

Flying Tigers 1942

Stagecoach 1939

Texas Terror 1935

Sagebrush Trail 1933

Ride Him, Cowboy 1932

Three Girls Lost 1931

The Big Trail 1930

In the early part of the twentieth century, as movies were becoming standardized entertainment based on mass appeal and the mastery of basic storytelling, the Western became synonymous with the United States, inasmuch as describing the great wide spaces of the Old West was useful for reflecting the modern condition. Also born in exactly this same moment of industrial consolidation and generic development, Marion Morrison took his first breaths in Iowa, where his family lived in marginal conditions before moving to Glendale, California.

Throughout his boyhood, Morrison was a good student and athlete, and he was usually seen with his pet dog "Duke," which eventually became his nickname, too. Graduating high school with a gift for football, he applied to the U.S. Naval Academy, was rejected, and earned a scholarship to the University of Southern California where he played for Howard Jones.

During downtime from school and practice, he began working around the Los Angeles movie studios. When an injury ended his football career, Morrison left U.S.C. and turned to Hollywood, picking up work as a prop man. At this time, he also made friends with the young John Ford.

RIGHT: Wayne with costars George Bancroft and Claire Trevor in John Ford's *Stagecoach*.

1900s

After numerous bit parts, Wayne earned his first starring role in *The Big Trail* (1930), for which he adopted the stage name John Wayne. Thereafter was begun one of the most enduring screen romances between a star and a genre. Wayne became a symbol of the American West, a bulwark of deliberateness in the face of the untamed wilds, a focus of decency in a chaotic environment, and the constant force of unassailable will in a world of increasing moral ambiguity. He was tall, handsome in his youth—although brutish and gristly in later years—and earnest to a fault. Working like an ambitious tradesman with no room to reject work, Wayne established a résumé that quickly filled with forgettable titles (*Three Girls Lost*, 1931; *Ride Him, Cowboy*, 1932; *Sagebrush Trail*, 1933; *Texas Terror*, 1935), alongside one singular masterpiece, *Stagecoach*, in 1939. By the

ABOVE: Wayne as Sean Thornton tries to tame Maureen O'Hara in *The Quiet Man*.

"Westerns are closer to art than anything else in the motion picture business."

American Patriot

John Wayne was a vocal right-wing patriot and political activist during his life. However, he became slightly more moderate in his views as he got older, and, interestingly, he supported President Carter and the Democrats over the Panama Canal issue in 1978—they felt that the canal belonged to the people of Panama rather than the United States.

- Unlike many other actors of his generation, Wayne did not serve in World War II. He requested deferment from the draft on the basis of being a married father of four children.
- Wayne lost a small fortune on his Vietnam movie *The Green Berets*, which he directed and starred in. Many commentators felt its optimistic gung ho patriotism was at odds with the images of the conflict being broadcast on television.
- Wayne supported blacklisting and assisted the House Un-American Activities Committee. He financed movies with an anticommunist message, like *Big Jim McLain* (1952). He is said to have been on the hit lists of Joseph Stalin and Mao Tse-tung.
- In 1968 the Republican Party allegedly asked Wayne to run for president of the United States. He turned the offer down because he thought the country would not take a movie star running for president seriously.

start of World War II, his type and persona were well formed and his audience perpetually ready for the next Western starring their favorite righteous man in the fields, prairies, and river valleys of the Old West; the actual filming location was typically Monument Valley in Arizona and Utah.

Moving away from Westerns

The years of World War II saw Wayne expand his filmography to include military parts, in movies such as *Flying Tigers* (1942) and *Sands of Iwo Jima* (1949), which earned him his first Oscar nomination. At the same time, he dabbled in thrillers but continued his mainstay in Westerns, as often as not directed by Ford (*Fort Apache*, 1948; *The Searchers*, 1956; *She Wore a Yellow Ribbon*, 1949; *Rio Grande*, 1950). In later years Wayne slowed down, having already worked in perhaps 200 films. But he also took on the job of direction, as in *The Alamo* (1960), in which he was producer and star, and the pro-Vietnam War military procedural *The Green Berets* in 1968.

By this time, age and declining health further diminished his capacity for work—but then a funny thing happened: *True Grit* (1969), his Oscar-winning role as the eye patch-wearing Rooster Cogburn in a revenge story that finally brought critical recognition to the table alongside long-standing popular attraction. A lifelong political conservative and smoker, Wayne died of lung and stomach cancer. **GCQ**

ABOVE: With *True Grit* Wayne won the approval of both critics and audiences.

ROSALIND RUSSELL

Born: Rosalind Russell, June 4, 1907 (Waterbury, Connecticut, U.S.); died 1976 (Los Angeles, California, U.S.).

Star qualities: Tall beauty; expressive eyes; versatile, witty, and sophisticated screwball comedienne; singer; stylish lead and character actress; humanitarian.

Rosalind Russell emerged from the Broadway stage and returned there in the 1950s, coming back to Hollywood to re-create her triumph in *Auntie Mame* (1958), for which she earned one of her four Oscar nominations. The movie career in between was a patchy one, with plenty of supporting roles and loan-outs. For all that, it is as the star of a small number of late 1930s and early 1940s titles that she is best remembered, usually as the "boss lady"—a spiky career woman with smart one-liners and big hats.

The daughter of a lawyer, Russell trained at New York's American Academy of Dramatic Arts before starting her stage career in her early twenties. She made her screen debut in *Evelyn Prentice* (1934). Although fine in serious drama she was clearly built for comedy, with her wide, expressive eyes and constantly mobile body, her performances frequently threatening to go over the top but skillfully reigned in at the last moment.

She was rarely the first choice for anything, including her two most celebrated roles, as the bitchiest of *The Women* (1939), and Hildy Johnson in Howard Hawks's *His Girl Friday* (1940). Yet it is hard indeed to imagine another actress attempting either character with such authority and abandon. In the first she manages to steal scenes from Norma Shearer, Joan Crawford, and Paulette Goddard, sometimes simultaneously; in the second she gives her finest performance as the reporter at her happiest trading wisecracks with the boys in the pressroom. Russell suffered from rheumatoid arthritis and devoted her last years to campaigning for arthritis research. In 1972 the Academy of Motion Picture Arts and Sciences awarded her the Jean Hersholt Humanitarian Award for her charity work. **MC**

Top Takes...

Gypsy 1962
Auntie Mame 1958 ☆
Picnic 1955
A Woman of Distinction 1950
Mourning Becomes Electra 1947 ☆
The Guilt of Janet Ames 1947
Sister Kenny 1946 ☆
Flight for Freedom 1943
My Sister Eileen 1942 ☆
Take a Letter, Darling 1942
Design for Scandal 1941
This Thing Called Love 1940
His Girl Friday 1940
The Women 1939
Night Must Fall 1937
Evelyn Prentice 1934

"Acting is standing up naked and turning around very slowly."

BARBARA STANWYCK

Born: Ruby Catherine Stevens, July 16, 1907 (Brooklyn, New York, U.S.); died 1990 (Santa Monica, California, U.S.).

Star qualities: Seductive beauty; chorus girl; workaholic; often played provocative parts but was a versatile performer.

Barbara Stanwyck made her screen debut as a fan dancer in *Broadway Nights* (1927). Surprisingly often cast as a stripper, she was the sexiest of the grand dames of Hollywood's golden age, in comic mode as the con woman ensnaring Henry Fonda's snake expert in *The Lady Eve* (1941) and dead serious as Phyllis Dietrichson tempting Fred MacMurray into murder in *Double Indemnity* (1944). Often dubbed "The Best Actress who never won an Oscar," Stanwyck received four Academy Award nominations, including one for *Double Indemnity*, but—apart from an honorary award in 1981—she never won.

After her mother's death when she was four, and the abandonment of her father, Stanwyck was raised in foster homes, working as a model and chorus girl from the age of thirteen. She had a flurry of provocative roles in pre-Code films, including *Baby Face* (1933), a frank, cynical picture about an amiably amoral tramp who sleeps her way to the top of a skyscraper. Proven as a star and a versatile actress who could play repressed spinsters (*The Bitter Tea of General Yen*, 1933) as well as uncorseted minxes, Stanwyck survived the arrival of heavier censorship in the mid-1930s to benefit from tailor-

Top Takes…

Forty Guns 1957

Cattle Queen of Montana 1954

Blowing Wild 1953

Clash by Night 1952

To Please a Lady 1950

The Furies 1950

The File on Thelma Jordon 1950

***Sorry, Wrong Number* 1948** ☆

Cry Wolf 1947

The Two Mrs. Carrolls 1947

The Strange Love of Martha Ivers 1946

Christmas in Connecticut 1945

***Double Indemnity* 1944** ☆

Lady of Burlesque 1943

***Ball of Fire* 1941** ☆

The Lady Eve 1941

The Mad Miss Manton 1938

***Stella Dallas* 1937** ☆

Annie Oakley 1935

A Lost Lady 1934

Baby Face 1933

The Bitter Tea of General Yen 1933

Shopworn 1932

Ten Cents a Dance 1931

Broadway Nights 1927

RIGHT: Stanwyck as the intense title character in the drama *Stella Dallas*.

made roles like *Annie Oakley* (1935), in which she shows for the first time how well she looks in Western duds, and *Stella Dallas* (1937), where she is more honestly affecting in soap opera than Joan Crawford in similar roles.

The sass of Stanwyck's early roles translated well into screwball comedy: she's a hoot in *The Mad Miss Manton* (1938) and *Christmas in Connecticut* (1945). After *Double Indemnity*, she made a few more films noirs, including *The Strange Love of Martha Ivers* (1946). In *The Two Mrs. Carrolls* (1947), *Cry Wolf* (1947), and *Sorry, Wrong Number* (1948), she is apparently or actually persecuted by husbands Humphrey Bogart, Errol Flynn, and Burt Lancaster, and works up a fine line in repressed hysteria. In the 1950s, she played middle-aged nymphomaniacs (*Clash by Night*, 1952; *Blowing Wild*, 1953) and cattle baronesses (*Cattle Queen of Montana*, 1954; *Forty Guns*, 1957), then in the mid-1960s Stanwyck retired to a successful career in TV. **KN**

ABOVE: Stanwyck as the scheming Phyllis Dietrichson in the noirish *Double Indemnity*.

On the Small Screen

When her movie career declined, Barbara Stanwyck made the successful transition from big to small screen. Although *The Barbara Stanwyck Show* (1961–1962) was not a hit, it earned her an Emmy. She did, however, achieve great popularity (and another Emmy) in her role as the Barkley family matriarch of the Western series *The Big Valley* (1965–1969). In the 1980s she struck TV gold once more as Constance Colby in *Dynasty* and its spin-off series *The Colbys*. (She had turned down the role of Angela Channing in *Falcon Crest*, which went to Jane Wyman instead.) She gained a final Emmy for *The Thorn Birds* in 1983.

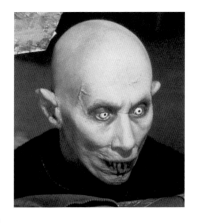

REGGIE NALDER

Born: Alfred Reginald Natzler, September 4, 1907 (Vienna, Austria); died 1991 (Santa Monica, California, U.S.).

Star qualities: "The Face That Launched a Thousand Trips"; scarred physiognomy; soft voice; character actor; horror movie icon.

Top Takes…

The Devil and Max Devlin 1981

Seven 1979

Dracula Sucks 1979

Dracula's Dog 1978

Crash! 1977

Il Casanova di Federico Fellini 1976 (*Fellini's Casanova*)

L'Uccello dalle piume di cristallo 1970 (*The Bird with the Crystal Plumage*)

Hexen bis aufs Blut gequält 1970 (*Mark of the Devil*)

The Manchurian Candidate 1962

The Man Who Knew Too Much 1956

Adventures of Captain Fabian 1951

Le signal rouge 1949

Jericho 1946

Reggie Nalder had one of the most unforgettable faces in the cinema, more closely resembling Gaston Leroux's description of the Phantom of the Opera than Lon Chaney in the silent film. Nalder offered wildly varying accounts of the accident in which his mouth was distinctively scarred, perhaps being disfigured from burns, and that led to his nickname "The Face That Launched a Thousand Trips."

Nalder had a colorful and rather mysterious past. He was born into an acting family: his mother, father, and uncle were all actors. His uncle owned a notorious cabaret in 1920s Vienna called Hölle, meaning "Hell." The young Nalder helped his uncle by painting backdrops and suggesting tableaux for the cabaret. When the Nazis arrived, he fled to Paris and worked in musical revues. When World War II was over he made his film debut in *Jericho* (1946). Active in French films in the 1950s, he was hired by Alfred Hitchcock to play the silent assassin in *The Man Who Knew Too Much* (1956), gaining a visibility that ensured he would remain in work for the rest of his life. His scars also meant that he was perpetually cast as the villain.

Nalder is one of the brainwashers in *The Manchurian Candidate* (1962), another hit man in *The Bird with the Crystal Plumage* (1970), an albino witch-hunter in *Mark of the Devil* (1970), and one of the parade in *Il Casanova di Federico Fellini* (1976) (*Fellini's Casanova*). He played a strange array of roles in vampire movies: as Dracula's devoted half-human servant in *Dracula's Dog* (1978), the Nosferatu-faced master fiend in TV's *Salem's Lot* (1979), and (under the name "Detlef van Berg") Dr. Van Helsing in the hard-core porno movie *Dracula Sucks* (1979), a spoof adaptation of Bram Stoker's *Dracula*, in which he does not take part in the sex scenes. **KN**

> "Hitchcock was responsible for my coming to America, and I owe him a great deal."

FAY WRAY

Born: Vina Fay Wray, September 15, 1907 (Cardston, Alberta, Canada); died 2004 (New York City, New York, U.S.).

Star qualities: Petite, brunette; "The Beauty who charmed the Beast"; queen of the scream; the shaking captive of the screen's biggest gorilla.

Fay Wray's Mormon family moved to the United States for work, first to Arizona and then to Los Angeles, where she got parts as an extra. She started out in Westerns at Universal Studios during the silent era. In 1926 she was one of 13 young starlets the Western Association of Motion Picture Advertisers selected as most likely to succeed in the movies. Director Erich von Stroheim elevated her from bit player to star in *The Wedding March* (1928), and she became a busy early talkie leading lady in the likes of *Dirigible* (1931), *Three Rogues* (1931), and *Stowaway* (1932), often as the girl fought over by two brawling male comrades.

She was a brunette in almost all her movies, but won lasting pop-culture fame as the blonde Ann Darrow clutched in the paw of the giant gorilla in *King Kong* (1933). Blessed with a piercing scream, Wray found herself in a blip of horror films: lovely in two-strip Technicolor in *Doctor X* (1932) and *Mystery of the Wax Museum* (1933), shrilly imperiled in *The Vampire Bat* (1933), and as the "prize" sought by mad Leslie Banks in *The Most Dangerous Game* (1932). After *King Kong* she had surprisingly few memorable roles, venturing to Britain for the interesting *The Clairvoyant* (1934) and the amusing *Bulldog Jack* (1935). From the late 1930s onward she only occasionally showed up in the cinema, although she worked steadily as a guest star in television shows, such as *Alfred Hitchcock Presents* (1958–1959), into the 1960s. Wray became friends with director Peter Jackson during his remake of *King Kong* (2005). She died on September 15, 2004, and two days after her death, the lights on New York's Empire State Building—the scene of the climax in *King Kong*—were dimmed for 15 minutes in her honor. **KN**

Top Takes...

Bulldog Jack 1935
Viva Villa! 1934
The Clairvoyant 1934
King Kong 1933
Mystery of the Wax Museum 1933
The Vampire Bat 1933
The Most Dangerous Game 1932
Doctor X 1932
Stowaway 1932
Dirigible 1931
Three Rogues 1931
The Four Feathers 1929
The Wedding March 1928

"When I shot my scenes Kong wasn't there at all. I had to use my imagination."

1900s

GENE AUTRY

Born: Orvon Gene Autry, September 29, 1907 (Tioga, Texas, U.S.); died 1998 (Los Angeles, California, U.S.).

Star qualities: "The Singing Cowboy"; veteran Westerns actor; best-selling country-music singer; composer; songwriter; producer; rodeo star; baseball fan.

Top Takes…

On Top of Old Smoky 1953
Gene Autry and The Mounties 1951
Beyond the Purple Hills 1950
Robin Hood of Texas 1947
Twilight on the Rio Grande 1947
Sioux City Sue 1946
Call of the Canyon 1942
Home in Wyomin' 1942
Cowboy Serenade 1942
Down Mexico Way 1941
Shooting High 1940
Rancho Grande 1940
Blue Montana Skies 1939
Oh, Susanna! 1936
In Old Sante Fe 1934

A pivotal figure both in the history of the B-Western and in the development of country music, Gene Autry began as a singer on radio in Oklahoma and became a popular recording star before making his movie debut in a Ken Maynard vehicle, *In Old Santa Fe* (1934). His singing, songwriting, and record career was phenomenal and included recording popular classics such as "Rudolph the Red-Nosed Reindeer" (1949).

In 1935 he appeared in the 13-part serial *The Phantom Empire*, a bizarre mixture of the Western and science fiction. Signing with Republic Pictures, Autry starred in scores of formulaic Westerns over the next two decades. In pictures such as *Oh, Susanna!* (1936) and *Sioux City Sue* (1946), always playing a character named "Gene Autry," he battled against crooks and outlaws in a never-never land where six-guns and horses coexisted with automobiles and airplanes. His pleasant singing voice and affable personality made him a favorite with women as well as men, and children appreciated the comedy in his films—usually supplied by Smiley Burnette—and the prowess of his horse Champion, "Wonder Horse of the West."

War service with Air Transport Command interrupted the flow of movies, but in the early 1950s Autry was one of the first Hollywood stars to see the potential of television. He formed his own company, Flying A Productions, which produced TV series such as *The Gene Autry Show* (1950), *The Adventures of Champion* (1955), and *Annie Oakley* (1954). Ever an astute man, when Autry retired from acting he became extremely wealthy from his investments in real estate, radio, and TV. He owned the California Angels baseball team from 1961 to 1997, then sold part of his share to The Walt Disney Company. He died at the age of ninety-one. **EB**

> "I'm not a good actor . . . or a particularly good singer, but they seem to like what I do."

BURGESS MEREDITH

Born: Oliver Burgess Meredith, November 16, 1907 (Cleveland, Ohio, U.S.); died 1997 (Malibu, California, U.S.).

Star qualities: Diminutive; director; producer; character actor in supporting roles; famed for his penguinlike quack.

Burgess Meredith has his place in popular culture as a meek little loser in several *Twilight Zone* episodes (1982–1983)—most memorably "Time Enough at Last"—and as The Penguin on TV's *Batman* (1966–1968). He achieved peer recognition in 1975 when he was nominated for an Academy Award for Best Supporting Actor for his work in *Day of the Locust* (1975). However, he is perhaps best remembered for playing the grouchy trainer Mickey Goldmill opposite Sylvester Stallone as boxer Rocky Balboa in *Rocky* (1976), for which he received another Academy Award nomination. He reprised the role in three of the four sequels.

Meredith had a long, distinguished career that unfortunately was interrupted by blacklisting in the 1950s because of his liberal political views, which kept him out of movies until the 1960s. His strongest early roles were in films of stage plays: *Winterset* (1936), *Idiot's Delight* (1939), and as George in *Of Mice and Men* (1939). He was well cast as war correspondent Ernie Pyle in *Story of G. I. Joe* (1945), and very good as the psychiatrist in *Mine Own Executioner* (1947).

He directed and costarred in *The Man on the Eiffel Tower* (1950) in France, then worked mostly on television until Otto Preminger offered him roles in movies such as *The Cardinal* (1963) and *Skidoo* (1968). After playing the Devil in *Torture Garden* (1966) and costarring with Elvis Presley in *Stay Away, Joe* (1968), he cornered a market on peppery old-timer roles in films such as *There Was a Crooked Man . . .* (1970), *The Day of the Locust* (1975), and *Grumpy Old Men* (1993). In the TV movie *Tail Gunner Joe* (1977), he evens a score by playing Joseph Welch, the lawyer who brought down Senator Joseph McCarthy. **KN**

Top Takes...

Grumpy Old Men 1993
***Rocky* 1976** ☆
***The Day of the Locust* 1975** ☆
There Was a Crooked Man . . . 1970
Skidoo 1968
Stay Away, Joe 1968
Torture Garden 1967
Batman 1966
The Cardinal 1963
L'Homme de la tour Eiffel 1950
    (*The Man on the Eiffel Tower*)
Mine Own Executioner 1947
Story of G. I. Joe 1945
Of Mice and Men 1939
Idiot's Delight 1939
Winterset 1936

"The main impetus to continue appearing on *Batman* . . . was that it was fashionable."

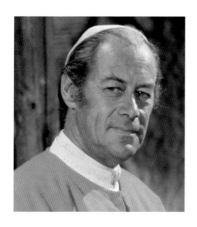

REX HARRISON

Born: Reginald Carey Harrison, March 5, 1908 (Huyton, Lancashire, England); died 1990 (New York City, New York, U.S.).

Star qualities: "Sexy Rexy"; comic timing; quick delivery; acidic air; producer; knighted; played the aristocrat, the cad, the doctor, and the professor.

Top Takes...

Doctor Dolittle 1967
The Honey Pot 1967
The Agony and the Ecstasy 1965
My Fair Lady 1964 ★
Cleopatra 1963 ☆
Midnight Lace 1960
Unfaithfully Yours 1948
Escape 1948
The Ghost and Mrs. Muir 1947
Anna and the King of Siam 1946
The Rake's Progress 1945
Blithe Spirit 1945
Major Barbara 1941
Night Train to Munich 1940

Sir Rex Harrison exuded hauteur as effortlessly as he tossed even the most elaborate dialogue. He was born to play cads or characters that combined a glacial air along with an inerasable gravitas. At times, he came across as the kind of personality for whom the phrase "high maintenance" was coined, even if his screen vehicles were invariably lightweight in the best sense.

Harrison made his stage debut in 1924 and his screen debut in 1930. He first grabbed hold of the cinematic audience with the Hitchcockean thriller *Night Train to Munich* (1940) and the film adaptation of George Bernard Shaw's *Major Barbara* (1941). Following service in the British navy in World War II, Harrison returned to form in Noel Coward's *Blithe Spirit* (1945) and *The Rake's Progress* (1945).

Hollywood beckoned, and Harrison's appearances were something of a hodgepodge; it was as though the dream factory could not altogether make a place for him. After a racial makeover for the leading role in *Anna and the King of Siam* (1946), he worked with two directors who understood and successfully employed his acidic air: Preston Sturges in *Unfaithfully Yours* (1948), and Joseph L. Mankiewicz in *The Ghost and Mrs. Muir* (1947) and *Escape* (1948). In the wake of these successes, the 1950s were largely a cinematic blind alley for Harrison, although his star became even more luminous with the stage success of *My Fair Lady* (1956). The movie version in 1964 transferred his most indelible performance to celluloid. Few other jobs tested his skills as successfully, although Mankiewicz called upon him twice more, in the notorious *Cleopatra* (1963) as Caesar, and as an eccentric tycoon in *The Honey Pot* (1967). He also had a stab at singing once more in *Doctor Dolittle* (1967). **DS**

"There is always a struggle, a striving for something bigger than yourself in all forms of art."

ANNA MAGNANI

Born: Anna Magnani, March 7, 1908 (Rome, Latium, Italy); died 1973 (Rome, Latium, Italy).

Star qualities: Icon of Italian postwar cinema; raven-haired; plump, sensual leading lady of Italian neorealism; famed for playing earthy roles; singer; writer.

Anna Magnani was the antithesis of an Italian *maggiorata*: she wasn't blessed with the looks of Gina Lollobrigida or Sophia Loren. Short in stature, with heavy features, her appeal came from her ability to portray the working-class Italian everywoman, struggling in postwar Italy.

An illegitimate child, Magnani was raised by her maternal grandmother in the slums of Rome. She financed her acting studies at Rome's Accademia Nazionale D'Arte Drammatica by singing in nightclubs, and made her film debut with a bit part in *Scampolo* (1928). Through the 1930s and 1940s she worked in the theater and kept moving up the movie cast list. She was most notable for a supporting role in director Vittorio De Sica's *Teresa Venerdì* (1941) (*Do You Like Women*). Her big break came as the lead in director Roberto Rossellini's vanguard neorealist film, *Roma, città aperta* (1945) (*Open City*), set in Nazi-occupied Italy. Her tour-de-force performance put her on the map both at home and abroad, and from there she went on to work with top directors in Italy and beyond.

She worked again with Rossellini in the contentious *L'Amore* (1948) (*Ways of Love*), and teamed with Jean Renoir to play an actress juggling too many lovers in *Le Carrosse d'or* (1953) (*The Golden Coach*). Her performance as a grieving widow in her first English-language movie, the screen adaptation of Tennessee Williams's *The Rose Tattoo* (1955), won her an Oscar for Best Actress. She returned to Hollywood for George Cukor's less successful drama *Wild Is the Wind* (1957), Stanley Kramer's *The Secret of Santa Vittoria* (1969), and Sidney Lumet's *The Fugitive Kind* (1959), but also continued to work in her native Italy. Her last role was, almost fittingly, as herself in a small part in Federico Fellini's *Roma* (1972). **CK**

Top Takes...

Roma 1972
The Secret of Santa Vittoria 1969
Mamma Roma 1962
The Fugitive Kind 1959
Nella città l'inferno 1959
  (*The Wild Wild Women*)
Wild Is the Wind 1957 ☆
The Rose Tattoo 1955 ★
Le Carrosse d'or 1953 (*The Golden Coach*)
Bellissima 1951
L'Amore 1948 (*Ways of Love*)
Roma, città aperta 1945 (*Open City*)
Teresa Venerdì 1941 (*Do You Like Women*)
Scampolo 1928

"Animals are good, better than humans really, animals do not betray you."

BUDDY EBSEN

Born: Christian Rudolph Ebsen Jr., April 2, 1908 (Belleville, Illinois, U.S.); died 2003 (Torrance, California, U.S.).

Star qualities: Tall, blue eyes; folksy image; shuffling dance style; vaudeville and musical performer; writer; composer; singer; producer.

Cast as the original Tin Man in the classic *The Wizard of Oz* (1939), Buddy Ebsen was replaced by Jack Haley when he suffered an almost fatal allergic reaction to the costume's aluminum dust. When Ebsen was ten his family moved to Florida, where his father operated a dance studio and subsequently taught his children to dance. After a few years of college and studying medicine, financial difficulties forced him to quit school. Ebsen left Orlando for New York, where he worked in vaudeville theaters; he and one of his sisters, Vilma Ebsen, later moved to Hollywood and debuted in a movie, *Broadway Melody of 1936* (1935), after which Ebsen's talent landed him roles in musical films throughout the 1930s, culminating in the ill-fated *Oz* part.

During the 1940s, Ebsen was cast in minor parts in Westerns; also, during World War II, he served in the U.S. Coast Guard. He lost another famous role when, originally picked as the lead in Disney's TV feature *Davy Crockett, King of the Wild Frontier* (1954), he was relegated to play Crockett's fictional friend George Russel when Disney replaced him with Fess Parker.

Ebsen then concentrated on straight acting. With his lead role as the hillbilly turned millionaire Jed Clampett in the comedy television series *The Beverly Hillbillies* (1962–1971), his career was finally ensured. When this show was canceled by CBS (despite its strong ratings), he landed another lead in the TV detective show *Barnaby Jones* (1973–1980). Ebsen remained active in cameo parts even into his eighties, and at the time of his death, at the age of ninety-five, he was writing novels, one of which was a murder mystery based on his Barnaby Jones sleuth character. He also wrote an autobiography, *The Other Side of Oz* (1994). **RU**

"There are a lot of mes."
——On having written a romance novel at the age of ninety-three

BETTE DAVIS

Born: Ruth Elizabeth Davis, April 5, 1908 (Lowell, Massachusetts, U.S.); died 1989 (Neuilly, France).

Star qualities: Strong and complex repertoire; fought hard for good roles; shares the record for the most consecutive Oscar nominations; legendary leading lady.

After studying at John Murray Anderson's acting school in New York, Bette Davis made her first appearance on Broadway in *Broken Dishes* in 1929. The following year she was dropped by Universal Studios, her first studio, because she had "as much sex appeal as Slim Summerville," but plugged away at Warner Brothers throughout the 1930s as a variety of pert, pretty, chic, urban girls. Like many young actresses, she knew that the best way to stand out from the pack was to play an outrageous tramp, and lobbied hard for the role of cockney "artist's model" Mildred, opposite Leslie Howard, in *Of Human Bondage* (1934). However, Warner Brothers tended to cast her as molls who wait at the ringside during fights (*Kid Galahad*, 1937) or at home during lengthy prison spells (*20,000 Years in Sing Sing*, 1932), bumping her up a little as a waitress smitten with intellectual drifter Howard in *The Petrified Forest* (1936) and the Mary Astor "scheming woman" role in *Satan Met a Lady* (1936), a version of *The Maltese Falcon*.

Against the odds, Davis won a Best Actress Oscar as a drunken actress in *Dangerous* (1935), but still had to fight for

Top Takes...

The Whales of August 1987
Return from Witch Mountain 1978
The Nanny 1965
Hush . . . Hush, Sweet Charlotte 1964
What Ever Happened to Baby Jane? 1962 ☆
The Virgin Queen 1955
The Star 1952 ☆
All About Eve 1950 ☆
Mr. Skeffington 1944 ☆
Old Acquaintance 1943
Now, Voyager 1942 ☆
The Man Who Came to Dinner 1942
The Little Foxes 1941 ☆
The Bride Came C.O.D. 1941
The Letter 1940 ☆
The Private Lives of Elizabeth and Essex 1939
The Old Maid 1939
Dark Victory 1939 ☆
Jezebel 1938 ★
Kid Galahad 1937
Satan Met a Lady 1936
The Petrified Forest 1936
Dangerous 1935 ★
Of Human Bondage 1934
20,000 Years in Sing Sing 1932

LEFT: Davis makes a comeback as fading actress Margot Channing in *All About Eve*.

A Formidable Woman

Bette Davis was a strong-minded woman and a star to be reckoned with. She once famously said, "Until you're known in my profession as a monster, you're not a star." Throughout her career, she fought for the roles she wanted, even bringing a lawsuit against Warner Brothers when they failed to produce such roles in the aftermath of her Best Actress Oscar.

- In October 1941, Davis was elected as the first female president of the American Academy of Motion Picture Arts and Sciences. She lasted less than two months, however, announcing publicly that she was too busy to fulfill her duties as president, while privately fuming that the Academy had expected her to act as a mere figurehead.

- Davis openly acknowledged that her relationships with men suffered as a result of her career and driven nature. She was married (and divorced) four times, and had numerous affairs—with George Brent and William Wyler, among others—believing, "An affair now and then is good for a marriage. It adds spice, stops it from getting boring. I ought to know."

- When Davis started out in Hollywood, Universal Pictures wanted to change her name to Bettina Dawes. She flatly refused, telling the studio that she would not go through life with a name that sounded like "Between the Drawers."

parts worthy of her talents. She didn't manage to land Scarlett O'Hara, the role she most hankered after, but gained a second Oscar in the consolation role as another Southern belle in Warner Brothers's GWTW "spoiler" *Jezebel* (1938). After that, she became Warner Brothers's in-house "great actress" and starred in high-profile pictures built around her suffering. She frequently found herself as a woman who sacrifices personal happiness for others or who finds love against the odds— terminally ill in *Dark Victory* (1939), mistreated by Miriam Hopkins in *The Old Maid* (1939) and *Old Acquaintance* (1943), forced to behead her lover in *The Private Lives of Elizabeth and Essex* (1939), more directly murdering another lover in *The Letter* (1940), gleefully ruining the lives of her whole family in *The Little Foxes* (1941), the neurotic spinster wooed by cigarette-brandishing Paul Henreid in *Now, Voyager* (1942), losing her looks to diphtheria only to find a devoted Claude Rains has gone blind in *Mr. Skeffington* (1944), and good-and-bad twins in *A Stolen Life* (1946). Amid all this, the pleasant comedy hijinks of *The Bride Came C.O.D.* (1941) and *The Man Who Came to Dinner* (1942) must have been a relief.

Diminishing star

Davis's career stalled in middle age, as the fashion for "women's pictures" faded after World War II. Her contract with Warner Brothers wound down with *Beyond the Forest* (1949), the trashy King Vidor movie in which she puffs on a cigarette and drawls "What a dump!" as quoted in *Who's Afraid of Virginia Woolf?* Joseph L. Mankiewicz put her back in the limelight in *All About Eve* (1950), in which she clearly channels herself as a theatrical diva challenged by a scheming, younger rival. Although an instant classic, *All About Eve* didn't restore Davis's fortunes, and she was reduced to reprising an old role (as Elizabeth I in *The Virgin Queen*, 1955).

By the 1960s Davis's career had come to a standstill. She was down to guest shots on *Wagon Train* when Robert Aldrich gifted her with the role of Baby Jane in *What Ever Happened to Baby Jane?* (1962), a Hollywood *guignol* that pits her against

her offscreen rival Joan Crawford in a venomous battle to the death. As deranged former child star Jane Hudson, Davis earned yet another Best Actress Oscar nomination, and the flames of her career were reignited. She gamely turned to more Gothics, flamboyant with Aldrich and Olivia de Havilland in *Hush . . . Hush, Sweet Charlotte* (1964), underplaying to terrifying effect as the cracked servant in *The Nanny* (1965), sporting a sequin eye patch as a monster matriarch in *The Anniversary* (1968), and a female Fu Manchu in *Madame Sin* (1972). She played Disney villainesses (*Return from Witch Mountain*, 1978) and horror hags (*Wicked Stepmother*, 1989) to the end, and had a last acting hurrah in *The Whales of August* (1987). The "First Lady of Film" took her final breath at the age of ninety-one. **KN** ·

ABOVE: *Whatever Happened to Baby Jane?* revived Davis's and Joan Crawford's careers.

"There was more good acting at Hollywood parties than ever appeared on the screen."

1900s

JAMES STEWART

Born: James Maitland Stewart, May 20, 1908 (Indiana, Pennsylvania, U.S.); died 1997 (Los Angeles, California, U.S.).

Star qualities: Mr. Nice Guy with an "aw shucks" demeanor; brought an honest and soft-spoken manner to his leading dramatic roles; an icon for all Hitchcock buffs.

Top Takes...

The Big Sleep 1978
Airport '77 1977
The Shootist 1976
Fools' Parade 1971
The Cheyenne Social Club 1970
Cheyenne Autumn 1964
The Man Who Shot Liberty Valance 1962
Two Rode Together 1961
Anatomy of a Murder 1959 ☆
Vertigo 1958
The Man Who Knew Too Much 1956
The Man from Laramie 1955
Rear Window 1954
The Naked Spur 1953
Bend of the River 1952
Harvey 1950 ☆
Winchester '73 1950
Rope 1948
Call Northside 777 1948
It's a Wonderful Life 1946 ☆
The Philadelphia Story 1940 ★
Destry Rides Again 1939
Mr. Smith Goes to Washington 1939 ☆
You Can't Take It with You 1938

James "Jimmy" Stewart graduated from Princeton University in 1932 with a degree in architecture. A member of the Princeton University Triangle Club, Stewart quickly discovered his thespian talents, and his acting career took off at the end of the 1930s. After some minor roles, he landed a major part as the only sane person in a family of screwballs in Frank Capra's *You Can't Take It with You* (1938). The following year, Stewart appeared in Capra's *Mr. Smith Goes to Washington*, excelling as the small-town innocent who unmasks the crooked politicians in the nation's capital. In the comedy Western *Destry Rides Again* (1939), Stewart played another seemingly naive hero who triumphs over the crooks. He won an Academy Award for Best Actor opposite Cary Grant and Katharine Hepburn in the sophisticated comedy *The Philadelphia Story* (1940), but his career was put on hold when he joined the U.S. air force, flying missions as a bomber pilot in World War II. He was the first Hollywood movie star to sign up for active duty.

His first movie after the war was again for Capra. *It's a Wonderful Life* (1946) had a darker tone, with Stewart as a

RIGHT: Stewart in *The Man Who Knew Too Much*, his third movie for Alfred Hitchcock.

ABOVE: Stewart stars as an eccentric with a fantasy rabbit friend in the comedy *Harvey*.

banker exploring the frustrations and disappointments of small-town life. Stewart's previous screen persona had been folksy, his gangling frame and slow drawl embodying an unsophisticated moral virtue. But now he extended his range. In *Call Northside 777* (1948) he is a tenacious reporter determined to put right a miscarriage of justice, and in 1950 he embarked on a series of Westerns for director Anthony Mann, beginning with *Winchester '73*. In these films, including *Bend of the River* (1952), *The Naked Spur* (1953), and *The Man from Laramie* (1955), Stewart's character is driven, obsessive, given to outbursts of almost murderous violence. The movies also offered Stewart the chance to break free of the studio star system and become one of the first Hollywood actors to participate in independent production.

"Sometimes I wonder if I'm doing a Jimmy Stewart imitation myself."

Jimmy and Politics

James Stewart was a staunch Republican who promoted right-wing causes, including blacklisting in Hollywood during the late 1940s. At one point, he even got into a fistfight with his best friend, the very liberal Henry Fonda, over politics. Rather than further jeopardize their friendship, the pair apparently agreed never to discuss politics again.

- President Harry S. Truman was an avid fan of Stewart's work. The president even went so far as to say that if he'd had a son, he'd have wanted him to be "just like Jimmy Stewart."
- During the 1940s, Stewart worked as an undercover agent for FBI leader J. Edgar Hoover, flushing out suspected communists from Hollywood. His status as a famous, decorated war hero gave him authority. By 1970, his views were unchanged: "I don't think there's any question that the communists are behind a great deal of unrest in the United States. In addition, I feel they are still a potential danger in show business."
- Stewart was at first dubious about supporting his friend Ronald Reagan's campaign for the governorship of California in 1966 because of Reagan's Democrat past, but he went on to campaign extensively for Reagan in the 1976 presidential primaries.
- He campaigned for Richard Nixon in the 1968 and 1972 elections.

Stewart made his first movie for Alfred Hitchcock, *Rope* (1948), in a role that sees him unmask a murder committed by two callous young men who are his former pupils. The relationship between actor and director developed and Stewart went on to become, along with Cary Grant, Hitchcock's most reliable leading man. Less of a romantic lead than Grant, Stewart plays characters more inwardly troubled than those of the debonair Grant. In *Rear Window* (1954) he is a photographer laid up with a broken leg who observes a murder from his apartment window while negotiating a tricky romance with Grace Kelly. In *The Man Who Knew Too Much* (1956), his child is kidnapped by an unscrupulous gang of spies. In one of his greatest roles, in Hitchcock's *Vertigo* (1958), Stewart is a policeman who becomes dangerously obsessed with a woman while trying to recover from a disabling fear of heights.

Taking a comic turn

Stewart was adept at comedy, one of his most successful films being *Harvey* (1950), in which he plays an eccentric with a fantasy rabbit as a friend. But he continued to give powerful performances in dramatic roles, such as *Anatomy of a Murder* (1959), a gripping courtroom drama, for which he received his fifth Academy Award nomination. Later in his career he made *Two Rode Together* (1961) for John Ford, playing a venal sheriff with an engagingly laconic manner; and in Ford's *The Man Who Shot Liberty Valance* (1962), he is a young lawyer out West who trades on his spurious celebrity as a gunfighter to become a senator. His cameo as Wyatt Earp in Ford's *Cheyenne Autumn* (1964) is delightfully comic. The Westerns he made after that, such as *The Cheyenne Social Club* (1970), are undemanding, with the exception of *The Shootist* (1976), where Stewart makes the most of a small part as John Wayne's doctor, forced to give him the unwelcome news that he is dying of cancer.

Stewart disliked the glamour of Hollywood and shunned the limelight; unlike many of his contemporaries, he steered clear of expensive tastes and fast cars. He was devoted to his wife, Gloria, and was devastated when she died in 1994. **EB**

RIGHT: Stewart was nominated for an Oscar for his performance in *It's a Wonderful Life*.

DON AMECHE

Born: Dominic Felix Amici, May 31, 1908 (Kenosha, Wisconsin, U.S.); died 1993 (Scottsdale, Arizona, U.S.).

Star qualities: Pencil-thin moustache; glittering smile; well groomed; versatile; leading man in romantic comedies and dramas followed by mature character roles.

Top Takes...

Corrina, Corrina 1994
Folks! 1992
Oscar 1991
Things Change 1988
Coming to America 1988
Cocoon 1985 ★
Trading Places 1983
The Boatniks 1970
Picture Mommy Dead 1966
Sleep, My Love 1948
Heaven Can Wait 1943
Swanee River 1939
The Story of Alexander Graham Bell 1939
Alexander's Ragtime Band 1938
Ramona 1936
Sins of Man 1936

Like all light leading men, Don Ameche was consistently underrated. Born to an Italian father and an Irish-German mother, he started out in vaudeville with singer and actress Texas Guinan until she dropped him from the act, saying he was "too stiff." After a dual role playing two sons in *Sins of Man* (1936), he became a Twentieth Century Fox leading man with *Ramona* (1936). Most often found in pleasant musicals such as *Alexander's Ragtime Band* (1938), he occasionally starred in musical biopics, for example as Stephen Foster in *Swanee River* (1939). His role as the inventor in the biopic *The Story of Alexander Graham Bell* (1939) even led to "Ameche" becoming the slang term of the day for the telephone. More charming than Tyrone Power, with whom he often competed for Alice Faye, his trademarks were a pencil moustache and a glittering smile. His best starring role came in Ernst Lubitsch's *Heaven Can Wait* (1943) as Henry Van Cleve, a likable but melancholy rogue on the road to hell, and he showed versatility as the villain in Douglas Sirk's *Sleep, My Love* (1948).

A star on radio with Frances Langford in "The Bickersons," he moved into TV in the 1950s, returning to the cinema with the odd B-feature such as *Picture Mommy Dead* (1966), or in crusty cameos as in *The Boatniks* (1970). A solid supporting role as an elderly millionaire in *Trading Places* (1983) reminded Hollywood that Ameche was still working. His last decade found him showcased in geriatric hits such as *Cocoon* (1985), which won him an Academy Award for Best Supporting Actor, and led to an affectionate, sharp picture built entirely around him, David Mamet's *Things Change* (1988). Ameche was happily married to Honore Prendergast until her death in 1986. The couple had six children. **KN**

> "I feel tremendous! I'm ready to take on the world!"
>
> —Art Selwyn, *Cocoon*

ROBERT CUMMINGS

Born: Charles Clarence Robert Orville Cummings, June 10, 1908 (Joplin, Missouri, U.S.); died 1990 (Los Angeles, California, U.S.).

Star qualities: Youthful good looks; comic timing; health-food fan; fit; writer, director, and producer; TV sitcom veteran.

Robert Cummings was one of those fresh-faced, likable actors who maintained a long career both on the big screen and TV. He appeared in *The Bob Cummings Show* (rerun under the title *Love That Bob*) from 1955 to 1959 as an unattached ladies' man photographer who bantered with his acerbic secretary, Schultzy, played by Ann B. Davis. Two other series followed, *The New Bob Cummings Show* (1961–1962) and *My Living Doll* (1964), yet it was the first program that established his persona as a suave, younger-than-his-years lothario.

Cummings's career took more turns than this image would indicate. He was taught to fly by his godfather, Orville Wright, and served as a pilot in World War II. He studied acting at the Carnegie Institute of Technology and American Academy of Dramatic Arts. Curiously, he initially appeared onstage and on film under two pseudonyms: "Blade Stanhope Conway" and "Bruce Hutchins." He was contracted by Paramount Pictures in 1935 and took minor roles until his breakthrough in a Deanna Durbin vehicle, *Three Smart Girls Grow Up* (1939).

If comedy marked Cummings's TV career, drama took precedence in his movie work, despite appearances in lightweight vehicles such as the Betty Grable musical *Moon over Miami* (1941). Alfred Hitchcock employed him twice as a stalwart hero: *Saboteur* (1942) and *Dial M for Murder* (1954), the latter his last film appearance before turning to the small screen. Other credits of note from Cummings in the 1940s include the moody film noir *The Chase* (1946), and a curious adaptation of Henry James's *The Aspern Papers*, *The Lost Moment* (1947). Cummings's few screen appearances in the 1960s are negligible, and his last outing on TV came in 1979. **DS**

Top Takes...

Five Golden Dragons 1967
Stagecoach 1966
Promise Her Anything 1965
What a Way to Go! 1964
Dial M for Murder 1954
For Heaven's Sake 1950
Paid in Full 1950
Reign of Terror 1949
Sleep, My Love 1948
The Lost Moment 1947
The Chase 1946
Saboteur 1942
Kings Row 1942
Moon Over Miami 1941
The Devil and Miss Jones 1941
Three Smart Girls Grow Up 1939

"I'd love to tell all those critics how well I feel today because of my diet. But they're all dead."

MILTON BERLE

Born: Mendel Berlinger, July 12, 1908 (New York City, New York, U.S.); died 2002 (Los Angeles, California, U.S.).

Star qualities: Comedian; joke teller and writer; child performer; "Mr. Television"; espoused charitable causes; mentored young comics.

Top Takes...

Storybook 1995
The Muppet Movie 1979
Lepke 1975
For Singles Only 1968
Where Angels Go, Trouble Follows 1968
Silent Treatment 1968
The Happening 1967
The Oscar 1966
The Loved One 1965
It's a Mad Mad Mad Mad World 1963
Let's Make Love 1960
Always Leave Them Laughing 1949
Margin for Error 1943
Over My Dead Body 1942
Birthright 1920
The Mark of Zorro 1920

There is probably no name more synonymous with the golden age of U.S. TV than Milton Berle, earning him the sobriquet "Mr. Television." The son of a salesman, Berle was encouraged in his stage ambitions when he won a lookalike contest with his impersonation of Charlie Chaplin in 1913. He went on to stage school and then hit Broadway. He became a child performer in a number of early silent movies such as *Birthright* (1920) and *The Mark of Zorro* (1920), but the comedian really made his name in the early days of radio. By the late 1940s, Berle was headlining his own radio variety shows. But it was NBC, in bringing Berle's *The Texaco Star Theater* to TV in 1948 (while the show was also running on ABC radio), that made "Uncle Miltie" a household name. Thanks to this success, Berle signed an unprecedented 30-year contract with NBC in 1951.

From 1948 until the early 1950s, Berle dominated Tuesday nights, with restaurants closing between 8:00 and 9:00 P.M. and rumors about dropping reservoir levels after 9:00 P.M., when avid TV watchers would finally go to the bathroom. Berle was also known for dressing in women's clothing as part of his shtick—somewhat ironic, perhaps, as he was a reportedly well-endowed ladies' man and was married five times (twice to Joyce Mathews). By 1953, however, the shine was beginning to be lost, and with a series of changes in the show's sponsors, dropping ratings, and networks beginning to look for the next big thing, Berle finally canceled *The Milton Berle Show* (*Texaco Star Theater*) in 1956. From the 1960s to the end of the century, he appeared in a number of movies, such as *It's a Mad, Mad, Mad, Mad World* (1963) and *The Oscar* (1966), mostly in cameo roles. Berle also made regular appearances on dozens of other TV series. **MK**

> "You have to keep the desire to forge ahead ... Success is just one long street fight."

LUPE VÉLEZ

Born: María Guadalupe Vélez de Villalobos, July 18, 1908 (San Luis Potosí, Mexico); died 1944 (Los Angeles, California, U.S.).

Star qualities: Petite sex symbol; glamorous long-haired beauty; brash; passionate; "The Mexican Spitfire"; played the exotic leading lady in melodramas and comedies.

Thanks largely to Kenneth Anger's TV series *Hollywood Babylon* (1992–1993), Lupe Vélez has now found the immortality she had despaired of ever achieving through her work. But the terribly sad circumstances surrounding her premature death, recounted by Anger with obvious pleasure, should not eclipse all memories of her movies, or of her undoubted popularity. She is surely owed that much.

A brash, tempestuous, voluptuous Mexican actress and renowned party girl, Vélez did bits in silents, supporting Charley Chase and others at the Hal Roach studios, before Douglas Fairbanks cast her in *The Gaucho* (1927) alongside Mary Pickford. This led her to MGM, where she played passionate and exotic roles in a series of pre-Code melodramas, including the still eye-opening *Kongo* (1932).

Hot Pepper (1933) revealed a hitherto untapped talent for comedy and initiated the second phase of her career, which led her, via an egg fight with Stan Laurel and Oliver Hardy in *Hollywood Party* (1934), to the very amusing *Mexican Spitfire* series at RKO Pictures (1939–1943). Vélez's likable screen presence found a home in these eight movies, costarring with comedian Leon Errol, but her mainstream career had fizzled out. She returned to Mexico for one last dramatic lead in an adaptation of Émile Zola's *Nana* (1944), but she was beset by financial and personal difficulties. She had married *Tarzan* movie star Johnny Weissmuller in 1933, but they divorced in 1939. Following a doomed romance with Westerns cowboy actor Gary Cooper, Vélez became pregnant by married Austrian actor Harald Maresch, who refused to leave his wife to marry her. Vélez killed herself by taking an overdose in December 1944. She was only thirty-six years old. **MC**

Top Takes...

Nana 1944
Mexican Spitfire's Blessed Event 1943
Ladies' Day 1943
Mexican Spitfire's Elephant 1942
Mexican Spitfire Sees a Ghost 1942
Mexican Spitfire at Sea 1942
Mexican Spitfire's Baby 1941
Mexican Spitfire Out West 1940
Mexican Spitfire 1940
Hollywood Party 1934
Laughing Boy 1934
Strictly Dynamite 1934
Palooka 1934
Hot Pepper 1933
Kongo 1932
The Gaucho 1927

"I prefer to take my life away and our baby's before I bring him shame." —Suicide note

FRED MacMURRAY

Born: Fredrick Martin MacMurray, August 30, 1908 (Kankakee, Illinois, U.S.); died 1991 (Santa Monica, California, U.S.).

Star qualities: Handsome, clean-cut looks; blue eyes; dark hair; musician; singer; vaudeville performer; affable screen persona; versatile leading man; producer.

Top Takes...

Charley and the Angel 1973
The Happiest Millionaire 1967
Follow Me, Boys! 1966
Kisses for My President 1964
Son of Flubber 1963
The Absent-Minded Professor 1961
The Apartment 1960
At Gunpoint 1955
The Caine Mutiny 1954
Father Was a Fullback 1949
The Egg and I 1947
Double Indemnity 1944
Take a Letter, Darling 1942
Hands Across the Table 1935
Alice Adams 1935
Grand Old Girl 1935

Fred MacMurray's father was a concert violinist, and Fred Jr. initially followed in his father's footsteps, playing saxophone. He sang and played in orchestras to earn his college-tuition fees, and had occasional roles as an extra in movies. He then joined a vocal ensemble, the California Collegians, and went to New York, where he started to get work on Broadway. He followed this with a stint as a vaudeville performer before making his film debut in *Grand Old Girl* (1935).

MacMurray went on to spend almost his entire career as a smiling, chin-dimpled collegiate nice guy, from preppy heirs, as in *Alice Adams* (1935), through to emasculated clods: as a male secretary in *Take a Letter, Darling* (1942), and "First Husband" to a female U.S. president in *Kisses for My President* (1964). He also did a turn as Disney scientists in *The Absent-Minded Professor* (1961) and *Son of Flubber* (1963), and had success on TV as the archetypal sitcom father in *My Three Sons* (1964–1972). He was so clean-cut that artist C. C. Beck used him as the model for the comic superhero Captain Marvel.

However, MacMurray's best screen work came in his all-too-rare heel roles: as the lecherous insurance salesman seduced into a murder scheme in Billy Wilder's *Double Indemnity* (1944); the glib-talking gutless instigator of *The Caine Mutiny* (1954); and the hideously amoral adulterous boss of Wilder's *The Apartment* (1960). Embodying a specifically U.S. style of slick, sleazy corruption, MacMurray is so strong in these roles that his lightweight, grinning regular chumps in the likes of *The Egg and I* (1947) ring false, as if the backstabbing, feral smile were barely held in check. He's good, too, as a Western storekeeper whose one lucky shot turns him into a marked man in *At Gunpoint* (1955). **KN**

"A cowboy actor needs two changes of expression— hat on and hat off."

CAROLE LOMBARD

Born: Jane Alice Peters, October 6, 1908 (Fort Wayne, Indiana, U.S.); died 1942 (Table Rock Mountain, Nevada, U.S.).

Star qualities: Beautiful; blonde; slim; sporty; sexy; petite; glamorous; witty; clear voice; screwball comedy queen; romantic lead.

Carole Lombard moved with her mother to Los Angeles following her parents' divorce. She was spotted by director Allan Dwan in the street; he cast her at age twelve in her movie debut, *A Perfect Crime* (1921). This whetted her appetite for acting and she joined a theater troupe. She was eventually signed by the Fox Film Corporation and had scattered bits as beautiful blondes in silent films such as *Hearts and Spurs* (1925). But in 1926 her face was left scarred after a car accident, and Fox canceled her contract. She found a new studio in Pathé, and when the talkies arrived she became a star.

Unaffected, clear-voiced, and reed-slender, Lombard was good in *No Man of Her Own* (1932), a rough romance with Clark Gable, but her real gift was for screwball comedy. She battles with John Barrymore in *Twentieth Century* (1934) and William Powell in *My Man Godfrey* (1936), for which she was nominated for an Oscar for Best Actress. Offscreen, her similarly uncompromising approach, love of parties, and inelegant language earned her the nickname "The Profane Angel."

Lombard turned to straighter, nearly tearjerking romance with James Stewart in *Made for Each Other* (1939), and tried heavy melodrama in *They Knew What They Wanted* (1940). But her final roles found her happily back in marital comedy, as the suddenly unmarried wife in *Mr. & Mrs. Smith* (1941). She died prematurely in a plane crash returning from a war-bond rally, and was posthumously awarded the Medal of Freedom by President Franklin D. Roosevelt as the first woman killed in the line of duty in World War II. Lombard was married twice, both times to costars. Her first marriage was to Powell, whom she divorced in 1933, and then to Gable in 1939, whom she was with until she died. **KN**

Top Takes...

To Be or Not to Be 1942
Mr. & Mrs. Smith 1941
They Knew What They Wanted 1940
Vigil in the Night 1940
In Name Only 1939
Made for Each Other 1939
Fools for Scandal 1938
True Confession 1937
Nothing Sacred 1937
My Man Godfrey 1936 ☆
Twentieth Century 1934
We're Not Dressing 1934
Supernatural 1933
No Man of Her Own 1932
Hearts and Spurs 1925
A Perfect Crime 1921

"I think marriage is dangerous. The idea of two people trying to possess each other is wrong."

LEW AYRES

Born: Lewis Frederick Ayre III, December 28, 1908 (Minneapolis, Minnesota, U.S.); died 1996 (Los Angeles, California, U.S.).

Star qualities: Director; producer; writer; musician; boyish good looks; moustache; confident; idealistic; character actor; committed pacifist.

Top Takes...

After dropping out of college, Lew Ayres got his lucky break when he was spotted by a talent scout in a Los Angeles nightclub. He started out in bit parts until he became Greta Garbo's love interest in *The Kiss* (1929). Then followed *All Quiet on the Western Front* (1930), which made him a star. Ayres's Paul Bäumer transforms from fresh-faced idealist to traumatized combat soldier, expiring while reaching for a butterfly on the barbed wire. His limited range exposed by *The Doorway to Hell* (1930), an early gangster movie that needed the strut of James Cagney, he soon turned to cheery juvenile roles, as in *State Fair* (1933). After leads in many minor films such as *Silk Hat Kid* (1935) and supporting roles in a few bigger pictures such as *Holiday* (1938), he was cast in *Young Dr. Kildare* (1938) and found a niche in the successful series as the earnest junior physician mentored by Lionel Barrymore's Dr. Gillespie.

In 1942, Ayres became a controversial figure when—having taken the antiwar message of *All Quiet* to heart—he became a conscientious objector during World War II. Having taken the *Kildare* films seriously too, he served valiantly in the Medical Corps in the Pacific and in New Guinea, but MGM dropped him and launched a Barrymore solo series with *Calling Dr. Gillespie* (1942). Besides his political beliefs, Ayres had apparently opposed the network's use of cigarette sponsorship to fund its programs. Later, he had solid, mature roles in *Johnny Belinda* (1948)—it won him an Oscar nomination for Best Actor—and *Donovan's Brain* (1953). He then worked mostly in TV playing dignified elder statesmen, but has a memorable death under ice in *Damien: Omen II* (1978). Ayres married three times, his second wife being actress Ginger Rogers, whom he married in 1934 and divorced in 1940. **KN**

> "You still think it's beautiful to die for your country."
>
> —Bäumer, *All Quiet on the Western Front*

JOSÉ FERRER

Born: José Vicente Ferrer de Otero y Cintrón, January 8, 1909 (Santurce, Puerto Rico); died 1992 (Coral Gables, Florida, U.S.).

Star qualities: Shakespearean stage actor; director; producer; writer; musician; intelligent; versatile; distinctive voice; the ultimate Cyrano de Bergerac.

José Ferrer won a Tony and an Oscar—and was nominated for an Emmy—as Cyrano de Bergerac, although the 1950 movie version now seems like an embalmed stage production, and his hard-won, great actor reputation dwindled with too many credits for such minor works as *Dracula's Dog* (1977).

A graduate of Princeton University and a member of the renowned Princeton University Triangle Club, Ferrer took to acting and hit Broadway in 1935. He had his first starring role on Broadway in 1940, the title character in *Charley's Aunt*. This was followed by an even greater success as Iago in the 1943 production of *Othello*. It became, and still is, the longest-running production of a Shakespeare play staged in the United States. He went on to direct Broadway productions.

Properly petulant as the dauphin in *Joan of Arc* (1948), his screen debut, Ferrer landed prize roles for a while: easy to caricature with shoes on his knees as Henri de Toulouse-Lautrec in *Moulin Rouge* (1952); emasculated and glumly obsessed with Rita Hayworth in *Miss Sadie Thompson* (1953); driving Humphrey Bogart mad on the witness stand and dashing wine in Fred MacMurray's face in the last reel of *The Caine Mutiny* (1954); an investigative reporter in the underrated gem *The Great Man* (1956), which he also directed; and suffering as Captain Alfred Dreyfus in *I Accuse!* (1958). After that, he reprised his signature role in the French *Cyrano et d'Artagnan* (1964), and did cameos such as Herod Antipas in *The Greatest Story Ever Told* (1965). Ferrer was married five times, twice to the same woman, actress Rosemary Clooney, whom he divorced and then remarried three years later. The couple had five children. He is also the uncle of actor George Clooney. **KN**

Top Takes...

Dune 1984
A Midsummer Night's Sex Comedy 1982
A Life of Sin 1979
Crash! 1977
The Greatest Story Ever Told 1965
Cyrano et d'Artagnan 1964
Lawrence of Arabia 1962
The High Cost of Loving 1958
I Accuse! 1958
The Great Man 1956
The Shrike 1955
The Caine Mutiny 1954
Miss Sadie Thompson 1953
Moulin Rouge 1952 ☆
Cyrano de Bergerac 1950 ★
Joan of Arc 1948 ☆

"The truth is, I made a few good movies in the fifties, then went into freefall."

CARMEN MIRANDA

Born: Maria do Carmo Miranda Da Cunha, February 9, 1909 (Marco de Canavezes, Portugal); died 1955 (Los Angeles, California, U.S.).

Star qualities: "The Brazilian Bombshell"; flamboyant exotic beauty; voluptuous; fresh-fruit hats; toothy smile; samba singer and dancer with a haunting high voice.

1900s

Top Takes...

Scared Stiff 1953
Nancy Goes to Rio 1950
A Date with Judy 1948
Copacabana 1947
If I'm Lucky 1946
Doll Face 1945
Four Jills in a Jeep 1944
Greenwich Village 1944
The Gang's All Here 1943
Springtime in the Rockies 1942
Down Argentine Way 1941
That Night in Rio 1941
Alô Alô Carnaval 1936
Estudantes 1935
Alô, Alô, Brasil 1935
A Voz do Carnaval 1933

A typical 1940s novelty act, atypical in that her name and memory endure to the present, Carmen Miranda survives as a handful of images and impressions: of impossibly long eyelashes; hats that look like a mountain of fresh fruit; songs with names such as "I, Yi, Yi, Yi, Yi (I Like You Very Much)" (1941); a scandalous penchant for performing high-kicking dance numbers without underwear (with photos to prove it); and an over-the-top look and performing style more typical of a cartoon character than a real woman—cartoon characters started to imitate her. There are novelty acts and novelty acts, but Miranda was startling.

Portuguese by birth, she moved with her family to Brazil. She started working in a boutique, where she learned how to make hats. She sang while she worked and was soon spotted, leading to work on local radio in Rio de Janeiro. She was a Brazilian recording superstar by the late 1920s, and made her movie debut in *A Voz do Carnaval* (1933). She was the most successful exponent of the 1940s craze for all things Latin American, heading first to Broadway, where she appeared in musicals, and eventually the big screen. She made a big impression in *Down Argentine Way* (1941) and similar revue-style entertainments at the beginning of the decade. A different proposition when not singing, she was not easy to cast, but consolidated her value as wartime morale booster as one of the *Four Jills in a Jeep* (1944) and holds her own opposite Groucho Marx in *Copacabana* (1947). Her last screen appearance was in *Scared Stiff* (1953), two years before a sudden and unexpected heart attack killed her at the age of forty-six. Her body was flown to Brazil, where her death was cause to declare a period of national mourning. **MC**

"Look at me and tell me if I don't have Brazil in every curve of my body."

JAMES MASON

Born: James Neville Mason, May 15, 1909 (Huddersfield, Yorkshire, England); died 1984 (Lausanne, Switzerland).

Star qualities: Stagecraft; subtle; versatile; soft voice; brooding good looks; character actor known for villains and antihero roles; director; writer; producer.

James Mason was an intelligent young man; he was educated at one of England's top schools, Marlborough, before heading to Cambridge University. He planned to become an architect but found himself drawn to the stage, and after a period in repertory he joined London's Old Vic theater. Subtle and persuasive, he was a versatile performer. In British movies from the mid-1930s onward, he was an interesting, anguished contemporary antihero in *The Night Has Eyes* (1942) and *Thunder Rock* (1943). But he gained popularity as a brooding, sexy semivillain in Gainsborough Pictures' bodice-rippers such as *The Man in Grey* (1943) and *The Wicked Lady* (1945).

Mason was a conscientious objector in World War II, a stance that created a lasting rift with his family. His general popularity endured, however, and after the war, he began to take varied leads in challenging movies: the fleeing IRA man in *Odd Man Out* (1947), the blackmailer in *The Reckless Moment* (1949), the Flying Dutchman in *Pandora and the Flying Dutchman* (1951), and Field Marshal Erwin Johannes Rommel in *The Desert Fox: The Story of Rommel* (1951). This was not the only time Mason played Rommel. The second time was two years later in Robert Wise's *The Desert Rats* (1953), which featured fellow British actor Richard Burton as Rommel's English enemy commander. As an older actor, Mason was sleek as the bisexual villain in *North By Northwest* (1959), and perfect as a velvet-voiced Professor Humbert Humbert in *Lolita* (1962). He then turned to domestic tyrants, as in *Spring and Port Wine* (1970), and sad, corrupt authority figures such as the film director in *The Last of Sheila* (1973). He is stalwart, loyal, dim, and sweet-natured as one of the screen's best Dr. Watsons in *Murder by Decree* (1979). **KN**

Top Takes...

***The Verdict* 1982** ☆
Murder by Decree 1979
The Last of Sheila 1973
Spring and Port Wine 1970
***Georgy Girl* 1966** ☆
Lolita 1962
North by Northwest 1959
20,000 Leagues Under the Sea 1954
***A Star Is Born* 1954** ☆
The Desert Rats 1953
The Prisoner of Zenda 1952
The Desert Fox: The Story of Rommel 1951
The Reckless Moment 1949
The Wicked Lady 1945
The Man in Grey 1943
The Night Has Eyes 1942

"[I wish to be remembered] just as a fairly desirable sort of character actor."

1900s

JESSICA TANDY

Born: Jessica Alice Tandy, June 7, 1909 (London, England); died 1994 (Easton, Connecticut, U.S.).

Star qualities: Twinkly blue eyes; graceful; leading lady of stage and screen in serious dramatic roles; late career renaissance.

Top Takes...

Nobody's Fool 1994
Camilla 1994
Fried Green Tomatoes 1991
Driving Miss Daisy 1989 ★
Cocoon: The Return 1988
The House on Carroll Street 1988
Cocoon 1985
The Bostonians 1984
Best Friends 1982
Still of the Night 1982
The Birds 1963
September Affair 1950
A Woman's Vengeance 1948
Dragonwyck 1946
The Green Years 1946
The Seventh Cross 1944

Jessica Tandy was born in London and became a U.S. citizen in 1954. She was a minor Hollywood player in the late 1930s and early 1940s, without much screen time in such movies as *The Seventh Cross* (1944) and *Dragonwyck* (1946). Her breakthrough came on Broadway, with a star turn as Blanche Du Bois in the initial production of Tennessee Williams's *A Streetcar Named Desire* (1947). Dumped for the screen version on the insistence of Warner Brothers executives, who wanted a more glamorous woman and a bigger name, Tandy more or less disappeared from Hollywood altogether (although she kept her career going on Broadway) until cast by Alfred Hitchcock as the mother driven by Oedipal jealousies and reduced to near catatonia by uncontrollable fear in *The Birds* (1963), a standout performance in an impressive ensemble cast.

Thereafter, Tandy delivered some excellent film work in supporting roles, such as the mother of a troubled psychiatrist in *Still of the Night* (1982) and the still attractive but nonetheless betrayed older woman in *Cocoon* (1985), one of many roles she played opposite her second husband, Hume Cronyn. Offered a rare chance at a starring role, in Bruce Beresford's acclaimed *Driving Miss Daisy* (1989), Tandy won a Best Actress Oscar for her portrayal of an elderly Southern Jewish widow, crusty and resentful of social change but with a heart of gold, who abuses yet depends absolutely on her loyal and long-suffering African-American chauffeur. She reprised this impersonation with equal success in yet another small movie with a Deep South connection, *Fried Green Tomatoes* (1991). Tandy's superb work as a silver-haired senior hints at what might have been had Hollywood found more juicy roles for her when she was in her prime. **BP**

"I found out what the secret to life is: friends. Best friends."
—N. Threadgoode, *Fried Green Tomatoes*

BURL IVES

Born: Burl Icle Ivanhoe Ives, June 14, 1909 (Hunt, Illinois, U.S.); died 1995 (Anacortes, Washington, U.S.).

Star qualities: Folk and country music singer; banjo player; tall; imposing screen presence; played roles as the Big Daddy or the lawman.

Although Burl Ives made his reputation as an easygoing singer of American folk songs, his screen career oscillated between avuncular characters, often sheriffs, and darker individuals that drew upon the potentially daunting characteristics of his sizable personality. He graduated from Eastern Illinois University and, after traveling the country working as a handyman, moved to New York. There, he broke into the public consciousness with his 1940 CBS radio series *The Wayfaring Stranger*.

In the latter part of the decade his recording career took off. In 1949 he began to mount the record charts with "Lavender Blue." Ives initiated his screen career in a Western, *Smoky* (1946), and appeared as a kindly blacksmith in the Disney pastoral feature *So Dear to My Heart* (1948). Elia Kazan elevated his cinematic posture when he cast Ives as Sam the sheriff in *East of Eden* (1955). He portrayed a cruel or domineering patriarch in adaptations of Eugene O'Neill's *Desire Under the Elms* (1958) and Tennessee Williams's *Cat on a Hot Tin Roof* (1958). In the latter, the role of Big Daddy was specially written for Ives.

William Wyler's epic Western *The Big Country* (1958) followed, for which he received an Oscar as Best Supporting Actor. Directors intuited the darker side of Ives's screen persona, yet imbued it with an undeniable degree of sympathy. Nicholas Ray cast him as Cottonmouth in *Wind Across the Everglades* (1958), a freewheeling, if inevitably doomed, force of nature, whereas in *Day of the Outlaw* (1959) director André de Toth made him a ripe and ruthless villain. The tail end of his credits illustrates the diversity of his talents. He portrayed a crusty but courageous animal trainer in Sam Fuller's little-seen *White Dog* (1982) and last appeared as a sheriff in the melodrama *Two Moon Junction* (1988). **DS**

Top Takes...

Two Moon Junction 1988
White Dog 1982
Just You and Me, Kid 1979
Baker's Hawk 1976
Rocket to the Moon 1967
Ensign Pulver 1964
Summer Magic 1963
The Spiral Road 1962
Let No Man Write My Epitaph 1960
Our Man in Havana 1959
The Big Country 1958 ★
Cat on a Hot Tin Roof 1958
East of Eden 1955
Sierra 1950
So Dear to My Heart 1948
Smoky 1946

"My heart jumped for joy. Life, excitement, experience was on this long road."

1900s

ERROL FLYNN

Born: Errol Leslie Flynn, June 20, 1909 (Hobart, Tasmania, Australia); died 1959 (Vancouver, British Columbia, Canada).

Star qualities: Tall, swashbuckling hero; troublemaker; charming ladies' man who was rumored to be very well endowed ("in like Flynn"); whiskey lover; writer.

Top Takes…

Cuban Rebel Girls 1959
Too Much, Too Soon 1958
The Sun Also Rises 1957
The Story of William Tell 1953
Against All Flags 1952
Kim 1950
That Forsyte Woman 1949
Adventures of Don Juan 1948
Silver River 1948
Never Say Goodbye 1946
San Antonio 1945
Objective, Burma! 1945
Uncertain Glory 1944
Edge of Darkness 1943
Deperate Journey 1942
They Died with Their Boots On 1941
The Sea Hawk 1940
The Private Lives of Elizabeth and Essex 1939
Dodge City 1939
The Adventures of Robin Hood 1938
The Prince and the Pauper 1937
The Charge of the Light Brigade 1936
Captain Blood 1935
The Case of the Curious Bride 1935
In the Wake of the Bounty 1933

RIGHT: Flynn's Robin Hood takes on Basil Rathbone in The Adventures of Robin Hood.

Errol Flynn liked to pretend that he took nothing seriously, least of all acting. A Tasmanian with a colorful early life that had a habit of catching up with him, he made his movie debut in a lead role as Fletcher Christian in the obscure Australian film In the Wake of the Bounty (1933), but began his Hollywood career as a murder victim in Michael Curtiz's The Case of the Curious Bride (1935). When Robert Donat dropped out of Captain Blood (1935), Warner Brothers needed a suitable replacement and Curtiz was persuaded to give his former bit player corpse a shot. With Olivia de Havilland as love interest and Basil Rathbone as scurvy villain, Captain Blood set the mold for subsequent Flynn vehicles. These were mostly directed by Curtiz, until he fell out with the star and Raoul Walsh took over as authority figure.

Flynn grinned, fought, and romanced throughout history in The Charge of the Light Brigade (1936), The Prince and the Pauper (1937), The Adventures of Robin Hood (1938), and The Sea Hawk (1940), delivering the odd straight hero line ("It's injustice I hate, not Normandy!") to demonstrate that tweaking the baddies' noses wasn't all a jolly lark.

ABOVE: Flynn fishing with his son, Sean, who would become a war correspondent.

When swashbuckling faltered, Flynn was just as comfortable in Westerns (cleaning up *Dodge City*, 1939; riding valiantly to doom as Custer in *They Died with Their Boots On*, 1941) or war movies (whether the romp of *Desperate Journey*, 1942, or the violent grit of *Objective, Burma!*, 1945). Declared 4F—unfit for military service—by the World War II draft board, he gamely appeared in *Thank Your Lucky Stars* (1943), playing himself as a saloon blowhard who brags of imaginary battlefield heroics.

Flynn's later career was littered with stodgy imitations of his earlier movies (*Against All Flags*, 1952; *The Story of William Tell*, 1953), but he was often better in haunted, flawed roles with which he made a personal connection: the breezy charmer who winds up with his neck on the chopping block in *The Private Lives of Elizabeth and Essex* (1939), a true-to-Hemingway alcoholic in *The Sun Also Rises* (1957), and his own unhappy predecessor John Barrymore in *Too Much, Too Soon* (1958). **KN**

Wicked, Wicked Ways

Errol Flynn led a colorful life and was often in trouble. In many ways, his own life mirrored that of his characters:

- Flynn was expelled from two schools for fighting and getting too friendly with members of the opposite sex.
- Early in his career, Flynn pretended to be Irish because he believed that few people had heard of Australia.
- When banned from boozing on set, Flynn would inject oranges with vodka to make his breaks more entertaining.
- Flynn died in the arms of his teenage lover Beverley Aadland while at a party.

RUBY KEELER

Born: Ethel Hilda Keeler, August 25, 1909 (Halifax, Nova Scotia, Canada); died 1993 (Rancho Mirage, California, U.S.).

Star qualities: Tap dancer; singer; showgirl; pretty child performer; wife of showbiz legend Al Jolson; played the sweet innocent ingénue.

Top Takes...

Beverly Hills Brats 1989
Sweetheart of the Campus 1941
Mother Carey's Chickens 1938
Ready, Willing and Able 1937
Colleen 1936
Shipmates Forever 1935
Go Into Your Dance 1935
Flirtation Walk 1934
Dames 1934
Footlight Parade 1933
Gold Diggers of 1933 1933
42nd Street 1933

No star ever received such prolonged and elaborate onscreen adoration as Ruby Keeler in the "I Only Have Eyes for You" number from Busby Berkeley's *Dames* in 1934, with its dozens upon dozens of rotating, gyrating cutouts of her face. In Berkeley's backstage musicals she was the good girl, less worldly-wise than Joan Blondell or Ginger Rogers; she looked as if she had gotten to the stage door without going twice around the block first. It was to her, in her movie debut *42nd Street* (1933), that the most legendary line in 1930s musicals was actually addressed: "You're going out a youngster, but you've got to come back a star!" No filmgoer could have been so cruel as to deny Keeler the same opportunity; unfortunately, there were only so many variations to be played on the formula, and in 1941 she wisely retired to raise her children.

Neither was she more than a good hoofer—the Berkeley films weren't really about dancing anyway—and although she usually got to be the star of the show and go home with Dick Powell, it was her appealingly naive personality that set Keeler apart from the rest of the chorus. A tap dancer from her young teens, she was only a sixteen-year-old chorus girl when she caught the eye of legendary singer, entertainer, and actor Al Jolson, who was 24 years her senior. They married two years later, in 1928. Unable to have children, the couple adopted a son, but the marriage was said to be a rocky one, and they divorced in 1939. Keeler remarried and went on to have four children with her second husband, John Homer Lowe. After 30 years in retirement, she made a Broadway comeback in 1971 when she appeared in the hugely successful revival of *No No Nanette*, directed by veteran Busby Berkeley. She died from cancer at age eighty-four. **MC**

"I think Al sensed that it wasn't easy for me being married to an American institution."

ROBERT RYAN

Born: Robert Bushnell Ryan, November 11, 1909 (Chicago, Illinois, U.S.); died 1973 (New York City, New York, U.S.).

Star qualities: Towering stature; handsome; piercing eyes; mean, rugged looks; played the stern but tender tough guy; character lead and supporting actor.

One of the United States's most underrated actors, Robert Ryan played a variety of archetypal tough guys throughout his career: hardened cops, nasty villains, everyone from boxers and soldiers to bullies and racists. He looked the part: a towering figure of imposing masculinity, he also possessed a commandingly stern countenance that undoubtedly served him well in his days as a Marine drill instructor in World War II. If Ryan never achieved the iconic status afforded some of his tough-guy contemporaries, it may be because the depth and complexity of his performances gave them a richness—more specifically, a sadness and tenderness—that is not easily reduced to the simplicity of idol standing.

A boxer at Dartmouth College, Ryan kicked around in many vocations throughout his twenties, including ranch hand and laborer. He tried to make it as a playwright, then, in the early 1940s, turned to acting to support himself. After several film appearances, it was *Crossfire* (1947)—an exploration of bigotry in the military—that elevated Ryan to a new level of stardom.

The world of film noir would give Ryan some of his best acting work, such as *Beware, My Lovely* (1952). Another remarkable performance can be found in Nicholas Ray's unique noir, *On Dangerous Ground* (1952), in which Ryan plays a brutal, self-loathing city cop caught up with blind Ida Lupino.

Ryan's career in the late 1950s and most of the 1960s is more uneven, and includes much TV work. Even so, there were strong performances in three key action films of the era: *The Professionals* (1966), *The Dirty Dozen* (1967), and, most memorably, *The Wild Bunch* (1969), a graphically violent Western. Prior to his early death from lung cancer, the actor went out on a series of high notes. **TC**

Top Takes...

The Iceman Cometh 1973
The Wild Bunch 1969
The Dirty Dozen 1967
The Professionals 1966
The Dirty Game 1965
The Longest Day 1962
God's Little Acre 1958
House of Bamboo 1955
Beware, My Lovely 1952
Clash by Night 1952
On Dangerous Ground 1952
The Racket 1951
Born to Be Bad 1950
The Set-Up 1949
Caught 1949
Crossfire 1947 ☆

> "What I like and what I need are two different things."
>
> —Deke Thornton, *The Wild Bunch*

DOUGLAS FAIRBANKS Jr.

Born: Douglas Elton Ulman Fairbanks, December 9, 1909 (New York City, New York, U.S.); died 2000 (New York City, New York, U.S.).

Star qualities: Son of a screen legend; producer; writer; athletic; handsome; tall; moustache; enthusiastic; charming; socialite; war hero; knighted; humanitarian.

Douglas Fairbanks Jr. was the son of a great star and a Rhode Island heiress, Anna Beth Sully. Ever surrounded by legendary names, he had Mary Pickford as a stepmother, Marlene Dietrich as a lover, was briefly married to Joan Crawford, and even featured in the Christine Keeler sex scandal. During World War II he was a lieutenant commander in the U.S. navy, and took part in several Anglo-U.S. operations for which he was made an Honorary Knight of the British Empire—an honor almost never granted to non-Britons. He also received the French Légion d'Honneur, Italian War Cross for Military Valor, the U.S. navy's Legion of Merit, and Knight Grand Officer of King George I of Greece. On top of this, he made more than 100 films, starting his movie career at the tender age of thirteen. Yet he never quite established an image in the film business beyond being handsome, enthusiastic, well-spoken, and turning up on time to get the scenes done.

Fairbanks Jr. was always the charming extra guest invited to spark an unpartnered woman, but among many unmemorable movies are some true highlights. In *Little Caesar* (1931), he plays Edward G. Robinson's best pal, a dancer modeled on George Raft and credible as the object of the hoodlum's lifelong crush. In *The Prisoner of Zenda* (1937), his best screen work, he dared trespass in his father's favored genre—not as a swashbuckling hero, but as the deftly villainous Rupert of Hentzau, a witty Ruritanian rogue who combines daring with utter ruthlessness. Otherwise, he tended to play the juvenile among bigger stars, as in *The Dawn Patrol* (1930), ora kitschy leading man, as in *Green Hell* (1940). After the 1950s, Fairbanks Jr. worked extensively in TV, and was the first victim in *Ghost Story* (1981). **KN**

> "I never tried to emulate my father ... that would be a second-rate carbon copy."

JOAN BENNETT

Born: Joan Geraldine Bennett, February 27, 1910 (Palisades, New Jersey, U.S.); died 1990 (Scarsdale, New York, U.S.).

Star qualities: Blonde who played the ingénue before she became the brunette femme fatale; glamorous; sexy; part of an acting dynasty; singer.

Joan Bennett, one of three acting daughters of silent-screen star Richard Bennett, was for a while less prominent a film star than her sister Constance, though over the long haul she became more famous. She made her first appearance onstage at age four, then made her film debut two years later in *The Valley of Decision* (1916), in which her father acted. After more bit parts in her father's films, she became a leading lady in early talkies, opposite Ronald Colman in *Bulldog Drummond* (1929), George Arliss in *Disraeli* (1929), and Spencer Tracy in *Me and My Gal* (1932). She survived being written into *Moby Dick* (1930) as Captain Ahab Ceely's love interest, and worked throughout the 1930s in ingénue roles such as Amy March in *Little Women* (1933) and the princess in *The Man in the Iron Mask* (1939).

After an against-type part as an implied streetwalker in Fritz Lang's *Man Hunt* (1941), Bennett delivered her best screen performances in subsequent Fritz Lang film noirs, dangerously bewitching Edward G. Robinson as the long-legged, cold-hearted, classy-on-the-outside-but-inwardly-a-tramp villainess of *The Woman in the Window* (1944) and *Scarlet Street* (1945). In 1951, her husband of 11 years, producer Walter Wanger, shot her new agent in a jealous rage over an alleged affair. Wanger was sent to prison for two years, but the couple remained married until 1965. The scandal that ensued almost ended Bennett's career. Her only notable screen role in later years was as a chic, malevolent witch in Dario Argento's horror fantasy *Suspiria* (1977). However, she worked steadily and successfully in TV, including the entire five-year run of the Gothic soap opera *Dark Shadows*, for which she received an Emmy Award nomination and that led to a movie spin-off, *House of Dark Shadows* (1970). **KN**

Top Takes…

Suspiria 1977
House of Dark Shadows 1970
Desire in the Dust 1960
We're No Angels 1955
Father of the Bride 1950
Scarlet Street 1945
The Woman in the Window 1944
Man Hunt 1941
The Man in the Iron Mask 1939
The Pursuit of Happiness 1934
Little Women 1933
Me and My Gal 1932
Moby Dick 1930
Disraeli 1929
Bulldog Drummond 1929
The Valley of Decision 1916

"The profession has given me an incredibly varied life . . . I've not a single regret for any of it."

DAVID NIVEN

Born: James David Graham Niven, March 1, 1910 (London, England); died 1983 (Château-d'Oex, Switzerland).

Star qualities: The archetypal English gentleman; upper-class accent; sophisticated, stylish, and well groomed; witty socialite; war hero; author; producer; director.

Top Takes...

King, Queen, Knave 1972
Casino Royale 1967
The Pink Panther 1963
The Guns of Navarone 1961
Separate Tables 1958 ★
Around the World in Eighty Days 1956
The Elusive Pimpernel 1950
Magnificent Doll 1946
A Matter of Life and Death 1946
The Way Ahead 1944
The First of the Few 1942
Raffles 1939
Wuthering Heights 1939
The Charge of the Light Brigade 1936
Thank You, Jeeves! 1936

David Niven came from a military family and attended Stowe School and Sandhurst Military Academy, serving for two years in Malta with the Highland Light Infantry. He arrived in Hollywood in the 1930s and had roles as a typical lightweight: Bertie Wooster in *Thank You, Jeeves!* (1936), doomed in *The Charge of the Light Brigade* (1936), Edgar Linton in *Wuthering Heights* (1939), and the gentleman thief in *Raffles* (1939). He rejoined the British army in World War II and served with distinction, receiving the Legionnaire of the Order of Merit— the highest U.S. award that can be earned by a foreigner. During the war he made only a few select propaganda films, *The First of the Few* (1942) and *The Way Ahead* (1944).

After the war, Niven returned to the big screen and was the poetic airman on trial in heaven in *A Matter of Life and Death* (1946), but tended to get stiff roles in postwar movies: Aaron Burr in *Magnificent Doll* (1946) and a lackluster Sir Percy Blakeney in *The Elusive Pimpernel* (1950).

Phoning it in as Phileas Fogg in the overstuffed *Around the World in Eighty Days* (1956), and back in the hero pack in *The Guns of Navarone* (1961), Niven showed acting muscles as a derelict officer in *Separate Tables* (1958), for which he won an Academy Award for Best Actor. He is likable as an aging roué amid mod surroundings as The Phantom in *The Pink Panther* (1963) and Sir James Bond in *Casino Royale* (1967). Later in life he won critical acclaim for his memoirs of his youth and acting career, *The Moon's a Balloon* (1971) and *Bring on the Empty Horses* (1975). Niven was twice married. His first wife, actress Primula Rollo, died in a tragic accident at the house of actor Tyrone Power. He was survived by his second wife and four children. **KN**

"Keep the circus going inside you, keep it going . . . it'll all work out in the end."

SIMONE SIMON

Born: Simone Thérèse Fernande Simone, April 23, 1910 (Marseille, Provence-Alpes-Côte d'Azur, France); died 2005 (Paris, Île-de-France, France).

Star qualities: Petite; Gallic charm; a sexy pout; dark eyes; arched eyebrows; seductive kittenish face; feline prowess.

Simone Simon made her movie debut in *On opère sans douleur* (1931) and soon became one of France's leading film stars. After seeing her in *Lac aux dames* (1934) (*Ladies' Lake*), director and producer Darryl F. Zanuck imported her to Hollywood to star in *Under Two Flags* (1936), only to be replaced by Claudette Colbert. She made an impression as Diane the Hooker in the Parisian romance *Seventh Heaven* (1937), and had a few ooh-la-la French roles in such productions as *Love and Hisses* (1937). But she had problems mastering English, and returned home to be remarkable as the sexy wife to Jean Gabin in Jean Renoir's *La bête humaine* (1938) (*The Human Beast*).

Simon's devilish trollop in *The Devil and Daniel Webster* (1941) led to her classic role in *Cat People* (1942) as a sad, frigid young wife who believes (with good cause) that if aroused she will turn into a black leopard. For producer Val Lewton, she reprised the role, in a very different tone, in the magical *The Curse of the Cat People* (1944), and also took a lead as the laundress in the Guy de Maupassant-derived *Mademoiselle Fifi* (1944). These were her greatest successes in English-language cinema, but they still didn't make the heart-faced, purring Simon a Hollywood star, and so—after a weird comedy with an imp, *Johnny Doesn't Live Here Any More* (1944)—she returned to Europe. There she played a number of roles, including the maid in the French *La Ronde* (1950) (*Roundabout*) and a movie star in the British *The Extra Day* (1956). After that film, her roles were few and she finally retired in 1973. Simon never married but had many relationships with fellow actors and musicians, among others. It was said she had a gold-plated key made, which she gave to special male friends to allow them access to her boudoir. **KN**

Top Takes...

The Extra Day 1956
Das Zweite Leben 1954 (*A Double Life*)
La Ronde 1950 (*Roundabout*)
Temptation Harbor 1947
Johnny Doesn't Live Here Any More 1944
The Curse of the Cat People 1944
Mademoiselle Fifi 1944
Tahiti Honey 1943
Cat People 1942
The Devil and Daniel Webster 1941
La bête humaine 1938 (*The Human Beast*)
Josette 1938
Love and Hisses 1937
Seventh Heaven 1937
Lac aux dames 1934 (*Ladies' Lake*)
On opère sans douleur 1931

"Oh, it's alright. It's just that cats don't seem to like me."

—Irena Dubrovna, *Cat People*

PAULETTE GODDARD

Born: Pauline Levy, June 3, 1910 (Long Island, New York, U.S.); died 1990 (Ronco, Switzerland).

Star qualities: Beautiful Goldwyn Girl; singer; dancer; intelligent; married to silent screen legend Charlie Chaplin; glamorous leading lady; producer.

Top Takes…

Anna Lucasta 1949
Bride of Vengeance 1949
An Ideal Husband 1947
The Diary of a Chambermaid 1946
Kitty 1945
So Proudly We Hail! 1943 ☆
Reap the Wild Wind 1942
North West Mounted Police 1940
The Great Dictator 1940
The Ghost Breakers 1940
The Cat and the Canary 1939
The Women 1939
Modern Times 1936
Roman Scandals 1933
The Kid from Spain 1932

Paulette Goddard was a child model who was part of the Ziegfeld Follies by the age of thirteen; she gained fame in the show as the girl on the prop crescent moon and was married to a screenplay writer by the time she was only sixteen. After her divorce she went to Hollywood in 1931. She became one of the anonymous Goldwyn Girls in movies such as *The Kid from Spain* (1932) and *Roman Scandals* (1933), had small parts in Laurel and Hardy short films, and appeared essentially as a beautiful ornament in movies for a variety of studios.

In 1932 she met actor and future second husband Charles Chaplin, who bought her contract from Hal Roach Studios and gave her the female leads in *Modern Times* (1936) and *The Great Dictator* (1940). These roles required her only to look pretty and keep out of the way while he was being funny, but they made her a star in the process.

A solid spot in the all-female cast of *The Women* (1939) led to more rewarding leads. She was sweet and glamorous opposite Bob Hope in *The Cat and the Canary* (1939) and her performance won her a ten-year contract with Paramount Pictures. She teamed up with Hope again in *The Ghost Breakers* (1940), and was a fetching Cecil B. DeMille adventure heroine in *North West Mounted Police* (1940) and *Reap the Wild Wind* (1942). Her role as a war nurse in *So Proudly We Hail!* (1943) won her an Oscar nomination for Best Supporting Actress. Goddard was spirited if shaky in *An Ideal Husband* (1947), *Bride of Vengeance* (1949), and *Anna Lucasta* (1949), but credits such as *Babes in Bagdad* (1952) suggested where she was heading. She retired to Europe to marry German novelist Erich Maria Remarque, but reappeared briefly as the murder victim in the TV pilot *The Snoop Sisters* (1972). **KN**

"… the most fascinating person in the world—actors or anybody—is yourself."

GLORIA STUART

Born: Gloria Frances Stewart, July 4, 1910 (Santa Monica, California, U.S.).

Star qualities: Slim, blonde, glamorous; played B-lead parts in her youth followed by mature character roles; stagecraft; career renaissance in her eighties that has featured an Oscar nomination; painter.

Gloria Stuart was spotted at the Pasadena Playhouse and signed by Universal Studios in 1932. She was then chosen as one of the 13 Western Association of Motion Picture Advertisers Baby Stars of 1932. These were young starlets thought most likely to make it in films. As a young woman, Stuart was slender, blonde, and shining in mostly forgotten films of the 1930s. Her most lasting credits, for James Whale, find her pursued by a hulking Boris Karloff in *The Old Dark House* (1932) and menaced by Claude Rains in *The Invisible Man* (1933). Stuart is fine as well-bred, slightly superior young misses in these films, but director and audience are more interested in the less-straight characters. She sparkles in *Gold Diggers of 1935* (1935) and suffers as the wife of the unjustly condemned man in *The Prisoner of Shark Island* (1936), but barely registers in Shirley Temple vehicles such as *Rebecca of Sunnybrook Farm* (1938).

After playing Queen Anne d'Autriche in the Ritz Brothers version of *The Three Musketeers* (1939) and the B-lead in *It Could Happen to You* (1939), Stuart retired for the first time. She became an accomplished painter, staging several one-woman shows in New York, Austria, and Italy during the 1960s. She came back in a few 1940s B-features, such as *The Whistler* (1944), and then retired again until *The Legend of Lizzie Borden* (1975), and once more after *Shootdown* (1988). She returned to play one hundred-year-old Rose De Witt in *Titanic* (1997), for which she was nominated for an Oscar for Best Supporting Actress, and became the oldest person ever nominated. Thanks to this movie, she enjoyed a career renaissance, and has stayed in work ever since, appearing in films such as Wim Wenders's *The Million Dollar Hotel* (2000) and in TV guest roles. **KN**

Top Takes...

The Million Dollar Hotel 2000
***Titanic* 1997** ☆
Shootdown 1988
My Favorite Year 1982
The Legend of Lizzie Borden 1975
The Whistler 1944
Here Comes Elmer 1943
It Could Happen to You 1939
Winner Take All 1939
The Three Musketeers 1939
Time Out for Murder 1938
Rebecca of Sunnybrook Farm 1938
The Prisoner of Shark Island 1936
Gold Diggers of 1935 1935
The Invisible Man 1933
The Old Dark House 1932

> "I saw my whole life as if I had already lived it."
> —Old Rose, *Titanic*

1910s

KINUYO TANAKA

Born: Kinuyo Tanaka, November 28, 1910 (Yamaguchi, Japan); died 1977 (Japan).

Star qualities: Icon of Japanese cinema; leading lady of dramas; one-time muse of Japanese director Kenji Mizoguchi; independent; trailblazing; Japan's first female director.

Kinuyo Tanaka was a major film star in Japan for around 50 years, appearing in every movie genre. She started out studying music, and appeared in light operas with Osaka's Biwa Shojo Kageki girls' revue. She made her film debut in the silent *Mura no bokujo* (1924) at the age of fourteen. She then joined Tokyo's Shochiku Kamata Studio and became its leading star. She was notable as a naive young girl in films such as Yasujiro Ozu's *Daigaku wa deta keredo* (1929) (*I Graduated But...*) and *Ojosan* (1930) (*Young Miss*), and went on to appear as the lead in Japan's first talkie, Heinosuke Gosho's comedy *Madamu to nyobo* (1931) (*The Neighbor's Wife and Mine*). The film won critical plaudits and established Tanaka as a box-office success and leading lady. She went on to tackle challenging roles for the rest of her career.

She was best known for her work with director Kenji Mizoguchi, who directed her outstanding performance in the story of a seventeenth-century samurai's daughter who falls in love with a man beneath her social class, in *Saikaku ichidai onna* (1952) (*The Life of Oharu*). She frequently appeared as the heroine in Mizoguchi's films, including the masterpieces *Ugetsu monogatari* (1953) (*Tales of Ugetsu*) as Miyagi, the wife of a peasant looking for a new life, and *Sanshô dayû* (1954) (*Legend of Bailiff Sansho*) as yet another suffering wife, this time of a governor fallen on hard times. The pair's collaboration spilled into their offscreen life. Mizoguchi asked Tanaka to marry him, but Tanaka rejected his offer because he tried to block her becoming Japan's first woman director. Undeterred, Tanaka made her directorial debut with *Koibumi* (1953) (*Love Letter*), in which she also starred; she went on to direct another five films during her career. **CK**

Top Takes...

Sandakan hachibanshokan bohkyo 1974
  (*Sandakan No. 8*)

Arupusu no wakadaishô 1966
  (*It Started in the Alps*)

Akahige 1965 (*Red Beard*)

Koge 1964 (*The Scent of Incense*)

Wakarete ikiru toki mo 1961 (*Eternity of Love*)

Sanshô dayû 1954 (*Legend of Bailiff Sansho*)

Koibumi 1953 (*Love Letter*)

Ugetsu monogatari 1953 (*Tales of Ugetsu*)

Saikaku ichidai onna 1952 (*The Life of Oharu*)

Madamu to nyobo 1931
  (*The Neighbor's Wife and Mine*)

Ojosan 1930 (*Young Miss*)

Daigaku wa deta keredo 1929
  (*I Graduated But...*)

Mura no bokujo 1924

> "[Tanaka's] subtle emotions color Miyagi"—On *Tales of Ugetsu*, *Entertainment Insiders*

VAN HEFLIN

Born: Emmett Evan Heflin Jr., December 13, 1910 (Walters, Oklahoma, U.S.); died 1971 (Hollywood, California, U.S.).

Star qualities: Redhead; freckled; deep voice; intense; athletic; seaman and swimmer; powerful screen presence; second lead and character actor.

The son of a dentist, Van Heflin started his acting career on Broadway in the early 1930s before being spotted by RKO Studios. He made his film debut in *A Woman Rebels* (1936) opposite Katharine Hepburn. Potato-faced, freckled, and intense, Heflin is a powerful presence in a surprising number of films, often—as in *Shane* (1953) or *3:10 to Yuma* (1957)— playing the hardworking second lead who survives after the glamour-boy hero such as Alan Ladd or Glenn Ford has passed out of the picture. He reached his peak as Jeff Hartnett in the melodrama *Johnny Eager* (1942), winning an Academy Award for Best Supporting Actor.

In films from the mid-1930s, Heflin proved he could do Westerns, as in *Santa Fe Trail* (1940), crime-fighting, as in *Kid Glove Killer* (1942), musicals, as in *Presenting Lily Mars* (1943), film noir, as in *The Strange Love of Martha Ivers* (1946), comedy, as in *Week-End with Father* (1951), and war hero, as in *Battle Cry* (1955). He even stretched creditably to Athos in *The Three Musketeers* (1948) and Charles Bovary in *Madame Bovary* (1949). He was at his best as regular guys being eaten up inside by appalling circumstances: the white-collar veteran stalked by the ex-soldier played by Robert Ryan, who knows he's a traitor, in *Act of Violence* (1948); the Confederate officer perpetrating a terrorist strike against a small town in *The Raid* (1954); and the young executive rising during a cutthroat boardroom battle in *Patterns* (1956). Throughout his career he regularly returned to the stage, and appeared on Broadway with Katharine Hepburn in *The Philadelphia Story*. His last major role was in *Airport* (1970) as loose cannon D. O. Guerrero, who hopes to blow up the plane so his wife can collect the life insurance. **KN**

Top Takes...

Airport 1970
3:10 to Yuma 1957
Patterns 1956
Battle Cry 1955
The Raid 1954
Shane 1953
Week-End with Father 1951
Madame Bovary 1949
Act of Violence 1948
The Three Musketeers 1948
The Strange Love of Martha Ivers 1946
Presenting Lily Mars 1943
Kid Glove Killer 1942
***Johnny Eager* 1942 ★**
Santa Fe Trail 1940
A Woman Rebels 1936

"I just didn't have the looks and if I didn't do a good acting job I looked terrible."

RONALD REAGAN

Born: Ronald Wilson Reagan, February 6, 1911 (Tampico, Illinois, U.S.); died 2004 (Los Angeles, California, U.S.).

Star qualities: Hollywood's most famous actor when he became U.S. president; played Westerns and action-adventure roles; survived an assassination attempt.

Top Takes...

The Killers 1964
Hellcats of the Navy 1957
Tennessee's Partner 1955
Cattle Queen of Montana 1954
Prisoner of War 1954
Hong Kong 1952
Bedtime for Bonzo 1951
The Last Outpost 1951
Storm Warning 1951
This is the Army 1943
Desperate Journey 1942
Kings Row 1942
Knute Rockne All American 1940
The Angels Wash Their Faces 1939
Secret Service of the Air 1939
Love Is on the Air 1937

"It's true hard work never killed anybody, but I figure, why take the chance?"

In 1981, at the age of sixty-nine, Ronald Reagan became president of the United States. During his political career, he was often lampooned for his supposed B-status as an actor, but in truth he was a pleasant, competent star. If he never made the first rank, he was rarely terrible. Reagan started his acting career while studying economics, and his first job in showbiz was as a sportscaster at an Iowa radio station. He moved to Hollywood, where he was signed by Warner Brothers, and made his film debut in *Love Is on the Air* (1937). He rose from bit parts to straight-up heroes in juvenile action movies such as *Secret Service of the Air* (1939), and more earnest melodramas such as *The Angels Wash Their Faces* (1939).

Reagan's signature roles were in support, as the Gipper in *Knute Rockne All American* (1940) and the young man whose legs are needlessly amputated by a sadistic surgeon in *King's Row* (1942). In World War II, he served as a noncombat captain in the Army Air Corps and produced training films. When he returned to Hollywood in 1947, he began a five-year stint as president of the Screen Actors Guild union. He was earnest in the anti-Klan melodrama *Storm Warning* (1951), a rare liberal Hollywood film of the 1950s, but surprisingly winning in the oft-derided silly comedy *Bedtime for Bonzo* (1951), where he played a college professor who befriends his science lab chimpanzee. In the 1950s he worked mostly in TV, but before abandoning acting for politics in 1964, he made a good villain in *The Killers* (1964). In manipulated stock footage, he appears in *Salvador* (1986), *Alien Nation* (1988), and the multiple Oscar-winning *Forrest Gump* (1994).

In 1991, Reagan's autobiography, *An American Hero*, was well received by critics. He died in 2004 from Alzheimer's. **KN**

RIGHT: Reagan with his second wife, Nancy, at the film premiere of *Moby Dick*.

Mocambo

MOBY DICK

MOBY DICK

JEAN HARLOW

Born: Harlean Harlow Carpenter, March 3, 1911 (Kansas City, Missouri, U.S.); died 1937 (Los Angeles, California, U.S.).

Star qualities: The original "Platinum Blonde"; green eyes; penciled-on arched eyebrows; pale complexion; clinging silky gowns; risqué dialogue; comic timing.

Jean Harlow fell into the movies by chance. She was spotted by a Fox Film Corporation executive while sitting in a parking lot waiting for an aspiring actress friend. She was invited for an audition and the rest is history. She became the leading blonde good-bad girl of the early talkies, constantly surrounded by scandal regarding her failed marriages and the numerous men in her life. Cast out of character as a proper English "Miss" by Howard Hughes in the huge hit *Hell's Angels* (1930), Harlow swiftly became a sex symbol.

The following year she was cast as the love interest, opposite James Cagney, in the gangster epic *The Public Enemy* (1931). Harlow really came into her own in partnership with virile Clark Gable in the MGM movies *Red Dust* (1932), *Hold Your Man* (1933), and *China Seas* (1935), typically portraying a loose-living tramp whose honest sexiness is refreshingly appealing to both costar and audience. Amusing in the ensemble *Dinner at Eight* (1933), she began playing showbiz roles that flirted with autobiography, such as *Bombshell* (1933), *The Girl from Missouri* (1934), and *Reckless* (1935). She showed flair for the just-invented screwball comedy genre in *Wife vs. Secretary* (1936) and *Libeled Lady* (1936), in which she strikes sparks off rival Myrna Loy. The Hays Code toned down her image, leading to less clingy gowns and cutting out risqué dialogue and situations. Her last film was a stuffy reunion with Gable in *Saratoga* (1937). It was during the filming of *Saratoga* that Harlow fell ill with uremic poisoning, and was hospitalized, dying only a few days later. She was just twenty-six years old. The film had to be finished with long angle shots using a double. Gable said he felt like he was in the arms of a ghost during the final parts of the movie. **KN**

Top Takes...

"Underwear makes me uncomfortable and besides, my parts have to breathe."

MAUREEN O'SULLIVAN

Born: Maureen Paula O'Sullivan, May 17, 1911 (Boyle, County Roscommon, Ireland); died 1998 (Scottsdale, Arizona, U.S.).

Star qualities: Fresh-faced beauty; flowing brunette locks; bikini-clad curvaceous figure; Tarzan heroine; played the young ingénue and the mature matriarch.

After finishing her education, Maureen O'Sullivan returned to her native Dublin to work with the poor. There, she was spotted by director Frank Borzage when both were at a horse show. She took up his invitation to move to Hollywood and made her debut in *So This Is London* (1930). She was then swiftly shuffled through musicals such as *Just Imagine* (1930) and *A Connecticut Yankee* (1931). She landed her signature role as Jane Parker in *Tarzan the Ape Man* (1932). Freshly beautiful, O'Sullivan's Jane looks as comfortable in Paris fashion jungle outfits as the minimal skin bikini of *Tarzan and His Mate* (1934). Her relationship with Johnny Weissmuller's Tarzan is complex: sexual but also maternal, because Jane is as intrepid in protecting her man from emotional complexities he is unequipped for as he is in defending her from rampaging wildlife, headhunters, and evil white hunters.

Censorship tamed the series and O'Sullivan got stuck with more motherly roles in later films, slipping out of the franchise after *Tarzan's New York Adventure* (1942). Sadly, she rarely got the roles she deserved. She was the second female lead in *The Barretts of Wimpole Street* (1934), *Anna Karenina* (1935), and *Pride and Prejudice* (1940); pretty but surplus in *The Devil-Doll* (1936) and *A Day at the Races* (1937). She retired from films in 1942 to devote her time to her husband, director John Farrow—who had just left the navy with typhoid—and her seven children, two of whom grew up to be actresses Mia Farrow and Tisa Farrow. She returned to the big screen in 1948 in films such as *The Big Clock* (1948), directed by her husband, and *Bonzo Goes to College* (1950), then retired again until the 1980s, when she played mother to her daughter Mia in *Hannah and Her Sisters* (1986). **KN**

Top Takes...

Peggy Sue Got Married 1986
Hannah and Her Sisters 1986
Bonzo Goes to College 1952
The Big Clock 1948
Tarzan's New York Adventure 1942
Pride and Prejudice 1940
A Day at the Races 1937
The Devil-Doll 1936
Anna Karenina 1935
The Barretts of Wimpole Street 1934
The Thin Man 1934
Tarzan and His Mate 1934
Tarzan the Ape Man 1932
A Connecticut Yankee 1931
Just Imagine 1930
So This Is London 1930

1910s

"I'm Jane Parker. Understand? Jane, Jane."

—Jane Parker, *Tarzan the Ape Man*

VINCENT PRICE

Born: Vincent Leonard Price Jr., May 27, 1911 (St. Louis, Missouri, U.S.); died 1993 (Los Angeles, California, U.S.).

Star qualities: Boris Karloff's American counterpart; sinister voice; expressive face; perfect as comic villains in horror classics; ironic; Yale art history graduate; gourmet.

Top Takes...

RIGHT: Price played the doomed scientist's brother, François Delambre, in *The Fly*.

Though his nasal purr, arched eyebrow, and maniacal gleam landed Vincent Price a secure position as an American horror star, he was always inclined to comedy—indeed, camp—and his most characteristic grotesques usually had an edge of velvety black humor. He started in tights and ruff as Sir Walter Raleigh in *The Private Lives of Elizabeth and Essex* (1939), drowned in malmsey in *Tower of London* (1939), and lent his voice to *The Invisible Man Returns* (1940).

Signed with Twentieth Century Fox as a character actor, Price made history as Joseph Smith (*Brigham Young*, 1940), Charles II (*Hudson's Bay*, 1941), and the Secretary of the Treasury (*Wilson*, 1944). After so many stick-up-the-fundament roles, Price was far better for Otto Preminger in *Laura* (1944) as a gigolo doubled over when Dana Andrews sucker punches him in the gut. He turned straight as the drug-addicted patroon of *Dragonwyck* (1946), was shady in film noirs (*The Web*, 1947; *The Bribe*, 1949), and worked a monumental confidence trick in *The Baron of Arizona* (1950) before turning to knockabout comedy (a crass soap tycoon in *Champagne for Caesar*, 1950; a skit on Errol Flynn in *His Kind of Woman*, 1951).

Horror beckoned with juicy roles in the successful *House of Wax* (1953) and *The Fly* (1958). His unique voice, looming six-foot, four-inch frame, and malevolent laugh were ideally suited to such parts and, having teamed up with William Castle (*House on Haunted Hill*, 1959) and Roger Corman (*House of Usher*, 1960; *Pit and the Pendulum*, 1961), it is in horror that Price's true legacy lies. Price took Corman toward laughs in *The Raven* (1963), but was up to the necrophile poesy of *The Masque of the Red Death* (1964) and *The Tomb of Ligeia* (1964). He turned up the chill again as *Witchfinder General* (1968).

In the early 1970s Price appeared twice as inventive fiend Dr. Phibes and once as a mad Shakespearean (*Theatre of Blood*, 1973), inflicting outlandish death traps on distinguished actors and reveling in unhinged monologues. After that he slowed, though he kept down with the kids in Michael Jackson's *Thriller* video and Tim Burton's *Edward Scissorhands* (1990). **KN**

ABOVE: Price in later years as The Inventor in Tim Burton's *Edward Scissorhands*.

A Rich, Full Life

In reality, creepy Uncle Vincent was a supportive father, the author of several cookbooks, an avid art collector, and a witty storyteller:

- Price founded an art gallery at Los Angeles College and selected and commissioned artworks to be sold to the public.
- Price's voice-over work included the Euro-Disney Phantom ride as well as Michael Jackson's *Thriller* video.
- A regular TV talk-show guest, Price once demonstrated on air how to poach a fish in a dishwasher.

GINGER ROGERS

Born: Virginia Katherine McMath, July 16, 1911 (Independence, Missouri, U.S.); died 1995 (Rancho Mirage, California, U.S.).

Star qualities: Hollywood's redheaded leading lady of the ballroom floor; dazzling dancing partner of Fred Astaire; lead of light comedy and romances.

Top Takes…

Oh, Men! Oh, Women! 1957

Monkey Business 1952

Dreamboat 1952

The Barkleys of Broadway 1949

Roxie Hart 1942

**Kitty Foyle: The Natural History
of a Woman 1940 ★**

Bachelor Mother 1939

Shall We Dance 1937

Swing Time 1936

Top Hat 1935

The Gay Divorcee 1934

Flying Down to Rio 1933

Professional Sweetheart 1933

Gold Diggers of 1933 1933

42nd Street 1933

1910s

History has decreed that Ginger Rogers must waltz into posterity arm in arm with Fred Astaire, her costar and dancing partner in a string of nine legendary musicals made between 1933 and 1939. Of these, *The Gay Divorcee* (1934) and *Top Hat* (1935) stand out especially, but all still dazzle with their skill, precision, and Art Deco elegance. They are exercises in pure style: their scripts frothy and trifling, and their backgrounds opulent and indistinct.

Though Astaire never quite clicked in the same way with another partner, Rogers was never merely the refined, elegant creature of these films. She had made 19 films before the partnership even began, including two for Busby Berkeley that more accurately convey her early 1930s persona. She was altogether spikier and sassier in *42nd Street* (1933) as the wise-mouth chorus girl Anytime Annie, and again in *Gold Diggers of 1933* (1933) dancing to avoid the breadline. She was funny and sexy as an uninhibited radio star who marries for a promotional stunt in *Professional Sweetheart* (1933).

After the Astaire years she concentrated on comedy and the occasional women's picture, winning an Oscar for Best Actress for her role as the confused middle-class girl in *Kitty Foyle: The Natural History of a Woman* (1940). She again registered strongly in *Bachelor Mother* (1939) and as the eponymous *Roxie Hart* (1942). By 1945 she was recorded as Hollywood's highest-paid female performer, but by the end of the decade, her career was in decline. She continued in films throughout the 1950s and took to Broadway in a successful run of *Hello! Dolly* (1965). She spent her later years doing guest spots on TV shows, and in 1985 she directed the musical stage comedy *Babes in Arms*. **MC**

"… cagey enough to realize that acting did not stop when dancing began."—John Mueller

HUME CRONYN

Born: Hume Blake Cronyn, July 18, 1911 (London, Ontario, Canada); died 2003 (Fairfield, Connecticut, U.S.).

Star qualities: Versatile leading actor; famous for film noir roles; stagecraft; one-half of a celebrity theatrical couple; director; writer; producer.

Hume Cronyn's family tree contained some of Canada's earliest settlers, as well as politicians and the founders of Labatt Breweries. He studied law at Canada's McGill University, but his dream was to be an actor, and he went on to study acting at New York's American Academy of Dramatic Arts.

He first appeared on Broadway playing the part of a janitor in *Hipper's Holiday* (1934) and soon became known for his versatility. He made his screen debut playing older than his years as a fussy, crime-obsessed gossip in Alfred Hitchcock's *Shadow of a Doubt* (1943). Hitchcock liked the Canadian actor and called him back as a survivor for *Lifeboat* (1944); he also hired him to adapt the screenplays for *Rope* (1948) and *Under Capricorn* (1949). Cronyn was nominated for an Academy Award for Best Supporting Actor for his performance in Fred Zinnemann's war drama, *The Seventh Cross* (1944).

Despite appearances in major films such as *Phantom of the Opera* (1943), *The Postman Always Rings Twice* (1946), and *Cleopatra* (1963), Cronyn was more committed to the stage than the movies. He is well cast as Doctor J. Robert Oppenheimer in *The Beginning or the End* (1947), but made his greatest screen impact as the sly, perverse, cultured prison captain in *Brute Force* (1947), administering punishment beatings with a sadistic feel.

From the 1970s onward, he started appearing more often in films, first in vivid character roles in titles such as *The Parallax View* (1974), then in geriatric whimsy such as *Cocoon* (1985) and **batteries not included* (1987). He played love interest for his second wife, Jessica Tandy, in *Camilla* (1994); was a Supreme Court justice in *The Pelican Brief* (1993); a juror in the TV remake of *12 Angry Men* (1997); and Saint Nicholas in *Santa and Pete* (1999). **KN**

Top Takes...

Santa and Pete 1999
Marvin's Room 1996
Camilla 1994
The Pelican Brief 1993
*batteries not included 1987
Cocoon 1985
The World According to Garp 1982
The Parallax View 1974
Cleopatra 1963
Brute Force 1947
The Beginning or the End 1947
The Postman Always Rings Twice 1946
The Seventh Cross 1944 ☆
Lifeboat 1944
Phantom of the Opera 1943
Shadow of a Doubt 1943

"To act you must have a sense of truth and some degree of dedication."

LUCILLE BALL

Born: Lucille Desiree Ball, August 6, 1911 (Jamestown, New York, U.S.); died 1989 (Los Angeles, California, U.S.).

Star qualities: Redhead; 1930s glamour girl; wacky comedienne; hardworking, astute businesswoman; winner of four Emmy Awards.

Top Takes…

At drama school redheaded Lucille Ball was outshone by her peers, who included Bette Davis, and told by a coach that she "had no future at all as a performer." Nevertheless, she started an acting career, appearing on Broadway before moving to Hollywood to pursue movie roles. Eventually contracted to RKO Pictures, she had a few good roles (*Top Hat*, 1935; *Dance, Girl, Dance*, 1940), but was mostly given small parts in B movies. In the 1940s she was signed to MGM but did not achieve much success there either, and she became known in Hollywood circles as "Queen of the Bs."

In 1940 Ball met the Cuban musician Desi Arnaz on the set of *Too Many Girls* (1940). After a whirlwind romance, the pair married. After a few years Ball landed a starring role on the radio comedy *My Favorite Husband*. In 1950, CBS offered to turn the show into a TV pilot. Ball and Arnaz wanted to play the central couple, but CBS did not think the American public would accept a Cuban husband of an all-American wife. The couple finally convinced programmers to let them play the roles, accepting an extraordinary amount of professional and financial risk in the process. *I Love Lucy* debuted in 1951 and became the standard for all TV sitcoms to follow. It lasted six years, through cast conflicts, location shoots, stiffer competition, and two Ball-Arnaz children. The couple divorced in 1960, but she went on to play largely the same role in *The Lucy Show* and *Here's Lucy*, with an occasional big-screen break (*Yours, Mine and Ours*, 1968; *Mame*, 1974), but the point was made: *I Love Lucy* is the stuff of legend, and every episode remains as fresh and funny as the day it was recorded. It also finally made Lucille Ball the star that movies had failed to do. **GCQ**

"Once in his life, every man is entitled to fall madly in love with a gorgeous redhead."

CANTINFLAS

Born: Mario Moreno Reyes, August 12, 1911 (Mexico City, Mexico); died 1993 (Mexico City, Mexico).

Star qualities: Legendary comic actor of Mexican cinema; moustache; tousled hair; large ears; slapstick style; dancer; singer; writer; producer; civic minded.

Cantinflas was the Charlie Chaplin of his native Mexico in more ways than one. An enormously popular comedian and actor, like Chaplin he was noted for his distinctive appearance: baggy pants, a moustache, tousled hair, big ears, and a small hat. Like Chaplin he was noted for his slapstick style of comedy in the vein of Buster Keaton and Harold Lloyd. And also like Chaplin, he was born into poverty, and was to become almost a folk hero in his depiction of the working-class everyman and underdog. However, unlike Chaplin, Cantinflas had talents seen after the silent-film era, and he was famous for his wit and fast-talking verbal dexterity.

Cantinflas started out as a singer and dancer in traveling-tent variety shows, progressing to become known as an acrobat and clown. He made his movie debut in *No te engañes corazón* (1937) (*Don't Fool Thyself, Heart*), and went on to make another 50 films during his career that were box-office hits in the Spanish-speaking world. He ventured into English-language films playing Passepartout, the valet to David Niven's Phileas Fogg in *Around the World in Eighty Days* (1956). But it seemed that Hollywood did not know what to do with Cantinflas, and his next English-language attempt, *Pepe* (1960), was a failure at the box office. He continued to star in Spanish-language films until the 1980s, although he spent much of his last 20 years working with charitable and humanitarian organizations, especially for Mexico City's poor. Cantinflas was one of the founding members, and served as president, of the Mexican actors' union, the Asociación Nacional de Actores, and as first secretary general of the Mexican independent filmworkers' union, Sindicato de Trabajadores de la Producción Cinematográfica. **CK**

Top Takes...

El barrendero 1982
El ministro y yo 1976 (*The Minister and Me*)
Su excelencia 1967
El señor doctor 1965
El padrecito 1964 (*The Little Priest*)
Agente XU 777 1963 (*Special Delivery*)
El extra 1962 (*The Extra*)
El analfabeto 1961 (*The Illiterate One*)
Pepe 1960
Around the World in Eighty Days 1956
Un día con el diablo 1945
  (*One Day with the Devil*)
Gran Hotel 1944
Los tres mosqueteros 1942 (*The Three Musketeers*)
No te engañes corazón 1937
  (*Don't Fool Thyself, Heart*)

"A new verb, 'cantinflear,' means to talk much, say little, indulge in wild non sequiturs."

ROY ROGERS

Born: Leonard Franklin Slye, November 5, 1911 (Cincinnati, Ohio, U.S.); died 1998 (Apple Valley, California, U.S.).

Star qualities: Country singer and composer; veteran of Westerns teamed with his horse, Trigger; "King of the Cowboys"; producer.

Top Takes…

Son of Paleface 1952
Down Dakota Way 1949
Night Time in Nevada 1948
Under California Stars 1948
Home in Oklahoma 1946
Roll on Texas Moon 1946
Under Nevada Skies 1946
My Pal Trigger 1946
Don't Fence Me In 1945
Sunset in El Dorado 1945
The Man from Oklahoma 1945
Sunset Serenade 1942
Dark Command 1940
Gallant Defender 1935
The Old Homestead 1935
Slightly Static 1935

Originally a singer under his real name of Leonard Slye, Roy Rogers changed his name to Dick Wesson when he became part of the Sons of the Pioneers singing group. The group first appeared onscreen in the Western *Slightly Static* (1935). By the end of the 1930s he had established himself in B Westerns under his screen name of Roy Rogers. When Gene Autry went into the military during World War II, Rogers succeeded him as the top Western star.

Together with his horse Trigger, dog Bullet, and his fourth wife, Dale Evans, Rogers appeared in nearly 100 movies from the late 1930s until the demise of the B Western in the early 1950s. He earned the sobriquet "King of the Cowboys," and Dale was known as "Queen of the West."

Representative titles include *Sunset Serenade* (1942), *Roll On Texas Moon* (1946), and *Night Time in Nevada* (1948). The formula never varied, alternating action in the form of fistfights, gunplay, and chases on horseback; comedy, often supplied by Gabby Hayes; and country-style singing by Rogers, frequently accompanied by the Sons of the Pioneers. Rogers made occasional appearances in A features, for example in the Bob Hope comedy Western *Son of Paleface* (1952) and in Raoul Walsh's classic *Dark Command* (1940). He also starred in his own TV program, *The Roy Rogers Show*, from 1951 to 1964. On Trigger's death, the thirty-three-year-old horse was stuffed and put on display in the Roy Rogers Museum. But Rogers's memory lived on in other ways, too. As a child, Hollywood actor Val Kilmer lived next door to Rogers, and, as an adult, bought Rogers's old ranch. In 1999, Kilmer led Trigger's grandson onto the stage at the Academy Awards ceremony in honor of Rogers and his equine sidekick. **EB**

"Cowboys weren't allowed to kiss girls in pictures . . . so I had to kiss Trigger instead."

JORGE NEGRETE

Born: Jorge Alberto Negrete Moreno, November 30, 1911 (Guanajuato, Mexico); died 1953 (Los Angeles, California, U.S.).

Star qualities: Handsome; moustache; dashing icon of Mexican cinema's golden age; popular singer; distinctive baritone voice; charismatic; suave; civic minded.

Jorge Negrete was as famous as a singer in his native Mexico as for being a movie idol of *la época de oro*, or golden age. His father was a lieutenant colonel in the army, and at the age of fourteen Negrete was sent to Mexico's prestigious El Colegio Militar military academy, rising to the rank of lieutenant. Classically trained in music, Negrete started his career as an opera singer, performing on the radio in 1931 in Mexico City. In 1935 he headed to the United States and found work on TV with popular Cuban and Mexican musicians. Such was the quality of Negrete's baritone voice that he was even invited to join New York's Metropolitan Opera House company.

But Negrete returned to Mexico and made his screen debut in *La madrina del diablo* (1937) (*The Devil's Godmother*). He had his first real success in the Latin American region starring in the musical comedy *¡Ay Jalisco, no te rajes!* (1941) (*Jalisco, Don't Backslide*). Along with setting Negrete on the road to stardom, the movie also brought him into contact with actress Gloria Marín for the first time. The pair became romantically attached and went on to star together in nine other films.

Marín was not the first actress Negrete was involved with, nor would she be the last. His first marriage was to his *La valentina* (1938) costar, Elisa Christy, with whom he had a daughter, and his second was to his costar in *El Peñón de las Ánimas* (1943) (*The Rock of Souls*), María Félix. Negrete remained a popular figure for the rest of his career, both as an actor and singer, notably performing with his band, Los Tres Calaveras. He was one of the founding members of the Mexican Actors Association, and won huge respect for his work for the union and entertainers' rights. He died of hepatitis, contracted in New York. **CK**

Top Takes...

El rapto 1954 (*The Kidnapping*)
Dos tipos de cuidado 1953
  (*Two Careful Fellows*)
Un gallo en corral ajeno 1952
  (*The Straying Rooster*)
Gran Casino 1947
Una carta de amor 1943 (*A Love Letter*)
El rebelde 1943 (*The Rebel*)
El Peñón de las Ánimas 1943 (*The Rock of Souls*)
Seda, sangre y sol 1942 (*Silk, Blood, and Sun*)
¡Ay Jalisco, no te rajes! 1941
  (*Jalisco, Don't Backslide*)
El cementerio de las águilas 1939
  (*The Eagles' Cemetery*)
La valentina 1938
La madrina del diablo 1937
  (*The Devil's Godmother*)

"I suffer hangovers badly and will almost certainly die a bachelor."

LEE J. COBB

Born: Leo Jacoby, December 8, 1911 (New York City, New York, U.S.); died 1976 (Los Angeles, California, U.S.).

Star qualities: Stagecraft; harmonica player; character actor; famed for playing menacing gangland villains and rumpled authority figures.

Top Takes…

1910s

Lee J. Cobb achieved his professional apotheosis in 1949 by creating the original stage role of Willy Loman in Arthur Miller's *Death of a Salesman* on Broadway, but Fredric March took over for the 1951 film version. Thanks to that slight, which was rectified too late in a 1966 TV production, Cobb's screen career never soared, and he was lazily cast as an endless succession of gangland villains and world-weary cops.

The son of a Jewish newspaper editor, Cobb found his first love in music, playing the violin and the harmonica. After breaking his wrist, he turned his attention to acting and made his professional debut at the Pasadena Playhouse in 1931. A number of Broadway productions followed, and his first film appearance was in the Western *The Vanishing Shadow* (1934).

Cobb became a powerhouse in a remarkable run of outwardly amiable but frequently brutal bad guys: the glad-handing fruit trader of *Thieves' Highway* (1949); the union racketeer who batters Marlon Brando to a standstill in *On the Waterfront* (1954), which won him an Oscar nomination for Best Supporting Actor; the Capone-like Prohibition crime boss who drips acid on a paper flower to show what he could do to Cyd Charisse's face in *Party Girl* (1958); and Gary Cooper's outlaw foster father in *Man of the West* (1958). He is the angriest of the *12 Angry Men* (1957), holding out until the last moment. In later years Cobb calmed down to take more genial roles, as James Coburn's character's stuffy spy boss in the two Derek Flint movies and the New York cop sneering at cowboy Clint Eastwood in *Coogan's Bluff* (1968). He also appeared as the Columbo-like homicide detective poking around the case in the Academy Award-winning horror *The Exorcist* (1973). **KN**

"…because I lost my hair I was stuck playing butchers and crooks."

BRODERICK CRAWFORD

Born: William Broderick Crawford, December 9, 1911 (Philadelphia, Pennsylvania, U.S.); died 1986 (Rancho Mirage, California, U.S.).

Star qualities: Hoarse and grating voice; weather-beaten face; small eyes; burly physique; played the brutal tough guy with a vulnerable inner core.

Broderick Crawford was the son and grandson of vaudeville performers. He joined his parents onstage, working for producer Max Gordon. With vaudeville in decline, he went to Harvard University but dropped out after only three months to work as a stevedore on the New York docks. He returned to acting, including working with the Marx Brothers, but came to prominence in 1937 when he played the half-wit Lennie in *Of Mice and Men* on Broadway.

Crawford got a start in movies as the burliest member of any given posse, outlaw gang, foreign legion platoon, or band of barroom loafers. Rarely mean enough to play the brutal thugs his physique suited him for, he gravitated toward comical bruisers, aptly as a Damon Runyon robber in *Butch Minds the Baby* (1942). He won the Best Actor Academy Award for his portrayal of the Huey Long-a-clef demagogue Willie Stark in *All the King's Men* (1949), but his bearlike bluster works better as the dim but powerful cuddly mobster in *Born Yesterday* (1950).

Despite such peaks, Crawford was typecast and got surprisingly few similar, challenging roles; highlights being the cuckolded engine driver in Fritz Lang's *Human Desire* (1954), and a trip to Italy to play an aging swindler in demise for Federico Fellini in *Il bidone* (1955) (*The Swindle*). He had a hit TV show as the police chief barking: "Send me black and whites" into a car radio in *Highway Patrol* (1955–1959). Crawford passed time in Westerns such as *Red Tomahawk* (1967), and TV guest spots and exploitation such as *Hell's Bloody Devils* (1970). But he got one more chance to shine, in Larry Cohen's *The Private Files of J. Edgar Hoover* (1977), where he gave a formidable performance as the sad but terrifying law-enforcement bulldog. **KN**

Top Takes...

The Private Files of J. Edgar Hoover 1977
Hell's Bloody Devils 1970
Red Tomahawk 1967
Square of Violence 1963
Between Heaven and Hell 1956
The Fastest Gun Alive 1956
Il bidone 1955 (The Swindle)
New York Confidential 1955
Human Desire 1954
Night People 1954
The Mob 1951
Born Yesterday 1950
All the King's Men 1949 ★
Butch Minds the Baby 1942
I Can't Give You Anything but Love, Baby 1940
Woman Chases Man 1937

1910s

"I've made upwards of a million bucks in the cops-and-robbers business."

KARL MALDEN

Born: Malden George Sekulovich, March 22, 1912 (Chicago, Illinois, U.S.).

Star qualities: Large cauliflower nose and memorably crumpled face; intelligent, versatile leading man and character actor; stoic demeanor; gravitas; Method acting style; stagecraft; writer; director.

Top Takes...

1910s

Chicago-born, Indiana-bred Karl Malden was born of Czech and Serbian parents. A character actor with the gravity, if not the face, of a leading man, he embodies a no-nonsense Midwestern panache little seen in today's chain-store-bland movie land. Yet there always seems to be something precariously simmering behind his stolid demeanor, even when he's playing a patented stand-up guy, which, it turns out, isn't that often.

Right up to his iconic guest spot as priest and presidential confessor, Father Thomas Cavanaugh in an episode of TV's White House drama *The West Wing* (2000), Malden has fearlessly essayed a variety of characters. He was clingy in his career-defining role as Harold "Mitch" Mitchell in Elia Kazan's *A Streetcar Named Desire* (1951), which won him an Oscar for Best Supporting Actor; gleefully sadistic as a sheriff in *One-Eyed Jacks* (1961) (Marlon Brando's one shot at directing); immoral in Ken Russell's *Billion Dollar Brain* (1967); and strident as a unionist in the failed TV series *Skag* (1980).

He can play the avuncular with the best of them too, as a police detective in his biggest mid-career hit, TV's reliable cop show *The Streets of San Francisco* (1972–1976), which benefited from his obvious rapport with his costar, the young Michael Douglas. Such mutable intensity is the Method actor in him, no doubt; he acted for New York's Group Theater, where he first worked with Elia Kazan, prior to serving in World War II. But along with an underlying whimsy and watchful intelligence, Method acting is what makes Malden so indelible a presence in every role he takes. Offscreen, he was elected president of the Academy of Motion Picture Arts and Sciences in 1988, a title he held for five years. He has been married to Mona Greenberg since 1938. **MH**

> "I love every movie I've been in, even the bad ones . . . because I love to work."

MARIA MONTEZ

Born: Maria Africa Antonia Gracia Vidal de Santo Silas, June 6, 1912 (Barahona, Dominican Republic); died 1951 (Paris, Île de France, France).

Star qualities: Exotic looks; redheaded Latina leading lady; famed for outrageous exotic costumes and jewelry; "The Queen of Technicolor"; socialite; writer.

The daughter of a Spanish diplomat, Maria Montez was one of the kitschier movie stars of the 1940s, commanding a huge audience for shoddy but entertaining exotic films in which she was cast as high priestesses, harem queens, and island girls. Such roles, combined with her talent for appearing bejeweled in outrageous camp costumes, led to her nickname "The Queen of Technicolor."

Montez taught herself English and traveled to New York, where she became a model. But she wanted to be an actress, and campaigned hard to be offered a contract by Universal Studios. Montez began with bit parts in *The Invisible Woman* (1940) and *Moonlight in Hawaii* (1941), rising up the cast list with *South of Tahiti* (1941) and *Bombay Clipper* (1942). In her first starring role, she was atypically cast as a Parisian murder victim in *Mystery of Marie Roget* (1942). Often teamed with Sabu, Jon Hall, or Turhan Bey, she headed a succession of Universal Studios quickies draped in backlit atmosphere and sporting skimpy outfits in roles from Scheherezade in *Arabian Nights* (1942) to Queen Antinea in *Siren of Atlantis* (1949).

Montez's star vehicles include *White Savage* (1943), *Ali Baba and the Forty Thieves* (1944), *Cobra Woman* (1944), *Gypsy Wildcat* (1944), *Bowery to Broadway* (1944), and *Tangier* (1946). Her vogue passed with the 1940s—post-World War II escapist fare was no longer called for—and she moved to Paris. In Europe, Montez turned out a few French, Italian, and German movies before suffering a heart attack and drowning in her bathtub at the age of thirty-nine. Her native country recognized her achievements in 1996 when it named the Barahona airport *Aeropuerto Internacional María Montez* (Maria Montez International Airport). **KN**

Top Takes...

Amore e sangue 1951 (*City of Violence*)
Hans le marin 1949 (*Wicked City*)
Siren of Atlantis 1949
The Exile 1947
Tangier 1946
Bowery to Broadway 1944
Gypsy Wildcat 1944
Cobra Woman 1944
Ali Baba and the Forty Thieves 1944
White Savage 1943
Arabian Nights 1942
Mystery of Marie Roget 1942
Bombay Clipper 1942
South of Tahiti 1941
Moonlight in Hawaii 1941
The Invisible Woman 1940

"When I look at myself, I am so beautiful I scream with joy!"

GENE KELLY

Born: Eugene Curran Kelly, August 23, 1912 (Pittsburgh, Pennsylvania, U.S.); died 1996 (Los Angeles, California, U.S.)

Star qualities: Iconic dancer; dazzling footwork; singer; innovative; musicals maestro; melodious voice; good looks; director; writer; composer; choreographer.

Top Takes...

What a Way to Go! 1964
Let's Make Love 1960
The Happy Road 1957
Invitation to the Dance 1956
It's Always Fair Weather 1955
Brigadoon 1954
Singin' in the Rain 1952
It's a Big Country 1951
An American in Paris 1951
On the Town 1949
Take Me Out to the Ball Game 1949
The Pirate 1948
Living in a Big Way 1947
Anchors Aweigh 1945 ☆
Cover Girl 1944
For Me and My Gal 1942

Gene Kelly was the only rival to Fred Astaire as Hollywood's greatest male dancer, although the men's dancing style and image were very different. Astaire sported top hat and tails, and Kelly was more famed for his casual dress. Kelly's style was more muscular and masculine than Astaire's, and his singing voice, husky and melodious, had a stronger presence.

As a child, Kelly performed in vaudeville with his four siblings. He went on to study law while working as a teacher at his family's dance studio. But he decided to pursue a career in showbiz full time, and in 1938 he dropped out of law school and moved to New York. He made his name on Broadway in Rogers and Hart's *Pal Joey,* and was brought to Hollywood to appear with Judy Garland in *For Me and My Gal* (1942). *Cover Girl* (1944) saw him costar with Rita Hayworth. He went on to receive an Academy Award nomination for Best Actor in *Anchors Aweigh* (1945), in which he danced with Jerry Mouse.

Together with director Stanley Donen, Kelly revitalized the film musical, taking such innovative pictures as *On the Town* (1949), *Singin' in the Rain* (1952), and *It's Always Fair Weather* (1955) out of the theater and film studios and into the streets. Kelly's work with Vincente Minnelli on *The Pirate* (1948) and *An American in Paris* (1951) was no less accomplished, if more stylized. *Invitation to the Dance* (1956), which Kelly directed himself, was an experiment, telling three separate stories through dance alone. His later directorial outings, including the Barbra Streisand vehicle *Hello, Dolly!* (1969), were more conventional. In 1951 Kelly was awarded a special Academy Award for his achievements in choreography. He was the ideal host for the compilation of MGM's greatest musicals, *That's Entertainment* (1974), and its sequels. **EB**

"Fred Astaire represented the aristocracy, I represented the proletariat."

RIGHT: Gene Kelly sings in the rain in his most famous film, *Singin' in the Rain*.

DALE EVANS

Born: Frances Octavia Smith, October 31, 1912 (Uvalde, Texas, U.S.); died 2001 (Apple Valley, California, U.S.).

Star qualities: "Queen of the Cowgirls"; pretty, fresh-faced brunette; horsemanship; country singer; leading lady of musical Westerns; pianist; composer; writer.

Top Takes…

Dale "Queen of the Cowgirls" Evans eloped with her high-school sweetheart to marry at the age of fourteen; she was divorced and a mother by the age of seventeen. She entered show business as a vocalist, singing with big bands such as the Anson Weeks Orchestra, before going solo as a radio station singer. Two marriages later, she arrived in Hollywood, and after minor roles, including an appearance with John Wayne in *In Old Oklahoma* (1943), she was cast opposite singing Western star Roy Rogers in *Cowboy and the Senorita* (1944). This proved the start of a long and successful partnership. A charming brunette with a melodious singing voice, Evans married Rogers in 1947. They acted and sang together in more than a score of films, and then on TV in *The Roy Rogers Show* (1951–1957). Evans was the composer of the couple's theme song, "Happy Trails," with which they closed the show each week.

Among their more successful pictures were *The Yellow Rose of Texas* (1944), *Don't Fence Me In* (1945), and *Twilight in the Sierras* (1950), with Evans usually riding her buckskin horse, Buttermilk. Their last appearance together on film was in *Pals of the Golden West* (1951). For many, the couple were the embodiment of the American dream, but their personal life was marred by tragedy, three of their children dying young. They became born-again Christians and opened a museum dedicated to their achievements, initially based in California and then relocated to Missouri. In the 1970s, Evans recorded several solo albums of religious music in the gospel vein, and the 1990s saw her host her own religious TV program, *A Date with Dale* (1996). She also wrote many books on her life and spiritual development through adversity, including the best seller *Angel Unaware* (1953). **EB**

"Some trails are happy ones, others are blue. It's the way you ride the trail that counts."

LORETTA YOUNG

Born: Gretchen Young, January 6, 1913 (Salt Lake City, Utah, U.S.); died 2000 (Los Angeles, California, U.S.).

Star qualities: Blue-eyed beauty; exquisite face; radiant skin; graceful; glamorous; stagecraft; versatile; lead in period pieces and dramas; writer, humanitarian.

Loretta Young began her career in silents and ended it on TV. The first major Hollywood star to defect to the upstart medium, she achieved a success rarely equaled by those who followed.

In between were three decades of stardom—begun when she successfully answered a casting call intended for her sister in 1927—but surprisingly few memorable films. Her reputation as a beauty among beauties ensured constant box-office appeal, although she went on strike for better parts at the end of the 1930s, tired of "being Mrs. Alexander Graham Bell," as she once put it in a reference to her appearing in period costume dramas such as *The Story of Alexander Graham Bell* (1939). Devoutly religious, she also resisted suggestions to play the kinds of bad-girl roles permissible in the pre-Hays Code era, and in fact did so only once, as the loose-living single mother in *Born to Be Bad* (1934).

Her best performance is probably as Gallagher, the one-of-the-boys journalist in Frank Capra's *Platinum Blonde* (1931), discreetly vying with rich girl Jean Harlow for the affections of Robert Williams. Of her later appearances, she is impressive in Orson Welles's *The Stranger* (1946), slowly realizing that the husband she idolizes is a renegade Nazi. The following year she won an Oscar, playing a Swedish maid in the comedy *The Farmer's Daughter* (1947). She also received an Academy Award nomination for her role in *Come to the Stable* (1949). In the 1950s her career on the big screen was fading, so she moved to the small screen, where she hosted the series *Letter to Loretta* (1953–1961), and then *The New Loretta Young Show* (1962–1963). In her later years she wrote a lonely hearts column for Roman Catholic newspapers and devoted much of her time to Catholic charities. **MC**

Top Takes...

It Happens Every Thursday 1953
Come to the Stable 1949 ☆
The Bishop's Wife 1947
The Farmer's Daughter 1947 ★
The Stranger 1946
A Night to Remember 1943
Eternally Yours 1939
The Story of Alexander Graham Bell 1939
Second Honeymoon 1937
Bulldog Drummond Strikes Back 1934
Born to Be Bad 1934
The Life of Jimmy Dolan 1933
Taxi! 1932
Platinum Blonde 1931
The Magnificent Flirt 1928
Sirens of the Sea 1917

"I've a full-length triple-panel mirror . . . and I spend quite a lot of time in front of it."

LLOYD BRIDGES

Born: Lloyd Vernet Bridges Jr., January 15, 1913 (San Leandro, California, U.S.); died 1998 (Los Angeles, California, U.S.).

Star qualities: Stagecraft; producer; director; young character actor followed by mature deadpan comic roles; head of an acting dynasty; scuba-diving TV fame.

Top Takes...

1910s

Lloyd Bridges started out in the Actors Lab in the mid-1930s before moving to Broadway to debut in *Othello* in 1939. He was signed by Columbia Pictures in 1941, and in the 1940s he racked up many bit parts in films, including *Here Comes Mr. Jordan* (1941), before showing heroic mettle in the serial *Secret Agent X-9* (1945). He served another five years in supporting roles, such as the younger brother in *Canyon Passage* (1946) and a weak-chinned juvenile in *Colt .45* (1950), with the occasional B lead, such as a space pilot in *Rocketship X-M* (1950), before the notable role of the spineless deputy in *High Noon* (1952) lifted him out of the posse. Then he loitered in Westerns, playing a character called Gar in *City of Bad Men* (1953) and one called Gyp in *Wichita* (1955).

In the 1950s, Bridges was graylisted after he admitted toying with communism to the House Un-American Activities Committee hearings. However, he was resurrected by producer Ivan Tors, who cast him as diver-for-hire adventurer Mike Nelson in the TV series *Sea Hunt* (1958–1961).

In the 1960s and 1970s Bridges was best served by TV movies, doing his finest screen work in the poignant *Silent Night, Lonely Night* (1969), featuring in the weirdly memorable *Haunts of the Very Rich* (1972), and strutting as Aramis in *The Fifth Musketeer* (1979). His career changed tack after the release of the comedy *Airplane!* (1980) in which he parodied the type of performance he had been giving for decades. Following the huge success of that film, Bridges's highest profile later work was in similar broad comedy, such as *Hot Shots!* (1991) and *Jane Austen's Mafia!* (1999). He was the father of actors Beau Bridges and Jeff Bridges, and grandfather of actor Jordan Bridges. **KN**

> "Looks like I picked the wrong week to quit drinking."
>
> —Steve McCroskey, *Airplane!*

VICTOR MATURE

Born: Victor John Mature, January 29, 1913 (Louisville, Kentucky, U.S.); died 1999 (Rancho Santa Fe, California, U.S.).

Star qualities: Tall; wavy hair; beefcake good looks; "The Hunk"; looked good in a loincloth and sandals; played in Biblical epics; producer.

The son of Swiss immigrants, Victor Mature tended to get laughed at for his wooden handsomeness and tendency to flex his chest in entertainingly terrible films such as Cecil B. DeMille's *Samson and Delilah* (1949), and just plain terrible films such as *The Bandit of Zhobe* (1959). However, "The Hunk" also made many good films—and was good in them.

He made his debut in Hal Roach's *The Housekeeper's Daughter* (1939), then grunted in caveman skins in *One Million B.C.* (1940), but in the 1940s he showed range. He was the sweaty, anguished fall guy in *I Wake Up Screaming* (1941); mysterious in cape and fez in *The Shanghai Gesture* (1941); likable in the musical biopic *My Gal Sal* (1942); and—best of all—drunkenly self-hating and consumptive, but showing mettle, as surgeon and gunfighter Doc Holliday in John Ford's *My Darling Clementine* (1946). He was in a few more good film noirs such as *Kiss of Death* (1947), but after *Samson* he got stuck in costume dramas, such as *The Robe* (1953). He was also excellent in 1950s Westerns such as *The Last Frontier* (1955).

In the 1960s his film career started to wane, and he turned his attention to golf. When he did appear in films, his roles were often comedic. Never one to take himself too seriously, Mature parodied his own screen image in films such as Bob Rafelson's *Head* (1968), where he epitomizes gargantuan Hollywood self-regard, with The Monkees pop group cast as his dandruff; Vittorio De Sica's *Caccia alla volpe* (1966) (*After the Fox*); and *Won Ton Ton, the Dog Who Saved Hollywood* (1976). He semiretired from acting in the late 1970s to run a TV shop in Hollywood and concentrate on his big love: golf. In 1984 he appeared in a TV remake of *Samson and Delilah*, playing Samson's father, before retiring permanently. **KN**

Top Takes...

Won Ton Ton, the Dog Who Saved Hollywood 1976
Head 1968
Caccia alla volpe 1966 (*After the Fox*)
The Last Frontier 1955
Violent Saturday 1955
The Robe 1953
Samson and Delilah 1949
Cry of the City 1948
Kiss of Death 1947
My Darling Clementine 1946
My Gal Sal 1942
The Shanghai Gesture 1941
I Wake Up Screaming 1941
One Million B.C. 1940
The Housekeeper's Daughter 1939

1910s

> "I'm not an actor, and I enclose my press cuttings to prove it."

GERT FRÖBE

Born: Karl-Gerhart Fröeber, February 25, 1913 (Zwickau, Saxony, Germany); died 1988 (Munich, Bavaria, Germany).

Star qualities: Tall; ruddy complexion; heavyset; character actor in dramas and lighthearted comedies; memorable Bond movie arch villain; musician.

Top Takes...

Strapped to a table with a laser aimed at his groin, James Bond snarls, "Do you expect me to talk?" "No, Mr. Bond," responds mastermind Auric Goldfinger, "I expect you to die." Gert Fröbe secured a place in movie history as the most genially threatening of Bond villains. For *Goldfinger* (1964), German Fröbe's English wasn't up to the mark, and so English actor Michael Collins dubbed his dialogue, impersonating the German actor. Later, using his own voice, he sounds exactly like Collins. Although Fröbe was a member of the Nazi Party both before and during World War II, he helped German Jews by hiding them from the Gestapo. Because of Fröbe's past affiliation with the Nazi Party, *Goldfinger* was banned in Israel until he was publicly thanked by a Jewish family he had aided.

A violinist and stage designer in his twenties, Fröbe turned to acting in the 1930s. A resemblance to 1930s actor Otto Wernicke ensured that he was cast as the archenemy of the master crook in Fritz Lang's *Die Tausend Augen des Dr. Mabuse* (1960) (*The Thousand Eyes of Dr. Mabuse*), although he didn't take over Wernicke's role as Inspector Lohmann until *Im Stahlnetz des Dr. Mabuse* (1961) (*The Return of Dr. Mabuse*). Fröbe worked in many European films, often as a trench-coated policeman, for Orson Welles in *Mr. Arkadin* (1955) and Ingmar Bergman in *The Serpent's Egg* (1977). After *Goldfinger*, he was in international family movies, often as a comic villain. He had a role in the British comedy *Those Magnificent Men in Their Flying Machines* (1965), and in its spin-off *Monte Carlo or Bust* (1969). He was Baron Bomburst in *Chitty Chitty Bang Bang* (1968), which was based on the book by James Bond author Ian Fleming. In *J'ai tué Raspoutine* (1967) (*Rasputin*), he is one of the screen's chubbier Rasputins. **KN**

"I am a big man, and I have a laugh to match my size."

JOHN GARFIELD

Born: Jacob Julius Garfinkle, March 4, 1913 (New York City, New York, U.S.); died 1952 (New York City, New York, U.S.).

Star qualities: Wavy dark hair; rugged good looks; chiseled features; character actor; often played brooding tough guys; producer.

John Garfield first came across acting when he attended a special school for problem children after his mother died when he was only seven years old. He went on to drama school, and worked for a number of years in the theater before making his screen debut as a cynical suitor among sugary sweethearts in *Four Daughters* (1938). He reprised the role in the sequel *Four Wives* (1939), and stuck around the Warner Brothers lot as a young tough in films such as *The Sea Wolf* (1941). But his brief heyday came after World War II, when his wounded, ethnic sensitivity suited him to melodrama, as in *Humoresque* (1946), film noir as in *The Postman Always Rings Twice* (1946), and social comment, as in *Gentleman's Agreement* (1947).

Garfield's best roles were as the blinded veteran in *Pride of the Marines* (1945), the boxer mixed up with the crooked fight racket in *Body and Soul* (1947), and the mob lawyer who turns against the system that kills his brother in *Force of Evil* (1948). A political liberal, he was unfairly targeted by anticommunists. He refused to name names when he gave testimony before the House Un-American Activities Committee in April 1951, and was blacklisted—barred from employment by studio bosses. For the rest of his career he struggled to land decent roles, although he aptly took the Humphrey Bogart part in *The Breaking Point* (1950), a remake of *To Have and Have Not* (1944), which returns to the Ernest Hemingway novel that Howard Hawks had ignored. Garfield was twice nominated for an Oscar, for both Best Supporting Actor and Best Actor. He died in 1952 of a heart complaint at the young age of thirty-nine. His funeral in New York was mobbed by 10,000 fans, the largest number to attend an actor's funeral since that of silent-screen icon Rudolph Valentino in 1926. **KN**

Top Takes...

He Ran All the Way 1951
The Breaking Point 1950
Force of Evil 1948
Gentleman's Agreement 1947
Body and Soul 1947 ☆
Humoresque 1946
The Postman Always Rings Twice 1946
Pride of the Marines 1945
Hollywood Canteen 1944
Destination Tokyo 1943
Air Force 1943
Tortilla Flat 1942
The Sea Wolf 1941
Castle on the Hudson 1940
Four Wives 1939
Four Daughters 1938 ☆

"Screen acting is my business but I get my kicks from Broadway."

STEWART GRANGER

Born: James Lablache Stewart, May 6, 1913 (London, England); died 1993 (Santa Monica, California, U.S.).

Star qualities: Tall, dark, and handsome; wavy hair; stagecraft; young romantic hero in costume dramas and swashbuckling action films; mature character actor.

Top Takes…

The grandson of an Italian comic actor, Stewart "Jimmy" Granger went to drama school and made his professional debut in 1935. He hit London's West End in 1938 in *The Sun Never Sets*. Around this time he adopted his professional name to avoid confusion with the U.S. movie star James Stewart. With the outbreak of World War II he joined the British army. But in 1942 he was wounded in action, and thus became available as a handsome leading man when most British actors his age were still in military service. With wavy hair and a tendency to wear tight pants, he impressed in period romances such as Gainsborough Pictures's *The Man in Grey* (1943)—his first starring role—and in *Fanny by Gaslight* (1944) . But he was also effective as the slacker who takes a righteous beating from John Mills in *Waterloo Road* (1945).

By the end of the 1940s Granger was one of Britain's top stars, and he moved to Hollywood to take up a contract with MGM. Then he went international in exciting versions of famous adventures: as Allan Quatermain in *King Solomon's Mines* (1950), the imposter and the king in *The Prisoner of Zenda* (1952), and the outlaw harlequin in *Scaramouche* (1952), triumphing in a terrific swordfight with Mel Ferrer. Solid in Fritz Lang's *Moonfleet* (1955), Granger made a fist of the colonial officer in *Bhowani Junction* (1956), then slid to German-Yugoslav Karl May Westerns such as *Unter Geiern* (1964) (*Frontier Hellcat*) and Edgar Wallace *krimis* such as *The Trygon Factor* (1966). After playing a poor Sherlock Holmes in the TV movie of *The Hound of the Baskervilles* (1972), he stuck to cameo dastards, as in *The Wild Geese* (1978).

Granger was married three times, including from 1950 to 1960 to actress and former costar Jean Simmons. **KN**

> "I was a good costume actor but I shortened my career by making the wrong choices."

PETER CUSHING

Born: Peter Wilton Cushing, May 26, 1913 (Kenley, Surrey, England); died 1994 (Canterbury, Kent, England).

Star qualities: Shakespearean stagecraft; cadaverous face; haunting eyes; thick gray hair; veteran master of British horror; imperious, energetic screen presence.

Peter Cushing studied drama at London's Guildhall School of Music and Drama. He went on to work as a clerk in a surveyor's office before making his first professional stage appearance in 1935. Four years later he went to the United States, where he picked up odd Hollywood credits, such as in Laurel and Hardy's *A Chump at Oxford* (1940). He then returned to Britain and the stage and bit parts such as Osric in Laurence Olivier's *Hamlet* (1948). He started to get leading roles as Mr. Darcy, Winston Smith, and Beau Brummell on British TV. It was as the icily fanatical Baron Frankenstein in Hammer Film Productions's *The Curse of Frankenstein* (1957) that he secured his position as a British horror star. He reprised Frankenstein, played Dr. Abraham Van Helsing in *Dracula* (1958), and was an outstanding Sherlock Holmes on film in *The Hound of the Baskervilles* (1959) and on TV. Amid many further Hammer horrors, including *The Mummy* (1959) and others, he essayed a dotty scientist in the two lively *Dr. Who* (1965, 1966) movies.

Among Cushing's best performances are the Scrooge-like bank manager menaced by a polite robber in *Cash on Demand* (1961); a radically evil Frankenstein in *Frankenstein Must Be Destroyed* (1969); a lonely old man who seeks revenge as a heart-ripping zombie in *Tales from the Crypt* (1972); and a wry scientist, teamed with frequent costar and close friend Christopher Lee, in *Horror Express* (1973). After a high-profile appearance in *Star Wars* (1977), he stuck to cameo roles, such as in *Top Secret!* (1984). Cushing retired from the screen in 1986. He went to live on Britain's south coast, where he pursued his hobbies, bird-watching and painting, and wrote his memoirs: *An Autobiography* (1986) and *Past Forgetting* (1988). **KN**

Top Takes...

Biggles 1986
Top Secret! 1984
Star Wars 1977
Horror Express 1973
Tales from the Crypt 1972
The House That Dripped Blood 1971
Frankenstein Must Be Destroyed 1969
Daleks' Invasion Earth: 2150 A.D. 1966
Dr. Who and the Daleks 1965
Cash on Demand 1961
The Mummy 1959
The Hound of the Baskervilles 1959
Dracula 1958
The Curse of Frankenstein 1957
Hamlet 1948
A Chump at Oxford 1940

1910s

"Actually, I'm a gentle fellow ... when I'm in the country, I'm a keen bird-watcher."

RED SKELTON

Born: Richard Bernard Skelton, July 18, 1913 (Vincennes, Indiana, U.S.); died 1997 (Rancho Mirage, California, U.S.).

Star qualities: Redhead clown; master of ad lib; comic sketch artist; created enduring comedy characters; writer; producer; composer; painter.

Top Takes…

Those Magnificent Men in Their Flying Machines 1965
Ocean's Eleven 1960
Around the World in Eighty Days 1956
The Clown 1953
Ziegfeld Follies 1946
Whistling in Brooklyn 1943
Du Barry Was a Lady 1943
Whistling in Dixie 1942
Panama Hattie 1942
Ship Ahoy 1942
Lady Be Good 1941
Dr. Kildare's Wedding Day 1941
Whistling in the Dark 1941
Flight Command 1940
Having Wonderful Time 1938

A success on stage, radio, film, and TV, Red Skelton was the son of a circus clown who died two months before his birth. He grew up poor and worked selling newspapers on street corners. His red hair gave him the nickname "Red." By the age of fifteen he had left home and begun his professional career, working such disparate venues as medicine shows, minstrel shows, vaudeville, burlesque, showboats, and circuses.

Skelton had his first professional break on the radio in *The Rudy Vallee Show,* making his debut in 1937, and becoming a regular on the NBC show *Avalon Time* in 1939. The network gave him his own program in 1941, and he remained with NBC until 1949, when he moved to CBS.

Skelton was signed to MGM in 1940 and appeared in a variety of comedies and musicals. He starred in a series of comedy-mysteries: *Whistling in the Dark* (1941), *Whistling in Dixie* (1942), and *Whistling in Brooklyn* (1943). The musicals include *Lady Be Good* (1941), *Panama Hattie* (1942), *Du Barry Was a Lady* (1943), and *Ziegfeld Follies* (1946).

By the mid-1950s, Skelton was more or less exclusively a TV star. CBS had moved him to the new medium in 1951, and he remained on the air for the next 20 years. He featured a number of recurrent characters, including the tramp Freddy the Freeloader, the wiseacre child Junior, the con artist San Fernando Red, and the country hick Clem. Skelton also frequently performed pantomime, at which he excelled. In the 1970s he retired from performing and developed a successful second career as a painter, particularly of clowns. His paintings fetched prices of more than $80,000. In the 1980s Skelton returned to live performances and appeared at New York's Carnegie Hall. **DS**

> "I just want to be known as a clown because to me that's the height of my profession."

ALAN LADD

Born: Alan Walbridge Ladd, September 3, 1913 (Hot Springs, Arkansas, U.S.); died 1964 (Palm Springs, California, U.S.).

Star qualities: Diminutive; icy good looks; blond hair; blue eyes; rich voice; charismatic; famous for lead tough guy and Western gunslinger roles.

Alan Ladd's life began in hardship and ended in tragedy. In between, he became one of Hollywood's most popular tough guys. Born in Arkansas, his English mother was left a widow when Ladd was only four years old. They moved to California, where the frail-looking Ladd surprisingly excelled in swimming and track at school. In 1931 he decided to train for the 1932 Olympics, but his hopes were dashed when he suffered an injury and couldn't participate in the Olympic trials. He performed a series of menial jobs, eventually working backstage at Warner Brothers while doing radio shows. His small stature seemed to disqualify him for movies, but Hollywood agent Sue Carol discovered him and started to promote him as star material; in 1942 the pair married.

His big break came when he played a ruthless killer in *This Gun for Hire* (1941), based on the novel by Graham Greene. The movie also starred Veronica Lake, who proved to be Ladd's ideal costar, not least because, at less than five feet tall, she was a good deal shorter than even he. They were reunited in *The Glass Key* (1942) and were teamed again in yet another film noir, the Raymond Chandler-scripted *The Blue Dahlia* (1946). Ladd's expressionless face, cold blue eyes, and blond hair made him appear sexy but unreachable, and for a time he enjoyed big box-office appeal. Westerns and other action films were his domain; two excellent Westerns for director Delmer Daves were *Drum Beat* (1954) and *The Badlanders* (1958). But before that came the role with which he is most closely identified, the buckskin-clad Shane in the 1953 film of that title, in which he is the nemesis of professional gunslinger Wilson, played by Jack Palance. Ladd died young, of alcohol-related illness, in 1964. **EB**

Top Takes...

The Carpetbaggers 1964
The Badlanders 1958
Drum Beat 1954
Saskatchewan 1954
Hell Below Zero 1954
Shane 1953
Desert Legion 1953
Thunder in the East 1952
The Iron Mistress 1952
Red Mountain 1951
Appointment with Danger 1951
The Great Gatsby 1949
Saigon 1948
The Blue Dahlia 1946
The Glass Key 1942
This Gun For Hire 1941

1910s

"If you can figure out my success on the screen, you're a better man than me."

TREVOR HOWARD

Born: Trevor Wallace Howard-Smith, September 29, 1913 (Cliftonville, Kent, England); died 1988 (Bushey, Hertfordshire, England).

Star qualities: Tall; stagecraft; romantic lead turned character actor; often played the restrained British gentleman in war films and period dramas.

Top Takes...

Gandhi 1982
Sir Henry at Rawlinson End 1980
Ludwig 1972
Ryan's Daughter 1970
The Charge of the Light Brigade 1968
Mutiny on the Bounty 1962
Sons and Lovers 1960 ☆
The Heart of the Matter 1953
Outcast of the Islands 1952
The Third Man 1949
They Made Me a Fugitive 1947
Green for Danger 1946
Brief Encounter 1945
The Way to the Stars 1945
The Way Ahead 1944

Trevor Howard went to top British school Clifton College, then on to the Royal Academy of Dramatic Art. He acted on the London stage for several years before World War II, when he joined the Royal Artillery. He was wounded in action in 1943. He entered British films as a navy man in *The Way Ahead* (1944) and an RAF flier in *The Way to the Stars* (1945), and stayed in uniform throughout his screen career. His breakthrough came in David Lean's *Brief Encounter* (1945), where he plays a doctor who has a hesitant romance with prim Celia Johnson, and brings affecting sincerity to a role that has often been parodied as the epitome of English repression.

Howard had good supporting parts in *Green for Danger* (1946) and *The Third Man* (1949), and interestingly essayed postwar confusion as the veteran turned bank robber in *They Made Me a Fugitive* (1947), the betrayer in *Outcast of the Islands* (1952), and the colonial official of *The Heart of the Matter* (1953). He received recognition from his peers for his performance as the drunken Walter Morel in the film adaptation of D. H. Lawrence's novel *Sons and Lovers* (1960) when he received an Academy Award nomination for Best Actor. Becoming craggier, he rose up the ranks and was best seen playing mad or malicious officers, such as Captain Bligh in *Mutiny on the Bounty* (1962) and a purple-faced, bewhiskered Lord Cardigan in *The Charge of the Light Brigade* (1968). In later life, although he worked steadily, he too rarely landed roles as good as Richard Wagner in *Ludwig* (1972) and Father Collins in *Ryan's Daughter* (1970). He was memorable as an eccentric peer in *Sir Henry at Rawlinson End* (1980). Truly British, Howard insisted on a clause in all his movie contracts that allowed him to attend cricket Test matches. **KN**

> "It's no use pretending it hasn't happened, 'cause it has."
> —Dr. Alec Harvey, *Brief Encounter*

BURT LANCASTER

Born: Burton Stephen Lancaster, November 2, 1913 (New York City, New York, U.S.); died 1994 (Century City, California, U.S.).

Star qualities: Tall; rugged good looks; athletic; larger-than-life screen presence; producer; director; writer; heavyweight lead roles in dramas and action films.

The son of a postal worker, the young Burt Lancaster had an interest in gymnastics that led him to a career as a circus acrobat. He did not break into the movies until 1946, in *The Killers*. His career took off in the 1950s, when his good looks and athleticism made him at home in a series of action films such as *The Flame and the Arrow* (1950) and *The Crimson Pirate* (1952), and Westerns such as *Apache* (1954) and *Gunfight at the O.K. Corral* (1957). But his sensitivity as an actor meant he was increasingly in demand for challenging dramatic roles, such as that of Sergeant Warden in *From Here to Eternity* (1953).

Lancaster was also one of the first actors in Hollywood to form his own production company, which he did in 1948 with Harold Hecht and James Hill, to help control his career. He memorably played a cynical journalist in *Sweet Smell of Success* (1957), a charlatan preacher in *Elmer Gantry* (1960)—for which the self-taught actor won an Academy Award for Best Actor—and a rehabilitated convict in *Birdman of Alcatraz* (1962). In 1962 he extended his artistic range by taking the lead role in *Il Gattopardo* (1963) (*The Leopard*), made in Italy by Luchino Visconti. As he grew older, increasing ill health prevented him from working as much as he would have liked. Lancaster's last great role was as an aging small-time crook in Louis Malle's *Atlantic City* (1980).

A lifelong political liberal and Democrat, Lancaster was also a member of the American Civil Liberties Union, but managed to avoid being blacklisted. However, he did appear on U.S. President Richard Nixon's "List of Enemies" because of his support for Senator George McGovern in the 1972 presidential election.

Lancaster was known for his prickly personality, and he guarded his private life fiercely. **EB**

Top Takes...

Field of Dreams 1989
***Atlantic City* 1980** ☆
The Swimmer 1968
Seven Days in May 1964
Il Gattopardo 1963 (*The Leopard*)
***Birdman of Alcatraz* 1962** ☆
Judgment at Nuremberg 1961
***Elmer Gantry* 1960** ★
Separate Tables 1958
Sweet Smell of Success 1957
Gunfight at the O.K. Corral 1957
Apache 1954
***From Here to Eternity* 1953** ☆
The Crimson Pirate 1952
The Flame and the Arrow 1950
The Killers 1946

"Tits and sand—that's what we used to call sex and violence in Hollywood."

VIVIEN LEIGH

Born: Vivian Mary Hartley, November 5, 1913 (Darjeeling, West Bengal, India); died 1967 (London, England).

Star qualities: Radiant petite beauty; blue-green eyes; brown hair; superb stagecraft; played the powerful and vulnerable with emotional intensity.

Top Takes...

Ship of Fools 1965
The Roman Spring of Mrs. Stone 1961
The Deep Blue Sea 1955
A Streetcar Named Desire 1951 ★
Anna Karenina 1948
Caesar and Cleopatra 1945
That Hamilton Woman 1941
Waterloo Bridge 1940
21 Days 1940
Gone with the Wind 1939 ★
Sidewalks of London 1938
A Yank at Oxford 1938
Storm in a Teacup 1937
Dark Journey 1937
Fire Over England 1937
The Village Squire 1935

Like that of Orson Welles, the nature of Vivien Leigh's Hollywood starring debut was so mythic that some degree of anticlimax thereafter was virtually inevitable. The story of her casting as Scarlett O'Hara is a fairy tale, stepping in at virtually the last minute after producer David O. Selznick had poured $50,000 into a two-and-a-half year-campaign to find the perfect actress. Leigh was on a visit to New York to see her lover and future second husband, actor Laurence Olivier, when the couple met Selznick, who invited her for a screen test. Not exactly unknown in Hollywood—several of her British films of the 1930s had been well received—Leigh was by no means a star, and it was a risk for Selznick to cast her. It helped that she was a perfect match for the character physically, and any problems of accent and style were carefully smoothed over in what is still an arresting and commanding performance.

Immediately after *Gone with the Wind* (1939), Hollywood tried hard to consolidate her Oscar-winning success in *Waterloo Bridge* (1940), in which she is equally radiant, yet she made only nine more screen appearances. Most of them were in historical or classical roles such as Lady Hamilton, Cleopatra, and Anna Karenina, and she also worked widely in theater. There was a second Oscar for Best Actress as another Southern belle in *A Streetcar Named Desire* (1951), but the second half of her career was clouded by mental and physical illness. She suffered from tuberculosis and was diagnosed as suffering from bipolar disorder, and she gained a reputation as a difficult person to work with. Her mental health and its accompanying mood swings and erratic behavior also cast a cloud over her marriage to Olivier, and in 1960 the couple eventually divorced. **MC**

> "As God is my witness, they're not going to lick me!"
>
> —Scarlett O'Hara, *Gone with the Wind*

RIGHT: Vivien Leigh tussles with hunk Marlon Brando in *A Streetcar Named Desire*.

HEDY LAMARR

Born: Hedwig Eva Maria Kiesler, November 9, 1913 (Vienna, Austria); died 2000 (Orlando, Florida, U.S.).

Star qualities: Blinding beauty; tall; glamorous; witty; determined; notoriously faked an orgasm in one of cinema's first nude scenes; played sex-kitten roles.

Throughout the 1940s Hedy Lamarr was the most beautiful woman on the planet, in a field with strong competition. She was also the threatening "exotic other woman." Betrayal, suicide attempts, and psychological instability were the hallmarks of many of the parts she played—Hollywood's way of ensuring that the hero would choose the all-American gal instead of the heavenly gorgeous foreigner.

Throughout her career Lamarr struggled to be respected as an actress, not just a bombshell. Her nude appearance in a ten-minute swimming sequence in the Czechoslovakian film *Ekstase* (1933) (*Ecstasy*) drew the world's attention, at least toward her body. She was recruited by MGM, changed her name, and starred in a series of adventure movies, of which *Algiers* (1938), *Lady of the Tropics* (1939), and *White Cargo* (1942) are the most memorable. Her entry in that last film, as Tondaleyo, is unforgettable and her beauty blinding.

In passing, Lamarr also showed what a talented actress she was, especially when twinned with Hollywood great Spencer Tracy in *I Take This Woman* (1940) and *Tortilla Flat* (1942), a surprisingly unglamorous performance. Her most epic role, as the seductive Delilah in *Samson and Delilah* (1949), would also be the last before a fast downfall. She retired at the age of forty-four, leaving her legacy as the woman who had injected wartime Hollywood with a dose of sensuality. Offscreen, Lamarr was married and divorced six times and had two children and one adopted son. Her first marriage was in 1933 to an Austrian arms dealer, Friedrich Mandl, who was a Nazi sympathizer. In a bid to escape from him, Lamarr drugged the maid hired by the obsessive Mandl to guard her, and fled to Paris. **EM**

Top Takes…

"Any girl can look glamorous. All you have to do is stand still and look stupid."

JANE WYMAN

Born: Sarah Jane Mayfield, January 4, 1914 (St. Joseph, Missouri, U.S.).

Star qualities: Petite; blonde; radio singer; a versatile performer on film and TV; shone in serious dramatic roles as well as comic roles; a participant, with Regis Toomey, in the longest ever recorded screen kiss.

Born in 1914 to the mayor of St. Joseph, Missouri, Manning J. Mayfield, and Le Jerne Pichelle, a struggling actress, Jane Wyman was destined for the limelight. She became a versatile actress capable of strong performances in a range of genres.

Following the death of her father, Wyman entered show business around 1930 as a radio singer named Jane Durrell. By age fifteen, she was in Hollywood. Her adopted stage name, Jane Wyman, coincided with her becoming a contract player at Warner Brothers in 1936; she had been billed once prior as Sarah Jane Fulks, the surname of her unofficial foster family back in Missouri. Established at Warner Brothers, Wyman met her future husband, Ronald Reagan, costarring with him in the comedy *Brother Rat* (1938) and its sequel, *Brother Rat and a Baby* (1940). They married in 1940, but divorced in 1948. They had two children and adopted a third.

Wyman won an Academy Award for Best Actress for her portrayal of the deaf-mute rape victim in *Johnny Belinda* (1948). She became as famous for her witty acceptance speech as for the role she played, saying: "I won this by keeping my mouth shut, and that's what I'm going to do now." Subsequently, she appeared primarily in tearjerkers, garnering yet another Oscar nomination for her performance opposite Rock Hudson in Douglas Sirk's improbable melodrama *Magnificent Obsession* (1954). That movie's success led to her again starring with Hudson, this time as the older woman in a May-to-September romance, Sirk's *All That Heaven Allows* (1955). After her final feature film, *How to Commit Marriage* (1969), she went into semiretirement, but years later made a triumphant return on TV, starring as Angela Channing on the prime-time soap opera *Falcon Crest* (1981–1990). **SU**

Top Takes...

How to Commit Marriage 1969
Pollyanna 1960
Holiday for Lovers 1959
Miracle in the Rain 1956
All That Heaven Allows 1955
Magnificent Obsession 1954 ☆
Just for You 1952
The Story of Will Rogers 1952
The Blue Veil 1951 ☆
The Glass Menagerie 1950
Stage Fright 1950
Johnny Belinda 1948 ★
The Yearling 1946 ☆
The Lost Weekend 1945
Brother Rat and a Baby 1940
Brother Rat 1938

"Some women just aren't the permanent marrying kind, and I'm one of them."

ARTHUR KENNEDY

Born: John Arthur Kennedy, February 17, 1914 (Worcester, Massachusetts, U.S.); died 1990 (Branford, Connecticut, U.S.).

Star qualities: Tall; steely-blue eyes; Shakespearean stagecraft; versatile premier character and support lead actor; often in Westerns.

Top Takes...

Ricco 1973
Lawrence of Arabia 1962
Elmer Gantry 1960
Some Came Running 1958 ☆
Peyton Place 1957 ☆
The Desperate Hours 1955
Trial 1955 ☆
The Man from Laramie 1955
Rancho Notorious 1952
Bend of the River 1952
Bright Victory 1951 ☆
Champion 1949 ☆
Boomerang! 1947
They Died with Their Boots On 1941
High Sierra 1941
City for Conquest 1940

Though rarely a leading man in movies, Arthur Kennedy was one of the most talented and reliable actors in Hollywood for several decades. The son of a dentist, he became involved in local theater groups. He started out on the stage in his early twenties and went on to do important work, appearing on Broadway in several Arthur Miller plays. He was discovered by James Cagney while performing on the stage and made his movie debut playing Cagney's character's younger brother in *City for Conquest* (1940). He had important roles in the thriller *High Sierra* (1941), in the Western *They Died with Their Boots On* (1941), and the war film *Air Force* (1943). After serving in World War II, Kennedy returned to Broadway to play Chris Keller in Miller's *All My Sons* (1947) and won fame in the role of Biff in *Death of a Salesman* (1948).

Kennedy was exceptionally versatile, able to play the hero's stalwart best friend or, as in *Champion* (1949), the decent brother of the ruthless boxer played by Kirk Douglas. But he was equally adept as a charming but devious villain, as in two Westerns with James Stewart, *Bend of the River* (1952) and *The Man from Laramie* (1955). In *Bright Victory* (1951) he had the lead, playing a blinded soldier, and was nominated for an Oscar for Best Actor. Throughout his career he received five Academy Award nominations and gained a reputation as one of Hollywood's finest actors. Another 1950s Western, *Rancho Notorious* (1952), offered him a meaty role opposite Marlene Dietrich. After this, notable performances included *The Desperate Hours* (1955), *Peyton Place* (1957), and *Some Came Running* (1958). In the 1970s Kennedy made numerous appearances in European melodramas and in crime films such as *Ricco* (1973). **EB**

"What attracts you personally to the desert?"

—Jackson Bentley, *Lawrence of Arabia*

ALEC GUINNESS

Born: Alec Guinness de Cuffe, April 2, 1914 (London, England); died 2000 (Midhurst, Sussex, England).

Star qualities: Shakespearean stagecraft; writer; played serious roles, often in war dramas, as well as comic characters; the ultimate TV spymaster; knighted.

Sir Alec Guinness's career spanned more than 60 years, his performances ranging from Shakespeare to Ealing Studios comedies. His movie roles included an Oscar-winning performance as Colonel Nicholson in *The Bridge on the River Kwai* (1957), where his brand of subtly unhinged Britishness is at the heart of David Lean's film.

He started out as an advertising copywriter before winning a scholarship at the Fay Compton Studio of Dramatic Art. He then joined London's Old Vic theater in his early twenties, and had his big break as Osric in the company's production of *Hamlet* in 1934. Directed by Lean, Guinness entered films by way of several Charles Dickens adaptations, playing Herbert Pocket in *Great Expectations* (1946) and Fagin in *Oliver Twist* (1948). After these, he became a fixture in gentle, barbed, endlessly pleasurable Ealing comedies: he was an entire family of murder victims, playing eight different characters, in *Kind Hearts and Coronets* (1949); a heist planner mild or mad in *The Lavender Hill Mob* (1951) and *The Ladykillers* (1955); and an unworldly inventor in *The Man in the White Suit* (1951).

Guinness personally scripted *The Horse's Mouth* (1958), gifting himself with the role of unconventional artist Gulley Jimpson. He then specialized in military commanders losing ground, being passed over for promotion in *Tunes of Glory* (1960) and committing suicide in *Hitler: The Last Ten Days* (1973). As Obi-Wan Kenobi in *Star Wars* (1977), he took a percentage of the profits, earning a retirement income. But the great role of his later career was on TV as John Le Carré's spymaster in *Tinker, Tailor, Soldier, Spy* (1979) and *Smiley's People* (1982). Guinness was awarded an honorary Oscar in 1979 in recognition of his achievements in screen acting. **KN**

Top Takes...

Little Dorrit 1988 ☆
A Passage to India 1984
Star Wars 1977 ☆
Hitler: The Last Ten Days 1973
Doctor Zhivago 1965
Lawrence of Arabia 1962
Tunes of Glory 1960
Our Man in Havana 1959
The Horse's Mouth 1958
The Bridge on the River Kwai 1957 ★
The Ladykillers 1955
The Man in the White Suit 1951
The Lavender Hill Mob 1951 ☆
Kind Hearts and Coronets 1949
Oliver Twist 1948
Great Expectations 1946

"An actor . . . can call on heaven and hell to mesmerize a group of innocents."

MARÍA FÉLIX

Born: María de los Ángeles Félix Güereña, April 8, 1914 (Alamos, Sonora, Mexico); died 2002 (Mexico City, Mexico).

Star qualities: Mexican screen legend; voluptuous beauty and femme fatale; leading lady of dramas, often portraying strong women; glamorous.

Top Takes...

La Generala 1971

La Bandida 1963 (*The Bandit*)

La estrella vacía 1960 (*The Empty Star*)

La fièvre monte à El Pao 1959 (*Fever Rises in El Pao*)

La Escondida 1956 (*The Hidden One*)

French Cancan 1954

Camelia 1954

Doña Diabla 1950

Río Escondido 1948 (*Hidden River*)

Enamorada 1946

La Monja alférez 1944 (*The Lieutenant Nun*)

La Mujer sin alma 1944 (*Woman Without a Soul*)

Doña Bárbara 1943

El Peñón de las Ánimas 1943 (*The Rock of Souls*)

Pale-skinned, dark-haired sex siren María Félix is to Spanish-language film audiences what blonde-haired Marilyn Monroe is to English-language moviegoers. Despite making more than 40 films during her career, Félix is little known outside of the Hispanic world because she never ventured to Hollywood. But, like Monroe, she was almost as famous for her life as a femme fatale offscreen as for her smoldering performances onscreen. She was married four times—including to singer/songwriter Agustín Lara and actor and singer Jorge Negrete—widowed twice, and divorced twice. Throughout her life her name was linked with various men, including the Mexican painter and muralist Diego Rivera.

Félix was born one of 16 children of a wealthy family. She studied at the University of Guadalajara, then moved to Mexico City, where she made her film debut in *El Peñón de las Ánimas* (1943) (*The Rock of Souls*). But it was her third movie, *Doña Bárbara* (1943), that catapulted her to stardom and earned her the sobriquet of "La Doña," or "The Dame." The role type of a strong, intelligent, sexy woman was one that Félix made her own, and one that she would return to often throughout her career. She went on to make a string of hit movies, and occasionally ventured into European films, such as Jean Renoir's comedy drama *French Cancan* (1954) and Luis Buñuel's political drama *La fièvre monte à El Pao* (1959) (*Fever Rises in El Pao*). Félix retired from acting in the early 1970s. In later life, she had a home in Paris, where she owned a racehorse stable, as well as her home in Mexico. She died of a heart attack on her eighty-eighth birthday. But even in death Félix hit the headlines when her body was exhumed for tests to investigate claims that she was poisoned. **CK**

> "I cannot complain about men. I have had tons of them and they have treated me fabulously well."

TYRONE POWER

Born: Tyrone Edmund Power Jr., May 5, 1914 (Cincinnati, Ohio, U.S.); died 1958 (Madrid, Spain).

Star qualities: Handsome, clean-cut pinup; swashbuckling in period roles; romantic hero in contemporary dramas; part of an acting dynasty; producer.

Tyrone Power was born into a famous acting dynasty. He was the son of identically named stage star Tyrone Power Sr. and the grandson of the first Tyrone Power, an Irish comedian. Power's parents divorced when he was young, but Power Sr. continued to encourage his son's interest in acting from a distance. In 1931, Power reunited with his father on the New York stage. Sadly, the father/son partnership was cut short that same year when Power Sr. died suddenly from a heart attack.

The young Power went on to pursue his acting dream, and was eventually signed by Twentieth Century Fox in 1936. The studio first starred him in *In Old Chicago* (1937), and kept him on top in lavish musicals such as *Alexander's Ragtime Band* (1938), Westerns such as *Jesse James* (1939), and costume dramas such as *Blood and Sand* (1941). Stiffer than Errol Flynn, he was nevertheless a dashing swordsman in hugely enjoyable swashbucklers—such as *The Mark of Zorro* (1940), *Son of Fury: The Story of Benjamin Blake* (1942), and *The Black Swan* (1942)— but Power soon grew frustrated that his pinup handsomeness barred him from winning more eccentric, demanding roles.

After a stint as a pilot for the Marine Corps during World War II, Power returned to Hollywood, where Twentieth Century Fox finally indulged his ambitions with *The Razor's Edge* (1946) and *Nightmare Alley* (1947). In his role as a bogus mystic, *Nightmare Alley* is Power's best screen work, showing great range. In the 1950s, he acted in a few good cowboy films such as *Rawhide* (1951), but by then he was past his peak. Even so, *The Sun Also Rises* (1957) and *Witness for the Prosecution* (1957) suggest that Power could have successfully switched to character roles if he hadn't been felled by a heart attack on the set of *Solomon and Sheba* in 1958. **KN**

Top Takes...

Witness for the Prosecution 1957
The Sun Also Rises 1957
Pony Soldier 1952
Rawhide 1951
Nightmare Alley 1947
The Razor's Edge 1946
The Black Swan 1942
Son of Fury: The Story of Benjamin Blake 1942
A Yank in the R.A.F. 1941
Blood and Sand 1941
The Mark of Zorro 1940
Brigham Young 1940
The Rains Came 1939
Jesse James 1939
Alexander's Ragtime Band 1938
In Old Chicago 1937

1910s

"I'm sick of all these knights in shining armor parts. I want to do something worthwhile."

LOUIS DE FUNÈS

Born: Louis Germain de Funès de Galarza, July 31, 1914 (Courbevoie, Hauts-de-Seine, France); died 1983 (Nantes, Loire-Atlantique, France).

Star qualities: Diminutive popular French slapstick comic; jazz pianist; balding; skinny; satirist; writer; director; famed for his many facial expressions.

Top Takes…

Le gendarme et les gendarmettes 1982
(Never Play Clever Again)

L'aile ou la cuisse 1976
(The Wing and the Thigh)

Les aventures de Rabbi Jacob 1973
(The Adventures of Rabbi Jacob)

Les grandes vacances 1967 (The Big Vacation)

La grande vadrouille 1966
(Don't Look Now—We're Being Shot At)

Le Grand restaurant 1966
(What's Cooking in Paris)

Fantômas 1964

Le gendarme de St. Tropez 1964
(The Gendarme of St. Tropez)

Un certain monsieur 1949 (A Certain Mister)

La Tentation de Barbizon 1946
(The Temptation of Barbizon)

It has taken the world a while to accept Louis de Funès, but his importance to the comedy genre is now finally acknowledged—and he has proven that bald, skinny, short men can become movie stars. The son of Spanish immigrants to France, de Funès dropped out of school to become a jazz pianist, playing in clubs in the Pigalle district in Paris. He started acting just after World War II, making his film debut in *La Tentation de Barbizon* (1946) (*The Temptation of Barbizon*), and going on to appear in more than 100 roles. His popular breakthrough came with the *Le gendarme de St. Tropez* (1964–1979) (*The Gendarme of St. Tropez*) series, five films centered on a short-tempered police corps commander whose conservative views clash with the mores of the St. Tropez resort holidaymakers.

Ridiculing dignitaries became a constant in de Funès's career. The police force, religion in *Les aventures de Rabbi Jacob* (1973) (*The Adventures of Rabbi Jacob*), and *l'art de cuisinerie*, which he attacked in *L'aile ou la cuisse* (1976) (*The Wing and the Thigh*), all fell victim to his sharp humor. He was also progressive: *La grande vadrouille* (1966) (*Don't Look Now—We're Being Shot At*) poked fun at World War II well before anyone else dared to. Like Peter Sellers, de Funès pushed screen gags beyond their immediate punch line and sustained them across scenes. His blundering Commissaire Juve in *Fantômas* (1964) practically coincided with Sellers's Inspector Clouseau. It enabled him to create characters whose surface might be crude and clumsy, but whose antics and inner conflicts also offer insights into the human psyche. Sadly, although de Funès was enormously successful throughout much of Europe and the former Soviet Union, he never became much of a star in the English-speaking world. **EM**

"Some people are comedians. But as for us, we are actors."

DOROTHY LAMOUR

Born: Mary Leta Dorothy Slaton, December 10, 1914 (New Orleans, Louisiana, U.S.); died 1996 (Los Angeles, California, U.S.).

Star qualities: Beautiful; long dark hair; exotic; singer; wartime forces pinup glamour girl; "The Sarong Girl"; comic timing; played decorative film roles.

In 1931, Dorothy Lamour won the Miss New Orleans title in a beauty contest and then moved to Chicago, Illinois, hoping to become a professional singer. She became a vocalist with the band of Herbie Kay, who also became her first husband. By 1935, she had her own weekly musical program on NBC Radio and also sang on the popular Rudy Vallee radio show. She made her film debut in *Footlight Parade* (1933), but her big break came wrapped tight in a revealing sarong in the title role of *The Jungle Princess* (1936). She then found herself as a succession of exotic native-girl types, usually with South Sea Island settings: *The Hurricane* (1937), *Moon Over Burma* (1940), *Aloma of the South Seas* (1941), and *Beyond the Blue Horizon* (1942), and she became a popular pinup girl.

Road to Singapore* (1940), with Bing Crosby and Bob Hope, gave Lamour essentially the same sarong part, but the Paramount Pictures programmer clicked and began a hugely successful series to which she was essential: "Bet you eight to four that we meet Dorothy Lamour," sing Bing and Bob in *Road to Morocco* (1942). Even though she wore the sarong in only six of her 59 movies, it came to define her career. At the time it was thought that Lamour was just the attractive straight woman, but when she was reduced to a cameo in *Road to Hong Kong* (1962), with Joan Collins in the lead, the formula failed.

Aside from the *Road to . . .* movies, Lamour was in crime films such as *Johnny Apollo* (1940), and musicals such as *Dixie* (1943). In the 1950s, her movie career petered out, but she returned to the Pacific Islands for John Ford's *Donovan's Reef* (1963). Until her death, Lamour was a successful nightclub entertainer and stage and TV actress. Her autobiography, *My Side of the Road*, was published in 1980. **KN**

Top Takes...

Creepshow 2 1987
Won Ton Ton, the Dog Who Saved Hollywood 1976
Donovan's Reef 1963
The Greatest Show on Earth 1952
The Girl from Manhattan 1948
Dixie 1943
Road to Morocco 1942
Aloma of the South Seas 1941
Chad Hanna 1940
Moon Over Burma 1940
Johnny Apollo 1940
Road to Singapore 1940
The Hurricane 1937
The Jungle Princess 1936
Footlight Parade 1933

"I was the happiest and highest paid straight woman in the business."

RICHARD WIDMARK

Born: Richard Widmark, December 26, 1914 (Sunrise, Minnesota, U.S.).

Star qualities: Blond; handsome; slight; character actor; meteoric rise to fame; often played the psychotic villain in film noir and tough characters in Westerns; stagecraft; director; producer.

Top Takes…

Twilight's Last Gleaming 1977
Madigan 1968
Cheyenne Autumn 1964
How the West Was Won 1962
Judgment at Nuremberg 1961
Two Rode Together 1961
The Alamo 1960
The Law and Jake Wade 1958
The Last Wagon 1956
Backlash 1956
The Cobweb 1955
No Way Out 1950
Night and the City 1950
Yellow Sky 1948
The Street with No Name 1948
Kiss of Death 1947 ☆

"You think a squealer can get away from me? Huh?"

—Tommy Udo, *Kiss of Death*

Richard Widmark studied acting before debuting on radio in 1938 in *Aunt Jenny's Real Life Stories*. He hit Broadway in 1943 in *Kiss and Tell*. His iconic film debut was as the sneering, giggling villain Tommy Udo in *Kiss of Death* (1947), for which he won a Best Supporting Actor Academy Award nomination. He also became the first recipient of the Hollywood Foreign Press Association's Golden Globe for Most Promising Newcomer.

Within two years, Widmark was placing his hands and feet in concrete outside Grauman's Chinese Theater. Yet his early success saw him typecast as the heavy in thrillers such as *The Street with No Name* (1948) and *No Way Out* (1950), and in Westerns such as *Yellow Sky* (1948) and *The Law and Jake Wade* (1958). But the blond, handsome Widmark could also play tough and resourceful heroes out West, as seen in *Backlash* (1956) and *The Last Wagon* (1956). A more subtle, demanding role was as the head of a psychiatric clinic in *The Cobweb* (1955).

Widmark appeared in a couple of late John Ford Westerns, in tandem with James Stewart in *Two Rode Together* (1961), in which they have some highly comic scenes, and in *Cheyenne Autumn* (1964). He had a major dramatic role in *Judgment at Nuremberg* (1961), as the prosecuting attorney, and a meaty one as the amoral police detective in Don Siegel's thriller *Madigan* (1968), a role that he retained in the subsequent TV series. Later parts, such as that of a general in *Twilight's Last Gleaming* (1977), and in *Murder on the Orient Express* (1974), were more in the nature of character roles, but he kept working until he retired in 1990 at the age of seventy-six. Widmark was married to Jean Hazlewood, a writer, for 55 years until her death in 1997. He married again, aged eighty-four, to Henry Fonda's ex-wife, Susan Blanchard. **EB**

ANN SHERIDAN

Born: Clara Lou Sheridan, February 21, 1915 (Denton, Texas, U.S.); died 1967 (Los Angeles, California, U.S.).

Star qualities: "The Oomph Girl"; sizzlingly sexy; versatile leading lady of dramas and comedies; glamorous pinup; magnetic screen presence; producer.

Born in Texas, Ann Sheridan was training as a teacher when she won the prize in a local beauty contest—a bit part in a Hollywood film. From 1934 to 1936 she continued in small roles at Paramount Pictures, but the studio made little effort to develop her career and she left. She went on to have her heyday at Warner Brothers between 1936 and 1948. Marketed as "The Oomph Girl," she certainly exuded glamour, but also indicated that she never entirely took such sobriquets seriously. Expert at both comedy and drama, she came across as smart yet sassy, a good-time girl with a head on her shoulders.

Warner Brothers employed Sheridan as the love interest in some notable crime films: *Angels With Dirty Faces* (1938), alongside James Cagney; *They Drive By Night* (1940) with Humphrey Bogart and George Raft; and *City for Conquest* (1940), once again with Cagney. She also appeared twice alongside Errol Flynn in Westerns: *Dodge City* (1939) and *Silver River* (1948), her final movie at Warner Brothers.

On the dramatic front, Sheridan ably appeared in *King's Row* (1942), as well as in two underrated women's pictures, *Nora Prentiss* (1947) and *The Unfaithful* (1947). Her facility with farce drew upon Sheridan's capacity to make fun of herself but never appear unattractive. She more than held her own among the fast-talking banter of Cagney and Pat O'Brien in *Torrid Zone* (1940); ably contributed to the ensemble in *The Man Who Came to Dinner* (1942); and along with Cary Grant galvanized the cross-dressing farce *I Was a Male War Bride* (1949). Sheridan concluded her career as a regular on the TV soap opera *Another World* (1964) and the Western comedy series *Pistols 'n' Petticoats* (1966). She was just experiencing a career revival when she died of cancer in 1967. **DS**

Top Takes…

The Opposite Sex 1956
Woman on the Run 1950
Stella 1950
I Was a Male War Bride 1949
Silver River 1948
The Unfaithful 1947
Nora Prentiss 1947
Shine on Harvest Moon 1944
Edge of Darkness 1943
King's Row 1942
The Man Who Came to Dinner 1942
City for Conquest 1940
They Drive by Night 1940
Torrid Zone 1940
Dodge City 1939
Angels with Dirty Faces 1938

"Being known by a nickname indicates that you're not thought of as a true actress."

ANTHONY QUINN

Born: Antonio Rudolfo Oaxaca Quinn, April 21, 1915 (Chihuahua, Mexico); died 2001 (Boston, Massachusetts, U.S.).

Star qualities: Tall; swarthy good looks; producer; character actor; his Irish and Mexican roots led him to be cast in ethnic roles in English-language films.

Top Takes...

The Shoes of the Fisherman 1968
A High Wind in Jamaica 1965
***Alexis Zorbas* 1964** ☆
(*Zorba the Greek*)
Lawrence of Arabia 1962
The Guns of Navarone 1961
The Savage Innocents 1960
Warlock 1959
***Wild Is the Wind* 1957** ☆
Notre Dame de Paris 1956
(The Hunchback of Notre Dame)
***Lust for Life* 1956** ★
Attila 1954
La Strada 1954 (The Road)
***Viva Zapata!* 1952** ★
They Died with Their Boots On 1941

"I have lived in a flurry of images, but I will go out in a freeze frame."

RIGHT: Quinn sported a false nose to play Auda abu Tayi in the epic *Lawrence of Arabia*.

Anthony Quinn was of Irish and Mexican extraction, but could credibly portray most ethnicities. He played in more than 150 films, and was best known for his lead role in *Alexis Zorbas* (1964) (*Zorba the Greek*), a part that he reprised 20 years later on Broadway. He won two Oscars for Best Supporting Actor: as Marlon Brando's sidekick in *Viva Zapata!* (1952) and as the painter Paul Gauguin in the biopic *Lust for Life* (1956).

He started out in the 1930s, playing thugs, minions, and Native Americans—often warring against the white-eyes, as seen in his portrayal of Crazy Horse in *They Died With Their Boots On* (1941). By the 1950s he was prominent enough to share the screen with heavyweights, and starred opposite Henry Fonda as his psychotic gunslinger devotee in *Warlock* (1959). Quinn ventured abroad to play the strongman for Federico Fellini in *La Strada* (1954) (*The Road*), ravage Europe in, and as, *Attila* (1954), and deliver a plug-ugly Quasimodo in *Notre Dame de Paris* (1956) (*The Hunchback of Notre Dame*).

Thereafter, he straddled the world in various "foreigner" roles in English-language movies, notably as the leader of the Howeitat tribe of Bedouin Arabs in David Lean's *Lawrence of Arabia* (1962). Quinn's personal life was also eventful. He married three times; first to actress Katherine DeMille, the adopted daughter of director Cecil B. DeMille. Tragically, the couple's first child drowned at age three in actor W. C. Fields's swimming pool. Quinn had nine children with his various wives, but fathered 13 children in all. His offscreen passion was art, and he was a successful painter and sculptor. In the 1980s, his artworks began to be exhibited internationally. He also wrote two volumes of memoirs, *The Original Sin* (1972) and *One Man Tango* (1997). **KN**

ORSON WELLES

Born: George Orson Welles, May 6, 1915 (Kenosha, Wisconsin, U.S.); died 1985 (Hollywood, California, U.S.).

Star qualities: Talented actor, director, and writer; child prodigy; conspicuously deep voice; tall; ample in later life.

Top Takes...

Although *Citizen Kane* (1941) is regularly branded one of the greatest movies ever made, and although Orson Welles was the true auteur of the piece, having been lead actor, cowriter, director, and producer, Welles himself is as likely to be remembered as the voice of Unicron in *The Transformers: The Movie* (1986) or the voice of Robin Masters in *Magnum P. I.* (1981). It is precisely this discrepancy between his value to film history on the one hand, and the kitsch of his straightforwardly bankable lesser roles on the other, that puts Welles in such a bad way outside the rarefied field of movie scholars.

It is no joke that the one-time hawker of coffee and narrator of numerous films (*King of Kings*, 1961; *Shogun*, 1980) is also the embodiment of a certain kind of overwrought performance (*Macbeth*, 1948; *Casino Royale*, 1967). That his career is a test case for artistic integrity run aground against the demands of a cutthroat business is a cautionary tale of legendary proportions.

Born in Wisconsin, the son of an inventor father and pianist mother, Welles was a creatively gifted child. Orphaned as a teenager, he made for the stage, finally establishing himself in New York in 1934. Soon afterward he formed the Mercury

RIGHT: Welles starred as a publishing tycoon in *Citizen Kane*, which he also directed.

Theatre with John Houseman, and they began producing a revolutionary series of stage productions and radio broadcasts, such as "The Voodoo Macbeth" and "The War of the Worlds."

Hollywood beckoned in the form of RKO Pictures, whence Welles produced *Citizen Kane* in 1941, a mixed critical success and commercial failure. The next year he made *The Magnificent Ambersons*, a box-office bomb and also his first experience of having work taken out of his hands and recut to suit studio needs. He married his second wife, Rita Hayworth, in 1943, but the relationship was a turbulent one and lasted just five years.

No longer the wunderkind, Welles spent the rest of his days performing in studio pictures (*Jane Eyre*, 1944) to fund his own projects (*Mr. Arkadin*, 1955), while also working in the occasional mainstream gem (*The Third Man*, 1949; *Catch-22*, 1970). In the 1970s his work was reevaluated, partially because of the friendship of Peter Bogdanovich. **GCQ**

ABOVE: Welles shone in the screen adaptation of Graham Greene's *The Third Man*.

The War of the Worlds

"2X2L calling CQ . . . . Isn't there anyone on the air? Isn't there . . . anyone?" On October 30, 1938, Orson Welles and John Houseman sparked a national panic with their radio broadcast of H. G. Wells's novel *The War of the Worlds*. Intended as a Halloween prank, the adaptation simulated a live news bulletin, revealing "events" as they unfolded. In the tense atmosphere surrounding the buildup to World War II, the U.S. public rapidly believed the news of a Martian invasion. Mass hysteria ensued. The broadcast brought Welles instant notoriety, and he was forced to issue a public apology the next day.

YUL BRYNNER

Born: Yuli Borisovich Bryner, July 11, 1915 (Vladivostok, Russia); died 1985 (New York City, New York, U.S.).

Star qualities: Bald shaved head; stagecraft; singer; musician; acrobat; athletic physique; director; producer; played the exotic leading man; iconic "King of Siam."

Top Takes...

"Now that I'm gone, I tell you: Don't smoke, whatever you do, just don't smoke."

The Russian-born Yul Brynner sometimes claimed to be the exotic half-Swiss and half-Japanese "Taidje Khan," although his real life was hardly unexciting. He worked as a musician, acrobat, TV talk show host, and TV director before being cast on Broadway as King Mongkut of Siam in the Rodgers and Hammerstein musical *The King and I* in 1951. He reprised the role in the 1956 film, for which he won the Best Actor Oscar, and was perennially onstage for the rest of his life.

When Brynner's father abandoned the family, his mother took him and his sister to Manchuria, where they went to a Young Men's Christian Association school. The family later moved to Paris, France, where Brynner dropped out of school to become a musician. In 1941, he immigrated to the United States to study acting, and made his stage debut the same year as Fabian in a New York production of *Twelfth Night*.

Bald, polyglot, and imposing, he was hard to cast. He played ancient monarchs in *The Ten Commandments* (1956) and *Solomon and Sheba* (1959), and Russians in *Anastasia* (1956) and *The Brothers Karamazov* (1958). He was amusing as the arrogant conductor in *Once More, With Feeling!* (1960), and did a cameo for old friend Jean Cocteau in *Le Testament d'Orphée ou Ne Me Demandez Pas Pourquoi!* (1960) (*The Testament of Orpheus*). However, he also won pop culture immortality as Chris Adams, most magnificent of *The Magnificent Seven* (1960), and returned in two sequels. Thereafter, he alternated exotic barbarians as in *Taras Bulba* (1962), super-villains such as The Deaf Man in *Fuzz* (1972), and cowboys—although even his Western roles are bizarre, such as an Apache among Mayans in *Kings of the Sun* (1963), and a robot in the science-fiction Western *Westworld* (1973). **KN**

INGRID BERGMAN

Born: Ingrid Bergman, August 29, 1915 (Stockholm, Sweden); died 1982 (London, England).

Star qualities: "Sweden's illustrious gift to Hollywood"; romantic leading lady; versatile performer; elegant, natural beauty; irresistible onscreen and off.

Ingrid Bergman was the protégée of Swedish director Gustaf Molander. In his film *Intermezzo* (1936), she played a young pianist who has an affair with a married man; the whiff of scandal that attended many of her screen roles was later to intrude into her personal life. She had already made around a dozen films in Sweden, but *Intermezzo* was the first in which she could realize her immense potential as an actress capable of both charm and intensity, and it brought her to the attention of Hollywood producer David O. Selznick. Her Hollywood career was launched with a remake of *Intermezzo* in 1939. Selznick lent her out to Warner Brothers to make *Casablanca* (1942), in which she also played a married woman having an affair, this time with Humphrey Bogart. The role established her as one of Hollywood's foremost romantic stars.

Bergman won her first Best Actress Oscar for *Gaslight* (1944), in which she played a wife persecuted by husband Charles Boyer. The next milestone in her career was being directed by Alfred Hitchcock, first in *Spellbound* (1945), then in *Notorious* (1946). In the latter, she costarred with Cary Grant and once

Top Takes...

Höstsonaten 1978 ☆
 (Autumn Sonata)
A Matter of Time 1976
Murder on the Orient Express 1974 ★
The Yellow Rolls-Royce 1964
The Inn of the Sixth Happiness 1958
Indiscreet 1958
Anastasia 1956 ★
Elena et les hommes 1956 (*Elena and her Men*)
Viaggio in Italia 1954 (*Journey to Italy*)
Europa '51 1952 (*The Greatest Love*)
Stromboli 1950
Under Capricorn 1949
Joan of Arc 1948 ☆
Arch of Triumph 1948
Notorious 1946
Saratoga Trunk 1945
The Bells of St. Mary's 1945 ☆
Spellbound 1945
Gaslight 1944 ★
For Whom the Bell Tolls 1943 ☆
Casablanca 1942
Dr. Jekyll and Mr. Hyde 1941
Intermezzo: A Love Story 1939
Intermezzo 1936

LEFT: Bergman gave an Oscar-winning performance as a tormented wife in *Gaslight*.

A Serious Career

Despite a sometimes scandalous private life, which included three marriages and an affair with the war photographer Robert Capa, Ingrid Bergman was nothing but serious about her acting career. "It's the talent and the passion that count in success," she said, and she trained her talent passionately.

- To prepare for her role of Israeli Prime Minister Golda Meir in the TV film *A Woman Called Golda*, Bergman traveled around Israel, interviewing those who had known her and studying old newsreels to master her mannerisms.

- She could speak Swedish, German, English, Italian, and French fluently. After appearing with her in *Murder on the Orient Express*, for which she won an Oscar, actor John Gielgud remarked, "She can speak five languages, but she can't act in any of them." Not jealous, surely?

- During her career, Bergman played Joan of Arc three times; once onstage and in two movies.

- In the 1940s, Bergman took acting lessons from famed Russian coach Michael Chekhov. Ironically, Chekhov's only Academy Award nomination was for his part in *Spellbound*, which also starred Bergman.

- Sweden's most successful actress was ranked the fourth greatest ever screen legend by the American Film Institute.

more played an adulterous wife, although motivated by patriotic impulses: at the instigation of the American secret service, she marries Claude Rains in order to penetrate a Nazi spy ring. It's a bittersweet romance in which Grant is reluctant to show his feelings for her, mistakenly believing she is a slut, and she is too proud to let him know he is wrong. The moment in which they embrace, while Grant makes a fateful phone call, is one of the longest kisses in screen history, and certainly one of the most erotic. Unfortunately her third outing with Hitchcock, *Under Capricorn* (1949), a period romance set in nineteenth-century Australia, was not a success.

Her radiance was overshadowed by scandal

If less classically beautiful than some of her Hollywood contemporaries, Bergman displayed a radiance and emotional integrity on the screen that audiences found irresistible. She was more natural than many other actresses; she had not changed her name for Hollywood, and she wore little makeup. Bergman played more spiritual roles, too: a nun in the very successful *The Bells of St. Mary's* (1945), costarring with Bing Crosby as a priest; St. Joan in *Joan of Arc* (1948); and later a missionary in *The Inn of the Sixth Happiness* (1958). But real-life scandal was to engulf her in 1949 when she traveled to Italy to make a film with director Roberto Rossellini. They fell in love and she became pregnant. Both were already married, Bergman to a Swedish dentist with whom she had a daughter. The relationship caused a huge scandal in the United States and Bergman was no longer welcome there. She moved to Italy to marry Rossellini; one of the children of the union is actress Isabella Rossellini. The pair made three films together: *Stromboli* (1950), *Europa '51* (1952) (*The Greatest Love*), and *Viaggio in Italia* (1954) (*Journey to Italy*), films that were generally disliked in America, where the self-righteous had not forgiven her for her adulterous relationship with the director.

Eventually Bergman's marriage to Rossellini broke down. Her return to American cinema with *Anastasia* (1956) brought her a second Best Actress Oscar, and her public embraced her

1910s

once more. In *Indiscreet* (1958), she renewed her partnership with Cary Grant. Though ill with cancer for the last eight years of her life, she continued to give a series of excellent performances in films both lighthearted—*The Yellow Rolls-Royce* (1964); *Murder on the Orient Express* (1974)—and more serious. Undoubtedly her greatest role in later life was that of Charlotte in *Höstsonaten* (1978) (*Autumn Sonata*)—for which she received an incredible seventh Academy Award nominaton—directed by her Swedish namesake, Ingmar Bergman. Here she plays a concert pianist who has, in the course of devoting herself to her art, neglected her two daughters. Now she is forced to confront them and her possible role in causing the mental breakdown of one of them. Ingrid Bergman died on her birthday at the age of sixty-seven. **EB**

ABOVE: Bergman and Cary Grant get intimate in Alfred Hitchcock's *Notorious*.

"I've gone from saint to whore and back to saint again, all in one lifetime."

ELI WALLACH

Born: Eli Wallach, December 7, 1915 (Brooklyn, New York, U.S.).

Star qualities: Swarthy looks; weather-beaten face; versatile character actor; method trained; famed for tough guy and bandit roles in spaghetti Westerns; makes a charming and plausible villain; stagecraft; producer; writer.

Eli Wallach always considered himself primarily a stage actor—he passed up the Academy Award-winning role eventually played by Frank Sinatra in *From Here to Eternity* (1953) in favor of a Tennessee Williams stage play—but he has had a distinguished film career playing character parts.

Wallach grew up Jewish in an Italian neighborhood of Brooklyn, and first dreamed of being an actor after appearing in a school play when he was fifteen years old. He went to college at the University of Texas, and later trained in Method acting at New York's The Actors Studio. After five years' service in the U.S. army's Medical Administrative Corps during World War II, Wallach returned to the stage. His Broadway debut was in the flop, *Skydrift* (1945), but he went on to success in plays such as *The Rose Tattoo* (1951), for which he won a Tony award.

He impressed in his first screen appearance, *Baby Doll* (1956), another Tennessee Williams adaptation in which he played a sly seducer. In Don Siegel's *The Lineup* (1958) he was a talkative and eccentric hit man, and he was outstanding as the wily bandit Calvera in *The Magnificent Seven* (1960). In *The Misfits* (1961) Wallach held his own against Marilyn Monroe and Clark Gable; whereas playing another villain, the rascally Tuco, opposite Clint Eastwood in Sergio Leone's *Il buono, il brutto, il cattivo* (1966) (*The Good, the Bad and the Ugly*), Wallach stole the picture. Other spaghetti Westerns followed, including *I Quattro dell'Ave Maria* (1968) (*Ace High*) and *Il bianco, il giallo, il nero* (1975) (*Shoot First . . . Ask Questions Later*). He has also worked frequently in TV. More recently, he had a substantial part as Don Altobello in *The Godfather: Part III* (1990), and an uncredited cameo in *Mystic River* (2003). Now in his ninth decade, Wallach is still working. **EB**

Top Takes...

Mystic River 2003
The Godfather: Part III 1990
Tough Guys 1986
Il bianco, il giallo, il nero 1975
  (*Shoot First . . . Ask Questions Later*)
I Quattro dell'Ave Maria 1968 (*Ace High*)
The Tiger Makes Out 1967
Il buono, il brutto, il cattivo 1966
  (*The Good, the Bad and the Ugly*)
The Moon-Spinners 1964
The Victors 1963
The Misfits 1961
The Magnificent Seven 1960
The Lineup 1958
Baby Doll 1956

"Having the critics praise you is like having the hangman say you've got a pretty neck."

FRANK SINATRA

Born: Francis Albert Sinatra, December 12, 1915 (Hoboken, New Jersey, U.S.); died 1998 (Los Angeles, California, U.S.).

Star qualities: The legendary king of swing; songwriter; musicals maestro; instinctive; spontaneous; character actor; leader of the "Rat Pack"; "Ol' Blue Eyes".

Frank Sinatra was important in practically every entertainment medium of the twentieth century: as a live singer, a recording artist, on radio, on film, and on TV. Born to a poor family in New Jersey, Sinatra started out as a singer, forming the Hoboken Four before joining the Harry James band and then the Tommy Dorsey Orchestra. Following numerous performances in nightclubs and on the radio, by 1942 he had established himself as an American idol and respected solo artist.

Sinatra's reputation as a singer made it easy for him to break into acting. His first movie roles were, naturally, in musicals, such as *Anchors Aweigh* (1945), but he lobbied hard for the role of the martyred Private Angelo Maggio in *From Here to Eternity* (1953), for which he won an Academy Award for Best Supporting Actor and emerged as a major character star. An instinctive performer, often dubbed "One-Take Charlie" for his approach to film acting, Sinatra played in high-profile musicals such as *Guys and Dolls* (1955) and *High Society* (1956), as well as taking more dramatically challenging roles in *Suddenly* (1954), as a would-be assassin, and *The Manchurian Candidate* (1962).

With *Ocean's Eleven* (1960), Sinatra began a series of movie romps with his "Rat Pack" colleagues Dean Martin, Sammy Davis Jr., Peter Lawford, and Joey Bishop. Humphrey Bogart, founder of the original "Rat Pack," nicknamed Sinatra "The Chairman of the Board," and the actors' gang's offscreen antics dominated showbiz news for much of the period 1958 to 1963.

His personal life was as interesting as his meteoric career, and as complex as his songs. He married four times, and two of his wives, Ava Gardner and Mia Farrow, were legendary actresses themselves. Sinatra was awarded the Academy's Jean Hersholt Humanitarian Award in 1970. **KN**

Top Takes...

Cannonball Run II 1984
The First Deadly Sin 1980
The Detective 1968
Von Ryan's Express 1965
The Manchurian Candidate 1962
Sergeants 3 1962
Ocean's Eleven 1960
Some Came Running 1958
Pal Joey 1957
High Society 1956
The Man with the Golden Arm 1955 ☆
Guys and Dolls 1955
Suddenly 1954
From Here to Eternity 1953 ★
On the Town 1949
Anchors Aweigh 1945

"'I'm not one of those complicated, mixed-up cats ... I just go on from day to day."

1910s

CURD JÜRGENS

Born: Curd Gustav Andreas Gottlieb Franz Jürgens, December 13, 1915 (Munich, Bavaria, Germany); died 1982 (Vienna, Austria).

Star qualities: Tall; stagecraft; director; writer; lead in serious dramas; Teutonic roots led him to play the villainous foreigner in English-language movies.

Top Takes...

The Spy Who Loved Me 1977

The Mephisto Waltz 1971

Battle of Britain 1969

The Longest Day 1962

Die Dreigroschenoper 1962
(*Three Penny Opera*)

Katia 1959 (*Adorable Sinner*)

The Blue Angel 1959

The Inn of the Sixth Happiness 1958

The Enemy Below 1957

Et Dieu ... créa la femme 1956
(*. . . And God Created Woman*)

Des Teufels General 1955 (*The Devil's General*)

The Mozart Story 1948

Wen die Götter lieben 1942
(*Whom the Gods Love*)

Königswalzer 1935 (*The Royal Waltz*)

"Observe, Mr. Bond, the instruments of Armageddon."
—Karl Stromberg, *The Spy Who Loved Me*

Curd Jürgens—usually billed as "Curt" in English-language films—started out as a journalist before his first wife, actress Louise Basler, persuaded him to try acting. He went on to land stage roles in Vienna, and made his film debut as Kaiser Franz Joseph of Austria in *Königswalzer* (1935) (*The Royal Waltz*). In World War II he was outspokenly critical of the Nazis, which led to Dr. Joseph Goebbels ordering him to be sent to a concentration camp in 1944. Jürgens survived, and he became an Austrian citizen when the war ended.

He had a long career in German films, often playing royalty: Emperor Joseph II in *Wen die Götter lieben* (1942) (*Whom the Gods Love*) and *The Mozart Story* (1948), and Czar Alexander II in *Katia* (1959) (*Adorable Sinner*). He came to international notice as Brigitte Bardot's German lover in the French, Roger Vadim-directed *Et Dieu ... créa la femme* (1956) (*. . . And God Created Woman*). Soon he started landing Nazi roles in English-language movies: a submarine commander in *The Enemy Below* (1957), a major general in *The Longest Day* (1962), and Baron von Richter in *Battle of Britain* (1969).

Jürgens also took on lead roles in forgotten remakes of German classics, such as the professor in *The Blue Angel* (1959) and Mack the Knife in *Die Dreigroschenoper* (1962) (*Three Penny Opera*). His stiff neck unbent a little for a couple of enjoyable horror movies, such as *The Mephisto Waltz* (1971), which starred Alan Alda, and he played one of the more extravagant James Bond villains, crazed shipping magnate Karl Stromberg, in *The Spy Who Loved Me* (1977). An international star who appeared in more than 100 movies, Jürgens was also a prolific stage actor, an occasional film director, and a writer of screenplays. **KN**

1910s

JACKIE GLEASON

Born: Herbert John Gleason, February 26, 1916 (Brooklyn, New York, U.S.); died 1987 (Fort Lauderdale, Florida, U.S.).

Star qualities: Nightclub comedian; composer; musician; writer; director; conductor; veteran TV variety-show performer; character actor in dramas.

Jackie Gleason is so identified with TV and his iconic character of Ralph Kramden and the antics featured on *The Honeymooners* (1955–1956) that it's easy to forget he possessed film credits. He appeared with virtually no professional success in nine films released in 1941 and 1942. They include two Warner Brothers releases: *All Through the Night* (1942) with Humphrey Bogart and *Larceny, Inc.* (1942) with Edward G. Robinson. He capped off this period with two releases featuring the Glenn Miller orchestra, which included Gleason playing the bass: *Orchestra Wives* (1942) and *Springtime in the Rockies* (1942).

Thereafter, Gleason rose to TV stardom, initially as the replacement for William Bendix on *The Life of Riley* (1949), then as the host of the Du Mont network *Cavalcade of Stars* (1950). CBS wooed him on board in 1952. The Kramden character first appeared on *Cavalcade*, but Gleason brought him over to CBS's *The Jackie Gleason Show*, with Art Carney as his sidekick, Ed Norton, and various women as his wife, Alice, until Audrey Meadows became identified with the part.

This meteoric success led to achievements in other media. Gleason received a Tony Award for Best Actor in a Musical in 1960, appearing in *Take Me Along*. Hollywood beckoned once again, as Robert Rossen cast Gleason as the pool champion Minnesota Fats in *The Hustler* (1961), for which he received an Academy Award nomination. He followed up these triumphs with the lauded dramatic performance in *Requiem for a Heavyweight* (1962). Gleason ended his long career with the commercially successful trio of Burt Reynolds's *Smokey and the Bandit* movies (1977, 1980, and 1983) and last appeared as an aging deadbeat father alongside Tom Hanks in *Nothing in Common* (1986). **DS**

Top Takes...

Nothing in Common 1986
Smokey and the Bandit Part 3 1983
The Sting II 1983
The Toy 1982
Smokey and the Bandit II 1980
Smokey and the Bandit 1977
Don't Drink the Water 1969
How to Commit Marriage 1969
Skidoo 1968
Soldier in the Rain 1963
Requiem for a Heavyweight 1962
Gigot 1962
The Hustler 1961 ☆
Orchestra Wives 1942
Larceny, Inc. 1942
All Through the Night 1942

"... don't make life difficult. Just play the melody—and do it the simplest way possible."

STERLING HAYDEN

Born: Sterling Relyea Walter, March 26, 1916 (Montclair, New Jersey, U.S.); died 1986 (Sausalito, California, U.S.).

Star qualities: "The Most Beautiful Man in the Movies!"; tall; blond; rugged good looks; action man of Westerns and film noir; writer.

The House Un-American Activities Committee witch hunts had a baleful effect on many Hollywood careers; one regrettable victim was Sterling Hayden who, having been blacklisted, subpoenaed, and forced to name names, never pursued his career with the enthusiasm he might have.

A sailor, Hayden came to Hollywood with his future first wife Madeleine Carroll in 1940. By 1941, Paramount Studios had started advertising him as "The Most Beautiful Man in the Movies!" and "The Beautiful Blond Viking God." But during World War II he became an undercover agent with the Office of Strategic Services—the predecessor of the CIA—and acted in few films before *Blaze of Noon* (1947). His service in the war included running guns through German lines to the Yugoslav partisans and parachuting into fascist Croatia. He won the Silver Star and a commendation from Yugoslavia's Marshal Tito. His admiration for the communist partisans was one reason for his interest in the communist party in later years.

His rugged virility ensured that he then appeared mainly in Westerns and crime films, notably *The Asphalt Jungle* (1950), *Johnny Guitar* (1954), *Crime Wave* (1954), *Suddenly* (1954), *The Killing* (1956), and *Terror in a Texas Town* (1958). Thereafter he acted sporadically but very effectively in mostly carefully chosen films: as the deranged colonel bringing about the end of the world in *Dr. Strangelove or: How I Learned to Stop Worrying and Love the Bomb* (1964); and as a corrupt police chief in *The Godfather* (1972). None, however, was as powerfully played as the self-loathing, alcoholic, Hemingway-like novelist in *The Long Goodbye* (1973), a magnificent performance for which Hayden clearly drew upon elements of his own life. **GA**

Top Takes...

The Outsider 1980
Winter Kills 1979
King of the Gypsies 1978
Novecento 1976 (*1900*)
The Long Goodbye 1973
The Godfather 1972
Ternos Caçadores 1969 (*Sweet Hunters*)
Dr. Strangelove or: How I Learned to Stop Worrying and Love the Bomb 1964
Terror in a Texas Town 1958
The Killing 1956
Suddenly 1954
Johnny Guitar 1954
Crime Wave 1954
The Asphalt Jungle 1950
Blaze of Noon 1947

"An actor is only a pawn— brilliant sometimes . . . but no less a pawn for that."

GREGORY PECK

Born: Eldred Gregory Peck, April 5, 1916 (La Jolla, California, U.S.); died 2003 (Los Angeles, California, U.S.).

Star qualities: Legendary heroic and romantic-lead actor; tall, athletic physique; stagecraft; charming; suave; producer; noted humanitarian and political liberal.

Gregory Peck entered movies in brooding, handsome, troubled roles, and emerged as one of the United States's most treasured movie stars, representing conviction, decency, intelligence, and moral fortitude. He wowed audiences with his strong physique and suave good looks, and, with four Oscar nominations and one Oscar win, the critical establishment did not fail to acknowledge his talents as an actor.

He made his big-screen debut in 1944, as a resistance fighter in *Days of Glory*, and then won his first Academy Award nomination for his second film role in the same year, as a priest in *The Keys of the Kingdom*. Peck went on to star—mostly as the good guy hero—in more than 60 movies. After worthy performances in *Cape Fear* (1962), *Spellbound* (1945), *Roman Holiday* (1953), and *Moby Dick* (1956), he stoically faced the end of the world in *On the Beach* (1959), and won the war in *The Guns of Navarone* (1961). But it was his role as the small-town defense lawyer Atticus Finch in *To Kill a Mockingbird* (1962) that finally won him an Oscar for Best Actor.

Peck remained a star into old age, and also stuck around to do cameos in remakes of his earlier vehicles *Cape Fear* (1991) and *Moby Dick* (1998). He always chose his roles with great care. Also noted for being civic-minded, for his Roman Catholic faith, and for his liberal politics, he served as president of the Academy Awards body, and was active in the Motion Picture and Television Relief Fund, American Cancer Society, National Endowment for the Arts, and other causes. He won many awards, including the Academy's Jean Hersholt Humanitarian Award in 1967, and a Lifetime Achievement Award from the American Film Institute in 1989, and the Presidential Medal of Freedom for his humanitarian work. **KN**

Top Takes...

Old Gringo 1989
The Boys from Brazil 1978
MacArthur 1977
The Omen 1976
***To Kill a Mockingbird* 1962 ★**
Cape Fear 1962
The Guns of Navarone 1961
Roman Holiday 1953
The Million Pound Note 1953
Captain Horatio Hornblower R.N. 1951
***Twelve O'Clock High* 1949** ☆
***Gentleman's Agreement* 1947** ☆
***The Yearling* 1946** ☆
Spellbound 1945
***The Keys of the Kingdom* 1944** ☆
Days of Glory 1944

"Playing the good guys is more challenging because it's harder to make them interesting."

GLENN FORD

Born: Gwyllyn Samuel Newton Ford, May 1, 1916 (Sainte-Christine, Quebec, Canada); died 2006 (Los Angeles, California, U.S.).

Star qualities: Rugged good looks; the fast gunman in Westerns; the complex guy in comedies; the tough guy hero in film noir; producer.

Top Takes...

Superman 1978
Advance to the Rear 1964
The Courtship of Eddie's Father 1963
Pocketful of Miracles 1961
It Started with a Kiss 1959
The Sheepman 1958 (Stranger with a Gun)
Cowboy 1958
3:10 to Yuma 1957
The Teahouse of the August Moon 1956
The Fastest Gun Alive 1956
Jubal 1956
Blackboard Jungle 1955
The Violent Men 1955 (The Bandits)
Human Desire 1954
The Big Heat 1953
Gilda 1946

Glenn Ford did stage work in California before signing for Columbia Pictures in 1939, but his early career was interrupted by wartime service. *Gilda* (1946), a film noir in which he costarred with Rita Hayworth, put him firmly back in the public eye. Hayworth played the archetypal femme fatale, married to a wealthy casino owner and aiming to settle scores with her former lover Ford, who believes that he hates her whereas he is in fact still in love with her. But despite the film's success, it was not until the 1950s that Ford truly got into his stride, playing a succession of tough, sometimes embittered heroes in a variety of genres. Westerns were a specialty, and he made a series of appearances for director Delmer Daves, including *3.10 to Yuma* (1957), in which he played a rare bad guy. In these and other Westerns, such as *The Violent Men* (1955), Ford gave a series of forceful, edgy performances lightened by flashes of humor.

He was equally at home in the thriller, playing in a brace of Fritz Lang movies, including *The Big Heat* (1953). One of Ford's most acclaimed performances was in the liberal *Blackboard Jungle* (1955), in which he plays a schoolteacher in a tough inner-city school who has to confront unruly pupils and charges of racism while receiving scant support from his peers.

Ford brought great intensity to his roles, but he also had a gift for comedy. *The Courtship of Eddie's Father* (1963) is a deft and charming film, in which Ford plays the father of child star Ron Howard. He was also notable in Frank Capra's *Pocketful of Miracles* (1961). A memorable late performance came in *Superman* (1978), where he played the Kansas farmer who becomes Superman's adoptive father. Each of Ford's four marriages ended in divorce. He had one son, Peter, with his first wife, the actress Eleanor Powell. **EB**

"I think the most ridiculous thing for me to do would be to try and play Shakespeare."

RIGHT: Ford shows he can get tough in the classroom in *Blackboard Jungle* 1955.

1910s

Pp Qq Rr
written (any, no)
y letter.
I wouldn't sa
the ball
barrow
dent.
the (hea
11.
12.
13.
14.
15.
16.

OLIVIA DE HAVILLAND

Born: Olivia Mary de Havilland, July 1, 1916 (Tokyo, Japan).

Star qualities: Beautiful; elegant; intelligent; ambitious; feisty; took on the studio system and won; played the ingenue and later more serious dramatic lead roles; gained five Academy Award nominations.

Top Takes...

Olivia de Havilland was the daughter of a British lawyer and his actress wife, and spent her early years in Tokyo, Japan. When her parents divorced, her family moved to Los Angeles, California. She entered movies as a beautiful teenager, luminous in black and white as Hermia in *A Midsummer Night's Dream* (1935) and Errol Flynn's ladylove in *Captain Blood* (1935), and a vision of pink and pastel loveliness in Technicolor opposite Flynn as Maid Marian in *The Adventures of Robin Hood* (1938), and out West in *Dodge City* (1939).

On loan to MGM from Warner Brothers, she died prettily in *Gone with the Wind* (1939), gaining an Oscar nomination for her trouble. In *The Strawberry Blonde* (1941) she is sweetly funny as a modern girl of the 1890s, trying to impress James Cagney by smoking a cigarette. She supported Bette Davis in *In This Our Life* (1942), but de Havilland grew frustrated by the damsel-in-distress parts offered to her at Warner Brothers, and she began to reject such scripts. At that time the law allowed studios to suspend contract players for rejecting a role, and to add the period of suspension to the contract period. On a six-month suspension, de Havilland sued Warners and won, setting a legal precedent. All performers were to be limited to a seven-year contract that would include any suspensions given out. The court's ruling was known as "De Havilland Law." After 1945 her roles improved, and she won Best Actress Oscars for both *To Each His Own* (1946) and *The Heiress* (1949), and wide acclaim for her depiction of a mentally ill woman in *The Snake Pit* (1948). Her rare later appearances include being menaced by thugs in *Lady in a Cage* (1964). De Havilland is now retired and lives in Paris, France. Her estranged younger sister is the actress Joan Fontaine. **KN**

"Famous people feel that they must perpetually be on the crest of the wave."

MARTHA RAYE

Born: Margaret Teresa Yvonne Reed, August 27, 1916 (Butte, Montana, U.S.); died 1994 (Los Angeles, California, U.S.).

Star qualities: "The Big Mouth"; brash and energetic comedienne; outrageous; powerful singer; dancer; patriotic; wartime forces entertainer; humanitarian.

"Brash" is probably the best way to describe Martha Raye: exuberant regular in the kind of broad, energetic comedies, with big-band interludes, that typified U.S. entertainment in the World War II years.

Her parents were a song-and-dance act, and she was literally born into vaudeville—her mother gave birth backstage. Raye was loud and funny, had rhythm, and could belt out a song. She was noted for her large mouth, which she used to comic effect, earning the sobriquet "The Big Mouth." (It also earned her an income when she became the spokesperson for Polident denture cleanser in the 1970s and 1980s.)

Rarely given a leading role, she upstaged most of the comics on Paramount Pictures's roster in the late 1930s, among them Bob Hope, Bing Crosby, Jack Benny, W. C. Fields, and George Burns and Gracie Allen. A move to Universal Studios in the early 1940s saw her turn up in *Hellzapoppin'* (1941), and she was delightful as identical twins confusing Bud Abbott and Lou Costello in *Keep 'Em Flying* (1941). As one of the eponymous *Four Jills in a Jeep* (1944)—cast on account of her extensive touring with the United Service Organizations (USO) that provided entertainment for troops in the war—she was spotted by Charlie Chaplin. This led to her best role, playing the grotesque and indestructible Annabella Bonheur in the Chaplin-directed *Monsieur Verdoux* (1947).

Her film career petered out after the war, but Raye kept busy on radio and TV. *The Martha Raye Show* ran from 1954 to 1956, and she appeared as a guest star on many other TV programs. Raye continued her work with the USO during the wars in Korea and Vietnam, and when she died, she was buried with full military honors at Fort Bragg, North Carolina. **MC**

Top Takes...

The Concorde: Airport '79 1979
Pufnstuf 1970
Billy Rose's Jumbo 1962
Monsieur Verdoux 1947
Pin Up Girl 1944
Hellzapoppin' 1941
Keep 'Em Flying 1941
Navy Blues 1941
The Boys from Syracuse 1940
The Farmer's Daughter 1940
Never Say Die 1939
The Big Broadcast of 1938 1938
Double or Nothing 1937
Waikiki Wedding 1937
The Big Broadcast of 1937 1936
Rhythm on the Range 1936

1910s

"I didn't have to work till I was three. But after that, I never stopped."

KIRK DOUGLAS

Born: Issur Danielovitch Demsky, December 9, 1916 (Amsterdam, New York, U.S.).

Star qualities: Distinctive cleft chin; rasping voice; edgy, alarming grin; made a convincing cowboy; usually played action villains or irritable characters; humanitarian; head of an acting dynasty.

Born into poverty in New York State to parents of Russian-Jewish ancestry, Kirk Douglas became one of Hollywood's leading men in action and dramatic roles. After some theater experience and war service, he got his big break in the film noir *The Strange Love of Martha Ivers* (1946). Another film noir, *Out of the Past* (1947) followed, along with one of his most striking performances as the ruthless boxer who will stop at nothing to win the title in *Champion* (1949).

Douglas, with his cleft chin and menacing grin, was ideal casting for cynical or edgy characters, or on occasion out-and-out villains, such as the exploitative newspaperman in Billy Wilder's *Ace in the Hole* (1951) or the out-of-control policeman in William Wyler's *Detective Story* (1951). He was compelling as the megalomaniac movie producer in *The Bad and the Beautiful* (1952), and convincing as Vincent van Gogh hovering on the edge of insanity in *Lust for Life* (1956). Westerns were something of a specialty: he played Doc Holliday opposite Burt Lancaster's Wyatt Earp in *Gunfight at the O.K. Corral* (1957); starred opposite Rock Hudson in *The Last Sunset* (1961); and was memorable as a modern-day cowboy in *Lonely Are the Brave* (1962).

Top Takes…

Oscar 1991
Tough Guys 1986
Saturn 3 1980
The Villain 1979
The Fury 1978
There Was a Crooked Man 1970
The Way West 1967
Cast a Giant Shadow 1966
In Harm's Way 1965
Seven Days in May 1964
For Love or Money 1963
Lonely Are the Brave 1962
The Last Sunset 1961
Spartacus 1960
The Vikings 1958
Paths of Glory 1957
Gunfight at the O.K. Corral 1957
Lust for Life 1956 ☆
The Bad and the Beautiful 1952 ☆
Detective Story 1951
Ace in the Hole 1951
Champion 1949 ☆
Out of the Past 1947
The Strange Love of Martha Ivers 1946

RIGHT: Douglas gave a strong performance as the rebellious title character in *Spartacus*.

Two of Douglas's outstanding performances came in films directed by Stanley Kubrick. In *Paths of Glory* (1957) he plays Colonel Dax of the French army, defending his men against charges of cowardice during World War I. And in the epic *Spartacus* (1960) he brought power and intensity to the title role of the slave who led a revolt against Imperial Rome. Douglas was instrumental in overturning the blacklisting policies that had plagued Hollywood throughout the 1950s, breeding suspicion and ruining numerous promising careers. When Kubrick tried to take credit for the *Spartacus* screenplay, Douglas rebelled, insisting that the blacklisted screenwriter, Dalton Trumbo, be given an onscreen acknowledgment.

Douglas could do comedy, too. He is delightfully devious in the Western *There Was a Crooked Man* . . . . (1970), and in *Tough Guys* (1986) he was reunited with Burt Lancaster. His son, Michael Douglas, is also a successful actor and producer. **EB**

Best Buddies?

Kirk Douglas and Burt Lancaster made seven movies together, and the actors were perceived to be good friends. But the "friendship" was not always rosy, and may have been invented for publicity's sake.

- Douglas, the shorter actor at five feet, nine inches, wore lifts in many of his movies to add stature onscreen. Once, as a prank, Lancaster hid Douglas's lifts during filming, causing great annoyance.

- Douglas on Lancaster: "I've finally gotten away from Burt Lancaster. My luck has changed for the better. I've got nice-looking girls in my films now."

BETTY GRABLE

Born: Elizabeth Ruth Grable, December 18, 1916 (St. Louis, Missouri, U.S.); died 1973 (Santa Monica, California, U.S.).

Star qualities: Iconic pinup beauty; "The Girl with the Million Dollar Legs"; curvaceous; wholesomely sexy; wartime forces sweetheart; singer; dancer.

Since the rigid implementation of the Hays Code in 1934, the goddess model typified by Greta Garbo had replaced earlier, franker depictions of female sexuality. World War II brought with it a need for a freer, less monumental kind of glamour, but the Hays Code still regulated how much blatant eroticism was permitted. The solution was the "sweater girl": healthy, fresh-scrubbed girls-next-door whose sportiness incidentally meant that they were often seen in tight sweaters and shorts. Betty Grable's good fortune was to personify this new archetype more wholly and entirely than any other star.

A performer since aged only thirteen, Grable could sing and dance and—an asset in the atmosphere of wartime gloom—project optimism. Careful gimmicks such as insuring her legs with Lloyd's of London for a million dollars, and hailing her as the favorite pinup of forces overseas, all meant that she swiftly became a totemic figure, whose actual films were of secondary importance. She was Hollywood's top draw in 1943, and was reported to be the highest paid woman in the United States, earning $300,000 a year. Ironically, her famous bathing suit pinup photo—in which she had her back to the camera, and glanced back over one shoulder—was posed in such a way out of necessity rather than sauciness, because she was several months' pregnant when the picture was taken. Her movies included a number of 1940s hits such as *Moon Over Miami* (1941), *Springtime in the Rockies* (1942), and *Coney Island* (1943).

After the war she was no longer of vital importance, but Twentieth Century Fox kept her busy to the point of working her to exhaustion. In her last major role, she was as good as her costars, Lauren Bacall and Marilyn Monroe, in *How to Marry a Millionaire* (1953). **MC**

Top Takes...

"There are two reasons why I'm in show business, and I'm standing on both of them."

ERNEST BORGNINE

Born: Ermes Effron Borgnine, January 24, 1917 (Hamden, Connecticut, U.S.).

Star qualities: Thick-set physique; grizzled looks; solid character actor and major supporting star; often played middle-aged heavies in dramas and Westerns; animation voice-over artist; producer.

The son of Italian immigrants, Ernest Borgnine spent ten years in the navy before going to drama school. His big break came in 1949, when he made his Broadway acting debut as a male nurse in *Harvey*. A few years later he made his movie debut, playing Bill Street in *The Whistle at Eaton Falls* (1951). With this and successive performances, Borgnine proved himself to be a capable and versatile character actor.

Borgnine won a Best Actor Academy Award for his personification of Paddy Chayefsky's inarticulate Italian butcher Marty Piletti in the film adaptation of *Marty* (1955), beating stiff competition from the likes of Spencer Tracy and James Dean. Broader and more sentimental than Rod Steiger's TV original—the Martys team as heavies in *Jubal* (1956)—the performance wears less well than Borgnine's many other supporting thugs, notably the sadistic Sergeant James "Fatso" Judson in *From Here to Eternity* (1953), Borgnine's big break; an outlaw in *Johnny Guitar* (1954); the cowboy thrown by Spencer Tracy's judo in *Bad Day at Black Rock* (1955); and the lusty chieftain jumping into a pit of wolves in *The Vikings* (1958).

He starred in the TV sitcom *McHale's Navy* (1962–1966), and its 1964 big-screen incarnation, and made a cameo appearance in the 1997 remake. But he also continued to work in strong roles for manly directors such as Robert Aldrich—as an officer in *The Dirty Dozen* (1967) and the brutal railroad bull in *Emperor of the North Pole* (1973). He was also enjoyable as the bullying boss eaten by rats in *Willard* (1971) and as a redneck demon in *The Devil's Rain* (1975). Borgnine continues to work, and has appeared in more than 100 feature films to date. He also does voice-over work, notably as Mermaid Man on TV's *SpongeBob SquarePants* (1999–2005). **KN**

Top Takes...

1910s

"Everything I do has a moral to it . . . . The moral was that, by golly, bad guys got it."

DEAN MARTIN

Born: Dino Paul Crocetti, June 7, 1917 (Steubenville, Ohio, U.S.); died 1995 (Beverly Hills, California, U.S.).

Star qualities: Iconic laid-back crooner; comedian; "Rat Pack" member; handsome; cool; stylish; trademark cigarette and glass of alcohol as a nightclub singer.

Top Takes...

Of all the relaxed ballad singers of the postwar period, Dean "Dino" Martin was the most laid-back. Though technically accomplished, he never seemed to take himself seriously, onstage or off. His film career had several distinct modes. First came his music/comedy partnership with comedian Jerry Lewis. The pair became known as "The Monkey and the Organ Grinder," and their nightclub act led to films such as *Artists and Models* (1955), *Pardners* (1956), and *Hollywood or Bust* (1956).

After ten years together, differences between the pair became intolerable and, in 1956, they parted. Martin lost no time in proving himself a serious actor of considerable talent, in *The Young Lions* (1958), *Some Came Running* (1958), and *Rio Bravo* (1959), in which he played John Wayne's deputy, trying to shake off alcoholism and an unhappy love affair. The scene where, stung by Wayne's disdain, he pours a drink of whiskey back in the bottle without spilling a drop, remains a classic.

In the heist movie *Ocean's Eleven* (1960) Martin appeared with other members of the so-called "Rat Pack," including Frank Sinatra and Sammy Davis Jr. After this his roles were mainly undemanding, in such unambitious films as the Western *Texas Across the River* (1966). One later performance stands out, however: his self-parody as the skirt-chasing Dino in Billy Wilder's *Kiss Me, Stupid* (1964). He also made a huge mark in TV with *The Dean Martin Show* (1965–1974), which won him a Golden Globe Award in 1965. The show format continued under different names until 1984. Martin was famed for the glass of alcohol that accompanied him onstage, but his son has since asserted that it actually contained apple juice. And, in spite of his reputation as a womanizer, Martin was devoted to his family. **EB**

"Hard work, perseverance, and discipline: the things you need when you have no talent."

SUSAN HAYWARD

Born: Edythe Marrener, June 30, 1917 (Brooklyn, New York, U.S.); died 1975 (Hollywood, California, U.S.).

Star qualities: Redheaded beauty; porcelain complexion; curvaceous; glamorous; drawling voice; ambitious; determined; played serious lead dramatic roles.

Susan Hayward began her career as a model before catching the attention of director George Cukor in 1937. Modeling pictures of the striking redhead in the *Saturday Evening Post* prompted his invitation to test for the role of Scarlett O'Hara in *Gone with the Wind* (1939), but, like hundreds of others, Hayward lost out to Vivien Leigh.

Deciding to stay in Hollywood, she landed a number of bit parts before being cast opposite Gary Cooper in *Beau Geste* (1939). This performance qualified her for a number of other leading-lady roles—twice opposite John Wayne, in *Reap the Wild Wind* (1942) and *The Fighting Seabees* (1944)—before receiving the first of five Oscar nominations for her role as an alcoholic nightclub singer in *Smash-Up: The Story of a Woman* (1947). In 1949, Hayward was nominated again for *My Foolish Heart* (1949), and in 1953 for *With a Song in My Heart* (1952).

Hayward was best playing tortured women. She earned her fourth Academy Award nomination for her portrayal of another alcoholic in *I'll Cry Tomorrow* (1955), before finally winning the coveted Best Actress Oscar in 1958 for her gritty performance of real-life killer Barbara Graham in *I Want to Live!* (1958), which is considered by many to be one of the finest screen performances of all time. Her last film was *The Revengers* (1972), before cancer-related pneumonia claimed her life in 1975 at the age of fifty-six. Her diagnosis of brain cancer three years earlier was allegedly the result of being exposed to radioactive toxins, from nuclear tests, on location in Utah while making *The Conqueror* (1956). All the leads in the movie—John Wayne, Agnes Moorehead, John Hoyt, Hayward, and the director Dick Powell—died of cancer. The validity of the claim is still being debated. **DW**

Top Takes...

The Revengers 1972
Valley of the Dolls 1967
Where Love Has Gone 1964
Ada 1961
I Want to Live! 1958 ★
I'll Cry Tomorrow 1955 ☆
With a Song in My Heart 1952 ☆
My Foolish Heart 1949 ☆
The Lost Moment 1947
They Won't Believe Me 1947
Smash-Up: The Story of a Woman 1947 ☆
The Fighting Seabees 1944
Jack London 1943
The Forest Rangers 1942
Reap the Wild Wind 1942
Beau Geste 1939

"I never thought of myself as a movie star. I'm just a working girl."

ROBERT MITCHUM

Born: Robert Charles Durman Mitchum, August 6, 1917 (Bridgeport, Connecticut, U.S.); died 1997 (Santa Barbara, California, U.S.).

Star qualities: Pinnacle of movie star cool; charismatic leading man; often played the antihero in Westerns and romantic dramas; film noir icon.

Top Takes…

Dead Man 1995
Cape Fear 1991
The Last Tycoon 1976
Ryan's Daughter 1970
The Longest Day 1962
Cape Fear 1962
The Night of the Hunter 1955
Second Chance 1953
Angel Face 1952
Where Danger Lives 1950
The Big Steal 1949
Blood on the Moon 1948
Rachel and the Stranger 1948
Out of the Past 1947
Crossfire 1947
Story of G.I. Joe 1945 ☆

"Listen. I got three expressions: looking left, looking right, and looking straight ahead."

Robert Mitchum is one of the quintessential cinematic representations of twentieth-century U.S. masculinity, in no small part because he embodies a series of complexities and apparent contradictions: Mitchum is laconic, lazy, disheveled, and brutish—just as he is also erudite, intelligent, sophisticated, and passionate—often in the same role. Mitchum is also a testament to the sheer power of natural charisma in the U.S. movie star, for he appeared only in a comparatively small number of worthwhile films throughout his career. Iconic roles, such as the demonic preacher in *The Night of the Hunter* (1955) and the psychopathic ex-con in the original *Cape Fear* (1962), are scarce in a filmography dominated by fairly undistinguished Westerns, thrillers, and war movies that rarely used Mitchum's unique screen presence to its fullest.

Mitchum began an acting career after he was discharged from the army during World War II. He appeared in several minor roles in the mid-1940s before achieving greater fame with his only Oscar-nominated performance in *Story of G.I. Joe* (1945). More significant films followed, such as the critically acclaimed *Crossfire* (1947) and the noir classic *Out of the Past* (1947). But Mitchum was at the peak of his stardom during the 1950s, after his rugged antisocial, antihero persona was enlivened by a pot-possession bust. However, even during this decade of success, the films were seldom as riveting as Mitchum himself, and he worked more infrequently, albeit still steadily, during the 1960s and 1970s, appearing in many forgettable international coproductions and television series. Although he often threatened retirement, Mitchum acted until his death, appearing in films such as Martin Scorsese's *Cape Fear* (1991) remake. **TC**

JUNE ALLYSON

Born: Eleanor Geisman, October 7, 1917 (The Bronx, New York, U.S.); died 2006 (Ojai, California, U.S.).

Star qualities: Petite blonde beauty; dancer; husky voice; determined; played girl-next-door roles in musicals, comedies, and dramas.

June Allyson was brought up in near poverty by her divorced mother. She was injured in a cycling accident when she was eight years old, and told by doctors that she would not walk again. She spent the next four years wearing a steel brace, and regained her health with a regimen of swimming and dancing. She started to enter dance competitions in her teens, and went on to make her Broadway debut in the 1938 musical *Sing Out the News*, and to appear in musical film shorts such as *Dime a Dance* (1937). She made her feature debut in a Lucille Ball vehicle, *Best Foot Forward* (1943).

After appearing as a peppy, good-humored ornament in the likes of *Two Girls and a Sailor* (1944) and *Good News* (1947), she rose to leading roles, most happily cast as Jo March in *Little Women* (1949). After playing the wife of James Stewart's baseball player in the biopic *The Stratton Story* (1949), she became typecast as the perfect 1950s wife—a military or sports widow—standing by her husband in two more biopics, Stewart again in *The Glenn Miller Story* (1953) and Alan Ladd in *The McConnell Story* (1955).

Allyson's throaty, sexy voice was slightly at odds with her starched blonde looks, which served her well in melodramas such as *Woman's World* (1954) and comedies such as *My Man Godfrey* (1957). A big star in the 1950s, in 1955 she was voted second-most-popular female star, behind Grace Kelly. In later decades, Allyson worked in TV with her first husband, actor and director Dick Powell, in *The Dick Powell Show* (1961–1963), and did guest spots on the likes of *The Incredible Hulk* (1979). Her most distinctive late career film role found her trashing her good-gal image by playing a psycho in *They Only Kill Their Masters* (1972). **KN**

Top Takes…

Blackout 1978
They Only Kill Their Masters 1972
My Man Godfrey 1957
The Opposite Sex 1956
The McConnell Story 1955
Strategic Air Command 1955
Woman's World 1954
Executive Suite 1954
The Glenn Miller Story 1953
Battle Circus 1953
The Stratton Story 1949
Little Women 1949
The Three Musketeers 1948
Good News 1947
Two Girls and a Sailor 1944
Best Foot Forward 1943

"I'm not a career woman … I'd just as soon stay home and raise babies."

JOAN FONTAINE

Born: Joan de Havilland, October 22, 1917 (Tokyo, Japan).

Star qualities: Beautiful; elegant; intelligent; ambitious; part of an acting family; played serious lead roles in melodramas; excelled in roles as innocent young women who suffer at the hands of others.

Top Takes…

The Witches 1966 (*The Devil's Own*)
Tender Is the Night 1962
Voyage to the Bottom of the Sea 1961
Beyond a Reasonable Doubt 1956
Ivanhoe 1952
Kiss the Blood Off My Hands 1948
Letter from an Unknown Woman 1948
Ivy 1947
The Affairs of Susan 1945
Frenchman's Creek 1944
Jane Eyre 1944
The Constant Nymph 1943 ☆
Suspicion 1941 ★
Rebecca 1940 ☆
The Women 1939
Gunga Din 1939

"I married first … and if I die first, [Olivia]'ll undoubtedly be livid because I beat her to it!"

Joan Fontaine changed her name to avoid comparison with her elder sister, the actress Olivia de Havilland. She was the daughter of a British patent lawyer and his actress wife, and spent her early years in Japan before moving to Los Angeles, California. She became a star as The Second Mrs. de Winter in Alfred Hitchcock's romantic drama *Rebecca* (1940), for which she received an Oscar nomination. But she had already served time as left-back-at-the-fort damsels, as in *Gunga Din* (1939), and in the shadow of divas, as in *The Women* (1939). Hitchcock cast her as another worried wife in *Suspicion* (1941), for which she won a Best Actress Oscar, which was widely, if unjustly, seen as a consolation prize for losing with *Rebecca*.

Ironically, the year Fontaine won her Oscar, her sister Olivia was also nominated, for her role as Emmy Brown in *Hold Back the Dawn* (1941). The rivalry between the two sisters was always reported to be intense, but Fontaine's win is said to have strained relations further. Several years later, de Havilland did win an Oscar, and famously snubbed her sister at the ceremony. By the 1970s the sisters had stopped speaking.

Throughout the 1940s, Fontaine was an A-list choice for leading female roles, often adaptations of best sellers: *The Constant Nymph* (1943); *Jane Eyre* (1944); and *Frenchman's Creek* (1944). Slightly nasal suffering seemed her note, but she did comedy too, as shown by her role in *The Affairs of Susan* (1945). Fontaine had an interesting period as femme fatale in films such as *Ivy* (1947) before landing the apotheosis of put-upon crinoline roles in Max Ophüls's widely acclaimed *Letter from an Unknown Woman* (1948). In the 1950s, Fontaine was rarely used well. She is now retired, and lives in seclusion in Carmel, California. **KN**

PEDRO INFANTE

Born: José Pedro Infante Cruz, November 18, 1917 (Mazatlán, Sinaloa, Mexico); died 1957 (Mérida, Yucatán, Mexico).

Star qualities: Icon of Mexican cinema; handsome; singer; prolific output; charming; leading man across a range of genres; often played the Mexican everyman.

Pedro Infante was a superstar, not just in his native Mexico, but throughout Latin America. He appeared in more than 60 movies, many of which are still watched on TV in Mexico today. Never typecast, he played in comedies and romances alike, one minute playing the macho, the next the romantic hero, and the next the clown.

His fame is also down to his singing talent, and he recorded hundreds of popular songs. These ranged from cha-cha-chas and waltzes to boleros, or ballads, such as "Así es la vida" (1943) ("Such Is Life"), and saw him work with popular composers and some of the region's foremost mariachi and ranchera bands. Music was in Infante's genes, since his father was a musician. Infante started out making a living as a carpenter, but encouraged by his father, he aspired to be a musician and used his carpentry skills to make his own guitar. He made his singing debut at a local festival in 1937, then headed toward Mexico City where he won a spot on a local radio station. He was soon playing concert halls, and won a recording contract.

His film debut came in *El Organillero* (1939), which led to a string of hits during the next two decades. He is perhaps most famous for the trilogy *Nosotros, los pobres* (1948) (*We the Poor*), *Ustedes, los ricos* (1948) (*You the Rich*), and *Pepe El Toro* (1953), which portrays the life of the Mexican working class. The character he created, Pepe "El Toro," has since become a symbol of Mexican culture.

Offscreen, Infante was a keen pilot, but this was also to lead to his tragic early demise, when he was killed in a plane crash near Mérida, Yucatán. His death was declared a national day of mourning in Mexico, and when his coffin arrived in Mexico City, many thousands of his fans besieged the airport. **CK**

Top Takes...

Escuela de rateros 1958
Tizoc 1957
Pablo y Carolina 1957
Escuela de música 1955 (*Music School*)
Escuela de vagabundos 1955
   (*School for Tramps*)
Cuidado con el amor 1954 (*Watch Out for Love*)
Dos tipos de cuidado 1953
Pepe El Toro 1953
¡¿Qué te ha dado esa mujer?! 1951
A.T.M.: ¡¡A toda máquina!! 1951 (*A.T.M.*)
Ustedes, los ricos 1948 (*You the Rich*)
Nosotros, los pobres 1948 (*We the Poor*)
Los Tres García 1947
Vuelven los García 1947
El Organillero 1939

1910s

"I am who I am, and that is like nobody else!"

OSSIE DAVIS

Born: Raiford Chatman Davis, December 18, 1917 (Cogdell, Georgia, U.S.); died 2005 (Miami Beach, Florida, U.S.).

Star qualities: African-American icon; stagecraft; outspoken civil rights activist; fought against limited African-American roles; writer; producer; director.

Top Takes...

She Hate Me 2004
Doctor Dolittle 1998
I'm Not Rappaport 1996
Get on the Bus 1996
The Client 1994
Grumpy Old Men 1993
Malcolm X 1992
Jungle Fever 1991
Joe Versus the Volcano 1990
Do the Right Thing 1989
School Daze 1988
The House of God 1984
Let's Do It Again 1975
The Hill 1965
Shock Treatment 1964
No Way Out 1950

A writer, playwright, activist, director, and actor with the talents to match his ambitions, Ossie Davis was a major presence on stage and screen (and behind the scenes) for several decades of his fruitful and productive life. Born in Cogdell, Georgia, Davis attended Howard University in Washington, D.C., before moving to New York and trying to get his start in theater. During World War II he worked as a surgical technician in the military, where he wrote plays for the troops. After the war, he made his Broadway debut in *Jeb* (1946). His leading lady was actress Ruby Dee, whom he married in 1948, and the couple would remain virtually inseparable until his death in 2005. Davis made his film debut in *No Way Out* (1950) alongside Sidney Poitier, and appeared in numerous movies, stage productions, and TV shows before making his directorial debut with *Cotton Comes to Harlem* (1970), which he also wrote for the screen and scored.

While he found regular work on stage and screen (both movies and TV), Davis also demonstrated his oratory prowess as a key force in the U.S. Civil Rights movement. He spoke at the funerals of both Martin Luther King and Malcolm X, and stayed politically active and outspoken throughout his career.

In the mid-1980s, Davis found a kindred spirit in director and fellow activist Spike Lee, lending his stature as an African-American icon to seven of the director's films, including a memorable turn as Da Mayor (sharing the screen with Dee) in Lee's *Do the Right Thing* (1989). His funeral was attended by a number of notable names, including former U.S. President Bill Clinton, who said of Davis, "He would have been a very good president of the United States. Like most of you here, he gave more to me than I gave to him." **JK**

> "Any form of art is a form of power . . . it can not only move us, it makes us move."

IDA LUPINO

Born: Ida Lupino, February 4, 1918 (Camberwell, London, England); died 1995 (Los Angeles, California, U.S.).

Star qualities: "The poor man's Bette Davis"; played serious dramatic lead roles; director; writer; producer; pioneering female filmmaker.

Although she would undoubtedly be familiar to anyone who watched films and television throughout the 1940s and 1950s, Ida Lupino is not nearly as recognizable to younger generations today, and that's both tragic and inexplicable. Lupino was not only one of the strongest female leads in films from that era—capable of matching her male costars Humphrey Bogart, Edward G. Robinson, Richard Widmark, and Robert Ryan in toughness and force—but also a pioneering female director, helming B-movie thrillers and socially conscious dramas that were as intense as her performances.

Lupino came to Hollywood in her late teens, and appeared in mostly minor roles throughout the 1930s. Interestingly, her career ascension mirrored the success of another prolific 1930s working actor who became a star at the onset of the 1940s and the emergence of film noir: Bogart. They appeared together twice, in *They Drive by Night* (1940) and *High Sierra* (1941), films that would prove to be significant advances for both actors.

Lupino continued to be a strong presence throughout thrillers and dramas of the 1940s, but as that decade drew to a close, she became unhappy with the roles being offered to her and decided to focus—notably courageously for a woman at that time—on directing. Both the rape drama *Outrage* (1950) and the riveting, outstanding, noirish thriller *The Hitch-Hiker* (1953) are among her best directing work.

During the 1950s, Lupino gradually turned her attentions—as both actor and director—to TV, where she largely worked until her retirement in the late 1970s. She was also rumored to have directed some of Nicholas Ray's brilliant *On Dangerous Ground* (1952) when he became ill during shooting. Her last screen appearance was in *My Boys Are Good Boys* (1978). **TC**

Top Takes...

My Boys Are Good Boys 1978
Junior Bonner 1972
While the City Sleeps 1956
Women's Prison 1955
Jennifer 1953
Beware, My Lovely 1952
On Dangerous Ground 1952
Woman in Hiding 1950
Road House 1948
The Hard Way 1943
Life Begins at Eight-Thirty 1942
Ladies in Retirement 1941
The Sea Wolf 1941
High Sierra 1941
They Drive by Night 1940
The Light That Failed 1939

"... at the tender age of thirteen, I set upon the path of playing nothing but hookers."

WILLIAM HOLDEN

Born: William Franklin Beedle Jr., April 17, 1918 (O'Fallon, Illinois, U.S.); died 1981 (Santa Monica, California, U.S.).

Star qualities: "The Golden Boy"; captivating; handsome clean-cut looks; witty; sexual magnetism; character actor and romantic lead in action films.

Top Takes…

The Earthling 1980
Network 1976 ☆
The Towering Inferno 1974
The Wild Bunch 1969
The World of Suzie Wong 1960
The Bridge on the River Kwai 1957
Picnic 1955
Love Is a Many-Splendored Thing 1955
The Country Girl 1954
Sabrina 1954
Executive Suite 1954
The Moon Is Blue 1953
Stalag 17 1953 ★
Born Yesterday 1950
Sunset Blvd. 1950 ☆
Golden Boy 1939

"Movie acting may not have a certain kind of glory as true art, but it is damn hard work."

At age twenty-one, William Holden's first major film role was in the boxing drama *Golden Boy* (1939), and that nickname stuck: much of Holden's career was spent playing charming, romantic leading men and daring heroes in often-formulaic adventure fare. Some have withstood the test of time, such as *Sabrina* (1954), *Love is a Many-Splendored Thing* (1955), and *The Bridge on the River Kwai* (1957), whereas many have been largely forgotten over the decades. But Holden was never less than a captivating, handsome, witty screen presence, the kind of actor who seems clearly destined for stardom.

True admirers of the actor probably respond more profoundly to the other Holden. In his most memorable performances, Holden displays a deep sadness, a sense of insecurity and self-loathing beneath the masculine magnetism. In retrospect, the complexity behind these roles could perhaps be linked to the inner distress Holden experienced in his personal life: he was significantly debilitated by alcoholism; numerous marriage-wrecking infidelities—with, rumor has had it, some of Hollywood's leading ladies of the time; and self-doubt regarding his abilities. Holden allowed a darker side of the U.S. male to creep into his acting, particularly as he grew older. The most remarkable of his performances are not the suave romantic leads, but rather characterizations such as the cynical sergeant in *Stalag 17* (1953), the hack writer in *Sunset Blvd.* (1950), the weary bandit leading Sam Peckinpah's *The Wild Bunch* (1969), and the defeated news producer of *Network* (1976). Sadly, Holden died in 1981 from head injuries incurred during a bout of heavy drinking. One suspects that his best performances could have been ahead of him in his later years. **TC**

ROBERT PRESTON

Born: Robert Preston Meservey, June 8, 1918 (Newton Highlands, Massachusetts, U.S.); died 1987 (Montecito, California, U.S.).

Star qualities: Charismatic; distinctive gravelly voice; versatile; comic timing; stagecraft; musician; mature character actor; booming vocalist of musicals.

Robert Preston is one of those performers who had a long and distinguished career, but would be unremembered if he hadn't landed one particular role. Preston is astonishing in his role as con man Professor Harold Hill in the hit movie *The Music Man* (1962). For the film, he recreated the star performance he had given on Broadway a few years earlier in the Meredith Willson musical, for which he won a Tony Award in 1958. Ironically, it was not only Preston's first performance in a musical, but the first time he had ever sung a note in public. It was this role that brought him into the limelight, and from then on he alternated between movies and the theater.

Born the son of a garment worker and a record store clerk, Preston was raised in Los Angeles. He trained as a musician—although he was never a singer—before becoming interested in acting. He studied drama at the Pasadena Community Playhouse and started to take part in plays there. It was during one such performance that Preston was spotted by a talent scout for Paramount Pictures and offered a contract.

From his movie debut in *King of Alcatraz* (1938), Preston spent a whole career on the big screen as a stalwart, welcome second-in-command: he was Digby Geste to Gary Cooper's *Beau Geste* (1939) and a cop on the case upstaged by the crook, Alan Ladd, in *This Gun for Hire* (1942). After his acclaimed performance in *The Music Man*, he got a few unusual older roles, and his gravelly tones were always welcome in roles like that of the rodeo father in *Junior Bonner* (1972). But Preston's finest hour was as a flamboyant, homosexual cabaret artist, opposite Julie Andrews, in Blake Edwards's *Victor/Victoria* (1982), for which he received an Academy Award nomination for Best Supporting Actor. **KN**

Top Takes...

The Last Starfighter 1984
Victor/Victoria 1982 ☆
Mame 1974
Junior Bonner 1972
How the West Was Won 1962
The Music Man 1962
The Dark at the Top of the Stairs 1960
The Last Frontier 1955
Wake Island 1942
This Gun for Hire 1942
Reap the Wild Wind 1942
Parachute Battalion 1941
Typhoon 1940
Beau Geste 1939
Union Pacific 1939
King of Alcatraz 1938

1910s

"I'd get the best role in every B picture and the second best in the A pictures."

RITA HAYWORTH

Born: Margarita Carmen Cansino, October 17, 1918 (Brooklyn, New York, U.S.); died 1987 (New York City, New York, U.S.).

Star qualities: "The Love Goddess"; dancer; intense sexual magnetism; inherent beauty; World War II forces pinup; comic timing; naturally timid.

Top Takes…

Trained as a dancer in the family tradition, Rita Hayworth was performing onstage from the age of eight. She worked for a time in "exotic" roles under the name "Rita Cansino"—as an Egyptian in *Charlie Chan in Egypt* (1935); and an Argentine in *Under the Pampas Moon* (1935)—often using her dance skills to brighten up tatty little movies. With her Spanish name anglicized, she rose to B leads (*The Shadow*, 1937; *Who Killed Gail Preston?*, 1938) before being reinvented by Columbia Pictures boss Harry Cohn as a glamour star. She endured electrolysis to raise her hairline, dyed her naturally black hair red, and emerged as the 1940s premier epitome of airbrushed gorgeousness.

Hayworth's first solid roles in major movies found her as the beautiful girl who the hero is initially more interested in than the heroine he eventually winds up with: losing Cary Grant to Jean Arthur in *Only Angels Have Wings* (1939) and James Cagney to Olivia de Havilland in *The Strawberry Blonde* (1941). Cohn built her up effectively as a leading lady in jolly, entertaining musicals: *You'll Never Get Rich* (1941) with Fred Astaire, who actually had to sweat a little to keep up with her on the dance floor; *My Gal Sal* (1942), one of several movies in

RIGHT: Hayworth reclines seductively in the film poster for *Gilda*, her most famous role.

1910s

1910s

which she is voluptuous in "gay nineties" fashions; and *Cover Girl* (1944), where she is well-matched with Gene Kelly. But her greatest screen moment came in *Gilda* (1946).

Hayworth's career was never quite the same after *Gilda*. Her marriage to Orson Welles was already over when she cropped her trademark hair and had it dyed blonde—to Cohn's horror—to play a dangerous woman in Welles's twisted *The Lady from Shanghai* (1947). A brief career break ensued, as Hayworth left Hollywood for life as a princess in Europe. Her marriage to Prince Aly Khan lasted less than four years, however, and soon she was back in cinemas with some "great temptress" roles (*Miss Sadie Thompson*, 1953). She took a fetching, mature role in *Pal Joey* (1957), queening it over her successor as Columbia Pictures's leading lady, Kim Novak. In the 1960s, Alzheimer's disease began to take hold, and Hayworth made only a few minor films after that. The disease finally killed her in 1987. **KN**

ABOVE: With cropped, blonde hair, Hayworth was no Gilda in *The Lady from Shanghai*.

Being Gilda

"Every man I have known has fallen in love with Gilda and awakened with me." Rita Hayworth's defining screen moment came in Charles Vidor's *Gilda* (1946), a noirish triangle melodrama in which she plays one of cinema's most iconic women. Gilda sings ("Put the Blame on Mame") and brings down the house in a striptease that involves little more than peeling off her elbow-length gloves. This scene was seductive enough to induce some protest from movie censors, and it made Gilda a cultural icon. But the character was hard to live up to; as Hayworth sighed, "No one can be Gilda twenty-four hours a day."

JACK PALANCE

Born: Volodymyr Palanyuk, February 18, 1919 (Lattimer Mines, Pennsylvania, U.S.); died 2006 (Montecito, California, U.S.).

Star qualities: Tall athletic physique; savage face; distinctive gravelly voice; intense screen presence; played bad-guy gunslingers in Westerns; writer; director.

Top Takes…

Jack Palance's savage face and fierce intensity easily earned him many bad-guy roles. His distinctive appearance was, in part, a result of both an early career in boxing and burns suffered as a bomber pilot during World War II when his B-24 plane crashed and he was knocked unconscious. After the war, he went on to study journalism at Stanford University, but dropped out to pursue a career on the stage. His acting breakthrough came when he was chosen as Marlon Brando's understudy in a 1947 Broadway production of *A Streetcar Named Desire*. It is said Palance made it on to the stage after accidentally punching Brando on the nose during a workout in the theater's boiler room.

In his early acting years, he received Oscar nominations for *Sudden Fear* (1952)—again stealing a part from Marlon Brando—and for the gunslinger in *Shane* (1953), and won an Emmy for Best Actor for *Requiem for a Heavyweight* (1956). But the promise of these roles never fully panned out, as Palance focused more on being a working actor than on receiving critical acclaim, and took parts that relied on his intimidating looks and not much else. A steady diet of historical adventures, Westerns, and crime films made in Europe ensued. He still managed, however, to impress the critics at periodic times with performances in such movies as *The Horsemen* (1971), and *Out of Rosenheim* (1987). Palance again grabbed critical attention when, at age seventy-three, he won the Best Supporting Actor Oscar for the comedy *City Slickers* (1991). His acceptance speech, when he performed one-armed pushups, is now part of Oscar show history. A published poet and painter, Palance also recorded a country and western album in 1969. **ML**

"The only two things you can truly depend upon are gravity and greed."

1910s

HOWARD KEEL

Born: Harry Clifford Keel, April 13, 1919 (Gillespie, Illinois, U.S.); died 2004 (Palm Desert, California, U.S.).

Star qualities: Tall; ruggedly handsome; booming voice; singer; athletic, heavy-built physique; powerful screen presence in musical extravaganzas.

Howard Keel was working as a mechanic when, at the age of twenty, he heard a classical singing recital at the Hollywood Bowl and resolved to take singing lessons. During World War II he worked for the Douglas Aircraft Company, where his booming voice led the company to employ him as a roving entertainer, touring its plants to raise workers' spirits. He went on to appear on Broadway, and in a succession of hit movie musicals such as *Show Boat* (1951) and *Kismet* (1955).

He had his greatest screen success in the kitsch-colored, wide-screen, stereophonic musicals of the 1950s, where the tall, wavy-haired athlete with a 42-tooth grin and powerful voice was seen as a refreshing change from the top-hat-and-tails look of stars such as Fred Astaire. He was especially good as buckskinned leading men in competition with feisty frontier gals: singing the numbers "Anything You Can Do" as Frank Butler with Betty Hutton's Annie Oakley in *Annie Get Your Gun* (1950), and "I Can Do Without You" as Wild Bill Hickok to Doris Day's *Calamity Jane* (1953). He is at his most amusing as the braggart Shakespearean actor in *Kiss Me Kate* (1953), where he relishes Cole Porter's intricate rhymes in "Where Is the Life that Late I Led?," and most enthusiastic belting out "Bless Yore Beautiful Hide" in *Seven Brides for Seven Brothers* (1954). He had a sideline in nonsinging Westerns such as *Ride, Vaquero!* (1953), and action movies such as *Floods of Fear* (1959). But by the 1970s Keel's movie career was over, and he returned to the stage. He struggled to earn a living for some years, working in cabaret and nightclubs, and briefly on Broadway. His later career was rejuvenated when he was approached to play Miss Ellie's husband, oil baron Clayton Farlow, on the hit TV series *Dallas* (1981–1991). **KN**

Top Takes...

My Father's House 2002
The War Wagon 1967
Red Tomahawk 1967
Waco 1966
The Day of the Triffids 1962
The Big Fisherman 1959
Floods of Fear 1959
Kismet 1955
Jupiter's Darling 1955
Seven Brides for Seven Brothers 1954
Rose Marie 1954
Kiss Me Kate 1953
Calamity Jane 1953
Ride, Vaquero! 1953
Show Boat 1951
Annie Get Your Gun 1950

> "You get your ups and downs but you just don't fall apart. You take another shot at it."

1910s

LOUIS JOURDAN

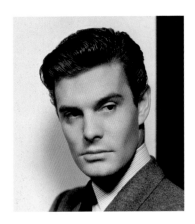

Born: Louis Gendre, June 19, 1919 (Marseille, Bouches-du-Rhône, France).

Star qualities: Tall; sophisticated; suave; urbane; classically handsome; stagecraft; cast as the romantic Frenchman in English-language films; character actor of costume dramas; singer.

Top Takes…

Year of the Comet 1992
Octopussy 1983
Cervantes 1967
Le Comte de Monte Cristo 1961
   (The Story of the Count of Monte Cristo)
The Best of Everything 1959
Gigi 1958
Escapade 1957
Julie 1956
Three Coins in the Fountain 1954
Bird of Paradise 1951
Madame Bovary 1949
Letter from an Unknown Woman 1948
The Paradine Case 1947
La vie de bohème 1945
Le corsaire 1939

French actor Louis Jourdan was educated in France, Turkey, and England, but trained as an actor in France. He made his film debut in *Le corsaire* (1939) with Charles Boyer. He continued to appear in films made in occupied France while also working for the Resistance. His big break came after the war, when his role in *La vie de bohème* (1945) brought him an offer from Hollywood producer David O. Selznick. He came to the United States to play in *The Paradine Case* (1947) with Gregory Peck, although director Alfred Hitchcock thought he was miscast. He had far more suitable roles as slightly weak, but not callous, objects of female desire in European-set romances, often in stiff collars: the recipient of the *Letter from an Unknown Woman* (1948), the lover in *Madame Bovary* (1949), an Italian prince in *Three Coins in the Fountain* (1954). He is best remembered for the jaded Parisian sophisticate who purrs his songs in *Gigi* (1958). These films had the effect of typecasting Jourdan as a continental lover, and he was never offered the challenging roles that would have developed his career.

Jourdan has played the hero and the villain in different versions of *The Count of Monte Cristo* (1961 and 1975), D'Artagnan in *The Man in the Iron Mask* (1977), and a lizardlike, seductive vampire in the BBC's miniseries *Count Dracula* (1977) (*Great Performances: Count Dracula*). In his later career, he has played poised, witty, pompous continental villains: a celebrity chef murderer on the TV series *Columbo* (1978), a mad scientist in Wes Craven's *Swamp Thing* (1982), and one of the less memorable James Bond villains, Kamal Khan, in *Octopussy* (1983). His swan song was as a villain searching for the fountain of youth in *Year of the Comet* (1992). He is now retired and lives in the south of France. **KN**

"I didn't want to be perpetually cooing in a lady's ear. There's not much satisfaction in it."

SLIM PICKENS

Born: Louis Bert Lindley Jr., June 29, 1919 (Kingsburg, California, U.S.); died 1983 (Modesto, California, U.S.).

Star qualities: Tall; portly; equestrian skill; rodeo cowboy turned Westerns cowboy; drawling accent; hoarse voice; played the comic sidekick and villain; composer.

A virtuoso horse rider, Slim Pickens began as a rodeo performer aged only twelve. He spent the next 20 years touring the United States on the rodeo circuit as a bull wrangler and rodeo clown. It was his rodeo career that is said to have given him his stage name, because he was told such work would earn him "slim pickings." His portly figure, hoarse voice, and folksy manner seemed to destine him for comedy roles from his first entry into movies, in Errol Flynn's *Rocky Mountain* (1950). But in the Marlon Brando-directed Western *One-Eyed Jacks* (1961) he is successfully cast against type as a sadistic deputy sheriff. This led to more villainous roles; in the opening scene of the Western *An Eye for an Eye* (1966), he shoots a baby in its crib.

Perhaps his most memorable role was a kind of caricature of himself playing a Westerner in Stanley Kubrick's *Dr. Strangelove or: How I learned to Stop Worrying and Love the Bomb* (1964). As Major T. J. "King" Kong, the gung-ho Texan air-force pilot, Pickens is last seen waving his Stetson while riding an atomic bomb.

In the remake of John Ford's *Stagecoach* (1966) he was cast as the driver, Buck, played in the original by the equally portly Andy Devine. A particular favorite of Western director Sam Peckinpah, Pickens appeared in *Major Dundee* (1965), *The Ballad of Cable Hogue* (1970), and most movingly as Sheriff Colin Baker in *Pat Garrett & Billy the Kid* (1973), where his death scene is accompanied by Bob Dylan's elegiac "Knockin' on Heaven's Door." He made frequent appearances on TV, including in such series as *The Lone Ranger* (1956), *Maverick* (1958), and *Alias Smith and Jones* (1971–1972). One of his last notable performances was as the henchman Taggart in Mel Brooks's Western spoof *Blazing Saddles* (1974). **EB**

Top Takes...

1910s

"After *Dr. Strangelove*, the roles, the dressing rooms, and the checks all started gettin' bigger."

LINO VENTURA

Born: Angiolino Giuseppe Pascal Ventura Lino Borrini, July 14, 1919 (Parma, Italy); died 1987 (Saint-Cloud, Hauts-de-Seine, France).

Star qualities: Legendary icon of French cinema; athletic, heavy-built physique; powerful screen presence as a tough guy in thrillers and film noirs.

Top Takes…

Le Ruffian 1983 (*The Ruffian*)
The Medusa Touch 1978
Cadaveri eccellenti 1976 (*Illustrious Corpses*)
L'emmerdeur 1973 (*A Pain in the A . . .*)
The Valachi Papers 1972
Boulevard du rhum 1971 (*Rum Runners*)
Le clan des Siciliens 1969 (*The Sicilian Clan*)
L'armée des ombres 1969
   (*Army in the Shadows*)
Les aventuriers 1967 (*The Last Adventure*)
Le deuxième souffle 1966 (*Second Breath*)
Cent mille dollars au soleil 1964
   (*Greed in the Sun*)
Un taxi pour Tobrouk 1960 (*Taxi for Tobruk*)
Ascenseur pour l'échafaud 1958
   (*Elevator to the Scaffold*)
Touchez pas au grisbi 1954 (*Grisbi*)

> "[I'm not a communist.] But I can still have comrades."
> —Philippe Gerbier, *Army in the Shadows*

Lino Ventura is sadly far less well known outside of France than his considerable talent deserves. Ventura was a Greco-Roman wrestler, winning the European championship in 1950, until he suffered an injury that forced him to look for work outside the ring. Stocky, and neither particularly tall nor handsome, he was spotted by director Jacques Becker as looking right for a film he was making. Ventura then made his screen debut in a supporting role as a gangster in the crime classic *Touchez pas au grisbi* (1954) (*Grisbi*), starring Jean Gabin. It was a fitting start, given that Ventura would go on to specialize in moody underworld film noir thrillers and develop an ordinary, but honorable, working-class criminal persona not unlike that of Gabin, with whom he became good friends.

He was very good in Louis Malle's *Ascenseur pour l'échafaud* (1958) (*Elevator to the Scaffold*), but his most memorable performances were for Jean-Pierre Melville, as the ex-con settling scores in *Le deuxième souffle* (1966) (*Second Breath*), and as the intense French Resistance fighter in *L'armée des ombres* (1969) (*Army in the Shadows*). Here, Ventura's subtle understatement transcended tough-guy heroics: his expressive, watchful eyes and immaculately controlled gestures brought both psychological and moral depth to roles hinged on deftly measured assessments of courage and cowardice, duty and responsibility, trust and honor. So good was he in these films that he tended to be typecast: *Le clan des Siciliens* (1969) (*The Sicilian Clan*) and *The Valachi Papers* (1972) were characteristic. In the hit-man farce *L'emmerdeur* (1973) (*Pain in the A . . .*) he revealed a brilliant talent for deadpan comedy, and a highlight of his later years was *Cadaveri eccellenti* (1976) (*Illustrious Corpses*). **GA**

VERONICA LAKE

Born: Constance Frances Marie Ockelman, November 14, 1919 (Brooklyn, New York, U.S.); died 1973 (Burlington, Vermont, U.S.).

Star qualities: Petite platinum blonde; shoulder-length hair; "The Peek-a-boo Girl"; lake-blue eyes; pinup sex symbol; played femme fatale roles.

If anyone requires proof that it takes only one or two great films to make a timeless screen legend, look no further than Veronica Lake. Working steadily for just a five-year period or so in the early to mid-1940s, Lake has nonetheless gone on to become an iconic figure in Hollywood history, and the irresistible charm and undeniable beauty displayed in her best work justifies the eternal fame.

After appearing in a few minor roles, Lake became a true star with her supporting role in *I Wanted Wings* (1941) and her comedic lead in Preston Sturges's classic *Sullivan's Travels* (1941). She rocketed immediately to stardom, becoming World War II's defining platinum blonde. Her famous "peek-a-boo" hairstyle became so imitated that the U.S. government asked her to pin it back because they feared female factory workers would have their tresses entangled in equipment. Sadly, she seemed to burn out just as fast. Only *I Married a Witch* (1942) used her natural comedic talents as effectively as the Sturges movie, and her only other career highlights are some of the film noir thrillers she starred in alongside her equally diminutive costar Alan Ladd, most notably *The Blue Dahlia* (1946), her last success.

Lake had developed a reputation for being difficult to work with and, after a string of flops, in 1948 she was dropped by Paramount Pictures. She appeared in a few mediocre films, and then retreated to TV and theater, but found little success in those arenas. Lake had been through three marriages and had an alcohol problem by the time she virtually disappeared from the public eye. In the 1960s, she was found living in a crumbling hotel and working as a cocktail waitress. She appeared in two largely forgotten low-budget films after this, before dying of hepatitis in 1973. **TC**

Top Takes...

Flesh Feast 1970
Footsteps in the Snow 1966
The Blue Dahlia 1946
Miss Susie Slagle's 1946
Hold That Blonde 1945
Out of This World 1945
The Hour Before the Dawn 1944
So Proudly We Hail! 1943
I Married a Witch 1942
The Glass Key 1942
This Gun for Hire 1942
Sullivan's Travels 1941
I Wanted Wings 1941
Young as You Feel 1940
All Women Have Secrets 1939
The Wrong Room 1939

1910s

"You could put all the talent I had into your left eye without suffering from impaired vision."

TOSHIRÔ MIFUNE

Born: Sanchuan Minlang, April 1, 1920 (Tsingtao, China); died 1997 (Mitaka City, Tokyo, Japan).

Star qualities: "The Wolf"; dynamic and intense screen presence; a powerful action guy with impressive speed of movement; prolific actor-director pairing with Kurosawa.

Top Takes...

Toshirô Mifune is officially Japan's greatest movie star, not excluding Godzilla. And this is despite the fact that he never even saw Japan until the age of twenty-one. After military service in World War II, Mifune turned to acting. He made his film debut in *Ginrei no hate* (1947) (*Snow Trail*) as a bank robber, but then went through a period of being typecast in the kind of roles Arthur Kennedy or Vic Morrow were getting in Hollywood—as the junior member of the gangster crew, with a chip on his shoulder and a greasy proto-Elvis pompadour.

　　Director Akira Kurosawa cast Mifune in *Yoidore tenshi* (1948) (*Drunken Angel*) as a tearaway who moderates his behavior under the influence of a derelict doctor (Takashi Shimura). The film was the first of what would become Japan's most renowned and prolific actor–director partnership. Kurosawa made 16 movies with Mifune (often in partnership with Shimura), all of which have found great popularity and critical acclaim outside Japan. For Kurosawa, Mifune was the swaggering bandit in *Rashômon* (1950) (*In the Woods*), the wannabe swordsman in *Shichinin no samurai* (1954) (*Seven Samurai*), and the crumpled, itchy, anonymous ronin in *Yojimbo*

RIGHT: Mifune played a ruthlessly ambitious Macbeth figure in Kurosawa's *Throne of Blood*.

(1961) (*The Bodyguard*) and its sequel *Tsubaki Sanjûrô* (1962) (*Sanjuro*). It is apt that *The Bodyguard* was remade as *A Fistful of Dollars* (1964): Mifune's emotional, disheveled, disreputable characters relate to the dignified samurai ideal much as Clint Eastwood's unshaven, mean-eyed bounty hunter does to the more typically clean-cut Western heroes that went before.

Mifune worked with other major directors (Kenji Mizoguchi in *Saikaku ichidai onna*, 1952 (*Diary of Oharu*)) and journeymen (frequent films for Hiroshi Inagaki and Ishirô Honda), but his career was so closely linked with Kurosawa that it seems odd that a personal rift separated the pair in 1965. They never worked together again. Mifune went international with a Mexican film, *Ánimas Trujano* (1962) (*The Important Man*), and appeared in English as a samurai out West in *Soleil rouge* (1971) (*Red Sun*), an enemy navy officer in *Midway* (1976), and feudal Japan personified as a lord in the miniseries *Shogun* (1980). **KN**

ABOVE: Mifune looks fierce next to the other six samurai in *Seven Samurai*.

Kurosawa on Mifune

"Mifune had a kind of talent I had never encountered before in the Japanese film world. It was, above all, the speed with which he expressed himself that was astounding. The ordinary Japanese actor might need ten feet of film to get across an impression; Mifune needed only three. The speed of his movements was such that he said in a single action what took ordinary actors three separate movements to express. He put forth everything directly and boldly, and his sense of timing was the keenest I had ever seen in a Japanese actor. And yet with all his quickness, he also had surprisingly fine sensibilities."

ALBERTO SORDI

Born: Alberto Sordi, June 15, 1920 (Rome, Italy); died 2003 (Rome, Italy).

Star qualities: Jovial icon of Italian cinema; comic timing; satirized the archetypal Italian—woebegone, mediocre, and uninterested; gave voice to the feelings of the Italian people; writer; director.

Top Takes...

Italian actor and director Alberto "Albertone" Sordi starred in more than 150 movies. He is commonly associated with the *commedia all'italiana* (comedy, Italian style) of the 1950s and 1960s, although his career dates back to the 1930s. He was also famous for being the Italian-dubbed voice of Oliver Hardy.

Sordi's star persona was cultivated as the proletarian Italian everyman—hopeless, mediocre, and apathetic—making him one of the most popular screen actors of the time, and representative of Italian masculinity during the economic boom in films such as *Un Americano a Roma* (1954) (*An American in Rome*) and *Una vita difficile* (1961) (*A Difficult Life*). A more audience-accessible alternative to fellow Italian actor Marcello Mastroianni, Sordi's characters were often marked by the prevailing satire and cynicism of the Italian comedy, and Sordi's star quality as the stereotypical Italian man was central in explaining, through cinema, an Italy in the throes of a rapid social and cultural transformation.

Sordi's career also cut across both the popular and art cinemas, with memorable performances in Federico Fellini's *Lo sceicco bianco* (1952) (*The White Sheik*) and *I vitelloni* (1953) (*The Young and the Passionate*). Working hard behind the camera as well as in front of it, Sordi directed 18 movies from 1966 onward. His direction in the episodic film *Le copie* (1970) (*The Couples*) is especially noteworthy, because it tries to continue the satirical Italian comedy tradition for which Sordi will always be remembered. The actor was genuinely loved by his countrymen, and when he died, some said it was "like losing a member of the family." A crowd of an estimated 250,000 packed Rome's San Giovanni square to pay their respects at his funeral. **GN**

> "I observe and reflect real life and ordinary people and sooner or later that raises a laugh."

1920s

SETSUKO HARA

Born: Masae Aida, June 17, 1920 (Yokohama, Japan).

Star qualities: "The Eternal Virgin"; elegant, charismatic allure; the embodiment of Japanese traditional values and beauty; graceful screen presence; played heroines in melodramas.

For the Japanese, Setsuko Hara was "The Eternal Virgin," an actress who was the perfect embodiment of traditional values and beauty. In the West—despite her roles in Akira Kurosawa's *Waga seishun ni kuinashi* (1946) (*No Regrets for Our Youth*), as well as Mikio Naruse's *Meshi* (1951) (*Repast*)—she will be forever linked with director Yasujiro Ozu. Her six roles for Ozu—she progressively played daughter, wife, and mother—are superb examples of focused and generous acting. Part and parcel of the ascetic and pure director's design, which reflects the ritualistic nature of Japanese society, Hara's behavior and carefully chosen expressions were privileged moments of those films' emotional profundity.

Hara achieved authentic melodrama without ever being melodramatic, most evidently in the *Noriko* trilogy: *Banshun* (1949) (*Late Spring*); *Bakushû* (1951) (*Early Summer*), and *Tokyo monogatari* (1953) (*Tokyo Story*). Partly because Ozu clearly shows sympathy for her trials, but mainly for her skillful performance, Hara's characters always retain their dignity and radiance, even in the most difficult circumstances. At the end of the Kyoto sequence in *Late Spring*, where father and daughter have their last trip together, sadness, tenderness, and the frailty of separation are beautifully realized in the interplay between Hara and Chishu Ryu, but especially in the shades of her face and smile: nobility in quiet suffering.

Her retirement and seclusion from the business in 1963 after Ozu's death, her silence and distance afterward, were another poignant element in creating the definitive Hara mystery and charisma. One suspects that she has actually taken some steps—the logical extension and conclusion of her screen persona—denied to her Ozu heroines. **AB**

Top Takes...

Kohayagawa-ke no aki 1961 (*Early Autumn*)
Fundoshi isha 1960 (*Life of a Country Doctor*)
Tokyo monogatari 1953 (*Tokyo Story*)
Tokyo no koibito 1952 (*Tokyo Sweetheart*)
Meshi 1951 (*Repast*)
Bakushû 1951 (*Early Summer*)
Hakuchi 1951 (*The Idiot*)
Banshun 1949 (*Late Spring*)
Waga seishun ni kuinashi 1946
   (*No Regrets for Our Youth*)

1920s

"… she played all social roles— daughter, wife, and mother— [but] only in her films."—D. Richie

MAUREEN O'HARA

Born: Maureen FitzSimons, August 17, 1920 (Ranelagh, County Dublin, Ireland).

Star qualities: Tall; slender; athletic; redheaded beauty; creamy complexion; haunting eyes; soprano voice; energetic, fiery screen presence; performed her own stunts; lead in romances and Westerns; writer.

Maureen O'Hara grew up in Ireland with a love of singing and performing, and was only fourteen when she was accepted to train at the Abbey Theatre in Dublin—Ireland's national theater. Three years later O'Hara had got herself an agent, and while in London to do a screen test at Elstree Studios, her agent telephoned her to say there was someone he wanted her to meet: that person was actor Charles Laughton. Together with Eric Pommer, Laughton owned film company Mayflower Pictures, and they were looking for a young girl to play in Alfred Hitchcock's period adventure *Jamaica Inn* (1939). Laughton liked her and offered O'Hara a contract.

She was later introduced to a U.S. audience as the gypsy dancer Esmeralda in *The Hunchback of Notre Dame* (1939). John Ford then put her in *How Green Was My Valley* (1941), and she became his favorite leading lady, partnered in brawling relationships with John Wayne, in roles as the Southern vixen in *Rio Grande* (1950), the definitive Irish colleen in *The Quiet Man* (1952), and a military wife in *The Wings of Eagles* (1957).

With her copious red hair, flashing eyes, and strong cheekbones, O'Hara was one of the screen's great amazons, memorable in Technicolor swashbucklers such as *The Black Swan* (1942). Without Ford, Wayne kept her on for *McLintock!* (1963) and *Big Jake* (1971); she was also well matched with Henry Fonda in *Spencer's Mountain* (1963). O'Hara withdrew from the screen after marrying aviator Charles Blair in 1968. Together they managed a commuter seaplane service in the Caribbean and published a magazine, for which she wrote a monthly column. After his death she returned to acting, appearing in TV movies and playing John Candy's smothering mother in *Only the Lonely* (1991). **KN**

Top Takes...

Only the Lonely 1991
Big Jake 1971
Spencer's Mountain 1963
McLintock! 1963
The Wings of Eagles 1957
The Quiet Man 1952
Rio Grande 1950
Sitting Pretty 1948
Miracle on 34th Street 1947
Sinbad the Sailor 1947
Sentimental Journey 1946
The Spanish Main 1945
The Black Swan 1942
How Green Was My Valley 1941
The Hunchback of Notre Dame 1939
Jamaica Inn 1939

> "I was tough. I was tall. I was strong. I didn't take any nonsense from anybody."

SHELLEY WINTERS

Born: Shirley Schrift, August 18, 1920 (East St. Louis, Illinois, U.S.); died 2006 (New York City, New York, U.S.).

Star qualities: Flamboyant blonde bombshell; brash; witty; outspoken; played early glamour roles and mature matronly character parts; producer.

Shelley Winters was raised in New York, where her family moved so her father, a tailor's cutter, could be close to the city's garment industry. She worked as a model and chorus girl to pay for acting lessons, making her Broadway debut in the comedy *The Night Before Christmas* (1941). She then had minor roles in several movies until she came to wider notice as a waitress smart enough to be scared—but dumb enough to be strangled—by Ronald Colman in the film noir *A Double Life* (1947). Ideally cast as Myrtle Wilson in a regrettably poor *The Great Gatsby* (1949), Winters played a succession of similar roles in film noirs such as *Johnny Stool Pigeon* (1949), and Westerns such as *Winchester '73* (1950).

Her acting trademark was a slight squint when she suspected, much too late, she was in horrible danger: she plays a factory girl who winds up dumped in a lake by Montgomery Clift in *A Place in the Sun* (1951), for which she garnered an Oscar nomination. She later followed this up with an Academy Award for Best Supporting Actress for her performance as Mrs. Van Daan in *The Diary of Anne Frank* (1959). Winters was Jewish, and fittingly donated this Oscar to the Anne Frank museum in Amsterdam. But she got to keep her second Oscar, which she won six years later in 1965 for her role as a manipulative matriarch in *A Patch of Blue*.

In the 1960s, a little blowsier, Winters was perfect as Charlotte Haze in *Lolita* (1962), and the middle-aged sexpot in *Alfie* (1966). Then she switched to monster mamas and gorgons: a scary concierge in Roman Polanski's *Le Locataire* (1976) (*The Tenant*), and Mrs. Touchett in *The Portrait of a Lady* (1996). Winters was married four times and had many relationships with fellow actors. She recounted her lively love life in two autobiographies. **KN**

Top Takes...

The Portrait of a Lady 1996
Pete's Dragon 1977
Le Locataire 1976 (*The Tenant*)
The Poseidon Adventure 1972 ☆
What's the Matter with Helen? 1971
Whoever Slew Auntie Roo? 1971
Bloody Mama 1970
Wild in the Streets 1968
Alfie 1966
A Patch of Blue 1965 ★
Lolita 1962
The Diary of Anne Frank 1959 ★
The Night of the Hunter 1955
A Place in the Sun 1951 ☆
Winchester '73 1950
A Double Life 1947

1920s

"My face was always so made up, it looked as though it had the decorators in."

MICKEY ROONEY

Born: Joe Yule Jr., September 23, 1920 (Brooklyn, New York, U.S.).

Star qualities: Legendary pint-sized performer; cheeky grin; longevity; singer and dancer; comic timing; lead juvenile character actor; dedication; has been in the movie business for eight decades.

Top Takes...

The Black Stallion 1979 ☆
Pulp 1972
It's a Mad Mad Mad Mad World 1963
Requiem for a Heavyweight 1962
Breakfast at Tiffany's 1961
Baby Face Nelson 1957
The Bold and the Brave 1956 ☆
Quicksand 1950
National Velvet 1944
The Human Comedy 1943 ☆
Babes on Broadway 1941
Young Tom Edison 1940
Babes in Arms 1939 ☆
The Adventures of Huckleberry Finn 1939
A Family Affair 1937
A Midsummer Night's Dream 1935

Mickey Rooney's parents were a comedian and a chorus girl who played on vaudeville, and he made his first appearance on the stage with them aged only seventeen months. He was a scrappy kid in the silent-era Mickey McGuire shorts (1927–1933), then played "lead character as a boy" roles—such as in *The World Changes* (1933) and *Manhattan Melodrama* (1934)—and Puck in *A Midsummer Night's Dream* (1935). A star turn as a good-natured, trouble-prone teen in *A Family Affair* (1937) led to a long series of folksy Andy Hardy pictures that represented MGM head Louis B. Mayer's ideal of the United States. This was followed by energetic musical teamings with fellow MGM property Judy Garland in *Babes in Arms* (1939) and *Babes on Broadway* (1941). He won an Academy Award nomination for Best Actor for his role in the former, and at nineteen years old was the first teenager to receive such a nomination. He landed other plum adolescent roles in *The Adventures of Huckleberry Finn* (1939) and *Young Tom Edison* (1940).

Like many child stars, Rooney never quite outgrew his pint-sized kid image, but tried hard in film noirs such as *Quicksand* (1950) and an especially vicious gangster biopic *Baby Face Nelson* (1957). In the 1960s he began touring nightclubs and theaters again, though he continued in occasional movie roles. He caricatured himself enjoyably as a movie star with underworld connections in *Pulp* (1972), and has since worked steadily in crusty old-timer roles such as in *The Black Stallion* (1979). In 1983, after 60 years' working as an actor, he received a Lifetime Achievement Academy Award. Rooney has been married eight times; his first wife was actress Ava Gardner. He has been married to his current wife, Jan Chamberlin, longer than all his other wives combined. **KN**

"The public made me. The public can break me. I owe them my life."

MONTGOMERY CLIFT

Born: Edward Montgomery Clift, October 17, 1920 (Omaha, Nebraska, U.S.); died 1966 (New York City, New York, U.S.).

Star qualities: Sensitive; sexual magnetism; vulnerable; stagecraft; played the neurotic young man in serious dramas; intense, brooding screen presence; writer.

Montgomery "Monty" Clift was a forerunner of Marlon Brando and James Dean in beautiful, wounded, neurotic male star roles. His signature acting tic was the twitch of a cheek muscle to imply roiling passions beneath his frozen, perfect face.

Clift made his Broadway debut aged only thirteen, and worked in the theater for ten years before moving to the big screen. He made his film debut as a sensitive G.I. in *The Search* (1948), for which he won the first of four Academy Award nominations. From then on he had roles perfectly tailored to his persona: the adopted son who defies John Wayne in *Red River* (1948); the worthless suitor left banging on the door in *The Heiress* (1949); the socially ambitious murderer who drowns Shelley Winters to get a shot at Elizabeth Taylor in *A Place in the Sun* (1951); the priest suspected of murder because he won't break the seal of confession in *I Confess* (1953); and the trumpet-playing soldier who goes absent without leave rather than box again in *From Here to Eternity* (1953).

A disfiguring car accident during the production of *Raintree County* (1957) is often blamed for stalling his career, but that movie was his first in four years. He turned down many starring roles, including those in *Sunset Blvd.* (1950) and *East of Eden* (1955). Instead, in his later career Clift applied himself in stiff earnestness to a few literary, poetic, or serious pictures, including *Judgment at Nuremberg* (1961).

Offscreen, Clift was a sadly troubled individual. A closet homosexual, he was addicted to alcohol and drugs. He suffered from dysentery and colitis for much of his career, and was beset by health problems. When he died aged only forty-five, a drama teacher at The Actors Studio, Robert Lewis, called Clift's death "the longest suicide in history." **KN**

Top Takes...

Freud 1962
***Judgment at Nuremberg* 1961** ☆
The Misfits 1961
Wild River 1960
Suddenly, Last Summer 1959
The Young Lions 1958
Lonelyhearts 1958
Raintree County 1957
***From Here to Eternity* 1953** ☆
Stazione Termini 1953
    (*Indiscretion of an American Wife*)
I Confess 1953
***A Place in the Sun* 1951** ☆
The Heiress 1949
Red River 1948
***The Search* 1948** ☆

"Failure and its accompanying misery is for the artist his most vital source of creative energy."

1920s

GENE TIERNEY

Born: Gene Eliza Tierney, November 19, 1920 (Brooklyn, New York, U.S.); died 1991 (Houston, Texas, U.S.).

Star qualities: Glamorously beautiful; tall; high cheekbones; gracefully elegant; intelligent; conscientious; poised; versatile; exotic leading lady of film noir.

Gene Tierney was the daughter of a successful insurance broker and a teacher, and had a fairly privileged upbringing and education, including two years traveling in Europe and attending a Swiss finishing school. By 1938, she was bored with society life, and decided to become an actress. She made her Broadway debut in *What a Life* (1939).

She went on to become an exceptionally glamorous leading lady at Twentieth Century Fox. The studio starred her from the first in history lessons, such as her screen debut, *The Return of Frank James* (1940). When she heard her voice in the movie, she was shocked by its "Minnie Mouse" sound, and started to smoke heavily to lower it. (This decision came to haunt her, because she later died of emphysema.) She gained a Best Actress Academy Award nomination for *Leave Her to Heaven* (1945), a huge hit for Fox. But Tierney is best remembered as *Laura* (1944), even though she appears in the film mostly in fragmentary flashbacks and as a portrait, before her astonishing return-from-the-dead entrance at the halfway point.

She got to be sexy as the barefoot Ellie May Lester in *Tobacco Road* (1941). Otto Preminger, director of *Laura*, was loyal, and gave her good film noir roles in movies such as *Whirlpool* (1949). But her private life was in turmoil throughout the 1940s and 1950s. Following a bout of German measles, she gave birth to a severely handicapped child, which brought on deep depression. Later she had doomed affairs with future U.S. president John F. Kennedy and playboy Prince Aly Khan. After a suicide attempt in 1957 she was admitted to hospital suffering from mental illness. Preminger gave her one last good cameo, as a Washington society hostess in *Advise & Consent* (1962). **KN**

Top Takes...

Advise & Consent 1962
The Egyptian 1954
Plymouth Adventure 1952
Way of a Gaucho 1952
Where the Sidewalk Ends 1950
Night and the City 1950
Whirlpool 1949
The Ghost and Mrs. Muir 1947
Dragonwyck 1946
Leave Her to Heaven 1945 ☆
Laura 1944
Heaven Can Wait 1943
The Shanghai Gesture 1941
Tobacco Road 1941
Hudson's Bay 1941
The Return of Frank James 1940

"I learned quickly at Columbia that the only eye that mattered was the one on the camera."

RICARDO MONTALBÁN

Born: Ricardo Gonzalo Pedro Montalbán Merino, November 25, 1920 (Mexico City, Mexico).

Star qualities: Tall; swarthy good looks; athletic physique; Latin leading man and character actor; dancer; civic minded.

Before coming to Hollywood, Ricardo Montalbán starred in films in his native Mexico, playing the bullfighter in *La hora de la verdad* (1945) (*The Hour of Truth*). He first came to Hollywood's attention as a dancer in the Esther Williams musicals *Fiesta* (1947), *On an Island With You* (1948), and *Neptune's Daughter* (1949). In the United States, he resisted the studio suggestion to change his name to Ricky Martin, but stayed around to be a Latin leading man anyway. He was an undercover agent posing as an illegal immigrant in *Border Incident* (1949), a soldier in *Battleground* (1949), a cop in *Mystery Street* (1950), and a boxer in *Right Cross* (1950). As one of only a few employed Hispanic actors, he took his share of stereotyped movie roles: as Chu Chu Ramirez in *My Man and I* (1952), Pepe Gonzalez in *Sombrero* (1953), and Roberto Santos in *Latin Lovers* (1953).

Aside from his typecast Latin roles, Montalbán was a talented character actor. His scattered film roles include a priest in *The Singing Nun* (1966), the villain of *The Naked Gun: From the Files of Police Squad!* (1988) and—still working into his eighties—the wheelchair-bound grandfather in the two *Spy Kids* sequels (2002, 2003). He combined film work with TV performances, playing the macho villain in the *Star Trek* episode "Space Seed" (1967)—a role he reprised in the cinema in *Star Trek II: The Wrath of Khan* (1982)—and Mr. Roarke, the mysterious host of *Fantasy Island* (1977–1984). In 1970, he founded the Nosotros nonprofit organization to improve the image of Latinos and Hispanics in the entertainment industry and expand their employment opportunities. Since 1993 he has used a wheelchair as the result of a spinal-cord injury incurred during filming of *Across the Wide Missouri* (1951). **KN**

Top Takes...

Spy Kids 3-D: Game Over 2003
Spy Kids 2: Island of Lost Dreams 2002
The Naked Gun: From the Files of Police Squad! 1988
Star Trek: The Wrath of Khan 1982
Conquest of the Planet of the Apes 1972
Escape from the Planet of the Apes 1971
The Singing Nun 1966
Sayonara 1957
Latin Lovers 1953
Sombrero 1953
My Man and I 1952
Right Cross 1950
Mystery Street 1950
Battleground 1949
Border Incident 1949

> "It is to TV that I owe my freedom from bondage of the Latin lover roles."

1920s

DONNA REED

Born: Donna Belle Mullenger, January 27, 1921 (Denison, Iowa, U.S.); died 1986 (Los Angeles, California, U.S.).

Star qualities: Tall; slender; beauty queen looks; dazzling smile; comic timing; played wholesome girl-next-door roles and the mature matriarch; feisty.

Top Takes...

For those of a certain age, Donna Reed seems synonymous with suburban maternity, as she ruled the roost of her TV household on *The Donna Reed Show* from 1958 to 1966, and later briefly played one of the notable dramatic matriarchs, Miss Ellie Ewing, on *Dallas* from 1984 to 1985. That same air of blissful domesticity is evident in her role as James Stewart's better half in Frank Capra's *It's a Wonderful Life* (1946), widely known through its recurrent appearances on TV.

Reed's film career is more diverse. She won a movie contract in a beauty contest, and joined MGM in 1941. She initially paid her dues in installments in the *Tin Man*, *Andy Hardy*, and *Dr. Kildare* series. More interesting and demanding work followed, most notably the lavish adaptation of Oscar Wilde's *The Picture of Dorian Gray* (1945), the stirring war film *They Were Expendable* (1945), and mystery drama *Chicago Deadline* (1949).

The 1950s saw her depart MGM and take on roles in B-features that often possess more lasting interest than the froth of the previous decade. A thriller such as *Scandal Sheet* (1952) or Westerns such as *The Far Horizons* (1955) and *Backlash* (1956) display hearty and energetic examples of Reed's skills as an actress. Her most notable role, which won her a Best Supporting Actress Academy Award, came in Fred Zinneman's *From Here to Eternity* (1953), where she broke type as a good-time girl who wooed Montgomery Clift. In later years, her stint in *Dallas* came to an ignominious end in 1985, when the actress who originally played Miss Ellie, Barbara Bel Geddes, was well enough to return to the series and Reed was fired. She sued the show's production company and received a $1 million settlement, but unfortunately it came only shortly before her death from cancer in 1986. **DS**

> "Forty pictures I was in, and all I remember is 'What kind of bra will you be wearing today . . . ?'"

1920s

LANA TURNER

Born: Julia Jean Mildred Frances Turner, February 8, 1921 (Wallace, Idaho, U.S.); died June 29, 1995 (Century City, California, U.S.).

Star qualities: "The Sweater Girl"; lively; flirtatious; beautiful; struggled for challenging roles; nominated for a Best Actress Oscar.

Lana Turner was a major movie star, but had little screen personality beyond her sheen of beauty and was only occasionally called upon to act (which she did, rather well). Ask anyone to name two of her movies and—after *The Postman Always Rings Twice* (1946)—they'll struggle; in official classics like *The Bad and the Beautiful* (1952), she tended to be overshadowed in ensemble casts.

Turner's singing was dubbed and she was stiff in comedy, but she was astonishingly beautiful and did unexpectedly well when Ingrid Bergman insisted she and Turner exchange roles in the Spencer Tracy-starring *Dr. Jekyll and Mr. Hyde* (1941). Bergman plays Hyde's abused mistress, the showy part, but Turner is equally good as Jekyll's prim, sensual, gorgeously garbed fiancée. Officially a big star, Turner was teamed with MGM's strongest leading men, and made four films with their king, Clark Gable. She rose to the demands of the slutty, sexy Cora in *Postman*—a hash slinger who still exudes Hollywood glamour—but film noir was an atypical genre for Turner, who was more often used in smart, modern romance or comedy.

After an insufficiently wicked Lady de Winter in *The Three Musketeers* (1948) and the alcoholic actress (modeled on Diana Barrymore) in *The Bad and the Beautiful* (1952), the still-gorgeous Turner found herself stranded in the 1950s, trussed in improbable costumes for musicals (*The Merry Widow*, 1952) and epics (*The Prodigal*, 1955). Offscreen scandal— including seven husbands and countless affairs—plagued her, though her career had an Indian summer in glossy, heavy-breathing soap opera (*Imitation of Life*, 1959). She faded out of sight, but not without a few late-career flukes, most notably *The Big Cube* (1969) and *Persecution* (1974). **KN**

Top Takes…

Persecution 1974
The Big Cube 1969
Madame X 1966
Bachelor in Paradise 1961
Portrait in Black 1960
Imitation of Life 1959
Peyton Place **1957** ☆
The Sea Chase 1955
The Prodigal 1955
The Bad and the Beautiful 1952
Green Dolphin Street 1947
The Postman Always Rings Twice 1946
Johnny Eager 1942
Honky Tonk 1941
Dr. Jekyll and Mr. Hyde 1941
Calling Dr. Kildare 1939

1920s

"I find men terribly exciting, and any girl who says she doesn't is an anemic old maid . . . ."

GIULIETTA MASINA

Born: Giulia Anna Masina, February 22, 1921 (San Giorgio di Piano, Bologna, Italy); died 1994 (Rome, Italy).

Star qualities: Federico Fellini's iconic muse; vulnerable eyes; expressive face; stylish; played both fantasy and comic roles with a sense of pathos.

Top Takes...

Aujourd'hui peut-être... 1991
  (*A Day to Remember*)
Ginger e Fred 1986 (*Ginger and Fred*)
Giulietta degli spiriti 1965 (*Juliet of the Spirits*)
Le notti di cabiria 1957 (*Nights of Cabiria*)
Il bidone 1955 (*The Swindle*)
Buonanotte... avvocato! 1955
La strada 1954 (*The Road*)
Lo sceicco bianco 1952 (*The White Sheik*)
Luci del varietà 1950 (*Variety Lights*)

Few artists in history have been fortunate enough to find so perfect a muse as Italian director Federico Fellini found in his wife, Giulietta Masina. In several collaborations Masina developed a unique screen persona: broad, often brash and loud, and defiantly unrealistic yet affectingly vulnerable and sincere. She could never be mistaken for any other actress, although comparisons have been made with such great silent performers as Charles Chaplin, Marcel Marceau, and Harpo Marx, the latter of whom she somewhat resembled.

Masina and Fellini spent almost their whole lives together. She studied drama at a university in Rome, and by 1943 was carving out a career as a radio actress when she starred in a radio serial, *Cico e Pallina*, that had been written by the young Fellini. The couple were married the same year.

She could be naturalistic when necessary, as is demonstrated in *Il bidone* (1955) (*The Swindle*). But her specialty was in playing the girl who belonged in the circus yet was somehow washed up in the tenements of postwar Rome; a misfit whose simplicity acted as a magnet for misfortune. As such, she became the perfect human vehicle for Fellini's part-fantasy, part-neorealist style. She was the living embodiment—physically, facially, vocally, and emotionally—of the eternally optimistic yet eternally misused prostitute in *Le notti di cabiria* (1957) (*Nights of Cabiria*), and the childlike eccentric sold by her mother to a traveling strongman in *La strada* (1954) (*The Road*). In each film she leaves an indelible impression, and her endlessly expressive, clownlike face remains one of the key icons of 1950s world cinema. Masina passed away in 1994, only months after her husband died, and they are buried together in Rimini cemetery. **MC**

> "What a funny face! Are you a woman, really? Or an artichoke?"
>
> —The Fool to Gelsomina, *The Road*

SIMONE SIGNORET

Born: Henriette Charlotte Simone Kaminker, March 25, 1921 (Wiesbaden, Germany); died 1985 (Eure, Haute Normandie, France).

Star qualities: Glowing beauty; sensual sex bomb; heavy-lidded eyes; seductive smile; young screen siren and mature matriarch roles; writer; liberal political activist.

Born in Germany, Simone Signoret grew up in Paris. At the start of World War II, her Jewish father fled to England to join General Charles de Gaulle, and she had to find work as an extra in films to support her family. She took her French-born mother's maiden name as a screen name to help conceal her Jewish roots.

In her youth, Signoret radiated a ripe sensuality that glowed from the screen. She moved with the indolent languor of a woman supremely confident in her own powers of attraction; the slow, sleepy smile and heavy-lidded eyes irresistibly evoked thoughts of warm bedrooms and rumpled sheets. Not surprising then that she was often cast as a prostitute: in Max Ophüls's carousel of love *La Ronde* (1950) (*Roundabout*), and as Serge Reggiani's lover in Jacques Becker's low-life period drama *Casque d'or* (1952) (*Golden Marie*). Her performance as the seductive older woman in Jack Clayton's *Room at the Top* (1959) won her an Academy Award for Best Actress.

There was a tenacity about Signoret that suited her to dangerous roles. She made a convincing murderess in Marcel Carné's *Thérèse Raquin* (1953) (*The Adultress*), and a devious accomplice in the homicidal labyrinth of Henri-Georges Clouzot's thriller *Les diaboliques* (1955) (*Diabolique*). For Jean-Pierre Melville she played a dedicated French Resistance fighter in *L'armée des ombres* (1969) (*Army in the Shadows*), and offscreen she also held staunchly to her convictions. The outspoken left-wing views she shared with her second husband, Yves Montand, often hampered her career. Later in life, rejecting conventional notions of glamour, Signoret let her face and figure grow heavy, and accepted grumpy, grandmotherly roles. But her smile could still light up her face with warmth and tenderness. **PK**

Top Takes...

L'Étoile du Nord 1982 (*The North Star*)
La chair de l'orchidée 1975 (*Flesh of the Orchid*)
L'aveu 1970 (*The Confession*)
L'armée des ombres 1969
  (*Army in the Shadows*)
Ship of Fools 1965 ☆
Room at the Top 1959 ★
Les Sorcières de Salem 1957 (*The Crucible*)
Die Windrose 1957 (*Rose of the Winds*)
Les diaboliques 1955 (*Diabolique*)
Thérèse Raquin 1953 (*The Adultress*)
Casque d'or 1952 (*Golden Marie*)
La Ronde 1950 (*Roundabout*)
Boléro 1942

"I collect all the reviews of the films I turned down. And when they're bad—I have to smile."

DIRK BOGARDE

Born: Derek Jules Gaspard Ulric Niven van den Bogaerde, March 28, 1921 (Hampstead, London, England); died 1999 (London, England).

Star qualities: British screen heartthrob; "The Idol of the Odeon"; handsome; sexy; suave; sophisticated; charismatic; versatile leading man; stagecraft; writer; artist.

Top Takes…

Despair 1978
A Bridge Too Far 1977
Il Portiere di notte 1974 (*The Night Porter*)
Le Serpent 1973 (*The Serpent*)
Morte a Venezia 1971 (*Death in Venice*)
La Caduta degli dei 1969 (*The Damned*)
Accident 1967
Modesty Blaise 1966
The Servant 1963
Victim 1961
Cast a Dark Shadow 1955
The Sea Shall Not Have Them 1954
The Sleeping Tiger 1954
Doctor in the House 1954
Appointment in London 1952
The Blue Lamp 1950

Incredibly handsome, suave, and sophisticated, Dirk Bogarde seemed cut out to become the Cary Grant of the postwar British cinema, but also played a more interesting, and varied, role. He first caught attention as a conscienceless, homicidal "spiv" in *The Blue Lamp* (1950), achieving such success that he immediately landed a number of featured roles. He offered stiff-upper-lip quietude in war films such as *The Sea Shall Not Have Them* (1954), and showed skill at genteel comedy as Dr. Simon Sparrow in one of the 1950s' most popular franchises, the *Doctor* series, starting with *Doctor in the House* (1954).

Bogarde's darker side was showcased in a number of second-rate—but because of his charismatic presence always interesting—melodramas. Among them is *Cast a Dark Shadow* (1955) in which he played a seductive *homme fatale* finally undone by his scheming. For Joseph Losey in *The Sleeping Tiger* (1954), he posed as a criminal not reformed by a psychiatrist's therapeutic efforts, who repays his benefactor by seducing his wife—a bad film, but made credible by Bogarde's considerable sex appeal. Bogarde did his best work in two other Losey films: *The Servant* (1963), playing a gentleman's gentleman who mentally overpowers his feckless upper-class employer; and *Accident* (1967), where he is an Oxford tutor embroiled in a romantic triangle. The sexual ambivalence of Bogarde's persona was well exploited by Luchino Visconti in *Morte a Venezia* (1971) (*Death in Venice*), a film that confirmed Bogarde's status as a star of the international art theater cinema, along with the notable *Il Portiere di notte* (1974) (*The Night Porter*). In middle age, he returned to war films, playing conventional roles in *A Bridge Too Far* (1977) and *Despair* (1978). Bogarde was knighted in 1992. **BP**

> "Cinema is just a form of masturbation. Sexual relief for disappointed people."

PETER USTINOV

Born: Peter Alexander Ustinov, April 16, 1921 (London, England); died 2004 (Los Genolier, Vaud, Switzerland).

Star qualities: Portly; prolific writer; witty talk-show raconteur; mimic; ad lib artist; imperious stage and screen presence; comic timing; director; producer; humanitarian.

Sir Peter Ustinov won the Best Supporting Actor Oscar twice, but arguably gave his best performances on TV talk shows as a highly sought-after raconteur. His assertion—"I was irrevocably betrothed to laughter, the sound of which has always seemed to me to be the most civilized music in the world"—perfectly sums up his approach to acting, and to life.

Ustinov was born in London soon after his artist mother emigrated from Russia to join her husband, a German journalist. He left school at sixteen to study drama at the London Theatre Studio, and was a professional actor by the age of eighteen. Supplementing his income from acting, he wrote his first play, *House of Regrets*, a year later, and saw it transfer to London's West End at the onset of World War II. The inevitable military service followed. He later said that the highlight of his army career was his time spent as batman for fellow actor David Niven. Ustinov spent part of the war with the Army Cinema Unit, where he was involved in making recruitment films.

A playwright, novelist, and occasional director of movies such as *Billy Budd* (1962), he was involved in such an eclectic mix of projects that he gave the impression of mere dabbling in acting. He began with wartime bit parts such as in *One of Our Aircraft Is Missing* (1942), followed by a rare star role as the title character in *Private Angelo* (1949), which he also wrote and codirected. His performance as Emperor Nero in *Quo Vadis* (1951) landed him a string of vivid supporting roles: he was especially good as the sad, bloated Prince Regent in *Beau Brummell* (1954), and won his first Best Supporting Actor Oscar for his portrayal of Roman toady Lentulus Batiatus in *Spartacus* (1960). Ustinov continued to perform into old age and was a particularly beguiling Hercule Poirot. **KN**

Top Takes...

Luther 2003
Charlie Chan and the Curse of the Dragon Queen 1981
Death on the Nile 1978
Logan's Run 1976
Viva Max! 1969
***Topkapi* 1964 ★**
Billy Budd 1962
***Spartacus* 1960 ★**
Lola Montès 1955 (*The Sins of Lola Montes*)
We're No Angels 1955
Beau Brummell 1954
***Quo Vadis* 1951 ☆**
Private Angelo 1949
The Goose Steps Out 1942
One of Our Aircraft Is Missing 1942

"I imagine hell like this: Italian punctuality, German humor, and English wine."

JANE RUSSELL

Born: Ernestine Jane Geraldine Russell, June 21, 1921 (Bemidji, Minnesota, U.S.).

Star qualities: Tall; voluptuous; beauty queen looks; cantilevered brassiere; feisty; comic timing; tough, sweater-girl leading lady; wartime forces pinup; producer; singer; civic minded.

Top Takes...

Darker Than Amber 1970
The Born Losers 1967
Waco 1966
The Fuzzy Pink Nightgown 1957
The Revolt of Mamie Stover 1956
Hot Blood 1956
Underwater! 1955
The French Line 1954
Gentlemen Prefer Blondes 1953
Montana Belle 1952
Son of Paleface 1952
Macao 1952
The Las Vegas Story 1952
His Kind of Woman 1951
The Paleface 1948
The Outlaw 1943

Jane Russell's father was a lieutenant in the U.S. army, and her mother was an actress with a traveling troupe. She grew up interested in music and drama, and started her career in modeling before going to drama school. Her big break came when she was discovered by Texan millionaire Howard Hughes. All of the publicity material for his steamy Western The Outlaw (1943) drew attention to Russell's prodigious bosoms, for which the genius Hughes allegedly designed a cantilevered brassiere. Russell's presence as Billy the Kid's squeeze is beardlike, since The Outlaw is one of the more homoerotic Hollywood movies and the Kid's real relationships are with male mentors. Even so, her smoldering, voluptuous looks led to her becoming a pinup for U.S. forces during World War II.

Russell's chief asset as a performer was her ironic sense of humor, much better served in comedy: as the heroic cowgirl who shores up coward Bob Hope's legend in The Paleface (1948) and Son of Paleface (1952), and as the brunette who gives the lie to the title in Gentlemen Prefer Blondes (1953). Otherwise, she was feisty out West in Montana Belle (1952), engaged her singing talents in film noirs such as His Kind of Woman (1951), and sported brief outfits in Hot Blood (1956). After The Revolt of Mamie Stover (1956) and The Fuzzy Pink Nightgown (1957), she more or less retired, returning only for a few cameo roles, such as in Darker Than Amber (1970). Unable to have children, Russell adopted three with her first husband, high school sweetheart Bob Waterfield. An active campaigner, in 1955 she founded the World Adoption International Fund, which has since placed more than 38,000 children with adoptive families. It pioneered adoptions from foreign countries by U.S. citizens. **KN**

> "The girl with the summer-hot lips . . . and the winter-cold heart."

FERNANDO FERNÁN GÓMEZ

Born: Fernando Fernández Gómez, August 28, 1921 (Lima, Peru).

Star qualities: Titan of Spanish cinema; craggy face; bulbous nose; comic timing; stagecraft; a mature performer able to play a wide range of roles; tour-de-force director and writer of comedies, poetry, and novels.

Although Fernando Fernández Gómez was born to theater actress Carola Fernán Gómez when she was on tour in Lima, Peru, in 1921, he was nationalized in Argentina and has since considered himself an Argentine citizen. Gómez is one of the giants of Spanish cinema and theater. Even in his young days his craggy face and bulbous nose were distinctive features, while a grounded sense of maturity and assuredness informed his performances. He moved to Spain in 1924 and first studied law before heading for a life in the theater and adopting his mother's surname as a stage name. Ever since he appeared in *Cristina Guzmán* (1943), he has starred in more than 200 movies, including comedies and dramas such as Carlos Saura's *Ana y los lobos* (1973) (*Anna and the Wolves*) and Víctor Erice's *El espíritu de la colmena* (1973) (*The Spirit of the Beehive*).

Gómez made his directorial debut with *Manicomio* (1954) (*Asylum*) and went on to direct 29 more films, frequently scripting them as well. In 1987 he accomplished an unheard-of feat by winning Spain's version of the Academy Award, the Goya, for Best Director and Best Screenplay for *El viaje a ninguna parte* (1986) (*Voyage to Nowhere*), which also won the Best Picture award, and for Best Actor for *Mambrú se fue a la guerra* (1986) (*Mambru Went to War*). Aside from his work in cinema, Gómez has been a playwright and director of plays, and has written poetry, novels, and memoirs that have met with as much success as his movies. In 1959 he scandalized Roman Catholic Spain when he divorced his wife, singer María Dolores Pradera, with whom he has a daughter. His romantic partner since 2000 has been Emma Cohen, an actress and author who gained fame in Spanish horror movies in the 1970s. **ML**

Top Takes...

Mia Sarah 2006
Para que no me olvides 2005
La Lengua de las mariposas 1999
(*Butterfly Tongues*)
Todo sobre mi madre 1999
(*All About My Mother*)
Así en el cielo como en la tierra 1995
(*On Earth as It Is in Heaven*)
Belle epoque 1992 (*The Age of Beauty*)
Mambrú se fue a la guerra 1986
(*Mambru Went to War*)
El amor del capitán Brando 1974
(*The Love of Captain Brando*)
Ana y los lobos 1973 (*Anna and the Wolves*)
El espíritu de la colmena 1973
(*The Spirit of the Beehive*)
Cristina Guzmán 1943

> "If they say about me that I'm impertinent and bad-mannered, well . . . it's true."

DEBORAH KERR

Born: Deborah Kerr-Trimmer, September 30, 1921 (Helensburgh, Scotland).

Star qualities: Tall, elegant beauty with a refined accent, ladylike manner, and poise; disciplined; stagecraft; played the prim-and-proper girl followed by serious dramatic lead roles.

Top Takes...

Deborah Kerr was the daughter of a soldier, Captain Arthur Kerr-Trimmer. She enjoyed acting from a young age, but trained first in ballet. Soon realizing that she was too tall to be a professional ballerina, Kerr made her stage debut in her teens. Her first appearance on London's West End stage was as Ellie Dunn in *Heartbreak House* in 1943. During World War II she performed in France, Belgium, and Holland with the British army's entertainment service, the Entertainments National Service Association (dubbed "Every Night Something Awful").

She made her screen debut in Michael Powell's *Contraband* (1940). After supporting roles in *Major Barbara* (1941) and *Love on the Dole* (1941), she reunited with Powell to play three incarnations of the love interest in *The Life and Death of Colonel Blimp* (1943). Ravishing in Technicolor, she worked surprisingly little in the next few years: as the spirited Irish girl who offers to fight the English for Hitler in *I See a Dark Stranger* (1946), and as the lead nun in Powell's *Black Narcissus* (1947).

In Hollywood, Kerr became a prim presence in such movies as *King Solomon's Mines* (1950) and *Julius Caesar* (1953). Tiring of propriety, she went blonde and tramplike in the adulterous surf clinch with Burt Lancaster in *From Here to Eternity* (1953). A run of significant leads followed in *The King and I* (1956), *Tea and Sympathy* (1956), and *The Night of the Iguana* (1964). After a funny Scots cameo in *Casino Royale* (1967) and performances in such late 1960s oddities as *Eye of the Devil* (1967), she retired, returning only briefly for a few movies including *The Assam Garden* (1985). Kerr received an Academy Award in 1993 for Lifetime Achievement. She is the only actress to have had six nominations for Best Actress, and not to have won an Oscar. **KN**

> "I am . . . like a beautiful Jersey cow; I have the same pathetic droop to the corners of my eyes."

YVES MONTAND

Born: Ivo Livi, October 13, 1921 (Pistoia, Tuscany, Italy); died 1991 (Oise, Picardie, France).

Star qualities: Tall; dark, Latin good looks; singer; nightclub performer; ladies' man who had many celebrity lovers, including Édith Piaf and Marilyn Monroe; charming; charismatic; suave; stylish; character actor.

"A handsome electrician sent out by the management to apologize for the absence of the star" was how English theater critic Kenneth Tynan described Yves Montand. This is quite apt considering Montand's breakthrough role was a disillusioned driver of a nitroglycerine truck in the French thriller *Le Salaire de la peur* (1953) (*Wages of Fear*). His career later led to a variety of roles, yet his character tended to side with the common man, often taking a political stance. This is evident in such movies as *Z* (1969) and *I . . . comme Icare* (1979) (*I as in Icarus*), in which he played respectively an assassinated politician and a rogue investigator from a Warren Commission-like entity.

Montand was born in Italy. His peasant family immigrated to France soon after his birth, and he was raised in Marseilles. He started out in showbiz as a music hall singer and, in 1944, was discovered by Édith Piaf in Paris. The *chanteuse* made him part of her act and the pair became lovers.

An early role in the film *Les Sorcières de Salem* (1957) (*The Crucible*), based on Arthur Miller's Pulitzer Prize-winning play comparing McCarthyism to the Salem witch trials, led to Montand's being cast opposite Marilyn Monroe in *Let's Make Love* (1960). Relationships with both Monroe and Hollywood were short lived, however. Back in France, Montand declined from Jean-Pierre Melville's *Le cercle rouge* (1970) (*The Red Circle*) to more common crime thrillers before being internationally rediscovered in one of his last roles, as the embittered wine farmer in Claude Berri's twin movies, *Jean de Florette* (1986) and *Manon des sources* (1986) (*Manon of the Spring*). He was married twice, first to the French actress Simone Signoret, until her death in 1985, and second to his then-assistant, Carole Amiel. **LL**

Top Takes...

IP5: L'île aux pachydermes 1992
  (IP5: The Island of Pachyderms)
Manon des sources 1986 (Manon of the Spring)
Jean de Florette 1986
I . . . comme Icare 1979 (I as in Icarus)
Tout va bien 1972 (All's Well)
Le cercle rouge 1970 (The Red Circle)
L'aveu 1970 (The Confession)
Z 1969
Grand Prix 1966
La guerre est finie 1966 (The War Is Over)
My Geisha 1962
Goodbye Again 1961
Let's Make Love 1960
Les Sorcières de Salem 1957 (The Crucible)
Le Salaire de la peur 1953 (The Wages of Fear)

"I think a man can have two, maybe three affairs . . . . But three is the absolute maximum."

CHARLES BRONSON

Born: Charles Dennis Buchinsky, November 3, 1921 (Ehrenfeld, Pennsylvania, U.S.); died 2003 (Los Angeles, California, U.S.).

Star qualities: Rugged macho looks; weather-beaten face; sinewy physique; played the hard-man hero and villain in Westerns, action films, and crime dramas

Top Takes...

Death Wish V: The Face of Death 1994
Death Wish 4: The Crackdown 1987
Death Wish 3 1985
Death Wish II 1982
Breakheart Pass 1975
Death Wish 1974
Città violenta 1970 (*The Family*)
Le passager de la pluie 1969 (*Rider on the Rain*)
C'era una volta il West 1968
  (*Once Upon a Time in the West*)
The Dirty Dozen 1967
The Great Escape 1963
The Magnificent Seven 1960
Machine-Gun Kelly 1958
House of Wax 1953
You're in the Navy Now 1951

Charles Bronson was one of 14 children born to Polish immigrants. He worked as a coal miner and served in World War II before becoming an actor. Rugged, sinewy, and short, with a face he described as: "Like a rock quarry that someone has dynamited," Bronson seemed destined to be stuck in secondary movie roles and guest spots on U.S. TV shows. Even after he earned notice with two popular films for John Sturges, *The Magnificent Seven* (1960) and *The Great Escape* (1963), and after being one of *The Dirty Dozen* (1967), Bronson was still not a big-name star until he accepted Sergio Leone's request to play the heroic lead in *C'era una volta il West* (1968) (*Once Upon a Time in the West*). He had previously declined to star in the director's *Per un pugno di dollari* (1964) (*A Fistful of Dollars*), a role that then went to Clint Eastwood.

The success of his movies with Leone meant Bronson became a celebrated actor in Europe, and he continued to build on his reputation on that continent with such action films as *Le passager de la pluie* (1969) (*Rider on the Rain*) and *Città violenta* (1970) (*The Family*). Soon U.S. studios were ready to use him as the tough lead in their crime B movies. The brutal *Death Wish* (1974) startled the liberal consciousness of a nation and made Bronson an institution, besides initiating a subgenre of violent vigilante movies. Four more *Death Wish* films followed from 1982 to 1994, with Bronson reprising his role as the one-man killing squad, Paul Kersey. Offscreen, Bronson was married three times, and his second wife, actress Jill Ireland, starred with him in many of his later films, including the Western *Breakheart Pass* (1975). The man with the dynamited, rock quarry face died in 2003 after suffering from Alzheimer's disease. **ML**

> "Acting is the easiest thing I've done, I guess that's why I'm stuck with it."

CHRISTOPHER LEE

Born: Christopher Frank Carandini Lee, May 22, 1922 (Belgravia, London, England).

Star qualities: Tallest ever lead actor; iconic as Count Dracula and master monster of horror genre; intimidating screen presence; versatile character actor specializing in villains; producer; classically trained singer.

At six feet five inches tall, British actor Christopher Lee was told early in his acting career that he could never achieve success because of his height. This seemed to be his fate until he was selected by Hammer Film Productions to play the Frankenstein monster in *The Curse of Frankenstein* (1957). This, in turn, led Lee to portray the titular role in Hammer's *Dracula* (1958), a role that would gain him worldwide fame. He appeared again as the Prince of Darkness in six Hammer sequels, and in Harry Alan Towers's production of *Nachts, wenn Dracula erwacht* (1970) (*Count Dracula*). He continued in this vein and became a familiar presence in horror movies and gruesome mysteries, many of which were shot in Europe.

In the 1970s, Lee made a decisive attempt to break away from the stereotypical blood-thirsty roles that had made his fame. In such films as the Western *Hannie Caulder* (1971), the James Bond entry *The Man with the Golden Gun* (1974), and Richard Lester's *The Three Musketeers* (1973) and its sequel, *The Four Musketeers* (1974), Lee solidified his reputation as a versatile character actor. It was during this time that he appeared in the cult sensation *The Wicker Man* (1973) as the poetic pagan, Lord Summerisle. He is a prolific and hardworking actor who has appeared in more than 200 movies; his greatest performance thus far is undoubtedly his portrayal of the founder of Pakistan, in the biopic *Jinnah* (1998), a film that has struggled to be seen in major markets worldwide. In recent years, he has maintained his position in the forefront of mainstream cinema by appearing in both the *Star Wars* series and the *Lord of the Rings* trilogy. Lee is something of an expert on J. R. R. Tolkien, and was the only member of the cast and crew to have met the author in person. **ML**

Top Takes…

Charlie and the Chocolate Factory 2005
Star Wars: Episode III—Revenge of the Sith 2005
The Lord of the Rings: The Return of the King 2003
The Lord of the Rings: The Two Towers 2002
Star Wars: Episode II—Attack of the Clones 2002
The Lord of the Rings: The Fellowship of the Ring 2001
Jinnah 1998
The Man with the Golden Gun 1974
The Wicker Man 1973
The Three Musketeers 1973
Nachts, wenn Dracula erwacht 1970 (*Count Dracula*)
The Hound of the Baskervilles 1959
Dracula 1958
The Curse of Frankenstein 1957

"In Britain, any degree of success is met with envy and resentment."

1920s

JUDY GARLAND

Born: Frances Ethel Gumm, June 10, 1922 (Grand Rapids, Minnesota, U.S.); died 1969 (Chelsea, London, England).

Star qualities: Good-girl image; an engaging performer with a soulful voice that resonates worldwide; "Miss Showbusiness" (her nickname) to the core.

Top Takes...

I Could Go on Singing 1963
Judgment at Nuremberg 1961 ☆
A Star Is Born 1954 ☆
Summer Stock 1950
In the Good Old Summertime 1949
Easter Parade 1948
The Pirate 1948
Ziegfeld Follies 1946
The Clock 1945
Meet Me in St. Louis 1944
Girl Crazy 1943
Presenting Lily Mars 1943
For Me and My Gal 1942
Babes on Broadway 1941
Life Begins for Andy Hardy 1941
Ziegfeld Girl 1941
Little Nellie Kelly 1940
Andy Hardy Meets Debutante 1940
Babes in Arms 1939
The Wizard of Oz 1939
Listen, Darling 1938
Love Finds Andy Hardy 1938
Thoroughbreds Don't Cry 1937
Broadway Melody of 1938 1937
Pigskin Parade 1936

RIGHT: Garland was nominated for an Oscar for her performance in *A Star Is Born*.

She was born for Hollywood and Hollywood killed her. Her fame came suddenly, at the age of seventeen, and by forty-seven it had become such a burden that it led her to take her own life through a drug overdose. And Hollywood was implicated in what happened, for better and for worse.

Judy Garland signed a contract with MGM when she was only thirteen years old. Her first appearance of note came when she started singing, first to "Dear Mr. Gable" (*Broadway Melody of 1938*, 1937), and subsequently as the innocent Dorothy in *The Wizard of Oz* (1939), in which she immortalized "Over the Rainbow." A star from then on, she excelled in the musical genre at a time when the world needed music more than ever. MGM showcased her petite demeanor and tender yet far-reaching voice and let her shine in the sophisticated *For Me and My Gal* (1942) and *Girl Crazy* (1943). Her performance in *Meet Me in St. Louis* (1944) is one of the best acting and singing achievements the world has ever seen; her renditions of "The Trolley Song" and "Have Yourself a Merry Little Christmas" are full of life and heartfelt emotion, sunlight and comfort, sung straight into the hearts of millions of war-weary viewers.

MGM's strong control over Garland's strict schedule led to physical and emotional fatigue and a gradual dependence on drugs. She married director Vincente Minnelli, with whom she made several more movies (*The Clock*, 1945; *Ziegfeld Follies*, 1946). It wasn't until after the couple divorced, and MGM had terminated her contract, that she was able to play "fuller" parts, and *A Star Is Born* (1954)—her attempt at a comeback after four years without a movie—demonstrates that she can carry a film dramatically, as well as dance and sing in it.

A Star Is Born was also dangerously close to Garland's own life, referencing alcohol addiction and studio manipulation. Whereas the movie is now a cult success, it was deemed a failure at the time and Garland never recovered. Although she kept acting, only her last picture, *I Could Go on Singing* (1963), is memorable. In it she proves once more that her singing voice is a true life force, though sadly not for herself. **EM**

ABOVE: Garland in her iconic role as Dorothy Gale in *The Wizard of Oz*.

Image Is Everything

Garland, the ultimate girl next door, was neither sexy nor elegant in Hollywood terms. She constantly fretted about her appearance, and in later years underwent several transformations to make herself more glamorous. Along with other child stars, she was given drugs by the studio so that they could maintain a frantic filming schedule. Her weight fluctuated and her health suffered as a result. At age nineteen, Garland was even forced to have an abortion in order to preserve her squeaky-clean image. In her own words, "Hollywood is a strange place if you're in trouble. Everybody thinks it's contagious."

1920s

DOROTHY DANDRIDGE

Born: Dorothy Jean Dandridge, November 9, 1922 (Cleveland, Ohio, U.S.); died 1965 (West Hollywood, California, U.S.).

Star qualities: "Dottie"; first African-American screen goddess; fragile beauty; magical nightclub diva; trailblazing character actress of dramas and musicals.

Top Takes…

Dorothy Dandridge began performing at four years old, a singer and dancer in the age of segregation whose drive and ambition led her to push at the artificial boundaries placed around her. She, her sister Vivian, and a friend, Etta Jones, formed the Dandridge Sisters. The trio appeared in the Marx Brothers's *A Day at the Races* (1937). The girls later performed at New York's famous Cotton Club, often on the same bill as Cab Calloway and Bill "Bojangles" Robinson. But Dandridge's subsequent movie work was strictly minor, and mostly under the umbrella of African-American targeted "race films." Yet those race films led to the title role in Otto Preminger's retelling of the *Carmen* opera with an African-American cast, *Carmen Jones* (1954). It was a historic performance that earned Dandridge an Oscar nomination for Best Actress, the first ever for an African-American actress. She also became the first African-American to appear on the cover of *Life* magazine.

Yet despite such a major breakthrough and strong performances in *Island in the Sun* (1957) and *Porgy and Bess* (1959), major roles were not forthcoming for Dandridge. She suffered abuse at the hands of her second husband and had some unhappy relationships with various suitors, and was found dead at the age of forty-two of an antidepressant overdose. Whether the overdose was accidental or intentional remains a mystery. Dandridge has since been a source of inspiration for countless African-American actors. Indeed, shortly after playing the actress in the TV biopic *Introducing Dorothy Dandridge* (1999), Halle Berry won a Best Actress Oscar for her performance in *Monster's Ball* (2001), the first African-American woman to do so. Dandridge was the first person Berry thanked as she accepted the award. **JK**

"Dottie came through the back door so I could go through the front."—Halle Berry

KIM HUNTER

Born: Janet Cole, November 12, 1922 (Detroit, Michigan, U.S.); died 2002 (New York City, New York, U.S.).

Star qualities: Petite; memorable, caring ape woman; versatile leading lady; witty, charming, and intelligent; political liberal; stagecraft; producer and writer.

After training at the prestigious Actors Studio, Kim Hunter started out on the stage at the age of seventeen with a small theater company in Miami. She made her screen debut four years later for producer Val Lewton (who helped invent her stage name) and director Mark Robson as the orphan heroine of the remarkable horror movie *The Seventh Victim* (1943). She had a scattering of good roles, such as in the unusual B thriller *When Strangers Marry* (1944) and as the girl next door in the Technicolor *A Matter of Life and Death* (1946).

Her work in *Tender Comrade* (1943), about a group of women living together during World War II, was cited by staunchly Republican costar Ginger Rogers as red propaganda. Writer Dalton Trumbo and director Edward Dmytryk were blacklisted as two of "The Hollywood Ten." By implication, Hunter was also blacklisted and driven to work in the theater and TV. But in 1956 she courageously took a role in *Storm Center*, the only U.S. film of the 1950s to be openly critical of the anticommunist witch hunt.

Despite being in official disfavor, Hunter recreated her 1947 Broadway stage success as Marlon Brando's wife, Stella Kowalski, in *A Streetcar Named Desire* (1951), for which she won an Academy Award for Best Supporting Actress. She appeared under makeup as the chimpanzee scientist Dr. Zira in *Planet of the Apes* (1968) and its first sequels, and was especially affecting in *Escape from the Planet of the Apes* (1971). Always busier on TV than in movies, she has good showings in *The Swimmer* (1968) and Dario Argento's *Due occhi diabolici* (1990) (*Two Evil Eyes*) segment of *The Black Cat*. She spent six years on the council of the Actor's Equity Association and was active in the Screen Actors Guild. **KN**

Top Takes...

The Hiding Place 2000
A Price Above Rubies 1998
Midnight in the Garden of Good and Evil 1997
Due occhi diabolici 1990 (*Two Evil Eyes*)
Escape from the Planet of the Apes 1971
Beneath the Planet of the Apes 1970
The Swimmer 1968
Planet of the Apes 1968
The Young Stranger 1957
Anything Can Happen 1952
A Streetcar Named Desire 1951 ★
A Matter of Life and Death 1946
When Strangers Marry 1944
A Canterbury Tale 1944
Tender Comrade 1943
The Seventh Victim 1943

"Don't you think your superior attitude is a little out of place?"

—Stella Kowalski, *A Streetcar Named Desire*

1920s

GÉRARD PHILIPE

Born: Gérard Philip, December 4, 1922 (Cannes, Alpes-Maritimes, France); died 1959 (Paris, France).

Star qualities: Legendary actor of French cinema and stage; handsome; sexy; suave; leading man across a range of genres; director.

Top Takes...

La fièvre monte à El Pao 1959
    (*Fever Rises in El Pao*)
Le joueur 1958 (*The Gambler*)
La vie à deux 1958 (*Life as a Couple*)
Montparnasse 19 1958
    (*Modigliani of Montparnasse*)
Pot-Bouille 1957 (*Lovers of Paris*)
Le rouge et le noir 1954 (*Rouge et noir*)
Si Versailles m'était conté 1954
    (*Royal Affairs in Versailles*)
Fanfan la tulipe 1952 (*Fan-Fan the Tulip*)
La ronde 1950 (*Roundabout*)
La beauté du diable 1950 (*Beauty and the Devil*)
Le diable au corps 1947 (*Devil in the Flesh*)
L'idiot 1946 (*The Idiot*)
Le pays sans étoiles 1946 (*Land Without Stars*)
Les petites du quai aux fleurs 1944

"Philipe is not only brilliant as a performer but has a hauntingly tragic face."—*New York Times*

RIGHT: Philipe looks dashing yet thoughtful in this publicity photograph from 1946.

Gérard Philipe studied acting at Paris's Conservatoire National Supérieur d'Art Dramatique. After graduation he took to the stage, and soon he became a member of the Théâtre National Populaire. He made his movie debut with a bit part in *Les petites du quai aux fleurs* (1944), and continued to work in films and onstage. Postwar France opened up greater opportunities for a young actor, and it was his role as the teenager François Jaubert in *Le diable au corps* (1947) (*Devil in the Flesh*) that shot him to fame, partly because of his good looks and performance, but also because the film itself achieved some notoriety in its depiction of an adulterous affair.

Philipe had caught the attention of audiences and directors alike, and he went on to appear in such movies as René Clair's *La beauté du diable* (1950) (*Beauty and the Devil*) as both Mephistopheles and a young Henri Faust, and as The Count in Max Ophüls's *La ronde* (1950) (*Roundabout*).

In 1951 Philipe married actress and writer Nicole Fourcade, and with his talent being acknowledged and his popularity as a screen idol increasing, his future looked bright. He had fun with a less serious role as the lead in the swashbuckling romantic comedy *Fanfan la tulipe* (1952) (*Fan-Fan the Tulip*), which saw him as a peasant soldier who manages to get the girl. Philipe also notably headed up Luis Buñuel's *La fièvre monte à El Pao* (1959) (*Fever Rises in El Pao*). He continued to work on the stage for the Théâtre National Populaire, and from 1950 to 1959 he played an impressive 605 times on its stages, including such significant parts as Don Rodrigue in Pierre Corneille's *Le cid* (1951). Sadly, Philipe's stardom was cut tragically short at the age of thirty-six, when he died soon after being diagnosed with liver cancer. **CK**

AVA GARDNER

Born: Ava Lavinia Gardner, December 24, 1922 (Brogden, North Carolina, U.S.); died 1990 (Westminster, London, England).

Star qualities: Legendary sultry beauty; screen goddess; the face of an angel; curvaceous; glamorous; famous husbands; often played the femme fatale.

Top Takes...

Regina Roma 1982
The Sentinel 1977
The Cassandra Crossing 1976
Earthquake 1974
Tam Lin 1970 (The Devil's Widow)
The Night of the Iguana 1964
Seven Days in May 1964
55 Days at Peking 1963
On the Beach 1959
The Sun Also Rises 1957
The Barefoot Contessa 1954
Mogambo 1953 ☆
Show Boat 1951
Pandora and the Flying Dutchman 1951
One Touch of Venus 1948
The Killers 1946

Ava Gardner was one of Hollywood's most beautiful female stars. She was married and divorced three times, and to three of Hollywood's top stars: Mickey Rooney, Artie Shaw, and Frank Sinatra. The seventh and youngest child of poor tobacco farmers, Gardner was invited for an interview at MGM on the grounds of her astonishing good looks. She moved to Hollywood in 1941, where, after five years busy in B parts, in everything from unbilled bits to romantic leads in East Side Kids movies, she was perfect as Kitty Collins, the film noir temptress of *The Killers* (1946), leaving Burt Lancaster such a shell that he doesn't resist being assassinated. Sadly, she didn't immediately get much interesting work; she was cast for her looks as a goddess in *One Touch of Venus* (1948) and dubbed among the chocolate box surroundings of *Show Boat* (1951). In *Pandora and the Flying Dutchman* (1951), she has her most rounded role, as a conflicted temptress who drives men to ruin but also yearns to join James Mason in the afterlife.

Gardner shimmers in *The Barefoot Contessa* (1954) as a star modeled on Rita Hayworth but channeling her own personal and career demons. She moved to Spain in 1955 following her divorce from Sinatra, and many of her subsequent movies were made abroad. Her perspiring, fraying glamour fits well into the all-star worlds of *The Sun Also Rises* (1957), *On the Beach* (1959), and *The Night of the Iguana* (1964). Wonderfully witchlike in the little-seen *Tam Lin* (1970) (*The Devil's Widow*), she also gamely shows up in *Earthquake* (1974) and *The Cassandra Crossing* (1976). In 1968 Gardner moved to London and spent her final years almost as a recluse. She suffered a stroke in 1989 that left her bedridden, and her third husband Sinatra paid all her medical expenses. **KN**

"What I'd really like to say about stardom is that it gave me everything I never wanted."

GLORIA GRAHAME

Born: Gloria Hallward, November 28, 1923 (Los Angeles, California, U.S.); died 1981 (New York City, New York, U.S.).

Star qualities: Sexy blonde bombshell; husky voice; voluptuous seductress; stagecraft; played lead bad-girl roles; mature, serious character actress.

Gloria Grahame's father was an architect and her mother an actress and drama teacher. She decided at a young age to follow her mother onto the stage and quit high school to head for Broadway. There, she was spotted performing in 1944 by Louis B. Mayer, who offered her a contract with MGM. The contract was short lived—Grahame did not really fit the rigid star profile demanded by MGM—and she moved across to RKO Pictures in 1947, where she had a brief career as a seductive star in a series of film noirs and melodramas. She made her mark opposite Humphrey Bogart in *In a Lonely Place* (1950), having married its director, Nicholas Ray, two years earlier. She was flirtatious as the wife of writer Dick Powell in *The Bad and the Beautiful* (1952), for which she won an Academy Award for Best Supporting Actress. In Fritz Lang's *The Big Heat* (1953), her husky voice and pouting lips make her perfect casting as a gangster's moll, and she appeared again for Lang as an errant wife caught up in murder in *Human Desire* (1954).

Grahame rarely played a good woman. In *The Cobweb* (1955) she is manipulative and disloyal to her hard-working husband, Richard Widmark. In *Not as a Stranger* (1955) she breaks up Robert Mitchum's marriage. Yet in the musical *Oklahoma!* (1955), as the girl "who can't say no," her waywardness is in a more lighthearted mode. Grahame was tone deaf, and her singing part in the musical apparently had to be pieced together note by note from recordings. After that the good parts seemed to dry up, and she worked in TV for several years. In the 1970s she made some low-budget horror movies such as *Blood and Lace* (1971). She was married four times; her fourth marriage was in 1960 to Anthony Ray, the son of her second husband, Nicholas Ray. **EB**

Top Takes...

The Nesting 1981
Melvin and Howard 1980
The Todd Killings 1971
Blood and Lace 1971
Ride Beyond Vengeance 1966
Odds Against Tomorrow 1959
Oklahoma! 1955
Not as a Stranger 1955
The Cobweb 1955
Human Desire 1954
The Big Heat 1953
The Bad and the Beautiful 1952 ★
The Greatest Show on Earth 1952
In a Lonely Place 1950
Crossfire 1947 ☆
It's a Wonderful Life 1946

"It wasn't the way I looked at a man, it was the thought behind it."

SABU

Born: Selar Shaik Sabu, January 27, 1924 (Karapur, Mysore, India); died 1963 (Chatsworth, California, U.S.).

Star qualities: The first Indian actor to make it big in Hollywood; played stereotypical Indian roles; athletic; charming; youthful good looks.

Top Takes...

Sabu was an eleven-year-old stable boy working for the maharajah of Mysore when documentary filmmaker Robert Flaherty chose him to star in *Elephant Boy* (1937), an adaptation of Rudyard Kipling's *Toomai of the Elephants*. It elevated the Indian youth to the position of English-language movie star. In Britain, producer Zoltan Korda cast him as Prince Azim in *The Drum* (1938), and then made him the lead in *The Thief of Bagdad* (1940). When that production shifted to Hollywood, Sabu went along and found himself as Mowgli in Korda's *Jungle Book* (1942). He was signed by Universal Studios and went on to costar in Maria Montez melodramas such as *Arabian Nights* (1942), *White Savage* (1943), and *Cobra Woman* (1944). In January 1944 Sabu became a U.S. citizen. Not long after, he joined the U.S. Army Air Corps, and went on to serve as a tail gunner for the remainder of World War II, flying more than 40 missions in the Pacific and winning the Distinguished Flying Cross, among other decorations.

Sabu's British-based films notably gave him more interesting characters than his U.S. quickies, which just made him a stock ethnic exotic. As a young man, he reunited with *Thief* codirector Michael Powell to play The Young General, drenched in the eponymous scent in *Black Narcissus* (1947). Sadly, after this charming and almost sinister role, it was back to regulation adventure (often playing a character called Sabu) in *Man-Eater of Kumaon* (1948), *Song of India* (1949), *Baghdad* (1952), *Jungle Hell* (1956), *The Black Panther* (1956), and *Sabu and the Magic Ring* (1957). Excluding Anglo-Indians Merle Oberon and Boris Karloff, Sabu was the first Indian to become an international movie star. He died from a heart attack at the age of thirty-nine. **KN**

"I am Abu the thief. Son of Abu the thief. Grandson of Abu the thief."—Abu, *The Thief of Bagdad*

LEE MARVIN

Born: Lee Marvin, February 19, 1924 (New York City, New York, U.S.); died 1987 (Tucson, Arizona, U.S.).

Star qualities: U.S. icon of cinematic masculinity; tall; white hair; grizzled looks; growling voice; lead man of action movies; stagecraft; singer; producer.

Not to imply that he wasn't appreciated during his life—he did win a Best Actor Oscar for his role in the comic Western *Cat Ballou* (1965)—but since his death, the Lee Marvin cult has been building with every successive year.

Marvin is that rare actor capable of conveying more with a simple facial expression or physical gesture than another actor could achieve with pages of dialogue. Like the other great U.S. icons of cinematic masculinity, Clint Eastwood and Robert Mitchum, among others, Marvin is a tough guy with depth and complexity of character. After receiving a Purple Heart medal in World War II, Marvin took up theater acting almost for fun, eventually going to Hollywood in 1950. He spent much of the following decade playing menacing heavies and lumbering villains in B movies and noir thrillers, such as the excellent *The Big Heat* (1953) and *Bad Day at Black Rock* (1955). Still, his best film work lay ahead when directors felt comfortable casting him as a leading man. Marvin sustained himself throughout the 1950s and much of the 1960s in episodic TV.

Don Siegel's *The Killers* (1964) was originally intended for TV but was deemed too violent at the time and released theatrically instead. It inaugurated a six-year period that is the highlight of Marvin's career. After winning his Oscar, Marvin went on to deliver a series of exceptional performances: *The Professionals* (1966), *The Dirty Dozen* (1967), and—the best work of his career—John Boorman's inventive thriller *Point Blank* (1967). In the 1970s Marvin's work became more uneven, and he made only a few good movies, such as *Prime Cut* (1972). With the perspective of time, however, it is possible to see just how much he is missed: there is not a contemporary male actor who comes anywhere close. **TC**

Top Takes...

The Delta Force 1986
The Big Red One 1980
Shout at the Devil 1976
The Iceman Cometh 1973
Prime Cut 1972
Point Blank 1967
The Dirty Dozen 1967
The Professionals 1966
Cat Ballou 1965 ★
The Killers 1964
The Man Who Shot Liberty Valance 1962
Bad Day at Black Rock 1955
The Caine Mutiny 1954
The Wild One 1953
The Big Heat 1953
You're in the Navy Now 1951

1920s

"If I have any appeal at all, it's to the fellow who takes out the garbage."

MARLON BRANDO

Born: Marlon Brando Jr., April 3, 1924 (Omaha, Nebraska, U.S.); died 2004 (Los Angeles, California, U.S.).

Star qualities: The yardstick against which all U.S. actors are measured; cultural icon with magnetic presence; intelligent and versatile performer; pure genius.

Top Takes...

The Island of Dr. Moreau 1996

Christopher Columbus: The Discovery 1992

The Freshman 1990

A Dry White Season 1989 ☆

Apocalypse Now 1979

Superman 1978

The Missouri Breaks 1976

Ultimo tango a Parigi 1972 ☆
(Last Tango in Paris)

The Godfather 1972 ★

Reflections in a Golden Eye 1967

The Appaloosa 1966

The Chase 1966

The Ugly American 1963

Mutiny on the Bounty 1962

One-Eyed Jacks 1961

The Fugitive Kind 1959

Sayonara 1957 ☆

Guys and Dolls 1955

On the Waterfront 1954 ★

The Wild One 1953

Julius Caesar 1953 ☆

Viva Zapata! 1952 ☆

A Streetcar Named Desire 1951

The Men 1950

RIGHT: Brando won his first Oscar for his performance in *On the Waterfront*.

Dying as one of the world's truly fat men and more prominent eccentrics, Marlon Brando's behavior in later life nearly overshadowed his earlier standard for postwar actors; a standard against which he often came up wanting. But during his glory period, from 1950 to 1972, he did manage to stamp himself the greatest screen actor of all time.

Born in Omaha, Nebraska, Brando had two sisters and alcoholic parents. His father was frequently absent and his mother, who was artistically inclined, was often broken down drunk. In 1943, after being expelled from high school and failing to join the army because of a damaged knee, he moved to New York with his sisters, partly to strike out on his own and partly to show up his father's low expectations for his future.

Enrolling in drama workshops at the New School, he was mentored by Stella Adler, who was then applying Stanislavsky technique and emphasizing an actor's ability to draw on important emotional experiences to imbue performances with authenticity. Undertaking the "Method," perhaps not as his true style but as a guiding influence, Brando made his

1920s

ABOVE: Brando revived his film career as the iconic Don Corleone in *The Godfather*.

Broadway debut in 1944 in *I Remember Mama*; terrific reviews brought him Hollywood invitations, which he declined due to the limitations of long-term contracts.

After six years, though, he relented and made his feature debut in *The Men* (1950), a story about paraplegic soldiers. Thereafter he forsook the stage for the screen and offered some of the most remarkable, galvanizing, and difficult performances any actor had yet presented to audiences. Titles in the early 1950s alone include *A Streetcar Named Desire* (1951); his first Oscar nomination, *Viva Zapata!* (1952); *Julius Caesar* (1953); *The Wild One* (1953); and *On the Waterfront* (1954), his first Oscar for Best Actor. From 1955 to 1962, Brando was box-office gold. Importantly, he was also among the best-paid actors in the industry, setting new records for a single-

"An actor's a guy who, if you ain't talking about him, ain't listening."

The Myth of Brando

Marlon Brando is widely recognized to be one of the greatest screen actors who has ever lived. By the age of thirty his style had revolutionized American acting. Many of his iconic characters—Stanley Kowalski and Don Corleone, among others—achieved this status as a result of Brando's improvisation on set. He was the role model for the likes of James Dean, Paul Newman, and Robert Redford, and the standard by which all U.S. actors are measured. Here are some of the things that have been said about the great man:

- "He gave us our freedom."—Jack Nicholson on Brando, the "Method," and his astonishing impact on acting styles.

- "He loves the light! See how the light shines through him? . . . I shouldn't be partial, but he is my favorite one."—Playwright Tennessee Williams.

- "I wanted either an Italian-American or an actor who's so great that he can portray an Italian-American. So, they said, 'Who do you suggest?' I said, 'Lookit, I don't know, but who are the two greatest actors in the world? Laurence Olivier and Marlon Brando . . . [And] Brando is my hero of heroes. I'd do anything to just meet him.'"—Francis Ford Coppola on casting the Godfather.

- "He and I had much in common. He too had made many enemies. He too is a perfectionist."—Bette Davis, thrilled that a like-minded being had won an Oscar.

picture salary with a staggering $1.25 million payout for *Mutiny on the Bounty* in 1962. The pressure generated by this high commercial esteem, combined with the license generally granted him as the recognized pioneer of "acting as serious craft," meant that he started behaving erratically. Such behavior led to the breakdown of productions (*One-Eyed Jacks*, 1961), hurt feelings among collaborators, and an overall sense that Brando was wasting himself in the pursuit of varied appetites—food and women foremost among them—and not in the further development of his prodigious talents.

Reviving the Brando "brand"

This critical attitude took firm hold with a batch of commercial flops in the 1960s (*The Ugly American*, 1963; *The Chase*, 1966). Then Brando was reborn in Francis Ford Coppola's adaptation of Mario Puzo's novel *The Godfather* (1972), which made his Don Corleone an instant icon and winner of another Oscar and a Golden Globe. Brando annoyed many of his Hollywood peers by refusing to accept this Academy Award. Even so, 1972 may be best remembered for his most significant performance of all, in *Ultimo tango a Parigi* (*Last Tango in Paris*).

In his final years, he worked sporadically in often laughable, extraordinarily overpaid roles (*Superman*, 1978; *The Formula*, 1980; *Christopher Columbus: The Discovery*, 1992; *The Island of Dr. Moreau*, 1996), alongside a few gems that acknowledged his age and outsider status (*The Missouri Breaks*, 1976; *Apocalypse Now*, 1979; *The Freshman*, 1990), and he even did one star turn in the TV miniseries *Roots* (1979). But the main theme running through his last decade, which included the much-publicized death of his daughter, is waste.

By recognizing the frustrating choices and habits of genius, we also have to acknowledge that Brando's truly earth-shattering influence over the performance arts is real. As standard bearer, he developed space not just for a distinctly American school of acting, but also for a distinctly American kind of manhood, one that combined masculine and feminine traits with class consciousness. **GCQ**

RIGHT: Brando smolders as the rebel-without-a-cause Johnny in *The Wild One*.

DORIS DAY

Born: Doris Mary Ann Von Kappelhoff, April 3, 1924 (Cincinnati, Ohio, U.S.).

Star qualities: Blonde, girl-next-door looks; squeaky-clean virginal image; dubbed "The Tomboy with a Voice" because of her powerful singing voice; leading lady of lighthearted comedies and romances.

Top Takes...

The Ballad of Josie 1967
Send Me No Flowers 1964
Move Over, Darling 1963
That Touch of Mink 1962
Lover Come Back 1961
Please Don't Eat the Daisies 1960
Pillow Talk 1959 ★
The Pajama Game 1957
The Man Who Knew Too Much 1956
Love Me or Leave Me 1955
Calamity Jane 1953
On Moonlight Bay 1951
Storm Warning 1951
Tea for Two 1950
Young Man with a Horn 1950
Romance on the High Seas 1948

The daughter of German immigrants, Doris Day was named "Doris" after silent movie actress Doris Kenyon, whom her mother liked. She started out as a dancer, turning to singing after injuring her leg in an auto accident in 1937. Day sang with the big bands of Barney Rapp and Bob Crosby and charted 12 popular music hits with Les Brown before setting out on her own in the late 1940s. It was Rapp who convinced her that "Kappelhoff" was an awkward name, and suggested "Day," after the song "Day After Day," which was part of her repertoire.

Day was signed to Warner Brothers in 1948 and appeared in musicals such as *Tea for Two* (1950), winning audiences with her girl-next-door looks and powerful voice. One of her early great performances was as a tomboy in love in *Calamity Jane* (1953). She is a prim blonde in Alfred Hitchcock's *The Man Who Knew Too Much* (1956), singing "Whatever Will Be, Will Be" ("Que Será, Será") to save her kidnapped son. The song won an Academy Award, and the tune became her signature piece.

Day was paired with some of Hollywood's biggest male stars, including Cary Grant and Clark Gable. She worked well with Rock Hudson in *Pillow Talk* (1959), a glossy romance, as well as *Lover Come Back* (1961) and *Send Me No Flowers* (1964), but soon the formula wore thin and Day's virginal screen character became a joke. The irony was that her own life was troubled: her first husband was violent and abusive, while her third husband, who was also her agent, was driving Day to do films she didn't want to make. She tried wilder roles, doing comedy thrills in *Caprice* (1967), but disappeared from the big screen, going on to success with TV's *The Doris Day Show* (1968–1973). She is now retired and runs the Doris Day Animal League in Carmel, California. **KN**

"The frightening thing about middle age is the knowledge that you'll grow out of it."

EVA MARIE SAINT

Born: Eve Marie Saint, July 4, 1924 (Newark, New Jersey, U.S.).

Star qualities: "The Helen Hayes of Television"; blonde, beautiful, and graceful; intelligent; stagecraft; successful in emotionally charged, lead heroine roles; Hitchcockian femme fatale; now a mature serious character actress.

After graduating from high school, Eva Marie Saint moved west to study acting at Bowling Green State University in Ohio. In the 1940s she started out doing work in radio and TV before winning the Drama Critics Award for her Broadway stage role in *The Trip to Bountiful* (1953). The next few years also saw her win two Emmy nominations for TV work, earning her the sobriquet "The Helen Hayes of Television." She then won the Best Supporting Actress Oscar (for playing a lead female role) in her screen debut, *On the Waterfront* (1954). A rare, beautiful character actress, Saint—as with many female Academy Award winners—had trouble finding worthy follow-ups to her breakthrough, and got stuck looking pretty next to Bob Hope in *That Certain Feeling* (1956), or frozen with the rest of the cast in *Raintree County* (1957) and *Exodus* (1960).

Saint is good in her *Waterfront* mode, as the addict's wife in *A Hatful of Rain* (1957), and superb as a Hitchcockian blonde, ensnaring Cary Grant on a train in *North By Northwest* (1959). At Alfred Hitchcock's insistence, Saint's waist-length hair was cut short for the role. Though drawn and lovely as Warren Beatty's object of desire in *All Fall Down* (1962), she spent most of the 1960s as a sidelined love interest in movies such as *Grand Prix* (1966), or overshadowed support, as in *The Sandpiper* (1965). She played a tough frontier woman in a good Western, *The Stalking Moon* (1968), and was terrific as George Segal's wife in *Loving* (1970), but found herself back with Bob Hope in *Cancel My Reservation* (1972). As an older actress finding less interesting film roles, she has returned mostly to the stage and TV. She played a mother in Wim Wenders's *Don't Come Knocking* (2005) and adoptive mother Martha Kent in *Superman Returns* (2006). **KN**

Top Takes...

Superman Returns 2006
Don't Come Knocking 2005
I Dreamed of Africa 2000
Time to Say Goodbye? 1997
Nothing in Common 1986
Cancel My Reservation 1972
Loving 1970
The Stalking Moon 1968
Grand Prix 1966
The Sandpiper 1965
All Fall Down 1962
Exodus 1960
North by Northwest 1959
Raintree County 1957
That Certain Feeling 1956
On the Waterfront 1954 ★

1920s

"I thought *North by Northwest* was as sexy as you can get and we had all our clothes on."

LAUREN BACALL

Born: Betty Joan Perske, September 16, 1924 (New York City, New York, U.S.).

Star qualities: Deep, sexy voice; the Humphrey Bogart–Lauren Bacall partnership was a massive box-office draw; powerful screen presence; enjoyed significant success across genres, but perhaps most famously in film noir.

Top Takes...

These Foolish Things 2006
Manderlay 2005
Dogville 2003
Presence of Mind 1999
The Mirror Has Two Faces 1996 ☆
Misery 1990
Mr. North 1988
Appointment with Death 1988
The Fan 1981
The Shootist 1976
Murder on the Orient Express 1974
Harper 1966
North West Frontier 1959
The Gift of Love 1958
Written on the Wind 1956
Blood Alley 1955
The Cobweb 1955
How to Marry a Millionaire 1953
Young Man with a Horn 1950
Key Largo 1948
Dark Passage 1947
The Big Sleep 1946
Confidential Agent 1945
To Have and Have Not 1944

In 1943, a *Harper's Bazaar* cover of Lauren Bacall caught the eye of Nancy, wife of Howard Hawks. The director put Bacall under personal contract and remodeled her, partially in Nancy's image. Publicists sold her as "The Look," stressing her silky hair, large eyes, and generous mouth. Hawks teamed her with Humphrey Bogart in *To Have and Have Not* (1944), a loose adaptation of the Ernest Hemingway novel. As much hardboiled romantic comedy as wartime adventure, Bacall's debut film was an instant classic, and her memorable banter ("You do know how to whistle") became a pop culture fixture. Besides matching Bogart for onscreen insolence, Bacall's character, Marie "Slim" Browning ("Slim" was Nancy's nickname), delivered several Hoagy Carmichael songs in a husky style, for many years mistakenly ascribed to overdubbing by Andy Williams.

Bacall earned the ultimate accolade of a Warner Brothers cartoon appearance, in *Bacall to Arms* (1946). Hawks reteamed Bogart and Bacall in *The Big Sleep* (1946), but then dropped her contract—purportedly because he disapproved of, or felt excluded by, their whirlwind romance and marriage. Bacall was less well served by director Herman Shumlin and costar Charles

RIGHT: Bacall with husband Humphrey Bogart and their pet dog, circa 1945.

Boyer in *Confidential Agent* (1945) and for the rest of the decade she appeared only in Bogart films, *Dark Passage* (1947) and *Key Largo* (1948). In *Young Man with a Horn* (1950), she was well cast as a predatory older woman, but subsequent roles in melodrama (*Written on the Wind*, 1956) or romantic comedy (*How to Marry a Millionaire*, 1953) tended to find her upstaged.

Widowed on Bogart's death in 1957, Bacall worked on Broadway, notably taking the lead in *Applause*, the musical version of *All About Eve* (1950). Cast for iconic noir associations in *Harper* (1966), she returned to the movies in character roles—funny in *Murder on the Orient Express* (1974) and affecting in *The Shootist* (1976). She was well teamed with James Garner in the horror film *The Fan* (1981), in which she caricatures herself as a Broadway diva stalked by a psychopath. Still in demand, she has worked with generations of interesting directors, including Robert Altman and Lars von Trier. **KN**

ABOVE: Bacall starred in her first film, *To Have and Have Not*, at age twenty.

Bacall on Marriage

Although Lauren Bacall was married twice—her first marriage to Humphrey Bogart lasted until his death in 1957—she was mostly cynical about the institution:

- "I never believed marriage was a lasting institution . . . I thought that to be married for five years was to be married forever."

- "I would hate now [2005] to be married. It does occur to me on occasion that, if I fall and hit my head, there will be no one to make the phone call."

- "I put my career in second place throughout both my marriages and it suffered. I don't regret it."

MARCELLO MASTROIANNI

Born: Marcello Vincenzo Domenico Mastrojanni, September 28, 1924 (Fontana Liri, Latium, Italy); died 1996 (Paris, Île-de-France, France).

Star qualities: Italian screen legend; handsome; stylish; powerful screen presence; versatile leading man; known for "Latin lover" roles; prolific output.

Top Takes...

Trois vies & une seule mort 1996
   (*Three Lives and Only One Death*)

Prêt-à-Porter 1994

***Oci ciornie* 1987** ☆
   (***Dark Eyes***)

Ginger e Fred 1986 (*Ginger and Fred*)

***Una giornata particolare* 1977** ☆
   (***A Special Day***)

8 ½ 1963

***Divorzio all'italiana* 1961** ☆
   (***Divorce—Italian Style***)

La notte 1961 (*The Night*)

La dolce vita 1960

I soliti ignoti 1958
   (*Big Deal on Madonna Street*)

Tempi nostri 1954 (*The Anatomy of Love*)

Vita da cani 1950 (*A Dog's Life*)

"In front of a camera, I feel solid, satisfied. Away from it I am empty, confused."

An Italian acting icon best known for his work with director Federico Fellini, Marcello Mastroianni is the rare international star whose reputation and talent transcended language barriers. Born the son of a carpenter, Mastroianni took his first stage roles at his parish church. During World War II, he was briefly interred in a labor camp in Germany by the Nazis before escaping and living as a refugee in Venice until 1945. After the war he went to Rome, where he worked as a clerk with the British film distribution company Eagle Lion (Rank) Films and acted in the evenings with a group of university students. Following his discovery by directing legend Luchino Visconti, Mastroianni made the rounds in Italian film circles before he connected with Fellini for his starring role in *La dolce vita* (1960) playing a jaded tabloid journalist among Rome's socialites.

Mastroianni and Fellini would work again in the latter's masterpiece, *8½* (1963), but lest the pair be too inextricably linked, Mastroianni also appeared in such Italian cinema classics as *I soliti ignoti* (1958) (*Big Deal on Madonna Street*), Michelangelo Antonioni's *La notte* (1961) (*The Night*), and the black comedy *Divorzio all'italiana* (1961) (*Divorce—Italian Style*). The third of these movies landed Mastroianni a Best Actor nomination at the Oscars, a feat he repeated with *Una giornata particolare* (1977) (*A Special Day*) and *Oci ciornie* (1987) (*Dark Eyes*). As Mastroianni grew older, his career intersected with Robert Altman, whose *Prêt-à-Porter* (1994) reunited him one more time with frequent screen partner Sophia Loren. His final role was in *Trois vies & une seule mort* (1996) (*Three Lives and Only One Death*). Mastroianni passed away shortly after its release, but his death was preceded by some of the best reviews of his career. **JK**

RIGHT: Mastroianni strides purposefully into the water as Romano in *Dark Eyes*.

CHARLTON HESTON

Born: John Charles Carter, October 4, 1924 (Evanston, Illinois, U.S.).

Star qualities: "Chuck"; tall and muscular; chiseled features and thick dark hair; deep voice; conservative family values; right-wing political activist and philanthropist; heroic performances in Biblical epics; cultured; director.

Top Takes...

Planet of the Apes 2001
Armageddon 1998
Hercules 1997
The Awakening 1980
Midway 1976
Soylent Green 1973
Antony and Cleopatra 1972
The Omega Man 1971
Julius Caesar 1970
Beneath the Planet of the Apes 1970
Planet of the Apes 1968
Khartoum 1966
Major Dundee 1965
The Greatest Story Ever Told 1965
El Cid 1961
Ben-Hur 1959 ★
The Big Country 1958
Touch of Evil 1958
The Ten Commandments 1956
The Private War of Major Benson 1955
The Naked Jungle 1954
The Greatest Show on Earth 1952
Dark City 1950
Julius Caesar 1950
Peer Gynt 1941

RIGHT: Heston as the Jewish prince turned slave in William Wyler's epic *Ben-Hur*.

A handsome man with a sculpted jaw and long forehead leading up to a mop of thick brown hair, with bushy eyebrows, a thin line for a mouth, and an inscrutable squint under bright sunlight, Charlton Heston began his performance career as a model but ended up an Oscar-winning actor. Following the divorce of his parents and his mother's remarriage to Chester Heston, young Heston and his family moved to a Chicago suburb. He participated in community theater, experimented with filmmaking while in high school, and earned a drama scholarship to Northwestern University. In 1944 he left school for the U.S. Army Air Corps, served two years, and married Lydia Clarke, a fellow Northwestern student and model.

After military service, Heston headed to New York, where he earned acclaim for his work in the Broadway play *Antony and Cleopatra*, along with his efforts on a number of TV shows, especially *Suspense* and *Studio One*. There were early movie roles in *Dark City* and *Julius Caesar*, both in 1950, but the breakout year was 1952, when he played the circus manager in *The Greatest Show on Earth* for director Cecil B. DeMille, who became one of his most important collaborators.

Afterward the six-foot, three-inch-tall actor appeared in such titles as *The Naked Jungle* (1954) and *The Private War of Major Benson* (1955) before doing the Biblical epic *The Ten Commandments* (1956), in which he played Moses. Now an annual rite for American Christians on their Easter celebration, this one performance concretely established Heston as a good man: an artistically sound, culturally centrist, morally and ethically upright actor of no ill repute, and a hunk. Two years later he lent his influence to Orson Welles for *Touch of Evil* (1958), a noirish masterpiece, but the pivotal role will always be *Ben-Hur* (1959). Although later years would see him undertake similarly large-scale historical epics like *El Cid* (1961), *Khartoum* (1966), and *Midway* (1976), his Judah Ben-Hur made Heston a shorthand statement for purity, silent suffering, and

ABOVE: Heston as Moses, parting the Red Sea in *The Ten Commandments*.

"The minute you feel you have given a faultless performance is the time to get out."

A Man of Conviction

"If you need a ceiling painted, a chariot race run, a city besieged, or the Red Sea parted, you think of me." The film roles chosen by Charlton Heston in many ways reflect his own strong political and religious convictions. His chiseled good looks were well suited to playing morally upright heroes—in fact, Cecil B. DeMille chose him for the role of Moses in *The Ten Commandments* (1956) because he bore an unnatural resemblance to the statue of Moses by Michelangelo.

- Heston was an active campaigner in the civil rights movement in the 1960s and marched with the Rev. Dr. Martin Luther King Jr. at the 1963 March on Washington. He was a narrator in the original, uncut version of *King: A Filmed Record . . . Montgomery to Memphis* (1970).

- A World War II veteran, Heston is fiercely patriotic. He visited troops in Vietnam in 1966 and offered words of support to soldiers during the invasion of Iraq in 2003: "There is no duty more noble than that which has called you across the world in defense of freedom. Yours is a mission of hope and humanity for the oppressed."

- Heston has been married to Lydia Clarke since 1944 and is keen to promote strong family values. The couple adopted their second child to ensure that they had one son and one daughter—"the perfect family."

loyalty to higher powers, be those powers God or otherwise. As if to gild his saintliness, Heston later appeared as John the Baptist in *The Greatest Story Ever Told* in 1965.

For many fans, Heston is better remembered for his work in less religiously dogmatic and more fantastic works like *Planet of the Apes* (1968), *Omega Man* (1971), and *Soylent Green* (1973). There are also those who favor his inclination to experimental and less popular fare like *Major Dundee* (1965), or his extensive TV work, including *Dynasty*, *The Colbys*, and *Treasure Island*.

Ever in the public eye

Heston is the flesh-and-blood center of all these performances, and he is a personality that exists far beyond them. He is also a father and activist-oriented, political risk taker, unafraid of wearing his beliefs on his sleeve, and to that extent he stepped beyond the mold of big-screen actor. Heston has headed the Screen Actors Guild and the National Rifle Association. Now a conservative, he supports free speech and racial integration while being against abortion and political correctness.

Take him or leave him, like him or hate him, Heston has been fearless in living up to this simple, though not simple-minded, point of view about being true to one's career and life direction. This for him has meant nearly 50 years of steady work before bouts with prostate cancer and onset Alzheimer's hampered his ability to be in the public eye. **GCQ**

RIGHT: Heston played Detective Robert Thorn in the futuristic *Soylent Green*.

1920s

GERALDINE PAGE

Born: Geraldine Sue Page, November 22, 1924 (Kirksville, Missouri, U.S.); died 1987 (New York City, New York, U.S.).

Star qualities: Versatile leading lady; often played emotionally fragile women; intense screen presence; selective role choice; offbeat; Method actress.

A sensation as a young actress on Broadway, Geraldine Page appeared in a number of notable productions, including a pairing with James Dean in André Gide's *L'Immoraliste* (1954) (*The Immoralist*). Although only in her early thirties, she was a sensation, thanks to her Method training under Lee Strasberg, in the role of the Princess, an aging movie queen, in Tennessee Williams's *Sweet Bird of Youth* (1962)—a part she reprised with equal success for Richard Brooks's screen version, gaining a Best Actress Academy Award nomination.

This began a quite remarkable trend as Page, despite appearing in only a limited number of movies because of her continuing career on Broadway—where she received a Tony nomination for her unforgettable neurotic nun in *Agnes of God* (1982—went on to garner seven Oscar nominations in leading and supporting categories, and finally one Best Actress win, as an old woman making a final journey home in one of her last movies, *The Trip to Bountiful* (1985). Some of these performances are among the most riveting and affecting of the era: as the repressed virgin seduced by Laurence Harvey in another Williams adaptation, *Summer and Smoke* (1961); as a touched-by-God evangelist in *The Day of the Locust* (1975); and as the manipulative wife abandoned by her husband in Woody Allen's *Interiors* (1978). Most interestingly, perhaps, Page showed her range in her bone-chilling incarnation of a psychopathic murderer of old women in *What Ever Happened to Aunt Alice?* (1969), a filmic riposte to Robert Aldrich's *What Ever Happened to Baby Jane?* (1962) in which she outdoes Bette Davis in self-theatricalizing Grand Guignol. Offscreen, she was married twice, the second time to leading Hollywood actor Rip Torn, with whom she had three children. **BP**

Top Takes...

My Little Girl 1987
Riders to the Sea 1987
Native Son 1986
The Trip to Bountiful 1985 ★
The Pope of Greenwich Village 1984 ☆
Interiors 1978 ☆
The Day of the Locust 1975
Pete 'n' Tillie 1972 ☆
The Beguiled 1971
What Ever Happened to Aunt Alice? 1969
You're a Big Boy Now 1966 ☆
The Three Sisters 1966
Dear Heart 1964
Sweet Bird of Youth 1962 ☆
Summer and Smoke 1961 ☆
Hondo 1953 ☆

1920s

"I wanted to be a Broadway actress who every so often does a movie."

PAUL NEWMAN

Born: Paul Leonard Newman, January 26, 1925 (Shaker Heights, Ohio, U.S.).

Star qualities: Legendary heartthrob and superstar sex appeal; enviable good looks and muscular body—for decades Newman won the hearts of women all over the world with his famous eyes; kind, caring, and generous; warm sense of humor.

Top Takes...

Road to Perdition 2002 ☆
Message in a Bottle 1999
Nobody's Fool 1994 ☆
The Hudsucker Proxy 1994
The Color of Money 1986 ★
Harry & Son 1984
The Verdict 1982 ☆
Absence of Malice 1981 ☆
Slap Shot 1977
Buffalo Bill and the Indians, or Sitting Bull's History Lesson 1976
The Towering Inferno 1974
The Sting 1973
Butch Cassidy and the Sundance Kid 1969
Cool Hand Luke 1967 ☆
Torn Curtain 1966
Hud 1963 ☆
Sweet Bird of Youth 1962
The Hustler 1961 ☆
Exodus 1960
Cat on a Hot Tin Roof 1958 ☆
The Left Handed Gun 1958
The Long, Hot Summer 1958
Somebody Up There Likes Me 1956
The Silver Chalice 1954

RIGHT: Newman demonstrates the power of "Old Blue Eyes" in *Cat on a Hot Tin Roof*.

Paul Newman, "Old Blue Eyes," spent his childhood in Shaker Heights, Ohio, where his father traded in sporting goods. During his early years he participated in school plays and caught the acting bug before logging time in the navy at the end of World War II. After his discharge, he went to Kenyon College in Gambier, Ohio, where he earned his degree, and married Jackie Witte. He then attended Yale for a year before making his way to New York and the Actors Studio. Stage work followed, along with roles on TV, and after a rough, somewhat embarrassing movie debut in *The Silver Chalice* (1954), he struck gold as boxer Rocky Graziano in *Somebody Up There Likes Me* (1956)—a role originally intended for James Dean, who died prematurely before filming began—with the first of many well-remembered performances.

So it was at the age of thirty-one that Newman emerged as blue-eyed beefcake with a cut body and charismatic personality with which to enfold fans of both sexes and propel him through the late 1950s—when he really hit his stride. At that time he also divorced his first wife and married Joanne

1920s

Woodward, his artistic peer and companion since 1958. Thereafter the pair became Hollywood royalty, frequently collaborating on projects as costars, though in later years with Newman behind the lens as director and Woodward as star (*Rachel, Rachel*, 1968; *Harry & Son*, 1984; *The Glass Menagerie*, 1987). Individually, Newman concluded the 1950s starring in such memorable vehicles as *The Long, Hot Summer* (1958), *The Left Handed Gun* (1958), and Richard Brooks's adaptation of Tennessee Williams's play *Cat on a Hot Tin Roof* (1958). But in the 1960s he became tops at the box office and year-end awards ceremonies with rich performances in *The Hustler* (1961), *Sweet Bird of Youth* (1962), *Hud* (1963), *Torn Curtain* (1966), *Cool Hand Luke* (1967), and *Butch Cassidy and the Sundance Kid* (1969), his first pairing with Robert Redford.

ABOVE: Newman with Robert Redford in the iconic *Butch Cassidy and the Sundance Kid*.

"The embarrassing thing is that my salad dressing is out-grossing my films."

Self-Parody

Paul Newman possesses the admirable quality of being able to laugh at his own misfortunes. He needed a sense of humor to deal with the critical savaging he received for his first movie, 1954's *The Silver Chalice*. Indeed, Newman was so mortified by his performance that he took out a full-page advertisement in the trade magazine *Variety*, apologizing to the film-going public. In his own words, "Good Lord, it was really bad. In fact, it was the worst film made in the 1950s." Here are some of his other witticisms:

- "I picture my epitaph: 'Here lies Paul Newman, who died a failure because his eyes turned brown.'"

- "When I realized I was going to have to be a whore, to put my face on the label, I decided that the only way I could do it was to give away all the money we make."—On Newman's Own.

- "I never ask my wife about my flaws. Instead I try to get her to ignore them and concentrate on my sense of humor. You don't want any woman to look under the carpet, guys, because there's lots of flaws underneath."

- "Why fool around with hamburger when you have steak at home?"—On adultery.

- Robert Redford gave his *Butch Cassidy and the Sundance Kid* costar no such credit: "He tells the worst jokes. And that wouldn't be so bad if he didn't keep repeating them over and over."

Age did little to blunt the basic Newman appeal. His eyes remained blue. The voice tended to go gravelly with more intense emotions. But the physique stayed lean and the persona was enriched with the scars of passing years, new roles, and the fundamental recognition that Newman has "it:" the thing cameras love and that we notice in the sly smile, seemingly embarrassed but really just playing our patience on the way to disarming our hearts and minds with characters so rich in psychological depth, so appealing as physical specimens, and so vivid in their onscreen existence, that they become flesh and blood.

Aging gracefully but still going strong

Hitting middle age improved Newman's stride with *The Sting* (1973), *The Towering Inferno* (1974), and *The Verdict* (1982), and in his sunset years he has been rejuvenated with a series of roles that variously meditate on aging. His Dodge Blake tries to give advice to a headstrong son in *Message in a Bottle* (1999) and his John Rooney deals with an awakening sense of regret concerning one of the hit men he employs in *Road to Perdition* (2002). But to the youth of today, Newman may be forever known as Doc Hudson, the one-time speedway champion automobile, in Pixar's animated adventure *Cars* (2006). For an automobile enthusiast who finished second in the 1979 Le Mans 24-hour race, this role seems particularly fitting.

For certain fans, though, Newman's legacy includes several unusual pictures, worthy of mention if only for their cult status. These roles include his Buffalo Bill in *Buffalo Bill and the Indians, or Sitting Bull's History Lesson* (1976), the hockey washout Reggie Dunlop in *Slap Shot* (1977), and the unscrupulous Sidney Mussburger in *The Hudsucker Proxy* (1994).

Nine times nominated for an Academy Award, he has taken home one competitive trophy for *The Color of Money* (1986) and two honorary awards for his career and good works. For it should also be remembered that the Newman's Own foundation, through its many food labels, has contributed tens of millions of dollars to charities since 1982. **GCQ**

RIGHT: Newman in fighting form as prisoner Lucas Jackson in 1967's *Cool Hand Luke*.

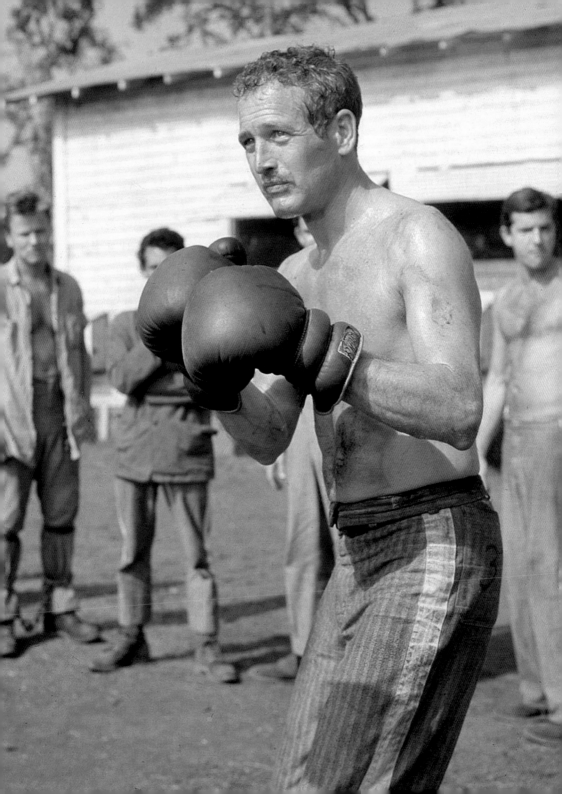

JACK LEMMON

Born: Jack Uhler Lemmon III, February 8, 1925 (Newton, Massachusetts, U.S.); died 2001 (Los Angeles, California, U.S.).

Star qualities: Superb stagecraft; ultimate character actor of serious and comic roles; portrayed the bewildered and neurotic; director; pianist; composer.

Top Takes...

The Harvard-educated only child of a doughnut manufacturer, Jack Lemmon came to personify the ultimate Hollywood character actor. Lemmon had dreamed of being an actor since he was four years old, after appearing with his father in an amateur production of *Gold in Them Thar Hills*. Following service as a navy ensign, Lemmon worked his way through New York's Off-Broadway circuit, eventually gaining radio and TV credits. He made his Broadway debut in *Room Service* (1953), in which he was spotted by Hollywood scouts and then signed by Columbia Pictures.

His first film role was in George Cukor's *It Should Happen to You* (1954). A year later, in only his fourth film outing, he won a Best Supporting Actor Oscar playing opposite Henry Fonda and James Cagney in *Mister Roberts* (1955). Critically, Lemmon's career was to peak with *Save the Tiger* (1973), for which he won the Best Actor Oscar—he received eight Academy Award nominations in all—although it was his performances in *Some Like It Hot* (1959), *The Apartment* (1960), *Days of Wine and Roses* (1962), *How to Murder Your Wife* (1965), and his typically fastidious Felix Ungar in *The Odd Couple* (1968) for which this prolific and popular actor will probably be best remembered.

After a movie career specializing in mannered, anxious performances, by turns mixing world-weary melancholy with a deft comic touch, in 1988 he was conferred with the American Film Institute's Life Achievement Award. Lemmon continued to work well into his seventies, winning renewed critical acclaim for his performances in *Glengarry Glen Ross* (1992), *Grumpy Old Men* (1993), *My Fellow Americans* (1996), and *Tuesdays with Morrie* (1999), in which he exploited his advancing years to excellent effect. **RH**

> "I won't quit until I get run over by a truck, a producer, or a critic."

ROD STEIGER

Born: Rodney Stephen Steiger, April 14, 1925 (Westhampton, New York, U.S.); died 2002 (Los Angeles, California, U.S.).

Star qualities: Method actor; character actor and leading man; played brooding complex brutes and historical figures; dynamic screen presence.

Rod Steiger ran away from home when he was fifteen years old to join the U.S. navy during World War II. After the war he returned to New York, where he studied at the New York Actors Workshop with fellow performers such as Marlon Brando. He went on to Broadway and built a reputation in live TV, originating the title role of *Marty* (1953). His big movie breakthrough came with *On the Waterfront* (1954), with its famous taxi-ride scene opposite Brando; Steiger's part earned him his first Oscar nomination as Best Supporting Actor.

After *Oklahoma!* (1955), in which Steiger was the brooding Jud Fry, he specialized in playing brutes: a bullying studio head modeled on Harry Cohn in *The Big Knife* (1955), a fight fixer in *The Harder They Fall* (1956), an Irish Confederate who joins with the Apache to keep fighting the Union in *Run of the Arrow* (1957), and a criminal ringleader in *Cry Terror!* (1958).

Steiger also impressed in subtler roles, for instance as the Holocaust survivor of *The Pawnbroker* (1964), for which he won his second Oscar nomination, this time for Best Actor. But he still cut loose on broad material, such as his role as Southern police chief in *In the Heat of the Night* (1967), for which he finally won an Oscar for Best Actor. Steiger suffered seriously from depression for a number of years, but later recovered and went on to lecture on mental health and to reestablish his career.

Steiger turned down the lead role in *Patton* (1970), a move he later regretted as George C. Scott went on to win an Oscar for the part. He played Benito Mussolini and W. C. Fields, and gave his hammiest performance as the fly-pestered priest in *The Amityville Horror* (1979). He then tended to be called in only when excess was demanded, as in *American Gothic* (1988) and *Mars Attacks!* (1996). **KN**

Top Takes...

End of Days 1999
Mars Attacks! 1996
American Gothic 1988
The Amityville Horror 1979
W. C. Fields and Me 1976
The Illustrated Man 1969
In the Heat of the Night 1967 ★
Doctor Zhivago 1965
The Loved One 1965
The Pawnbroker 1964 ☆
Cry Terror! 1958
Run of the Arrow 1957
The Harder They Fall 1956
The Big Knife 1955
Oklahoma! 1955
On the Waterfront 1954 ☆

> "Method acting is anything that gets you involved personally in the part."

TONY CURTIS

Born: Bernard Schwartz, June 3, 1925 (the Bronx, New York, U.S.).

Star qualities: Thick, black hair and prominent forelock; pretty-boy good looks; teen idol; dazzling smile; charming; comic timing; the lead across a range of genres; writer; producer; painter; head of an acting dynasty.

Top Takes...

Tony Curtis is the oldest of three sons of Hungarian immigrants. His father was a tailor and the family was poor; Curtis had become a member of a street gang in the Bronx by the age of eleven. After serving a tour in the U.S. navy, he attended City College of New York and the Dramatic Workshop in Greenwich Village, where he got his first taste of acting. He was spotted by Universal Studios and offered a contract.

By the early 1950s Curtis was in movies as a pouting pretty boy with a curly forelock in a style that became known as a "Tony Curtis haircut." In comedy swashbucklers, such as *Son of Ali Baba* (1952), his Bronx tones seem ludicrously out of place. He was brilliant as the hustling press agent in *Sweet Smell of Success* (1957), paid serious drama dues in *The Defiant Ones* (1958), and secured his screen immortality in drag, and with a Cary Grant skit, in *Some Like It Hot* (1959). He even took time to revisit the sword-and-sandal genre in high style opposite Kirk Douglas in *The Vikings* (1958) and *Spartacus* (1960).

Thereafter, Curtis tended to relax in movies such as *The Great Race* (1965) and he joined Roger Moore in the chintzy jet-set TV series *The Persuaders!* from 1971 to 1972. However, he also proved himself capable in more demanding and complex roles, playing Albert de Salvo in *The Boston Strangler* (1968) and the Senator McCarthy figure in *Insignificance* (1985). Since the 1980s, Curtis has slowed down his prolific output—he played more than 150 roles in 50 years—limiting his appearances to bit parts and TV work. He now has a second career as a successful artist. Curtis has been married six times; his first wife was the actress, and sometime costar, Janet Leigh. Three of his children are also actresses: Jamie Lee Curtis, Kelly Curtis, and Allegra Curtis. **KN**

> "Comedy is the most honest way for an actor to earn his living."

1920s

PETER SELLERS

Born: Richard Henry Sellers, September 8, 1925 (Southsea, Hampshire, England); died 1980 (London, England).

Star qualities: Huge comic talent; sense of the absurd; impressionist; genius mimic; dancer; musician; ability to play multiple roles; writer; director; producer.

Peter Sellers dissipated his talent with too many laughless comedies such as *The Fiendish Plot of Dr. Fu Manchu* (1980). Nevertheless, he was an enormous comic talent and an underrated screen actor.

His parents worked in variety, and Sellers made his first appearance on stage only two days after his birth, when his father brought him out during an encore. He joined the Royal Air Force during World War II and was part of a troupe of entertainers who performed at air force camps. It was at this time that he met Spike Milligan, Sir Harry Secombe, and Michael Bentine, whom he would later collaborate with on the hit BBC comedy radio series *The Goon Show* (1951–1960).

Sellers began making astonishingly varied film appearances in the 1950s: as a young hell-raiser in comedy *The Ladykillers* (1955); as hero, villain, and dowager duchess in *The Mouse That Roared* (1959), and as the Indian doctor opposite Sophia Loren in *The Millionairess* (1960). Sellers and Loren recorded the song "Goodness Gracious Me" to promote the movie, and it became a Top Ten hit on the British charts in 1960.

Under Stanley Kubrick's direction, Sellers was the mercurial, sinister Clare Quilty in *Lolita* (1962), and three contrasting and memorable characters in *Dr. Strangelove or: How I Learned to Stop Worrying and Love the Bomb* (1964), which earned him an Oscar nomination for Best Actor. He is perhaps best known and loved by audiences, however, as the gloriously inept Inspector Jacques Clouseau of *The Pink Panther* (1963) and its four sequels. His last great performance was as the near-autistic gardener Chance in *Being There* (1979), which won him his second Academy Award nomination for Best Actor. **KN**

Top Takes...

The Fiendish Plot of Dr. Fu Manchu 1980
Being There 1979 ☆
Revenge of the Pink Panther 1978
The Pink Panther Strikes Again 1976
The Return of the Pink Panther 1975
What's New, Pussycat 1965
A Shot in the Dark 1964
Dr. Strangelove or: How I Learned to Stop Worrying and Love the Bomb 1964 ☆
The Pink Panther 1963
Lolita 1962
Two Way Stretch 1960
The Millionairess 1960
The Mouse That Roared 1959
I'm All Right Jack 1959
The Ladykillers 1955

"There used to be a me behind the mask, but I had it surgically removed."

ANGELA LANSBURY

Born: Angela Brigid Lansbury, October 16, 1925 (London, England).

Star qualities: Shapely; singer; dancer; stagecraft; character actress; leading lady of stage musicals; mature roles as twinkling old lady and detective; producer; institution of U.S. theater and television.

Top Takes...

The daughter of an actress, Angela Lansbury was evacuated to the United States as a teenager at the start of World War II and became a U.S. citizen in 1951. She was Oscar-nominated for her debut as the flirty maid in *Gaslight* (1944), and again as the doomed Sybil Vane in *The Picture of Dorian Gray* (1945). As Sybil, she also warbled a ditty, signaling later success in stage musicals such as *Sweeney Todd: The Demon Barber of Fleet Street* (1979), for which she received one of her four Tony awards. Lovely, shapely, and smart, she tended to get roles as "the other woman" in such movies as *The Harvey Girls* (1946) and *The Court Jester* (1955).

Lansbury then switched profitably to parts as the smothering mother, an act she tried out initially—with surprising success—on Elvis Presley in *Blue Hawaii* (1961) before more acclaimed turns with Warren Beatty in *All Fall Down* (1962) and with Laurence Harvey in *The Manchurian Candidate* (1962). As Mrs. Senator Iselin in *The Manchurian Candidate*, she abandoned her usual geniality, cooing semi-incestuously over the son she has had brainwashed into a zombie assassin for the communists so that her idiot husband can be swept into government with "powers that will make martial law look like anarchy." In later years, Lansbury graduated to playing sprightly, twinkling old ladies, as in *Bedknobs and Broomsticks* (1971), *The Lady Vanishes* (1979), and *The Mirror Crack'd* (1980). It's an act she successfully took to television as mystery writer Jessica Fletcher in the long-running popular series *Murder, She Wrote* (1984–1996), the role for which she is probably most famous. She is Granny in *The Company of Wolves* (1984), and voices a teapot in *Beauty and the Beast* (1991). **KN**

> "I just stopped playing bitches on wheels and peoples' mothers."

RICHARD BURTON

Born: Richard Walter Jenkins Jr., November 10, 1925 (Pontrhydyfen, Wales); died 1984 (Céligny, Geneva, Switzerland).

Star qualities: Legendary talent; beautiful voice; twice-married to Hollywood's ultimate leading lady; Shakespearean stagecraft; mesmerizing.

Richard Burton let his turbulent private life in the form of five marriages—two to Elizabeth Taylor—and a battle with alcoholism overshadow his acting career. He regarded the cinema as a lesser medium than the stage, which explains his seemingly indiscriminate filmography. When fully engaged, he was mesmerizing; when let off the leash, he was frequently very entertaining. He was one of Britain's greatest-ever actors and was nominated seven times for the Best Actor Oscar.

Born the son of a coal miner, Burton was both inspired and legally adopted by a local schoolteacher, Philip Burton. During World War II he was an air force cadet but was able to study at Oxford University for six months. He worked on the stage and in radio and film to critical acclaim, but despite a khaki role in *The Desert Rats* (1953), he didn't fit into the war-obsessed British cinema of the 1950s. He was then given the lead in *My Cousin Rachel* (1952) opposite Olivia de Havilland, which established him as a Hollywood leading man.

When he decamped to Hollywood he played breastplate-and-skirt warriors such as Marc Antony opposite Elizabeth Taylor in *Cleopatra* (1963). He went on to costar with Taylor in ten more films, including *Who's Afraid of Virginia Woolf?* (1966) and *The Taming of the Shrew* (1967). But he was compelling alone in historical drama (*Becket*, 1964), downbeat espionage (*The Spy Who Came in from the Cold*, 1965), and action film (*Where Eagles Dare,* 1968). The shoddiness of some of his later movies became a joke, but he was still powerful as a gangster in *Villain* (1971), the psychic misanthrope of *The Medusa Touch* (1978), the psychiatrist in *Equus* (1977)—which earned him his seventh and last Oscar nomination—and the torturer in *Nineteen Eighty-Four* (1984). **KN**

Top Takes…

Nineteen Eighty-Four 1984
The Medusa Touch 1978
Equus 1977 ☆
Villain 1971
Anne of a Thousand Days 1969 ☆
Where Eagles Dare 1968
The Taming of the Shrew 1967
Who's Afraid of Virginia Woolf? 1966 ☆
The Spy Who Came in from the Cold 1965 ☆
Hamlet 1964
The Night of the Iguana 1964
Becket 1964 ☆
Cleopatra 1963
The Robe 1953 ☆
The Desert Rats 1953
My Cousin Rachel 1952 ☆

"You may be as vicious about me as you please. You will only do me justice."

1920s

ROCK HUDSON

Born: Roy Harold Scherer Jr., November 17, 1925 (Winnetka, Illinois, U.S.); died 1985 (Los Angeles, California, U.S.).

Star qualities: Tall hunk; thick dark hair; sparkling smile; deep voice; charming, stylish sex symbol; leading man of action films and lighthearted comedies.

Top Takes...

The Ambassador 1984
Pretty Maids All in a Row 1971
The Undefeated 1969
Ice Station Zebra 1968
Seconds 1966
Strange Bedfellows 1965
Send Me No Flowers 1964
Man's Favorite Sport? 1964
Lover Come Back 1961
Pillow Talk 1959
A Farewell to Arms 1957
Giant 1956 ☆
All That Heaven Allows 1955
Magnificent Obsession 1954
Bright Victory 1951
Winchester '73 1950

"I have no philosophy about acting or anything else. You just do it. And I mean that."

Rock Hudson epitomized the U.S. male self-image of the 1950s: big, grinning, good looking, confident, not overly bright but always competent. After he left high school he worked as a postal employee, and served as an airplane mechanic in the U.S. navy during World War II. After the war he worked as a truck driver, but he always hoped to become an actor. Talent scout Henry Willson, who spotted Hudson's looks and appeal, suggested his new name, a combination of the Rock of Gibraltar and the Hudson River.

He rose from the ranks after war films, such as *Bright Victory* (1951), and Westerns, such as *Winchester '73* (1950), to be cast by Douglas Sirk as the object of Jane Wyman's affections in *Magnificent Obsession* (1954) and *All That Heaven Allows* (1955). In *Giant* (1956), he plays a Texas oilman from vigorous youth to tough old age. It was a performance that played well, and he received an Oscar nomination for Best Actor.

In *Pillow Talk* (1959), he was effectively teamed with Doris Day in a bickering, glossy, cosmopolitan, widescreen romance. Hudson went on to make two more movies with Day, *Lover Come Back* (1961) and *Send Me No Flowers* (1964). He reprised the same pleasant, self-mocking comedy style in *Man's Favorite Sport?* (1964) and *Strange Bedfellows* (1965). In later years he moved successfully into television, starring in the detective series *McMillan & Wife* (1971–1976). Hudson was one of the first major celebrities to reveal that he had AIDS, an announcement that drew attention to his homosexuality, which he had managed to keep secret for most of his career, given that it may have ruined it at that time. His long-time partner, Marc Christian, successfully sued Hudson's estate after the actor's death. **KN**

SAMMY DAVIS Jr.

Born: Sammy Davis Jr., December 8, 1926 (Harlem, New York, U.S.); died 1990 (Beverly Hills, California, U.S.).

Star qualities: Singer; dancer; musician; raconteur; impressionist; comic timing; "Rat Pack" member; fought against racial segregation; director; producer; writer.

There may, somewhere, be people to whom Sammy Davis Jr. does not appeal. But even they would have trouble arguing that he was not the most purely talented entertainer of the twentieth century. Not only were his talents so many in number—singer, dancer, musician, raconteur, actor, and impressionist just for starters—he was so supernaturally gifted at each that he could have restricted himself to any one and still been a show-business giant.

The son of a vaudeville entertainer, Sammy Davis Sr., Davis worked with his father from the age of four. He often performed in cities with strict child labor laws. To circumvent them, he was billed as "Silent Sammy, the Dancing Midget," and walked around backstage with a rubber cigar in his mouth and a woman on each arm. He made his movie debut tap dancing in the 1933 short *Rufus Jones for President*.

On Broadway, on TV, or in cabaret, with or without his pals in the "Rat Pack," Davis was unmatched and unmatchable. On film he is less well commemorated, mainly because leading roles for black performers were not easy to come by in the decades in which he was at his height, and it was difficult to find supporting roles that could contain his energy and personal magnetism. So he turned up here and there, larking about with his mates in *Ocean's Eleven* (1960), *Salt and Pepper* (1968), and *The Cannonball Run* (1981), or propping up the leads in *Porgy and Bess* (1959) and *Sweet Charity* (1969). His one major solo vehicle, *A Man Called Adam* (1966), was not well received, but it may simply have been ahead of its time. Davis helped to break down racial barriers during the 1950s and 1960s; his marriage to Swedish-born actress May Britt in 1968 caused great controversy. **MC**

Top Takes...

Broadway Danny Rose 1984
The Cannonball Run 1981
Sammy Stops the World 1978
Sweet Charity 1969
Salt and Pepper 1968
A Man Called Adam 1966
Nightmare in the Sun 1965
Robin and the 7 Hoods 1964
Johnny Cool 1963
Of Love and Desire 1963
Sergeants 3 1962
Pepe 1960
Ocean's Eleven 1960
Porgy and Bess 1959
Sweet and Low 1947
Rufus Jones for President 1933

> "Man, I am a one-eyed, black Jew! *That's* my handicap!"
> —On being asked his golf handicap

HILDEGARD KNEF

Born: Hildegard Frieda Albertine Knef, December 28, 1925 (Ulm, Württemberg, Germany); died 2002 (Berlin, Germany).

Star qualities: Icon of German cinema; "The Voice of Berlin"; versatile leading lady of drama; composed screen presence; stagecraft; singer; writer.

Pretty and blonde, Hildegard Knef appeared in more than 50 movies throughout her career, but she is better known to audiences in Europe than the United States. She reportedly turned down producer David O. Selznick's offer of a Hollywood studio contract after being told she would have to change her name and claim she was Austrian, not German.

Knef grew up in Berlin. During World War II she worked at the Universum Film AG studios as a painter and cartoonist in the animation department while studying acting at the Babelsberg Film Institute. She made her film debut in Harald Braun's *Träumerei* (1944), but her scenes were deleted. She became a star in the first film produced by the German Democratic Republic's Deutsche Film-Aktiengesellschaft studio, Wolfgang Staudte's noir *Die Mörder sind unter uns* (1946) (*Murderers Among Us*). She played a former Nazi concentration-camp inmate returning home. It was a role played from the heart: to escape being raped by the advancing Soviet army, Knef had adopted the guise of a young man and was sent to a prisoner of war camp.

Knef then turned to postwar Berlin's stage before leaving for the United States. She found some success, such as a supporting role in *The Snows of Kilimanjaro* (1952), but decided to return to Germany. She soon hit the headlines, scandalizing the Roman Catholic Church when she did a brief nude scene while playing a prostitute in *Die Sünderin* (1951) (*The Story of a Sinner*). The rest of her career was spent in European cinema, with the occasional foray into U.S. productions. She found acclaim in middle age as a singer with a smoky voice, appearing on Broadway from 1954 to 1965 as Ninotchka in Cole Porter's musical comedy *Silk Stockings*. **CK**

Top Takes...

Fedora 1978
The Lost Continent 1968
The Dirty Dozen 1967
Mozambique 1965
Landru 1963 (*Bluebeard*)
Caterina di Russia 1963
    (*Catherine of Russia*)
Lulu 1962
Die Dreigroschenoper 1962
    (*Three Penny Opera*)
The Man Between 1953
The Snows of Kilimanjaro 1952
Die Sünderin 1951
    (*The Story of a Sinner*)
Die Mörder sind unter uns 1946
    (*Murderers Among Us*)

"Success and failure are greatly overrated. But failure gives you . . . more to talk about."

JERRY LEWIS

Born: Jerome Levitch, March 16, 1926 (Newark, New Jersey, U.S.).

Star qualities: "The King of Comedy"; squeaky voice; rubbery face; goofy comedian; slapstick movements; master of zany improvisation and ad lib; singer; director; producer; writer; humanitarian.

The son of vaudeville performers, Jerry Lewis first appeared on stage at the age of only five. His break came in 1946 when he teamed up with Dean Martin. The pairing began when Lewis was performing at the 500 Club in Atlantic City and one of the other entertainers quit suddenly. Lewis suggested Martin as a replacement, and the pair soon devised a zany comedy act improvising insults and jokes. In less than 18 weeks their salaries soared from $250 a week to $5,000. The duo parlayed their stage success into a film career with supporting roles in the *My Friend Irma* movies (1949, 1950) and buddy comedies for Paramount Pictures. With interchangeable plotlines, films such as *Scared Stiff* (1953) and *Pardners* (1956) featured Martin as the smooth songster tolerating Lewis's manic excess.

Following the duo's acrimonious breakup, Lewis stayed at Paramount, filming such titles as *The Delicate Delinquent* (1957) and *Cinderfella* (1960). Beginning with *The Bellboy* (1960), Lewis worked as director, producer, cowriter, and lead actor in several roles. The pinnacle of this period is *The Nutty Professor* (1963).

Lewis departed from Paramount in 1965 and released several films through Columbia Pictures. The 1970s saw little activity, with Lewis's *The Day the Clown Cried* (1972) remaining unfinished. The early 1980s, however, brought about a career resurgence with the moneymakers *Hardly Working* (1980) and *Cracking Up* (1983). Building on these successes, he turned in a rare but memorable dramatic performance in Martin Scorsese's *The King of Comedy* (1983). Lewis is also known for hosting the yearly Labor Day Telethon for the Muscular Dystrophy Association, a duty he has performed since 1966. He was nominated for the Nobel Peace Prize in 1977 for his charity work. **WW**

Top Takes...

Mr. Saturday Night 1992
Cracking Up 1983
The King of Comedy 1983
Hardly Working 1980
The Day the Clown Cried 1972
The Disorderly Orderly 1964
The Nutty Professor 1963
Cinderfella 1960
The Bellboy 1960
The Delicate Delinquent 1957
Pardners 1956
Scared Stiff 1953
The Stooge 1952
That's My Boy 1951
My Friend Irma Goes West 1950
My Friend Irma 1949

1920s

> "[Dean Martin and I] had that X factor—the powerful feeling between us."

MARILYN MONROE

Born: Norma Jean Mortensen, June 1, 1926 (Los Angeles, California, U.S.); died 1962 (Los Angeles, California, U.S.).

Star qualities: "The Blonde Bombshell"; quintessential blue-eyed, blonde movie star with a breathless voice and enviable figure; natural comedy talent.

Top Takes…

The Misfits 1961

Some Like It Hot 1959

The Prince and the Showgirl 1957

Bus Stop 1956

The Seven Year Itch 1955

There's No Business Like Show Business 1954

River of No Return 1954

How to Marry a Millionaire 1953

Gentlemen Prefer Blondes 1953

Niagara 1953

O. Henry's Full House 1952

Monkey Business 1952

Don't Bother to Knock 1952

We're Not Married! 1952

Clash by Night 1952

Let's Make It Legal 1951

Love Nest 1951

As Young as You Feel 1951

Home Town Story 1951

All About Eve 1950

The Asphalt Jungle 1950

Marilyn Monroe spent much of her career trying to shrug off the label "comic actress"—despite which, she was one of the most instinctive comediennes ever to light up the screen. Her two finest comedies, *The Seven Year Itch* (1955) and *Some Like It Hot* (1959), were directed by Billy Wilder. The daughter of a mentally ill mother who left her to abusive foster homes and an orphanage, Monroe grew up very insecure. Drug addiction and uterine disorders made things worse. She could be hell to work with—showing up hours late, incapable of learning the simplest lines. After *Itch*, Wilder swore never to work with her again: "But whenever I saw her, I always forgave her."

John Huston gave Monroe her first worthwhile role as a childlike mistress in *The Asphalt Jungle* (1950). A decade later, he cast her again in her last completed movie, *The Misfits* (1961), as a lonely divorcee who links up with a trio of down-on-their-luck cowboys. She was battling addiction and her marriage to the film's screenwriter, Arthur Miller, was falling apart. In between, she had become perhaps the most famous movie star and greatest sex symbol in the world. The blonde hair, little-girl voice, and air of wide-eyed innocence gave her

RIGHT: *The Misfits*, Monroe's last film, was popular with critics and public alike.

global appeal. Fans raved over her voluptuous curves, enhanced by the famous Monroe wiggle. Ironically, Monroe loathed what gave her stardom—the sex appeal, the naive but sensual image—deployed so well in the Wilder comedies, and in such films as Howard Hawks's *Gentlemen Prefer Blondes* (1953). Even greater public attention was focused on the sexy star in 1954 during her short-lived marriage to baseball star Joe DiMaggio. Yearning to be taken seriously as an actress, she starred with Laurence Olivier in *The Prince and the Showgirl* (1957). They disliked each other and the film flopped.

Although she was an icon, Monroe's insecurities deepened; and her unreliability on set worsened. Affairs with both Jack and Robert Kennedy ended in rejection. There had been earlier suicide attempts, and the overdose that killed her may have been the final one—although dark rumors of murder have dogged her memory. She was thirty-six years old. **PK**

ABOVE: One of the most famous moments in movie history, from *The Seven Year Itch*.

Ditching the Ditz

For Monroe there was always a painful gap between how she saw herself and how others perceived her. She aspired to improve herself even before the trajectory of her stardom began, taking literature courses at UCLA, accumulating hundreds of books (including works by Tolstoy, Milton, and Whitman), and listening to Beethoven. Desperate to be taken more seriously as an actress in the 1950s, she studied with acting guru Lee Strasberg. In 1956, the same year that she stunned the public by wedding playwright Arthur Miller, Marilyn showed in *Bus Stop* that she could play a straight dramatic part.

MEL BROOKS

Born: Melvin Kaminsky, June 18, 1926 (Brooklyn, New York, U.S.).

Star qualities: A natural ham; comic timing; sense of the absurd; slapstick humor; master of cinematic spoof and parody; lover of wacky song-and-dance routines; director; composer; producer; writer.

Top Takes...

The Producers 2005
The Prince of Egypt 1998
Dracula: Dead and Loving It 1995
The Little Rascals 1994
Robin Hood: Men in Tights 1993
Life Stinks 1991
Look Who's Talking Too 1990
Spaceballs 1987
To Be or Not to Be 1983
History of the World: Part I 1981
The Muppet Movie 1979
High Anxiety 1977
Silent Movie 1976
Young Frankenstein 1974
Blazing Saddles 1974
The Producers 1968

"I cut my finger. That's tragedy. A man walks into an open sewer and dies. That's comedy."

Mel Brooks grew up in Brooklyn, New York, the son of Russian-Jewish parents. He served in the U.S. army in World War II as an engineer stationed in North Africa. After the war, he took to the stage as a stand-up comedian, and then became a comedy writer for television. He later moved across into movies; some would argue most notably as a director and producer.

It has been commented, not unfairly, that the films Brooks writes and/or directs are funnier when he has minimal or no screen time. Certainly, *The Producers* (1968) and *Young Frankenstein* (1974), to which he contributes only brief voiceovers, are his best work, and some of the films in which he takes lead roles, as the grumpy millionaire in *Life Stinks!* (1991) or Dr. Abraham Van Helsing in *Dracula: Dead and Loving It* (1995), are almost endurance tests.

A natural ham who wanted to cast himself as the Nazi playwright eventually played by Kenneth Mars in *The Producers*, Brooks is amusing as the groveling peasant in *The Twelve Chairs* (1970), but less so as Governor Le Petomaine in *Blazing Saddles* (1974), Yoghurt in *Spaceballs* (1987), or Rabbi Tuckman in *Robin Hood: Men in Tights* (1993). Taking center screen, he sweet-naturedly skewers himself as Mel Funn in *Silent Movie* (1976); has one great scene in the Alfred Hitchcock parody *High Anxiety* (1977) as his paranoid psychoanalyst who suddenly has a burst of confidence and delivers a show-stopping Sinatra-style lounge number; and doesn't disgrace the memory of Jack Benny in the remake of *To Be or Not to Be* (1983). Brooks has had significant success on the stage with his production of *The Producers*—the Broadway version won a record-breaking 12 Tony awards. He was married to actress Anne Bancroft from 1964 until her death in 2005. **KN**

KLAUS KINSKI

Born: Nikolaus Günther Nakszynski, October 18, 1926 (Zoppot, Danzig, Poland); died 1991 (Lagunitas, California, U.S.).

Star qualities: Cult German actor; distinctive voice; wild eyes; hot tempered; intense screen presence; creative partnership with Werner Herzog; director; writer.

It is impossible to determine whether Klaus Kinski was just maniacally intense or clinically insane. After drawing attention with his role in *Doctor Zhivago* (1965), Kinski gained cult status as a range of Aryan madmen, usually raging revolutionaries, fanatic officers, or haunted doctors in European genre films such as *Per qualche dollaro in più* (1965) (*For a Few Dollars More*), *El Chuncho, quién sabe?* (1967) (*A Bullet for the General*), and *Il dito nella piaga* (1969) (*Salt in the Wound*). Symptomatically, he is one of the only actors to have portrayed both Renfield and Dracula, in Jess Franco's *Nachts, wenn Dracula erwacht* (1970) (*Count Dracula*) and Werner Herzog's *Nosferatu: Phantom der Nacht* (1979) (*Nosferatu the Vampyre*), respectively.

Three of Kinski's other films with Herzog—the only director to match his extreme behavior—ensured his place in film history. *Aguirre, der Zorn Gottes* (1972) (*Aguirre: the Wrath of God*), *Fitzcarraldo* (1982) and *Cobra Verde* (1987) (*Slave Coast*) rank among cinema's rawest and most beautiful explorations of men's missions under extreme pressure. Both egomaniacs, Herzog and Kinski often clashed, and they pushed each other to excellence and exhaustion—and even threatened to kill each other. Herzog's tribute to their partnership, *Mein liebster Feind—Klaus Kinski* (1999) (*My Best Fiend*), also captures tender moments of understanding; Kinski's taunting and flirting with a butterfly during a pause in shooting *Fitzcarraldo* reveals his compelling ambiguity, both cute and cruel. After he split from Herzog following arguments during the filming of *Cobra Verde*, Kinski never recovered. He was married several times, and three of his children have gone on to become actors: Nastassja Kinski, Pola Kinski, and Nikolai Kinski. **EM**

Top Takes…

Cobra Verde 1987 (*Slave Coast*)
The Secret Diary of Sigmund Freud 1984
Fitzcarraldo 1982
Haine 1980
Woyzeck 1979
Nosferatu: Phantom der Nacht 1979
  (*Nosferatu the Vampyre*)
Aguirre, der Zorn Gottes 1972
  (*Aguirre: The Wrath of God*)
Nachts, wenn Dracula erwacht 1970
  (*Count Dracula*)
Il dito nella piaga 1969 (*Salt in the Wound*)
El Chuncho, quién sabe? 1967
  (*A Bullet for the General*)
Doctor Zhivago 1965
Per qualche dollaro in più 1965
  (*For a Few Dollars More*)

1920s

"I choose films with the shortest schedule and the most money."

SIDNEY POITIER

Born: Sidney Poitier, February 20, 1927 (Miami, Florida, U.S.).

Star qualities: Respected and likable leading actor; brought integrity and charm to his roles; first black actor to win a Best Actor Oscar; prominent onstage, onscreen, and in the civil rights movement; received a knighthood in 1974.

Top Takes...

The Jackal 1997
Sneakers 1992
Shoot to Kill 1988
Uptown Saturday Night 1974
The Organization 1971
They Call Me MISTER Tibbs! 1970
Guess Who's Coming to Dinner 1967
In the Heat of the Night 1967
To Sir, with Love 1967
A Patch of Blue 1965
Lilies of the Field 1963 ★
A Raisin in the Sun 1961
All the Young Men 1960
Porgy and Bess 1959
The Defiant Ones 1958 ☆
Band of Angels 1957
The Blackboard Jungle 1955
Cry, the Beloved Country 1951
No Way Out 1950

Born in Florida during a stateside visit by his Bahamian parents, Sidney Poitier grew up in poverty, the son of a farmer. By the age of fifteen, with little education and a bent toward delinquency, he was sent to Miami to live with his brother, where, presumably, he would build a better life for himself. Confrontation with the U.S. racial caste system and a string of menial jobs eventually led him to New York. After a brief stint in the army he returned to Harlem. There he suffered through an unsuccessful and impulsive audition that ignited a passion for acting, along with the immediate task of changing his native accent and educating himself. Overcoming these limitations, he eventually earned acceptance into the American Negro Theatre, where his talents led to more high-profile work on Broadway and, finally, Hollywood by the early 1950s.

From there began a string of roles that perfectly positioned Poitier between differing points of view about how to represent American blackness during the civil rights movement, when representation, or lack of black representation specifically, was central to the cultural experience. For example, there are his remarkable turns as a mainstream lead in such popular films as

RIGHT: Poitier with costar Katherine Houghton in *Guess Who's Coming to Dinner.*

Porgy and Bess (1959), *The Defiant Ones* (1958), *A Patch of Blue* (1965), and his Academy Award-winning role in *Lilies of the Field* (1963). This line continues through *In the Heat of the Night* (1967) and *Guess Who's Coming to Dinner* (1967), after which Poitier began directing (*Uptown Saturday Night*, 1974; *Stir Crazy*, 1980) and appearing less often onscreen.

ABOVE: *The Defiant Ones* gave Poitier his first Oscar nomination for Best Actor.

Critics, however, argue that he is an Uncle Tom; brown-skinned, yes, but culturally "white" in the midst of a racist mainstream, and seemingly unable to tackle this condition through his work as an actor. Responses to Poitier's image and status as a mainstream icon here include films like *Sweet Sweetback's Baadasssss Song* (1971) and *Super Fly* (1972). Yet this hostile, or at least alternative, perspective generally ignores Poitier's own pioneering works on the subject of racial identity,

"If you apply reason and logic to this career of mine, you're not going to get very far."

Stranger than Fiction

In the 1980s, a young African-American man conned his way into the lives of rich and famous New Yorkers by claiming to be the son of Sidney Poitier. The story provided the inspiration for a play, *Six Degrees of Separation* by John Guare, and was later made into a movie of the same name in 1993 starring Will Smith.

Con artist David Hampton first pretended to be Poitier's son in 1983 when he and a friend got into the exclusive New York club Studio 54 by claiming to be the sons of Sidney Poitier and Gregory Peck, respectively. Assuming the name David Poitier and armed with fabricated tales, Hampton went on to con meals in restaurants and to persuade prominent New Yorkers to let him into their homes and give him money; those who fell prey to Hampton's ruse included Gary Sinise, Melanie Griffith, and Calvin Klein. Playwright John Guare became interested in the story because of the involvement of his friends Osborn and Inger Elliot.

The title of the play and movie comes from the idea that everyone in the world is connected to everyone else by a chain of no more than six other people. After the play's success, Hampton harassed Guare and tried to sue him for a share of the profits; he was later imprisoned. But it still remains incredible how easily Hampton convinced so many privileged New Yorkers that he was Poitier's son.

like *A Raisin in the Sun* (1961), or his civil rights activism. So the real trouble dogging Poitier is that he is a true artistic and political pioneer, demonstrating the need for social change in his moment of greatest impression, while participating within mainstream culture rather than ignoring it or foolishly trying to revolt against it with only limited influence.

Opening the door for black performers

It must be remembered, however, that before Poitier there really weren't any black Hollywood leads. Whereas history shows us that the subsequent chapter hasn't been particularly welcoming to nonwhite types either, his example has led the way for such performers as Bill Cosby, Richard Pryor, Eddie Murphy, and Denzel Washington, each of whom can trace a connection to Poitier's work in the 1950s and 1960s.

To hear Poitier speak in person, then, is to hear a refinement of the word at all levels: technical, cultural, and acoustic. There's a precision to how he enunciates syllables, how he strings together words, how he controls volume and pitch, all to capture our attention. Then there's the employment of gesture, always graceful, and silence. Finally, there's a genuine sense that a capable mind is grappling with big thoughts while respecting the importance of speech to communicate through the most accessible language possible, and that there is pleasure in succeeding to entertain and provoke. **GCQ**

RIGHT: Poitier in *Porgy and Bess*, the movie based on George Gershwin's famous opera.

1920s

GINA LOLLOBRIGIDA

Born: Luigina Lollobrigida, July 4, 1927 (Subiaco, Rome, Italy).

Star qualities: "La Lollo"; "The World's Most Beautiful Woman"; iconic Italian beauty; earthy looks and short wavy hair; curvaceous, beauty-queen glamour; artist; photographer.

Like many of her Italian postwar contemporaries, Gina "La Lollo" Lollobrigida's stardom is constructed around her earthiness as a rustic and untouched beauty standing in contrast to the artificial glamour often associated with female stardom in Hollywood. She studied sculpture at university but began her career in beauty contests, where she came third in 1947's Miss Italy. Lollobrigida was soon cast in numerous French-Italian coproductions such as René Clair's *Les belles de nuit* (1952) (*Beauties of the Night*), and in her native land she shot to fame through the two "pink neorealism" films *Pane, amore e fantasia* (1953) (*Bread, Love and Dreams*), and *Pane, amore e gelosia* (1954) (*Bread, Love and Jealousy*). Her appearance in *La donna più bella del mondo* (1956) (*Beautiful But Dangerous*) led to her being called "The World's Most Beautiful Woman" after the title of the film.

Her career also took off in Hollywood as she costarred with Yul Brynner in the biblical epic *Solomon and Sheba* (1959), but it was her part in *Come September* (1961) opposite Rock Hudson and Sandra Dee that warmed U.S. audiences to her as well as Jerry Lewis, with whom she had a brief affair. Although still connected to cinema throughout the 1970s, Lollobrigida's career took a different turn when she became a successful photojournalist; she achieved considerable respect within the media when she gained an exclusive interview with Fidel Castro. Although now retired, Lollobrigida followed the fate of many other female stars of her generation by appearing in trashy 1980s soap operas, in her case, *Falcon Crest*. In 1999 she ventured into politics and ran, unsuccessfully, for one of Italy's European Parliament seats from her native town of Subiaco. **GN**

Top Takes...

XXL 1997
Buona Sera, Mrs. Campbell 1968
Hotel Paradiso 1966
Come September 1961
Solomon and Sheba 1959
Notre Dame de Paris 1956
  (*The Hunchback of Notre Dame*)
Trapeze 1956
La donna più bella del mondo 1956
  (*Beautiful But Dangerous*)
Pane, amore e gelosia 1954
  (*Bread, Love and Jealousy*)
Pane, amore e fantasia 1953
  (*Bread, Love and Dreams*)
Beat the Devil 1953
Les belles de nuit 1952
  (*Beauties of the Night*)

"Popularity has a bright side, it unlocks many doors. But the truth is that I don't like it."

JANET LEIGH

Born: Jeanette Helen Morrison, July 6, 1927 (Merced, California, U.S); died 2004 (Beverly Hills, California, U.S.).

Star qualities: Petite blonde beauty; flawless complexion; married a teen idol; legendary role in *Psycho*; played youthful ingénues and later character parts.

Top Takes...

Janet Leigh was a student at the University of the Pacific, studying music and psychology when she was discovered while visiting her parents in Northern California, where they were working at a ski resort. Retired MGM star Norma Shearer saw a photo of her and recommended her to talent agent Lew Wasserman. She was offered a contract by MGM following a screen test, and went on to make her screen debut as a lovely ingénue in *The Romance of Rosy Ridge* (1947).

She worked steadily, first in sweet teenage roles such as Meg March in *Little Women* (1949), and then in colorful costume pictures such as *Scaramouche* (1952). In her starlet phase, Leigh landed a few good dramatic parts: in very tight jeans as the Western wildcat of *The Naked Spur* (1953), a 1920s flapper in *Pete Kelly's Blues* (1955), and vivacious in *My Sister Eileen* (1955).

After Howard Hughes's bizarre production *Jet Pilot* (1957), in which she is a Russian lady flier, she played key roles in a variety of major films opposite such stars as Gary Cooper, Errol Flynn, Orson Welles, and James Stewart. Leigh's most notable part, however, was as the iconic Marion Crane in Alfred Hitchcock's *Psycho* (1960). At the end of her 45 minutes onscreen she was unforgettably stabbed to death in the shower by cross-dressing lunatic Norman Bates. The role earned her an Academy Award nomination for Best Supporting Actress and a place in movie history. After her star years, she gamely faced giant killer rabbits in *Night of the Lepus* (1972) and wrote some books. Leigh is the mother of actresses Jamie Lee Curtis and Kelly Curtis by her third husband, actor Tony Curtis. Leigh worked with Jamie Lee in her last two films, *The Fog* (1980) and *Halloween H20: 20 Years Later* (1998). **KN**

> "[*Psycho*] gave me very wrinkled skin. I was in that shower for seven days."

ROBERT SHAW

Born: Robert Shaw, August 9, 1927 (Westhoughton, Lancashire, England); died 1978 (Tourmakeady, County Mayo, Ireland).

Star qualities: Man of action; tough-guy looks; stagecraft; prolific writer; award-winning novelist; versatile character actor; played villains and historical characters.

The son of a doctor, Robert Shaw trained at London's Royal Academy of Dramatic Art. Onscreen and off, Shaw was at once a boozing, brawling man of action, and appeared well qualified to hunt sharks or assassinate 007. Yet he was also an intellectual artist of some depth who maintained a parallel career as a serious novelist and playwright. His novel *The Man in the Glass Booth* (1967) tells the story of a Jewish industrialist who is accused of being a Nazi war criminal; it was adapted into a stage play and, in 1975, into a film.

In the movies, it was his role as Donovan "Red" Grant, the bleached-blond psycho of the James Bond film *From Russia with Love* (1963), that put him on the map. By contrast, he was also in the film version of Harold Pinter's *The Caretaker* (1963) at the same time. He was a presence in big, literary, historical films: as King Henry VIII in *A Man for All Seasons* (1966), General George Custer in *Custer of the West* (1967), and Spanish explorer Francisco Pizarro in *The Royal Hunt of the Sun* (1969).

Shaw did a few adventurous films such as *The Hireling* (1973), and then went to the United States as an intense, grim supporting actor. He was the patsy in *The Sting* (1973) and the mastermind in *The Taking of Pelham One Two Three* (1974). But his most memorable role is probably as the coarse shark hunter Captain Quint in *Jaws* (1975); many of Quint's lines were improvisations by Shaw himself. The enormous success of *Jaws* got him lead roles once again, such as the cold-eyed Sheriff of Nottingham in *Robin and Marian* (1976)—once again playing villain to Sean Connery's hero—and a formidable Israeli antiterror operative in *Black Sunday* (1977). In tribute to the actor and his love of the bottle, the town of his birth has a pub named The Robert Shaw. **KN**

Top Takes...

Force 10 from Navarone 1978
The Deep 1977
Black Sunday 1977
Robin and Marian 1976
Jaws 1975
The Taking of Pelham One Two Three 1974
The Golden Voyage of Sinbad 1974
The Sting 1973
The Hireling 1973
The Royal Hunt of the Sun 1969
The Birthday Party 1968
Custer of the West 1967
A Man for All Seasons 1966 ☆
Battle of the Bulge 1965
From Russia with Love 1963
The Caretaker 1963

1920s

"I drink too much. Will you tell me one great actor who doesn't drink?"

ROGER MOORE

Born: Roger George Moore, October 14, 1926 (Stockwell, London, England).

Star qualities: Tall, suave, and handsome; slick, cool persona; comic interpretation of 007; played the playboy and the spy; perfected the raised eyebrow look; writer; composer; producer; director; knighted.

Top Takes…

Spice World 1997
The Quest 1996
A View to a Kill 1985
Curse of the Pink Panther 1983
Octopussy 1983
For Your Eyes Only 1981
The Cannonball Run 1981
Moonraker 1979
The Wild Geese 1978
The Spy Who Loved Me 1977
Shout at the Devil 1976
The Man with the Golden Gun 1974
Live and Let Die 1973
The Man Who Haunted Himself 1970
Crossplot 1969
The Last Time I Saw Paris 1954

Born the son of a policeman, Sir Roger Moore wanted to be an artist but instead served in the British military during World War II. He went to London's Royal Academy of Dramatic Art and became a bit player in movies before moving to the United States in 1953 and signing with MGM.

Moore worked frequently and had a few notable screen roles, including in *The Last Time I Saw Paris* (1954) and *Crossplot* (1969). By middle age he had a modicum of fame based on his TV work as gambler cousin Beau in *Maverick* (1957–1962), and as benevolent thief Simon Templar in *The Saint* (1962–1969). *The Saint* made him a major star, although less so in the United States. To remedy this he starred opposite Tony Curtis in the TV series *The Persuaders!* (1971–1972); the show was hugely popular in Europe, but the U.S. version had to be canceled.

In 1973, history changed shape as Sean Connery retired from the role of a lifetime as James Bond and ceded the field to Moore in *Live and Let Die* (1973). Although audiences were jolted by the change, Moore quickly won popular support and finished the 1970s with more Bond vehicles (*The Man with the Golden Gun*,1974; *The Spy Who Loved Me*, 1977; and *Moonraker*, 1979), as well as the occasional nonfranchise role such as in *Shout at the Devil* (1976). After turning fifty, he began doing comic turns (*Curse of the Pink Panther*, 1983) while concluding his foray as Ian Fleming's superspy in *For Your Eyes Only* (1981), *Octopussy* (1983), and *A View to a Kill* (1985). Passing 007 to Timothy Dalton, he entered the final phase of his career, offering performances that largely reflected on his smooth, handsome, calm-as-a-cucumber persona in roles such as Lord Edgar Dobbs in *The Quest* (1996). He has been a United Nations Children's Fund ambassador since 1991. **GCQ**

> "My acting range? Left eyebrow raised, right eyebrow raised."

1920s

JEANNE MOREAU

Born: Jeanne Moreau, January 23, 1928 (Montmartre, Paris, France).

Star qualities: French New Wave love goddess; dark eyes; sensual screen presence; played lead femme fatale roles; singer; great stage actress; documentary filmmaker; director; producer; writer.

By the time she was consecrated in the early 1960s as the love goddess of the French New Wave, Jeanne Moreau was already in her thirties with more than a score of films behind her. She offered a ripe, frank sensuality, enhanced by the intelligence of her gaze. In repose, her face could seem forbidding. The sulky pout of her mouth and dark, unsmiling eyes hinted at reserves of anger, making her sudden smile all the more enchanting.

Moreau grew up in Paris, the daughter of a French restaurateur and a former Folies-Bergère dancer from England. She studied acting at the Paris Conservatoire. By the time she was twenty, she became the youngest full-time member in the history of the Comédie-Française theatrical company.

By the time Louis Malle launched her glory years in film, she was already a premier star of the stage. Malle cast her in *Ascenseur pour l'échafaud* (1958) (*Elevator to the Gallows*) as the lover of her husband's killer, and as an unashamedly adulterous wife in *Les Amants* (1958) (*The Lovers*). She was the apex of a love triangle in François Truffaut's *Jules et Jim* (1962); disenchanted in Michelangelo Antonioni's study of alienation, *La Notte* (1961) (*The Night*); an archetypal femme fatale in Joseph Losey's *Eva* (1962); and went blonde as a compulsive gambler for Jacques Demy's *La Baie des anges* (1963) (*Bay of the Angels*). She made three films with Orson Welles, including a suitably sluttish Doll Tearsheet in his Shakespearean *Campanadas a medianoche* (1966) (*Chimes at Midnight*). Welles called Moreau "the greatest actress in the world."

In recent years the roles have grown rarer, but she can still illuminate the screen, as in François Ozon's *Le temps qui reste* (2005) (*Time to Leave*). She has directed two well-received features and a documentary about Lillian Gish. **PK**

Top Takes…

Le temps qui reste 2005 (*Time to Leave*)
Map of the Human Heart 1993
Querelle 1982
Les valseuses 1974 (*Going Places*)
Nathalie Granger 1972
Great Catherine 1968
Campanadas a medianoche 1965
  (*Chimes at Midnight*)
Viva Maria! 1965
La Baie des anges 1963 (*Bay of the Angels*)
Eva 1962
Jules et Jim 1962
La Notte 1961 (*The Night*)
Les Amants 1958 (*The Lovers*)
Ascenseur pour l'échafaud 1958
  (*Elevator to the Gallows*)

1920s

"Each time an actor acts he does not hide; he exposes himself."

MICHEL SERRAULT

Born: Michel Serrault, January 24, 1928 (Brunoy, Essonne, France).

Star qualities: Gallic charm; rubbery face; doe-eyed; comedian; stagecraft; character actor; singer; prolific output; versatile player of both comic and dramatic lead roles; producer.

Top Takes...

Une hirondelle a fait le printemps 2001
  (One Swallow Brought Spring)
Les Acteurs 2000 (Actors)
Les Enfants du marais 1999
  (The Children of the Marshland)
Nelly & Monsieur Arnaud 1995
  (Nelly and Mr. Arnaud)
La cage aux folles 3—'Elles' se marient 1985
  (La Cage aux Folles 3: The Wedding)
Garde à vue 1981 (The Inquisitor)
La cage aux folles II 1980
Pile ou face 1980 (Heads or Tails)
La cage aux folles 1978 (Birds of a Feather)
La Belle américaine 1961 (The American Beauty)
Assassins et voleurs 1957 (Lovers and Thieves)
Les diaboliques 1955 (Diabolique)

There is something about Michel Serrault that words cannot fully describe: his uncontrollable laugh, full of irony, self-mockery, and desperation. It might well be this ambiguity that enables him to appear comfortable in both comic and dramatic parts. Serrault had originally wanted to be a priest, and spent a few months in a seminary until he fell in love with a girl. He then joined a song and comedy cabaret act, and later was part of Robert Dhery's theater troupe.

Serrault made his first onscreen appearance in 1954; at first he mostly alternated between successful comedies such as *Assassins et voleurs* (1957) (*Lovers and Thieves*) and *La Belle américaine* (1961) (*The American Beauty*) and dispensable humorous pieces, often alongside Jean Poiret, with whom he debuted on the stage. A respected actor in the French theater, he encountered huge success doing a play that became a hit in the cinema a few years later: in *La cage aux folles* (1978) (*Birds of a Feather*), he was Zaza Napoli the drag artist, a highly caricatured character for which he won the first of his three Best Actor Césars and became widely known outside France. However, at the beginning of the 1980s, with *Pile ou face* (1980) (*Heads or Tails*) and *Garde à vue* (1981) (*The Inquisitor*), he was increasingly offered serious and subtle parts such as disenchanted detectives and murderers, which finally enabled him to demonstrate the full range of his talent. He tends to stay within the realm of French cinema. But Serrault's career is not only the story of a comedian who suddenly became respectable. Since 1966, his fruitful collaboration with maverick director Jean-Pierre Mocky—more than ten films so far—keeps proving one thing: you can be a star and still not worry about your image. **FL**

> "This film has . . . a great deal to do with the craft of acting."
>
> —Pauline Kael on *La cage aux folles II*

HARDY KRÜGER

Born: Franz Eberhard August Krüger, April 12, 1928 (Berlin-Wedding, Germany).

Star qualities: Tall, rugged, matinee idol looks; blond hair; producer; director; frequently plays character roles as the foreigner in English-language action films; fluent in English, French, and German.

Hardy Krüger first appeared on screen as a fifteen year old in *Junge Adler* (1944). His career ground to a halt, however, when he was drafted into the German infantry the following year. It is said that during the war he was taken prisoner by the Americans but managed to escape successfully on the third attempt. He did not take up acting again until 1949, when he had some success in his native Germany. His emerging reputation, combined with his rugged good looks and James Dean-like hauteur, led to a contract with the British movie mogul J. Arthur Rank in 1957 and a subsequent career as an international star in English-language films.

Two of the films Krüger did for Rank endure. Roy Ward Baker's *The One That Got Away* (1957) features him as a fearless yet sympathetic Nazi flyer prisoner of war who repeatedly escapes British incarceration, whereas Joseph Losey's *Blind Date* (1959) draws upon his matinee-idol appearance as a foreigner caught in a romantic relationship with an older woman and subsequent implication in her murder. His best roles in the 1960s were in multinationally cast action features. He played a cocky but caring big game hunter opposite John Wayne in Howard Hawks's *Hatari!* (1962), and a dour but dauntingly intelligent engineer trapped after a plane crash in the desert in Robert Aldrich's *The Flight of the Phoenix* (1965). Stanley Kubrick cast him as Captain Potzdorf in the historical drama *Barry Lyndon* (1975), and his most recent role of note took his life full circle as he played Field Marshal Erwin Rommel in the television miniseries *War and Remembrance* (1988). During the 1970s and 1980s, Krüger directed a number of European TV documentaries. He is the father of actors Christiane Krüger and Hardy Krüger Jr. **DS**

Top Takes...

The Wild Geese 1978
A Bridge Too Far 1977
Barry Lyndon 1975
Paper Tiger 1975
The Secret of Santa Vittoria 1969
The Defector 1966
The Flight of the Phoenix 1965
Hatari! 1962
Blind Date 1959
Bachelor of Hearts 1958
The One That Got Away 1957
Junge Adler 1944

1920s

"I'd rather sit out a picture than take a role I don't think is right for me."

SHIRLEY TEMPLE

Born: Shirley Jane Temple, April 23, 1928 (Santa Monica, California, U.S.).

Star qualities: Magical Hollywood sparkle; bright singing and incredible tap dancing; cheerful and energetic; box-office champion; most famous child star; respected diplomat.

Perhaps the most famous and talented of the child stars Hollywood has produced—a children's drink is even named after her—Shirley Temple began her career in 1932, appearing in a series of one-reel comedies for Educational Pictures. A truly precocious child, her sweet, startlingly doll-like features, complete with dimples and curls, enhanced the appeal of her acting, dancing, and singing abilities. She appeared in bit and minor roles in many films, mostly shorts, during 1933, finally catching the attention of talent scouts at both Fox Film Corporation and Paramount Pictures. Her ascent to stardom began when she was featured in the song-and-dance number "Baby, Take a Bow" in the Fox Film Corporation musical *Stand Up and Cheer!* (1934) with James Dunn, with whom she would be paired in several subsequent pictures. By 1935, she was Fox's biggest star, appearing in the sentimental comedies *Our Little Girl, Curly Top, The Little Colonel,* and *The Littlest Rebel*—the latter two being Civil War-era dramas that featured her in complex, syncopated dance numbers with Bill "Bojangles" Robinson, which she executed to near perfection. By 1938, she was the top-grossing U.S. box-office star.

Top Takes…

Fort Apache 1948
The Bachelor and the Bobby-Soxer 1947
Kiss and Tell 1945
I'll Be Seeing You 1944
Since You Went Away 1944
Miss Annie Rooney 1942
Kathleen 1941
Young People 1940
The Blue Bird 1940
Susannah of the Mounties 1939
The Little Princess 1939
Little Miss Broadway 1938
Rebecca of Sunnybrook Farm 1938
Heidi 1937
Wee Willie Winkie 1937
Stowaway 1936
Poor Little Rich Girl 1936
The Littlest Rebel 1935
Curly Top 1935
Our Little Girl 1935
The Little Colonel 1935
Bright Eyes 1934
Now and Forever 1934
Baby Take a Bow 1934
Stand Up and Cheer! 1934

RIGHT: The nine-year-old Shirley Temple playing little Swiss girl Heidi in 1937.

Temple's massive popularity resulted in the creation of product tie-ins, including dolls, a line of dresses, movie novelizations, coloring books, and sheet music of film songs, among them "On the Good Ship Lollipop" (*Bright Eyes*, 1934), "Animal Crackers in My Soup" (*Curly Top*, 1935), and "Goodnight, My Love" (*Stowaway*, 1936). By 1940, Temple's box-office appeal had begun to decline, and thus her period of greatest popularity coincided with the Great Depression. Even so, she appeared in some successful pictures as a teenager in the 1940s, including *Since You Went Away* and *I'll Be Seeing You* (both 1944), *The Bachelor and the Bobby-Soxer* (1947), and *Fort Apache* (1948), in which she appeared with her first husband, John Agar, whom she had married at age seventeen. Temple's autobiography, *Child Star: An Autobiography*, was published in 1988; it in turn became the basis of a biopic, *Child Star: The Shirley Temple Story* (2001). **SU**

ABOVE: At work in the film *The Littlest Rebel*. Temple could do it all: act, sing, and dance.

Change of Direction

In 1950, Shirley Temple married California businessman Charles Alden Black and as Shirley Temple Black she began a second career in politics. In 1969, President Richard Nixon appointed her as U.S. representative to the United Nations; she later served as U.S. ambassador to Ghana (1974–1976), and subsequently became chief of protocol, in charge of U.S. State Department ceremonies. During the years 1989 to 1992 she served as ambassador to Czechoslovakia. Temple brought the same degree of professionalism to politics that had made her career in the movie world such a great success.

RODDY McDOWALL

Born: Roderick Andrew Anthony Jude McDowall, September 17, 1928 (Herne Hill, London, England); died 1998 (Studio City, California, U.S.).

Star qualities: Child actor turned mature character actor; stagecraft; prolific output; socialite; photographer; film preservationist; director; producer.

Top Takes…

A Bug's Life 1998
Funny Lady 1975
Battle for the Planet of the Apes 1973
The Life and Times of Judge Roy Bean 1972
The Poseidon Adventure 1972
Conquest of the Planet of the Apes 1972
Escape from the Planet of the Apes 1971
Planet of the Apes 1968
It! 1966
Lord Love a Duck 1966
Cleopatra 1963
The Keys of the Kingdom 1944
Lassie Come Home 1943
My Friend Flicka 1943
Son of Fury: The Story of Benjamin Blake 1942
How Green Was My Valley 1941

Roddy McDowall was a rare child actor who achieved lasting success as an adult, and appeared in more than 150 films. His mother—who wanted to be in movies herself—moved McDowall and his sister Virginia to the United States at the beginning of World War II. McDowall soon landed the key role of Huw Morgan, youngest child in a family of Welsh coal miners, in John Ford's *How Green Was My Valley* (1941), acting alongside Maureen O'Hara and Walter Pidgeon. He then took on other child roles, as a friend to animals in *My Friend Flicka* (1943) and *Lassie Come Home* (1943), before going on to play characters "as a boy" in *Son of Fury: The Story of Benjamin Blake* (1942) and *The Keys of the Kingdom* (1944).

After doing TV work in the 1950s, McDowall returned to movies as Octavian in *Cleopatra* (1963) and hyperactive high school mastermind Alan "Mollymauk" Musgrave in *Lord Love a Duck* (1966). For some time, he drifted toward fey, gay, or psycho roles such as museum assistant Arthur Pimm in the British horror film *It!* (1966). However, he then had considerable success in a monkey mask as Cornelius in the sci-fi classic *Planet of the Apes* (1968), returning as the heart of the franchise for three sequels and a TV series. In later life McDowall became a respected stills photographer and published five books of photographs. He was also an avid collector of movies, a hobby that got him into trouble with the Federal Bureau of Investigation in 1974. The agency raided his home and seized his collection during an investigation of copyright infringement and movie piracy. The Academy of Motion Picture Arts and Sciences named its photo library The Roddy McDowall Photograph Archive at the Margaret Herrick Library in his honor. **KN**

> "My whole life I've been trying to prove I'm not just yesterday."

GEORGE PEPPARD

Born: George Peppard Jr., October 1, 1928 (Detroit, Michigan, U.S.); died 1994 (Los Angeles, California, U.S.).

Star qualities: Tall, blue-eyed, blond; handsome lead actor; elegant manner; charming; stagecraft; cult TV show action hero; producer; director.

George Peppard was born the son of a building contractor and an opera singer. He studied at New York's Actors Studio with famous acting coach Lee Strasberg. After experience on Broadway and in television, Peppard made his film debut in *The Strange One* (1957). He benefited from an old-fashioned studio build-up and was given solid lower rank roles in such films as *Pork Chop Hill* (1959), followed by a key supporting part as Robert Mitchum's illegitimate son in the popular melodrama *Home from the Hill* (1960).

After famously starring opposite Audrey Hepburn in *Breakfast at Tiffany's* (1961)—one of his finest performances—Peppard started getting featured parts in all-star movies such as *How the West Was Won* (1962) and *The Victors* (1963). He finally landed a lead in *The Carpetbaggers* (1964), in which he played industrialist Jonas Cord. His best work on the big screen, however, came in his portrayal of the chilly, ambitious, World War I German ace pilot, Bruno Stachel, who challenges the Prussian aristocracy in *The Blue Max* (1966).

Yet Peppard was too remote to become a lasting star and he started losing ground, and roles, to other cool cats of the time, such as Steve McQueen and James Coburn. He was also suffering from alcoholism. Unfortunately, he was then found in shakier vehicles such as *Cannon for Cordoba* (1970) and *One More Train to Rob* (1971). Aside from playing a space cowboy in *Battle Beyond the Stars* (1980), his later career was spent on the small screen, headlining as the Polish-American detective Thomas Banacek in the clever series *Banacek* (1972–1974) and as the cigar-chomping squadron leader Colonel John "Hannibal" Smith in the enormously popular cult series *The A-Team* (1983–1987). **KN**

Top Takes...

Battle Beyond the Stars 1980
Newman's Law 1974
One More Train to Rob 1971
Cannon for Cordoba 1970
The Executioner 1970
Tobruk 1967
The Blue Max 1966
Operation Crossbow 1965
The Carpetbaggers 1964
The Victors 1963
How the West Was Won 1962
Breakfast at Tiffany's 1961
The Subterraneans 1960
Home from the Hill 1960
Pork Chop Hill 1959
The Strange One 1957

"Mine isn't a string of victories. It's no golden past. I'm no George Peppard fan."

MAX von SYDOW

Born: Max Carl Adolf von Sydow, April 10, 1929 (Lund, Skåne län, Sweden).

Star qualities: Discerning and intellectual performer; tall with imposing presence; consummate villain; idol of the international art theater; one of few actors to be nominated for an Oscar for a foreign-language film.

Top Takes...

RIGHT: Von Sydow striking a lighter note as Ming the Merciless in *Flash Gordon*.

Max von Sydow came to prominence for his work with Ingmar Bergman in Sweden: as the knight who plays chess with Death in *Det Sjunde inseglet* (1957) (*The Seventh Seal*), the garage mechanic whose dazzling smile seems at odds with the auteur's worldview in *Smultronstället* (1957) (*Wild Strawberries*), the snake-oil salesman/conjurer of *Ansiktet* (1958) (*The Face*), and the avenging father of *Jungfrukällan* (1960) (*The Virgin Spring*). Von Sydow was cast as Jesus in *The Greatest Story Ever Told* (1965) and survived that all-star Hollywood embarrassment with two parallel careers: as Bergman's gloomy alter ego in increasingly spare, ascetic Swedish films (*Nattvardsgästerna* (*Winter Light*), 1962; *Vargtimmen* (*Hour of the Wolf*), 1968; and so on) and as a major international character actor.

In this latter mode, von Sydow specialized in wry, menacing Nazis (*The Quiller Memorandum*, 1966) and communists (*The Kremlin Letter*, 1970), until he had another breakout role as Father Merrin in *The Exorcist* (1973). In a rare instance (compare Orson Welles as old Kane with old Orson), von Sydow has aged to look exactly as makeup man Dick Smith made him look in *The Exorcist*, although he turns up as young Merrin in *Exorcist II:*

The Heretic (1977). He continued to play sinister figures in international intrigues (*Three Days of the Condor*, 1975; *Cadaveri eccellenti* (*Illustrious Corpses*), 1976), and developed another specialty as shaggy futuristic gurus (*The Ultimate Warrior*, 1975; *La mort en direct* (*Deathwatch*), 1980; *Bis ans Ende der Welt* (*Until the End of the World*), 1991). A few too many suffering Swedish peasant roles (*Nybyggarna* (*The New Land*), 1972; *Pelle erobreren* (*Pelle the Conqueror*), 1987; *Oxen*, 1991) confirmed von Sydow as the movies' greatest wet blanket. Even when Bergman started to use him less, Woody Allen cast him for his miserabilist associations in *Hannah and Her Sisters* (1986). But von Sydow strongly established a more fun-loving mode as Ming the Merciless in *Flash Gordon* (1980), which landed him roles in boys' adventures like *Victory* (1981), *Conan the Barbarian* (1982), and (as Blofeld) *Never Say Never Again* (1983). He continues to work regularly in Europe and Hollywood. **KN**

ABOVE: Playing chess against the Grim Reaper in Bergman's *The Seventh Seal*.

Behind the Camera

During a fruitful international career spanning more than 50 years, Max von Sydow has also tried his hand at directing. He made his debut with *Ved vejen* in 1988. The movie earned him the Guldbagge Best Director award. Von Sydow considers filmmaking to be more of a director's medium than an actor's because the director has ultimate control of how a role is portrayed onscreen, whereas onstage the performance is the responsibility of the actor. He thinks that the one great advantage film has over theater, however, is proximity to the audience.

AUDREY HEPBURN

Born: Audrey Kathleen Ruston, May 4, 1929 (Brussels, Belgium); died 1993 (Tolochenaz, Switzerland).

Star qualities: Stunningly beautiful and effortlessly funny; fashion icon; adolescent charm; humanitarian; won an Oscar, a Tony, an Emmy, and a Grammy Award.

Top Takes...

Always 1989
They All Laughed 1981
Robin and Marian 1976
Wait Until Dark 1967 ☆
Two for the Road 1967
How to Steal a Million 1966
My Fair Lady 1964
Charade 1963
The Children's Hour 1961
Breakfast at Tiffany's 1961 ☆
The Unforgiven 1960
The Nun's Story 1959 ☆
Green Mansions 1959
Love in the Afternoon 1957
Funny Face 1957
War and Peace 1955
Sabrina 1954 ☆
Roman Holiday 1953 ★
The Lavender Hill Mob 1951

Among the grandes dames of Hollywood, Audrey Hepburn is the fragile saint with the incorruptible heart—vulnerable, but also exquisitely elegant. Frail though she appeared, she never cracked under pressure, and when she became a children's ambassador for UNICEF after she retired from acting (at a time when celebrity charity work was not yet fashionable), she did so with such solid commitment and dedication that it impressed even hardened politicians. That vocation as an international diplomat was the logical culmination of her life and her acting career.

Hepburn was the prototype of the true cosmopolitan. Born in Brussels of Dutch and Anglo-Irish parents (her mother was a baroness, her father a banker), she grew up in Belgium, the Netherlands, and England, spending World War II under the Nazi occupation. She is said to have witnessed such hardship during the occupation that she later turned down a role in *The Diary of Anne Frank* (1959) because it would bring up too many painful memories. It is also often suggested that her later problems with anorexia started with the malnutrition she

RIGHT: Hepburn in *Roman Holiday*, the film that shot her to international stardom.

suffered during the war (she once confessed to eating tulip bulbs). She moved from a modeling career in Amsterdam to small acting parts in Paris and London (most notably in *The Lavender Hill Mob*, 1951), until she was recruited for the role of the princess in William Wyler's *Roman Holiday*, shot on location in Rome, in 1953. *Roman Holiday* cashes in on her cosmopolitan background by incorporating stylish footage of her in several European cities, including Amsterdam, and she speaks a few words of Dutch in the audition ceremony at the end of the movie, a nice acknowledgment of her European roots. (Hepburn was fluent in five languages, a talent that would later assist her humanitarian work.)

The success of *Roman Holiday* catapulted Hepburn on to the world stage and won her an Academy Award for Best

ABOVE: Costar Rex Harrison cited Hepburn in *My Fair Lady* as his favorite leading lady.

"I never thought I'd land in pictures with a face like mine."

That Little Black Dress

In *Breakfast at Tiffany's* Holly Golightly is seen wearing it as she gracefully emerges from a New York cab and gazes into Tiffany's window while she eats breakfast from a paper bag. In December 2006 the very same little black dress worn by Audrey Hepburn (right) sold for £410,000 at Christie's auction house in London, making it the most expensive—as well as the most famous—dress ever worn in a movie.

Designed by Givenchy, the dress was instrumental in shaping Hepburn's image as an enduring style icon. Hepburn was the muse for fashion designer Hubert de Givenchy. He dressed her for many of her most famous films, including *Sabrina* (1954), *Funny Face* (1957), *Charade* (1963), and *How to Steal a Million* (1966). The black floor-length cocktail dress, size six, has a fitted bodice and rear décolletage, with a slit up the thigh. Fittingly, bearing in mind Hepburn's sterling humanitarian work, the proceeds of the dress's sale went to the City of Joy Aid, a charity that helps India's poor.

Always modest, Hepburn once suggested: "My look is attainable. Women can look like Audrey Hepburn by flipping out their hair, buying the large sunglasses, and the little sleeveless dresses." After her first hit movie, *Roman Holiday* (1953), millions of women worldwide aspired to the Hepburn look, as they still do today.

RIGHT: Hepburn as Holly Golightly, one of the definitive roles of her career.

Actress at the age of only twenty-four. This was soon followed by a Tony Award for Best Actress (Dramatic) in 1954 for her portrayal in *Ondine*. Her burgeoning fame also won her the everlasting adoration of a generation of female baby-boomers, who made her a role model for the modern young woman. While the Dutch, Belgian, and British press tried to claim her as one of their own, it was clear she now belonged to the world.

Hepburn's subsequent film career was neither lengthy nor particularly intense—she played only 15 major parts between 1953 and 1967—but it was so beautifully consistent that it forms a unity seldom seen in cinema. All of Hepburn's film roles are about education in one form or another. Whereas she may seem to run away from her strict training in favor of leisurely distractions in *Roman Holiday*, costar Gregory Peck still educates her in the ways of the world. Similarly, her most successful parts, in *Sabrina* (1954), *The Nun's Story* (1959), *The Children's Hour* (1961), *Breakfast at Tiffany's* (1961), and *My Fair Lady* (1964), emphasize how the glamour of her characters is always associated with training, effort, and proper manners. It should come as no surprise that Hepburn is every schoolteacher's favorite actress.

From Hollywood star to international diplomat

In 1958 she turned down the lead in *Gigi* (which went to French-born actress Leslie Caron), having helped create the character on Broadway. From the late 1960s onward, Hepburn gradually moved away from acting, and into international diplomacy, working with UNICEF in Africa and Latin America. She achieved such proficiency in that calling, and such respect, that it is far from pretentious that when she returned to the big screen one final time (a few years before her passing away of cancer in 1993), in Steven Spielberg's *Always* (1989), she played God. Not surprisingly, she did so with the disarming wit and charm of a true angel.

The gamine actress was married twice, to actor Mel Ferrer and Dr. Andrea Dotti, and she had a son from each marriage. In 1990 a tulip was named after her. **EM**

1920s

GRACE KELLY

Born: Grace Patricia Kelly, November 12, 1929 (Philadelphia, Pennsylvania, U.S.); died 1982 (Monacoville, Monaco).

Star qualities: Flawless beauty, poise, and glamour; one of Hitchcock's leading actresses; dated many of her costars before her fairytale wedding to Prince Rainier.

Top Takes...

High Society 1956

The Swan 1956

To Catch a Thief 1955

The Bridges at Toko-Ri 1955

Green Fire 1954

The Country Girl 1954 ★

Rear Window 1954

Dial M for Murder 1954

Mogambo 1953 ☆

High Noon 1952

Fourteen Hours 1951

One of the most beautiful women ever to become a major movie star, Grace Kelly was born into a wealthy family. Beginning her career as a model, she worked on Broadway and in television before landing a minor role in a Hollywood thriller, *Fourteen Hours* (1951). A year later she was cast as Gary Cooper's Quaker wife in the Western *High Noon*, which became a big hit. After costarring with Clark Gable and Ava Gardner in *Mogambo* (1953), an adventure film set in Africa, she went on to make two films for Alfred Hitchcock, *Dial M for Murder* (1954), with Ray Milland, and *Rear Window* (1954), in which her costar was James Stewart. Just the sort of cool, blonde type that Hitchcock favored, outwardly reserved but smoldering underneath, Kelly was much in demand.

Green Fire (1954), another adventure film, set this time in South America, was a waste of Kelly's talents; but for her meaty dramatic role in *The Country Girl* (1954), in which she played the loyal wife of washed-up alcoholic singer Bing Crosby, she received the Oscar for Best Actress. Set in Korea, *The Bridges at Toko-Ri* (1955) was not an especially remarkable war film, but then Hitchcock cast her again, this time opposite Cary Grant, in

RIGHT: Kelly's role as Lisa Fremont in *Rear Window* brought her Hollywood fame.

To Catch a Thief (1955). The moment when, having been icily distant with him all evening, Kelly suddenly kisses Grant on the mouth before firmly closing her bedroom door in his face, is one of the most sophisticatedly erotic in cinema history.

It was while filming this project on the French Riviera that Kelly first met Prince Rainier of Monaco. As if life were imitating art, Kelly's subsequent film, *The Swan* (1956), was a comedy set among European royalty. And her next movie proved to be her swan song. *High Society* (1956) was a musical remake of the Hollywood comedy *The Philadelphia Story* (1940), in which Kelly, playing opposite Frank Sinatra and Bing Crosby, takes the role originally played by Katharine Hepburn. After this she married Prince Rainier, retiring from the screen after a mere half a dozen years. Princess Grace was rarely out of the limelight after that. And then, in 1982, when she was only fifty-two, came tragedy—a fatal car crash on a mountain road. **EB**

ABOVE: Grace Kelly and Cary Grant giving stylish performances in *To Catch a Thief*.

Perfect Princess

Born the sole heir to the throne of the tiny French enclave of Monaco, Prince Rainier was the richest bachelor in the world. He was eager to marry a movie star in the hope that it would boost tourism in his principality. Marilyn Monroe and Gina Lollobrigida were considered as possible choices before he settled on Grace Kelly. (She was deemed suitable because she was Catholic and could bear children.) After they married in 1956, Princess Grace reluctantly gave up her acting career. No longer keen on the publicity his new wife attracted, Prince Rainier ordered that her films should not be shown in Monaco.

JOHN CASSAVETES

Born: John Nicholas Cassavetes, December 9, 1929 (New York City, New York, U.S.); died 1989 (Los Angeles, California, U.S.).

Star qualities: Character actor; improvisation advocate; creative partnership with Gena Rowlands; pioneering director of U.S. independent film; producer; writer.

Top Takes...

John Cassavetes was more interested in working as a director than an actor, giving his friends Ben Gazzara and Peter Falk the best roles in his personal films. He studied at the American Academy of Dramatic Arts in New York. After some Marlon Brando-like Method work in the 1950s, he incidentally became a movie star to finance his off-Hollywood independent films. In the 1950s he did a lot of TV work, including the jazzman detective show *Johnny Staccato* (1959–1960). He also played neurotic, violent delinquents in *The Night Holds Terror* (1955), *Crime in the Streets* (1956), and the Western *Saddle the Wind* (1958) while showing a more sensitive, if wounded, side in the film noir *Edge of the City* (1957).

The first movie he directed was *Shadows* (1959), and from then on he concentrated on directing, making noteworthy films such as *Faces* (1968) and *Gloria* (1980). But he still appeared in some box-office hits, usually in sinister roles such as the mobster in *The Dirty Dozen* (1967), the husband in *Rosemary's Baby* (1968), and the government spook who detonates at the end of *The Fury* (1978). Taking a few prominent roles in his own films such as *Love Streams* (1984), he also sometimes acted for his friends, brilliantly parodying Leonard Bernstein in a *Columbo* episode, "Étude in Black" (1972). He also partnered with Falk in six films for the big screen, including Elaine May's *Mikey and Nicky* (1976). Cassavetes was married to actress Gena Rowlands until his death in 1989, and the pair worked together on ten of his films. They also appeared together in Paul Mazursky's *Tempest* (1982), where Cassavetes played the Prospero equivalent. The couple had three children, Nick, Alexandra, and Zoe, all of whom have become actors and directors. **KN**

> "As an artist, I feel that we must try many things—but above all we must dare to fail."

GENE HACKMAN

Born: Eugene Allen Hackman, January 30, 1930 (San Bernardino, California, U.S.).

Star qualities: Tall; intelligent; veteran leading man and versatile actor who completely immerses himself in his characters; portrays the complex villain or unlikely hero; prolific output; stagecraft; producer.

Was Gene Hackman ever young? He always seemed mature, even in movies as early as *Lilith* (1964) and *Bonnie and Clyde* (1967). It's not merely a question of his never having had matinee-idol looks; it's the sense of doubt, anxiety, an awareness of life's complications born of experience that underlies even his most brashly confident characters. Even his role as Detective Jimmy "Popeye" Doyle in *The French Connection* (1971), for which he won an Academy Award for Best Actor, is one where the character has some kind of chip on his shoulder, arising perhaps from insecurity.

Hackman left home at the age of sixteen to join the U.S. Marine Corps. After a three-year tour, he returned to civilian life and went to study TV production and journalism at the University of Illinois under the G.I. Bill. Hackman then embarked on an acting career in his thirties. He joined California's Pasadena Playhouse, where he became friends with another hopeful, actor Dustin Hoffman. Discouragingly voted "The Least Likely to Succeed" by their classmates, both dropped out after a short time and worked for a while doing various menial jobs.

By the time Hackman really hit his stride in the mid-1970s, he was at his best exploring the middle-aged male's crisis in *The Conversation* (1974), *French Connection II* (1975), and *Night Moves* (1975). Despite regularly taking more routine parts in movies like *A Bridge Too Far* (1977) and *Superman* (1978), he has always been most persuasive and effective in darker, more complex, or watchful roles, as in *Reds* (1981), *Mississippi Burning* (1988), *Unforgiven* (1992), and *Absolute Power* (1997). However, he has also exhibited a flair for comedy in the movies *Get Shorty* (1995), *Twilight* (1998), and *The Royal Tenenbaums* (2001). **GA**

Top Takes...

The Royal Tenenbaums 2001
Twilight 1998
Absolute Power 1997
Get Shorty 1995
***Unforgiven* 1992** ★
***Mississippi Burning* 1988** ☆
Reds 1981
Superman 1978
A Bridge Too Far 1977
Night Moves 1975
French Connection II 1975
The Conversation 1974
***The French Connection* 1971** ★
***I Never Sang for My Father* 1970** ☆
***Bonnie and Clyde* 1967** ☆
Lilith 1964

"I wanted to act, but I'd always been convinced that actors had to be handsome."

1930s

STEVE McQUEEN

Born: Terence Steven McQueen, March 24, 1930 (Beech Grove, Indiana, U.S.); died 1980 (Juárez, Mexico).

Star qualities: "The King of Cool"; rugged good looks; blue-eyed rebel; legendary action hero and leading man; athletic; racing-car driver; director; producer.

Top Takes...

Steve McQueen was the movie hero James Dean might have become in the 1960s: cool, laconic, and capable, but tense with a deeply suppressed neurosis. After a troubled youth spent in reform schools, McQueen joined the U.S. Marine Corps in 1947, serving until 1950. He then studied acting and was accepted by New York's Actors Studio in 1955. His first star film role was as an overage teenager fighting a monster in *The Blob* (1958). After a TV series, *Wanted: Dead or Alive* (1958–1961), he registered as a presence in movies such as *Never So Few* (1959) and the iconic Western *The Magnificent Seven* (1960).

He is best remembered for leaping over barbed wire on a motorbike while being pursued by Nazi troops in the prisoner-of-war movie *The Great Escape* (1963). Although McQueen was a motorbike and racing-car enthusiast, the leap was done by a stuntman for insurance purposes, given that McQueen was one of the highest-paid stars of the 1960s—he earned $400,000 for his role in *The Great Escape*. But McQueen did do many of his own stunts, notably the chase sequence in *Bullitt* (1968).

As a star, McQueen essayed near-psychotic war heroes in films such as *Hell Is for Heroes* (1962), played a cocky card player in *The Cincinnati Kid* (1965), was a cool criminal mastermind in *The Thomas Crown Affair* (1968), and a scheming prisoner in *Papillon* (1973). Later in life he was diagnosed with a form of lung cancer related to asbestos exposure. It has been suggested that this may have been caused by the asbestos-insulated suits he wore when racing. He became reclusive, returning to the big screen only occasionally and bowing out as a bounty hunter in *The Hunter* (1980). McQueen had been married to his third wife, Barbara Minty, for less than a year when he died at age fifty. **KN**

"There's something about my shaggy-dog eyes that makes people think I'm good."

1930s

JEAN ROCHEFORT

Born: Jean Raoul Robert Rochefort, April 29, 1930 (Dinan, Côtes-du-Nord, France).

Star qualities: Handsome with a roguish smile; long face; moustache; leading man and character actor of French comedies and dramas; cabaret artist; stagecraft; prolific output; writer; director; keen horseman.

Jean Rochefort studied drama at Paris's Conservatoire National Supérieur d'Art Dramatique. He had to interrupt his studies to do national service in the French military, after which he began to perform in theater and cabaret in Paris. He made his movie debut with a small role in *Rencontre à Paris* (1956) (*Meeting in Paris*), and through the 1950s he worked in films, TV, and on the stage. By the 1960s he started to become a fixture in films as the sidekick to Jean-Paul Belmondo in such works as director Philippe De Broca's comedy adventure *Cartouche* (1962) (*Swords of Blood*) and *Les tribulations d'un Chinois en Chine* (1965) (*Chinese Adventures in China*). He also found success in films *sans* Belmondo, such as De Broca's comedy thriller *Le diable par la queue* (1969) (*The Devil by the Tail*).

His reputation as a character actor of comedies grew, and by the 1970s he was headlining movies such as *Le grand blond avec une chaussure noire* (1972) (*The Tall Blond Man with One Black Shoe*), in which he played a member of the French secret service. The movie was a hit and spawned a successful sequel.

But Rochefort did not rest on his comedy laurels and engaged in more serious fare, such as Bertrand Tavernier's thriller *L'horloger de Saint-Paul* (1974) (*The Clockmaker of St. Paul*) as the murder investigator Inspector Guilboud. Since then he has moved between comedies and dramas, both in his native France and abroad, including Robert Altman's all-star fashion ensemble *Prêt-à-Porter* (1994). His most notable role of late was as Don Quixote in his ill-fated version of the adaptation of the classic tale. Rochefort suffered a back injury during the shoot, one of many setbacks that meant the movie was never finished, only to make the big screen in documentary form in *Lost in La Mancha* (2002). **CK**

Top Takes...

L'homme du train 2002 (*The Man on the Train*)
Lost in La Mancha 2002
Ridicule 1996
Prêt-à-Porter 1994
Le Crabe-tambour 1977 (*Drummer-Crab*)
Le fantôme de la liberté 1974
   (*The Phantom of Liberty*)
L'horloger de Saint-Paul 1974
   (*The Clockmaker of St. Paul*)
Le grand blond avec une chaussure noire 1972
   (*The Tall Blond Man with One Black Shoe*)
Le diable par la queue 1969
   (*The Devil by the Tail*)
Les tribulations d'un chinois en Chine 1965
   (*Chinese Adventures in China*)
Cartouche 1962 (*Swords of Blood*)
Rencontre à Paris 1956 (*Meeting in Paris*)

"I try picking a fight and find someone who likes me."

—M. Manesquier, *The Man on the Train*

1930s

CLINT EASTWOOD

Born: Clinton Eastwood Jr., May 31, 1930 (San Francisco, California, U.S.).

Star qualities: Quintessential macho movie star; tall, with chiseled good looks; tough guy icon of the Western genre; all his characters have trademark expressions; international legend as actor and director; his career has spanned 50 years so far.

Top Takes...

Million Dollar Baby 2004 ☆

Absolute Power 1997

The Bridges of Madison County 1995

A Perfect World 1993

In the Line of Fire 1993

Unforgiven 1992 ☆

The Rookie 1990

White Hunter Black Heart 1990

City Heat 1984

Tightrope 1984

Escape from Alcatraz 1979

Every Which Way But Loose 1978

The Outlaw Josey Wales 1976

High Plains Drifter 1973

Dirty Harry 1971

Play Misty for Me 1971

The Beguiled 1971

Kelly's Heroes 1970

Coogan's Bluff 1968

Hang 'Em High 1968

Il buono, il brutto, il cattivo 1966
  (*The Good, the Bad and the Ugly*)

Per qualche dollaro in più 1965
  (*For a Few Dollars More*)

Per un pugno di dollari 1964 (*A Fistful of Dollars*)

RIGHT: Eastwood as the laconic antihero
in Sergio Leone's *For a Few Dollars More*.

Arguably U.S. cinema's single most important representation of that country's masculine image—with all of the gender's complexities and conflicts—Eastwood can do macho swagger and ice-cold toughness better than any other performer, but there's much more to his onscreen persona (and his directorial talents) than just that. It would seem that many U.S. critics had to wait until this icon's septuagenarian years to finally catch on, whereas European cineasts saw Eastwood's depth decades ago. Regardless, Clint Eastwood is now the very definition of a movie star. And if the Europeans appreciated his talents first, it's only fitting that a European was the first filmmaker to really utilize Eastwood's steely gaze and laconic charm effectively.

Twenty-five when he began acting, Eastwood appeared in minor film roles before finding success in TV Westerns, such as *Rawhide* (1959–1966). He worked on this level for nine years until Italian director Sergio Leone cast him in the *Dollars* trilogy— *Per un pugno di dollari* (1964) (*A Fistful of Dollars*), *Per qualche dollaro in più* (1965) (*For a Few Dollars More*), and *Il buono, il brutto, il cattivo* (1966) (*The Good, the Bad and the Ugly*). The films turned Eastwood into an international superstar, and he

found further fame on home turf with adventures like *Hang 'Em High* (1968), *Kelly's Heroes* (1970), and—the film that really catapulted him into movie legend status—1971's *Dirty Harry*.

ABOVE: Eastwood played unruly cop Harry Callahan in the classic movie *Dirty Harry*.

It speaks volumes that within the same year of *Dirty Harry's* controversial release, Eastwood would make two of his most commendably odd and unique career choices: making his directing debut with *Play Misty for Me*, and appearing in *Dirty Harry* director Don Siegel's bizarre Gothic, *The Beguiled*. In both films Eastwood plays a superficially seductive lothario who is gradually weakened and dominated by the affections of his female conquests. The subtle inquiry into the definition of masculine strength would continue as a theme throughout his work, be it in the form of thrillers, or in tender romances like *The Bridges of Madison County* (1995).

"I've actually had people come up to me and ask me to autograph their guns."

Making a Mark

There are numerous ways to identify a Clint Eastwood movie, aside from the obvious presence of the man himself. For starters, his films usually begin and end with the death of a character. Harry Callahan is a particularly dangerous man to hang around with—in *Dirty Harry* (1971) and all of the sequels, Harry's partner is either injured or killed. Further, although many of Eastwood's signature characters look much the same, sporting trademark cowboy hat, poncho, and grimace in true Western fashion, they have delivered some memorable lines. Here are a few things to look out for:

- Eastwood was so keen to stay in character that he wore the same poncho through all three of Sergio Leone's *Dollars* movies, without ever washing or replacing it. How authentic!

- On foiling a bank robbery in *Dirty Harry* (1971), Eastwood first utters the immortal line: "Do you feel lucky, punk?"

- The camera zooms away from the action at the end of every *Dirty Harry* movie. In *Magnum Force* (1973), the action fades as Harry walks away from the burning car of his superior, Lieutenant Briggs.

- "You forgot the rule. Now, what is the rule? . . . Is to protect yourself at all times. Now, what is the rule?"— Eastwood as Frankie Dunn in *Million Dollar Baby* (2004), hammering home the importance of self-preservation.

Through the 1970s and into much of the 1980s Eastwood's work is frustratingly uneven: some great (*High Plains Drifter*, 1973; *Escape from Alcatraz*, 1979), interesting experiments (*Bronco Billy*, 1980), but ultimately a lot of forgettable fodder (*City Heat*, 1984 and *Pink Cadillac*, 1989, among others). None of the *Dirty Harry* sequels, including those directed by Eastwood himself, came close to matching the impact of the original film. One interesting, underrated gem during these lean years is *Tightrope* (1984), a perverse cop thriller that further explores male insecurities and the strength of women.

Finding maturity and true recognition

Then in the late 1980s, something shifted. Although he had already directed a dozen movies—many of them excellent— in 1988 Eastwood directed the Charlie Parker biopic *Bird*, inaugurating a new phase in his career, one in which directing would finally take precedence over acting. He is strong and commanding as ever directing himself in the Oscar-winning projects *Unforgiven* (1992) and *Million Dollar Baby* (2004), along with more neglected films like *A Perfect World* (1993), *Letters from Iwo Jima*, and *Flags of Our Fathers* (both 2006).

Age is indeed just a number—Eastwood is as hot, and even more talented, now in a way that hasn't been as exciting since his *Dirty Harry* heyday. Only now he's calling the shots—literally. It's only a shame he can't live for another 75 years. **TC**

RIGHT: Eastwood directed and starred in the romance *The Bridges of Madison County*.

GENA ROWLANDS

Born: Virginia Cathryn Rowlands, June 19, 1930 (Madison, Wisconsin, U.S.).

Star qualities: Cool blonde beauty; lead character actress of independent cinema; magnificent in complex roles; legendary creative partnership with husband John Cassavetes (the pair made ten movies together); writer.

Cinema boasts many actress-director romances that profoundly shaped the career trajectories of both partners, but few are as memorable as the collaboration between the beautiful Gena Rowlands and her director and husband, John Cassavetes.

Married from 1954 until Cassavetes's death in 1989, the two of them are responsible for some of the most extraordinary U.S. independent film work from the 1960s through to the 1980s. In the process, Rowlands delivered one of the most remarkable, fearless performances ever given by an American actress: as the unbalanced homemaker Mabel Longhetti in the searing *A Woman Under the Influence* (1974), incarnating a complex character as perfectly as one could ever hope to see committed to film.

Prior to her Cassavetes collaborations, Rowlands began in the mid-1950s on Broadway and in TV, appearing in many of the era's most popular programs and a small handful of noteworthy movies such as *Lonely Are the Brave* (1962). Rowlands's first feature for her husband was *A Child Is Waiting* (1963), which was a rare mainstream effort for the director. Many more followed, including *Faces* (1968) and *Gloria* (1980). They also acted together in films and TV. Throughout this body of work, the trust and affection that Cassavetes clearly had for Rowlands is visible in every frame, and many of their collaborations are landmarks in independent, naturalistic, actor-driven filmmaking. Rowlands's work after Cassavetes's death contains other excellent projects, such as *Night on Earth* (1991). She continues to be one of the few actresses of her age to work consistently in movies. Her three children with Cassavetes, Nick, Alexandra, and Zoe, are all talented actors and directors in their own right. **TC**

Top Takes...

Broken English 2007
The Skeleton Key 2005
The Notebook 2004
The Weekend 1999
Hope Floats 1998
The Neon Bible 1995
Something to Talk About 1995
Night on Earth 1991
Another Woman 1988
Gloria 1980 ☆
Opening Night 1977
A Woman Under the Influence 1974 ☆
Minnie and Moskowitz 1971
Faces 1968
A Child Is Waiting 1963
Lonely Are the Brave 1962

"I can never have a poker face. Anybody looking at me can tell exactly what I'm thinking."

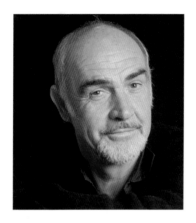

SEAN CONNERY

Born: Thomas Sean Connery, August 25, 1930 (Edinburgh, Scotland).

Star qualities: Chivalrous and sophisticated portrayal of British Agent 007; still lives up to his sex symbol status; surly good looks and attractive Scottish accent; received a Crystal Globe for outstanding artistic contribution to world cinema.

Top Takes…

Entrapment 1999
The Rock 1996
Dragonheart 1996
Rising Sun 1993
Robin Hood: Prince of Thieves 1991
Indiana Jones and the Last Crusade 1989
The Untouchables 1987 ★
The Name of the Rose 1986
Highlander 1986
Never Say Never Again 1983
A Bridge Too Far 1977
Robin and Marian 1976
The Man Who Would Be King 1975
The Offence 1972
Diamonds Are Forever 1971
You Only Live Twice 1967
Thunderball 1965
The Hill 1965
Goldfinger 1964
Marnie 1964
From Russia with Love 1963
Dr. No 1962
The Frightened City 1961
Another Time, Another Place 1958
Hell Drivers 1957

If fidelity to the novels of Ian Fleming were first priority, Sean Connery would not have been cast in *Dr. No* (1962). Fleming describes James Bond as looking like Hoagy Carmichael and expressed a preference for Cary Grant or David Niven. Connery, a working-class Scots milkman who came into show business after bodybuilding, had Bond's charisma and the muscle, but was a classless hero for the 1960s rather than a throwback to Bulldog Drummond or The Saint.

Before Bond, Connery had served his time in British crime films (*Hell Drivers*, 1957; *The Frightened City*, 1961), done serious TV (a British version of Rod Serling's *Requiem for a Heavyweight*, 1957), tasted stardom opposite Lana Turner (*Another Time, Another Place*, 1958), and sung in an approximate Irish accent (*Darby O'Gill and the Little People*, 1959). *Dr. No* made him a star—but for a while mostly as 007, taking vodka martinis, shaken, not stirred, quipping "shocking" after his enemies have perished, and bandying words with suave masterminds. Also, he demonstrated callous virility with a range of Continental starlets and hinted at a preening self-regard in his immaculate dinner jackets and calculated cigarette dangling—which led

RIGHT: Connery played a Franciscan monk turned investigator in *The Name of the Rose*.

1930s

Alfred Hitchcock to cast him in *Marnie* (1964) as the perverse millionaire who forces a frigid thief to marry him.

Bond continued (*From Russia with Love*, 1963; *Goldfinger*, 1964; and so on), but Connery finally broke free, though not before *Diamonds Are Forever* (1971), which feels more like the first of smirking Roger Moore than the last of Connery's brutal Bond. Otherwise, he set out to prove himself as an actor— terrific as the soldier convict in *The Hill* (1965) and the burned-out cop in *The Offence* (1972). He has kept busy and remained a star, winning an Academy Award for *The Untouchables* (1987), but hasn't made a film he really cares about since *The Name of the Rose* (1986). Still, he is fun in *Highlander* (1986) and *The Rock* (1996). Connery has gotten older, but his love interests still tend to be the age Ursula Andress was in *Dr. No*—which seems especially jarring when he canoodles with Catherine Zeta-Jones in the comedy romance *Entrapment* (1999). **KN**

ABOVE: Connery looks stern and ready for action in the second Bond film, *Goldfinger*.

Being James Bond

Sean Connery was legendary in his personification of the British spy, and successive actors have found it a hard act to follow. Here are some classic Bond quips:

- In response to Honey Ryder's innocent question, "Are you looking for shells too?" Bond replies, "No, I'm just looking." (*Dr. No*)
- "Shocking! Positively shocking!"—On a villain meeting a nasty end (*Goldfinger*).
- "I think he got the point."—On shooting Vargas with a spear gun (*Thunderball*).
- "Oh the things I do for England."—Bond makes love to yet another beautiful woman (*You Only Live Twice*).

RICHARD HARRIS

Born: Richard St. John Harris, October 1, 1930 (Limerick, Ireland); died 2002 (London, England).

Star qualities: Irish screen legend; versatile character actor and tall leading man; dangerous screen presence; stagecraft; hell-raiser; glamorous; director; writer.

Top Takes...

Richard Harris was born one of eight children to a rich flour miller. After his father's firm collapsed, he spent much of his childhood in poverty. His first love was rugby, and he was on the verge of being chosen to play that sport for his native Ireland. But his hopes were dashed when he contracted tuberculosis. He later said, "It was the luckiest thing that ever happened to me." Forced to convalesce, he began to read works by such Irish authors as Samuel Beckett and James Joyce, which whetted his appetite to become an actor. He moved to London in 1954, where he studied at the London Academy of Music and Dramatic Art.

After a long period on the stage he moved into films and was a virile Irish presence under arms in *The Guns of Navarone* (1961) and on sea in *Mutiny on the Bounty* (1962). But he broke out as the battered rugby player Frank Machin in the "kitchen-sink" British film *This Sporting Life* (1963). It won him a Best Actor Oscar nomination and caught Hollywood's attention. He then took roles that rarely stretched him, such as King Arthur in the adaptation of the Broadway musical *Camelot* (1967).

As well known for hell-raising as acting, Harris went through periods of indiscriminately accepting any role on offer: for example, he grates interestingly on Sean Connery in *The Molly Maguires* (1970), and was an aristocrat tortured by Apaches in the cult movie *A Man Called Horse* (1970). But his career had a renaissance when his performance as "Bull" McCabe in *The Field* (1990) brought him another Best Actor Oscar nomination. He impressed again only a few years later as gunfighter English Bob in Clint Eastwood's Western *Unforgiven* (1992). In his last years he was a twinkly-eyed Albus Dumbledore in the first two *Harry Potter* screen adaptations. **KN**

"But I made people laugh. I don't want immortality. I've lived it all. I've done it all."

1930s

PHILIPPE NOIRET

Born: Philippe Noiret, October 1, 1930 (Lille, Nord, France); died 2006 (Paris, France).

Star qualities: Tall, with hangdog features; grizzled face; nightclub entertainer turned leading man and character actor of European cinema; affecting and affable screen presence; stagecraft; hedonist and gourmet.

Philippe Noiret is most widely known to international audiences for two memorable roles. The first was his portrayal of Alfredo, a movie projectionist in a small Sicilian village who becomes a mentor and father figure to a young boy and future filmmaker in Giuseppe Tornatore's tear-jerking but heartwarming *Nuovo cinema Paradiso* (1988) (*Cinema Paradiso*). The second was his equally affecting portrayal of the exiled Chilean poet Pablo Neruda in *Il postino* (1994) (*The Postman*), where he poignantly brings to life the pain of a man cast out of his native country, bringing touching warmth to his character's relationship with the love-struck postman who becomes his friend.

In each film, Noiret's capacity to captivate an audience with his significant acting skills raises the movie into the league of the memorable. And in each, his hangdog looks add to the charm of his characters. It was almost as if the very lack of handsomeness that disqualified him from playing romantic heroes in his youth gradually became more of an asset.

Noiret trained at Rennes's Centre Dramatique de l'Ouest before going on to tour with the Théâtre National Populaire and working as a stand-up comic in nightclubs. He made his film debut with a bit part in *Gigi* (1949) and continued to work in films and TV through the 1950s. He first attracted attention playing an uncle to a wayward niece in Louis Malle's comedy *Zazie dans le métro* (1960) (*Zazie in the Subway*). He went on to win acclaim in his native France for his lead role in *Alexandre le bienheureux* (1968) (*Alexander*), and as one of a hedonist group of men who indulge in an orgy of gluttony in *La grande bouffe* (1973) (*Blow-Out*). His skills as a character actor established, he went on to play a diverse range of award-winning roles through the rest of his career. **CK**

Top Takes...

Il postino 1994 (*The Postman*)
J'embrasse pas 1991 (*I Don't Kiss*)
La vie et rien d'autre 1989
　(*Life and Nothing But*)
Nuovo cinema Paradiso 1988
　(*Cinema Paradiso*)
Les ripoux 1984 (*My New Partner*)
L'Etoile du Nord 1982 (*The North Star*)
Le vieux fusil 1975 (*The Old Gun*)
La grande bouffe 1973 (*Blow-Out*)
Alexandre le bienheureux 1968 (*Alexander*)
La vie de château 1966 (*A Matter of Resistance*)
Thérèse Desqueyroux 1962 (*Thérèse*)
Zazie dans le métro 1960 (*Zazie in the Subway*)
La pointe-courte 1956
Gigi 1949

"When you explain poetry, it becomes banal."
—Pablo Neruda, *The Postman*

MAXIMILIAN SCHELL

Born: Maximilian Schell, December 8, 1930 (Vienna, Austria).

Star qualities: Stagecraft; part of an acting family; has achieved rare international success as a German-speaking actor; versatile lead and character actor; writer; award-winning director; documentary filmmaker; producer.

Top Takes...

Das Haus der schlafenden Schönen 2006
  (*House of the Sleeping Beauties*)

Coast to Coast 2004

Deep Impact 1998

Vampires 1998

The Chosen 1981

Julia 1977 ☆

A Bridge Too Far 1977

Cross of Iron 1977

The Man in the Glass Booth 1975 ☆

The Odessa File 1974

The Desperate Ones 1968

Counterpoint 1968

Judgment at Nuremberg 1961 ★

The Young Lions 1958

Reifende Jugend 1955 (*Ripening Youth*)

"When you were a baby I once dropped you on your head."
—Jason Lerner, *Deep Impact*

Along with Marcello Mastroianni, Maurice Chevalier, and Emil Jannings, Maximilian Schell is one of the most renowned European film actors. The son of actress Margarethe Noe von Nordberg and writer/poet Hermann Ferdinand Schell, Maximilian was born in Vienna in 1930. He was raised during World War II in neutral Zurich, Switzerland, and was a committed anti-Nazi as a teenager. His sister, Maria Schell, was already an international movie star when Schell made his Hollywood film debut in the war drama *The Young Lions* (1958), opposite Marlon Brando. But he is perhaps best known for his role as defense attorney Hans Rolfe in *Judgment at Nuremberg* (1961), a part he had first played in a live TV broadcast two years earlier. Schell won an Oscar for Best Actor for his portrayal of Rolfe, beating his costar Spencer Tracy.

He has a wide range of credits to his name and has appeared in such movies as *The Odessa File* (1974), *Cross of Iron* (1977), *Julia* (1977), Richard Attenborough's *A Bridge Too Far* (1977), *The Chosen* (1981), and in the science-fiction thriller *Deep Impact* (1998). Schell is also an accomplished director; his film *Der Fussgänger* (1973) (*The Pedestrian*) was nominated for an Academy Award for Best Foreign Language film, and his documentary portrait of actress Marlene Dietrich, *Marlene* (1984), was nominated for the Feature Documentary Oscar. He also directed a documentary film about his sister, *Meine Schwester Maria* (2002) (*My Sister Maria*), to much critical acclaim. Since the 1990s he has appeared in many German-language made-for-TV films, such as *Alles Glück dieser Erde* (2003) (*All the Luck in the World*). More recently he appeared onstage in London in Robert Altman's production of Arthur Miller's *Resurrection Blues* (2006). **MK**

ARMIN MUELLER-STAHL

Born: Armin Mueller-Stahl, December 17, 1930 (Tilsit, East Prussia, Germany).

Star qualities: Sad eyes; versatile leading man and character actor of dramas; icon of German contemporary cinema; a respected concert violinist as a teenager; stagecraft; director; writer; painter.

A musical child prodigy growing up in the early years of the German Democratic Republic (GDR), Armin Mueller-Stahl turned to acting in his early twenties and quickly became one of East Germany's leading performers of stage and screen. Though Mueller-Stahl won a coveted GDR state prize for his contributions to the arts, his career collapsed as quickly as it had developed when he was blacklisted for protesting against government interference in the performing arts. The silver lining of this cloud was that he moved to West Germany, where his talent for creating complex characters was noted by several leading directors, including Werner Fassbinder and Andrzej Wajda. He was particularly good in the World War II morality piece *Eine Liebe in Deutschland* (1983) (*A Love in Germany*).

Moving to the United States, Mueller-Stahl achieved great recognition in *Music Box* (1989) for his portrayal of a former Hungarian Nazi collaborator, whose daughter, played by Jessica Lange, is forced to acknowledge the truth about a man she had always known as loving and kind. Mueller-Stahl also landed juicy roles in important independent films, including Steven Soderbergh's *Kafka* (1991) and Jim Jarmusch's *Night on Earth* (1991). Perhaps his most notable performance in a U.S. film is in *Avalon* (1990), where he plays a Russian-Jewish immigrant gradually and movingly coming to grips with the bitter ironies of historical change and aging.

Despite Hollywood success, he has never severed ties with European production. He was a talented but neurotic Thomas Mann in the German TV historical family saga *Die Manns—Ein Jahrhundertroman* (2001). He appeared on U.S. TV in yet another cultural, historical guise, as the prime minister of Israel in a series of episodes of *The West Wing* (2004). **BP**

Top Takes...

The X Files 1998
12 Angry Men 1997
Shine 1996 ☆
The House of the Spirits 1993
Utz 1992
Night on Earth 1991
Kafka 1991
Avalon 1990
Music Box 1989
Bittere Ernte 1985 (*Angry Harvest*)
Oberst Redl 1985 (*Colonel Redl*)
Eine Liebe in Deutschland 1983
　(*A Love in Germany*)
Die Sehnsucht der Veronika Voss 1982
　(*Veronika Voss*)
Lola 1981

"No one will love you like me, no one like me."

—Peter Helfgott, *Shine*

JAMES DEAN

Born: James Byron Dean, February 8, 1931 (Marion, Indiana, U.S.); died 1955 (Cholame, California, U.S.).

Star qualities: Legendary status for portraying troubled youth; 1950s heartthrob and enduring cultural icon; only actor to be nominated posthumously for two Oscars.

Top Takes...

Giant 1956 ☆
Rebel Without a Cause 1955
East of Eden 1955 ☆

Though he starred in only three films, James Dean was one of the key movie figures of the 1950s. He followed Montgomery Clift and Marlon Brando in male beauty, showing a more sensitive, agonized style than previous manly icons like Clark Gable or Errol Flynn. But Dean was much younger—in their first film roles, Clift and Brando played damaged World War II veterans, whereas Dean was a postwar young man, his traumas not picked up on D-Day or Guadalcanal. In *Rebel Without a Cause* (1955), Dean's finest picture, he plays his most archetypal role as Jim Stark, a man troubled by tensions within an affluent, peaceful 1950s American social scene, bereft of anything worth fighting for and desperate for his parents to be more than sitcom caricatures. Directed by Nicholas Ray, *Rebel* is a major film—a widescreen Technicolor melodrama that doesn't tut-tut over juvenile delinquents like *Blackboard Jungle* (1954) and iterates that some of the most troubled kids come from "good" homes rather than poverty.

Dean did a great deal of work in live TV from 1952 to 1953 (*The Kate Smith Hour*, *Studio One*, *Robert Montgomery Presents*) and near-invisible, uncredited bits in a handful of movies (*Fixed*

RIGHT: Dean as Jett Rink in *Giant*, his last film. The star died just before filming ended.

Bayonets!, 1951; *Sailor Beware*, 1952; *Has Anybody Seen My Gal?*, 1952), but his star oeuvre consists of three roles—Cal Trask in Elia Kazan's *East of Eden* (1955), from the John Steinbeck novel; Jim Stark in *Rebel*; and Jett Rink in George Stevens's *Giant* (1956). Of the three performances, only *Rebel* really lasts: *Eden* is lopsided by Kazan's indulgence of Dean's method, and *Giant* offers a handful of iconic images and moments (Dean crucified on a rifle, his distinctive farewell wave), but flounders in an unconvincing later section in which Dean awkwardly plays a talcum-haired old Jett. But *Rebel* is enough to secure him screen immortality, and his premature death in a car crash probably added to the film's stature and poignancy—though it isn't Jim Stark who dies in the film's daredevil race or Griffith Park Observatory climax. Dean was set to play the role taken by Paul Newman in *Somebody Up There Likes Me* (1956)—but after that, who knows what would have happened? **KN**

ABOVE: Dean immortalized teenager Jim Stark in *Rebel Without a Cause*, his best film.

Songs About Dean

James Dean's tragic death ensured his immortality on the screen. It also inspired a number of lyrical tributes to the legend:

- "You were too fast to live, too young to die, bye-bye."—"James Dean," The Eagles.
- "The Boy with the Thorn in His Side" —song title, The Smiths.
- "Jackie is just speeding away; thought she was James Dean for a day . . . ." —"Walk on the Wild Side," Lou Reed.
- "When the jester sang for the king and queen, in a coat he borrowed from James Dean . . . ."—"American Pie," Don McLean.

MARTIN LANDAU

Born: Martin Landau, June 20, 1931 (Brooklyn, New York, U.S.).

Star qualities: Tall, with large eyes and a thin face; chameleonlike versatility; character actor; stagecraft; prolific output; popular star of 1960s TV show *Mission: Impossible*; early villain roles; producer.

Top Takes...

Martin Landau started his working life at the age of seventeen on the *New York Daily News* as a cartoonist and illustrator. But he was drawn to acting and made his stage debut in *Detective Story* (1951) at Maine's Peak Islands Playhouse. He joined New York's Actors Studio in 1955, and went on to make his Broadway debut in *Middle of the Night* (1957). He first came to the movies in *Pork Chop Hill* (1959), and was memorable as the gay spy in Alfred Hitchcock's *North by Northwest* (1959).

However, he did his most notable early work on TV, on series such as *The Twilight Zone* (1959–1964). He also showed chameleonlike versatility as the master of disguise Rollin Hand in *Mission: Impossible* (1966–1969), for which he won a Golden Globe Best Male TV Star award. He starred alongside his wife, Barbara Bain, in this series, and in the 1970s show *Space: 1999*.

Landau played a supporting role as a flamboyant eccentric in *They Call Me MISTER Tibbs!* (1970), and was an impressive lead in the TV movie *Welcome Home, Johnny Bristol* (1972). But somehow, he started to slide to credits in minor TV films such as *The Harlem Globetrotters on Gilligan's Island* (1981).

A role as the money man in Francis Ford Coppola's *Tucker: The Man and His Dream* (1988) put Landau back on the Hollywood map when he was nominated for an Oscar as Best Supporting Actor. He scored a further Academy Award nomination—essentially for a leading role—as Woody Allen's doppelgänger in *Crimes and Misdemeanors* (1989), and then finally had an Oscar win playing a washed-up Béla Lugosi in Tim Burton's biopic *Ed Wood* (1994). He has since played old-timers in movies such as *The X-Files* (1998). Landau continues to work in TV and film and is executive director of the Actors Studio's west coast branch. **KN**

"Aren't you scared, little boy? I'm going to drink your blood!"

—Béla Lugosi, *Ed Wood*

1930s

LESLIE CARON

Born: Leslie Claire Margaret Caron, July 1, 1931 (Boulogne-Billancourt, Hauts-de-Seine, France).

Star qualities: Gamine Gallic charm; dancer; balletic grace; chic; played the youthful ingénue followed by romantic lead and mature character roles; writer.

A trained ballet dancer, Leslie Caron has always moved—even in nondancing roles—with a balletic grace. Discovered by Gene Kelly when she was dancing with a ballet troupe, she found international fame in her first screen role, partnering with Kelly in Vincente Minnelli's *An American in Paris* (1951). A string of MGM musicals followed, all requiring her to project innocence, Frenchness, and gamine charm: *Lili* (1953), *Daddy Long Legs* (1955), with Fred Astaire, and *Gigi* (1958), again for Minnelli, were the best of them. But she grew tired of being typecast in roles as waifs, orphans, and teenagers; she disliked the constraints of the studio system and returned to Europe when her contract expired.

Bryan Forbes's *The L-Shaped Room* (1962) called attention to a new, mature Caron, playing a lonely pregnant girl in a one-room London bedsit, and got her a second Academy Award nomination for Best Actress. But since then she has rarely found roles worthy of her abilities. She played a sinister housekeeper in Edouardo de Gregorio's enigmatic *Sérail* (1976) (*Surreal Estate*) and was in a lesser François Truffaut film, *L'homme qui aimait les femmes* (1977) (*The Man Who Loved Women*), as one of Charles Denner's many love objects. But given a halfway decent script she can still bring poise and sophistication to a role, as in Peter Chelsom's oddball *Funny Bones* (1995), where she went back to her roots and got to dance and sing a song. She took a cameo role as a sweet widow in Lasse Hallström's *Chocolat* (2000) and was a scheming mother-in-law in Merchant Ivory's social comedy *Le Divorce* (2003). Caron has been married four times and has two children from her marriage to British theater and film director Peter Hall. **PK**

Top Takes...

Le Divorce 2003
Chocolat 2000
Funny Bones 1995
La diagonale du fou 1984 (*Dangerous Moves*)
L'homme qui aimait les femmes 1977
  (*The Man Who Loved Women*)
Sérail 1976 (*Surreal Estate*)
Paris brûle-t-il? 1966 (*Is Paris Burning?*)
Father Goose 1964
The L-Shaped Room 1962 ☆
The Man Who Understood Women 1959
Gigi 1958
Daddy Long Legs 1955
Lili 1953 ☆
The Story of Three Loves 1953
An American in Paris 1951

"I think it's the end of progress if you stand still and think of what you've done in the past."

TAB HUNTER

Born: Arthur Andrew Kelm, July 11, 1931 (New York City, New York, U.S.).

Star qualities: "The Sigh Guy"; blond; tanned; athletic physique; American teen idol of the 1950s; singer; writer; youthful boy-next-door heartthrob roles and mature cult comic actor; producer.

Tab Hunter left school to join the Coast Guard at the age of fifteen but was later discharged because he had lied about his age. He then took a job at a riding academy, but his good looks led him to think about acting, and he headed for California, where he met agent Henry Willson, who renamed him—the "Hunter" referring to his horse-riding skills. Muscular, often shirtless, with crew-cut hair, and handsome, Hunter was popular with teenage girls and had a career as a recording star, topping the charts with the single "Young Love" in 1957.

Marketed for his immense sex appeal, the studios called Hunter "The Sigh Guy." He became the romantic interest in movies such as *Saturday Island* (1952) and third lead in Westerns such as *Track of the Cat* (1954). He is at his best as the old man supernaturally rejuvenated as baseball whiz Joe Hardy in *Damn Yankees!* (1958), and did well as the paratrooper lead opposite Sophia Loren in *That Kind of Woman* (1959). He also found early success on TV when he was nominated for an Emmy award for his performance as Donald Bashor in an episode of *Playhouse 90*, "Portrait of a Murderer" (1958).

But come the 1960s Hunter's appeal started to wane. He abandoned his contract with Warner Brothers and turned to TV, starring in the sitcom *The Tab Hunter Show* (1960). The series lasted just one season. In later years he turned to self-mocking comedy as transvestite Divine's love interest in John Waters's *Polyester* (1981) and Paul Bartel's Western spoof *Lust in the Dust* (1985). In his youth, Hunter often suffered at the hands of the press, which tried to "out" him as a homosexual; in the 1950s that would have ruined his career. Now working as a producer, Hunter published his memoirs in 2005, in which he reveals his homosexuality. **KN**

Top Takes…

1930s

"John Wayne treated me fine, but that macho stuff turns me off. It's not real."

ANNE BANCROFT

Born: Anna Maria Italiano, September 17, 1931 (Bronx, New York, U.S.); died 2005 (New York City, New York, U.S.).

Star qualities: Dark-browed Latin features; played the middle-aged femme fatale; leading lady and character actress playing strong women; director; writer.

In a career lasting more than 50 years, Anne Bancroft played almost 100 roles, but she'll always be best remembered as the predatory suburban housewife making a move on her daughter's boyfriend in the screen adaptation of Charles Webb's novel *The Graduate* (1967), giving Dustin Hoffman the infamous line: "Mrs. Robinson, are you trying to seduce me?"

Born in the Bronx, her dark-browed Latin features ruled her out for romantic leads but made her ideal for strong, emphatic roles. She attended the Actors Studio in New York and went on to get parts on Broadway, having changed her name to make it sound less "ethnic." She won her first Tony award opposite Henry Fonda in *Two for the Seesaw* (1958).

She found fame on the stage, and then on film, as Annie Sullivan, Helen Keller's tireless teacher, in *The Miracle Worker* (1962), both times directed by Arthur Penn. The role won her an Oscar, and she was to receive another four Academy Award nominations during her career. For Jack Clayton she was a baby-obsessed wife in *The Pumpkin Eater* (1964), having a spectacular breakdown in Harrods food hall, and as the down-to-earth doctor in John Ford's final movie, *7 Women* (1966), she sacrificed herself to save the other hostages. After her role as Mrs. Robinson, she was cast mostly in character parts, opposite other strong female leads such as Shirley MacLaine in *The Turning Point* (1977) and Jane Fonda in *Agnes of God* (1985), and she often lifted poor movies beyond their merits. She married the actor and director Mel Brooks in 1964, costarring with him in his ill-advised remake of *To Be or Not to Be* (1983), and herself directed one movie, *Fatso* (1980). She played for laughs in one of her last roles in *Heartbreakers* (2001). Bancroft died of cancer at age seventy-three. **PK**

Top Takes...

Heartbreakers 2001
How to Make an American Quilt 1995
Point of No Return 1993
84 Charing Cross Road 1987
Agnes of God 1985 ☆
To Be or Not to Be 1983
The Elephant Man 1980
Fatso 1980
The Turning Point 1977 ☆
Lipstick 1976
The Graduate 1967 ☆
7 Women 1966
The Pumpkin Eater 1964 ☆
The Miracle Worker 1962 ★
Nightfall 1957
Don't Bother to Knock 1952

"When men meet me, there's always that movie in the back of their mind."—On *The Graduate*

1930s

SHINTARÔ KATSU

Born: Toshio Okumura, November 29, 1931 (Fukagawa, Tokyo, Japan); died 1997 (Kashiwa, Chiba, Japan).

Star qualities: Iconic lead of Japanese sword and samurai movies; swordsman; prolific output; intense screen presence; singer; writer; director; producer.

Top Takes...

Rônin-gai 1990

Teito monogatari 1988
(Tokyo: The Last Megalopolis)

Shin Zatôichi monogatari: Oreta tsue 1972
(Zatoichi in Desperation)

Zatôichi rôyaburi 1967 (Zatoichi Breaks Jail)

Heitai yakuza 1965 (The Hoodlum Soldier)

Zatôichi sekisho yaburi 1964
(Adventures of Zatoichi)

Zatôichi senryô-kubi 1964
(Zatoichi and the Chest of Gold)

Zatôichi kenka-tabi 1963
(Zatoichi's Fighting Journey)

Zatôichi monogatari 1962 (The Tale of Zatoichi)

Akumyô 1961 (Tough Guy)

Bara ikutabika 1955
(A Girl Isn't Allowed to Love)

> "Katsu makes a grim, agile hero, about whom we get to know very little . . . ."—*New York Times*

Shintarô Katsu was a Japanese actor/producer/director who starred in more than 100 features but is best known for his characterization of the blind swordsman Zatoichi, the most popular screen hero in Japanese movie history. Katsu was born into a theatrical family; his father, Katsutôji Kineya, was a *kabuki* performer and master of the Japanese singing style known as *nagauta*. Katsu entered the film industry under contract to Daiei Studios, making his debut in *Bara ikutabika* (1955) (*A Girl Isn't Allowed to Love*). He then starred in *Zatôichi monogatari* (1962) (*The Tale of Zatoichi*) as a blind masseur who enjoys gambling and sword fighting. Katsu displayed a brooding emotional intensity that made Zatoichi his career-defining character—he showed that Zatoichi was an honorable man, even if he was a ruthless killer. The movie was an enormous success, spawning 25 sequels and a TV series.

Amazingly prolific, Katsu starred in two other long-running series for Daiei Studios during this period. The *Akumyô* (1961) (*Tough Guy*) series resulted in 16 films in 13 years, and the *Heitai yakuza* (*The Hoodlum Soldier*) series (1965–1972) featured nine films, with Katsu singing the themes to both. Katsu debuted as a producer on the twentieth *Zatôichi* movie in 1970 and made his directorial debut with *Kaoyaku* (1971). In addition to the *Zatôichi* series, Katsu produced the *Kozure Ôkami* (*Lone Wolf and Cub*) *jidaigeki* period drama series (1972–1974), starring his older brother Tomisaburo Wakayama. Offscreen, his life was troubled. He had a five-year affair with renowned geisha Mineko Iwasaki, but she ended it, realizing that she would always come second to his wife, the actress Tamao Nakamura. Katsu died in 1997 and was honored posthumously with a Japanese Academy Award. **WW**

PIPER LAURIE

Born: Rosetta Jacobs, January 22, 1932 (Detroit, Michigan, U.S.).

Star qualities: Pretty, petite redhead; milky skin and green eyes; played the youthful ingénue, followed by more demanding character roles; cult status developed from double role in TV's *Twin Peaks*.

Piper Laurie's father was a furniture dealer who moved his family to Los Angeles, California, when his daughter Rosetta was six years old. She attended elocution lessons and studied acting at a local drama school, which led to her being signed by Universal Studios when she was just seventeen.

Laurie was a beautiful starlet in the 1950s, stuck in the likes of *Francis Goes to the Races* (1951), *Son of Ali Baba* (1952), *Johnny Dark* (1954), and *Smoke Signal* (1955). Dissatisfied with the roles she was being offered, she dropped her Universal contract and went to New York to work onstage and on TV, performing in "Twelfth Night" (1957) and "Winterset" (1959) on *Hallmark Hall of Fame*, and "The Days of Wine and Roses" (1958) on *Playhouse 90*. She returned to film as the crippled, alcoholic love interest opposite Paul Newman in *The Hustler* (1961). An Oscar nomination for Best Actress didn't cancel out her break of contract with Universal, so she was essentially out of work until Brian De Palma cast her as the charismatic mad mother in *Carrie* (1976), which earned her another Oscar nomination, this time for Best Supporting Actress.

A sexy older woman and powerhouse actress, Laurie at last started getting worthy roles. She played a horror diva in *Ruby* (1977); wife of Nazi Joseph Goebbels, Magda, in *The Bunker* (1981); the mother in *Children of a Lesser God* (1986), which won her another Oscar nomination; woman of mystery Catherine Martell/Mr. Tojamura in David Lynch's TV series *Twin Peaks* (1990–1991), which gained her two Emmy nominations; a Truman Capote eccentric in *The Grass Harp* (1995); and a woman possessed by an alien in *The Faculty* (1998). Laurie divorced her husband Joe Morgenstern in 1981. The couple have one child, a daughter, Anne Grace. **KN**

Top Takes...

The Dead Girl 2006
The Mao Game 1999
The Faculty 1998
A Christmas Memory 1997
The Crossing Guard 1995
The Grass Harp 1995
Trauma 1993
Children of a Lesser God 1986 ☆
Return to Oz 1985
The Bunker 1981
Carrie 1976 ☆
The Hustler 1961 ☆
Smoke Signal 1955
Johnny Dark 1954
Son of Ali Baba 1952
Francis Goes to the Races 1951

"And if real life was like the movies, I should have lived happily ever after."

ELIZABETH TAYLOR

Born: Elizabeth Rosemond Taylor, February 27, 1932 (Hampstead, London, England).

Star qualities: Flawless complexion and violet eyes; her beauty mesmerized her audience and her costars; expensive tastes reflected in her choice of husbands and lifestyle; undoubtedly a movie legend.

Top Takes...

The Flintstones 1994
Zee and Co. 1972
The Only Game in Town 1970
Doctor Faustus 1967
The Taming of the Shrew 1967
Who's Afraid of Virginia Woolf? 1966 ★
The Sandpiper 1965
Cleopatra 1963
Butterfield 8 1960 ★
Suddenly, Last Summer 1959 ☆
Cat on a Hot Tin Roof 1958 ☆
Raintree County 1957 ☆
Giant 1956
Beau Brummell 1954
Elephant Walk 1954
Ivanhoe 1952
A Place in the Sun 1951
Father's Little Dividend 1951
Father of the Bride 1950
Little Women 1949
Julia Misbehaves 1948
Life with Father 1947
National Velvet 1944
Jane Eyre 1944
Lassie Come Home 1943

Elizabeth Taylor made her screen debut at the age of ten in *There's One Born Every Minute* (1942), but soon passed from a proletarian Universal Studios contract to the classier confines of MGM, where she was cast alongside sleekly beautiful animals in *Lassie Come Home* (1943) and *National Velvet* (1944). Her performance as Velvet Brown, a young girl with a love of horses who goes on to win the Grand National, was a huge box-office hit, and launched Taylor as MGM's biggest child star. With her long-term film contract established, she literally grew up onscreen, taking respectable, cute teenage roles in *Life with Father* (1947), *Cynthia* (1947), *Julia Misbehaves* (1948), and *Little Women* (as Amy, 1949), then necessarily maturing as Spencer Tracy's married-off-and-soon-expecting daughter in *Father of the Bride* (1950) and *Father's Little Dividend* (1951).

One of cinema's greatest beauties in the 1950s and blessed with clear, expressive Anglo-American tones—she was born in England to American parents—Taylor is an icon of everything poor-boy Montgomery Clift aspires to in George Stevens's *A Place in the Sun* (1951). Her evident classiness inclined her to

RIGHT: Taylor shot to fame at age twelve as girl-jockey Velvet Brown in *National Velvet*.

period pictures: as the Jewess in *Ivanhoe* (1952)—so devastating that costar Robert Taylor insisted he be shot from above the waist lest the camera notice the bulge she produced in his tights in their scenes together—a Regency lady in *Beau Brummell* (1954), and a Southern belle in *Raintree County* (1957). She gravitated toward more "important" movies with Stevens's *Giant* (1956), in which the whole cast gets to grow old with layers of makeup, and—playing up her much-discussed offscreen love life—began to specialize in steaminess. Her turn as a planter's wife in *Elephant Walk* (1954), misty behind mosquito nets, was just a warm-up for two major Tennessee Williams nymphomaniacs: slutty in a slip as Maggie in *Cat on a Hot Tin Roof* (1958) and mentally unstable in a white bathing suit in *Suddenly, Last Summer* (1959).

ABOVE: Taylor drew parallels with her own turbulent love life in *Cat on a Hot Tin Roof*.

"Some of my best leading men have been dogs and horses."

Le Scandale

"You find out who your real friends are when you're involved in a scandal." Of all people, Elizabeth Taylor should know. She began her career as a serial bride at age eighteen, thus starting a lifetime of gossip columns, adultery, and lots of husbands:

- Conrad Hilton Jr. (1950–1951). Taylor was married to the hotel heir for just nine months. It was an abusive relationship.
- Michael Wilding (1952–1957) was 20 years older, and Taylor soon got bored.
- Michael Todd (1957–1958). Todd's death in a plane crash cut short an extravagant marriage marked by lavish gifts.
- Eddie Fisher (1959–1964) was a friend of Todd and knew Taylor well. Debbie Reynolds was unceremoniously ditched by Fisher for the forceful femme fatale.
- Richard Burton (1964–1974; 1975–1976). In what Burton later dubbed "le scandale," the pair began an intense, alcohol-fueled love affair on the set of *Cleopatra*. Taylor was condemned by the Vatican for her actions. Both were notoriously hot-tempered and the marriage failed. Twice.
- John Warner (1976–1982). Suffering chronic back pain and weight problems, Taylor adopted a sedentary lifestyle during her marriage to the U.S. Senator.
- Larry Fortensky (1991–1996) was a construction worker who refused to be "polished" by Taylor. Plagued by illness, she soon grew tired of the effort.

RIGHT: Taylor played the title character in 1963's lavish production of *Cleopatra*.

Taylor won a Best Actress Academy Award as another disreputable woman in *Butterfield 8* (1960), and was then cast in the title role of *Cleopatra* (1963), which teamed her with Richard Burton for the first time. This film became a watchword for all manner of excesses, though Taylor's attempt at a performance was buried under all the costumes and décor. Taylor and Burton began a very public affair during the filming of *Cleopatra*, even though both were married to other people at the time. It was the start of an on-off relationship that saw the pair married and divorced twice in 11 years. She went on to star with Burton in a run of overheated, fairly kitschy vehicles ranging from glossy soap (*The Sandpiper*, 1965) to bizarre art efforts like *Boom* (1968), as another Tennessee Williams madwoman, and *Doctor Faustus* (1967), in which she was silent as a vision of Helen of Troy.

From drama queen to dame

Playing on their notoriously tempestuous offscreen romance, Taylor and Burton were archly cast in *The Taming of the Shrew* (1967) and *Who's Afraid of Virginia Woolf?* (1966). To rub in the ascendance of a star over an actor, Taylor won another Oscar for her impressively monstrous turn as Martha in *Virginia Woolf*, whereas often-nominated Burton never did. She was good in little-seen movies such as *Secret Ceremony* (1968) and *The Only Game in Town* (1970), in which she plays well with next-generation stars Mia Farrow and Warren Beatty, and *Zee and Co.* (1972), another riff on her gossip-column homewrecker image. However, the 1970s brought only feeble star vehicles (*Night Watch*, 1973; *Identikit*, 1974) and camp cameos (*The Blue Bird*, 1976; *Victory at Entebbe*, 1976; *The Mirror Crack'd*, 1980).

Never out of the tabloids, with more marriages and weight fluctuations, Taylor finally retired to TV—to play Louella Parsons in *Malice in Wonderland* (1985), more Tennessee Williams in *Sweet Bird of Youth* (1989), an ensemble with Shirley MacLaine, Debbie Reynolds, and Joan Collins in *These Old Broads* (2001). A Dame of the British Empire since 1999, Taylor was last sighted in cinemas as Pearl Slaghoople in *The Flintstones* (1994). **KN**

DEBBIE REYNOLDS

Born: Mary Frances Reynolds, April 1, 1932 (El Paso, Texas, U.S.).

Star qualities: Pretty beauty-queen looks; petite; down-home screen presence; played youthful girl-next-door and ingénue roles; singer; dancer; comedienne; nightclub performer; producer; writer.

Top Takes...

With her clean good looks, prim respectability, and irrepressible vim, Debbie Reynolds, perhaps inevitably, spent most of her Hollywood career in roles designed for that most characteristic of U.S. female types: the girl next door. Attractive yet obviously chaste, energetic yet not threateningly masculinized, assertive yet willing to accept male authority, this version of Reynolds proved eminently successful, and appealing, in the postwar musicals and light comedies for which her singing and dancing talents eminently qualified her: *Singin' in the Rain* (1952) and *Susan Slept Here* (1954), among others.

Reynolds's gritty likability allowed her to occasionally escape such typecasting, for example as the self-possessed and unapologetically low-class heroine of *The Unsinkable Molly Brown* (1964), which won her an Oscar nomination for Best Actress. Her characterization of the all-American girl is more nuanced when exploited by talented directors, especially Blake Edwards in *This Happy Feeling* (1958). Working with the less talented, Reynolds managed something like unintentional self-parody in *Tammy and the Bachelor* (1957) and *The Mating Game* (1959). Homely (in the best sense of the term), she proved a natural for the cool medium of TV; her lightly comedic TV series *The Debbie Reynolds Show* (1969–1970) enjoyed two successful seasons. She is the mother of actress and writer Carrie Fisher and producer Todd Fisher from her first marriage to actor and singer Eddie Fisher, who had an affair with, and later married, Hollywood's ultimate leading lady, Elizabeth Taylor. However, Reynolds and Taylor buried the hatchet to play with Shirley MacLaine and Joan Collins as screen divas reunited for a show in the TV movie *These Old Broads* (2001), which was cowritten by Carrie Fisher. **BP**

"I stopped making movies because I don't like taking my clothes off."

1930s

ANTHONY PERKINS

Born: Anthony Perkins, April 4, 1932 (New York City, New York, U.S.); died 1992 (Hollywood, California, U.S.).

Star qualities: Gaunt face; thin frame; famed for playing psychotic characters, most notably as Norman Bates in *Psycho*; director; writer.

Anthony Perkins was the only child of U.S. stage and movie actor Osgood Perkins and Janet Esseltyn Rane. Even before Alfred Hitchcock cast him as cross-dressing madman Norman Bates in *Psycho* (1960), Perkins specialized in playing nervous young men. He impressed as the Quaker son in *Friendly Persuasion* (1956), for which he received his only Oscar nomination; the psychologically fragile baseball player in *Fear Strikes Out* (1957); and the young sheriff in *The Tin Star* (1957). He moved on to portraying more normal guys in *The Matchmaker* (1958), *On the Beach* (1959), and *Tall Story* (1960).

After investing a split-personality murderer with tragic depth, Perkins tended to get creepy freak parts, as in *How Awful About Allan* (1970) and *Murder on the Orient Express* (1974). He is used cleverly in Orson Welles's *Le Procès* (1962) (*The Trial*), Noel Black's *Pretty Poison* (1968), and Alan Rudolph's *Remember My Name* (1978). *Psycho II* (1983), a surprisingly sensitive sequel, allowed him to revisit his Bates character interestingly, and he stayed with the series for *Psycho III* (1986), which he also directed, and *Psycho IV: The Beginning* (1990).

In his later career, Perkins delivered another classic study in dementia, as the mad street preacher in Ken Russell's *Crimes of Passion* (1984), and tried hard to play Dr. Jekyll as a proto-crack addict in *Edge of Sanity* (1989). He cowrote the waspish script for *The Last of Sheila* (1973) with fellow puzzle addict Stephen Sondheim.

Perkins was bisexual and had affairs with a number of men, including actor Tab Hunter, dancer Rudolf Nureyev, and dancer/choreographer Grover Dale, with whom Perkins had a six-year relationship before his marriage to actress, model, and photographer Berry Berenson. He died of complications from AIDS. **KN**

Top Takes...

Psycho IV: The Beginning 1990
Edge of Sanity 1989
Psycho III 1986
Crimes of Passion 1984
Psycho II 1983
Remember My Name 1978
Murder on the Orient Express 1974
How Awful About Allan 1970
Pretty Poison 1968
Le Procès 1962 (*The Trial*)
Psycho 1960
On the Beach 1959
The Matchmaker 1958
The Tin Star 1957
Fear Strikes Out 1957
Friendly Persuasion 1956 ☆

"I found it really scary. I was just as frightened as anybody else."

—On the shower scene in *Psycho*

1930s

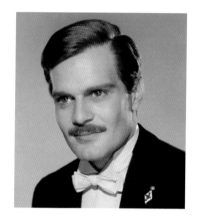

OMAR SHARIF

Born: Michael Shalhoub, April 10, 1932 (Alexandria, Egypt).

Star qualities: Egyptian movie icon; strikingly handsome; sexy but sensitive screen presence; moustache; leading man of romances and historical dramas; world-renowned bridge player; writer; producer.

Top Takes...

One Night with the King 2006

Monsieur Ibrahim et les fleurs du Coran 2003
(Monsieur Ibrahim)

The 13th Warrior 1999

Funny Lady 1975

The Tamarind Seed 1974

Mayerling 1968

Funny Girl 1968

Doctor Zhivago 1965

La fabuleuse aventure de Marco Polo 1965
(Marco the Magnificent)

Genghis Khan 1965

The Fall of the Roman Empire 1964

Lawrence of Arabia 1962 ☆

Siraa Fil-Wadi 1954 (The Blazing Sun)

"I don't know what sex appeal is. I don't think you can have sex appeal knowingly."

An established star in the Egyptian cinema, famed for his hypnotic effect on that country's female filmgoers, Omar Sharif moved to Hollywood in the hope of becoming a truly international star. But no one was more surprised than Sharif himself when David Lean decided on him for the crucial part of Sherif Ali in Lawrence of Arabia (1962). His bravura performance as an Arab nationalist whose admiration for the English hero turns eventually, although never completely, to profound misgiving, won him a Best Supporting Actor Oscar nomination, and made him a name to be reckoned with in the industry.

For years, however, like other male stars who sought to work outside their native market, Sharif found himself mired in supporting roles that called for a good-looking, somewhat dark-skinned, obviously "foreign" performer: The Fall of the Roman Empire (1964), La fabuleuse aventure de Marco Polo (1965) (Marco the Magnificent), and Genghis Khan (1965) chief among them. Lean gave Sharif yet another chance for international stardom by casting him in the title role of Doctor Zhivago (1965), the romantic pairing with Julie Christie succeeding in establishing him as a sexy, and sensitive, leading man. He reprised this role less successfully in Mayerling (1968), The Tamarind Seed (1974), and especially Funny Girl (1968) and its sequel, Funny Lady (1975). These latter two movies, in which Sharif strikes sparks with Barbra Streisand, boosted his popularity for a time, but no more really good projects were forthcoming. Sharif has spent the latter part of his career cast in inferior roles and forgettable films, including the embarrassing Oh Heavenly Dog (1980).

Sharif was once a professional bridge player, and would postpone any shootings that coincided with major games. **BP**

PETER O'TOOLE

Born: Peter Seamus O'Toole, August 2, 1932 (Connemara, County Galway, Ireland).

Star qualities: Tall; good looks; hell-raiser; Shakespearean stagecraft; leading man and character actor; often plays historical figures, including several kings and emperors; director; producer; keen sports fan.

Peter O'Toole was born the son of an Irish bookmaker and a Scottish nurse. After doing National Service as a radioman in the British Royal Navy, he applied to Dublin's Abbey Theatre Drama School but was rejected because he couldn't speak Irish. He went on to win a scholarship to London's Royal Academy of Dramatic Art. Initially he worked in the theater doing Shakespearean productions at Bristol's Old Vic. He then started to get film work, and was well down the cast list in *Kidnapped* (1960) and *The Savage Innocents* (1960).

He was instantly established as a major movie star in the title role of David Lean's *Lawrence of Arabia* (1962), which won him an Academy Award nomination for Best Actor. Tall, good-looking, and capable of fanaticism and disillusion, O'Toole's T. E. Lawrence was a romantic ideal rather than a true historical figure, but the role provided the actor with a screen image that he continued to explore in a variety of blueblood maniacs; O'Toole has produced two different takes on King Henry II in *Becket* (1964) and *The Lion in Winter* (1968), and played Don Quixote in *Man of La Mancha* (1972).

Medical problems threatened to destroy his career in the 1970s, but he later returned to the screen, switching to showy, well-spoken cameos and playing the Scottish academic and teacher Sir Reginald Fleming Johnston in Bernardo Bertolucci's biopic *The Last Emperor* (1987). His turn as the still-lecherous older actor in *Venus* (2006) won O'Toole his eighth Best Actor Oscar nomination. In 2003, the Academy gave him an Honorary Award in recognition of his lifelong contribution to film. He was initially reluctant to accept the honor, arguing that he was "still in the game," and would like more time to "win the lovely bugger outright." **KN**

Top Takes...

Venus **2006** ☆
Troy 2004
The Last Emperor 1987
Supergirl 1984
My Favorite Year **1982** ☆
The Stunt Man **1980** ☆
Man of La Mancha 1972
The Ruling Class **1972** ☆
Goodbye, Mr. Chips **1969** ☆
The Lion in Winter **1968** ☆
Lord Jim 1965
Becket **1964** ☆
Lawrence of Arabia **1962** ☆
The Day They Robbed the Bank of England 1960
The Savage Innocents 1960
Kidnapped 1960

"I can't stand light . . . . My idea of heaven is moving from one smoke-filled room to another."

TATSUYA NAKADAI

Born: Tatsuya Nakadai, December 13, 1932 (Tokyo, Japan).

Star qualities: Japanese screen legend; samurai superstar; tall; baritone voice; hollow-cheeked with expressive eyes; swordsman; stagecraft; leading man and versatile character actor.

Top Takes...

Yiu sau dou si 1992 (The Wicked City)

Ran 1985

Kagemusha 1980
  (Kagemusha the Shadow Warrior)

Jôi-uchi: Hairyô tsuma shimatsu 1967
  (Samurai Rebellion)

Kaidan 1964 (Kwaidan)

Tengoku to jigoku 1963 (High and Low)

Seppuku 1962 (Harakiri)

Tsubaki Sanjûrô 1962 (Sanjuro)

Yojimbo 1961 (Yojimbo the Bodyguard)

Ningen no joken III 1961
  (The Human Condition III)

Ningen no joken II 1959
  (The Human Condition II)

Kagi 1959 (The Key)

Ningen no joken I 1959 (The Human Condition I)

Tatsuya Nakadai has never achieved the international renown of fellow Japanese actor Toshirô Mifune, although his career has often seemed to shadow that of the older star. As a young man he was cast as Mifune's nemesis in director Akira Kurosawa's samurai dramas Yojimbo (1961) (Yojimbo the Bodyguard) and Tsubaki Sanjûrô (1962) (Sanjuro), a worthy opponent to be cut down in the final reel. Later in his film career, after Kurosawa and Mifune had irrevocably quarreled, Nakadai took the lead roles that would otherwise most likely have gone to Mifune in Kagemusha (1980) (Kagemusha the Shadow Warrior) and Ran (1985).

Nakadai trained as a stage actor specializing in Shingeki, the Japanese New Theater movement, which rejected the traditions of Noh and Kabuki in favor of Western realism. But he was discovered, it is said, working behind a shop counter by young Shochiku Studios director Masaki Kobayashi. He starred him in several of Kobayashi's movies: in the samurai revenge drama Seppuku (1962) (Harakiri), another Mifune-like role; the brilliantly stylized, ghost story anthology Kaidan (1964) (Kwaidan); and most notably as the tormented, principled hero of his epic nine-hour World War II trilogy, Ningen no joken (1959–1961) (The Human Condition). With his distinctive features, hollow cheeks, and large, expressive eyes, Nakadai has often been cast as characters in the grip of an obsession. For Kurosawa again he was a dogged police detective in Tengoku to jigoku (1963) (High and Low), and Kon Ichikawa cast him in Kagi (1959) (The Key) as a doctor fatally overinvolved with a female patient. His career has remained active well into his seventies, and he still works in Japanese movies, on TV, and on the stage. **PK**

> "I will do anything to rule this country. War is everywhere."
>
> ——Shingen Takeda, *Kagemusha*

KIM NOVAK

Born: Marilyn Pauline Novak, February 13, 1933 (Chicago, Illinois, U.S.).

Star qualities: "The Lavender Blonde"; youthful pinup; beautiful; slim; model poise; refined sex appeal; enigmatic, sensual screen presence; Columbia Pictures's leading lady of the 1950s and the studio's answer to Marilyn Monroe.

Despite being the daughter of two teachers, Kim Novak did not do well at high school and started out her working life as a teen model before taking a screen test and being signed by producer Harry Cohn. She soon became Columbia Pictures's 1950s leading lady, built up as a replacement for Rita Hayworth and a rival for Marilyn Monroe. Her acting career began with undemanding support roles in movies such as *Pushover* (1954). She then handled more substantial vehicles, playing the small-town princess in *Picnic* (1955), the devoted girlfriend in *The Man with the Golden Arm* (1955), biopic roles in *The Eddy Duchin Story* (1956) and *Jeanne Eagels* (1957), and a musical lead with Rita Hayworth and Frank Sinatra in *Pal Joey* (1957).

Though pinup beautiful, and about as good an actress as Monroe, Novak was a fairly bland star until Alfred Hitchcock cast her in the complex role of haunted ice maiden and remodeled shop girl in *Vertigo* (1958). This role was enough by itself to elevate her to cinematic greatness. Novak was teamed again with her *Vertigo* costar James Stewart in the lighter, still-magical *Bell Book and Candle* (1958). When the studio era came to an end, she was in a couple of underrated movies about stardom, such as Robert Aldrich's *The Legend of Lylah Clare* (1968), but struggled in *The Amorous Adventures of Moll Flanders* (1965). As her success began to fade, she moved over to TV, where she played Kit Marlowe in the TV series *Falcon Crest* (1986–1987). Ironically, the name of her character was the same one that had been suggested to her as a screen name when she started out with Columbia Pictures. At that time Novak refused, only agreeing to change her first name from "Marilyn" to "Kim," since the public associated her own name with her rival, Marilyn Monroe. **KN**

Top Takes...

Liebestraum 1991
The Mirror Crack'd 1980
The Legend of Lylah Clare 1968
The Amorous Adventures of Moll Flanders 1965
Kiss Me, Stupid 1964
Of Human Bondage 1964
Bell Book and Candle 1958
Vertigo 1958
Pal Joey 1957
Jeanne Eagels 1957
The Eddy Duchin Story 1956
The Man with the Golden Arm 1955
Picnic 1955
5 Against the House 1955
Phffft! 1954
Pushover 1954

"I had a lot of resentment for a while toward Kim Novak. But I don't mind her anymore."

MICHAEL CAINE

Born: Maurice Joseph Micklewhite, March 14, 1933 (Rotherhithe, London, England).

Star qualities: Tall; good looks; trademark glasses; distinctive voice and Cockney accent; witty and charming; stagecraft; leading man and extremely versatile character actor; prolific output; producer.

Top Takes...

Children of Men 2006
Batman Begins 2005
***The Quiet American* 2002** ☆
Austin Powers in Goldmember 2002
***The Cider House Rules* 1999** ★
Little Voice 1998
***Hannah and Her Sisters* 1986** ★
***Educating Rita* 1983** ☆
Dressed to Kill 1980
The Man Who Would Be King 1975
***Sleuth* 1972** ☆
Get Carter 1971
The Italian Job 1969
***Alfie* 1966** ☆
The Ipcress File 1965
Zulu 1964

> "I am in so many movies that are on TV at 2:00 A.M. that people think I am dead."

RIGHT: Noel Coward comforts Caine during the funeral scene in *The Italian Job*.

Michael Caine was born the son of a fish-market porter and a cleaning lady. After leaving school he took a series of menial jobs before doing National Service with the British army in Germany and Korea. When he returned to England he decided he wanted to be an actor and got a job as an assistant stage manager, working in repertory theaters. His stage name was originally "Michael Scott," but when he was offered a TV role he had to join Equity, the British actors' trade union, which already had a Michael Scott on its books. Caine's agent called him and gave him 30 minutes to come up with a name. At the time Caine was in London's cinema Mecca, Leicester Square. *The Caine Mutiny* (1954) was showing, starring Humphrey Bogart, one of Caine's favorite actors, and "Michael Caine" was born.

He played many bit parts before getting his break in *Zulu* (1964). Here, Caine moderated his Cockney accent to play an upper-crust officer, but his signature tones returned as glum spy Harry Palmer in *The Ipcress File* (1965) and the lothario *Alfie* (1966). Such roles made him a big movie star and led to iconic crime roles in *The Italian Job* (1969) and *Get Carter* (1971).

Since the 1970s, Caine has played a variety of characters. He was an academic and educator in *Educating Rita* (1983); excellent as the adulterous husband in Woody Allen's *Hannah and Her Sisters* (1986), for which he won an Academy Award for Best Supporting Actor; doctor and abortionist in the screen adaptation of John Irving's *The Cider House Rules* (1999), for which he won his second Oscar; and Alfred the butler in *Batman Begins* (2005). Knighted in 2000, Caine maintains a hectic filming schedule. He has been happily married to his second wife, actress and model Shakira Caine, since 1973. They have one daughter, Natasha. **KN**

JEAN-PAUL BELMONDO

Born: Jean-Paul Belmondo, April 9, 1933 (Neuilly-sur-Seine, Hauts-de-Seine, France).

Star qualities: "Bébel"; iconic French sex symbol, with charm and macho looks; proficient stuntman; winning smile; athletic; early roles in action films and mature comic parts; stagecraft; producer.

The son of famous sculptor Paul Belmondo, Jean-Paul "Bébel" Belmondo made his screen debut in 1957. He became an important figure of the French New Wave for his part in Jean-Luc Godard's *À bout de souffle* (1960) (*Breathless*). Next to the lovely Jean Seberg, he showed casualness, cynicism, and even coarseness: a new type of character was born.

Belmondo didn't really have movie star looks, but his manliness and somewhat insolent charm distinguished him from Alain Delon—in many ways his alter ego—and seduced some of the most influential directors of the time, such as Claude Chabrol, François Truffaut, and Alain Resnais. He could play almost anything; he was even a convincing priest for Jean-Pierre Melville in *Léon Morin, prêtre* (1961) (*The Forgiven Sinner*). However, from the mid-1960s onward, with films such as *Les tribulations d'un chinois en Chine* (1965) (*Chinese Adventures in China*), a successful blend of action and comedy to which he was well suited, he turned to commercial cinema, and soon became the most popular French actor of his time.

Full of energy, and always performing his own stunts—he was an accomplished sportsman before taking acting classes at Paris's Conservatoire National Superieur d'Art Dramatique—Belmondo has unfortunately stuck to increasingly similar characterizations of public entertainers, although he is also capable of showing self-mockery. In 1989 he received a César Award for his interpretation in Claude Lelouch's *Itinéraire d'un enfant gâté* (1988). Sadly, his later movies have rarely lived up to his sterling reputation. In recent years Belmondo has preferred to concentrate on stage work, but since suffering a stroke in 2001, he has been absent from both stage and screen. **FL**

Top Takes...

"I don't want to be a flying grandpa of the French cinema."

GIAN MARIA VOLONTÈ

Born: Gian Maria Volontè, April 9, 1933 (Milan, Italy); died 1994 (Florina, Greece).

Star qualities: Legendary Italian actor; spaghetti Westerns supremo; tall, rugged looks and menacing screen presence made him ideal for villainous characters; often took on controversial roles; left-wing political activist.

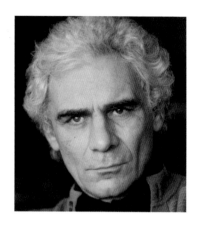

Gian Maria Volontè goes down in history as one of Europe's leading actors and is best known for the villains he has played. After studying drama at the Accademia Nazionale d'Arte Drammatica in Rome, he went on to play the king of Sparta in *Ercole alla conquista di Atlantide* (1961) (*Hercules Conquers Atlantis*) and artist Michelangelo Buonarroti in Italian TV's *Vita di Michelangelo* (1964). His break came when Sergio Leone cast him alongside Clint Eastwood as Ramón Rojo, the chief heavy of *Per un pugno di dollari* (1964) (*A Fistful of Dollars*). Billed for a while as "Johnny Wels," Volontè went on to make more spaghetti Westerns. He was a superb, dope-smoking psychotic El Indio in Leone's sequel *Per qualche dollaro in più* (1965) (*For a Few Dollars More*), and the Eastern Professor Brad Fletcher who exchanges places with outlaw Tomas Milian in Sergio Sollima's *Faccia a faccia* (1967) (*Face to Face*).

Face to Face was one of a run of politicized Westerns that relate to another strand of Volontè's career as a committed leftist. He was a Sicilian activist in Paolo Taviani's *Un uomo da bruciare* (1962) (*A Man for Burning*); the fascist cop in Elio Petri's *Indagine su un cittadino al di sopra di ogni sospetto* (1970) (*Investigation of a Citizen Above Suspicion*), which won an Oscar for Best Foreign Film; and the internal exile in Francesco Rosi's *Cristo si è fermato a Eboli* (1979) (*Christ Stopped at Eboli*). Volontè also played real-life controversial Italians: anarchist Bartolomeo Vanzetti in *Sacco e Vanzetti* (1971) (*Sacco and Vanzetti*), Nazi freedom fighter and politician Enrico Mattei in *Il caso Mattei* (1972) (*The Mattei Affair*), and murdered political leader Aldo Moro in *Il caso Moro* (1986) (*The Moro Affair*). Busy to the last, he died in Greece at the start of filming for *To Vlemma tou Odyssea* (1995) (*Ulysses' Gaze*). **KN**

Top Takes...

Il caso Moro 1986 (*The Moro Affair*)
Cristo si è fermato a Eboli 1979
  (*Christ Stopped at Eboli*)
Il caso Mattei 1972 (*The Mattei Affair*)
Sacco e Vanzetti 1971 (*Sacco and Vanzetti*)
Indagine su un cittadino al di sopra di ogni sospetto 1970 (*Investigation of a Citizen Above Suspicion*)
Faccia a faccia 1967 (*Face to Face*)
Per qualche dollaro in più 1965
  (*For a Few Dollars More*)
Vita di Michelangelo 1964
Per un pugno di dollari 1964
  (*A Fistful of Dollars*)
Un uomo da bruciare 1962 (*A Man for Burning*)
Ercole alla conquista di Atlantide 1961
  (*Hercules Conquers Atlantis*)

1930s

"Go ahead and shoot me, Colonel. Just try."

——El Indio, *For a Few Dollars More*

JAYNE MANSFIELD

Born: Vera Jayne Palmer, April 19, 1933 (Bryn Mawr, Pennsylvania, U.S.); died 1967 (Slidell, Louisiana, U.S.).

Star qualities: Natural brunette turned blonde, busty bombshell; typecast in sex kitten and bimbo roles but rarely taken seriously as an actor; multilingual; musician.

Top Takes...

Jayne Mansfield was a pneumatic "blonde bombshell" whose few substantial film roles tended to use her as a living cartoon. Below Marilyn Monroe and Kim Novak but above Sheree North and Mamie Van Doren in the 1950s pinup pecking order, Mansfield was a limited but likable screen performer, lucky enough to feature in one bona fide movie classic, Frank Tashlin's rock 'n' roll-packed exercise in visual va-va-voom, *The Girl Can't Help It* (1956). Here, she sends up her own celebrity as a gangster's girl promoted as a singing star by press agent Tom Ewell. She wobbles down the street to Little Richard's title song, driving men into Tex Avery Wolf-like frenzies of lust with her mere presence, and gamely poses for a series of juvenile sight gags (holding a pair of milk bottles to her breasts) that exploit her image as an American sex fantasy.

Mansfield's first film roles were as dumb blonde underworld hangers-on or murder victims (*Illegal*, 1955) but she was relaunched as a comedy star after her Broadway success in *Will Success Spoil Rock Hunter?*, which Tashlin filmed in 1957. Wonderful as Mansfield was in Tashlin's duo, there wasn't much more she could actually *do* in Hollywood movies. Soon after being uncomfortably pursued by Cary Grant in the archly titled *Kiss Them for Me* (1957), she left for Europe, appearing as a striptease queen in *Too Hot to Handle* (1960) before making *It Happened in Athens* (1962) and *Heimweh nach St. Pauli* (1963) (*Homesick for St. Pauli*). Back home, she appeared discreetly nude in *Promises! Promises!* (1963), and was one of the "Technical Advisors" in *A Guide for the Married Man* (1967). Mansfield played a prostitute in the tawdry drama *Single Room Furnished* (1968), which wasn't completed until after her tragic death in a car crash. **KN**

> "I don't particularly enjoy publicity, it seems to just follow me around."

GENE WILDER

Born: Jerome Silberman, June 11, 1933 (Milwaukee, Wisconsin, U.S.).

Star qualities: Unruly mop of curly hair; piercing blue eyes; rubbery features; expressive face; the original Willy Wonka; a comedian famed for comic caper roles; civic minded; political activist; producer; director; writer.

Gene Wilder established himself as a screen actor with a perfectly performed scene in *Bonnie and Clyde* (1967), where he played a terrified abductee nevertheless flattered by the attentions of the celebrity criminals. But it was a Broadway production of *Mother Courage and Her Children* (1963) that altered the course of his career. In its cast was Anne Bancroft, who was dating Mel Brooks at the time (they married in 1964). The two men struck an instant chord, and the friendship led to Wilder's becoming part of Brooks's "stock company."

Wilder—against all odds—held his own onscreen as erratic accountant Leo Bloom for the bravura first third of Brooks's comedy *The Producers* (1968). He was nominated for a Best Supporting Actor Oscar for this performance. Too sweet for *Quackser Fortune Has a Cousin in the Bronx* (1970) and *Willy Wonka & the Chocolate Factory* (1971), he reunited with Brooks for a turn as the burned-out gunslinger in *Blazing Saddles* (1974) and as a splendid parody of Basil Rathbone in *Young Frankenstein* (1974), the movie that made him a major star.

Having cowritten *Frankenstein*, Wilder directed himself in his next script, *The Adventure of Sherlock Holmes' Smarter Brother* (1975), and then continued to mine the spoof vein, with less amusing results, in *The World's Greatest Lover* (1977) and *Haunted Honeymoon* (1986). A genial partnership with Richard Pryor in the comic caper *Silver Streak* (1976) led to more fitfully funny vehicles such as *Stir Crazy* (1980) and *See No Evil, Hear No Evil* (1989). In *The Woman in Red* (1984), which he directed, and *Funny About Love* (1990), directed by Leonard Nimoy, Wilder overdoses appallingly on self-love. He retired from the movies in 1991 and published his memoirs, *Kiss Me Like a Stranger*, in 2005. **KN**

Top Takes...

Funny About Love 1990
See No Evil, Hear No Evil 1989
The Woman in Red 1984
Stir Crazy 1980
The World's Greatest Lover 1977
Silver Streak 1976
The Adventure of Sherlock Holmes' Smarter Brother 1975
Young Frankenstein 1974
Blazing Saddles 1974
Everything You Always Wanted to Know About Sex But Were Afraid to Ask* 1972
Willy Wonka & the Chocolate Factory 1971
Quackser Fortune Has a Cousin in the Bronx 1970
The Producers 1968 ☆
Bonnie and Clyde 1967

1930s

"I love movies because you have another shot at it. Let me try something else."

ALAN ARKIN

Born: Alan Wolf Arkin, March 26, 1934 (New York City, New York, U.S.).

Star qualities: Versatile character actor of drama and comedy; talent for playing the eccentric with panache; improvisation; stagecraft; director, writer, musician, and composer.

Top Takes...

Little Miss Sunshine 2006 ★
The Novice 2004
Jakob the Liar 1999
Grosse Pointe Blank 1997
Glengarry Glen Ross 1992
Coupe de Ville 1990
The In-Laws 1979
The Seven-Per-Cent Solution 1976
Freebie and the Bean 1974
Little Murders 1971
Catch-22 1970
The Heart Is a Lonely Hunter 1968 ☆
Wait Until Dark 1967
**The Russians Are Coming
  the Russians Are Coming 1966** ☆

Playing a heroin-using, porn-loving, foul-mouthed, aging-rocker grandfather in an offbeat comedy seems an unlikely role to win a Best Supporting Actor Oscar, yet Alan Arkin's tour-de-force turn in the dysfunctional family-on-the-road movie *Little Miss Sunshine* (2006) did just that. And rightly so, because it was his captivating and brilliant incarnation of the grandpa, who trains his granddaughter to do a striptease performance, and give a new meaning to the dance segment of a kids' beauty-pageant competition that was the performance audiences were talking about as they left the movie theater.

Arkin's Oscar win must have seemed like a lost dream come true, given it came 40 years after his first Oscar nod for Best Actor for his role as a Russian lieutenant in his debut feature, the Cold War comedy *The Russians Are Coming the Russians Are Coming* (1966). The young Arkin followed this up with a compelling portrayal of a doomed deaf mute in *The Heart Is a Lonely Hunter* (1968) that won him another Oscar nomination, but after this the golden statue looked set to elude him.

Yet over the years Arkin has brought a touch of brilliance to both the big and small screen in roles such as the war-weary pilot Captain John Yossarian in the Joseph Heller adaptation *Catch-22* (1970); an unscrupulous estate agent in *Glengarry Glen Ross* (1992); and an eccentric sculptor and long-lost father to his son in real life, Adam Arkin, in the TV hospital drama *Chicago Hope* (1994). Arkin brings his flair for playing the eccentric and unconventional to roles in both dramas and comedies, and his talent raises the bar of any ensemble cast. One hopes there are still many more lines of dialogue such as "I can say what I want. I've still got Nazi bullets in my ass" awaiting him. **CK**

> "I know that if I can't move people, then I have no business being an actor."

SHIRLEY MacLAINE

Born: Shirley MacLean Beaty, April 24, 1934 (Richmond, Virginia, U.S.).

Star qualities: Thick, curly, red hair; tall; singer and ballet dancer; witty; leading lady of drama and comedy; firm believer in out-of-body experiences and reincarnation; writer; director; producer.

"I guess I'm happiest," Shirley MacLaine once remarked, "when I'm looking like a slob." Her screen debut in Alfred Hitchcock's deadpan black comedy *The Trouble with Harry* (1955) brought something new to the Hollywood scene. Soignée high glamour in the old studio style clearly wasn't her thing, but at the same time she was too offbeat and droll to be the girl-next-door type. There was a hint of bohemian what-the-hell about her, but mixed with an appealing vulnerability. Given a script that made the most of both those sides of her, as did Billy Wilder's *The Apartment* (1960), she could be at once irresistibly funny and heartbreaking. Inevitably, she was often cast in tart-with-a-heart roles: for Wilder again with *Irma la Douce* (1963), and in Bob Fosse's *Sweet Charity* (1969). But she could bring a sweet, slightly daffy charm to them.

MacLaine's mother was a drama teacher and enrolled her daughter in a ballet class as a toddler to strengthen her weak ankles. After her junior year in high school, she moved to New York to pursue her studies. Auditions were being held for the revival of Oscar and Hammerstein's musical *Oklahoma*. MacLaine auditioned and got a part in the chorus. From then on her sights were set on Broadway, and in 1955 she was spotted and signed to Paramount Pictures.

As she's grown older she has moved into more imperious roles, for example, in James Brooks's *Terms of Endearment* (1983) or John Schlesinger's *Madame Sousatzka* (1988), playing women who, while often willful and infuriatingly eccentric, are redeemed by their emotional intelligence. Alongside her acting, MacLaine has sustained a career as a writer, tirelessly promoting her beliefs in spiritualism and reincarnation. Her younger brother is actor and director Warren Beatty. **PK**

Top Takes...

Rumor Has It . . . 2005
In Her Shoes 2005
These Old Broads 2001
The Evening Star 1996
Postcards from the Edge 1990
Steel Magnolias 1989
Madame Sousatzka 1988
Terms of Endearment 1983 ★
Being There 1979
The Turning Point 1977 ☆
Sweet Charity 1969
Irma la Douce 1963 ☆
Ocean's Eleven 1960
The Apartment 1960 ☆
Some Came Running 1958 ☆
The Trouble with Harry 1955

1930s

"Some people think I look like a sweet potato. I consider myself a spud with a heart of gold."

SOPHIA LOREN

Born: Sofia Villani Scicolone, September 20, 1934 (Rome, Lazio, Italy).

Star qualities: Voluptuous sex goddess of the 1960s; astonishing natural beauty; widely respected internationally as a dramatic and comedic actress; discerning, witty, and insightful; a treasure of world cinema.

Top Takes...

Prêt-à-Porter 1994

Una giornata particolare 1977 (A Special Day)

The Cassandra Crossing 1976

Man of La Mancha 1972

La moglie del prete 1971 (The Priest's Wife)

A Countess from Hong Kong 1967

Matrimonio all'italiana 1964 ☆
  (Marriage Italian-Style)

Ieri, oggi, domani 1963
  (Yesterday, Today, and Tomorrow)

La ciociara 1960 ★
  (Two Women)

The Millionairess 1960

It Started in Naples 1960

Heller in Pink Tights 1960

Houseboat 1958

The Pride and the Passion 1957

Boy on a Dolphin 1957

Attila 1954

L'oro di Napoli 1954 (The Gold of Naples)

Aïda 1953

Quo Vadis 1951

In her heyday, Sophia Loren was considered to be one of many natural Italian beauties of humble origin, untouched by artifice and foreign glamour, a star who was at the heart of the Italian nation from her impoverished beginnings near Naples, which she often recounts, through to her high-profile international reputation with a five-film contract at Paramount Pictures and a Best Actress Oscar for *La ciociara* (1960) (*Two Women*). A national poll in the 1980s also revealed Loren to be Italy's most important icon, and an attempt was even made to erect a giant statue in her honor near her Neapolitan hometown.

Along with Claudia Cardinale, Loren started her career in beauty contests, where she was quickly noticed by movie producers—in her case by Carlo Ponti, whom she later married. Early on, she had numerous uncredited roles, and can be briefly glimpsed as a slave girl in *Quo Vadis* (1951) while still in her teens. Loren was also a popular model in Italian photo-story magazines. Her first notable role was in the operatic *Aïda* (1953), although her singing voice was dubbed, but it was in the late 1950s and the 1960s that her fame became truly international, with numerous starring roles opposite Hollywood

RIGHT: Loren dazzles as Valeria Billi in Dino Risi's comedy, *The Priest's Wife*.

leading men, from Cary Grant in *Houseboat* (1958) to Marlon Brando in *A Countess from Hong Kong* (1967).

However, it was through Loren's collaboration with esteemed Italian director and actor Vittorio de Sica that her reputation was secured, not so much as one of cinema's most beautiful stars (that was already proven), but as a serious and versatile actress whose body might be international but whose heart belonged only to Italy. Her role as the pizza girl (*la pizzaiola*) in *L'oro di Napoli* (1954) (*The Gold of Naples*), one of her most cherished among Italian audiences, and her impressive performances alongside Marcello Mastroianni—the pair made 13 films together—as three different characters in *Ieri, oggi, domani* (1963) (*Yesterday, Today, and Tomorrow*) are career highlights. Her last reputable movie role, in which she wears a monstrously oversized hat (symbolic of her stardom?), is in Robert Altman's *Prêt-à-Porter* (1994). **GN**

ABOVE: Loren teamed up with Marcello Mastroianni for the last time in *Prêt-à-Porter*.

Beauty Incarnate

Sophia Loren set the standard of beauty against which all other stars of the period were measured. A term was even coined in Italy to describe Loren and her peers, such as Gina Lollobrigida, as new postwar embodiments of female stardom, defined by the presence of the body as having a star quality all its own. This term was *maggiorate fisiche*, meaning physically and very amply endowed. Loren was modest about her glorious physique, claiming, "Everything you see, I owe to spaghetti." Her beauty endures to this day: Loren features in the 2007 Pirelli calendar at age seventy-two.

BRIGITTE BARDOT

Born: Brigitte Bardot, September 28, 1934 (Paris, France).

Star qualities: Iconic French beauty; explosive sexuality; long blonde hair; cute pouting face; curvaceous; the definitive sex kitten; cast in pinup roles; singer; animal rights campaigner; right-wing political activist.

Top Takes...

L'histoire très bonne et très joyeuse de Colinot Trousse-Chemise 1973
  (*The Edifying and Joyous Story of Colinot*)

Shalako 1968

Histoires extraordinaires 1968
  (*Spirits of the Dead*)

Viva Maria! 1965

Le Mépris 1963 (*Contempt*)

Vie privée 1962 (*A Very Private Affair*)

La bride sur le cou 1961 (*Please, Not Now!*)

La Vérité 1960 (*The Truth*)

Voulez-vous danser avec moi? 1959
  (*Come Dance with Me!*)

En cas de malheur 1958 (*Love Is My Profession*)

Et Dieu . . . créa la femme 1956
  (*And God Created Woman*)

Helen of Troy 1956

"I have been very happy, very rich, very beautiful . . . very famous and very unhappy."

RIGHT: Bardot played Maria I alongside Jeanne Moreau's Maria II in *Viva Maria!*

Brigitte Bardot, or "BB," as she became known, was born the daughter of a wealthy industrialist. She was studying ballet when she was offered a modeling contract, and by the age of fifteen she was on the cover of *Elle* magazine. There she was spotted by director Marc Allegret, whose assistant, Roger Vadim, contacted Bardot. Although Allegret did not cast Bardot in a movie, Vadim fell in love with her, and they married in 1952.

She achieved worldwide fame with her starring role in Vadim's *Et Dieu . . . créa la femme* (1956) (*And God Created Woman*), in which she marries a young man while lusting after his brother. Her curvaceous figure and pretty, pouting face, her air of innocence combined with a constant suggestion of promiscuity, projected an uninhibited sexuality far removed from the primness of contemporary Hollywood stars.

Bardot's marriage to Vadim was only the first of a series of high-profile liaisons that kept her name constantly in the news, and the frequent nudity in her movies ensured the box-office success of such films as *En cas de malheur* (1958) (*Love Is My Profession*), in which she costarred with Jean Gabin. In the 1960s she worked with some important directors, such as Henri-Georges Clouzot in *La Vérité* (1960) (*The Truth*), Louis Malle in *Vie privée* (1962) (*A Very Private Affair*), and Jean-Luc Godard in *Le Mépris* (1963) (*Contempt*). In *Viva Maria!* (1965), also directed by Malle, she costarred with Jeanne Moreau in a witty and entertaining Western. She retired from the cinema in 1973 on the eve of her fortieth birthday; since then she has devoted herself to animal rights and flirted with the extreme right-wing politics of Jean-Marie Le Pen. Bardot's fourth husband, Bernard d'Ormale, whom she married in 1992, is a Front National politician. **EB**

JUDI DENCH

Born: Judith Olivia Dench, December 9, 1934 (York, North Yorkshire, England).

Star qualities: Diminutive British dame of the stage and screen; versatile character actress; penetrating glare; cracked voice; frequently plays historical figures and the strong-willed mature woman; prolific output.

In her mature years, Dame Judi Dench has played so many queens, matriarchs, and grandes dames it's hard to remember she was ever young, but her distinctively cracked voice, piercing looks, and blocky hauteur are evident as early as her gangster's girlfriend in *He Who Rides a Tiger* (1965) and Victorian social worker in *A Study in Terror* (1965).

Dench studied at London's Central School of Speech and Drama and has had a prolific stage career, having performed with the Royal Shakespeare Company, the National Theatre, and at London's Old Vic Theatre. For decades, her screen work was simply an extension of her stage career, but from the mid-1980s onward she has more often graced the big screen.

She has supported her contemporaries Vanessa Redgrave and Maggie Smith with eccentric turns in David Hare's *Wetherby* (1985) and James Ivory's *A Room with a View* (1985) and contributed cameos to Kenneth Branagh's Shakespeare films as Mistress Quickly in *Henry V* (1989) and Hecuba in *Hamlet* (1996). Dench began her run of noteworthy queens with Victoria in *Mrs. Brown* (1997) and Elizabeth I in *Shakespeare in Love* (1998). Her eight-minute performance in the latter won her an Oscar for Best Supporting Actress. A flinty spy mistress, M, in the Pierce Brosnan James Bond films since *GoldenEye* (1995), she is the sole regular to survive into Daniel Craig's tenure with *Casino Royale* (2006). Among her formidable lady characters are the writer Iris Murdoch in *Iris* (2001), Laura Henderson in *Mrs. Henderson Presents* (2005), and Lady Catherine de Bourg in *Pride & Prejudice* (2005). Her recent performance as a lonely, manipulative teacher in *Notes on a Scandal* (2006) has earned her yet another Academy Award nomination, her sixth. **KN**

Top Takes...

Notes on a Scandal **2006** ☆
Casino Royale 2006
Pride & Prejudice 2005
Mrs. Henderson Presents **2005** ☆
Ladies in Lavender 2004
The Shipping News 2001
Iris **2001** ☆
Chocolat **2000** ☆
Shakespeare in Love **1998** ★
Mrs. Brown **1997** ☆
GoldenEye 1995
Henry V 1989
A Room with a View 1985
Wetherby 1985
He Who Rides a Tiger 1965
A Study in Terror 1965

1930s

> "I don't think anybody can be told how to act . . . you have to find your own way through it."

MAGGIE SMITH

Born: Margaret Natalie Smith, December 28, 1934 (Ilford, Essex, England).

Star qualities: British dame of the stage; slim, elegant, steely leading lady of dramas and comedies; comic timing; shrill voice; idiosyncratic style; Triple Crown winner of Oscar, Tony, and Emmy.

One of the most beloved comediennes of London's West End theaters, Dame Maggie Smith never managed to find a niche in cinema truly befitting her talents. Her early roles were technically interesting and she seemed to be molding herself effectively as a popular type: the independent-minded, witty, self-possessed single English lady, probably much sexier than she at first appears. This was best incarnated in the music hall singer she played in *Oh! What a Lovely War* (1969).

On the strength of this work, she landed two plum starring roles. She was the lead in *The Prime of Miss Jean Brodie* (1969), and the *carpe diem* modernism of the virginal girls' school teacher suited the tradition-breaking morality of the era. Yet, strangely, Smith does not project what she might have about this fascinating character: her own desperation at the prospect of being permanently bypassed by Eros. An Academy Award for Best Actress was her reward. The second lead role was in the Graham Greene adaptation *Travels with My Aunt* (1972), displacing an unhappy Katharine Hepburn, which won her an Oscar nomination for Best Actress.

Smith remained adept at the brilliantly executed cameo, as in Neil Simon's *California Suite* (1978), another Oscar-winning part, this time for Best Supporting Actress. Otherwise she has been part of the British brigade's usual suspects, playing well, but with limited interest, in productions ranging from stagy Agatha Christie films such as *Death on the Nile* (1978) to the *Harry Potter* films. Sadly, Smith's best screen performance was for Alan Bennett's seldom-seen *Talking Heads* (1987), a TV anthology of monologues; her richly textured performance as a bitter woman hints at the even more illustrious film career that has eluded her. **BP**

Top Takes...

Harry Potter and the Goblet of Fire 2005
Ladies in Lavender 2004
Harry Potter and the Prisoner of Azkaban 2004
Harry Potter and the Chamber of Secrets 2002
Gosford Park 2001 ☆
Harry Potter and the Sorcerer's Stone 2001
The Secret Garden 1992
Sister Act 1992
The Lonely Passion of Judith Hearne 1987
A Room with a View 1985 ☆
California Suite 1978 ★
Death on the Nile 1978
Travels with My Aunt 1972 ☆
Oh! What a Lovely War 1969
The Prime of Miss Jean Brodie 1969 ★
Othello 1965 ☆

"One went to school, one wanted to act, one started to act, and one's still acting."

ELVIS PRESLEY

Born: Elvis Aron Presley, January 8, 1935 (Tupelo, Mississippi, U.S.); died 1977 (Memphis, Tennessee, U.S.).

Star qualities: Rock 'n' roll icon; an original and legendary entertainer; his films became a genre of their own and were immensely profitable; versatile singer.

Top Takes...

Elvis on Tour 1972
Elvis: That's the Way It Is 1970
Change of Habit 1969
Charro! 1969
Speedway 1968
Clambake 1967
Paradise, Hawaiian Style 1966
Harum Scarum 1965
Tickle Me 1965
Girl Happy 1965
Roustabout 1964
Viva Las Vegas 1964
Kissin' Cousins 1964
Fun in Acapulco 1963
It Happened at the World's Fair 1963
Girls! Girls! Girls! 1962
Kid Galahad 1962
Blue Hawaii 1961
Wild in the Country 1961
Flaming Star 1960
G.I. Blues 1960
King Creole 1958
Jailhouse Rock 1957
Loving You 1957
Love Me Tender 1956

RIGHT: The King doing what he did best: performing, in *Elvis: That's the Way It Is*.

Elvis Presley was one of the most important popular entertainers of the twentieth century and a major movie attraction for more than a decade, yet he never fulfilled his potential in films. Colonel Tom Parker, his manager, turned down *West Side Story* (1961) and other opportunities, essentially confining his cash cow to undemanding, colorful, clean-spirited musicals that, unforgivably, tended to stick the King of Rock 'n' Roll with terrible, unmemorable songs ("No Room to Rhumba in a Sports Car").

On a rising wave of popularity as a recording artist and notorious from his first TV appearances, Presley made his film debut in the post-Civil War Western *Love Me Tender* (1956), swiveling his hips as he strummed guitar in a hastily written-in number. He fared better in films that drew on his own biography (*Loving You*, 1957; *Jailhouse Rock*, 1957; *King Creole*, 1958), which also benefited from good directors, strong stories, and numbers "The King" could let loose with, such as "Got a Lot o' Livin' to Do" and "(You're So Square) Baby I Don't Care."

After his stint in the army, Presley appeared in *G.I. Blues* (1960), which set the mold for most of his subsequent vehicles,

1930s

then tentatively branched out as an actor, playing a renegade half-Indian in a good Don Siegel Western (*Flaming Star*, 1960) and a would-be writer in a Clifford Odets script (*Wild in the Country*, 1961). However, after *Blue Hawaii* (1961), Elvis was stuck in a run of cookie-cutter musicals with interchangeable plots, leading ladies, settings, and songs (*Girls! Girls! Girls!*, 1962; *Fun in Acapulco*, 1963; *Roustabout*, 1964; *Kissin' Cousins*, 1964; *Girl Happy*, 1965; *Tickle Me*, 1965; *Paradise, Hawaiian Style*, 1966; *Clambake*, 1967; *Stay Away, Joe*, 1968; *Speedway*, 1968). *Viva Las Vegas* (1964) is cut from the same cloth, but uniquely pairs Elvis with a partner (Ann-Margret) who can match his dance moves and gets some sex back into the act, saving him from total emasculation. In the late 1960s, after *Charro!* (1969) and *Change of Habit* (1969), he called it quits. However, he can be seen as himself, working hard in his Vegas lounge period in *Elvis: That's the Way It Is* (1970) and *Elvis on Tour* (1972). **KN**

ABOVE: Presley in *Jailhouse Rock,* his third and, some argue, his best movie.

Actor in Waiting

Elvis blamed the poor quality of the movies he starred in on his manager Colonel Tom Parker, with whom he had a turbulent relationship. Yet the serious acting potential of the rock 'n' roll star struck many in the world of Hollywood, including respected director Elia Kazan. Elvis was allegedly approached for some big movies (which Parker invariably rejected), including *The Defiant Ones* (1958), *Cat on a Hot Tin Roof* (1958), *Midnight Cowboy* (1969), and *A Star Is Born* (1976). Elvis's favorite actors were Marlon Brando and James Dean. He liked *King Creole* the best out of his own repertoire.

DONALD SUTHERLAND

Born: Donald McNichol Sutherland, July 7, 1935 (New Brunswick, Canada).

Star qualities: Tall, gaunt, wiry frame; slouch; deep, distinctive voice; extraordinarily versatile character actor; prolific output; political activist and counterculture icon; producer; head of an acting family.

One of the most consistently working supporting players with dozens of credits in movies and TV, while also being the father of actor Kiefer Sutherland, Donald Sutherland is a native Canadian and the heart and soul of countless beloved films.

He grew up in Nova Scotia and first studied drama and engineering at the University of Toronto. After graduating, he went to England to study at the London Academy of Music and Dramatic Art. After some small parts in British films and TV, he gained widespread recognition for his role as a killer in Robert Aldrich's star-studded *The Dirty Dozen* (1967). His second significant role was as surgeon Captain Benjamin Franklin "Hawkeye" Pierce in Robert Altman's classic comedy about medics in the field during the Korean War, *M*A*S*H* (1970).

It was at this time that Sutherland became a counterculture idol because of his antiwar stance. He was vocal in protesting against the Vietnam War and, with the participation of fellow protestor and *Klute* (1971) costar Jane Fonda, made the antiwar documentary *F.T.A.* (1972). But his career's overall flavor is a mix of widely popular entertainments with more challenging works, often featuring him as the pivotal villain. Along the first line there's *Kelly's Heroes* (1970), *JFK* (1991), and *Cold Mountain* (2003). Along the second line of more experimental work there's *Don't Look Now* (1973) and *Six Degrees of Separation* (1993). He has also worked occasionally in TV, most notably as Nathan Templeton in *Commander in Chief* (2005–2006). In every role, Sutherland is a type. He's physically tall, frequently changing from merely gaunt and therefore unusual to being outright nasty. His smile is lined with thin lips, and his blue eyes alternately sparkle with intrigue or malign intent. He's a master craftsman, too. **GCQ**

Top Takes…

Pride & Prejudice 2005
Cold Mountain 2003
Six Degrees of Separation 1993
JFK 1991
A Dry White Season 1989
Ordinary People 1980
Invasion of the Body Snatchers 1978
The Eagle Has Landed 1976
Il Casanova di Federico Fellini 1976
 (*Fellini's Casanova*)
Don't Look Now 1973
Steelyard Blues 1973
Klute 1971
Kelly's Heroes 1970
*M*A*S*H* 1970
The Dirty Dozen 1967

"I was always cast as an artistic homicidal maniac."
—On his early roles

JULIE ANDREWS

Born: Julia Elizabeth Wells, October 1, 1935 (Walton-on-Thames, Surrey, England).

Star qualities: Beloved screen icon; popular performer of musicals; early prim-and-proper screen image; stagecraft; pure-sounding singing voice with incredible range; writer; theater director.

An English stage actress, Dame Julie Andrews made the leap to cinema with a pair of prominent early roles in *Mary Poppins* (1964) and *The Sound of Music* (1965). They not only earned her two Academy Award nominations and a Best Actress win for the former, but also established her as one of the most adored screen icons of all time.

Andrews made her mark as a singer and actress in various stage and radio productions, including the London West End musical *My Fair Lady* (1956). Alan Jay Lerner and Frederick Loewe, the composers of *My Fair Lady*, went on to write *Camelot*, in which Andrews starred as Guenevere in the 1960 Broadway production. At a performance of *Camelot*, Walt Disney was in the audience and went backstage after the show to offer Andrews the lead in *Mary Poppins*. She went on to appear in the satire *The Americanization of Emily* (1964) and the screen version of Rodgers and Hammerstein's *The Sound of Music*, but dramatic roles in Alfred Hitchcock's *Torn Curtain* (1966) and *Hawaii* (1966) failed to match her early musical performances in popularity.

Andrews married writer/director Blake Edwards in 1969, appearing in several of his films, including *10* (1979), *S.O.B.* (1981), and *Victor/Victoria* (1982), the last earning her another Academy Award nomination. Sadly, an operation on her vocal chords left her singing voice badly damaged in 1998. While her film output slowed, Andrews began a second career as a children's book author. It was back to children that her most recent parts have taken her, with roles in *The Princess Diaries* (2001) and *The Princess Diaries 2: Royal Engagement* (2004), and as the voice of Queen Lillian in the animated film *Shrek 2* (2004). **JK**

Top Takes...

The Princess Diaries 2: Royal Engagement 2004
Shrek 2 2004
The Princess Diaries 2001
Duet for One 1986
Victor/Victoria 1982 ☆
S.O.B. 1981
Little Miss Marker 1980
10 1979
The Tamarind Seed 1974
Star! 1968
Thoroughly Modern Millie 1967
Hawaii 1966
Torn Curtain 1966
The Sound of Music 1965 ☆
The Americanization of Emily 1964
Mary Poppins 1964 ★

"Films are much more my level. Onstage I never feel quite enough."

ALAIN DELON

Born: Alain Delon, November 8, 1935 (Sceaux, Hauts-de-Seine, France).

Star qualities: Sexy, smoldering good looks; stagecraft; singer; edgy leading man of European thrillers and action films; often plays schizoid villains; writer; director; producer.

Alain Delon was the child of a broken home; he was sent to a series of boarding schools, several of which he was expelled from. At the age of seventeen he joined the French Marines, serving as a parachutist in Indochina. On his return to civilian life he made a visit to the Cannes Film Festival, where he was spotted by a Hollywood talent scout. He turned down a movie contract, choosing to stay in France, where he started to get film parts. He was the first actor to play Patricia Highsmith's Tom Ripley onscreen, in René Clément's *Plein soleil* (1960) (*Purple Noon*), which won him international recognition.

His brand of minimalist callousness, air of inner torment, and good looks swiftly made him an in-demand European star for major directors, frequently as an intriguing blank upon which an audience could project their own interpretations of events and character. In this mode, Delon works especially well with Luchino Visconti in *Rocco e i suoi fratelli* (1960) (*Rocco and His Brothers*), Michelangelo Antonioni in *L'Eclisse* (1962) (*Eclipse*), and Jean-Pierre Melville in *Le Samouraï* (1967) (*The Godson*).

In 1968 Delon and his first wife Nathalie were at the center of a scandal when their bodyguard was found shot dead in a dumpster outside their home. The ensuing investigation threatened to implicate many of France's celebrities and politicians in an intrigue of murder, drugs, and sex. Cleared of all charges, Delon saw his career bounce back. The enormous success of *Borsalino* (1970), a gangster film in which he teams with Jean-Paul Belmondo in a Humphrey Bogart and James Cagney manner, secured him a lasting place in the canon of entertaining French thrillers.

Delon started producing in the 1960s and made his directorial debut in 1981 with *Pour la peau d'un flic* (*For a Cop's Hide*). **KN**

Top Takes...

Les Acteurs 2000 (*Actors*)
Le jour et la nuit 1997 (*Day and Night*)
Un crime 1993 (*A Crime*)
Un amour de Swann 1984 (*Swann in Love*)
Pour la peau d'un flic 1981 (*For a Cop's Hide*)
Monsieur Klein 1976 (*Mr. Klein*)
Flic Story 1975 (*Cop Story*)
Zorro 1975
Borsalino 1970
Le Samouraï 1967 (*The Godson*)
Mélodie en sous-sol 1963
   (*Any Number Can Win*)
L'Eclisse 1962 (*Eclipse*)
Rocco e i suoi fratelli 1960
   (*Rocco and His Brothers*)
Plein soleil 1960 (*Purple Noon*)

"I do very well three things: my job, stupidities, and children."

WOODY ALLEN

Born: Allen Stewart Konigsberg, December 1, 1935 (Brooklyn, New York, U.S.).

Star qualities: Epitome of the neurotic New Yorker; thick black glasses; often plays himself in various guises; small physique; prolific director, writer, actor, musician, playwright, and comedian.

Woody Allen is a moviemaker and comic actor who has produced a feature film a year, often with himself as star, in a virtually unbroken streak dating back to the 1960s. Key to the stereotype he embodies is his slight, balding, and bespectacled physique with a tendency toward pantomime and perpetual worry—so much so, that worry forms the basis of his humor. Verbally dexterous, he isn't leading man material, but he's often center stage in movies, where his neurosis is simultaneously endearing and irritating.

Allen began his career writing jokes and TV shows before his feature debut with *What's Up, Tiger Lily?* in 1966. Never far from the stand-up stage, where he's long been comfortable channeling strong observation through his unimposing person, his smart lines and attitude are what make his movies so memorable, whether he is in front of or behind the camera.

Highlights as an actor include *Bananas* (1971), *Everything You Always Wanted to Know About Sex * But Were Afraid to Ask* (1972), and *Sleeper* (1973), before he reached his mature phase with *Annie Hall* in 1977. That picture earned him an Oscar for writing and direction, and his lone acting nomination on its way to being named Best Picture. It showcased Allen's lifelong concerns with cleverness, wordplay, East versus West Coast sensibilities, the problems of true love, and complications of career success and self-actualization.

A tendency toward darkness (*Manhattan*, 1979) is luckily just one shade in his pictures, which remain memorable because of their humor and strong acting, including *Hannah and Her Sisters* (1986) and *Husbands and Wives* (1992). This tendency is also what allows him to work as an actor on other projects, including a TV remake of *The Sunshine Boys* (1995). **GCQ**

Top Takes…

Scoop 2006
Deconstructing Harry 1997
Mighty Aphrodite 1995
Husbands and Wives 1992
Crimes and Misdemeanors 1989
Radio Days 1987
Hannah and Her Sisters 1986
Broadway Danny Rose 1984
Manhattan 1979
Annie Hall 1977 ☆
Sleeper 1973
*Everything You Always Wanted to Know About Sex * But Were Afraid to Ask* 1972
Play It Again, Sam 1972
Bananas 1971
What's Up, Tiger Lily? 1966

"If my film makes one more person miserable, I'll feel I've done my job."

LEE REMICK

Born: Lee Ann Remick, December 14, 1935 (Quincy, Massachusetts, U.S.); died 1991 (Los Angeles, California, U.S.).

Star qualities: Pretty; svelte; heart-shaped face; wide-eyed; sexy; intelligent; determined; charming; comic timing; versatile leading and character actress.

Top Takes...

Lee Remick was bright-eyed, intelligent, and sexy, but signaled her refusal to go the starlet route—although she was briefly considered as Marilyn Monroe's replacement on the unfinished *Something's Got to Give* (1962)—by not changing her name and seeking out challenging, troubled roles. She studied acting in New York, at Barnard College and the Actors Studio, and made her Broadway debut in *Be Your Age* in 1953.

She made an impression with her film debut as the cunning, ambitious majorette in Elia Kazan's *A Face in the Crowd* (1957), and her dedication was already evident: when they filmed the movie in Arkansas, she lived with a local family and practiced baton twirling so that she would be credible as the teenager. She then followed up with roles in *The Long, Hot Summer* (1958), as the small-town wife, Eula Varner; in the Western melodrama *These Thousand Hills* (1959); and put in an ambiguous, provocative turn as the supposed rape victim who has to be persuaded to wear a girdle on the witness stand in *Anatomy of a Murder* (1959). Her finest moment, however, came when she played a memorable crash-diving alcoholic opposite Jack Lemmon in *Days of Wine and Roses* (1962), for which she earned an Academy Award nomination for Best Actress. As a star, Remick clinched with Montgomery Clift in *Wild River* (1960), was kidnapped as Temple Drake in *Sanctuary* (1961), was cattily funny with James Garner in the screwball *The Wheeler Dealers* (1963), and got together with ex-con Steve McQueen in yet another steamy small town in *Baby the Rain Must Fall* (1965). Most of Remick's best work of her later career was on television (*Hustling*, 1975; *The Women's Room*, 1980; and *The Letter*, 1982), although many remember her in the horror feature *The Omen* (1976). **KN**

"As an actress I feel crazy [but] I would feel far more crazy if I were not an actress."

BURT REYNOLDS

Born: Burton Leon Reynolds Jr., February 11, 1936 (Lansing, Michigan, U.S.).

Star qualities: Male sex symbol; rugged looks; hairy chest; muscular physique; leading man of action films; number one box-office draw; enduring Hollywood star; writer; producer; director.

Appearing as a male centerfold in *Cosmopolitan* magazine in April 1972, Burt Reynolds was a thirty-six-year-old pinup, celebrated for his performance as Lewis Medlock, the macho outdoorsman in John Boorman's backwoods adventure movie *Deliverance* (1972). A onetime football star at Florida State, he suffered a knee injury that ended his prospects with the Baltimore Colts. With his muscled, hairy chest and squinty face, Reynolds personified a new turn to overt sexuality in mainstream cinema, his intelligent yet action-oriented persona fitting the bill perfectly.

Having spent the previous 13 years performing on television in series such as *Riverboat* (1959–1960) and *Gunsmoke* (1962–1965) and in a few movies (*100 Rifles*, 1969), Reynolds progressed from *Deliverance* to become one of the most popular stars of the late 1970s and early 1980s. His best-known vehicles from this period include *The Longest Yard* (1974), *Smokey and the Bandit* (1977), *The Cannonball Run* (1981), and *The Best Little Whorehouse in Texas* (1982).

For a while Reynolds could do no wrong: he was the number one box-office star in the world for five years in a row, and ranked among the Top Ten box-office stars in the world for 13 years. But then his name suddenly became synonymous with box-office flops, and Reynolds returned to his original medium, television. He was reborn on the small screen with the sitcom *Evening Shade* (1991–1993), for which he won an Emmy Award. Subsequently, he appeared in hits such as *The Dukes of Hazzard* (2005). The gem of his later years has been his role as porn film director Jack Horner in *Boogie Nights* (1997), which gained him an Academy Award nomination for Best Supporting Actor. **GCQ**

Top Takes…

The Dukes of Hazzard 2005
The Longest Yard 2005
***Boogie Nights* 1997** ☆
Striptease 1996
Heat 1986
City Heat 1984
The Best Little Whorehouse in Texas 1982
Sharky's Machine 1981
The Cannonball Run 1981
Smokey and the Bandit 1977
Nickelodeon 1976
Lucky Lady 1975
Hustle 1975
The Longest Yard 1974
Deliverance 1972
Fuzz 1972

1930s

"If you hold on to things long enough, they get back into style. Like me."

DEAN STOCKWELL

Born: Robert Dean Stockwell, March 5, 1936 (Hollywood, California, U.S.).

Star qualities: Photogenic cute child actor; one of the few child stars to have a lifelong career; natural acting style; mature versatile character actor playing eccentrics and outcasts; designer and artist; writer; producer; director.

Top Takes...

Dean Stockwell comes from an acting family: his father, Harry Stockwell, was a singer and actor, the voice of the Prince in Walt Disney's animated classic *Snow White and the Seven Dwarfs* (1937), and his stepmother, Nina Olivette, was a singer and dancer in vaudeville. Olivette took Dean and his brother, Guy, to a Broadway audition for *The Innocent Voyage* (1943), which was looking to hire about a dozen children. Both boys were cast in the show.

Photogenic, and with fair, curly hair, Dean was soon signed up by MGM and became a busy child actor in the 1940s and 1950s. He played the eleven-year-old son of Gregory Peck in *Gentleman's Agreement* (1947) and the privileged lad thrown into the company of men in the Western *Cattle Drive* (1951). He successfully segued to heavy dramatic adult roles such as one of the killers in *Compulsion* (1959), underplaying powerfully beside more flamboyant costars.

He then spent the next 20 years on television doing shows such as *Dr. Kildare* (1965), and occasional movies like the spooky *The Dunwich Horror* (1970). Then, in an inspired piece of casting, Wim Wenders picked him to play Walt in *Paris, Texas* (1984), and reminded Hollywood how versatile an actor Stockwell was. Since the success of that movie, Stockwell has been cool casting in a wide range of film and television projects. He is an unforgettable sleaze miming to "In Dreams" in David Lynch's *Blue Velvet* (1986), and his role as genial mafia boss in the comedy *Married to the Mob* (1988) led to an Academy Award nomination for Best Supporting Actor. He also went on to achieve cult TV-show star status as hologram Rear Admiral Al Calavicci in the U.S. series *Quantum Leap* (1989–1993). **KN**

> "I hate to admit it but you can't do a role unless it's somewhere in your psyche."

1930s

DENNIS HOPPER

Born: Dennis Lee Hopper, May 17, 1936 (Dodge City, Kansas, U.S.).

Star qualities: Infamous *enfant terrible*; hero of counterculture; comeback kid; character actor *par excellence*; plays psychotic villains; unconventional; intense screen presence; writer; director; painter and photographer.

Dennis Hopper has had so many careers that it's difficult to select which to analyze: Hopper as 1950s young Hollywood hotshot, 1960s hippie counterculture cine-revolutionary, 1970s drug burnout, 1980s comeback superstar, or 1990s (and beyond) clichéd, crazed villain-for-hire?

Hopper has had a fascinatingly varied livelihood, although his manic intensity has faded with age. He began as a friend of James Dean, appearing in *Rebel Without a Cause* (1955) and *Giant* (1956), before going on to spend much of the 1950s and 1960s in episodic TV and B movies. He made his directing debut with the celebrated hippie biker road-trip opus *Easy Rider* (1969) before then exploding into ego supernova with the infamous follow-up *The Last Movie* (1971). Hopper spent much of the 1970s and early 1980s battling a serious drug and alcohol addiction. Yet this period contains some of his best work, both as an actor in films such as Wim Wenders's *Der amerikanische Freund* (1977) (*The American Friend*), and as director of *Out of the Blue* (1980), in which he also stars.

Hopper made a comeback in the mid-1980s with a remarkable quartet of performances: completely unnerving as Frank Booth in *Blue Velvet* (1986); the town drunk in *Hoosiers* (1986), which won him an Academy Award nomination; another great role as Feck in *River's Edge* (1986); and memorably over-the-top in *The Texas Chainsaw Massacre 2* (1986). Hopper's work since then—as both actor and director—has been largely undistinguished, consisting principally of stock bad guys in genre films both good, such as *Speed* (1994), and bad, such as *Waterworld* (1995). Offbeat supporting roles in edgy fare such as *Basquiat* (1996) seem to be this unconventional star's remaining niche of interest. **TC**

Top Takes...

Basquiat 1996
Speed 1994
True Romance 1993
Hoosiers 1986 ☆
River's Edge 1986
Blue Velvet 1986
The Texas Chainsaw Massacre 2 1986
Rumble Fish 1983
Out of the Blue 1980
Apocalypse Now 1979
Der amerikanische Freund 1977
   (*The American Friend*)
The Last Movie 1971
True Grit 1969
Easy Rider 1969
Rebel Without a Cause 1955

"There is no evil in me, I just wear tight underwear."

—On why he plays such bad characters

ROBERT REDFORD

Born: Charles Robert Redford Jr., August 18, 1936 (Santa Monica, California, U.S.).

Star qualities: Pinup good looks and all-around sex appeal; a top box-office draw; famous pairings with Paul Newman; genuine environmentalist and lover of nature; an inspiration to innovative and independent filmmakers; director.

Top Takes...

Spy Game 2001
The Horse Whisperer 1998
Indecent Proposal 1993
Sneakers 1992
Out of Africa 1985
The Natural 1984
Brubaker 1980
The Electric Horseman 1979
A Bridge Too Far 1977
All the President's Men 1976
Three Days of the Condor 1975
The Great Waldo Pepper 1975
The Great Gatsby 1974
The Sting 1973 ☆
The Way We Were 1973
Jeremiah Johnson 1972
The Candidate 1972
The Hot Rock 1972
Downhill Racer 1969
Butch Cassidy and the Sundance Kid 1969
Barefoot in the Park 1967

Born in California, the original golden boy was a teen athlete who won a baseball scholarship to the University of Colorado, which he subsequently lost because of public drunkenness. He studied at the Pratt Institute of Art and at the American Academy of Dramatic Arts in New York, where he met Lola Van Wagenen, his wife and the mother of his four children. They would eventually divorce, one of his children would die in infancy, and much of his private life would be carefully preserved behind a sheen of mystery and near secrecy, so much so that he is often depicted as a recluse when not otherwise engaged in film-related activities, often through intermediaries acting on his behalf.

Typifying a certain vision of southern California—the sandy-haired beachcomber, comfortable in his skin, obviously handsome but not hung up on his looks, reserved, slow to speak, clean—Redford first found his way on the stage and into television, and finally into movies by the 1960s. His breakthrough was *Butch Cassidy and the Sundance Kid* (1969), his first pairing with Paul Newman, a lifelong friend and

RIGHT: Redford and Newman in the timeless classic *Butch Cassidy and the Sundance Kid*.

collaborator whose ascendance into the pantheon of movie actors may be a source of envy for Redford, whose own skills in front of the camera have rarely been celebrated beyond comments about his physique. Regardless, box-office success followed, along with global popularity, in *The Way We Were* (1973) with Barbra Streisand, *Jeremiah Johnson* (1972), *All the President's Men* (1976), and another run alongside Newman, as Johnny Hooker in the Best Picture Oscar-winning movie *The Sting* (1973). By the end of the 1970s Redford had become a mature performer, the envy of many men for his natural good looks and ease with the ladies, and the fantasy mate of many women for exactly the same reason.

ABOVE: Uncovering the Watergate scandal in *All the President's Men*.

"I've always been an extremely impatient actor . . . . Waiting around drove me nuts."

Despite this apparent plateau in his chosen career—not to overlook his commercial appeal and varying levels of artistic

The Outdoors Man

Despite his status as one of the world's most well-known movie stars, Robert Redford has consciously channeled his energies away from Hollywood toward his interests in conservation, environmental issues, and Native American rights.

- The center of his activism has been in Utah, where he has lived since 1963. He built his first home there using the proceeds from his work on *Butch Cassidy and the Sundance Kid* and *Downhill Racer*. He chose an area near Provo, called "Timphaven" (which he renamed "Sundance" after his character in the movie) to build a ranch and modest ski resort. In 1980, he set up the Sundance Institute for budding independent filmmakers in Park City, Utah.

- Redford is a founding board member of the Natural Resources Defense Council and has been involved in raising public awareness and lobbying the government about environmental issues such as solar energy. He has won many awards for this work, including the United Nations Global 500 Award, the Audubon Medal, and the Earth Day International Award.

- A very private person, Redford has always tended to shun the spotlight and tried to keep his movie star persona and his private persona apart. The passionate lover of the outdoors has commented: "Some people have analysis. I have Utah."

integrity in films, including *The Electric Horseman* (1979), *The Natural* (1984), *Out of Africa* (1985), *Sneakers* (1992), and the all-but-laughable *Indecent Proposal* (1993)—Redford's surprise turn was a two-pronged attempt to carve a unique niche in history. First off was his move from the actor's life under the spotlight to the director's chair, first demonstrated to great acclaim in *Ordinary People* (1980), a story of family disaster and an Oscar winner for both Best Picture and Director. This was followed by *A River Runs Through It* (1992), in which he directed the golden boy heir-apparent, Brad Pitt; *Quiz Show* (1994), another highly lauded film critical of the mass media's influence on ethics; and *The Horse Whisperer* (1998), a kind of Western.

Setting up Sundance

Redford's second surprise turn was an altruistically motivated interest in fostering a true filmmaking community of amateur and professional craftspeople who would exchange ideas in a commune-like workshop setting, to develop a less crassly commercial product than that produced by Hollywood. So the Sundance Institute was established in 1980 to assist aspirant filmmakers to create and fund their projects, although by the mid-1990s this genuinely benevolent organization finally devolved into being just another marketplace for buying and selling product. In 1997 Redford set up a cinema chain, Sundance Cinemas, with a major distributor to screen independent films. In 2002 he was given an Honorary Academy Award as "creator of Sundance, inspiration to independent and innovative filmmakers everywhere."

In the end, Redford is an enigma, a movie star whose success has long rested on being larger than life, while at the same time remarkably shy and reluctant to participate in the public relations process so central to the fame and fortune of his peers. Perhaps this is a lesson about discretion. Or maybe it's a sign of an ego that has had its fill of adulation. Most importantly, it may be sanity and humility requesting us to judge an artist on his merits and good works rather than on gossip and "personality." **GCQ**

RIGHT: Redford successfully renewing his partnership with Paul Newman in *The Sting*.

1930s

VANESSA REDGRAVE

Born: Vanessa Redgrave, January 30, 1937 (London, England).

Star qualities: Auburn hair; tall and lean; husky voice; stagecraft; part of a famous acting dynasty; opts for challenging roles over box-office draws; intelligent; brave; outspoken political and human rights activist; producer.

Top Takes…

"I am misrepresented very often, but so is everybody who has got something to say."

Vanessa Redgrave is part of a theatrical dynasty. Her parents were Sir Michael Redgrave and Rachel Kempson. Her sister, Lynn Redgrave, and her brother, Corin Redgrave, are also acclaimed actors. Vanessa Redgrave's daughters, Natasha Richardson and Joely Richardson, are respected actresses, and her son, Carlo Nero, is a writer and film director. Redgrave studied drama at London's Central School of Speech and Drama and made her first appearance on the West End stage in 1958, playing opposite her father.

She established herself as an exciting screen actress and an intellectual pinup with a flurry of varied roles, most of which required her to let her long red hair down in one way or another. She played a wary ex-wife seduced back into an infantile relationship in *Morgan: A Suitable Case for Treatment* (1966), a flirtatious Anne Boleyn in *A Man for All Seasons* (1966), a neurotic woman of mystery in *Blowup* (1966), a beheaded monarch in *Mary, Queen of Scots* (1971), and a possessed hunchbacked nun in *The Devils* (1971).

Always drawn to dramatic gestures and period settings, Redgrave also became renowned as a political activist; among her heavyweight items was *Julia* (1977), about a woman murdered by the Nazi regime prior to World War II for her antifascist activism. The film won her an Academy Award for Best Supporting Actress; she has had five other nominations throughout her career. Nonetheless, she has also slipped in some more entertaining features such as *Murder on the Orient Express* (1974). In mature years, she has taken acidic cameos that can utilize her distinctive croaky voice, such as in *Prick Up Your Ears* (1987), and sailed indomitably through literary adaptations such as *Howards End* (1992). **KN**

1930s

WARREN BEATTY

Born: Henry Warren Beaty, March 30, 1937 (Richmond, Virginia, U.S.).

Star qualities: Clean-cut looks; tall, slim, handsome; charisma; intelligent; ladies' man; dramatic and romantic lead actor; activist in liberal politics; writer; producer; Oscar-winning director.

The brother of actress Shirley MacLaine, the boyishly beautiful Warren Beatty is now probably better known for his past offscreen love life than for the sensitively nuanced characterizations scattered throughout a frustratingly uneven acting and directing career.

His mother was a drama teacher and his father an academic. Not to be outdone by his sister, he went to study acting under Stanislavsky Method proponent Stella Adler. After a stint on Broadway and TV, he first made a mark with Method-like performances in *Splendor in the Grass* (1961), *All Fall Down* (1962), and *Lilith* (1964). Beatty then hit his stride in two movies for Arthur Penn: *Mickey One* (1965), then *Bonnie and Clyde* (1967), which he also produced. The latter film was nominated for a staggering ten Academy Awards. The success and influence of that fashionably antiestablishment gangster yarn made him a major Hollywood player, and the 1970s saw him at his peak: note perfect as the shy, lovelorn gambler in *McCabe & Mrs. Miller* (1971); deeply ambiguous as the investigative journalist in *The Parallax View* (1974); and interrogating his own reputation as a lothario in *Shampoo* (1975), which he cowrote.

Beatty directed himself in the deft comedy *Heaven Can Wait* (1978) and the ambitious political biopic *Reds* (1981), which won him an Oscar for Best Director; but thereafter he has acted, produced, and directed only fitfully—and with scant artistic or commercial success. Only his genuinely unsettling playing of the gangster protagonist in *Bugsy* (1991) and of the disillusioned Democratic senator in his own political satire *Bulworth* (1998) have shown traces of the acutely alert intelligence of his earlier work. He married actress Annette Bening in 1992, and the couple have four children. **GA**

Top Takes...

Bulworth 1998
***Bugsy* 1991** ☆
Dick Tracy 1990
***Reds* 1981** ☆
***Heaven Can Wait* 1978** ☆
Shampoo 1975
The Parallax View 1974
McCabe & Mrs. Miller 1971
***Bonnie and Clyde* 1967** ☆
Mickey One 1965
Lilith 1964
All Fall Down 1962
The Roman Spring of Mrs. Stone 1961
Splendor in the Grass 1961

1930s

"I'm old, I'm young, I'm intelligent, I'm stupid. My tide goes in and out."

JACK NICHOLSON

Born: John Joseph Nicholson, April 22, 1937 (Manhattan, New York, U.S.).

Star qualities: Intelligent, charming, and a good sport; shark-like grin teamed with sunglasses; has given many of the most memorable movie performances; an arresting presence onscreen; ardent basketball fan.

Top Takes...

The Departed 2006

Something's Gotta Give 2003

Anger Management 2003

About Schmidt 2002 ☆

As Good as It Gets 1997 ★

Mars Attacks! 1996

The Crossing Guard 1995

Hoffa 1992

A Few Good Men 1992 ☆

Batman 1989

Ironweed 1987 ☆

Prizzi's Honor 1985 ☆

Terms of Endearment 1983 ★

Reds 1981 ☆

The Postman Always Rings Twice 1981

The Shining 1980

One Flew Over the Cuckoo's Nest 1975 ★

Tommy 1975

Chinatown 1974 ☆

The Last Detail 1973 ☆

Five Easy Pieces 1970 ☆

Easy Rider 1969 ☆

Psych-Out 1968

Ensign Pulver 1964

The Little Shop of Horrors 1960

RIGHT: Nicholson is terrifying as insane hotel caretaker Jack Torrance in *The Shining*.

If calm means being free of agitation, and if cool means the state of being fashionable and attractive, then Jack Nicholson possesses calmness and cool in the same way that oceans are filled with cups of water. He has long been (and still is) the definition of Hollywood manhood.

Yet a single glance fails to recommend him. He's got a receding hairline and black hair that refuses the straight lines of comb or brush. He generally looks unkempt, even when clothed in the finest wardrobe and with makeup applied by the surest hand. He's not particularly tall. Nor is he muscular. His dominant feature is a rakish smile, accompanied by intense, drilling eyes that are often covered by sunglasses. And he's given to a soft belly, easy anger, and a general sense of intelligent superiority that serves him equally as a whip and a magnet for the people around him.

Nicholson was raised as his grandmother's son, with his mother playing the part of the older sister, or so the story goes. He was married once for six years in the 1960s, but since then he has managed a smart bachelorhood, dating different women, having children with several of them, but always

keeping his home to himself without the legal demands of so-called connubial bliss.

ABOVE: Nicholson on Oscar-winning form in *One Flew Over the Cuckoo's Nest*.

He's written, produced, and directed a handful of movies, and he is reputed to have one of the sharpest minds in the industry. One story recounts an avid fan approaching him in a restaurant and passing a note of praise, only to have the note returned with corrections about misused syntax. So Nicholson is both star and thinker, a celebrity and a curiosity, which is easy enough to see in his annual devotion to the Los Angeles Lakers, an accepted series of interruptions in the production schedules of several movies over the years. But Nicholson is most of all an actor of unusually high regard.

"With my sunglasses on, I'm Jack Nicholson. Without them, I'm fat and seventy."

His early career featured mostly forgettable roles in mostly forgettable movies (Dolan in *Ensign Pulver*, 1964), although there

Jack Trivia

Jack Nicholson's popularity as an actor has spanned five decades, and he has been nominated for an Oscar in each of those decades, starting in the 1960s. With his seventh nomination for *As Good as It Gets* (1997), he overtook Laurence Olivier as the most-nominated actor ever (he now has 12 nominations). The enduring star remains in demand with filmmakers and is a surefire draw at the box office.

- Nickname is Mulholland Drive—where he lives—aka "Bad Boys' Drive" because residents there have included Marlon Brando and Warren Beatty.

- Childhood friend of actor and director Danny DeVito. Relatives of both actors ran a hairdressing business together.

- Owns a substantial art collection that includes works by Pablo Picasso and Tamara de Lempicka.

- An avid Los Angeles Lakers fan, he never misses a home game. Producers on his movies have to work the shooting schedule around that of the actor's favorite basketball team.

- His longest relationship was with actress Anjelica Huston; they were together for 17 years. The relationship ended when the media reported that Rebecca Broussard was pregnant with his child.

- Although his role in *The Shining* failed to attract an Oscar nomination, it remains one of his best performances.

were TV spots (*Dr. Kildare*, 1966) and a few films now reconsidered as cult classics for his involvement through the rosy lens of hindsight (*The Little Shop of Horrors*, 1960; *Psych-Out*, 1968). Falling in with a certain independent fervor then sweeping through the film industry in the 1960s, Nicholson saw his star finally begin its historic rise in 1969 with his supporting turn as George Hanson in *Easy Rider* (Academy Award and Golden Globe nominee).

Classic performances

Nicholson quickly cemented his personality in the changing world of U.S. movies, signaling a new golden age; he starred in some of the most memorable and major films of that period. Titles include *Five Easy Pieces* (1970), *The Last Detail* (1973), *Chinatown* (1974), *Tommy* (1975), *One Flew Over the Cuckoo's Nest* (1975), and *The Shining* (1980), after which this golden age dissolved beneath the resurgence of studios now controlled by newly formed mass-media conglomerates.

Still, Nicholson's position atop the talent hierarchy continued unabated. In movies as varied as *Reds* (1981), *Terms of Endearment* (1983), *Prizzi's Honor* (1985), *Batman* (1989), *A Few Good Men* (1992), *Mars Attacks!* (1996), *As Good as It Gets* (1997), and *Something's Gotta Give* (2003), he has proven to be versatile—both sinister and sensitive—while helping earn box-office dollars and critical accolades. **GCQ**

RIGHT: Winning his third Oscar as neurotic author Melvin Udall in *As Good as It Gets*.

MORGAN FREEMAN

Born: Morgan Freeman, June 1, 1937 (Memphis, Tennessee, U.S.).

Star qualities: Huge talent who has crossed the racial divide; gravitas and calm demeanor; mellifluous voice; respected lead and character actor; often plays wise characters; director; producer.

A former children's TV personality turned Best Supporting Actor Academy Award winner for his role as the old-timer ex-boxer Eddie "Scrap Iron" Dupris in *Million Dollar Baby* (2004), Morgan Freeman is a singular figure in modern Hollywood for having crossed both the color and age barriers on his way to a highly regarded acting career.

Stage trained, Freeman first tasted fame on TV but became truly memorable as a cruel pimp in *Street Smart* (1987), which won him an Oscar nomination for Best Supporting Actor. Having explored the career path of most African-American actors up to that time, he was now more fully able to widen his range. From the late 1980s onward he capitalized on new opportunities to maximum effect: *Glory* (1989), in which he played a Union soldier during the U.S. Civil War; *Lean on Me* (1989), where he was an inner-city educator; *Driving Miss Daisy* (1989), playing the chauffeur for an aged Southern woman, which garnered him another Oscar nomination, this time for Best Actor; and *The Shawshank Redemption* (1994), in which he played a prison mate who befriends a falsely accused banker portrayed by Tim Robbins. Freeman earned his third Oscar nomination for this role. These important roles opened a new world, making Freeman synonymous with quality screen acting, a remarkable achievement not only for a black actor, but also for an actor past fifty years of age.

Since then he has alternated a mix of sinister roles, as in *Dreamcatcher* (2003), with more heroic fare such as *Se7en* (1995), once even playing God in *Bruce Almighty* (2003). Freeman works constantly and has enjoyed a secondary career narrating such films as *La Marche de l'empereur* (2005) (*March of the Penguins*) and *Slavery and the Making of America* (2005). **GCQ**

Top Takes...

Million Dollar Baby 2004 ★
The Big Bounce 2004
Bruce Almighty 2003
Dreamcatcher 2003
Along Came a Spider 2001
Amistad 1997
Kiss the Girls 1997
Se7en 1995
The Shawshank Redemption 1994 ☆
Unforgiven 1992
The Bonfire of the Vanities 1990
Glory 1989
Driving Miss Daisy 1989 ☆
Lean on Me 1989
Street Smart 1987 ☆
Brubaker 1980

"I've been living with myself all of my life . . . . So when I watch me, all I see is me. It's boring."

DUSTIN HOFFMAN

Born: Dustin Lee Hoffman, August 8, 1937 (Los Angeles, California, U.S.).

Star qualities: Immensely versatile actor; renowned for taking on difficult and less glamorous roles; youthful looks; extensive playing range; a diligent, and often perfectionist, character actor who carefully researches his roles.

Top Takes...

Meet the Fockers 2004
Finding Neverland 2004
Confidence 2003
Moonlight Mile 2002
Wag the Dog 1997 ☆
American Buffalo 1996
Hook 1991
Billy Bathgate 1991
Dick Tracy 1990
Family Business 1989
Rain Man 1988 ★
Ishtar 1987
Tootsie 1982 ☆
Kramer vs. Kramer 1979 ★
Agatha 1979
Straight Time 1978
Marathon Man 1976
All the President's Men 1976
Lenny 1974 ☆
Papillon 1973
Straw Dogs 1971
Little Big Man 1970
Midnight Cowboy 1969 ☆
The Graduate 1967 ☆
The Tiger Makes Out 1967

RIGHT: Hoffman based his shy character in *Papillon* on the movie's screenwriter.

Dustin Hoffman was the epitome of baby boomer naivete directly after *The Graduate* in 1967, when he somehow captured the essence of a generation despite being a bit too old for the part in actual fact. His slight build, short stature, unconventionally handsome features, and brown eyes opening into a nervous soul have all served him well in a career that has spanned 40 years and numerous important roles that have made him a critical favorite and audience magnet.

After graduating from high school, Hoffman attended junior college and performed at the Pasadena Playhouse. Dissatisfied, he moved to New York City and became a proponent of the Method during his time with the Actors Studio. Some theater work and commercials led to a few bit parts in TV shows (*Naked City*, 1961–1963; *The Defenders*, 1962–1965) and a movie (*The Tiger Makes Out*, 1967), when up-and-coming director Mike Nichols cast him as Benjamin Braddock in *The Graduate*, his first Oscar nomination. The part proved career making, firmly planting Hoffman in the bedrock of the zeitgeist, then consumed with countercultural lifestyles and expressions, and finding a way to rejuvenate a moribund industry in Hollywood.

1930s

ABOVE: Hoffman in 1974 portraying the controversial stand-up comic Lenny Bruce.

Awash with popularity, he finished the 1960s with a showy performance as Ratso Rizzo in *Midnight Cowboy* (1969), another Oscar nod, and began a 20-year run of almost absolute critical luminescence until *Rain Man* in 1988, his second Academy Award win. In between, he notched up performances in *Little Big Man* (1970), *Straw Dogs* (1971), *Papillon* (1973), *Lenny* (1974), *All the President's Men*, *Marathon Man* (both 1976), *Kramer vs. Kramer* (1979), his first Oscar win, *Tootsie* (1982), and the unexpected critical and commercial failure of *Ishtar* (1987).

Having established his bona fides in both comedy and drama, his career since 1990 has been a careful give and take between the two styles. Continuing in the mold of the intense young man he was, he's been in *Billy Bathgate* (1991), *American Buffalo* (1996), and *Moonlight Mile* (2002). He's also enjoyed remarkable traction as a funny man in *Hook* (1991), *Wag the Dog* (1997), and especially in *Meet the Fockers* (2004). **GCQ**

Struggling Young Actors

Dustin Hoffman is close friends with actor Gene Hackman. They met at the Pasadena Playhouse in 1956, where they were both voted by their class as "The Least Likely to Succeed." After three months, Hackman left for New York to pursue stage acting. Following in Hackman's footsteps, Hoffman went and stayed at Hackman's one-bedroom apartment, sleeping on the kitchen floor. It was meant to be for only a few nights, but Hoffman wouldn't leave. Hackman had to help him find his own apartment in the end. Despite their long friendship, they did not appear onscreen together until *Runaway Jury* (2003).

VIRNA LISI

Born: Virna Lisa Pieralisi, September 8, 1937 (Ancona, Marches, Italy).

Star qualities: Grande dame of Italian cinema; blonde, blue-eyed beauty; slim and sexy; gravitas; stagecraft; youthful romantic lead and mature lead character actress and supporting player.

Top Takes...

Va' dove ti porta il cuore 1996
 (*Follow Your Heart*)
La Reine Margot 1994 (*Queen Margot*)
Ernesto 1979
Bluebeard 1972
Un beau monstre 1971 (*Love Me Strangely*)
The Statue 1971
If It's Tuesday, This Must Be Belgium 1969
Not with My Wife, You Don't! 1966
Assault on a Queen 1966
Casanova '70 1965
How to Murder Your Wife 1965
La Tulipe noire 1964 (*The Black Tulip*)
Eva 1962
Romolo e Remo 1961 (*Duel of the Titans*)

More than 50 years since her screen debut in *E Napoli canta* (1953), Virna Lisi has established herself as the grande dame of Italian cinema. Lisi quickly developed into one of Italy's leading female talents, eventually coming to a wider public fame with her work on *Romolo e Remo* (1961) (*Duel of the Titans*), in Joseph Losey's *Eva* (1962), starring opposite Alain Delon in *La Tulipe noire* (1963) (*The Black Tulip*), and working with Marcello Mastroianni in *Casanova '70* (1965).

Having made her U.S. film debut working with Jack Lemmon on *How to Murder Your Wife* (1965), the blonde, slim Lisi was not a stereotypical statuesque Italian *maggiorata*, and her stint in Hollywood was to be neither long nor overly successful. Despite having starred opposite the likes of Frank Sinatra in *Assault on a Queen* (1966) and Tony Curtis in *Not with My Wife, You Don't!* (1966), she found herself typecast as the blue-eyed, blonde love interest. In 1968 she was offered the title role of *Barbarella*, but she turned it down, deciding instead to return to her native Italy in the hope of finding more interesting work. (The role was later filled by Jane Fonda.) Once in Italy, Lisi divided her energies between theater, film, and television, and successfully found work in pan-European coproductions. A continued screen presence, she has used the passing years to add depth and gravitas to her craft, garnering acclaim for *Al di là del bene del male* (1977) (*Beyond Good and Evil*), *Ernesto* (1979), and for the role of her career as the cruel, scheming Catherine de Medici in the historical drama *La Reine Margot* (1994) (*Queen Margot*), for which she won the Cannes Film Festival Best Actress Award, a César for Best Supporting Actress, and a David di Donatello, the Italian version of an Oscar. **RH**

> "[As Medici] Lisi exudes venom ... in a performance that is so convincingly spiteful."—*DVD Times*

JANE FONDA

Born: Lady Jayne Seymour Fonda, December 21, 1937 (New York City, New York, U.S.).

Star qualities: "Hanoi Jane"; youthful, blonde sex symbol; mature leading lady playing character roles; fitness guru; outspoken political activist; part of an acting dynasty; writer; producer.

Jane Fonda is the daughter of legendary movie star Henry Fonda and New York socialite Frances Seymour Brokaw. She entered movies in the 1960s in a string of blonde sex-kitten roles, often modeling revealing, fetishist outfits such as the outer-space fashions of *Barbarella* (1968). An accomplished light comedienne in *Barefoot in the Park* (1967) and, later, wonderfully wry and smart in *Fun with Dick and Jane* (1977), Fonda worked hard in heavier dramatic roles, damping down her effervescence for Oscar bait such as *They Shoot Horses, Don't They?* (1969), *Klute* (1971), *Julia* (1977), *Coming Home* (1978), and *On Golden Pond* (1981).

Offscreen, Fonda has always been in the news. She has a reputation as a political radical, and her vehement opposition to the United States's involvement in the Vietnam War earned her the sobriquet "Hanoi Jane." In the 1980s she became an exercise guru, initiating the aerobic-exercise craze with her book and video cassette, *Jane Fonda's Workout*. She now admits to having suffered from the eating disorder bulimia from the ages of thirteen to thirty-seven. She has been married and divorced three times: to director Roger Vadim, politician Tom Hayden, and CNN founder Ted Turner. All of this has tended to cloud appreciation of her performances. Despite working with Jean-Luc Godard in *Tout va bien* (1972) (*All's Well*) and the occasional art film such as *Steelyard Blues* (1973), Fonda's left-wing politics has been inclined to come through onscreen in tidy, entertaining liberal movies such as *The China Syndrome* (1979), *The Electric Horseman* (1979), and *Nine to Five* (1980). After appearing old-fashioned in earnest vehicles such as *Stanley & Iris* (1990), she retired but made a comeback as a diva wannabe in *Monster-in-Law* (2005). **KN**

Top Takes...

Monster-in-Law 2005
Stanley & Iris 1990
The Morning After 1986 ☆
On Golden Pond 1981 ☆
Nine to Five 1980
The Electric Horseman 1979
The China Syndrome 1979 ☆
Coming Home 1978 ★
Julia 1977 ☆
Fun with Dick and Jane 1977
Steelyard Blues 1973
Tout va bien 1972 (*All's Well*)
Klute 1971 ★
They Shoot Horses, Don't They? 1969 ☆
Barbarella 1968
Barefoot in the Park 1967

"Working in Hollywood does give one a certain expertise in the field of prostitution."

ANTHONY HOPKINS

Born: Philip Anthony Hopkins, December 31, 1937 (Margam, Port Talbot, West Glamorgan, Wales).

Star qualities: Natural style of delivery belies the immense amount of preparation he puts into his roles; soft-spoken, intense, and distinguished British actor.

Top Takes...

RIGHT: Hopkins in his most infamous role as Hannibal Lecter in *The Silence of the Lambs*.

Anthony Hopkins didn't really emerge as a fully-fledged movie star until his Oscar-winning turn as Hannibal Lecter in *The Silence of the Lambs* (1991). Suddenly, his sucking noises and nonspecific evil accent were being imitated, and the long-serving character actor was a bogeyman to set beside Freddy Krueger. However, he had been working with distinction since the 1960s—with important early work as Richard the Lion-Heart in *The Lion in Winter* (1968) and Pierre Bezuhov in an epic BBC TV production of *War & Peace* (1972).

Hopkins tried being an action hero in *When Eight Bells Toll* (1971), but stayed mostly on the stage or TV for the 1970s, doing serious courtroom miniseries efforts as the plaintiff in *QB VII* (1974) and the accused in *The Lindbergh Kidnapping Case* (1976), and making occasional oddball movies such as *Audrey Rose* (1977). He is remarkably good as the mad ventriloquist in *Magic* (1978) and the dedicated, self-doubting doctor in *The Elephant Man* (1980).

Despite a smattering of self-consciously "small," put-upon characters in the sincere likes of *The Good Father* (1985), *84 Charing Cross Road* (1987), and *Spotswood* (1992), Hopkins has

1930s

ABOVE: Hopkins giving a very restrained performance in *The Remains of the Day*.

mostly sought out larger-than-life, bigger-than-history roles like Lloyd George (*Young Winston*, 1972), Yitzhak Rabin (*Victory at Entebbe*, 1976), Adolf Hitler (*The Bunker*, 1981), Quasimodo (*The Hunchback of Notre Dame*, 1982), Captain Bligh (*The Bounty*, 1984), traitor spy Guy Burgess (*Blunt*, 1985), Richard Nixon (*Nixon*, 1995), Pablo Picasso (*Surviving Picasso*, 1996), John Quincy Adams (*Amistad*, 1997), Zorro (*The Mask of Zorro*, 1998), and Titus Andronicus (*Titus*, 1999). His great strength in these big roles is his wry underplaying—he only rarely succumbs to the temptation to ham (notably as Van Helsing in *Bram Stoker's Dracula*, 1992).

After Lecter—reprised as a comedy turn in sequels *Hannibal* (2001) and *Red Dragon* (2002)—Hopkins was in demand, often bringing inner fire to repressed Brits (*Howards End*, 1992; *Shadowlands* and *The Remains of the Day*, both 1993). In tribute to his acting talents, he was knighted in 1993. **KN**

Being Hannibal

Many of Hannibal Lecter's mannerisms in *The Silence of the Lambs* were improvised by Hopkins himself: the unnerving effect on Jodie Foster when he mocks her character's West Virginia accent, his distortion of the word "chianti," and the vile slurping sound he makes. Hopkins won an Oscar for his unforgettable performance, even though he was only onscreen for 15 minutes, the shortest ever to win a Best Actor Oscar. Hopkins has remarked of the serial killer character, "I think he might be a very interesting person to have lunch with, provided that 'you' weren't the lunch."

OLIVER REED

Born: Robert Oliver Reed, February 13, 1938 (Wimbledon, London, England); died 1999 (Valletta, Malta).

Star qualities: Muscular macho man; deep voice; animal magnetism; electric screen presence; outspoken hell-raiser; extraordinary raconteur.

Top Takes…

1930s

Evaluating the careers of actors such as Oliver Reed is a difficult task, as with other cinematic eccentrics like Klaus Kinski and Christopher Walken. Reed loved to work regularly, no matter the role, and he took on many projects that were beneath his talents. There's also Reed's larger-than-life, off-camera persona with which to contend: he was a drunk, a fighter, a clown, a raconteur. He was also a great actor.

Reed began with minor roles in the late 1950s before finding a niche with menacing leads in Hammer Film Productions' movies of the early 1960s, most notably *The Curse of the Werewolf* (1961). But it was toward the end of that decade when Reed truly became one of England's most interesting actors of the era, with Ken Russell's *Women in Love* (1969); his nude wrestling scene with Alan Bates in that film is one of the defining moments in Reed's career.

Reed would continue to collaborate with Russell throughout the 1970s in movies such as *Tommy* (1975). But as the decade progressed, Reed's work became more variable. There are highlights: he was excellently understated in David Cronenberg's early thriller *The Brood* (1979). But one can definitely sense that Reed had lost interest in actively seeking out quality projects. This mind-set would continue throughout the 1980s and 1990s, despite a few highlights such as Nicolas Roeg's *Castaway* (1986) and Terry Gilliam's *The Adventures of Baron Munchausen* (1988). More than ten years later, Reed was back in the spotlight of a significant role in a major film with Ridley Scott's *Gladiator* (2000), but it was, sadly, to be his last. He died during production, after drinking several young sailors under the table in a Malta bar, in 1999. **TC**

> "I have made many serious statements—I just can't remember any of them."

CLAUDIA CARDINALE

Born: Claude Joséphine Rose Cardinale, April 15, 1938 (Tunis, Tunisia).

Star qualities: Italian screen icon; charismatic beauty; dark eyed and curvaceous; beauty-queen looks; unusually deep voice; sexual magnetism; fiery screen presence; versatile leading lady; writer.

Born in Tunisia to Sicilian parents, Claudia Cardinale initially wanted to be a teacher. But in 1957, she won "The Most Beautiful Italian Girl in Tunisia" contest. Her prize was a trip to Venice, where she came to the attention of the Italian film industry and was offered a seven-year contract with Vides Films. Her stardom was initially engineered by Vides Films's movie producer Franco Cristaldi, whom she married in 1966, and subsequently divorced. Appearing in a small role in her future husband's production, the successful Italian comedy *I soliti ignoti* (1958) (*Big Deal on Madonna Street*), Cardinale exhibited a magnetic presence that launched her career as an Italian screen icon. This was the beginning of an enormously eclectic career in which she starred in more than 100 films that demonstrated her sensational and charismatic beauty, as well as her incredible versatility as an actress.

Cardinale has worked almost exclusively in European cinema, appearing in several of the most prestigious films of the 1960s, including Luchino Visconti's *Rocco e i suoi fratelli* (1960) (*Rocco and His Brothers*) and *Il Gattopardo* (1963) (*The Leopard*); Federico Fellini's *8½* (1963); and Sergio Leone's *C'era una volta il West* (1968) (*Once Upon a Time in the West*). While her popularity in commercial cinema was beginning to wane by the 1970s, Cardinale reestablished herself in the 1980s through several difficult art-theater films, including Liliana Cavani's *La Pelle* (1981) (*The Skin*) and Werner Herzog's *Fitzcarraldo* (1982). More recently, Cardinale has been seen starring in several European television miniseries, including *Nostromo* (1997), and will appear in the most recent entry in the French *Astérix* movie series alongside Gérard Depardieu and Alain Delon. **GN**

Top Takes...

Astérix aux jeux olympiques 2008
  (*Asterix at the Olympic Games*)
Le cadeau 1982 (*The Gift*)
Fitzcarraldo 1982
La Pelle 1981 (*The Skin*)
The Salamander 1981
I Guappi 1973 (*Blood Brothers*)
C'era una volta il West 1968
  (*Once Upon a Time in the West*)
The Pink Panther 1963
Il Gattopardo 1963 (*The Leopard*)
8½ 1963
Senilità 1962 (*Careless*)
Rocco e i suoi fratelli 1960
  (*Rocco and His Brothers*)
I soliti ignoti 1958 (*Big Deal on Madonna Street*)

1930s

"I never felt scandal and confession were necessary to be an actress."

NATALIE WOOD

Born: Natalia Nikolaevna Zakharenko, July 20, 1938 (San Francisco, California, U.S.); died 1981 (Santa Catalina Island, California, U.S.).

Star qualities: Popular child actress, then versatile leading lady of comedy and serious drama; petite dark-haired beauty; luminous eyes; balletic poise; graceful.

Top Takes…

Brainstorm 1983

Bob & Carol & Ted & Alice 1969

Love with the Proper Stranger 1963 ☆

Gypsy 1962

West Side Story 1961

Splendor in the Grass 1961 ☆

All the Fine Young Cannibals 1960

Cash McCall 1960

Marjorie Morningstar 1958

The Searchers 1956

Rebel Without a Cause 1955 ☆

Father Was a Fullback 1949

Scudda Hoo! Scudda Hay! 1948

The Ghost and Mrs. Muir 1947

Miracle on 34th Street 1947

Happy Land 1943

Natalie Wood was the daughter of Russian immigrants who later changed their surname to "Gurdin." She was a child actor and made her film debut at only four years of age in *Happy Land* (1943). She was prominent in important movies such as *Miracle on 34th Street* (1947) and *The Ghost and Mrs. Muir* (1947), but also glided through lesser films such as *Scudda Hoo! Scudda Hay!* (1948) and *Father Was a Fullback* (1949).

As a young woman, Wood was iconic as Judy, the mixed-up teenage heroine of *Rebel Without a Cause* (1955)—a pivotal role in her career and one for which she earned her first Academy Award nomination—and Debbie, abducted by Native Americans, in *The Searchers* (1956). She matured into a leading lady, impressive in ordinarily good films such as *Marjorie Morningstar* (1958), *Cash McCall* (1960), and *All the Fine Young Cannibals* (1960). She was outstanding as the girl who goes mad for the love of Warren Beatty in *Splendor in the Grass* (1961), but was poorly cast as Maria in *West Side Story* (1961), classy as Gypsy Rose Lee in *Gypsy* (1962), and breezily believable as a modern girl in *Love with the Proper Stranger* (1963). She also performed well in the comedy of sexual mores *Bob & Carol & Ted & Alice* (1969), but fell out of fashion in the 1970s. In response, Wood turned to television, appearing in *Cat on a Hot Tin Roof* (1976) and *From Here to Eternity* (1979). She died during the production of the film *Brainstorm* (1983) when she was sailing on the yacht she shared with her husband Robert Wagner (she married him twice) and their friend, actor Christopher Walken. Wood fell into the sea while trying to board the dinghy that was tied up alongside the yacht, and drowned. She was just forty-three years old, and had always feared death by drowning. **KN**

"I spent all my time in the company of adults. I was very withdrawn."—On being a child actor

ROMY SCHNEIDER

Born: Rosemarie Magdelena Albach-Retty, September 23, 1938 (Vienna, Austria); died 1982 (Paris, France).

Star qualities: Fragile, dark-haired beauty; almond-shaped eyes; intelligent leading lady of historical and contemporary dramas; enigmatic; sensual screen presence.

Romy Schneider's life was one of failing to shed pasts. She was introduced to the world of acting at a young age by her German mother, Magda Schneider, a renowned actress herself, who oversaw the beginnings of her career. In fact, Magda played Romy's mother in her first major role, as Sissi, Princess Elisabeth of Bavaria, the angelic bride of the Austrian kaiser and savior of the Hapsburg Empire. The immensely successful *Sissi* trilogy of films (1955–1957) became such a beacon of hope for Europeans recovering from World War II that the role would haunt Schneider forever.

She tried to break away from the image by embracing art cinema and making brave choices, such as *Mädchen in Uniform* (1958) (*Maedchen in Uniform*) and Luchino Visconti's *Ludwig* (1972), in which she tried to deconstruct Sissi by approaching the exact same role from a less romantic angle. Her widely acclaimed performances in *La piscine* (1969) (*The Swimming Pool*), *L'important c'est d'aimer* (1975) (*That Most Important Thing: Love*)—for which she won her first Best Actress César— *Une histoire simple* (1978) (*A Simple Story*), and *Clair de femme* (1979) (*Womanlight*) did eventually give her a screen persona of her own. But the regained momentum was cut short in 1981 by the sudden death of her fourteen-year-old son, David, who was found impaled on a fence that he had attempted to climb. Succumbing to sorrow and depression, Schneider died shortly afterward, aged only forty-three. The official cause of death was a heart attack, yet many believe that she committed suicide from an overdose of sleeping pills and alcohol. Schneider left behind about a dozen acting gems—some still waiting for recognition—but these were all overshadowed by that one Sissi cult. **EM**

Top Takes...

Clair de femme 1979 (*Womanlight*)
Une histoire simple 1978 (*A Simple Story*)
L'important c'est d'aimer 1975
  (*That Most Important Thing: Love*)
Le trio infernal 1974 (*The Infernal Trio*)
Le train 1973 (*The Train*)
Ludwig 1972
The Assassination of Trotsky 1972
La piscine 1969 (*The Swimming Pool*)
What's New, Pussycat 1965
The Cardinal 1963
Mädchen in Uniform 1958
  (*Maedchen in Uniform*)
Sissi—Schicksalsjahre einer Kaiserin 1957
Sissi—Die junge Kaiserin 1956
Sissi 1955

> "Sissi sticks to me just like oatmeal."
> —On her role as Elisabeth of Bavaria

JEAN SEBERG

Born: Jean Seberg, November 13, 1938 (Marshalltown, Iowa, U.S.); died 1979 (Paris, France).

Star qualities: Blonde; svelte; iconic actress of French New Wave cinema; magnetic screen presence; intelligent; civil-rights activist; writer; director; producer.

Top Takes...

Ballad for Billy the Kid 1974

Airport 1970

Paint Your Wagon 1969

Les Oiseaux vont mourir au Pérou 1968
  (*Birds in Peru*)

A Fine Madness 1966

Lilith 1964

Les plus belles escroqueries du monde 1964
  (*The Beautiful Swindlers*)

In the French Style 1963

L'amant de cinq jours 1961
  (*Five Day Lover*)

À bout de souffle 1960 (*Breathless*)

La Récréation 1960

The Mouse That Roared 1959

Bonjour tristesse 1958

Saint Joan 1957

"Money doesn't buy happiness. But happiness isn't everything."

RIGHT: Seberg and Jean-Paul Belmondo stroll down the Champs-Élysées in *Breathless*.

Although she made her screen debut after besting some 18,000 other hopeful actresses for the opportunity to star as the title character, Joan of Arc, in Otto Preminger's *Saint Joan* (1957), it was her role as the pixieish newspaper vendor Patricia Franchini in Jean-Luc Godard's seminal French New Wave film *À bout de souffle* (1960) (*Breathless*) that cemented Jean Seberg's status as an international film icon. Alternately vibrant and melancholic, her performance as the witty paramour turned opportunistic foil to Jean-Paul Belmondo revealed an emotional range that would bring a distinctive energy to 32 additional movies in her tragically brief career. Included among her more notable contributions to cinema history are prominent roles in the Peter Sellers cold war farce *The Mouse That Roared* (1959), Joshua Logan's popular musical *Paint Your Wagon* (1969), and George Seaton's prototypical disaster film *Airport* (1970).

Sadly, Seberg's turbulent life offscreen rivaled, and at times eclipsed, the tumultuous fates of her most memorable dramatic roles. Married four times, Seberg was the subject of perpetual scrutiny by both rumor-mongering paparazzi and the Federal Bureau of Investigation, the latter of which targeted her for her support of the National Association for the Advancement of Colored People and the Black Panthers. In 1970, while distraught over public speculation (allegedly initiated by J. Edgar Hoover) that the father of her unborn child was a Black Panther movement leader, Seberg gave birth prematurely and the baby girl lived for less than two days. Seberg never recovered from the trauma, attempting suicide on several occasions. In 1979, her body was found with a suicide note after an overdose. **JM**

LIV ULLMANN

Born: Liv Johanne Ullmann, December 16, 1938 (Tokyo, Japan).

Star qualities: "The Norwegian Angel"; iconic leading lady of art-theater cinema; director Ingmar Bergman's favorite actress and muse; serious screen presence; writer; director; multilingual; down-to-earth.

Top Takes...

Höstsonaten 1978 (Autumn Sonata)

The Serpent's Egg 1977

Ansikte mot ansikte 1976 (Face to Face) ☆

The Abdication 1974

Zandy's Bride 1974

Scener ur ett äktenskap 1973
   (Scenes from a Marriage)

Lost Horizon 1973

Viskningar och rop 1972 (Cries and Whispers)

Pope Joan 1972

Nybyggarna 1972 (The New Land)

Utvandrarna 1971 (The Emigrants) ☆

En Passion 1969 (The Passion of Anna)

Skammen 1968 (Shame)

Vargtimmen 1968 (Hour of the Wolf)

Persona 1966

Are there any film performances greater than those given by Liv Ullmann for Swedish director Ingmar Bergman? Not just the magnificent series from *Persona* (1966) to *Höstsonaten* (1978) (*Autumn Sonata*), which also takes in *Vargtimmen* (1967) (*Hour of the Wolf*), *Skammen* (1968) (*The Shame*), *En Passion* (1969) (*The Passion of Anna*), *Viskningar och Rop* (1972) (*Cries and Whispers*), *Scener ur ett äktenskap* (1973) (*Scenes from a Marriage*), *Ansikte mot ansikte* (1975) (*Face to Face*), and *The Serpent's Egg* (1977), but also the late TV masterpiece *Saraband* (2003). The Norwegian actress is uniformly superb in these movies, her beautiful, sensuous, serious face framed in revealing close-up as it expresses the many nuances of the human tragedy as envisaged by the writer/director who was her onetime lover and father of her daughter, author Linn Ullmann. The wordless role of the actress struck dumb by the horrors of the modern world in *Persona* is arguably the most eloquent of all. In real life, Ullmann gives the impression of being surprisingly jolly, and is much given to laughter.

Although she has had a distinguished theatrical career, Ullmann's other films are mostly minor compared with her work with Bergman. She was impressive in Jan Troell's *Utvandrarna* (1970) (*The Emigrants*), for which she received an Oscar nomination for Best Actress; *Nybyggarna* (1972) (*The New Land*); and *Zandy's Bride* (1974). Nevertheless, she floundered in unworthy English-language fare such as *Pope Joan* (1972), *Lost Horizon* (1973), and *The Abdication* (1974). Indeed, her finest recent work has been as director, most notably of the Bergman-scripted *Trolösa* (2000) (*Faithless*), where she proved fully equal to the uncompromising, unsentimental sensibility of the master. **GA**

> "I've worked with more bad directors than good directors; you learn by the bad ones."

SAL MINEO

Born: Salvatore Mineo Jr., January 10, 1939 (Bronx, New York, U.S.); died 1976 (Hollywood, California, U.S.).

Star qualities: "The Switchblade Kid"; exotic good looks; edgy screen presence; teen idol; youthful bad-boy roles; mature character actor.

Sal Mineo was born the son of Sicilian immigrants. He was an authentic juvenile delinquent: a member of a street gang when he was only eight years old, and busted for robbery by the age of ten. He was given a choice of reform school or acting lessons, and chose the latter. He went on to small parts in theater and TV before entering movies as a young hoodlum who grows up to be Tony Curtis in *Six Bridges to Cross* (1955). His big break came when he landed an iconic role in *Rebel Without a Cause* (1955) as Plato, the sensitive, mixed-up kid who yearns to be adopted by James Dean and Natalie Wood but winds up being gunned down by the cops. He garnered an Oscar nomination for Best Supporting Actor for the role. It was back to poor boys struggling with bad backgrounds for *Crime in the Streets* (1956) and *The Young Don't Cry* (1957).

In his brief starring period, Mineo played a plethora of different roles. He was a Native American in *Tonka* (1958), a jazz drummer in *A Private's Affair* (1959), and the Zionist freedom fighter/terrorist Dov Landau in another Oscar-nominated role in *Exodus* (1960). Past his rebel youth phase, he did a lot of television guest spots, and his swan song movie was playing a chimp scientist in *Escape from the Planet of the Apes* (1971).

His later years were fraught with financial problems as his stardom declined, and he returned to work in the theater. He had positive reviews for his last performance as a homosexual burglar in a San Francisco production of the comedy *P.S. Your Cat Is Dead* (1976), and the play transferred to Los Angeles. While walking home from a rehearsal of the show at the Westwood Playhouse, Mineo was attacked and stabbed to death by a mugger in 1976. He was thirty-seven years old. **KN**

Top Takes...

Escape from the Planet of the Apes 1971
The Greatest Story Ever Told 1965
Cheyenne Autumn 1964
The Longest Day 1962
***Exodus* 1960** ☆
A Private's Affair 1959
Tonka 1958
The Young Don't Cry 1957
Dino 1957
Rock, Pretty Baby 1956
Giant 1956
Somebody Up There Likes Me 1956
Crime in the Streets 1956
***Rebel Without a Cause* 1955** ☆
The Private War of Major Benson 1955
Six Bridges to Cross 1955

1930s

"No one ever said movies are for developing your range. [Few get] that opportunity."

SONNY CHIBA

Born: Sadao Maeda, January 23, 1939 (Fukuoka, Kyushu, Japan).

Star qualities: Legendary martial arts actor of Asian movies; multiple black belt holder; swordsmanship; menacing screen presence; plays tough guys; stuntman; director; producer.

Top Takes...

The Fast and the Furious: Tokyo Drift 2006
Kill Bill: Vol. 1 2003
Sheng zhe wei wang 2000 (Born to Be King)
Codename: Silencer 1995 (Body Count)
Immortal Combat 1994
Itsuka giragirasuruhi 1992 (Double Cross)
Saigo no bakuto 1985 (The Last Gambler)
Fukkatsu no hi 1980 (Day of Resurrection)
Okinawa jū-nen sensō 1978
   (Okinawa: The Ten-Year War)
Gekisatsu! Judo ken 1977 (Soul of Bruce Lee)
Gyakushū! Satsujin ken 1974
   (Revenge! The Killing Fist)
Onna hissatsu ken 1974 (Sister Street Fighter)
Satsujin ken 2 1974 (Return of the Street Fighter)
Gekitotsu! Satsujin ken 1974 (The Street Fighter)

There are action stars. And then there are action stars. And then there's Shinichi "Sonny" Chiba. Until his recent performance as swordsmith Hattori Hanzo in Quentin Tarantino's *Kill Bill: Vol. I* (2003)—in yet another of that epic's postmodern winks, Chiba's character is named after an earlier role the actor played—Chiba was best known to Western audiences as Takuma Tsurugi in the infamously brutal *Gekitotsu! Satsujin ken* (1974) (*The Street Fighter*) and its series of sequels, such as *Satsujin Ken 2* (1974) (*Return of the Street Fighter*), and spin-offs such as *Onna Hissatsu Ken* (1974) (*Sister Street Fighter*). The infamy is justified: Chiba's success outside Japan is largely connected to the world's new appetite for martial-arts movies following the international popularity of Bruce Lee in the 1970s. However, not only could Chiba stand alongside Lee in martial arts abilities—he holds black belts in judo, ninjutsu, kendo, and kempo—but also he is one of cinema's all-time top tough guys. Chiba was supposed to work with Lee in the early 1970s, but the star's death quashed the project.

With a face that even when grinning—and Chiba can also be quite funny—seems to be caught between a scowl and a snarl, Chiba could not only wipe the floor with Jackie Chan and Jet Li, he could then drag Lee Marvin and Charles Bronson back from the afterlife to have drinks and laugh about it. Nonetheless, Chiba has also enjoyed a long and successful career outside the *Street Fighter* films, across a variety of genres. He began his career as a television actor and contract player for Toei Studios in 1960 and his credit list is as long as his lethal arms, including work for director Kinji Fukasaku, numerous science fiction and *yakuza* gangster pictures, and even comedies. **TC**

> "What I'm doing as an action star is what every actor should be doing. Action is drama."

HARVEY KEITEL

Born: Harvey Keitel, May 13, 1939 (Brooklyn, New York, U.S.).

Star qualities: Versatile character actor; fierce intelligence; often plays the tough guy; grim, melancholic expression; intense screen presence; keen to offer support to young filmmakers; producer.

Brutish intensity and fierce intelligence are not necessarily mutually exclusive qualities in an actor, but they rarely intersect with the level of passion displayed by the performances of Harvey Keitel. He is a doubly riveting presence; triply riveting, if you incorporate his coarse but handsome appearance. He looks like he's always thinking with every word of dialogue or facial expression, and he also appears to be ready to pounce with rage as a result of his inner contemplation. Keitel toiled for a decade as a court stenographer while also working in theater before finally landing his breakthrough with several early films from director Martin Scorsese: *I Call First* (1967), *Mean Streets* (1973), *Alice Doesn't Live Here Anymore* (1974), and *Taxi Driver* (1976). Keitel appeared in Scorsese's debut and he seems to have had a gift for predicting superlative filmmaking talent at its infancy. He has also starred in the feature debuts of directors like Ridley Scott in *The Duellists* (1977), James Toback in *Fingers* (1978), Paul Schrader in *Blue Collar* (1978), and Quentin Tarantino in *Reservoir Dogs* (1992).

His Tarantino projects, *Reservoir Dogs* and *Pulp Fiction* (1994), helped ignite a return to fame. Despite some interesting work, he was largely unknown through the 1980s, appearing in offbeat European productions but little solid fare. The 1990s brought Keitel's long-overdue comeback, a prolific period in both mainstream projects (*Thelma & Louise*, 1991; *Bugsy*, 1991; *From Dusk Till Dawn*, 1996); and independent projects such as *The Piano* (1993), *Smoke* (1995), and *To Vlemma tou Odyssea* (1995) (*Ulysses' Gaze*). His career-best performance is probably in Abel Ferrara's searing *Bad Lieutenant* (1992), making it all the more regrettable that he has recently appeared more in a supporting capacity. **TC**

Top Takes...

From Dusk Till Dawn 1996
Clockers 1995
To Vlemma tou Odyssea 1995 (*Ulysses' Gaze*)
Smoke 1995
Pulp Fiction 1994
The Piano 1993
Bad Lieutenant 1992
Reservoir Dogs 1992
***Bugsy* 1991** ☆
Thelma & Louise 1991
Fingers 1978
The Duellists 1977
Taxi Driver 1976
Alice Doesn't Live Here Anymore 1974
Mean Streets 1973
I Call First 1967

1930s

"Fear is a marker I need to rise above, otherwise I would drown in my fear of myself."

LILY TOMLIN

Born: Mary Jean Tomlin, September 1, 1939 (Detroit, Michigan, U.S.).

Star qualities: Expressive face; chameleonlike character actress; acerbic delivery; witty; intelligent; energetic; often plays larger-than-life characters; veteran stand-up comedienne; writer; producer.

Lily Tomlin has been such a chameleon that no one role epitomizes the breadth of her talent for drilling inside disparate personalities and conveying their core. To call her a comedienne would be to overlook her dramatic roles, yet even in the lightest vehicles she manages to impart something of human behavior, even if the part doesn't call for it.

Tomlin attended Wayne State University and honed her stand-up skills in nightclubs. She debuted on TV in *The Garry Moore Show* (1958) and later joined the ensemble cast of *Rowan & Martin's Laugh-In* (1969–1973), to which she contributed some of her signature characters: the wisecracking five-year-old Edith Ann and the nasal-voiced officious telephone operator Ernestine.

She made an auspicious movie debut among the crowd of characters in Robert Altman's *Nashville* (1975) as the mother of deaf children, followed by a sterling appearance alongside Art Carney as a pair of mismatched shamuses in *The Late Show* (1977). A string of less successful starring vehicles followed: *Moment by Moment* (1979) and *The Incredible Shrinking Woman* (1981). Nonetheless, Tomlin was impressive alongside Dolly Parton and Jane Fonda in the feminist farce *Nine to Five* (1980), and alongside Steve Martin in *All of Me* (1984). A decade of TV and stage work followed, notably as the presidential secretary Deborah Fiderer in *The West Wing* (2002–2006), although she also filmed her award-winning theatrical production *The Search for Signs of Intelligent Life in the Universe* (1991). She worked again with Altman in *Short Cuts* (1993) and in *A Prairie Home Companion* (2006). Of Tomlin's latest appearances, her role in the metaphysical comedy *I ♥ Huckabees* (2004) is a standout. **DS**

Top Takes…

A Prairie Home Companion 2006
I ♥ Huckabees 2004
Tea with Mussolini 1999
Blue in the Face 1995
The Beverly Hillbillies 1993
Short Cuts 1993
Shadows and Fog 1992
The Search for Signs of Intelligent Life
  in the Universe 1991
All of Me 1984
The Incredible Shrinking Woman 1981
Nine to Five 1980
Moment by Moment 1978
The Late Show 1977
Nashville 1975 ☆

"There will be sex after death—we just won't be able to feel it."

JOHN CLEESE

Born: John Marwood Cleese, October 27, 1939 (Weston-super-Mare, Somerset, England).

Star qualities: Tall, lanky, comic genius; silly walks; expressive face; brilliant mimic; member of the Monty Python team; writer; producer; director.

John Cleese went to Cambridge University, England, to study law, and there became involved in the legendary Footlights group that launched the careers of actors such as Peter Cook, Dudley Moore, and Jonathan Miller. He wrote and performed in comedy reviews, often in collaboration with future fellow Monty Python member Graham Chapman. After he graduated, he went on to write for the BBC, and in 1964 toured New Zealand and the United States with the "Cambridge Circus" comedy revue. He has starred in and written several successful movies and found a niche as a valued cameo player, but his cinema work has never eclipsed his double-dip of TV genius, first as the most prominent member of the cast of the smash-hit comedy series *Monty Python's Flying Circus* (1969–1974), and then as the monstrous, frustrated hotelier Basil Fawlty in *Fawlty Towers* (1975–1979).

In the 1960s and 1970s, Cleese popped into films for funny parts in *The Magic Christian* (1969) and *The Love Ban* (1973). With the Monty Python troupe he made *And Now for Something Completely Different* (1971) and later offered support to comrades Terry Gilliam in *Time Bandits* (1981), Graham Chapman in *Yellowbeard* (1983), and Terry Jones in *Erik the Viking* (1989).

Clockwise (1986), Cleese's first star role, was Fawlty-lite, but he managed a perfect vehicle with *A Fish Called Wanda* (1988), which he also cowrote. A follow-up, *Fierce Creatures* (1997), didn't quite click, but Cleese donated his brain to Robert De Niro in *Frankenstein* (1994), which should have made a funny film, and earned slots as Q's replacement in the James Bond series starting with *The World Is Not Enough* (1999). His most successful recent comic turn has been as the ghost Nearly Headless Nick in the *Harry Potter* films. **KN**

Top Takes...

Shrek 2 2004
Harry Potter and the Sorcerer's Stone 2001
The World Is Not Enough 1999
Fierce Creatures 1997
Frankenstein 1994
Erik the Viking 1989
A Fish Called Wanda 1988
Clockwise 1986
The Meaning of Life 1983
Time Bandits 1981
Life of Brian 1979
Monty Python and the Holy Grail 1975
The Love Ban 1973
And Now for Something Completely Different 1971
The Magic Christian 1969

1930s

"I never enjoyed *The Meaning of Life*. I always regarded that entire film as a bit of a cock-up."

JOHN HURT

Born: John Vincent Hurt, January 22, 1940 (Chesterfield, Derbyshire, England).

Star qualities: Sonorous voice; serious character actor; plays historical figures convincingly; Shakespearean stagecraft; frequent narrator; excels at playing outsider and villain roles.

Top Takes…

1940s

John Hurt was born the son of a vicar and an amateur actress. Initially he trained as an artist and studied painting at London's St. Martin's School for Art, but he turned to his first love, acting, in 1962, winning a scholarship to the Royal Academy of Dramatic Art. He later played with the Royal Shakespeare Company. He is remembered vividly for the chest-bursting scene from *Alien* (1979), in which his character, Kane, is killed birthing the spawn of an otherworldly monster. However, Hurt is an actor of wide range, long service, and deep skill who first drew attention for a small role in the film version of *A Man for All Seasons* (1966) when the film won six Oscars. He went on to play a mixture of film and TV roles, winning critical acclaim as the Roman emperor Caligula in the BBC TV series *I, Claudius* (1976). Since then, his career is cleaved in two parts: one devoted to his sonorous voice, as in *Watership Down* (1978), *The Lord of the Rings* (1978), *The Tigger Movie* (2000), and *Manderlay* (2005), the other employing him onscreen in a mix of heroic and villainous roles.

Along the hero model, *The Elephant Man* (1980), his Oscar-nominated turn as the disfigured John Merrick, is the early template, echoed later on by such films as *Nineteen Eighty-Four* (1984), *Contact* (1997), and *Hellboy* (2004). But it's the villain side of the equation where Hurt has really made his mark. One premonition was Porfiry on TV's *Crime and Punishment* (2002), but the real proof has arrived with middle age, perhaps most wickedly in *Rob Roy* (1995) and *V for Vendetta* (2005), where Hurt's Englishness makes his baddies particularly fascistic, two-dimensional, and all the more terrifying as symbols of social ills rather than mere flesh and blood people. **GCQ**

> "I've done some stinkers in the cinema. You can't regret it."

PETER FONDA

Born: Peter Henry Fonda, February 23, 1940 (New York City, New York, U.S.).

Star qualities: Tall, cool icon of 1960s counterculture; member of an acting dynasty; versatile character actor; chooses widely contrasting character types; intelligent; innovative; writer; director; producer.

Peter Fonda is part of a prestigious acting family: he is the son of legend Henry Fonda, the younger brother of Jane Fonda, and the father of Bridget Fonda. Jane and Peter had a strained relationship with their father. After studying acting Peter joined the Omaha Community Playhouse in Nebraska, where many actors such as his father and Marlon Brando began their careers. He worked on Broadway before going to Hollywood.

He put in a solid apprenticeship with trivial romantic leads in such films as *Tammy and the Doctor* (1963) and mixed-up-youth supporting roles as in *Lilith* (1964) before director Roger Corman cast him in a pair of counterculture quickies that established his rebel image. After the Hell's Angel biker of *The Wild Angels* (1966) and the acid experimenter of *The Trip* (1967), Fonda took things a little further with Dennis Hopper in the classic 1960s counterculture movie *Easy Rider* (1969). He cowrote the movie with Hopper and Terry Southern, and it won him an Academy Award nomination for Best Screenplay. Fonda's hog-straddling, pinup boy Captain America was every college-girl's dream and the contemporary incarnation of his father's Tom Joad character in *The Grapes of Wrath* (1940).

Fonda directed himself in the melancholy hippie Western *The Hired Hand* (1971) and went back to exploitation (albeit politically charged exploitation) for cool credits such as *Dirty Mary Crazy Larry* (1974), *Race with the Devil* (1975), *Fighting Mad* (1976), and *Outlaw Blues* (1977). He drifted in the 1980s, reappearing in roles that related to his earlier work: a burned-out Dracula/Doctor Van Helsing in *Nadja* (1994); a future surfer in *Escape from L.A.* (1997); and a jungle fighter who settles down to keep bees in *Ulee's Gold* (1997), which won him a Best Actor Oscar nomination. **KN**

Top Takes...

The Limey 1999
***Ulee's Gold* 1997** ☆
Escape from L.A. 1996
Nadja 1994
The Cannonball Run 1981
Outlaw Blues 1977
Fighting Mad 1976
Race with the Devil 1975
Dirty Mary Crazy Larry 1974
The Last Movie 1971
The Hired Hand 1971
Easy Rider 1969
The Trip 1967
The Wild Angels 1966
Lilith 1964
Tammy and the Doctor 1963

1940s

"Whenever I hear 'Mr. Fonda,' I look over at the door, figuring he's come back."

RAÚL JULIÁ

Born: Raúl Rafael Juliá y Arcelay, March 9, 1940 (San Juan, Puerto Rico); died 1994 (Manhasset, New York, U.S.).

Star qualities: Tall, darkly handsome, and suave; Shakespearean stagecraft; charismatic screen presence; exuberant; extremely versatile character actor.

Top Takes...

Addams Family Values 1993
The Addams Family 1991
Frankenstein Unbound 1990
Presumed Innocent 1990
Mack the Knife 1990
Romero 1989
Tequila Sunrise 1988
Moon Over Parador 1988
The Morning After 1986
Kiss of the Spider Woman 1985
Tempest 1982
One from the Heart 1982
Othello 1979
Eyes of Laura Mars 1978
Been Down So Long It Looks Like Up to Me 1971
The Panic in Needle Park 1971

Raúl Juliá was discovered while performing in a nightclub in San Juan, Puerto Rico, by actor Orson Bean. He encouraged Juliá to move to New York to pursue an acting career. Juliá soon found work in small and supporting roles in Off-Broadway shows. By the 1970s he had built a major reputation for his electrifying theater work as well as roles in Shakespearean films, playing Edmund in TV's *King Lear* (1973) and the title role in *Othello* (1979). He began taking gigs in counterculture films such as *The Panic in Needle Park* (1971) and *Been Down So Long It Looks Like Up to Me* (1971). Then director Francis Ford Coppola cast Juliá as Teri Garr's crooner/waiter lover in *One from the Heart* (1982), and he began getting more demanding roles. He was the Caliban character in *Tempest* (1982) and the political prisoner sharing a cell with a drag queen played by William Hurt in *Kiss of the Spider Woman* (1985).

Juliá was occasionally typecast in roles as a Hispanic actor: South American secret policemen, drug lords, gigolos, or priests. He also worked up a sideline in heroic martyrs, including Archbishop Óscar Romero of El Salvador in *Romero* (1989) and Brazilian rainforest activist Chico Mendes in the TV film *The Burning Season* (1994). He was the powerhouse lawyer in *Presumed Innocent* (1990) and re-created one of his great stage roles as MacHeath in *Mack the Knife* (1990). In more cartoonish mode, Juliá was Dr. Victor Frankenstein in *Frankenstein Unbound* (1990) and videogame villain General M. Bison in *Street Fighter* (1994). His best success in this line was as the pinstriped, grinning semisadist Gomez Addams in two *Addams Family* movies (1991, 1993). He was diagnosed with stomach cancer in 1993 and, his health in decline, died after a stroke in 1994. **KN**

> "I knew there was something special about the theater for me ... that I could transcend."

JAMES CAAN

Born: James Edmund Caan, March 26, 1940 (Bronx, New York, U.S.).

Star qualities: Tall, lean, masculine; athletic; tough-guy appearance; manly appeal; karate black belt; versatile character actor and leading man; edgy screen persona; director.

James Caan was born in New York to German Jewish immigrant parents. The young Caan was a keen sportsman; he played football, studied karate, and took part in the rodeo circuit under the nickname "The Jewish Cowboy." He became interested in acting while at Hofstra University and joined New York City's Neighborhood Playhouse, where he studied with Sanford Meisner. After serving his apprenticeship in TV and Off-Broadway productions, he broke into movies as a sailor in *Irma la Douce* (1963). More upmarket films soon followed: first a Western, *The Glory Guys* (1965), scripted by Sam Peckinpah, then Howard Hawks's motor-racing saga *Red Line 7000* (1965), and another Western, Hawks's *El Dorado* (1966), in which he costarred with John Wayne and Robert Mitchum.

Caan was given the lead as a brain-damaged football player in Francis Ford Coppola's romantic drama *The Rain People* (1969). Coppola cast him again in *The Godfather* (1972), in which he has the substantial role of the edgy, hot-tempered Santino "Sonny" Corleone. Two other performances stand out in Caan's career. He played the title role in *The Gambler* (1974) as a man whose compulsive gambling gets him deeper and deeper into debt and danger. And in Michael Mann's film noir *Thief* (1981) he plays a professional burglar who falls into the clutches of the mob. He plays the veteran sergeant preparing soliders for Vietnam in Coppola's *Gardens of Stone* (1987). Tall, lean, and tough-looking, Caan has acted in comedy and musicals, costarring with Barbra Streisand in *Funny Lady* (1975), but drama suits him best. He's excellent as a novelist trapped in a room by an obsessive stalker brilliantly played by Kathy Bates in *Misery* (1990), and in a character role in the crime thriller *The Yards* (2000). **EB**

Top Takes...

Elf 2003
The Yards 2000
For the Boys 1991
Misery 1990
Gardens of Stone 1987
Thief 1981
Comes a Horseman 1978
Funny Lady 1975
The Godfather: Part II 1974
The Gambler 1974
The Godfather 1972 ☆
The Rain People 1969
El Dorado 1966
The Glory Guys 1965
Red Line 7000 1965
Irma la Douce 1963

1940s

"Anyone of my generation who tells you he hasn't 'done' [Marlon] Brando is lying."

AL PACINO

Born: Alfredo James Pacino, April 25, 1940 (South Bronx, New York, U.S.).

Star qualities: A legend among film buffs; the godfather of gritty realism and gravelly-voiced gangsters; made many brave choices of role that challenged him personally and professionally; won one Oscar and eight nominations; director.

Top Takes...

The Merchant of Venice 2004
Insomnia 2002
Any Given Sunday 1999
The Insider 1999
The Devil's Advocate 1997
Donnie Brasco 1997
City Hall 1996
Looking for Richard 1996
Heat 1995
Carlito's Way 1993
Scent of a Woman 1992 ★
Glengarry Glen Ross 1992 ☆
Frankie and Johnny 1991
The Godfather: Part III 1990
Dick Tracy 1990 ☆
Sea of Love 1989
Revolution 1985
Scarface 1983
Cruising 1980
... And Justice for All 1979 ☆
Dog Day Afternoon 1975 ☆
The Godfather: Part II 1974 ☆
Serpico 1973 ☆
The Godfather 1972 ☆
The Panic in Needle Park 1971

RIGHT: Pacino in another classic role playing a real-life bank robber in *Dog Day Afternoon*.

Born in the Bronx, New York, Al Pacino is the gold standard against which most American actors—indeed, most world actors—are judged. A lifelong bachelor, occasional film director (*Looking for Richard*, 1996), and performer inclined toward artistically varied pursuits, although one owing a tremendous debt to Hollywood's deep pockets, Pacino is quintessentially American. An ethnic type who succeeded beyond the usual bounds to help define the mainstream, he has prospered despite numerous obstacles.

With age, his once pretty face has begun to droop, taking away the initial shine of youth. But his face is cut with a rich, dangerous smile and bright, orbital eyes that frequently give his performances a sense of caricature, inasmuch as Pacino has so wholly embodied cartoon-style villains (*Dick Tracy*, 1990), leading men (*The Godfather: Part II*, 1974), monsters (*The Devil's Advocate*, 1997), and working-class nobodies (*Frankie and Johnny*, 1991) with equal panache. His body also has a tendency to softness and is hunched, almost plodding, whereas his voice is explosive and angry. His dynamic range quickly changes, but

ABOVE: As "The Godfather," one of the most sought-after parts in movie history.

it is the more minute details of his performances we often admire—typically the pair of overlarge hands he uses with great expressivity. In short, his physical vessel is not easily categorized as "handsome" in a field replete with handsome men. But perhaps it is because of this refreshing contrast with the elitist WASP type that Pacino has been movie royalty for nearly two generations.

More remarkably, his roles are where words and actions truly leave the stage or screen, as the case may be, and it is here that Pacino has always made his mark. Trained as a Method actor under the tutelage of Lee Strasberg, he has honed his technique to a point. His style is therefore concerned with capturing emotional states and embodying them through physical performance, as well as in the employment of setting, décor, and lights—the

"I hope the perception is that I'm an actor; I never intended to be a movie star."

Stagestruck

Although Al Pacino has enjoyed a highly successful career onscreen, he has also made a huge contribution to theater. As a child he found relief from boredom in school plays. He later went into stage acting full time, but initially struggled on the verge of poverty, borrowing his bus fare to get to auditions. When he broke into film, his early roles echoed the gritty, realistic turns that first made him stand out on the stage, like his junkie portrayal in *The Panic in Needle Park* (1971). Over the years Pacino has concentrated on movies, but theater remains his first love.

- He studied with famed Method acting coach Lee Strasberg, who later worked alongside Pacino in *The Godfather: Part II* as Hyman Roth.

- He made his first real mark onstage in *The Indian Wants the Bronx* (1966–1967), for which he won an Obie Award. He has since won two Tony awards.

- He was a longtime member of David Wheeler's Theater Company of Boston.

- While he appeared in Bertolt Brecht's *The Resistable Rise of Arturo Ui* for Off-Broadway scale pay in 2002, the ticket price (at $115) was the highest in Off-Broadway history.

- An avid Shakespeare fan, he directed, produced, and starred in the highly acclaimed *Looking for Richard* (1996), in which he attempts to bring the Bard to a wider audience.

RIGHT: Pacino's role as the irascible colonel in *Scent of a Woman* finally won him an Oscar.

purview of important collaborators like Sidney Lumet, Norman Jewison, Francis Ford Coppola, and Michael Mann. Consequently, Pacino is central to the golden period of Hollywood in the 1970s, and it's his career-long association with quality work, with one or two exceptions (*Cruising*, 1980; *Revolution*, 1985), that makes him such a respected performer.

Over the decades he has become a legend, a performer *sui generis* while miraculously continuing a seemingly never-ending career prime, and all this despite originally possessing a rather effeminate voice now made gruff with age, a slight presence, and being Italian during a period when such traits were normally the stuff of support players at best. Pacino is therefore a working-class hero and gentleman's model both, which is a testament to his skill and the application of thoughtful craftsmanship.

Moving on from *The Godfather*

Witness his eponymous hero in *Serpico* (1973), the sad-sack bank robber Sonny in *Dog Day Afternoon* (1975), hanger-on Lefty Ruggiero in *Donnie Brasco* (1997), or the maniacal Tony Montana in *Scarface* (1983). Yet all roads flow through *The Godfather* (1972), that bedrock of modern U.S. cinema, because Al Pacino will be forever remembered as Michael Corleone.

In one performance—indeed the role of a lifetime—Pacino embodies the American dream of "hard work wins out" and the nightmare of loyalty to tribe, with the entire twentieth-century immigrant experience providing a backdrop of fratricide, murder, dashed love, and the accumulation of power. Still, he can cater for those who are partial to the "hoo-aah" of Lt. Col. Frank Slade in *Scent of a Woman* (1992), his Academy Award and Golden Globe Award-winning performance. But for others, the standout performances lie off to one side in such projects as *Heat* (1995), *The Insider* (1999), *Carlito's Way* (1993), and his Emmy Award-winning, electrifyingly nasty Roy Cohn in the HBO adaptation for television of Tony Kushner's *Angels in America* (2003). Pacino stands out as one of the most original and influential actors of his generation. **GCQ**

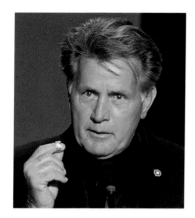

MARTIN SHEEN

Born: Ramón Gerardo Antonio Estévez, August 3, 1940 (Dayton, Ohio, U.S.).

Star qualities: Stagecraft; played intense young men and later roles in serious dramas; gravitas; prolific performer; liberal political activist; head of an acting family; producer; director.

Top Takes…

1940s

"I love my country enough
to suffer its wrath."

—On his political activism and arrests

A stage career led Martin Sheen to Hollywood, where in the early years he had to satisfy himself with small parts, often strikingly conceived and thus memorable. Sheen played a conventional angry young man, trying to break free of parental control in *The Subject Was Roses* (1968), reprising the role he had created on Broadway. In *Catch-22* (1970), he plays one of the deluded, and self-deluding, ensemble of air warriors. This was a study for the more extended portrayal of James Dean wannabe Charles Starkweather, who also happens to be a remorseless killer, in Terrence Malick's *Badlands* (1973). It is a riveting portrayal, slightly mannered and entirely effective.

For Francis Ford Coppola, Sheen extended the range of his rebel male, now a man driven close to insanity and moral outrage by his complicity in the attempt to make Vietnam safe for U.S. democracy in *Apocalypse Now* (1979). His Captain Benjamin L. Willard is capable of incredible sangfroid, finishing off without compunction a villager mistakenly shot by his men, but he can also return inspiringly to the primitive, the fascination with death and power he is asked, in some sense, to murder in himself. Sadly, no other director demanded so much, and Sheen's career faltered. However, even in limited roles in less than first-rate movies, he was often memorable, for example, as the fascist candidate in *The Dead Zone* (1983). Since the 1990s, Sheen's roles have taken a different turn. He was a sedate but firm and contrite General Robert E. Lee in *Gettysburg* (1993), and perhaps, the role he will be best remembered for, a compassionate U.S. president modeled on Bill Clinton, in the prime-time TV series *The West Wing* (1999–2006). He is the father of actors Charlie Sheen and Emilio Estévez. **BP**

RAQUEL WELCH

Born: Jo Raquel Tejada, September 5, 1940 (Chicago, Illinois, U.S.).

Star qualities: Curvaceous and statuesque; cult screen sex siren; beauty-queen looks; auburn hair; dazzling smile; stylish; played youthful pinup and mature character roles.

Raquel Welch was the sex symbol of the mid-1960s, most often found smoldering in ridiculous circumstances: in a white wetsuit and attacked by antibodies in *Fantastic Voyage* (1966), and in a fur bikini and plucked by a pterodactyl in *One Million Years B.C.* (1966). She took dancing lessons as a child, and her voluptuous looks helped her win a number of beauty pageants as a teenager. She set her sights on acting and studied theater arts at San Diego State College, but quit when she became a local TV weather presenter in San Diego. By this time she had married her childhood sweetheart and had two children. She divorced the first of her four husbands and moved to Los Angeles in 1964. She then started to get bit parts in TV series, such as *The Virginian* (1964) and *Bewitched* (1964), before she came to public attention in her early movies.

She continued in pinup roles during the 1960s and early 1970s: in a bikini and parachuting in *Fathom* (1967), in a stars-and-stripes swimsuit as a transsexual cultural revolutionary in *Myra Breckinridge* (1970), and naked beneath a poncho as a Western avenger in *Hannie Caulder* (1971).

But being seen as a joke even in good films must have been annoying, and Welch sought grittier roles, acting as well as posing for the posters. She acquitted herself admirably as a roller derby hellcat in *Kansas City Bomber* (1972), peasant maid in *The Three Musketeers* (1973), scandalous hostess in *The Wild Party* (1975), black-comedy paramedic in *Mother, Jugs & Speed* (1976), and Native American heroine in the TV film *The Legend of Walks Far Woman* (1982). In her later years, she still takes on cameo roles in films and on TV. But she has also ventured into the beauty business, most successfully with a signature line of wigs. **KN**

Top Takes...

Legally Blonde 2001
Mother, Jugs & Speed 1976
The Wild Party 1975
The Four Musketeers 1974
The Three Musketeers 1973
Kansas City Bomber 1972
Fuzz 1972
Bluebeard 1972
Hannie Caulder 1971
Myra Breckinridge 1970
The Beloved 1970
Bandolero! 1968
Bedazzled 1967
Fathom 1967
One Million Years B.C. 1966
Fantastic Voyage 1966

"Being a sex symbol was rather like being a convict."

ANNA KARINA

Born: Hanne Karen Blarke Bayer, September 22, 1940 (Copenhagen, Denmark).

Star qualities: Fashion-model looks; graceful; huge eyes; leading lady of French New Wave cinema; muse of Jean-Luc Godard, whom she married; singer; composer; writer; director.

Top Takes...

L'assassin musicien 1976 (*The Musician Killer*)
Pane e cioccolata 1973 (*Bread and Chocolate*)
Justine 1969
The Magus 1968
Lo Straniero 1967 (*The Stranger*)
Made in U.S.A. 1966
La religieuse 1966 (*The Nun*)
Pierrot le fou 1965
Alphaville, une étrange aventure de Lemmy Caution 1965 (*Alphaville, a Strange Adventure of Lemmy Caution*)
Bande à part 1964 (*Band of Outsiders*)
Le petit soldat 1963 (*The Little Soldier*)
Vivre sa vie: Film en douze tableaux 1962 (*My Life to Live*)
Une femme est une femme 1961 (*A Woman Is a Woman*)

> "I like that, being his muse."
>
> —On her cinematic relationship with director Jean-Luc Godard

Although she has since worked for many important filmmakers such as Luchino Visconti, Raul Ruiz, Volker Schlöndorff, Benoît Jacquot, Werner Fassbinder, and herself, there's little point in denying that the name "Anna Karina" will always have another name mentioned in the same sentence: Jean-Luc Godard. During their seven-year marriage, Karina and Godard shared more than an actress/director relationship, and she was more than simply Godard's muse during what remains arguably the most fertile, significant period of his career. Karina was the female face of France's *Nouvelle Vague* cinema movement: its very own radiant and magnetic Audrey Hepburn for the streets of Paris. Karina also acted in films by Godard contemporaries Jacques Rivette and Agnès Varda during this period.

Born and raised in Denmark, Karina came to Paris at the age of eighteen and took up with Godard shortly after, first collaborating with him on *Une femme est une femme* (1961) (*A Woman Is a Woman*); she had been offered Jean Seberg's role in *À bout de souffle* (1960) (*Breathless*) the previous year but turned it down. Six movies together would follow throughout the 1960s: *Vivre sa vie*: *Film en douze tableaux* (1962) (*My Life to Live*); *Le petit soldat* (1963) (*The Little Soldier*); *Bande à part* (1964) (*Band of Outsiders*); *Alphaville, une étrange aventure de Lemmy Caution* (1965) (*Alphaville, a Strange Adventure of Lemmy Caution*); *Pierrot le fou* (1965); and *Made in U.S.A* (1966). Karina is much more than beauty and charm in these films, for some of her performances are extraordinarily rich and complex, particularly in *Pierrot*. Karina and Godard moved on following their separation, and each continued to do fascinating work, but this was the most creative and exciting period for both. **TC**

BRUCE LEE

Born: Bruce Jun Fan Lee, November 27, 1940 (San Francisco, California, U.S.); died 1973 (Hong Kong).

Star qualities: Enduring international icon of martial arts movies; handsome; athletic; charismatic; inventive; tough, hot-tempered hero; writer; director.

There may be younger viewers who look at the tragically small body of work completed by actor/director Bruce Lee before his death, and then wonder why he has become such a legend. After all, most of Lee's movies are, frankly, rather mediocre and martial arts moves have been displayed with much more stylized panache in the years after Lee's passing by actors like Jackie Chan, Jet Li, and Tony Jaa. But none of his successors would have their movie careers if it weren't for the path cut by Lee. To put it simply—Lee was an international icon in the 1970s, and one of the most influential actors of that era.

Lee was a child actor in the 1940s and 1950s in Hong Kong before he exploded on to the scene in the 1970s; his most notable early role was in *Ren hai gu hong* (1960) (*The Orphan*). Lee's parents sent him back to the United States (he reportedly had a troubled adolescence), and Lee opened up kung-fu schools there before landing a role on the TV series *The Green Hornet* (1966–1967). He continued to work in TV during the 1960s and developed his own fighting style, Jeet Kune Do.

As the 1970s began, Lee returned to Hong Kong, starring in two movies by actor/director Lo Wei, *Tang shan da xiong* (1971) (*Fists of Fury*) and *Jing wu men* (1972) (*The Chinese Connection*). Both films were huge hits in Hong Kong and gave Lee a new career, but it was to be among the most tragically short-lived in cinema. He made his popular movie *Enter the Dragon* in 1973, and one year earlier directed himself in his behind the camera debut, *Meng long guojiang* (*Return of the Dragon*). Much of Lee's fame in the West came posthumously; he died suddenly of a cerebral edema in 1973, unaware of the impact he had on international action cinema—or on his dozens of cinematic imitators. **TC**

Top Takes...

Enter the Dragon 1973
Meng long guojiang 1972
  (*Return of the Dragon*)
Jing wu men 1972
  (*The Chinese Connection*)
Tang shan da xiong 1971 (*Fists of Fury*)
Marlowe 1969
Ren hai gu hong 1960 (*The Orphan*)
Lei yu 1957 (*The Thunderstorm*)
Er nu zhai 1955 (*We Owe It to Our Children*)
Ai xia ji 1955 (*Love Part 2*)
Ai 1955 (*Love*)
Ci mu lei 1953 (*A Mother's Tears*)
Ku hai ming deng 1953 (*The Guiding Light*)
Ren zhi cu 1951 (*Infancy*)
Xi lu xiang 1950 (*My Son, Ah Chung*)

1940s

"The key to immortality is first living a life worth remembering."

RICHARD PRYOR

Born: Richard Franklin Lennox Thomas Pryor III, December 1, 1940 (Peoria, Illinois, U.S.); died 2005 (Los Angeles, California, U.S.).

Star qualities: Influential, controversial stand-up comedian; mimic; cutting-edge sketches and profane language; social insight; acerbic wit; writer; producer; director.

Top Takes...

1940s

Born the son of a prostitute and her pimp, Richard Pryor was raised in his grandmother's brothel. He was molested twice, first at age six by a neighbor, and later on by a priest. To help escape his troubles, he became a frequent moviegoer. He was expelled from school at age fourteen, and after a series of menial jobs he joined the army in 1958. On returning to civilian life in 1960, he worked as a musician and singer in nightclubs and discovered his comic abilities.

He earned fame as a writer on the TV series *The Flip Wilson Show* (1970) and *Sanford and Son* (1972). By then also established as a caustic stand-up comedian famed for his profane language, he became a screen actor in films such as *The Mack* (1973) and *Uptown Saturday Night* (1974). By the mid-1970s he had cowritten the hit comedy *Blazing Saddles* (1974) and attracted attention for hosting *Saturday Night Live* (1975) and for his short-lived but brilliant turn on the TV series *The Richard Pryor Show* (1977).

Having shown dramatic abilities in *Lady Sings the Blues* (1972) and *Blue Collar* (1978), the 1980s saw him become a box-office success in *Stir Crazy* (1980) and *Superman III* (1983). He wrote and directed the autobiographical film *Jo Jo Dancer, Your Life Is Calling* (1986), but his drug abuse and ill health slowed him down. Although he was once known for being the most viciously funny and politically astute of U.S. comics, his final years were spent in a series of medical emergencies after he was diagnosed with multiple sclerosis; divorces (he was married seven times, twice to the same woman, and divorced six times); and supporting roles in *Lost Highway* (1997) and the TV series *The Norm Show* (1999). **GCQ**

> "I never met anybody who said when they were a kid, 'I wanna grow up and be a critic.'"

FAYE DUNAWAY

Born: Dorothy Faye Dunaway, January 14, 1941 (Bascom, Florida, U.S.).

Star qualities: Strikingly beautiful; sexy; dominating screen presence; refined looks; leading lady of dramas, she often plays strong-willed women; stagecraft; writer; producer; director.

If you have to have your sterling acting career ruined by a single role—as Faye Dunaway claims her career was—then you might as well go out kicking and screaming. Dunaway's turn as actress Joan Crawford in the notorious child-abuse biopic *Mommie Dearest* (1981) is, despite the scorn heaped upon the movie at the time of release, one of cinema's great over-the-top performances: a two-hour, tormented, Kabuki-theater-style howl that was Crawford as if done by Crawford herself. Dunaway was the icon of 1970s U.S. film womanhood—in that decade her performances defined female strength and drive more than any other actress—but sadly her career never quite rebounded.

Dunaway was catapulted to stardom as one half of the eponymous *Bonnie and Clyde* (1967) couple in Arthur Penn's groundbreaking film, and it was a role that won Dunaway her first Academy Award nomination for Best Actress. A series of career highs came in the decade after. She was elegance personified in *Chinatown* (1974), and then brilliantly narcissistic and neurotic as a TV executive in *Network* (1976), which finally won her a coveted Oscar. She was still a strong, commanding presence in *The Thomas Crown Affair* (1968), *The Towering Inferno* (1974), and *Eyes of Laura Mars* (1978).

It wouldn't be entirely accurate to claim that *Mommie Dearest* killed off a brilliant career alone: for one thing, she has done excellent work since, most notably as an alcoholic opposite Mickey Rourke in *Barfly* (1987). But Dunaway is reportedly a difficult collaborator, and sexist Hollywood can be less than kind to women of even lesser temperament as they near middle age. Her recent work has been of little note, but a comeback could certainly be waiting in the wings. **TC**

Top Takes...

The Rules of Attraction 2002
Don Juan DeMarco 1995
The Two Jakes 1990
The Handmaid's Tale 1990
Barfly 1987
The Wicked Lady 1983
Mommie Dearest 1981
The Champ 1979
Eyes of Laura Mars 1978
Network 1976 ★
Three Days of the Condor 1975
The Towering Inferno 1974
Chinatown 1974 ☆
Little Big Man 1970
The Thomas Crown Affair 1968
Bonnie and Clyde 1967 ☆

"I'm still the little Southern girl . . . who really didn't feel like she belonged."

BRUNO GANZ

Born: Bruno Ganz, March 22, 1941 (Zürich-Seebach, Switzerland).

Star qualities: Important figure of German New Wave cinema; prominent player in contemporary European theater; introspective leading man of serious dramas; director.

Top Takes...

Der Untergang 2004 (*The Downfall: Hitler and the End of the Third Reich*)

The Manchurian Candidate 2004

Luther 2003

In weiter Ferne, so nah! 1993 (*Faraway, So Close!*)

The Last Days of Chez Nous 1992

Der Himmel über Berlin 1987 (*Wings of Desire*)

Dans la ville blanche 1983 (*In the White City*)

Nosferatu: Phantom der Nacht 1979 (*Nosferatu the Vampyre*)

The Boys from Brazil 1978

Der Amerikanische Freund 1977 (*The American Friend*)

Die Wildente 1976 (*The Wild Duck*)

Die Marquise von O . . . 1976 (*The Marquise of O*)

Although Swiss-born, Bruno Ganz is best known to those outside that region for his performances in many of the most significant German films of the past three decades. He has also appeared in movies from Greece, Italy, and the United States, among other countries. He made his theater debut in 1961 and gained a good reputation as a solid young actor. In 1970 he cofounded the Schaubühne theater company in Berlin, and continues to enjoy success on the stage today.

Ganz is most recognizable to international movie audiences for his leading roles in several films directed by Wim Wenders, most notably *Der Himmel über Berlin* (1987) (*Wings of Desire*) and its sequel, *In weiter Ferne, so nah!* (1993) (*Faraway, So Close!*). But the two first collaborated on the excellent *Die Amerikanische Freund* (1977) (*The American Friend*), one of Ganz's early significant film roles. Aside from Wenders, Ganz has worked for some of contemporary world cinema's preeminent filmmakers over the years: Éric Rohmer in *Die Marquise von O . . .* (1976) (*The Marquise of O*), Alain Tanner in *Dans la ville blanche* (1983) (*In the White City*), and Theo Angelopoulos in *Mia Aioniotita kai Mia Mera* (1998) (*Eternity and a Day*), among numerous others. Handsome in a modest, unassuming, everyday sense, Ganz is oddly instantly familiar despite his subtle, reserved screen presence. This understated quality made him an unlikely, but ultimately ideal, choice to portray one of history's most reviled figures, Adolf Hitler, in *Der Untergang* (2004) (*The Downfall: Hitler and the End of the Third Reich*), a depiction of Hitler's final days during World War II. It is one of Ganz's finest performances and was a role that made him the first German-speaking actor to play Hitler. **TC**

> "As Hitler [he] ignites the screen with every appearance."
>
> —James Wegg

JULIE CHRISTIE

Born: Julie Frances Christie, April 14, 1941 (Chabua, Assam, India).

Star qualities: Petite blonde and blue-eyed beauty; versatile leading lady of romantic dramas; sexy icon of swinging sixties London; animal rights and environmental activist.

Julie Christie was raised in India on her father's tea plantation. She went to England and France for her education before studying acting at London's Central School of Speech and Drama. She was first impressive on TV as the alien in the BBC science-fiction series *A for Andromeda* (1961). In films Christie was initially cast in English gamine and pretty-girl roles, appearing as a modern Audrey Hepburn opposite Tom Courtenay in John Schlesinger's British classic *Billy Liar* (1963). Christie worked again for Schlesinger as the free-living girl in *Darling* (1965), which won her an Oscar for Best Actress, and as Everdene Bathsheba in *Far from the Madding Crowd* (1967). She grew to become an international leading lady, adventurous actress, and welcome presence, winning substantial film leads such as Lara Antipova in David Lean's *Doctor Zhivago* (1965).

Christie sought less mainstream challenges, producing classics with directors François Truffaut in *Fahrenheit 451* (1966), Richard Lester in *Petulia* (1968), Joseph Losey in *The Go-Between* (1970), Robert Altman in *McCabe & Mrs. Miller* (1971), and Nicolas Roeg in *Don't Look Now* (1973). Involvement with her *McCabe* costar Warren Beatty found her in the ensemble of his comedy *Shampoo* (1975) and as a rare bland love interest in his romantic fantasy *Heaven Can Wait* (1978). After a spell away from movies, she returned as an older, still lovely, woman, taking the odd part in films such as *Memoirs of a Survivor* (1981) and *Afterglow* (1997). Her fun side reemerged in *Belphégor—Le fantôme du Louvre* (2001) (*Belphegor, Phantom of the Louvre*), and as Madame Rosmerta in *Harry Potter and the Prisoner of Azkaban* (2004). Offscreen, she is politically active in animal rights, environmental protection, and the antinuclear power movement. **KN**

Top Takes…

Harry Potter and the Prisoner of Azkaban 2004
Belphégor—Le fantôme du Louvre 2001
   (*Belphegor, Phantom of the Louvre*)
***Afterglow* 1997** ☆
Memoirs of a Survivor 1981
Heaven Can Wait 1978
Shampoo 1975
Don't Look Now 1973
***McCabe & Mrs. Miller* 1971** ☆
The Go-Between 1970
Petulia 1968
Far from the Madding Crowd 1967
Fahrenheit 451 1966
Doctor Zhivago 1965
***Darling* 1965** ★
Billy Liar 1963

"All that concentrated adulation is terribly corroding."
—On fame

1940s

BARBRA STREISAND

Born: Barbara Joan Streisand, April 24, 1942 (Brooklyn, New York, U.S.).

Star qualities: Popular singer; versatile leading lady of light comedies and romances; feisty; witty; comic timing; political liberal; director; producer; composer; writer.

Top Takes...

"I am simple, complex, generous, selfish, unattractive, beautiful, lazy, and driven."

More famous perhaps as a singer, Barbra Streisand has nonetheless made a significant mark on Hollywood filmmaking. Neither conventionally attractive nor particularly sexy, she was happily forced to take on roles in which these limitations would prove advantages. Impersonating Fanny Brice in both *Funny Girl* (1968) and *Funny Lady* (1975), Streisand proved talented at light comedy and romantic pathos. Although neither role required complicated acting, Streisand proved immensely popular as Brice, an easy choice for the Best Actress Oscar in *Funny Girl. Hello, Dolly!* (1969) perhaps tried too hard to work the same kind of magic.

On a Clear Day You Can See Forever (1970) showed clearly what Streisand could not do: convincingly portray a reincarnated Englishwoman. But two screwball comedies, *The Owl and the Pussycat* (1970) and *What's Up, Doc?* (1972) offered her ideal opportunities to display a talent for pure wackiness. She then went on to make one of the most profitable films of the 1970s, *The Way We Were* (1973), as her left-wing concerns and Jewish charm convincingly won over Robert Redford's priggish WASP. That same serious effervescence, and the fact that she looked good dressed in boys' clothes, made *Yentl* (1983) a smash success, but she was less impressive as an abused woman turned bitter prostitute in *Nuts* (1987). She successfully impersonated a Jewish psychiatrist in *The Prince of Tides* (1991), and more recently, in perhaps her best performance since *Yentl*, Streisand reprises the ethnically stereotypical role as psychiatrist for laughs in *Meet the Fockers* (2004), a film that allowed her to send up her intensity and her Jewishness as she became the cinema's most unabashed and celebrated sex therapist for seniors. **BP**

1940s

RICHARD ROUNDTREE

Born: Richard Roundtree, July 9, 1942 (New Rochelle, New York, U.S.).

Star qualities: Handsome and suave; coolly stylish; athletic action hero; leading man and versatile character actor; icon of 1970s "blaxploitation" movies; magnetic screen presence.

"Who's the black private dick that's a sex machine to all the chicks?" It's John Shaft. But, more importantly, it's actor Richard Roundtree. Identification with a single character can be a blessing and a curse for an actor, and that couldn't be truer than in Roundtree's case. He's a gifted and complex actor who has appeared in dozens of movies and TV episodes since his breakthrough role in *Shaft* (1971), but he will always be remembered for that iconic performance. To those who didn't experience the film's presence in the early 1970s, the importance of *Shaft* may be difficult to understand, but it is a groundbreaking movie. It was arguably the first time that a sexy, strong, confident African-American male dominated the screen in an action film released by a big Hollywood studio.

Shaft was one of the earliest and most significant "blaxploitation" movies of the 1970s, and Roundtree was at its center, just as he continued to reprise his eponymous role in the two sequels, *Shaft's Big Score!* (1972) and *Shaft in Africa* (1973). Unfortunately, *Shaft* is not a particularly good film; originally a generic detective movie written for a white lead, it is plodding and dull. But Roundtree brings a charismatic presence and playful wit to the proceedings, and he deserved to be a bigger star. Much of his work following the *Shaft* trio is not memorable, but he has remained a solid working actor. He also has an underrated gift for comedy, a quality more evident in his TV work than in his big screen roles. But his filmography is proof that an actor is not always able to capitalize on a spectacular debut role. Other than sporadic supporting turns in titles such as *Se7en* (1995), the Samuel L. Jackson revival of *Shaft* (2000), and *Brick* (2005), much of Roundtree's work is in fare unworthy of his talents. **TC**

Top Takes...

Brick 2005
Boat Trip 2002
Shaft 2000
Original Gangstas 1996
Theodore Rex 1995
Se7en 1995
Once Upon a Time . . . When We Were Colored 1995
Miami Cops 1989
City Heat 1984
Diamonds 1975
Man Friday 1975
Earthquake 1974
Shaft in Africa 1973
Shaft's Big Score! 1972
Shaft 1971

"Number one, it put me on the map . . . . To this day that film still works."—*On Shaft*

1940s

HARRISON FORD

Born: Harrison Ford, July 13, 1942 (Chicago, Illinois, U.S.).

Star qualities: Adventure roles are his trademark; rugged good looks blended with charm, sincerity, and an enviable physique; modestly performs many of his own stunts; universal appeal.

Top Takes...

K-19: The Widowmaker 2002

Sabrina 1995

Clear and Present Danger 1994

The Fugitive 1993

Patriot Games 1992

Regarding Henry 1991

Presumed Innocent 1990

Indiana Jones and the Last Crusade 1989

Working Girl 1988

Frantic 1988

The Mosquito Coast 1986

Witness 1985 ☆

Indiana Jones and the Temple of Doom 1984

Star Wars: Episode VI—Return of the Jedi 1983

Blade Runner 1982

Raiders of the Lost Ark 1981

Star Wars: Episode V—The Empire Strikes Back 1980

The Frisco Kid 1979

Apocalypse Now 1979

Force 10 from Navarone 1978

Star Wars 1977

American Graffiti 1973

Journey to Shiloh 1968

A Time for Killing 1967

RIGHT: *Star Wars*'s wisecracking hero Han Solo was Ford's breakthrough action role.

It's hard to describe the appeal of Harrison Ford. He's handsome, but not devastatingly so. He's tall, quiet, and reactive. Built like an athlete, he wears a scar across his chin that dates to a car accident in early adulthood. He carries himself well and he smiles in a way that seems honest and warm. In many ways, his persona doesn't involve deception, concealment, or any of the other masks of many performers who see their purpose in undertaking other personalities as the very heart of their craft. It may be that Ford is always playing versions of himself, reminding us of simpler times when a few reliable heroes stayed within the boundaries of their own comfort and ease.

Having been involved with two of the most profitable movie franchises ever, *Star Wars* and the *Indiana Jones* trilogy, Ford is also one of the industry's more reliable commercial talents. That a degree of this charm has waned in recent years is partly because Ford is known for action—but being an action star beyond your sixtieth birthday isn't as believable as it once was, given the demands of modern audiences.

Groomed in feature film bit parts (*A Time for Killing*, 1967; *Journey to Shiloh*, 1968) and TV appearances (*The Virginian*,

1967; *Gunsmoke*, 1972–1973), he was first noticed playing Bob Falfa in *American Graffiti* in 1973. That he was noticed by George Lucas in particular resulted in Ford's being cast in the pivotal role of Han Solo in the 1977 landmark, *Star Wars*.

Then, as if he had always been a star, Ford vaulted through the follow-up work (*Force 10 from Navarone*, 1978; *The Frisco Kid*, 1979) before reprising Solo in *The Empire Strikes Back* (1980) and starring as Indy in *Raiders of the Lost Ark* (1981). Later came more success with Solo and Indy, a spate of other popular titles (*Witness*, 1985; *Patriot Games*, 1992; *The Fugitive*, 1993; *Air Force One*, 1997), a few commercial failures (*The Mosquito Coast*, 1986; *Frantic*, 1988; *K-19: The Widowmaker*, 2002), and at least one overlooked classic (*Blade Runner*, 1982).

Now a sometime recluse, living part of each year on his Jackson Hole ranch in Wyoming, Ford's best years may still be ahead of him. **GCQ**

ABOVE: Ford making Indiana Jones one of cinema's best-loved adventure heroes.

Harrison the Hero

He has often played heroes in his movies, not least the fearless (aside from a snake phobia) Indiana Jones, but in real life actor Harrison Ford is not without his own personal share of manly skills.

- His willingness to perform many of his own stunts made Indiana Jones a more believable adventure hero.
- A qualified pilot, he once flew his own helicopter from his ranch in Wyoming in a rescue mission.
- Before acting he worked as a carpenter and cabinet maker. He put these skills to use in *The Mosquito Coast* and *Witness*.

AMITABH BACHCHAN

Born: Amit Shrivastava, October 11, 1942 (Allahabad, India).

Star qualities: Icon of Indian cinema; busy star of Bollywood, nicknamed "the big B"; tall, handsome; baritone voice; versatile leading man; angry young man roles; intense screen presence; producer.

Top Takes...

Dev 2004
Baghban 2003
Kabhi Khushi Kabhie Gham . . . 2001 (*Happiness & Tears*)
Mohabbatein 2000 (*Love Stories*)
Bade Miyan Chote Miyan 1998
Shakti 1982
Silsila 1981
Kaala Patthar 1979
Don 1978
Amar Akbar Anthony 1977
Sholay 1975 (*Embers*)
Chupke Chupke 1975
Deewaar 1975 (*I'll Die for Mama*)
Zanjeer 1973 (*The Chain*)

To simply call Amitabh Bachchan India's biggest movie star would be like calling Clint Eastwood a recognizable working actor. A justifiable legend in Indian film, Bachchan could be the most authoritative presence in cinema history: he commands the screen at all times, and hearing his famous sonorous tone boom from the screen is like hearing the voice of God—whether someone speaks Hindi or not.

Bachchan's career arc also reflects the path of Bollywood film since his explosion on to the screen in the 1970s. Just as actors such as Robert De Niro and Jack Nicholson reflected changes in U.S. society, Bachchan was the angry young man figure of the era, a powerful presence in his breakthrough drama *Zanjeer* (1973) (*The Chain*), and such classics as the action landmark *Sholay* (1975) (*Embers*) and the moving tragedy *Deewaar* (1975) (*I'll Die for Mama*). Yet while his piercing eyes and intense energy are perfectly suited for melodramas and gangster pictures, Bachchan proved equally adept at comedy in *Amar Akbar Anthony* (1977) and *Don* (1978).

Throughout the 1980s and 1990s, Bachchan's career was sidetracked. He left films in 1984 to become a Congress party candidate, as a favor to his friend Indian Prime Minister Rajiv Gandhi. But a report of involvement in financial irregularities—he was later found innocent—made him give up politics and return to film. His career is now as strong as ever, because he has aged into commanding elder roles in hits like *Mohabbatein* (2000) (*Love Stories*) and *Kabhi Khushi Kabhie Gham . . .* (2001) (*Happiness & Tears*). He *is* Indian cinema. And if India has the largest film industry in the world, and Bachchan is its biggest star, doesn't that make him essentially the world's greatest movie star? **TC**

> "I have never really been confident about my career at any stage."

LYNN REDGRAVE

Born: Lynn Rachel Redgrave, March 8, 1943 (London, England).

Star qualities: Tall; member of an illustrious acting dynasty; Shakespearean stagecraft; versatile character actress; well-cast in "ordinary girl" roles; feisty; witty; comic timing; writer.

Lynn Redgrave was born into one of the acting profession's most famous dynasties: her father is Sir Michael Redgrave, her mother Rachel Kempson, and her siblings are Corin Redgrave and Vanessa Redgrave. She trained at London's Central School of Speech and Drama and made her stage debut in *A Midsummer Night's Dream* (1962) at the Royal Court Theatre. She went on to work for Britain's National Theatre before making her film debut in *Tom Jones* (1963). She was truly established as a screen performer in the title role of *Georgy Girl* (1966), in which she is the large, ordinary nice girl contrasted with a beautiful bitch played by Charlotte Rampling. The role won her an Oscar nomination for Best Actress. She teamed with Rita Tushingham, another unconventional 1960s face, in *Girl with Green Eyes* (1964) and the amusing skit on the swinging London vogue *Smashing Time* (1967).

Redgrave has always been at her best in slightly dark-hued comedy such as *The National Health* (1973) and *The Big Bus* (1976). An attempt to play up her Englishness in *Every Little Crook and Nanny* (1972) didn't work well, but she turned up the neurotic dramatics for a TV version of *The Turn of the Screw* (1974). Strong character roles in *Shine* (1996) and *Gods and Monsters* (1998) reminded casting directors of her talents, lifting her out of oddball efforts like *Midnight* (1989), in which she played a horror hostess. She was aptly cast with her sister Vanessa in the small screen remake of *What Ever Happened to Baby Jane?* (1991), chewing on the plum Bette Davis role. In 2002 Redgrave was diagnosed with breast cancer and had a mastectomy. With her photographer daughter Annabel, she has written a book about her experience. She continues to work on both the stage and screen. **KN**

Top Takes...

Kinsey 2004
Anita and Me 2002
Gods and Monsters 1998 ☆
Shine 1996
Midnight 1989
The Big Bus 1976
The Happy Hooker 1975
The National Health 1973
*Everything You Always Wanted to Know About Sex * But Were Afraid to Ask* 1972
Every Little Crook and Nanny 1972
The Virgin Soldiers 1969
Smashing Time 1967
Georgy Girl 1966 ☆
Girl with Green Eyes 1964
Tom Jones 1963

"Looking at my horrible ugly bulk on a huge screen was the turning point in my life."

CHRISTOPHER WALKEN

Born: Ronald Walken, March 31, 1943 (Queens, New York, U.S.).

Star qualities: Lanky, pale, and nervous-looking; highly versatile leading man and character actor; haunting screen presence; flair for playing psychotic roles; comic timing; dancing skills; writer; director; producer.

Top Takes...

There's a unique and ironic dichotomy to the cinematic presence of Christopher Walken: although he is remembered largely for his intense portrayals of the tormented in *The Deer Hunter* (1978) and *The Dead Zone* (1983); the vicious in *King of New York* (1990) and *True Romance* (1993); and the psychotically evil in *At Close Range* (1986) and *The Comfort of Strangers* (1990), mentioning Walken's name is likely to raise an immediate smile from almost anyone.

Are they recalling his more comedic work, such as in *Annie Hall* (1977), *Pulp Fiction* (1994), and *Wedding Crashers* (2005)? His occasional sympathetic role, such as the father in *Catch Me If You Can* (2002)? His musical performances in everything from *Pennies from Heaven* (1981) to *Hairspray* (2007) to a Fatboy Slim video? Or even his participation in family fare such as *Sarah, Plain and Tall: Winter's End* (1999) and a voice in *Antz* (1998)? No. The answer is that people love those who take pride and pleasure in their work, no matter what the job, and Walken possesses this quality in abundance. He lights up any scene in which he appears with his offbeat energy, and it is fortunate that he continues to be so prolific, for many movies would be a little bit better with a little bit of Walken. He began as a child actor in television, breaking into film in the early 1970s with *The Anderson Tapes* (1971) and achieving stardom with *The Deer Hunter* later in that decade. Although leading roles have appeared (he is riveting in both *The Dead Zone* and *King of New York*), Walken has mainly specialized in eccentric supporting characterizations in recent years. He works frequently and claims to have never refused a role, and for everyone who savors Walken's unconventional allure, that is a good thing. **TC**

"I don't need to be made to look evil. I can do that on my own."

1940s

MALCOLM McDOWELL

Born: Malcolm John Taylor, June 13, 1943 (Leeds, Yorkshire, England).

Star qualities: Sexy; charming; piercing blue eyes; witty; dynamic leading man and character actor; performer of iconic villain roles, especially in *A Clockwork Orange*; electrifying screen presence; producer.

Malcolm McDowell studied acting at the London Academy of Music and Dramatic Art. He went on to work at his parents' pub, but lost his job when the pub went bankrupt; his alcoholic father drank away the profits. He then had a variety of menial jobs, including one as a sales representative for a coffee company, before he found work as an extra with Britain's prestigious Royal Shakespeare Company.

He first gained prominence when director Lindsay Anderson cast him as rebellious student Mick Travis in his landmark film of teenage alienation, *If...* (1968). The performance caught the attention of director Stanley Kubrick, who picked him to play the psychotic and gratuitously violent Alex de Large in the controversial *A Clockwork Orange* (1971). It was a performance so powerful and memorable—even when raping and murdering, he could be witty and charming—that decades later McDowell would still be typecast as a villain.

McDowell reprised his Mick Travis role for Anderson in *O Lucky Man!* (1973), and again in *Britannia Hospital* (1982). He also tackled the starring role in the controversial epic romp *Caligola* (1979) (*Caligula*), financed by *Penthouse* magazine founder Bob Guccione and directed by Tinto Brass. His first U.S. film was *Time After Time* (1979), where he effectively shunned his devilish image to play a gentle, shy, and romantic H. G. Wells, but in subsequent years he is most remembered for his supporting roles playing villains in *Cat People* (1982) and *Blue Thunder* (1983). In recent years he is best known for his role as another villain, Dr. Tolian Soran, who famously kills off the beloved Captain James T. Kirk in *Star Trek: Generations* (1994). McDowell still works steadily and remains one of Britain's most popular actors. **DW**

Top Takes...

Bye Bye Benjamin 2006
Between Strangers 2002
Gangster No. 1 2000
Star Trek: Generations 1994
Bopha! 1993
Blue Thunder 1983
Britannia Hospital 1982
Cat People 1982
Look Back in Anger 1980
Time After Time 1979
Caligola 1979 (*Caligula*)
Aces High 1976
Royal Flash 1975
O Lucky Man! 1973
A Clockwork Orange 1971
If... 1968

1940s

"It's a remarkable film ... I'd be a raving idiot not to be thrilled with that."—On *A Clockwork Orange*

ROBERT DE NIRO

Born: Robert Mario De Niro Jr., August 17, 1943 (New York City, New York, U.S.).

Star qualities: Astute choice of roles; superstar status although ultra-private; meticulously researches his characters; prolific and respected actor over four decades; known for playing violent disturbed characters; comic talent; director.

Top Takes...

Meet the Fockers 2004
Analyze This 1999
Jackie Brown 1997
Wag the Dog 1997
Cop Land 1997
Sleepers 1996
Heat 1995
Casino 1995
Frankenstein 1994
Cape Fear 1991 ☆
Backdraft 1991
Awakenings 1990 ☆
Goodfellas 1990
Midnight Run 1988
The Untouchables 1987
Brazil 1985
The King of Comedy 1983
Once Upon a Time in America 1984
Raging Bull 1980 ★
The Deer Hunter 1978 ☆
New York, New York 1977
Novecento 1976 (*1900*)
Taxi Driver 1976 ☆
The Godfather: Part II 1974 ★
Mean Streets 1973

RIGHT: De Niro enters the Hollywood mainstream in *The Godfather: Part II*.

Currently recognized for his endorsement of American Express, which is one of many ways he helps promote his film production company, the TriBeCa Film Center, and its related film festival, Robert De Niro has come to epitomize New York City life through his movies over the last 35 years. With a persona built upon coiled, repressed intensity that literally explodes in operatic bouts of frustration and anger, and with a thin body given to easy movement, he's a courageous and mesmerizing performer who has worked steadily for decades in film after film after film.

Born in New York City's Manhattan to artist parents, he trained at the Stella Adler Conservatory and the American Workshop. After making friends with individuals in the group of young filmmakers orbiting the producer and director Roger Corman in the late 1960s, early performances he turned in demonstrated the live-wire sense of things to come, first truly showcased in *Bang the Drum Slowly* in 1973. Then there followed *Mean Streets*, also in 1973, and his first collaboration with longtime friend and constant source for creative alchemy,

Martin Scorsese. A speedy ascent to the height of Hollywood's acting ranks followed, with a surprise Best Supporting Actor Academy Award for *The Godfather: Part II* (1974).

ABOVE: The alienated and disturbed Travis Bickle practices his moves in *Taxi Driver*.

Never conventionally handsome, De Niro is unusual for having opened a seam in the Hollywood type, and this with a persona enclosed in the shadows of brooding and thoughtful observation. He's also got a pronounced mole and slim good looks, and he has been historically willing to dramatically alter his body for roles and believable performances while he has painstakingly researched the parts. This

"There is a mixture of anarchy and discipline in the way I work."

may be part of his Method training, but the tendency has allowed him to portray an aristocrat (*Novecento (1900)*, 1976), a saxophonist (*New York, New York*, 1977), a Vietnam vet (*The Deer Hunter*, 1978), Al Capone (*The Untouchables*, 1987), an

New York Guys

Robert De Niro is renowned for his enduring and fruitful collaboration with director and fellow New Yorker Martin Scorsese. They first worked together in 1973 when the young De Niro played smalltime Mafia hood "Johnny Boy" in *Mean Streets*. Scorsese has said that their creative relationship is so strong that they can often understand each other without even talking. Although their combined creative sparks have not lit up the screen in recent years, Scorsese says that he still shows almost every script he writes or considers directing to De Niro to get the actor's opinion regardless of whether he ends up getting involved.

- The pair worked on another seven movies after *Mean Streets*: *Taxi Driver* (1976); *New York, New York* (1977); *Raging Bull* (1980); *The King of Comedy* (1983); *Goodfellas* (1990); *Cape Fear* (1991); and *Casino* (1995).

- De Niro and Scorsese were brought up blocks away from each other in Manhattan. When introduced at a party in 1972, they realized that they had seen each other many times before but never spoken.

- Many actors are very keen to work with Scorsese because he often draws award-winning performances out of them (witness De Niro). Nominated for a Best Director Oscar five times, Scorsese finally won for *The Departed* (2006).

RIGHT: As Jake La Motta De Niro punches his way to his second Oscar in *Raging Bull*.

encephalitis victim (*Awakenings*, 1990), a priest (*Sleepers*, 1996), and the voice of a gangster shark (*Shark Tale*, 2004), all without causing his audience to lose sight of the overall story in which he is but one performer.

His second Oscar was earned for the electrifying and terrifying *Raging Bull* (1980), a truly memorable horror of personality. Over the course of two hours devoted to the autobiographically derived story of Jake La Motta, De Niro so fully embodied working-class paranoia, rage, and limitation as to render all other cinematic sports figures two-dimensional shadows in comparison. But audiences largely stayed away, probably due to the film's overall tone and violence, meaning De Niro's high standing has been more the stuff of legend than the basis for screenings outside the critical establishment.

Stalwart performer

Subsequently recognized for his artistic integrity and willingness to work year-in, year-out in projects of all genres (*Once Upon a Time in America*, 1984; *Frankenstein*, 1994; *The Adventures of Rocky & Bullwinkle*, 2000), all levels of production value (*Hi, Mom!*, 1970; *Cop Land*, 1997; *The Score*, 2001), and all resulting levels of meritorious achievement (*Goodfellas*, 1990 vs. *The Fan*, 1996), De Niro has also seen his fortunes rise according to the dictates of popular taste. Where he once earned a relatively modest $35,000 for *Taxi Driver* (1976), his regular salary now runs in the multiple millions, as evidenced by the $20 million he was paid for both *Analyze That* (2002) and *Meet the Fockers* (2004). De Niro isn't solely motivated by dollar signs, though, and has given time to fund-raisers and movies with smaller budgets (*Flawless*, 1999).

But De Niro's greatest attribute is probably the work ethic that has kept him employed long after it was necessary to prove himself or earn another paycheck. He is, simply put, an actor, and he's enriched the cinema in countless ways, from *Bloody Mama* (1970) to *Brazil* (1985), and *Backdraft* (1991) to *Wag the Dog* (1997), giving new meaning to the term "body of work" while building our expectations for what's next. **GCQ**

1940s

CATHERINE DENEUVE

Born: Catherine Fabienne Dorléac, October 22, 1943 (Paris, France).

Star qualities: An unforgettable femme fatale; fabled beauty; the archetypal ice maiden; has won international acclaim though managed to avoid making many films in Hollywood; brought up in an acting family.

Top Takes…

Rois et reine 2004 (Kings & Queen)
8 femmes 2002 (8 Women)
Dancer in the Dark 2000
Le temps retrouvé 1999 (Time Regained)
Belle maman 1999 (Beautiful Mother)
Place Vendôme 1998
Les Voleurs 1996
Ma saison préférée 1993 (My Favorite Season)
Indochine 1992 (Indochina) ☆
The Hunger 1983
Le dernier métro 1980 (The Last Metro)
Hustle 1975
Un flic 1972 (Dirty Money)
Tristana 1970
La sirène du Mississippi 1969
   (Mississippi Mermaid)
Mayerling 1968
Belle de jour 1967
Les demoiselles de Rochefort 1967
   (The Young Girls of Rochefort)
Les Créatures 1966 (The Creatures)
Repulsion 1965
Les parapluies de Cherbourg 1964
   (The Umbrellas of Cherbourg)
Le Vice et la vertu 1963 (Vice and Virtue)

Very often, Catherine Deneuve (she took her mother's maiden name to avoid confusion with her elder sister Françoise, also an actress until her death in 1967) seems hardly to be acting at all, so understated is her performance. Yet it has been argued, not without justification, that in doing "less," Deneuve actually conveys considerably more than most other screen actresses. But if so, what, precisely, is she conveying? There's the question: whatever the role, Deneuve tends to remain an enigma. There is always something mysterious about her characters, which is why she manages to hold our attention. And her greatness as an actress lies in that very mystery, because her air of secretiveness, suggestive of private inner thoughts and feelings, allows us to project more fully on to her characters.

A pity, then, that this reputedly cool and reticent blonde never got to work with Hitchcock (though there were plans in the 1970s for such a collaboration). Not that her resume is lacking in great directors; after a few roles in her teens—one of which (Le Vice et la vertu (Vice and Virtue), 1963) led to a relationship with and a child by Roger Vadim—she first achieved international fame in Jacques Demy's all-sung

RIGHT: Deneuve and Nino Castelnuovo play young lovers in The Umbrellas of Cherbourg.

romantic melodrama *Les parapluies de Cherbourg*, (1964) (*The Umbrellas of Cherbourg*). Next came another magical collaboration with Demy (*Les demoiselles de Rochefort* (*The Young Girls of Rochefort*), 1967), along with films for Roman Polanski (*Repulsion*, 1965), Luis Buñuel (*Belle de jour*, 1967; *Tristana*, 1970), and François Truffaut (*Le dernier métro* (*The Last Metro*), 1980). All three directors made her "unknowability" key to these films, hinting at perverse, even dangerous, desires behind the seductive veneer of her seemingly innocent face.

Nominated for an Oscar for her performance in *Indochine* (1992) (*Indochina*), Deneuve is a prolific, hardworking actress. Her versatility and quiet expertise have made for fine performances for Jean-Pierre Melville (*Un flic* (*Dirty Money*), 1972), Robert Aldrich (*Hustle*, 1975), André Téchiné (*Les Voleurs*, 1996), Lars von Trier (*Dancer in the Dark*, 2000), and François Ozon (*8 femmes* (*8 Women*), 2002). **GA**

ABOVE: Deneuve exudes low-lidded sexuality as Séverine Serizy in *Belle de jour*.

1940s

The Deneuve Factor

Sexy, beautiful, and elegant, Gallic actress Catherine Deneuve remains an iconic figure in world cinema and fashion.

- The face of Chanel No. 5 in the 1970s, Deneuve has even had a perfume named after her.
- She was once the muse of fashion designer Yves St. Laurent.
- She currently models for MAC Cosmetics and L'Oréal Paris.
- On her looks: "I know that if I didn't look the way I looked, I would never have started in films. That, I remember, and I know I have to accept it."

BEN KINGSLEY

Born: Krishna Bhanji, December 31, 1943 (Scarborough, Yorkshire, England).

Star qualities: Bald; slight frame; Shakespearean stagecraft; versatile leading man and character actor who has avoided being typecast; chameleon-like quality; sonorous voice; singer; knighted; producer.

Top Takes...

Lucky Number Slevin 2006
Oliver Twist 2005
House of Sand and Fog 2003 ☆
Sexy Beast 2000 ☆
Twelfth Night: Or What You Will 1996
Death and the Maiden 1994
Schindler's List 1993
Bugsy 1991 ☆
Romeo-Juliet 1990
Pascali's Island 1988
Maurice 1987
Turtle Diary 1985
Betrayal 1983
Gandhi 1982 ★
Fear is the Key 1972

English-born of mixed Indian and Jewish parentage, Sir Ben Kingsley is supremely qualified by birth to play a wide range of darker-skinned males, from a very convincing Meyer Lansky in the *Godfather*-light drama *Bugsy* (1991), which won him an Oscar nomination for Best Supporting Actor, to the most famous of British-educated Indians, Mahatma Gandhi in Richard Attenborough's hagiography *Gandhi* (1982), which won him an Oscar for Best Actor. Neither part demanded much in the way of a layered performance, but Kingsley has shown his considerable acting gifts in more demanding roles, such as a betrayed husband caught in the Pinteresque restrained hysterics of *Betrayal* (1983), and as the canny but suspicious Jewish businessman of *Schindler's List* (1993).

He made his London stage debut as the singing narrator of The Beatles's manager Brian Epstein's *A Smashing Day* (1966), and went on to join the Royal Shakespeare Company. He appeared in TV series such as the soap opera *Coronation Street* (1960) and his first film role was in *Fear is the Key* (1972), before he garnered international fame with *Gandhi*.

In the last decade or so, working in both TV and theatrical films, Kingsley has had fewer opportunities to shine. He was impressive enough as terrifying gangster Don Logan in *Sexy Beast* (2000) and as a proud Iranian exile struggling to keep his family together in *House of Sand and Fog* (2003) to win Oscar nominations for Best Supporting and Best Actor respectively. Otherwise, he's added a touch of exotic competence to minor productions: a slimy former policeman guilty of political torture in *Death and the Maiden* (1994); a more than adequate Fagin in *Oliver Twist* (2005); and another Jewish gangster in *Lucky Number Slevin* (2006). **BP**

"If I knew I was going to win, I would not have gone dressed as a waiter." — On winning his Oscar

1940s

RUTGER HAUER

Born: Rutger Oelsen Hauer, January 23, 1944 (Breukelen, Utrecht, Holland).

Star qualities: "The Dutch Paul Newman"; tall, blond, blue-eyed, and ruggedly handsome; leading man who plays action heroes and sinister villains; environmentalist; producer; director.

An immensely gifted, intense actor with a reputation undoubtedly tarnished by slumming through dozens of low-budget projects that occupy the dire direct-to-video hinterlands for the past 15 years or so, Rutger Hauer looked to be a potential superstar at one point in his career.

Reflect back to the 1980s: already a huge star in his native Holland for his work in, among other high-profile projects, Paul Verhoeven hits such as *Turks fruit* (1973) (*Turkish Delight*) and *Soldaat van Oranje* (1977) (*Soldier of Orange*), Hauer began working in the United States in villainous roles for major movies such as *Nighthawks* (1981), *Blade Runner* (1982), and *The Hitcher* (1986); and more complex characterizations for other big titles such as *Ladyhawke* (1985) and Verhoeven's English-language debut *Flesh+Blood* (1985). He has an instantly unforgettable face capable of registering rage, sexuality, and tenderness in equal measure; and a natural presence that immediately illuminates any scene in which he appears.

So what happened? Hauer tried on the generic action movie leading man role in the cheesy but amusing *Wanted: Dead or Alive* (1987), and then rapidly plummeted into the straight-to-video wasteland thereafter, only recently resurfacing in supporting roles in major films such as *Sin City* (2005) and *Batman Begins* (2005). Examine Hauer's list of credits from 1988 to, say, 2003, and ask who has seen more than one or two out of the dozens of movies in which he appeared then. This is perhaps the biggest waste of an actor's talent since Klaus Kinski cashed so many paychecks for garbage in the latter half of his career. Come back, Rutger: your steely gaze and magnetic charisma have been missed. All is forgiven. **TC**

Top Takes...

Batman Begins 2005
Sin City 2005
Tempesta 2004
Confessions of a Dangerous Mind 2002
Buffy the Vampire Slayer 1992
La leggenda del santo bevitore 1988
 (*The Legend of the Holy Drinker*)
Wanted: Dead or Alive 1987
The Hitcher 1986
Flesh+Blood 1985
Ladyhawke 1985
Eureka 1984
Blade Runner 1982
Nighthawks 1981
Soldaat van Oranje 1977 (*Soldier of Orange*)
Turks fruit 1973

> "I [know I] don't look like the Hunchback of Notre Dame but I can't understand the fuss."

JEAN-PIERRE LÉAUD

Born: Jean-Pierre Léaud, May 28, 1944 (Paris, France).

Star qualities: Vulnerable, romantic male face of French New Wave cinema; lean Gallic good looks; floppy dark hair; rebellious; outspoken political activist; writer; director.

Top Takes...

The Dreamers 2003

Ni neibian jidian 2001
    (What Time Is It Over There?)

Les keufs 1987 (Lady Cops)

L'amour en fuite 1979 (Love on the Run)

La maman et la putain 1973
    (The Mother and the Whore)

Ultimo tango a Parigi 1972 (Last Tango in Paris)

Os Herdeiros 1970 (The Heirs)

Domicile conjugal 1970 (Bed & Board)

Porcile 1969 (Pigpen)

Baisers volés 1968 (Stolen Kisses)

Dialóg 20-40-60 1968 (Dialogue)

Masculin Féminin: 15 faits précis 1966
    (Masculine, Feminine: In 15 Acts)

L'amour à vingt ans 1962 (Love at Twenty)

Les Quatre cents coups 1959 (The 400 Blows)

> "[Léaud] provokes extremes of identification and irritation in his audience."—Philippa Hawker

Along with fellow actor Jean-Paul Belmondo, Jean-Pierre Léaud emerged as the male face of the French New Wave movement of the 1960s. From his performance as the young Antoine Doinel in François Truffaut's classic *Les Quatre cents coups* (1959) (*The 400 Blows*) to his recent iconic cameos in contemporary films such as Ming-liang Tsai's exquisite *Ni neibian jidian* (2001) (*What Time Is It Over There?*) and Bernardo Bertolucci's nostalgic *The Dreamers* (2003), Léaud occupies an important position as one of French cinema's most recognizable, enduring, and, at times, outspoken stars.

Léaud was born to scenarist Pierre Léaud and the actress Jacqueline Pierreux, and grew up in front of the camera. Such a claim seems particularly appropriate when one considers Léaud's career in the years spanning the 1960s and 1970s. As the fifteen-year-old Doinel, his climactic expression of panicked disillusionment mixed with courageous defiance would prove prophetic, because all-too-similar countenances eventually etched their way onto many a young person's face in the decades to follow. Fittingly, in his work with Truffaut's fellow New Wave auteur, Jean-Luc Godard, Léaud portrayed an eclectic array of angry young men searching to effect social change in films such as *Masculin Féminin: 15 faits précis* (1966) (*Masculine, Feminine: In 15 Acts*). In 1968, a tumultuous year across the globe, Léaud was a major social and political activist. He braved armed police to read an open letter calling for the reinstatement of the recently ousted Henri Langlois as director of the Cinémathèque Française. Delivered before a crowd of disenchanted students, outraged film lovers, and striking laborers, his address remains one of the most important documents in the history of French cinema. **JM**

KLAUS MARIA BRANDAUER

Born: Klaus Georg Steng, June 22, 1944 (Alt Aussee, Austria).

Star qualities: Stocky, versatile leading man of serious dramas; character actor; highly respected actor of the German stage; charisma; imposing screen presence; director.

Born in Austria, Klaus Maria Brandauer studied theater in Germany at the Stuttgart Academy of Music and Dramatic Arts. After graduation, he started working in repertory theater until he was hired into the cast of the renowned Burgtheater in Vienna. By 1970, Brandauer had become a resounding success on the stage in the German-speaking world, famous for his versatility and charisma. He made his film debut as a villain in the espionage thriller *The Salzburg Connection* (1972).

Brandauer attracted international attention with his galvanizing performance as the showy actor Hendrik Hoefgen corrupted by Nazi power in István Szabó's adaptation of Heinrich Mann's novel *Mephisto* (1981). The picture won an Oscar for Best Foreign Language Film. Brandauer then capitalized on his international recognition by starring as nemesis Maximilian Largo in *Never Say Never Again* (1983), Sean Connery's return to the 007 franchise. In 1985, he received a Best Supporting Actor Oscar nomination for his portrayal of Meryl Streep's unchaste husband Baron Bror Blixen in *Out of Africa* (1985). Brandauer also teamed with Szabó on the movies *Oberst Redl* (1985) (*Colonel Redl*) and *Hanussen* (1988).

The next few years offered a series of well-essayed roles, including *Streets of Gold* (1986) as a Russian expatriate boxing coach; *Burning Secret* (1988) as the womanizing Baron Alexander von Hauenstein; a reunion with Connery as a Soviet scientist in *The Russia House* (1990); and a role in the Disney Jack London adaptation *White Fang* (1991). Splitting his time between stage and screen, Brandauer has also stepped behind the camera. His directorial debut was the biopic *Georg Elser—Einer aus Deutschland* (1989) (*Georg Elser*), in which he also stars as the lone would-be assassin of Adolf Hitler. **WW**

Top Takes...

Poem—Ich setzte den Fuss in die Luft und sie trug 2003 (*Poem: I Set My Foot Upon the Air and It Carried Me*)
Jedermanns Fest 2002 (*Everyman's Feast*)
Rembrandt 1999
White Fang 1991
The Russia House 1990
Georg Elser—Einer aus Deutschland 1989 (*Georg Elser*)
Burning Secret 1988
Hanussen 1988
Streets of Gold 1986
Out of Africa 1985 ☆
Oberst Redl 1985 (*Colonel Redl*)
Never Say Never Again 1983
Mephisto 1981
The Salzburg Connection 1972

"What do they want from me now? After all, I am just an actor."—Hendrik Hoefgen, *Mephisto*

MICHAEL DOUGLAS

Born: Michael Kirk Douglas, September 25, 1944 (New Brunswick, New Jersey, U.S.).

Star qualities: Member of Hollywood royalty; high-profile celebrity marriage to Catherine Zeta-Jones; leading man of romances and dramas; astute choice of films; gravitas; director; producer.

Top Takes...

You, Me and Dupree 2006
Traffic 2000
Wonder Boys 2000
The American President 1995
Disclosure 1994
Falling Down 1993
Basic Instinct 1992
The War of the Roses 1989
Black Rain 1989
***Wall Street* 1987 ★**
Fatal Attraction 1987
Romancing the Stone 1984
The China Syndrome 1979
Coma 1978

After so many years a leading man in the industry, Michael Douglas has recently become a frequent focus of gossip because of his second marriage to Welsh beauty and Oscar-winning actress Catherine Zeta-Jones, who is 25 years his junior. But youth has been kind to Douglas, the son of the star Kirk Douglas. Even with such a long shadow to overcome, Douglas has accomplished the feat admirably.

He first earned recognition and success playing a police detective on TV's *The Streets of San Francisco* (1972). The young Douglas also proved himself a showbiz mind by optioning the rights to Ken Kesey's *One Flew Over the Cuckoo's Nest* (1975), and then produced the Oscar-winning picture starring Jack Nicholson. At the same time he worked steadily in front of the camera in such movies as *Coma* (1978) and *The China Syndrome* (1979); but it was *Romancing the Stone* (1984) that made him a big star, which he soon capped with a Best Actor Academy Award win as the epitome of 1980s financial greed, Gordon Gekko, in Oliver Stone's *Wall Street* (1987).

Since then there have been hits such as *Basic Instinct* (1992), misses such as *One Night at McCool's* (2001), and misfires such as *The Game* (1997). Along the way he has continued producing successful and interesting movies such as *Flatliners* (1990), *The Rainmaker* (1997), and *Face/Off* (1997). But he is still putting in rich performances such as the beleaguered English professor Grady Tripp in the dark comedy *Wonder Boys* (2000), while ceding a certain sphere of activity to emerging, younger talents, reserving his energies for prestige projects such as *Traffic* (2000). Offscreen, Douglas is a notable supporter of the U.S. Democratic Party. In 1998, he was appointed a United Nations Messenger of Peace. **GCQ**

> "[L.A.] is one of the most frustrating and depressing places to be an actor."

UDO KIER

Born: Udo Kierspe, October 14, 1944 (Cologne, Germany).

Star qualities: Cult European leading man of horror and art theater films; villainous good looks; piercing blue eyes; vampire player; longtime collaborator with director Lars von Trier; sinister; director.

In his long and distinguished, but also terribly uneven, career, Udo Kier has never played the devil. He should have. There is no actor who looks as possessed as him, and the many diabolic parts he has played in otherwise forgettable movies, from the Pilgrim of Death in *Pan* (1973), through Jack the Ripper in *Lulu* (1980) and Baron Tante Teufel in *Egomania—Insel ohne Hoffnung* (1986), to Erich von Stroheim in *Dog Daze* (1995), could probably earn him a doctoral degree in Satanism.

Kier first came to be noticed in *Hexen bis aufs Blut gequält* (1970) (*Mark of the Devil*). He became infamous through a chance meeting with director Paul Morrissey on an airplane flight from Rome to Munich. Kier was sitting next to a man who asked him what he did, and Kier said he was an actor. The man was Morrissey, and he wrote Kier's telephone number down in his passport because he didn't have a piece of paper. Kier one day got a call asking him to play Baron Frankenstein in Morrissey's Andy Warhol-sponsored picture *Flesh for Frankenstein* (1973). Kier then followed this up with another Morrissey picture, *Blood for Dracula* (1974), and the cinematic bible of sadomasochism, Just Jaeckin's *Histoire d'O* (1975) (*The Story of O*). His subsequent roles include demonic maniacs in far-out exploitation movies such as *Spermula* (1976) and *Suspiria* (1977), but also more muted, thoughtful parts in Rainer Werner Fassbinder's *Lili Marleen* (1981), and occasional Hollywood cameos in *Blade* (1998) and *Armageddon* (1998).

Kier has also appeared in nearly all Lars von Trier's films, including *Dogville* (2003), and is good friends with the Danish director. Kier's lust for playing in vampire movies seems insatiable; his best performance has been in *Shadow of the Vampire* (2000). **EM**

Top Takes...

Dogville 2003
Shadow of the Vampire 2000
Blade 1998
Armageddon 1998
Dog Daze 1995
Egomania—Insel ohne Hoffnung 1986
Lili Marleen 1981
Lulu 1980
Suspiria 1977
Spermula 1976
Histoire d'O 1975 (*The Story of O*)
Blood for Dracula 1974
Flesh for Frankenstein 1973
Pan 1973
Hexen bis aufs Blut gequält 1970
   (*Mark of the Devil*)

"Only an angel can play the devil because the devil was a fallen angel."

1940s

DANNY DeVITO

Born: Daniel Michael DeVito Jr., November 17, 1944 (Asbury Park, New Jersey, U.S.).

Star qualities: Italian-American diminutive funny man; rotund; balding; riotous screen presence; versatile character actor; plays comic and sleazy villain roles; writer; producer; director.

Top Takes...

1940s

"I've got lawyers. They are like nuclear weapons: I've got em coz everyone else has."

Danny DeVito enrolled at New York's American Academy of Dramatic Arts to learn more about cosmetology, because he was working as a hairdresser and cosmetician at his sister's beauty salon. It was at this point that he changed his career course and decided to pursue acting. He went on to have small parts on the stage and in movies, and first came to notice as a background crazy in *One Flew Over the Cuckoo's Nest* (1975). But he achieved fame in the role of the peppery taxicab company dispatcher, Louie DePalma, in the TV sitcom *Taxi* (1978–1983). James L. Brooks, creator of *Taxi*, spotlighted DeVito in a comic cameo in *Terms of Endearment* (1983), and the actor raised his profile with funny villainy in *Romancing the Stone* (1984), one of the *Ruthless People* (1986), and a chip-on-his-shoulder, aluminum-siding salesman in *Tin Men* (1987).

As a director of movies such as *Throw Momma from the Train* (1987), *The War of the Roses* (1989), *Matilda* (1996), and *Death to Smoochy* (2002), DeVito gravitates toward comedy so black it hurts, but he tends not to play the worst of the films' monstrous people. When director Tim Burton cast him as a total freak, the Penguin, in *Batman Returns* (1992), DeVito created a human toon who still manages some poignance. Partnered with the hulking Arnold Schwarzenegger in *Twins* (1988) and *Junior* (1994), DeVito remained an A-list comedy performer. But he was more interesting in secondary roles such as a movie star in *Get Shorty* (1995) or the scandal publisher in *L.A. Confidential* (1997), although he was convincing as a cynical lawyer starring alongside Matt Damon in *The Rainmaker* (1997). He runs Jersey Films production company with his wife, the actress Rhea Perlman. The company's production credits include *Pulp Fiction* (1994) and *Erin Brockovich* (2000). **KN**

MIA FARROW

Born: Maria de Lourdes Villiers-Farrow, February 9, 1945 (Los Angeles, California, U.S.).

Star qualities: Waiflike beauty; slender, sexy, vulnerable screen presence; comic timing; intelligent; one-time muse of Woody Allen; advocate for children's rights.

Mia Farrow has always been a showbiz creature. She is the daughter of director John Farrow and actress Maureen O'Sullivan, former Jane to Tarzan. She has also been either married to or associated with some high-profile men: actor and crooner Frank Sinatra, composer and conductor André Previn, and actor and director Woody Allen. After a stint in the hit TV series *Peyton Place* (1964–1966), she came to movies in fragile, kooky waif roles, and was one of the faces of the 1960s. She was frazzled as the Antichrist's expectant mother in Roman Polanski's *Rosemary's Baby* (1968), and appeared in major studio attempts to click with the free-spirited youth market such as *John and Mary* (1969) opposite Dustin Hoffman.

Adrift in the 1970s, despite playing the gauche socialite Daisy Buchanan opposite Robert Redford in *The Great Gatsby* (1974), Farrow was funny and topless as the sister-in-law pregnant by the groom in Robert Altman's *A Wedding* (1978). But she then slipped in disasters such as *Avalanche* (1978). Her offscreen pairing with Allen offered her excellent, interesting onscreen material: *A Midsummer Night's Sex Comedy* (1982), *Zelig* (1983), *Broadway Danny Rose* (1984), *The Purple Rose of Cairo* (1985), *Hannah and Her Sisters* (1986), *Radio Days* (1987), *Another Woman* (1988), *New York Stories* (1989), *Crimes and Misdemeanors* (1989), *Alice* (1990), *Shadows and Fog* (1992), and *Husbands and Wives* (1992). But the relationship ended in very public acrimony, and Farrow has since produced little of note: it has been aged kooks such as in *Widows' Peak* (1994) and cameos such as the evil nanny in *The Omen* (2006). However, her return to the New York stage to appear Off-Broadway in the play *Fran's Bed* (2005) won her critical acclaim. **KN**

Top Takes...

The Omen 2006
Widows' Peak 1994
Husbands and Wives 1992
Shadows and Fog 1992
Crimes and Misdemeanors 1989
New York Stories 1989
Another Woman 1988
Radio Days 1987
Hannah and Her Sisters 1986
The Purple Rose of Cairo 1985
Broadway Danny Rose 1984
Zelig 1983
A Midsummer Night's Sex Comedy 1982
A Wedding 1978
The Great Gatsby 1974
Rosemary's Baby 1968

"I wondered if, after all the things I'd been through, could I really act again?"

HELEN MIRREN

Born: Ilyena Vasilievna Mironov, July 26, 1945 (Chiswick, London, England).

Star qualities: A class act; sensual, sophisticated beauty; virtuoso elegant leading lady of dramas; brave performer; stagecraft; feisty good humor; famous for doing nude scenes.

Top Takes...

The Queen 2006 ★
Calendar Girls 2003
Gosford Park 2001 ☆
Last Orders 2001
The Passion of Ayn Rand 1999
Critical Care 1997
Some Mother's Son 1996
The Madness of King George 1994 ☆
Where Angels Fear to Tread 1991
The Comfort of Strangers 1990
The Cook, the Thief, his Wife & her Lover 1989
The Mosquito Coast 1986
Excalibur 1981
The Long Good Friday 1980
Caligola 1979
O Lucky Man! 1973

"All you have to do is to look like crap on film and everyone thinks you're a brilliant actress."

To international audiences, Dame Helen Mirren is perhaps most known for her Best Actress Oscar-winning role as Queen Elizabeth II in *The Queen* (2006). Her tour de force performance as the British monarch under siege after the death of her daughter-in-law Diana, Princess of Wales, in 1997 was shockingly vivid in its realism. Mirren managed to veer away from caricature in a part playing one of the most famous people on the planet. Her voice, her mannerisms, and even her gait resembled the royal. What is even more surprising is that Mirren herself is known for her beauty, feisty sexuality, and propensity for doing nude scenes.

Born the granddaughter of a Russian aristocrat, Mirren's ancestral roots have always been obvious in what the British perceive as her sense of class: her elegant bearing, self confidence, and wry humor. Perhaps such innate qualities have led to her being cast as a monarch on more than just one occasion. She played two other queens of England: Elizabeth I in the TV series *Elizabeth I* (2005), and Queen Charlotte, the wife of George III, in *The Madness of King George* (1994). Yet Mirren can move down the social ladder, too, as with her poignant portrayal of the housekeeper in *Gosford Park* (2001).

Trained at London's National Youth Theatre, by the age of twenty Mirren was already a star of the stage. Her career has moved between stage, film, and TV ever since. Her stunning performance in the British gangster movie *The Long Good Friday* (1980) showed that she can deliver grit, and she revealed her flair for comedy in *Calendar Girls* (2003). Unlike many women who reach middle age in showbiz, Mirren's career has not floundered, and it seems unlikely that she has reached her peak even yet. **CK**

STEVE MARTIN

Born: Stephen Glenn Martin, August 14, 1945 (Waco, Texas, U.S.).

Star qualities: Tall, white-haired funny man; expressive face; stand-up comedian; king of spoof; master of improvisation and ad lib; intelligent; talented musician; composer; prolific performer; writer; director; producer; vegetarian.

White-haired funny man extraordinaire and often confused for being an alumnus of the TV variety show *Saturday Night Live* (1976–2006) after his 20 show appearances, Steve Martin began his performance career as a high-school cheerleader and entertainer at Disneyland and Knott's Berry Farm. It was during these stints that he developed his unusual talents for magic, juggling, playing the banjo, and creating balloon animals that he would use in his live comedy act.

His first professional splash was on the staff of *The Smothers Brothers Show* (1975), for which he won an Emmy Award as writer. More TV writing work followed, along with a few big-screen appearances in movies such as *Sgt. Pepper's Lonely Hearts Club Band* (1978) and *The Muppet Movie* (1979), before he became a leading comic actor with films such as *The Jerk* (1979), *All of Me* (1984), and *¡Three Amigos!* (1986).

Martin first offered a dramatic performance in *Pennies from Heaven* (1981), and he renewed the experiment years later with greater success in *Roxanne* (1987). Ever since then he has alternated outright comedy in films such as *Planes, Trains & Automobiles* (1987) with mixed comedy drama such as *Parenthood* (1989) and more poignant, straight dramatic roles in films such as *Grand Canyon* (1991).

Always productive, he has never stopped writing stage plays—*Picasso at the Lapin Agile* (1993) and its adapted screenplay, for one—and movie scripts, such as *The Pink Panther* (2006). He welcomed the twenty-first century as a box-office draw, with films such as *Cheaper by the Dozen* (2003) and its sequel; and a niche artist who can conjure ideas, bring them to the screen, and deliver the resulting film performance, as he demonstrates in *Shopgirl* (2005). **GCQ**

Top Takes...

The Pink Panther 2006
Cheaper by the Dozen 2 2005
Shopgirl 2005
Cheaper by the Dozen 2003
The Spanish Prisoner 1997
Grand Canyon 1991
Father of the Bride 1991
Parenthood 1989
Dirty Rotten Scoundrels 1988
Planes, Trains & Automobiles 1987
Roxanne 1987
¡Three Amigos! 1986
All of Me 1984
The Jerk 1979
The Muppet Movie 1979
Sgt. Pepper's Lonely Hearts Club Band 1978

1940s

"What is comedy? Comedy is the art of making people laugh without making them puke."

CARMEN MAURA

Born: Carmen García Maura, September 15, 1945 (Madrid, Spain).

Star qualities: Grande dame of contemporary Spanish cinema; leading lady of dramas and comedies; comic timing; TV show hostess; strong woman; gay icon following her characterization of a transsexual; cabaret artist; stagecraft.

Top Takes...

Carmen Maura started out her career running an art gallery and appearing in Madrid's nightclubs as a cabaret artist. After the death of Spain's General Francisco Franco in 1975, the arts and nightlife in Madrid exploded as its more liberal inhabitants felt free of the shackles of dictatorship. It was against this atmosphere of experimentation that Maura came to the fore. She made her film debut in the short, *El espíritu* (1969), but her first real break came with *Tigres de papel* (1977) (*Paper Tigers*).

Outside of her native Spain, she is most recognized for her collaborations with Spanish director Pedro Almodóvar. The pair first worked together on *Folle...folle...fólleme Tim!* (1978), which they followed up with *Pepi, Luci, Bom y otras chicas del montón* (1980) (*Pepi, Luci, Bom and Other Girls Like Mom*). At this time, Maura was also making a name for herself appearing as a host on TV talk shows such as *Esta Noche* (1981).

The first time Maura came to international attention was also the first time Almodóvar hit the world map, with the scatty comedy *Mujeres al borde de un ataque de nervios* (1988) (*Women on the Verge of a Nervous Breakdown*). The film won an Oscar nomination for Best Foreign Language Film, and arts theater lovers worldwide hunting down Almodóvar's earlier films soon discovered the acting talents of Maura, and her *Women on the Verge of a Nervous Breakdown* costar, Antonio Banderas, in the films *Matador* (1986) and *La ley del deseo* (1987) (*Law of Desire*). In the 1990s Maura branched out to work with directors such as Carlos Saura in *¡Ay, Carmela!* (1990), in which she played an actress traveling with a theater troupe during the Spanish Civil War. The millennium saw her team up with Almodóvar once more in *Volver* (2006) (*To Return*) to play a ghostly mother back from the dead. **CK**

> "To see a script where the most important characters are women is very special."

DIVINE

Born: Glen Harris Milstead, October 19, 1945 (Baltimore, Maryland, U.S.); died 1988 (Los Angeles, California, U.S.).

Star qualities: Larger-than-life comic camp performer; icon of cult bad-taste movies; transgressive; flamboyant; singer; diva disco performer; writer.

Divine started out as a hairdresser and ran his own salon, which was a gift from his indulgent parents. Ever plump and often moody, he had a difficult time fitting into his social surroundings and also his family. At one point his behavior led to a nine-year estrangement from his parents. It was a high-school friendship with director John Waters that led to him becoming the flamboyant diva for which he was famous. Waters suggested he rename himself "Divine," and in his new persona he went on to become Waters's star performer in a series of cult films in the 1970s and 1980s.

He was often shocking, but always funny, his most notable performances being in *Pink Flamingos* (1972) and *Female Trouble* (1974). Mistakenly dubbed as a drag queen or transvestite, Divine was an altogether different cinematic creation prone to bouts of outrage, glamour, and the use of camp all embodied in a performance that can only be described as terrorism against normality, conservatism, and the thin. Probably the act for which Divine is most famous is the scene that concludes *Pink Flamingos*: Divine scoops up fresh dog excrement, eats it, gags, and smiles for Waters's camera. After the suburban milieu of *Polyester* (1981), in which Divine plays a bored alcoholic housewife, his performances began to exhibit method and maturity, culminating with the character of Edna Turnblad in *Hairspray* (1988). A pop career also emerged in the 1980s with a string of disco hits including the track "You Think You're a Man" (1984).

Divine tragically died at the age of forty-two of sleep apnea, a result of his obesity. It was only two weeks after *Hairspray*'s premiere, and a sadly brief period to soak up the glorious career-defining reviews. **GR**

Top Takes...

Out of the Dark 1989
Hairspray 1988
Trouble in Mind 1985
Lust in the Dust 1985
Polyester 1981
Female Trouble 1974
Pink Flamingos 1972
The Diane Linkletter Story 1970
Multiple Maniacs 1970
Mondo Trasho 1969
Eat Your Makeup 1968
Roman Candles 1966

1940s

"All my life I wanted to look like Elizabeth Taylor. Now Elizabeth Taylor looks like me."

GOLDIE HAWN

Born: Goldie Jeanne Hawn, November 21, 1945 (Washington, D.C., U.S.).

Star qualities: Petite blue-eyed beauty; sexy; dizzy blonde image; giggly laugh; incredible comic timing; funny; endearing; ballet dancer; singer; writer; director; producer; devout Buddhist.

Top Takes...

The Banger Sisters 2002
The Out-of-Towners 1999
Everyone Says I Love You 1996
The First Wives Club 1996
Death Becomes Her 1992
HouseSitter 1992
Deceived 1991
Overboard 1987
Wildcats 1986
Swing Shift 1984
Private Benjamin **1980** ☆
Foul Play 1978
Shampoo 1975
Butterflies Are Free 1972
There's a Girl in My Soup 1970
Cactus Flower **1969** ★

Now more than sixty years old and seemingly retired, Goldie Hawn has left behind an appealing and groundbreaking filmography. Yet Hawn started out as a dancer. She began taking ballet and tap dance lessons at the age of three, and went on to dance in the chorus of the Ballet Russe de Monte Carlo production of *The Nutcracker* (1955). She studied drama at American University in Washington, D.C., but dropped out to run a ballet school. By 1964, she was working as a professional dancer. Her good looks and talent led her to start out on TV with small parts, and soon she was cast as a pretty laugh machine on the comedy show *Rowan & Martin's Laugh-In* (1968–1970). Her film debut in *Cactus Flower* (1969) alongside Walter Matthau and Ingrid Bergman won her a come-from-nowhere Oscar for her supporting performance.

In the early 1970s, Hawn continued doing comedy in such films as *Butterflies Are Free* (1972), *Shampoo* (1975), and *Foul Play* (1978), but also exposed a more serious side in *The Sugarland Express* (1974). With *Private Benjamin* (1980), the two halves collided in a singular role concerning a high-maintenance woman who joins the army only to find herself truly remade through discipline and hard work. Four years on, the twice-married and divorced Hawn made her first film with Kurt Russell, *Swing Shift* (1984). The pair began an offscreen romance and have been partners ever since. Her mature work has largely stuck to the tried and true: she's done mostly comedy such as *Wildcats* (1986), *The First Wives Club* (1996), and *Everyone Says I Love You* (1996), mixed with an occasional dramatic thriller such as *Deceived* (1991). Hawn's three children have followed her on to the big screen: Oliver Hudson, Kate Hudson, and Wyatt Russell. **GCQ**

"We should let men go off and have affairs ... and we [women] should run the world."

DIANE KEATON

Born: Diane Hall, January 5, 1946 (Los Angeles, California, U.S.).

Star qualities: Natural good looks; sexy, self-assured screen presence; comic timing; late-1970s style icon; unisex clothing; intelligent; one-time muse of Woody Allen; director; producer.

Diane Keaton had her stage debut in 1968 as the only fully-clothed member of the cast of the Broadway rock musical *Hair*. She later joined the Broadway cast of Woody Allen's *Play It Again, Sam* (1970), and then transferred to the film version in 1972. This was the beginning of a personal and professional involvement with the director that stretched to eight films, from the very amusing idiotic heroines of *Sleeper* (1973) and *Love and Death* (1975), to the Best Actress Oscar-winning showcase of *Annie Hall* (1977), which Allen wrote for her (her real surname is "Hall" and her nickname is "Annie.") Her role in the latter showed her worth as a breathy torch singer, and saw Keaton establish a ditzy style, as she became an offbeat fashion icon and girls emulated her unisex garb of ties and waistcoats. She collaborated again with Allen in more dramatic, chilly roles in *Interiors* (1978) and *Manhattan* (1979).

Although primarily associated with comedy, Keaton refused to be typecast and became a rare female presence in Francis Ford Coppola's *The Godfather* trilogy. She also demonstrated that she is a heavyweight actress in *Looking for Mr. Goodbar* (1977), *Shoot the Moon* (1982), *The Little Drummer Girl* (1984), and *Mrs. Soffel* (1984). After her partnership split with Allen she became involved with Warren Beatty, and appeared in his film *Reds* (1981) as the journalist Louise Bryant. The role confirmed she was more than simply a comedienne when she received an Oscar nomination for Best Actress. Lately Keaton has returned to scattiness, albeit with melodrama on the side, in *Crimes of the Heart* (1986). She reunited with Woody Allen for *Manhattan Murder Mystery* (1993), and played equally well with Jack Nicholson in the romantic comedy *Something's Gotta Give* (2003). **KN**

Top Takes...

Something's Gotta Give **2003** ☆
Marvin's Room **1996** ☆
Radio Days 1987
Crimes of the Heart 1986
Mrs. Soffel 1984
The Little Drummer Girl 1984
Shoot the Moon 1982
***Reds* 1981** ☆
Manhattan 1979
Interiors 1978
Looking for Mr. Goodbar 1977
***Annie Hall* 1977** ★
Love and Death 1975
Sleeper 1973
Play It Again, Sam 1972
The Godfather Trilogy 1972, 1974, 1990

1940s

"I think that [famous people] tend to be underdeveloped in their humanity skills."

LIZA MINNELLI

Born: Liza May Minnelli, March 12, 1946 (Los Angeles, California, U.S.).

Star qualities: Sexy, glamorous icon of U.S. cinema; singer; dancer; elegant; often plays eccentric dramatic roles; daughter of Hollywood legend Judy Garland and movie director Vincente Minnelli.

Top Takes...

The OH in Ohio 2006
Stepping Out 1991
Arthur 2: On the Rocks 1988
Rent-a-Cop 1987
Pinocchio and the Emperor of the Night 1987
Arthur 1981
New York, New York 1977
A Matter of Time 1976
Lucky Lady 1975
Journey Back to Oz 1974
Cabaret 1972 ★
Tell Me That You Love Me, Junie Moon 1970
The Sterile Cuckoo 1969 ☆
Charlie Bubbles 1967
In the Good Old Summertime 1949

"My mother gave me my drive but my father gave me my dreams."

One of the best-known showbiz personalities, Liza Minnelli's film career has been a distinct disappointment in later decades because of continuing personal problems. She made an impressive debut as Albert Finney's mistress, more interested in sex than the confused, anomic protagonist, in *Charlie Bubbles* (1967), a late British New Wave movie. Her talent for playing eccentrics was exploited more fully in one of the most interesting youth movies that followed in the wake of the smash success *The Graduate* (1967). As "Pookie" Adams in *The Sterile Cuckoo* (1969), Minnelli played a student who doesn't fit in with late-1960s college life. Eventually coupling with a straitlaced young man, who is at first attracted to her unconventionality, she finds herself rejected after an unplanned pregnancy. An attempt to reprise the character the next year in *Tell Me That You Love Me, Junie Moon* (1970) met with less success.

A talented singer and dancer, Minnelli landed a career-making part as Sally Bowles—yet another unconventional young woman making her way uncertainly through an unfamiliar moral landscape—in the film version of the smash Broadway musical *Cabaret* (1972). Her performance was a standout in a star-studded cast, and she received a well-deserved Oscar for Best Actress. Since *Cabaret*, good film roles have been few and far between for Minnelli. Paired with Robert De Niro in the retro musical homage to the Big Apple, *New York, New York* (1977), she did a first-rate job in a film that unfortunately flopped. She was an effective love interest for Dudley Moore in the two *Arthur* films (1981, 1988), playing straight to his inebriated wackiness. More recently she has had a much-applauded role in the TV sitcom *Arrested Development* (2003–2005). **BP**

SYLVESTER STALLONE

Born: Sylvester Enzio Stallone, July 6, 1946 (New York City, New York, U.S.).

Star qualities: Muscular good looks; "The Italian Stallion"; iconic hero of action movies; plays the underdog hero; physical fitness; known for few words; writer; director; producer.

Sly-Rocky-Rambo-Cobra-Dredd-Stallone is a post-Vietnam star because his mythos so closely mirrors a 1970s turn from masculinity in crisis into the 1980s affirmation of the male body as object of affection. Along a similar arc, his filmography begins with marshmallow porn in *The Party at Kitty and Stud's* (1970), continues on through little charmers such as *Deathrace 2000* (1975), and then flowers with the box-office hit *Rocky* (1976), the story of a nobody who succeeds in the boxing arena because he has heart. Stallone played the title role in his own screenplay for the film, which won an Oscar in 1976 for Best Picture, and he has never looked back. He reprised the role in 2006, the latest in an almost never-ending list of sequels: *Rocky II* (1979), *Rocky III* (1982), *Rocky IV* (1985), *Rocky V* (1990), and *Rocky Balboa* (2006).

Several wives, many children, an interest in painting, a self-titled magazine, and years of dedication to physical fitness have left him the holder of many distinctions, perhaps foremost a plethora of B-grade comedy and action films that occasionally satisfy, alongside a few gems that really work. Here one must put *Rhinestone* (1984), *Lock Up* (1989), and *Driven* (2001) to one side, so as to relish *Tango & Cash* (1989), *Demolition Man* (1993), *Cobra* (1986), and Stallone's other famous feature series as John J. Rambo. That series began with *First Blood* (1982) and Stallone is still lining up new vehicles for his Vietnam veteran role. *First Blood* and *Cop Land* (1997) are rare efforts to really act, but the Stallone machine is really about underdogs, and the lowest common denominator action and violence. That he's been so successful is a shock since such a brilliant commercial artist has survived any number of copycats, further signifying his uniqueness in Hollywood. **GCQ**

Top Takes...

Rocky Balboa 2006
Cop Land 1997
Judge Dredd 1995
Demolition Man 1993
Cliffhanger 1993
Rocky V 1990
Tango & Cash 1989
Lock Up 1989
Rambo III 1988
Cobra 1986
Rocky IV 1985
Rambo: First Blood Part II 1985
First Blood 1982
Rocky III 1982
Rocky II 1979
Rocky 1976 ☆

"I know people will think *Rocky* is my story, but it's also my generation's story."

1940s

CHEECH AND CHONG

Cheech: Born Richard Anthony Marin, July 13, 1946 (Los Angeles, California, U.S.).
Chong: Born Thomas B. Kin Chong, May 24, 1938 (Edmonton, Alberta, Canada).

Star qualities: Comedy duo of 1970s and 1980s counterculture movies; irreverent; stand-up comics; recording artists; writers; directors; producers.

Top Takes...

Grass 1999
FernGully: The Last Rainforest 1992
Far Out Man 1990
Get Out of My Room 1985
After Hours 1985
Cheech & Chong's The Corsican Brothers 1984
Group Madness 1983
Still Smokin 1983
Yellowbeard 1983
Things Are Tough All Over 1982
It Came from Hollywood 1982
Nice Dreams 1981
Cheech & Chong's Next Movie 1980
Up in Smoke 1978

Richard "Cheech" Marin and Tommy Chong were a popular comedy duo in the 1970s and 1980s, famous for their stand-up routines, which were based upon the hippie, free-love, and drug culture movements of the time. The pair started to work together at a nightclub in Vancouver, Canada, in 1970. They were spotted by a record executive when they were performing at Los Angeles's Troubadour Club. Their first album, *Cheech & Chong* (1972), went gold, and their second, *Big Bambu* (1972), was voted number one comedy album of 1972. They made their movie debut with *Up in Smoke* (1978), and it instantly established them as comedy legends. Playing stoners who just want to buy some marijuana, their search takes them from Los Angeles to Mexico and back to the United States, unwittingly driving a van made of pure marijuana.

Cheech and Chong's Next Movie (1980) featured the continuing adventures of these characters and repeated the box-office success, making them cinema's most successful comedy team of all time. Their popular personas clearly have mature interests in sex, drugs, and rock and roll, but are more like harmless kids looking for fun. Those who are part of the establishment culture—the rich and the police in particular—try to thwart their pursuits, yet they always manage to unconsciously defeat these attempts and carry on their merry way. Cheech and Chong's later efforts—*Nice Dreams* (1981), *Things Are Tough All Over* (1982), *Still Smokin* (1983), and *Cheech and Chong's The Corsican Brothers* (1984)—gradually pulled away from these characters and saw dwindling box-office returns. The duo broke in 1985 because of creative differences. They steadily work as solo artists, but it is the strength of their early work that gave them enduring fame. **DW**

> "No stems no seeds that you don't need Acapulco gold is bad ass weed." —*Up in Smoke*

DANNY GLOVER

Born: Danny Lebern Glover, July 22, 1946 (San Francisco, California, U.S.).

Star qualities: Handsome; stagecraft; comic timing; versatile lead and character actor; commanding screen presence; champion of social conscience films; civil rights activist; director; producer.

Now established as one of a handful of mature black performers in Hollywood, Danny Glover has been tops at the box office in movies such as the *Lethal Weapon* series (1987–1998) as Sergeant Roger Murtaugh; the force behind little-seen experimental works such as *To Sleep with Anger* (1990); and a voice for various political campaigns, including continued support for civil rights action. With a career now spanning three decades, he has worked in theater, on television, and in the movies, but his greatest strength has always been his ability to play the occasional cruel villains to counterbalance a steady stream of sympathetic heroes.

Glover enrolled in the Black Actors Workshop at the American Conservatory Theater, a regional training program in San Francisco, in his late twenties. Deciding that he wanted to be an actor, he abandoned his job in city administration. He soon began working as a stage actor, which eventually took him to Los Angeles and led him to bit parts in TV and films.

Prominently made an evil black man in *The Color Purple* (1985), the persona was doubled that year in *Witness* (1985) when he played a corrupt and homicidal cop. Still, his more typical role is as a calming force—a supportive father figure, police officer, or social outsider—as in *A Raisin in the Sun* (1989) and *ER* (2005) on TV; or *Grand Canyon* (1991), *Bopha!* (1993), and *Beloved* (1998) on film. There have also been many comedies, letting Glover play for laughs such as in *Operation Dumbo Drop* (1995), along with voice-only parts such as *Barnyard* (2006). Not bad for an actor who made his film debut playing an inmate in *Escape from Alcatraz* (1979), and ended up bridging genres and racial stereotypes in a career many regard with great fondness. **GCQ**

Top Takes...

Dreamgirls 2006
Barnyard 2006
The Royal Tenenbaums 2001
Beloved 1998
Antz 1998
Lethal Weapon 4 1998
The Rainmaker 1997
Operation Dumbo Drop 1995
Bopha! 1993
Lethal Weapon 3 1992
To Sleep with Anger 1990
Lethal Weapon 2 1989
Lethal Weapon 1987
The Color Purple 1985
Silverado 1985
Witness 1985

1940s

"Every day of my life I walk with the idea I am black no matter how successful I am."

TOMMY LEE JONES

Born: Tommy Lee Jones, September 15, 1946 (San Saba, Texas, U.S.).

Star qualities: Rugged good looks; chiseled features; serious screen presence; gravitas; deadpan delivery; physical fitness; intelligent; liberal political activist; writer; director; producer.

Top Takes…

A Prairie Home Companion 2006
The Three Burials of Melquiades Estrada 2005
The Hunted 2003
Men in Black II 2002
Rules of Engagement 2000
Double Jeopardy 1999
Small Soldiers 1998
Men in Black 1997
Batman Forever 1995
Blue Sky 1994
The Client 1994
Blown Away 1994
The Fugitive 1993 ★
JFK 1991 ☆
Coal Miner's Daughter 1980
Eyes of Laura Mars 1978

Rugged, lean, stern: three words often used to describe Tommy Lee Jones, the one-time Harvard roommate of the then future U.S. Vice President Al Gore, and partial inspiration for his former teacher Erich Segal for the character of Oliver in *Love Story* (1970), which was also his film debut. To the list of adjectives could be added handsome, steely-eyed, and intense, with a deadpan delivery and athletic build. But the proof of his screen appeal is usually rooted in steadfastness of purpose and controlled action, as in *The Fugitive* (1993), his Best Supporting Actor Oscar-winning turn as Marshal Samuel Gerard.

Jones earned his stripes on TV in shows such as *Barnaby Jones* (1975), *Baretta* (1976), and *Charlie's Angels* (1976). He notably switched to movies in a high-concept thriller *Eyes of Laura Mars* (1978), found respect back on TV in *The Executioner's Song* (1982) as the convicted murderer Gary Mark Gilmore, and became a viable lead after his Oscar win in the 1990s. Along the way he has amassed critically acclaimed parts in memorable movies such as *JFK* (1991) and *Blue Sky* (1994); stand-out parts in disposable movies such as *Blown Away* (1994) and *Double Jeopardy* (1999); and showy parts in blockbusters such as *Batman Forever* (1995) and *Men in Black* (1997). Never more convincing than when playing a reluctant hero, troubled by puzzling out a solution to difficult problems as in *Rules of Engagement* (2000) and *The Hunted* (2003), he also recently made his directorial debut with *The Three Burials of Melquiades Estrada* (2005), a well-received modern-day Western, in which he also acted. Offscreen, Jones's friendship with Gore has lasted, and he nominated Gore, as the Democratic Party's nominee for U.S. president at the 2000 Democratic National Convention. **GCQ**

> "It's no mean calling to bring fun into the afternoons of large numbers of people."

SUSAN SARANDON

Born: Susan Abigail Tomalin, October 4, 1946 (New York City, New York, U.S.).

Star qualities: Sexy, slim, leading lady; often plays strong women; selective choice of roles; one half of a famous Hollywood celebrity partnership; outspoken political liberal; producer.

Susan Sarandon—born Susan Abigail Tomalin and retaining her stage name from her marriage to actor Chris Sarandon—appeared first in film as the hippie waif in *Joe* (1970). She went to a casting call for the film with her then husband; he did not get a part, but she won the major role of the disaffected teenager. However, Sarandon made her first real impression in her underwear as the heroine of the camp, cult rock movie, *The Rocky Horror Picture Show* (1975), which showed off her too rarely used singing voice and daffy sexiness. She played a pale, lovely whore, and mother to twelve-year-old Brooke Shields, in Louis Malle's *Pretty Baby* (1978); and the would-be croupier rubbing lemons into her arms and breasts in a memorable, affecting scene from Malle's *Atlantic City* (1980).

In middle age, Sarandon became an icon of mature, often intellectual sensuality: succumbing to Catherine Deneuve playing a vampire in *The Hunger* (1983), drawn to Jack Nicholson as one of *The Witches of Eastwick* (1987), and putting the moves on Kevin Costner in *Bull Durham* (1988). In *White Palace* (1990) and *Thelma & Louise* (1991), she was wholly convincing as hash-slinger goddesses. After four Oscar nominations in the 1990s, she finally got a Best Actress win for playing the liberal nun Sister Helen Prejean in *Dead Man Walking* (1995), which was directed by her partner, actor and director Tim Robbins. In recent years, she has taken very varied, often maternal leading roles: as a terminally ill mother in *Stepmom* (1998), an irresponsible mother in *Anywhere But Here* (1999), grown-up groupie in *The Banger Sisters* (2002), and grieving mother in *Moonlight Mile* (2002).

She and Robbins, with whom she has two children, are both notable supporters of numerous liberal causes. **KN**

Top Takes...

Moonlight Mile 2002
The Banger Sisters 2002
Anywhere But Here 1999
Stepmom 1998
Dead Man Walking 1995 ★
Little Women 1994
The Client 1994 ☆
Lorenzo's Oil 1992 ☆
Thelma & Louise 1991 ☆
White Palace 1990
Bull Durham 1988
The Witches of Eastwick 1987
The Hunger 1983
Atlantic City 1980 ☆
Pretty Baby 1978
The Rocky Horror Picture Show 1975

1940s

"I think the only reason I remain an actor is that you can never quite get it right."

PEI-PEI CHENG

Born: Pei-pei Cheng, December 4, 1946 (Shanghai, China).

Star qualities: "The Queen of Swords"; elegant beauty; expert swordswoman of *wuxia* films of the 1960s; legendary leading lady of Hong Kong cinema; icon of martial arts movies.

Top Takes...

The Counting House 2006

Shadow Mask 2001

Wo hu cang long 2000
(*Crouching Tiger, Hidden Dragon*)

Zhong hua ying xiong 1999
(*A Man Called Hero*)

The Spirit of the Dragon 1998

Luan shi chao ren 1994 (*From Zero to Hero*)

Fei dao shou 1969 (*The Flying Dagger*)

Jin yan zi 1968 (*Golden Swallow*)

Shen jian zhen jiang hu 1967
(*The Thundering Sword*)

Tie shan gong zhu 1966 (*Princess Iron Fan*)

Da zui xia 1966 (*Come Drink with Me*)

Xiang jiang hua yue ye 1966
(*Hong Kong Nocturne*)

> "Your master ... deserved to die by a woman's hand!"
>
> —Jade Fox, *Crouching Tiger, Hidden Dragon*

Hong Kong cinema has had its share of action film heroines—Angela Mao, Brigitte Lin, Michelle Yeoh—but Pei-pei Cheng is one of the most memorable and one of the earliest actresses in contemporary Hong Kong cinema to make an impression as a driving force in genre films, largely a male-driven arena.

Cheng was a contract player for the renowned Shaw Brothers Studio in the 1960s, and it was in 1966 that the actress, aged only twenty at the time, had a major breakthrough. She performed in several significant films—including the musical *Xiang jiang hua yue ye* (1966) (*Hong Kong Nocturne*) and the fantasy *Tie shan gong zhu* (1966) (*Princess Iron Fan*)—but it was her role in director King Hu's martial arts classic *Da zui xia* (1966) (*Come Drink with Me*), one of the key films of the decade, that made her an icon. Cheng reprised her role as *Come Drink*'s Golden Swallow in Cheh Chang's film *Jin yan zi* (1968) (*Golden Swallow*), and she would continue to be a major presence in the Shaw Brothers's movies throughout the 1960s, appearing in *Fei dao shou* (1969) (*The Flying Dagger*) and others.

Cheng retired from the screen to get married in the early 1970s, but made a significant comeback throughout the late 1980s and into the 1990s. Her role as Jade Fox in Ang Lee's *Wo hu cang long* (2000) (*Crouching Tiger, Hidden Dragon*) was understandably regarded as her true return to form, but Cheng had already been back in the Hong Kong movie scene for more than a decade by the time of that film's release. Much of Cheng's comeback work is not especially noteworthy, although she certainly can move into non-action dramatic roles with ease: like Lin, Cheng is a premier actress first and a martial arts icon second, and she still has the elegant beauty and talent to continue her career. **TC**

TAKESHI KITANO

Born: Takeshi Kitano, January 18, 1947 (Tokyo, Japan).

Star qualities: Stocky; leading actor of Japanese action movies; outrageous comedian; stand-up comic; athletic; dancer; TV personality; director; producer; writer; poet; painter.

If one were to compare Japanese superstar Takeshi Kitano to Woody Allen, most of his Western admirers would likely be baffled by the analogy—after all, Kitano is the stoic, hardened antihero responsible for some of the most violent *yakuza* gangster films in recent memory. But this underlines the differences in celebrity status in the international marketplace: in Japan, Kitano is "Beat" Takeshi—outrageous comedian and popular TV personality—first, and Takeshi Kitano, acclaimed film fest-circuit auteur and brooding actor, second.

Kitano started his career as a stand-up comic long before he turned to directing himself in increasingly eccentric films, becoming famous in Japan for being one of the Two Beats stand-up comedy team during the 1970s, and hosting countless TV programs in that country through to the present day. Although he had appeared in a few films before directing himself in *Sono otoko, kyôbô ni tsuki* (1989) (*Violent Cop*), that picture marked a new phase in Kitano's career, in which he shifted from comedy to brutal, bloody gangster films in which his tough-guy poker-faced demeanor was served by deadpan explosions of sudden violence. Yet in the best of these films, *Sonatine* (1993) and *Hana-bi* (1997) (*Fireworks*), there is also much wit on display, and Kitano has continued to work in this genre on TV, also directing several nonviolent comic films such as *Minnâ-yatteruka!* (1995) (*Getting Any?*) and *Kikujirô no natsu* (1999).

In addition to acting and directing, Kitano is a prolific writer, poet, and painter, and he recently followed up the biggest mainstream success of his filmmaking career by appearing as a dyed-blond version of *Zatôichi* (2003) (*The Blind Swordsman: Zatoichi*) in his own story starring this popular samurai figure, *Takeshis'* (2005). **TC**

Top Takes…

Takeshis' 2005

Izo 2004

Zatôichi 2003 (*The Blind Swordsman: Zatoichi*)

Batoru rowaiaru 2000 (*Battle Royale*)

Brother 2000

Kikujirô no natsu 1999

Tokyo Eyes 1998

Hana-bi 1997 (*Fireworks*)

Johnny Mnemonic 1995

Minnâ-yatteruka! 1995 (*Getting Any?*)

Sonatine 1993 (*Sonachine*)

Sakana kara daiokishin!! 1992

Sono otoko, kyôbô ni tsuki 1990 (*Violent Cop*)

Kanashii kibun de joke 1985

Jukkai no mosquito 1983

Merry Christmas Mr. Lawrence 1983

"I wanted to make a movie that can't be pigeonholed."
—On *Takeshis'*

BILLY CRYSTAL

Born: William Jacob Crystal, March 14, 1947 (Long Island, New York, U.S.).

Star qualities: Academy Awards host; leading man of comedies; stand-up comedian and king of ad lib; sketch artist; master of mimicry; singer; writer; producer; director.

Top Takes...

Cars 2006
Analyze That 2002
Monsters, Inc. 2001
America's Sweethearts 2001
Analyze This 1999
Deconstructing Harry 1997
Fathers' Day 1997
City Slickers II 1994
Mr. Saturday Night 1992
City Slickers 1991
When Harry Met Sally . . . 1989
Throw Momma from the Train 1987
The Princess Bride 1987
Running Scared 1986
This Is Spinal Tap 1984

Billy Crystal was born and raised on Long Island, New York. His father was a concert promoter, so his youth was filled with celebrity guests such as Billie Holiday and Pee Wee Russell in the family home. He began doing a stand-up comedy act in the early 1960s, graduated from New York University in film and TV direction (where he studied under director Martin Scorsese), and got married. He started to earn a reputation for his comic impersonations and became the opening act for musicians such as Barry Manilow. Leaving New York for Hollywood in 1976, he made a splash on the TV sitcom *Soap* (1977–1981) as the gay character Jodie Dallas, and later capitalized on this exposure when he became a cast member of the TV show *Saturday Night Live* (1984–1985).

Such national recognition eventually led to the big screen, although his success has largely depended upon a good costar. First up was as a cop in *Running Scared* (1986), opposite Gregory Hines; then as a student in *Throw Momma from the Train* (1987), opposite Danny DeVito; and, finally, the love-struck best friend in *When Harry Met Sally . . .* (1989), opposite Meg Ryan, which made him a bankable box-office success. He went on to star as a salesman hit by a midlife crisis in *City Slickers* (1991), while at the same time establishing himself as preferred host for the annual Oscars telecast, for which he has won several Emmy Awards. In the years since, he has been in a few small experiments such as the devil in Woody Allen's *Deconstructing Harry* (1997); a few bombs such as a Hollywood agent in *My Giant* (1998); a few hits such as a shrink to a mobster in *Analyze This* (1999) and its sequel *Analyze That* (2002); and one beloved masterpiece as a kindly monster in *Monsters, Inc.* (2001). **GCQ**

> "Women need a reason to have sex. Men just need a place."

MEIKO KAJI

Born: Masako Ota, March 24, 1947 (Tokyo, Japan).

Star qualities: Haunting eyes; slinky beauty; elegant; cult leading lady of Japanese action films; plays femme fatale roles, often women in prison; stylish screen presence; singer.

If looks could indeed kill, then Meiko Kaji's piercing gaze should be registered as a weapon of mass destruction. Many actors are blessed with a specific physical attribute that sets them apart from the pack, but few have eyes as distinctively fierce and haunting as the optic orbs possessed by Kaji: her imposing strength in three continuing series of Japanese action films (among other individual appearances) rests largely in her take-no-prisoners, fearless stare.

Kaji worked only briefly in Japanese cinema of the 1970s, but she had the fortune to appear in several of its most enduring genre favorites. After only a few films, she hit stardom with her appearances in Nikkatsu Studios's girl-gang *Nora-neko rokku* (*Stray Cat Rock*) series beginning in 1970. But it was two years later that Kaji became an international femme fatale icon who will forever live in infamy. Kaji took on the role of Nami Matsushima, better known as "Sasori," meaning "scorpion," in Toei Studios's legendary *Joshuu 701-gô: Sasori* (1972) (*Female Prisoner #701: Scorpion*) series, adapted from a popular *manga*. The initial three entries, all directed by Shunya Ito, show Kaji at her best: a ferocious, beautiful, near-wordless instrument of violence and vengeance slicing her way through a delirious Pop Art landscape of stylized, colorful lighting, and *kabuki*-influenced set pieces. Ito left after the first three; the actress stayed on for one more entry, and then left.

Kaji is also famous for her roles in two period piece swordplay dramas *Shurayukihime* (*Lady Snowblood*) (1973, 1974), which apparently inspired Quentin Tarantino's *Kill Bill* films (2003, 2004). Yet she opted to virtually retire during the heyday of her mid-1970s success. Also a singer, Kaji's music can be heard in the *Kill Bill* films. **TC**

Top Takes...

Daichi no komoriuta 1976 (*Lullaby of the Earth*)

Shura-yuki-hime: Urami Renga 1974 (*Lady Snowblood 2: Love Song of Vengeance*)

Joshuu sasori: 701-gô urami-bushi 1973 (*Female Prisoner Scorpion: #701's Grudge Song*)

Joshuu sasori: Kemono-beya 1973 (*Female Prisoner Scorpion: Beast Stable*)

Shurayukihime 1973 (*Lady Snowblood*)

Joshuu sasori: Dai-41 zakkyo-bô 1972 (*Female Convict Scorpion Jailhouse 41*)

Joshuu 701-gô: Sasori 1972 (*Female Prisoner #701: Scorpion*)

Nora-neko rokku: Bôsô shudan '71 1971 (*Beat '71*)

Nora-neko rokku: Sekkusu hanta 1970 (*Stray Cat Rock: Sex Hunter*)

1940s

"You and I have some business to take care of . . . ."
—Yuki Kashima, *Lady Snowblood*

JAMES WOODS

Born: James Howard Woods, April 18, 1947 (Vernal, Utah, U.S.).

Star qualities: Tall, lean, extremely intelligent; intense screen presence; incredibly versatile lead and character actor; famous for playing unnerving villains; writer; producer; director.

James Woods is one of those actors who has become so identified with a type of character—wiry, manic, hyper-intelligent, strangely charismatic, and vaguely mercenary-cum-seedy—that a viewer is not only content to see him repeat such a portrayal, but disappointed when he doesn't. Since the 1980s, he has worked so frequently in film and TV that he has taken many roles that are more sedate and normal simply by volume of appearances, but fans of the actor always look to Woods for the zenith of cinematic nervy intensity.

A high academic achiever, he dropped out of Massachusetts Institute of Technology in the late 1960s to pursue acting and spent much of the decade after in minor film and TV roles—albeit in some notable movies such as *The Way We Were* (1973) and *Night Moves* (1975)—before truly breaking through in 1979 with his role in *The Onion Field*. Indeed, the 1980s found Woods at the top of his game, with one memorable role after another, in films both significant such as *Once Upon a Time in America* (1984) and *Salvador* (1986); and comparatively generic such as *Cop* (1988) and *The Boost* (1988).

Woods uneasily shifted into more conventional leading man portrayals at the onset of the 1990s, with disappointing results. The only thing more distasteful than seeing Woods do action comedy in fodder such as *The Hard Way* (1991) is watching him play a romantic figure opposite Dolly Parton in *Straight Talk* (1992). Unusual supporting roles in films such as *Nixon* (1995), *Casino* (1995), and *The Virgin Suicides* (1999) seem to be Woods's strength in recent years, although worthwhile leading roles still appear in movies both accomplished such as *Another Day in Paradise* (1997) and merely shamefully entertaining such as *Vampires* (1998). **TC**

> "I called up Marty and said, 'Any part, anytime, any place, anywhere.'"—On his role in *Casino*

ARNOLD SCHWARZENEGGER

Born: Arnold Alois Schwarzenegger, July 30, 1947 (Thal, Styria, Austria).

Star qualities: Muscular good looks; iconic leading man of action movies; ambitious; world-class bodybuilder; married into the Kennedy family; politician; producer; director.

Larger than life and literally pulsing, a giant among men, Arnold Schwarzenegger began his performance career as a bodybuilder. He still holds the record for winning the most major bodybuilding events in history: 13 titles (one Mr. Junior Western Europe, seven Mr. Olympias, and five Mr. Universes). He was transformed into the embodiment of Robert E. Howard's fantastic Conan in *Conan the Barbarian* (1982), and unforgettably said, "I'll be back." His biceps are usually considered the high points of his performances but, in the end, Schwarzenegger is crazy like a fox; witness his foresight to see that James Cameron's cyborg thriller *The Terminator* (1984) would make his career. There's also the fact that he rode the long tail of California electoral unrest as a Republican candidate to land the governorship in 2003. He won reelection in 2006, proving he was a savvy politician, not just a celebrity face.

Along the way he married into the Kennedy clan (his wife Maria Shriver is the niece of President John F. Kennedy, and Senators Robert F. Kennedy and Ted Kennedy), directed a movie for television, sired several children, and grew fabulously wealthy. Schwarzenegger's riches were accumulated not just from his movie roles but his line of weightlifting accessories and wise choice of real estate investments.

Among his more memorable adventure roles are *Predator* (1987), *Total Recall* (1990), *True Lies* (1994), and *Batman & Robin* (1997); and from the world of comedy, *Twins* (1988) and *Kindergarten Cop* (1990). Not bad for the son of an Austrian police officer who barely spoke English when he migrated to the United States in the 1960s. Not bad at all for the megalomaniac centerpiece of the bodybuilding documentary *Pumping Iron* (1977). **GCQ**

Top Takes...

Terminator 3: Rise of the Machines 2003
Collateral Damage 2002
Batman & Robin 1997
Junior 1994
True Lies 1994
Last Action Hero 1993
Terminator 2: Judgment Day 1991
Kindergarten Cop 1990
Total Recall 1990
Twins 1988
The Running Man 1987
Predator 1987
Commando 1985
The Terminator 1984
Conan the Destroyer 1984
Conan the Barbarian 1982

1940s

"There's a lot of people who want me to get out of acting … mostly movie critics."

RICHARD DREYFUSS

Born: Richard Stephen Dreyfus, October 29, 1947 (Brooklyn, New York, U.S.).

Star qualities: Diminutive; spectacles; versatile leading man; stagecraft; comic timing; the comeback kid; thoughtful screen presence; intelligent; civic rights activist; writer; director; producer.

Top Takes...

Considered Steven Spielberg's alter ego throughout their collaborations on the box-office hits *Jaws* (1975) and *Close Encounters of the Third Kind* (1977), Richard Dreyfuss has had a roller-coaster career that is back on the up. Dreyfuss spent his early years in New York, until his family moved to Los Angeles when he was nine years old. He started acting in his youth and learned his craft through bit parts on TV in shows such as *Ben Casey* (1965), *The Big Valley* (1967), and *The Mod Squad* (1970–1973), and in movies such as John Milius's *Dillinger* (1973), before seeing his big break in George Lucas's *American Graffiti* (1973). In the latter film he played Curt Henderson, a thoughtful and frightened small-town boy coming to manhood at the end of the 1950s, which helped form the Dreyfuss type: bookish aesthete filled with great curiosity.

He won a Best Actor Oscar for his first romantic lead as an out-of-work actor in *The Goodbye Girl* (1977). He then lived through a series of commercial disappointments such as *Whose Life Is It Anyway?* (1981), overcame a drug problem, and then reemerged in the mid-1980s as a comic lead. *Down and Out in Beverly Hills* (1986) announced his return, along with *Tin Men* (1987), *Stakeout* (1987), and *Nuts* (1987), but it was *What About Bob?* (1991) that tweaked the old Dreyfuss type, turning it inside out; now he could be a self-centered despot, or a sensitive friend. In middle age, he has alternated between portraying villains as in *The American President* (1995), and heroes as in *Mr. Holland's Opus* (1995), the latter winning him a Best Actor Oscar nomination. Although he's no longer the loud-laughing free spirit of youth, his maturity allows him to turn stereotype on edge and find the humanity within as he showed in *Poseidon* (2006). **GCQ**

> "Living is the process of going from complete certainty to complete ignorance."

KATHY BATES

Born: Kathleen Doyle Bates, June 28, 1948 (Memphis, Tennessee, U.S.).

Star qualities: Nicknamed "Bobo"; short and plump; versatile supporting actress and sometime leading lady; determination; stagecraft; imposing screen presence; director; producer; composer.

Although Kathy Bates's first film appearance stretches back to 1971, the actress was for many years best known for her notable roles onstage, where she anchored several award-winning productions. Born in Memphis, Tennessee, Bates studied theater at college before entering the business professionally. Much to her frustration, several prominent roles originated by Bates onstage went to better-known—and perhaps more glamorous—actresses when they were adapted to the screen. For example, she played the lead as the jaded waitress in the Off-Broadway production of the romance *Frankie and Johnny in the Clair De Lune* (1987), a part written by playwright Terrence McNally with her in mind, but the screen role went to Michelle Pfeiffer. However, Bates finally broke into Hollywood with a menacing performance as the scarily obsessed Annie Wilkes, who holds her favorite author captive, in an adaptation of Stephen King's *Misery* (1990). The role won her an Academy Award for Best Actress, and Bates began to get deservedly meatier roles on the big screen.

Bates continued to stand out in movies such as *Fried Green Tomatoes* (1991), *Titanic* (1997), and *Primary Colors* (1998), the latter earning her another Oscar nomination. Bates spent a good part of her time honing her directing and acting skills in TV as well, resulting in seven Emmy nominations. Yet her colorful appearance in *About Schmidt* (2002), in which she was enlisted as brash comic relief to shock the generally unflappable Jack Nicholson, served as a reminder of her particular talents, and garnered Bates yet another barrage of acclaim, including a third Academy Award nomination. Although neither a traditional lead nor a strict character actor, Bates still thrives making the most of even small parts. **JK**

Top Takes...

Charlotte's Web 2006
Failure to Launch 2006
The Bridge of San Luis Rey 2004
Around the World in 80 Days 2004
About Schmidt 2002 ☆
Primary Colors 1998 ☆
Titanic 1997
Dolores Claiborne 1995
North 1994
Shadows and Fog 1992
Fried Green Tomatoes 1991
At Play in the Fields of the Lord 1991
Misery 1990 ★
White Palace 1990
Dick Tracy 1990
The Morning After 1986

1940s

"The Oscar changed everything. Better salary ... more exposure, less privacy."

JEAN RENO

Born: Juan Moreno Errere y Rimenes, July 30, 1948 (Casablanca, Morocco).

Star qualities: Tall; handsome; large frame; mournful brown eyes; sexy, deep voice; stagecraft; versatile and inventive leading man of European cinema; often plays villains.

Top Takes...

The Da Vinci Code 2006
The Pink Panther 2006
La tigre e la neve 2005 (*The Tiger and the Snow*)
Just Visiting 2001
Les Rivières pourpres 2000 (*The Crimson Rivers*)
Ronin 1998
Godzilla 1998
Roseanna's Grave 1997
Le Jaguar 1996
Mission: Impossible 1996
Léon 1994 (*The Professional*)
Les visiteurs 1993 (*The Visitors*)
Nikita 1990 (*La Femme Nikita*)
Le grand bleu 1988 (*The Big Blue*)
Subway 1985
Le dernier combat 1983 (*The Final Combat*)

"I only have a few friends in real life … those people who I've known since the 1960s."

Tall, dark, with sad eyes, Jean Reno is one of the few contemporary actors to successfully maintain an active career both in Europe and Hollywood. Reno was born in Morocco to Spanish parents, who moved to North Africa to escape the fascist regime of General Francisco Franco. As a child he was asthmatic and spent long hours in front of the TV, which is when he first became interested in acting. Reno moved to France when he was seventeen years old. He trained in theater, making his stage debut in a Parisian production of *Ecce Homo* (1974), and eventually moved into films.

Reno first gained fame working with director Luc Besson in *Le dernier combat* (1983) (*The Final Combat*). The pair formed a creative attachment, and went on to work together in *Subway* (1985), *Le grand bleu* (1988) (*The Big Blue*), and *Nikita* (1990) (*La Femme Nikita*). He finally came to international prominence for his compelling performance as the stoic hit man Léon in Besson's *Léon* (1994) (*The Professional*). This led to higher profile Hollywood films such as *French Kiss* (1995), *Mission: Impossible* (1996), *Godzilla* (1998), and *Ronin* (1998).

Reno has demonstrated his multifaceted skill with comedies such as *Le Jaguar* (1996), *Roseanna's Grave* (1997), and *Les visiteurs* (1993) (*The Visitors*)—a role he re-created in a 1998 sequel and the U.S. remake *Just Visiting* (2001). In France, Reno scored another hit with *Les Rivières pourpres* (2000) (*The Crimson Rivers*) and its sequel. In demand because of his great versatility, Reno played an Iraqi in Italian director Roberto Benigni's *La tigre e la neve* (2005) (*The Tiger and the Snow*); the straight man to Steve Martin's Inspector Clouseau in *The Pink Panther* (2006); and a detective in *The Da Vinci Code* (2006). **WW**

SAMUEL L. JACKSON

Born: Samuel Leroy Jackson, December 21, 1948 (Washington, D.C., U.S.).

Star qualities: "King of Cool"; bald; deep voice; cool screen persona; stagecraft; box-office gold; leading man of action movies; often plays violent characters; authoritative screen presence; producer.

Samuel Leroy Jackson's films have grossed more money in box-office sales than any other actor in the history of filmmaking. He went to Morehouse College in Atlanta, Georgia, where he studied drama, and cofounded the Just Us Theater. After the 1968 assassination of the leader of the U.S. civil rights movement, Dr. Martin Luther King Jr., Jackson attended the funeral in Atlanta as one of the ushers. Upon graduation Jackson found bit parts on TV and spent years on the New York stage in productions for the Negro Ensemble Company and the New York Shakespeare Company.

In his younger years, Jackson himself suffered the lot of too many talented African-American actors on the big screen, playing a string of typecast roles such as Gang Member Number Two in *Ragtime* (1981) and Hold-Up Man in *Coming to America* (1989). Director Spike Lee used him in bit parts as in *School Daze* (1988), and then gave him the plum role of crack addict Gator Purify in *Jungle Fever* (1991).

In the 1990s, more prominent roles came along. In *Loaded Weapon 1* (1993), he spoofed the kind of action hero he would later become in Steven Spielberg's *Jurassic Park* (1993), in which he is a chain-smoker eaten by a dinosaur. Director Quentin Tarantino gifted him with reams of pithy, witty, profane dialogue as Jules Winnfield in the hit *Pulp Fiction* (1994), and he won an Oscar nomination for Best Supporting Actor in the process. Jackson then capitalized on the fact that producers at last knew who he was with big action paydays such as *Die Hard: With a Vengeance* (1995). He returned to Tarantino for *Jackie Brown* (1997); secured spots in the *Star Wars* (1999, 2002, 2005) and *xXx* franchises (2002, 2005); and played the lead in *Shaft* (2000). **KN**

Top Takes...

xXx: State of the Union 2005
The Incredibles 2004
Kill Bill: Vol. 2 2004
S.W.A.T. 2003
xXx 2002
Changing Lanes 2002
Shaft 2000
Rules of Engagement 2000
Star Wars: Episodes I, II, III 1999, 2002, 2005
The Negotiator 1998
Jackie Brown 1997
The Long Kiss Goodnight 1996
Die Hard: With a Vengeance 1995
Pulp Fiction 1994 ☆
Jurassic Park 1993
Jungle Fever 1991

1940s

"I was a square for so long and it totally amazes me that people think I am cool."

GÉRARD DEPARDIEU

Born: Gérard Xavier Marcel Depardieu, December 27, 1948 (Châteauroux, Indre, France).

Star qualities: Hardworking; very popular actor; leading light of French cinema; holds the record (14) for the most nominations for a Best Actor César.

Top Takes...

Quand j'étais chanteur 2006 (The Singer)

Unhook the Stars 1996

Le garçu 1995

My Father the Hero 1994

1492: Conquest of Paradise 1992

Tous les matins du monde 1991
  (All the Mornings of the World)

Mon père, ce héros 1991

Green Card 1990

Cyrano de Bergerac 1990 ☆

Trop belle pour toi 1989 (Too Beautiful for You)

Camille Claudel 1988

Sous le soleil de Satan 1987 (Under Satan's Sun)

Jean de Florette 1986

Danton 1983

Le retour de Martin Guerre 1982
  (The Return of Martin Guerre)

Le dernier métro 1980 (The Last Metro)

Loulou 1980

Mon oncle d'Amérique 1980
  (My American Uncle)

Maîtresse 1976 (Mistress)

Novecento 1976 (1900)

Les valseuses 1974 (Going Places)

By 2006, it seemed as if Gérard Depardieu might have run out of steam. Recent films—one need only think of *102 Dalmatians* (2000), *Le Placard* (2001) (*The Closet*), *Nathalie . . .* (2003)— seemed chores unworthy of someone who was a leading light of French cinema for more than two decades. It was well known that Depardieu attached great importance to his wine-growing business; he'd even at one point announced his retirement. Then he surprised everyone with his performance in *Quand j'étais chanteur* (2006) (*The Singer*), as complex, subtle, and deeply affecting as anything in his distinguished career.

His portrait of a small-time nightclub crooner is typical of his finest work in that it embraces, generously but never sentimentally, the many contradictions of the character's makeup. Even in his early work, which often echoed the actor's own rough and humble origins, the amoral, uncouth, even faintly thuggish types in *Les valseuses* (1974) (*Going Places*), *Novecento* (1976) (*1900*), *La dernière femme* (1976) (*The Last Woman*), *Préparez vos mouchoirs* (1978) (*Get Out Your Handkerchiefs*), and *Loulou* (1980) were endowed with an underlying intelligence and sensitivity. Those qualities allowed

RIGHT: The boastful poet-soldier Cyrano secretly woos Roxane in *Cyrano de Bergerac*.

ABOVE: Creating onscreen chemistry with costar Cécile De France in *The Singer*.

1940s

him to play characters more remote from his own experience: *Mon oncle d'Amérique* (1980) (*My American Uncle*), *Le dernier métro* (1980) (*The Last Metro*), *Danton* (1983), *Jean de Florette* (1986), the priest in *Sous le soleil de Satan* (1987) (*Under Satan's Sun*), and the sculptor Rodin in *Camille Claudel* (1988). It seemed no part was beyond him: he even brought *Cyrano de Bergerac* (1990) gloriously back to life, reveling in the role of a nasally afflicted beast blessed with a poet's beautiful heart.

Green Card (1990) proved he could pass muster working in English, after which he combined fine roles in French fare—*Tous les matins du monde* (1991) (*All the Mornings of the World*) and *Le garçu* (1995)—with less satisfying work in English-language films like *1492: Conquest of Paradise* (1992), *My Father the Hero* (1994), and *The Man in the Iron Mask* (1998). It is hoped that with his masterwork *The Singer*, Depardieu has rediscovered his love of the cinema. **GA**

Bon Vivant

When it comes to wine and food, Gérard Depardieu has epicurean taste. In fact, the bulky French actor (he readily admits to his ample love handles) is so passionate about wine that he has become an accomplished winemaker. He even describes himself on his passport as "acteur-vigneron" (actor-winemaker). As well as a dozen vineyards, he also owns two restaurants in Paris. His love of fine wines and food may be taking its toll, however; he underwent surgery in 2000 after a heart attack. As he has confessed: "I'm happy with very little on this earth, but I do like to have a lot in my glass."

JOE DALLESANDRO

Born: Joe Dallesandro, December 31, 1948 (Pensacola, Florida, U.S.).

Star qualities: Iconic gay pinup; erotic nude sex symbol of underground U.S. 1970s; discovered by pop artist and avant-garde filmmaker Andy Warhol; androgynous good looks; charismatic.

Before his fame with Andy Warhol's Factory at the end of the 1960s with *San Diego Surf* (1968) and *Lonesome Cowboys* (1969), Joe Dallesandro was already a star as a popular beefcake pinup for the gay physique scene. Appearing in many Athletic Model Guild photographs and short films during the 1960s, his pinup qualities became a recurring feature of his star persona throughout his Warhol career that, for the most part, required him to be naked. Such was his iconic status; he was immortalized as the hustler "Little Joe" by Lou Reed in his classic song "Walk on the Wild Side" (1972).

As the muse of director Paul Morrissey, Dallesandro was at the forefront of breaking taboos on male nudity in U.S. cinema in the cult Warhol-produced trilogy *Flesh* (1968), *Trash* (1970), and *Heat* (1972). After the trilogy, Dallesandro and Morrissey both went on to make *Flesh for Frankenstein* (1973) and *Blood for Dracula* (1974) in Europe. Tired of the Warhol scene, Dallesandro stayed in Europe throughout the 1970s to notably star alongside Jane Birkin in Serge Gainsbourg's sexually provocative *Je t'aime moi non plus* (1976) (*I Love You, I Don't*) in which he plays a gay garbage truck driver. In all, he would make 18 feature films in Europe, including roles in Louis Malle's dreamscape *Black Moon* (1975) and Jacques Rivette's gangster movie *Merry-Go-Round* (1978). He returned to the United States in the 1980s, playing a number of minor roles in cheap action movies. But there were highlights during this period. He played Charles "Lucky" Luciano in Francis Ford Coppola's *The Cotton Club* (1984), and John Waters cast him in a small part as a religious zealot alongside Johnny Depp in *Cry-Baby* (1990)—a nod to his cult reputation as the underground's only male pinup. **GN**

Top Takes...

The Limey 1999
Guncrazy 1992
Cry-Baby 1990
The Cotton Club 1984
Merry-Go-Round 1981
La Marge 1976 (*Emmanuelle '77*)
Je t'aime moi non plus 1976 (*I Love You, I Don't*)
L'ultima volta 1976 (*Born Winner*)
Black Moon 1975
Blood for Dracula 1974
Flesh for Frankenstein 1973
Heat 1972
Trash 1970
Lonesome Cowboys 1969
Flesh 1968
San Diego Surf 1968

1940s

"The gay world ... gave me a whole other attitude, a calmer attitude."

JOHN BELUSHI

Born: John Adam Belushi, January 24, 1949 (Chicago, Illinois, U.S.); died 1982 (Hollywood, California, U.S.).

Star qualities: Thick set comedian; wild man of comedy and improvisation; impersonator; one half of the Blues Brothers; writer.

John Belushi was born the son of an Albanian immigrant restaurant owner. He developed an interest in acting at high school, appearing in its variety show. He helped found the West Compass Players improvisation comedy troupe, and by 1971 was performing with Chicago's Second City Comedy Troupe. He then became part of the Off-Broadway *National Lampoon*-backed rock-musical show *Lemmings* (1973). His big break came when he joined the ensemble cast of the TV show *Saturday Night Live* (1975–1979), creating a range of memorable characters, including, with Dan Aykroyd, the Blues Brothers.

Belushi made his film debut in a supporting role in Jack Nicholson's Western *Goin' South* (1978), but became an iconic figure in the showy, purportedly autobiographical part of John "Bluto" Blutarski in John Landis's *Animal House* (1978). Reveling in slobbishness, crude behavior, and cartoonish anarchy (snatching away an unctuous folk singer's guitar and smashing it to pieces), Belushi became the official wild man of comedy, essentially reprising his Bluto act in Steven Spielberg's comedy spectacle *1941* (1979).

An instant star, he was hard to cast. He was uncomfortable in a light romance, *Continental Divide* (1981), and awkward as a straight man in a slightly darker comedy, *Neighbors* (1981). Before his premature death at age thirty-three, he delivered one further classic role as the porkpie hat and sunglasses sporting Jake Blues in Landis's *The Blues Brothers* (1980). The role gave him the chance to sing and dance (in his unique fashion) along with musical legends such as Ray Charles and Aretha Franklin. A party animal and drug user, Belushi died after a lethal injection of cocaine and heroin. His younger brother is actor and comedian James Belushi. **KN**

Top Takes...

Neighbors 1981
Continental Divide 1981
The Blues Brothers 1980
1941 1979
Old Boyfriends 1979
Goin' South 1978
Animal House 1978
Lemmings 1973

1940s

"I give so much pleasure to so many people. Why can I not get some pleasure for myself?"

JESSICA LANGE

Born: Jessica Phyllis Lange, April 20, 1949 (Cloquet, Minnesota, U.S.).

Star qualities: Tall, blonde; model looks; stagecraft; leading lady of serious dramas; intense screen presence; chooses her roles carefully and avoids mainstream films; intelligent; liberal political activist; producer.

Top Takes...

Don't Come Knocking 2005
Broken Flowers 2005
Big Fish 2003
Titus 1999
Rob Roy 1995
Blue Sky 1994 ★
Cape Fear 1991
Music Box 1989 ☆
Crimes of the Heart 1986
Sweet Dreams 1985 ☆
Country 1984 ☆
Frances 1982 ☆
Tootsie 1982 ★
The Postman Always Rings Twice 1981
All That Jazz 1979
King Kong 1976

Jessica Lange grew up wanting a career in painting or dance, until a screening of the French film *Children of Paradise* (1945) persuaded her to study mime with the renowned mime teacher Etienne Decroux in 1971. She moved to New York and became a model with the Wilhelmina Agency. It was at Wilhelmina in 1975 that Lange came to the attention of producer Dino De Laurentiis, who was seeking a female lead for his much-hyped remake of the 1930s classic *King Kong*. Lange was cast as Dwan, the love interest of the gigantic gorilla. Although Lange's film debut in the new *King Kong* (1976) was certainly high profile, the movie's lukewarm critical reception and the publicity circus regarding her unknown status seemed to have an initially detrimental effect on Lange's cinematic career. She did not work in film for two years, until she was cast in Bob Fosse's *All That Jazz* (1979).

Lange's critical redemption occurred when she played Cora, a waitress who conspires with her lover, played by Jack Nicholson, to kill her husband, in the erotic thriller *The Postman Always Rings Twice* (1981). Her performances in *Frances* (1982) and *Tootsie* (1982) brought her two Oscar nominations, as Best Actress and Best Supporting Actress, winning in the latter category. She was nominated for three further Oscars in the 1980s, for roles in *Country* (1984), *Sweet Dreams* (1985), and *Music Box* (1989). Since then, Lange has consistently picked complex, rich roles that have only increased her critical credibility. She tends to eschew blockbuster parts to play only those characters that interest her. She excels in playing regional characters, especially Midwestern and Southern women. Also active in theater and in politics, she is the longtime partner of playwright Sam Shepard. **PS**

> "To stay interested in acting, I have to keep trying stuff I've never done before."

PAM GRIER

Born: Pamela Suzette Grier, May 26, 1949 (Winston-Salem, North Carolina, U.S.).

Star qualities: Queen of 1970s blaxploitation movies; tall, beautiful, voluptuous sex symbol; leading lady and character actress; feminist icon; singer; specializes in playing strong women.

One could debate which male star defined the so-called "blaxploitation" African-American film explosion of the 1970s—Fred Williamson, Richard Roundtree, or Ron O'Neal—but there's no disputing who reigned as the queen of this film movement: Pam Grier.

The daughter of a U.S. air force mechanic, she was raised on military bases in England and Germany. During her teens her family settled in Denver, Colorado, where, at age eighteen, Grier entered the Miss Colorado Universe contest and attracted the attention of Hollywood agent David Baumgarten, who signed her to a contract. She began her career inauspiciously with a series of women-in-prison exploitation movies: *The Big Doll House* (1971), *Women in Cages* (1971), *The Big Bird Cage* (1972), and *Black Mama, White Mama* (1972). Then her *Doll House* director, Jack Hill, catapulted her to stardom with *Coffy* (1973) and *Foxy Brown* (1974), two of the most memorable and entertaining blaxploitation movies of the era.

Grier continued to be an icon in the 1970s, but her films became tamer and weaker. Of course, Grier reentered the public spotlight with her eponymous role in Quentin Tarantino's most underrated film to date, *Jackie Brown* (1997). (Tarantino renamed his central character in homage to Grier's Foxy Brown role.) But rather than launching her into a major comeback, her career seems to have changed little since *Jackie Brown*. She has worked consistently since the decline of the 1970s black genre film. But Hollywood barely seems to know what to do with strong African-American actresses in general, let alone middle-aged ones, so the fact that Grier works regularly (even in projects that are beneath her talents) is, alas, an accomplishment. **TC**

Top Takes...

Bones 2001
Ghosts of Mars 2001
Holy Smoke 1999
In Too Deep 1999
Jawbreaker 1999
Jackie Brown 1997
Mars Attacks! 1996
Escape from L.A. 1996
Friday Foster 1975
"Sheba, Baby" 1975
Foxy Brown 1974
Scream Blacula Scream 1973
Coffy 1973
The Big Bird Cage 1972
Women in Cages 1971
The Big Doll House 1971

1940s

"If you're an independent woman, every woman is Foxy Brown."

MERYL STREEP

Born: Mary Louise Streep, June 22, 1949 (Summit, New Jersey, U.S.).

Star qualities: A movie legend known for heart-wrenching, intelligent, versatile, and pitch-perfect performances; she's received more Oscar nominations for acting than any other (14, with two wins); meticulous preparation for roles; producer.

Top Takes...

The Devil Wears Prada **2006** ☆
A Prairie Home Companion 2006
The Manchurian Candidate 2004
The Hours 2002
Adaptation. **2002** ☆
Music of the Heart **1999** ☆
One True Thing **1998** ☆
Dancing at Lughnasa 1998
Marvin's Room 1996
The Bridges of Madison County **1995** ☆
The River Wild 1994
Death Becomes Her 1992
Postcards from the Edge **1990** ☆
Evil Angels **1988** ☆
Ironweed **1987** ☆
Heartburn 1986
Out of Africa **1985** ☆
Plenty 1985
Silkwood **1983** ☆
Sophie's Choice **1982** ★
The French Lieutenant's Woman **1981** ☆
Kramer vs. Kramer **1979** ★
The Seduction of Joe Tynan 1979
Manhattan 1979
The Deer Hunter **1978** ☆

RIGHT: Clad in black cape as the Victorian outcast in *The French Lieutenant's Woman*.

By now the conventional portrait is simply stated: Meryl Streep is the most brilliant actress of her generation. Insert your preferred superlative here. Quake in the presence of genius. Bend a knee, bow your head, and genuflect, genuflect, genuflect. You may now recognize greatness, but if it is not clear enough from personal experience, consider the evidence of the critical establishment.

Across a career that now spans three decades and includes celebrated work in television, movies, and on the stage, Streep has received 12 Academy Award nominations with two additional wins for *Sophie's Choice* (1982) and *Kramer vs. Kramer* (1979). She has won two Emmy Awards from three nominations for *Holocaust* (1978) and *Angels in America* (2003). She has also won six Golden Globe Awards from among 20 nominations for *Angels in America, Adaptation.* (2002), *Sophie's Choice, The French Lieutenant's Woman* (1981), *Kramer vs. Kramer*, and *The Devil Wears Prada* (2006). Throughout this body of work, she has starred, costarred, or voiced roles that have sampled most genres, allowing her to perform as a bug in *The Ant Bully* (2006),

a harridan from beyond in *Death Becomes Her* (1992), an action star in *The River Wild* (1994), a monstrous fashion magazine editor in *The Devil Wears Prada*, an adventuress in *Out of Africa* (1985), and a small-town survivor in *The Deer Hunter* (1978), all taken from a much longer and diverse list.

ABOVE: Streep playing the nuclear-plant worker turned whistleblower in *Silkwood*.

Simultaneously, and in almost total contrast to most other important actors and actresses, she's been a devoted wife and mother, married since 1978 to Don Gummer, with whom she has had four children, some of whom have been involved with their mother's career while *in utero*, if only at awards presentations at which their mother is a perennial favorite. This commitment to family is unusual. It suggests a personal set of priorities that promotes stability, care, and loyalty, characteristics that have also served her

"Sometimes under-preparation is very good, because it instills fear and fear is galvanizing."

Queen of the Oscars

Meryl Streep holds the record for the most Academy Award nominations. She has been nominated 14 times, and won twice, as a Supporting Actress for *Kramer vs. Kramer* and as an Actress in a Leading Role for *Sophie's Choice*. When she first won in 1979, she was so caught up in the Oscar brouhaha that she accidentally left her statuette in a bathroom.

- She was admired in her early career by Bette Davis but was apparently disliked by Katharine Hepburn. Interestingly, Streep, Davis (ten nominations, two wins), and Hepburn (twelve nominations, four wins) are the three actresses who top the list for the most Oscar nominations.

- She is a good loser. When she and Cher were both nominated for Best Actress in 1987 and Cher won (for *Moonstruck*), Streep instantly leaped to her feet to applaud the winner. Cher thanked Streep in her acceptance speech for her support as a costar in *Silkwood*.

- She also holds the record as the actress with the most Golden Globe wins (six).

- The longest she has gone without an Oscar nomination is five years, between *Postcards From the Edge* in 1990 and *The Bridges of Madison County* in 1995.

- On accepting an Emmy for her role in the television miniseries *Angels in America* (2003), she said: "There are some days when even I think I'm overrated, but not today."

RIGHT: Streep as the formidable fashion magazine editor in *The Devil Wears Prada*.

preparation for the work that has made her synonymous with high-quality movie acting and a kind of perfectionist craftsmanship that is easily overlooked.

Streep is an East Coaster by grooming and a one-time operatic wannabe turned thespian, via turns at Vassar and Yale, as if by destiny. Gifted with a robotlike ability to mimic accent and dialect, and being genuinely able to physically transform through the combination of costume and makeup, the results of her labors are remarkably complete. In fact, one line of criticism evokes machinery to describe her performances—a feeling that Streep churns acting "product" because her performances always have a new style of speech and emotional framework, as if designed by computer.

Always the subtle performer

Shibboleth of critical and popular respect that she is, and magnet for those interested in knocking the great from worshipful pedestals, Streep's true brilliance lies in the subtleties of her performances, the kinds of detail that extend offscreen and haunt the imagination in moments of thoughtful consideration. Witness her emotional breakdown in the center of *The Hours* (2002), in which her Clarissa Vaughan prepares a dinner party for an ailing friend intent on dying. Or the nervous fingers of Lindy Chamberlain in *A Cry in the Dark* (1988) as she defends herself against charges of murdering her child. Or the façade of maternal care slowly cracking around Kate Gulden in *One True Thing* (1998). Or Karen Silkwood's blue-collar defiance in *Silkwood* (1983). The list could go on, but suffice it to say that Streep is unlike other performers in that we never forget we're watching Streep perform, even as we are transported into the universe of her performances and allowed to watch her characters convincingly become three-dimensional people. Middle age has neither diminished her abilities, nor—despite the dearth of major roles for maturer actresses—reduced the level of her appearances on the big screen. Having been nominated regularly for Academy Awards for more than two decades, she truly is a superstar. **GCQ**

RICHARD GERE

Born: Richard Tiffany Gere, August 31, 1949 (Philadelphia, Pennsylvania, U.S.).

Star qualities: Sexy leading actor; charisma; physical fitness; sensual screen presence; leading man of drama and comedy; singer; dancer; humanitarian; producer; composer.

Top Takes...

The Hoax 2006
Chicago 2002
Unfaithful 2002
The Mothman Prophecies 2002
First Knight 1995
Sommersby 1993
Final Analysis 1992
Hachi-gatsu no kyôshikyoku 1991
 (*Rhapsody in August*)
Pretty Woman 1990
Internal Affairs 1990
The Cotton Club 1984
An Officer and a Gentleman 1982
American Gigolo 1980
Days of Heaven 1978
Looking for Mr. Goodbar 1977

Richard Gere's smoldering good looks and onscreen air of sexual confidence win female fans, but excite male envy. A musician and athlete in his high school years, he won a gymnastics scholarship to the University of Massachusetts–Amherst, where he majored in philosophy. He dropped out of college after two years to pursue his dream of acting, and landed a lead role in the London production of the rock musical *Grease* (1973). He followed this up with Broadway stage success as a concentration camp prisoner in *Bent* (1980).

He first attracted attention on the big screen as one of Diane Keaton's pickups in the thriller *Looking for Mr. Goodbar* (1977). But his breakthrough came in *American Gigolo* (1980), where the male escort's eager-to-please charm frays as his private world is invaded by a murder investigation. Gere cemented his position as a leading man loved by the ladies, dressed in whites, in the romantic drama *An Officer and a Gentleman* (1982). He drifted through the rest of the 1980s in flops such as *King David* (1985). But he reestablished himself as more than just a beautiful body in two contrasting roles in 1990. He was the corrupt but charismatic cop in *Internal Affairs* (1990) and the repressed but wealthy businessman who takes Julia Roberts's hooker on a shopping spree in *Pretty Woman* (1990). Subsequently, Gere has proved his versatility in many movies: as a peace lover in legendary Japanese director Akira Kurosawa's *Hachi-Gatsu no Kyôshikyoku* (1991) (*Rhapsody in August*); a widowed journalist in the thriller *The Mothman Prophecies* (2002); and a tap-dancing lawyer, Billy Flynn, in the hit musical *Chicago* (2002). Offscreen, Gere devotes significant time to his Buddhist beliefs and humanitarian causes. **KN**

"I honestly do not think about celebrity or image or sexual expectations on me."

SIGOURNEY WEAVER

Born: Susan Alexandra Weaver, October 8, 1949 (New York City, New York, U.S.).

Star qualities: Tall, slender beauty; dark hair and eyes; thin elfin face; gravitas; versatile leading lady and character actress; serious screen presence; stagecraft; environmentalist; producer.

Daughter of NBC TV executive Pat Weaver and his actress wife, Sigourney Weaver grew up in comfort. She spent some time in an Israeli kibbutz, and then graduated in English from Stanford University. Having changed her name to "Sigourney," Weaver went on to attend Yale School of Drama in New York, and ended up in the New York theater world in the 1970s. Nearly six feet tall, she had trouble landing movie roles until earning the right to play Warrant Officer/Lieutenant Ellen Ripley in Ridley Scott's classic science-fiction horror movie, *Alien* (1979).

Very quickly becoming bankable as a dramatic female lead, she turned a corner as a comic actress in *Ghost Busters* (1984) and reprised Ripley in *Aliens* (1986), which won her an Oscar nomination for Best Actress. She rounded out the 1980s with two juicy roles: the gorilla conservationist in *Gorillas in the Mist: The Story of Dian Fossey* (1988) and the ice queen Katharine Parker in *Working Girl* (1988). Both roles won her Academy Award nods, for Best Actress and Best Supporting Actress, respectively. With firm popular appeal, she lent her talents to *Ghostbusters II* (1989), *1492: Conquest of Paradise* (1992), and *Dave* (1993). She gave two vivid performances about desperation in *Death and the Maiden* (1994) and *Copycat* (1995).

Recognizing how age is cruel to most actresses, Weaver has since taken on stereotypic matron roles, but with chancy gusto, especially in *The Ice Storm* (1997) and *Galaxy Quest* (1999), each of which reflects the bittersweet tragedy of growing older. Always working, she is fast becoming a reliable support performer in such movies as *Tadpole* (2002), *Holes* (2003), and *The Village* (2004). At the same time, Weaver is a committed environmentalist, and is the honorary chairperson of the Dian Fossey Gorilla Fund. **GCQ**

Top Takes...

The Village 2004
Holes 2003
Galaxy Quest 1999
Alien: Resurrection 1997
The Ice Storm 1997
Copycat 1995
Death and the Maiden 1994
Dave 1993
Alien³ 1992
Working Girl 1988 ☆
Gorillas in the Mist: The Story of Dian Fossey 1988 ☆
Aliens 1986 ☆
Ghost Busters 1984
The Year of Living Dangerously 1982
Alien 1979

"I've always regretted having such a serious career because I'm really more of an idiot."

1940s

JEFF BRIDGES

Born: Jeffrey Leon Bridges, December 4, 1949 (Los Angeles, California, U.S.).

Star qualities: Handsome; sexy; part of Hollywood acting family; affable charm; versatile lead and character actor; convincing screen presence; outspoken political liberal; producer; composer.

Top Takes...

Son of Hollywood titan Lloyd Bridges, and brother of actor Beau Bridges, Jeff Bridges began acting on *Sea Hunt* (1958), a TV series centered on his father. TV jobs and movie walk-ons followed. Then, aged only twenty-two, Bridges landed the plum part of Duane Jackson in Peter Bogdanovich's adaptation of the Larry McMurtry novel *The Last Picture Show* (1971). Nominated for a Best Supporting Actor Oscar, and considered a force to be reckoned with, he worked with Clint Eastwood on *Thunderbolt and Lightfoot* (1974), another Oscar nod, and tackled a giant gorilla in the remake of *King Kong* (1976).

Then Bridges took on a pair of unusual roles: the Michael Cimino epic Western *Heaven's Gate* (1980) and the Disney-inspired *Tron* (1982). By the mid-1980s, he settled into a groove of charismatic performances in *Starman* (1984) and *Jagged Edge* (1985) before reprising his *Last Picture Show* character Duane Jackson in *Texasville* (1990) and becoming another version of himself, this time both more experimental and entertaining. *The Fisher King* (1991) illustrates his style, which includes *Fearless* (1993), *The Big Lebowski* (1998), and even the dramatic turns of *The Contender* (2000) and *Seabiscuit* (2003). *American Heart* (1992) and *Lebowski* demonstrate that his strengths lie as much within independent movies as in mainstream Hollywood. Having been happily married for decades, an oddity in his field, and having now become believably sexy, even comfortable in his skin, Bridges is an Old Hollywood star in New Hollywood: suave without arrogance, talented without too much attitude, able and convincing. He is also an accomplished cartoonist and photographer. His drawings appeared in *The Door in the Floor* (2004), in which he plays a children's novelist. **GCQ**

"I have played everything from psychopathic killers to romantic leading men."

1940s

SISSY SPACEK

Born: Mary Elizabeth Spacek, December 25, 1949 (Quitman, Texas, U.S.).

Star qualities: Petite; wispily beautiful; eternally youthful looks; versatile leading lady; plays real-life strong women in dramas; Oscar-winning and nominated actress; country music singer.

Sissy Spacek attended Quitman High School, where she was named homecoming queen, presaging the role she would eventually famously play in the classic horror movie *Carrie* (1976) about a disturbed teenage girl with telekinetic powers. She first became interested in acting when she was visiting her cousin, actor and Hollywood heartthrob Rip Torn, and after graduating, "Sissy" (her childhood nickname) moved to New York to stay with him. There she hung out and had a bit part in Andy Warhol's cult movie *Trash* (1970). She tried careers in both modeling and singing before joining the Actors Studio, where she studied under the legendary Lee Strasberg.

A versatile, gifted actress, her first Hollywood role was in Michael Ritchie's *Prime Cut* (1972), in which she played a young girl drugged, kidnapped, and about to be sold into white slavery. But it was her performance in Terrence Malick's *Badlands* (1973), in which the then twenty-four-year-old actress played an introverted, disturbed fifteen-year-old on a crime spree with her boyfriend, that she first gained critical notice. By the end of the decade she would win an Academy Award for Best Actress for *Coal Miner's Daughter* (1980), a dramatization of the life of the country singer Loretta Lynn. She was also nominated for a Grammy Award for her singing on the movie's soundtrack album.

In 1974, she married art director Jack Fisk, a frequent collaborator of director David Lynch. In the 1980s, her output was less prolific while she raised her two children on the family's ranch in Virginia. However, she reappeared on the big screen toward the end of the 1990s, demonstrating her considerable abilities once more in films like *The Straight Story* (1999) and *In the Bedroom* (2001), which won her yet another Oscar nomination. **SU**

Top Takes...

North Country 2005
In the Bedroom 2001 ☆
The Straight Story 1999
Affliction 1997
JFK 1991
Crimes of the Heart 1986 ☆
The River 1984 ☆
The Man with Two Brains 1983
Missing 1982 ☆
Raggedy Man 1981
Coal Miner's Daughter 1980 ★
3 Women 1977
Carrie 1976 ☆
Badlands 1973 ☆
Prime Cut 1972
Trash 1970

> "I enjoyed the sequel, but hated my role in the first film. I was awful."—On *Carrie*

DANIEL AUTEUIL

Born: Daniel Auteuil, January 24, 1950 (Algiers, Algeria).

Star qualities: Dark hair; well built; crumpled face, with sad eyes; adept leading man of French contemporary cinema across a range of genres; especially suited to portraying emotionally fragile characters.

Top Takes…

Caché 2005 (*Hidden*)
36 quai des Orfèvres 2004
L'Adversaire 2002 (*The Adversary*)
Le Placard 2001 (*The Closet*)
La Veuve de Saint-Pierre 2000
  (*The Widow of Saint-Pierre*)
The Lost Son 1999
La Fille sur le pont 1999 (*The Girl on the Bridge*)
Le huitième jour 1996 (*The Eighth Day*)
La Séparation 1994 (*The Separation*)
La Reine Margot 1994 (*Queen Margot*)
Ma saison préférée 1993 (*My Favorite Season*)
Romuald et Juliette 1989
  (*Mama, There's a Man in Your Bed*)
Manon des sources 1986 (*Manon of the Spring*)
Jean de Florette 1986

"I like working with directors who tell me where to enter, where to exit, how fast I should go."

One of France's best contemporary leading men, Daniel Auteuil is a versatile actor. He was born in Algeria to French parents who were both opera singers. His family moved back to France, and Auteuil was raised in Avignon. Auteuil trained at the French national theater, the Théâtre National Populaire, and after graduation found work in Parisian theater, followed by early screen roles in comedy and crime films.

Auteuil garnered acclaim and international recognition as the duplicitous farmer Ugolin in Claude Berri's dramas set in the idyllic French Provençal countryside: *Jean de Florette* (1986) and *Manon des sources* (1986) (*Manon of the Spring*). On set he met costar Emmanuelle Béart for the first time, with whom he would have a ten-year relationship that produced a daughter, Nelly, born in 1992. The role also won him the French equivalent of an Oscar, a César, for Best Actor, an award he has received ten nominations for over his career thus far. He had a second win for his performance as Gabor, the knife thrower, in the romance *La Fille sur le pont* (1999) (*The Girl on the Bridge*).

Auteuil proved his versatility, moving naturally from comedy in *Romuald et Juliette* (1989) (*Mama, There's a Man in Your Bed*), to historical performances in *La Reine Margot* (1994) (*Queen Margot*), and to drama in *La Séparation* (1994) (*The Separation*). He brought an everyman quality to the character of Harry in the drama *Le huitième jour* (1996) (*The Eighth Day*). Auteuil starred in the thrillers *The Lost Son* (1999), his only English-speaking role to date, and the true crime film *L'Adversaire* (2002) (The Adversary). He teamed up again with his *Jean de Florette* costar, Gérard Depardieu, in the Francis Veber comedy *Le Placard* (2001) (*The Closet*) and the cop movie *36 quai des Orfèvres* (2004). **WW**

WILLIAM HURT

Born: William Hurt, March 20, 1950 (Washington, D.C., U.S.).

Star qualities: Tall; almost handsome; versatile leading man of dramas and character actor; 1980s sex symbol; often plays the complex and flawed; always credible; stagecraft; producer.

Just shy of handsome, William Hurt's success has been in bringing his acting skills to complex and flawed character roles, more than romantic heroes or action roles. His filmography is diverse bar one strand, in that he continually makes whatever character he plays appear entirely credible, which is always an asset to whatever film he appears in.

Hurt found a flair for acting while at high school, but went on to study theology at Massachusetts's Tufts University before switching to study drama at New York's Juilliard Drama School. He started out on the stage and in TV series such as *Kojak* (1977) before making his film debut in Ken Russell's *Altered States* (1980) in the lead role as a research scientist, whose experiments with mind-altering drugs and sensory deprivation lead him back through stages of man's evolution.

He first attracted wide attention in Lawrence Kasdan's steamy thriller *Body Heat* (1981) as a lusting lawyer manipulated by a femme fatale. This led to a clutch of impressive roles through the remainder of the decade in movies such as *The Big Chill* (1983). Hurt's crowning glory was his powerhouse role as a homosexual prisoner in the critically acclaimed *Kiss of the Spider Woman* (1985), which won him an Oscar for Best Actor. Now on a roll, Hurt reaped more Best Actor nominations: one for his role as a speech teacher who poignantly falls in love with a deaf pupil in *Children of a Lesser God* (1986), and one for his role as a reporter juggling with morality in *Broadcast News* (1987).

The 1990s and millennium have seen Hurt take on challenging roles, most notably as an unsettling mob boss in David Cronenberg's psychological thriller *A History of Violence* (2005), which proved he had not lost his edge, or gravitas, by garnering him another Oscar nomination. **CK**

Top Takes...

The Good Shepherd 2006
Syriana 2005
A History of Violence 2005 ☆
The Village 2004
Artificial Intelligence: AI 2001
The Big Brass Ring 1999
One True Thing 1998
Lost in Space 1998
Dark City 1998
The Doctor 1991
Broadcast News 1987 ☆
Children of a Lesser God 1986 ☆
Kiss of the Spider Woman 1985 ★
The Big Chill 1983
Body Heat 1981
Altered States 1980

"All I know is that my best work has come out of being committed and happy."

1950s

NASEERUDDIN SHAH

Born: Naseeruddin Shah, July 20, 1950 (Delhi, India).

Star qualities: Icon of modern Indian cinema; leading actor of Bollywood and art theater movies; slight frame; stagecraft; intellectual; uncompromising; penchant for comedy; director; producer.

Top Takes...

Iqbal 2005
The Great New Wonderful 2005
Maqbool 2003
The League of Extraordinary Gentlemen 2003
The Tragedy of Hamlet 2002
Monsoon Wedding 2001
China Gate 1998
Mandi 1983 *(Market Place)*
Umrao Jaan 1981
Aakrosh 1980 *(Cry of the Wounded)*
Junoon 1978 *(A Flight of Pigeons)*
Bhumika: The Role 1977
Nishaant 1975 *(Night's End)*

Perhaps best known in the West for playing Lalit Varma, the stressed-out father in Mira Nair's *Monsoon Wedding* (2001), Naseeruddin Shah was born in Delhi, India. He is one of a number of actors from that subcontinent who have been able to sustain an acting career across both art cinema and the popular Bollywood film industry without diminishing their reputation as performers of some substance.

Now with more than 130 movie credits to his name, Shah came to prominence in several roles for the important Indian director Shyam Benegal. Their long association began in 1975 with *Nishaant* (1975) (*Night's End*), and continued with works such as *Bhumika: The Role* (1977), *Junoon* (1978) (*A Flight of Pigeons*), and *Mandi* (1983) (*Market Place*). For Bollywood producers and directors, Shah has appeared in a number of highly successful, and indeed influential, films. These have included *Umrao Jaan* (1981), by Bollywood's standards a rather risqué tale of prostitution, where he starred alongside Rekha; and *China Gate* (1998), where he played one of an over-the-hill magnificent ten who help a village battle against bandits.

Shah's more recent high profile has led to appearances in U.S. movies, including the rather ill-fated *The League of Extraordinary Gentlemen* (2003) and the more independent-feeling *The Great New Wonderful* (2005). His more thespian profile has been maintained by an appearance in Peter Brook's *The Tragedy of Hamlet* (2002), in which he played Rosencrantz. Shah also continues to work on the stage, giving performances with his theater troupe across India. As his varied career illustrates, Shah is a dependable, adaptable, and above all, skilled performer, whatever the context. **AW**

"I am happy with what I get and make the most of what is offered to me."

1950s

BILL MURRAY

Born: William James Murray, September 21, 1950 (Wilmette, Illinois, U.S.).

Star qualities: Comedian; master of ad lib; TV-sketch artist; wry humor; plays comic and ever more serious roles; tendency to improvise on the script; writer; producer; director; keen golfer and baseball supporter.

TV variety show *Saturday Night Live* (1977–1999) alumnus, star of several great comedies and a few poignant dramatic turns, Bill Murray is an unusual funny man. He started out with Chicago's Second City Comedy Troupe, then became a featured player on *The National Lampoon Radio Hour* (1973–1975).

His movie career was built on much-loved performances in *Meatballs* (1979) and *Caddyshack* (1980), with *Stripes* (1981) proving the point on the way to *Ghost Busters* (1984), his first outright box-office smash. *Little Shop of Horrors* (1986) and *Ghostbusters II* (1989) led to *What About Bob?* (1991). But it was the truly extraordinary *Groundhog Day* (1993) that furthered his persona and ended the first phase in his comic career. Since then, his work has been darker and more thoughtful, first taking shape around *Mad Dog and Glory* (1993) and *Rushmore* (1998), with further refinements in *The Royal Tenenbaums* (2001) and *The Life Aquatic with Steve Zissou* (2004).

Perhaps starting with *Where the Buffalo Roam* (1980), but certainly reaching back to *The Razor's Edge* (1984), Murray has been slowly developing a serious side, not given to deadpan delivery, sarcasm, madness, and snappy one-liners. In that vein, his work in *Cradle Will Rock* (1999) and his Polonius in *Hamlet* (2000) set the foundation for director Sofia Coppola's acclaimed independent film *Lost in Translation* (2003). His role as a washed-up U.S. actor on a visit to Japan who strikes up a friendship with a young woman won him an Oscar nomination for Best Actor. He followed this up with another sensitive role as a lonely middle-aged man who discovers he may have a son, in Jim Jarmusch's *Broken Flowers* (2005). These latter roles have marked him out as an important serious dramatic actor in the twenty-first century. **GCQ**

Top Takes...

Broken Flowers 2005
The Life Aquatic with Steve Zissou 2004
Lost in Translation 2003 ☆
The Royal Tenenbaums 2001
Hamlet 2000
Cradle Will Rock 1999
Mad Dog and Glory 1993
Groundhog Day 1993
What About Bob? 1991
Ghostbusters II 1989
Little Shop of Horrors 1986
The Razor's Edge 1984
Ghost Busters 1984
Stripes 1981
Caddyshack 1980
Meatballs 1979

1950s

"Movie acting suits me because I only need to be good for ninety seconds at a time."

KURT RUSSELL

Born: Kurt Vogel Russell, March 17, 1951 (Springfield, Massachusetts, U.S.).

Star qualities: Disney child actor who made a successful transition to adult roles; rugged good looks; one half of a Hollywood celebrity partnership; had a brief career as a professional baseball player; writer; producer.

Top Takes…

Poseidon 2006
Sky High 2005
Dark Blue 2002
Vanilla Sky 2001
Stargate 1994
Backdraft 1991
Tango & Cash 1989
Overboard 1987
Big Trouble in Little China 1986
The Best of Times 1986
Silkwood 1983
The Thing 1982
Escape from New York 1981
Elvis 1979
The Strongest Man in the World 1975
Follow Me, Boys! 1966

"If it hadn't been for video cassette, I may not have had a career at all."

Acting is in Kurt Russell's blood: his father, Bing Russell, in addition to being a big league baseball player, was also an actor best known for his role as the sheriff Deputy Clem Foster on the hit TV Western series *Bonanza* (1961–1973). Russell has shared the screen with his father on numerous occasions during his long career. A child star groomed in the Disney machine, Kurt Russell's career has an often overlooked juvenile phase, and a more varied adult second act that has shaped him into being one of modern Hollywood's more reliable performers. In the former phase belong ten movies for Disney, including *Follow Me, Boys!* (1966) and *The Strongest Man in the World* (1975); and in the latter belong a mix of dramatic, comic, and adventure roles that first began with his TV work as the lead in the biopic *Elvis* (1979).

Not often considered a first-rate actor but instead a genuinely pleasant onscreen presence, Russell has been impressive in genre works (*The Thing*, 1982; *Breakdown*, 1997), dramas (*Silkwood*, 1983; *Backdraft*, 1991), actioners (*Escape from New York*, 1981; *Tango & Cash*, 1989), and comedies (*The Best of Times*, 1986; *Sky High*, 2005). But his lasting fame will always be tied to his longtime love, actress Goldie Hawn—neither has seen fit to marry after previous failed relationships—and the friendly persona he had established, with her help, by the time of *Overboard* (1987). Still, to see Russell in *Dark Blue* (2002) is to watch a marquee good guy transformed into an antihero, cut through with an amoral code that flouts law and order, good and evil, kindness and hostility—all in the service of a presumed greater good.

Offscreen, Russell is a prominent member of the U.S. Libertarian Party. **GCQ**

ROBIN WILLIAMS

Born: Robin McLaurin Williams, July 21, 1951 (Chicago, Illinois, U.S.).

Star qualities: Legendary comic genius known for mimicry and off-the-wall humor; talented ad libber; big, warm smile; stagecraft; writer, producer, and director; versatile leading man and support player.

The critical perspective is clear. He's an Academy Award, Golden Globe Award, Grammy Award, and Emmy Award-winning actor with roles as impressive as the marquee is long: *Mork & Mindy* (1978–1982), *The World According to Garp* (1982), *Moscow on the Hudson* (1984), *Good Morning, Vietnam* (1987), *Dead Poets Society* (1989), *Awakenings* (1990), *The Fisher King* (1991), *Mrs. Doubtfire* (1993), *Good Will Hunting* (1997), *Robots* (2005), and *Happy Feet* (2006). But Robin Williams is, first and foremost, a comic genius.

His mind is electric and connects apocrypha instantaneously. His wit is all-consuming and energetic, the full-court press to defensive costars and lazy audiences. Yet it is his constant stream of caricatures and impressions that are legendary.

Growing up in Michigan and Northern California, he had a natural ability to make people laugh. With an improvisational style modeled on Jonathan Winters, and a mind constantly archiving character types for perfect mimicry, Williams harnessed topical news to become a moving comedy show after passing through Juilliard. His willingness to work, and work constantly, has also made him a widely recognized lead actor and support player in TV, movies, and the occasional play. Not bad for a hirsute guy with a stout chest, big gestures, and a warm smile. Quirkily, he is usually clean shaven in comic roles and bearded in serious ones.

A notable philanthropist, and an activist liberal supporter of the U.S. Democratic Party, Williams was outspoken about his opposition to the war in Iraq, yet he became the most consistent entertainer of U.S. troops. He has also sired several children, famously battled with addictions to cocaine and alcohol, and hosted various international telecasts. **GCQ**

Top Takes...

Man of the Year 2006
Robots 2005
Patch Adams 1998
Good Will Hunting 1997 ★
Flubber 1997
Jumanji 1995
Mrs. Doubtfire 1993
Aladdin 1992
Hook 1991
The Fisher King 1991 ☆
Awakenings 1990
Cadillac Man 1990
Dead Poets Society 1989 ☆
Good Morning, Vietnam 1987 ☆
Moscow on the Hudson 1984
The World According to Garp 1982

"Cocaine is God's way of telling you you are making too much money."

MICHAEL KEATON

Born: Michael John Douglas, September 5, 1951 (Coraopolis, Pennsylvania, U.S.).

Star qualities: Rugged good looks; dark hair; blue eyes; appealing leading man; athletic; iconic as the caped crusader; comic timing; an acting style tinged with desperation; producer; composer.

Top Takes…

Cars 2006
White Noise 2005
Desperate Measures 1998
Jackie Brown 1997
Much Ado About Nothing 1993
Batman Returns 1992
One Good Cop 1991
Pacific Heights 1990
Batman 1989
Beetle Juice 1988
The Squeeze 1987
Touch and Go 1986
Gung Ho 1986
Johnny Dangerously 1984
Mr. Mom 1983
Night Shift 1982

"Have you ever danced with the devil by the pale moonlight?"

—Batman, *Batman*

A college dropout, Michael Keaton at first tried out life as a stand-up comedian but found little success. After working as a TV cameraman in a cable station, he decided he wanted to be an actor. But that involved a name change: while auditioning for one of his first acting roles, he realized there was already a Michael Douglas (Keaton's birth name) in Hollywood. When reading the newspaper earlier that day, he had seen an article about actress Diane Keaton. Liking the name, he wrote it down on the audition paperwork. The name stuck. Keaton found bit parts in TV before earning a role in the short-lived comedy series *Working Stiffs* (1979). This led directly to *Night Shift* (1982), which marked him as an oddly appealing, acquired taste.

Mr. Mom (1983) followed, along with the mob spoof *Johnny Dangerously* (1984) and the culture-clash comedy *Gung Ho* (1986), until Keaton met director Tim Burton and was cast in the comedy horror *Beetle Juice* (1988). At this point known for odd humor built on being an everyman confronted with out-of-control experiences, Keaton was cast in Burton's *Batman* (1989) as the caped crusader, a choice without precedent, and much debated until the picture became one of the biggest box-office smashes of the 1980s. Audiences accepted Keaton, supporting him through a blockbuster sequel *Batman Returns* (1992). Since then he has done a mix of interesting movies including *Much Ado About Nothing* (1993) and *Jackie Brown* (1997), and forgettable entertainments such as *Jack Frost* (1998) and *White Noise* (2005). Through it all, Keaton has proven not exactly versatile, but appealing in a variety of stories that continue to make the audience realize that although the shoe may not at first seem to fit, the right shoehorn goes a long way toward eventual comfort. **GCQ**

LIAM NEESON

Born: William John Neeson, June 7, 1952 (Ballymena, County Antrim, Northern Ireland).

Star qualities: Crumpled handsome looks; trademark broken nose; smooth Irish voice; tall; sexy; versatile leading man; charismatic; mesmerizing screen presence.

Liam Neeson was an award-winning boxer as a teenager, gaining the broken nose that remains his trademark. He studied at college to become a teacher, but was drawn to the stage and joined the Belfast Lyric Players Theatre in 1976. After two years, Neeson moved to Dublin's Abbey Theatre where he performed the classics. It was while at the Abbey that he was spotted onstage by director John Boorman, and was given a part in the film *Excalibur* (1981).

He went on to be cast as minor members of manly crews in movies such as *Krull* (1983), *The Bounty* (1984), and *The Mission* (1986), and showed a sensitive side as the Christian drawn ambiguously to a young lad in *Lamb* (1986) and the mute accused in *Suspect* (1987). Then followed a few obligatory roles for the budding Irish actor, encompassing all the stereotypes: an IRA man in *A Prayer for the Dying* (1987); a trash filmmaker in *The Dead Pool* (1988); a superhero in *Darkman* (1990); a boxer in *The Big Man* (1990); a private eye in *Under Suspicion* (1991); and a literary lead in *Ethan Frome* (1993).

Neeson rose magnificently to the challenge of portraying the character Oskar Schindler in Steven Spielberg's *Schindler's List* (1993), which won him an Academy Award nomination for Best Actor. For a while he then slacked off entertainingly with regulation rebel heroes, such as those in *Rob Roy* (1995) and *Michael Collins* (1996), or mentors like those in *Star Wars: Episode I—The Phantom Menace* (1999) and *Batman Begins* (2005). He landed another substantial, challenging biopic lead as the initially repressed sex researcher in *Kinsey* (2004). In *The Chronicles of Narnia: The Lion, the Witch and the Wardrobe* (2005), Neeson's beautiful Irish brogue provides the voice of the lion and God figure, Aslan. **KN**

Top Takes...

The Chronicles of Narnia: The Lion, the Witch and the Wardrobe 2005
Batman Begins 2005
Kingdom of Heaven 2005
Kinsey 2004
Gangs of New York 2002
Star Wars: Episode I—The Phantom Menace 1999
Rob Roy 1995
Schindler's List 1993 ☆
Ethan Frome 1993
The Dead Pool 1988
Suspect 1987
A Prayer for the Dying 1987
Lamb 1986
Krull 1983
Excalibur 1981

1950s

"I never did think of myself as handsome, terribly attractive yes, but not handsome."

JEFF GOLDBLUM

Born: Jeffery Lynn Goldblum, October 22, 1952 (Christopher, Illinois, U.S.).

Star qualities: Very tall and lanky; geeky looks; large eyes; hesitant style of delivery; famous for playing eccentric and intellectual roles; intense; star of several 1990s blockbusters; intelligent; stagecraft; producer; director.

Top Takes...

Igby Goes Down 2002
The Lost World: Jurassic Park 1997
Independence Day 1997
Jurassic Park 1993
Deep Cover 1992
The Tall Guy 1989
Earth Girls Are Easy 1988
The Fly 1986
Silverado 1985
The Right Stuff 1983
The Big Chill 1983
Between the Lines 1977
Annie Hall 1977
Nashville 1975
California Split 1974
Death Wish 1974

"Well, of course I would choose to be the top scientist in my field."

RIGHT: Goldblum breaks through to fame in Cronenberg's classic remake of *The Fly*.

"How's the weather up there?" one might ask of Jeff Goldblum, a dizzily tall actor with big eyes, a nervous and stuttering style of delivery, and a peculiar charm. He made his big-screen debut as a rapist and thug in *Death Wish* (1974). In more than 30 years of performances since then, his best work usually stems from a showcase of eccentricities. Aside from his obvious intelligence and unusual good looks, Goldblum uses disarming gestures while delivering dialogue with great urgency, which distracts the viewer and leaves the characters he plays with little chance of being heard.

Goldblum studied acting at New York's prestigious Neighborhood Playhouse, and initially worked on the stage. He collected small parts in movies through the 1970s, such as in *Nashville* (1975) and *Annie Hall* (1977). He was an ensemble player in films like *The Big Chill* (1983), *The Right Stuff* (1983), and *Silverado* (1985), and finally became a leading man with David Cronenberg's remake of *The Fly* (1986). After costarring with Geena Davis in *Earth Girls Are Easy* (1988)—the pair were married briefly—Goldblum found his way back into more ensemble hits (*Jurassic Park*, 1993; *Independence Day*, 1997; *The Lost World: Jurassic Park*, 1997). Yet for those acquainted with his career, the important works are little seen and marvelous. Here, titles include *The Tall Guy* (1989), *Deep Cover* (1992), and *Igby Goes Down* (2002), in which Goldblum plays shades of good and evil, always convincing and brimming with magic. Away from films, Goldblum maintains his interest in the stage and is a founding member of the New York theater company, The Fire Dept. His talents extend to music, too. He is a jazz piano singer, and plays in The Mildred Snitzer Orchestra with fellow actor Peter Weller. **GCQ**

ISABELLE HUPPERT

Born: Isabelle Ann Huppert, March 16, 1953 (Paris, France).

Star qualities: Renowned for movie-defining roles; gives intelligent and considered performances that evoke empathy; glamorous, successful, and award-winning actress without the Hollywood tag.

Top Takes...

Isabelle Huppert began acting as a teenager and had been in numerous movies before she took the lead role in *La Dentellière* (1977) (*The Lacemaker*), the film that transformed her career. Although Claude Goretta's script and direction were excellent, the film's success was undoubtedly because of Huppert's portrayal of a shy hairdresser embarking on a first, doomed affair. At once exquisitely subtle and extremely powerful, her performance suggested both an emotional warmth and a lively intelligence underlying the girl's withdrawn, fragile façade; aptly, the critic Tom Milne wrote of "a mysterious inner radiance glowing behind her patient suffering."

No mean achievement for an actress barely out of her teens; Huppert went on to display her versatility by playing a murderess in Chabrol's *Violette Nozière* (1978), for which she won the Cannes Best Actress prize. Since then, she's worked often with Chabrol—her cool, clear-eyed intelligence and air of faintly ironic detachment are well suited to the beady vision of human behavior in movies like *Une affaire de femmes* (1988) (*Story of Women*) and *L'Ivresse du pouvoir* (2006) (*Comedy of Power*). Although she has acted in U.S. films (*Amateur*, 1994), she has

RIGHT: Huppert makes a convincing scam artist in the black comedy *Rien ne va plus*.

ABOVE: Huppert as the ex-nun turned porn writer Isabelle in Hal Hartley's *Amateur*.

never pursued stardom, preferring to collaborate with directors whose work interests her, like Diane Kurys and Michael Haneke.

Her readiness to take on daring or difficult roles makes for a body of work remarkable for its range and dramatic brilliance. She never does anything flashy or scene-stealing, but her superb sense of detail means her performances are compellingly watchable; even in *8 femmes* (2002) (*8 Women*), her often-overlooked talent for comedy quietly outshines the contributions of her far from negligible costars. Her greatest strength lies in her ability—and willingness—to arouse our sympathy for characters who might seem marginal or monstrous: the cold, masochistic protagonist in *La Pianiste* (2001) (*The Piano Teacher*), where uncompromising closeups reveal her extraordinary control of facial expression. Without doubt, it is one of the greatest film performances of recent times; then again, Huppert is arguably the finest actress of her generation. **GA**

A Family Affair

The youngest of five children, the talented Ms. Huppert is not the only member of her family involved in the film world. One of her older sisters, Caroline, is a director for television, and another, Elisabeth, is an actress who wrote, directed, and starred in her own movie, *Le Rat* (1981). Isabelle is married to the director Ronald Chammah; he directed his wife in *Milan noir* (1987) (*Black Milan*). They have three children, one of whom is the actress Lolita Chammah. Mother and daughter have worked together on three movies—*La Vie moderne* (2000), *Malina* (1991), and *Une affaire de femmes* (1988).

1950s

JOHN MALKOVICH

Born: John Gavin Malkovich, December 9, 1953 (Christopher, Illinois, U.S.).

Star qualities: Sexy, balding, and tall; versatile leading man; famed for playing psychotic characters; charismatic; deadpan delivery; distinctive voice; threatening screen presence; stagecraft; writer; producer; director.

Top Takes...

"I'm drawn to a character with a lack of humanity ... I'm good at them because I don't like them."

John Malkovich made his reputation in the theater. In 1976, he quit college to work at Chicago's Steppenwolf Theater before heading for New York and Broadway. His first major roles in film and TV tended to be theatrical in origin: Biff Loman (to Dustin Hoffman's Willy) in *Death of a Salesman* (1985), Tom Wingfield in *The Glass Menagerie* (1987), Vicomte Sébastien de Valmont in *Dangerous Liaisons* (1988). Oscar-nominated as Best Supporting Actor as the blind lodger in *Places in the Heart* (1984), he took acting challenges such as the repressed scientist and innocent robot in *Making Mr. Right* (1987), the Bilko-esque Sergeant in *Empire of the Sun* (1987), Port Moresby in *The Sheltering Sky* (1990), Lennie Small in *Of Mice and Men* (1992), and Kurtz in the TV film *Heart of Darkness* (1994).

A certain cerebral detachment hung about Malkovich's early work, but he clicked into his movie-acting groove as Clint Eastwood's master of disguise, psychotic nemesis Mitch Leary in *In the Line of Fire* (1993), and began to enjoy himself more onscreen. The role led to his second Oscar nomination for Best Supporting Actor. This opened the door to more pleasurable Malkovich performances such as Dr. Jekyll and Mr. Hyde in *Mary Reilly* (1996), the worthless Gilbert Osmond in *The Portrait of a Lady* (1996), Cyrus "The Virus" Grissom in *Con Air* (1997), and the swashbuckling Athos in *The Man in the Iron Mask* (1998). Malkovich famously played himself in Spike Jonze's off-the-wall and innovative *Being John Malkovich* (1999). He went on to play Herman J. Mankiewicz in *RKO 281* (1999), Friedrich Wilhelm Murnau in *Shadow of the Vampire* (2000), and Tom Ripley in *Ripley's Game* (2002).

Acting is not Malkovich's only line of business. He designs and sells clothes via his web site, UncleKimono.com. **KN**

JOHN TRAVOLTA

Born: John Joseph Travolta, February 18, 1954 (Englewood, New Jersey, U.S.).

Star qualities: Handsome; tall; toothy smile; cleft-chinned; the comeback kid; legendary disco dancer; stage musical performer; singer; versatile leading man; writer; producer.

A one-time sweat hog on the TV sitcom *Welcome Back, Kotter* (1975–1979), a punk in *Carrie* (1976), and the essential working-class ethnic wannabe in the smash hit *Saturday Night Fever* (1977), his first Best Actor Academy Award nomination, John Travolta emerged from the efflorescence of U.S. cinema in the 1970s as the poster boy for the triumph of youth. His Danny Zuko in *Grease* (1978) showed off his singing voice, beyond his already established dance moves. He performed several songs on the *Grease* soundtrack album, which went on to sell more than 10 million copies. His occasional forays into adult material such as *Blow Out* (1981) demonstrated acting muscles on the man otherwise known for being cleft-chinned and handsome.

But sometime after *Perfect* (1985) and *Look Who's Talking* (1989), Travolta fell out of popular favor. Beached and approaching forty, the comeback kid regenerated his career and once again became a superstar with *Pulp Fiction* (1994), his second Best Actor Oscar nod. Since then he has done high-concept pap such as *Broken Arrow* (1996), successful big-budget movies such as *Swordfish* (2001), and a handful of limited-appeal experiments, including *She's So Lovely* (1997).

Also known for being a Scientologist, one of Travolta's career missteps was *Battlefield Earth: A Saga of the Year 3000* (2000), which was based on a science-fiction work by Scientology founder L. Ron Hubbard. Generally, he's been savvy and attuned to the masses, collecting respectable credits in films such as *Get Shorty* (1995), *Phenomenon* (1996), *The General's Daughter* (1999), *Basic* (2003), and *Ladder 49* (2004). Offscreen, Travolta is married to actress Kelly Preston, and they have two children. His big passion is flying, and he is a licensed jet pilot. **GCQ**

Top Takes...

Be Cool 2005
Swordfish 2001
The General's Daughter 1999
The Thin Red Line 1998
Primary Colors 1998
Face/Off 1997
Michael 1996
Broken Arrow 1996
Get Shorty 1995
Pulp Fiction 1994 ☆
Look Who's Talking 1989
Perfect 1985
Blow Out 1981
Grease 1978
Saturday Night Fever 1977 ☆
Carrie 1976

"It's hard to make a cultural phenomenon every time."

1950s

JACKIE CHAN

Born: Kong-Sang Chan, April 7, 1954 (Victoria Peak, Hong Kong).

Star qualities: Legendary icon of Hong Kong action cinema; innovative master of martial arts; athletic; accomplished stuntman and stunt director; always plays the good guy; comedy skills; slapstick king; singer.

Top Takes...

"I never wanted to be the next Bruce Lee. I just wanted to be the first Jackie Chan."

Jackie Chan's career as Hong Kong action cinema's preeminent superstar essentially reached its peak in the middle of his fame, which is troubling when one ponders how he may ultimately be remembered. It's doubtful that his early work in the 1970s, when his comedic skills were minimized in order to groom him as a Bruce Lee imitator, will be recalled by those outside of die-hard martial arts fans. But it is hoped that his legacy will not be defined by his post-*Hong faan kui* (1995) (*Rumble in the Bronx*) U.S. work such as the inane *Rush Hour* (1998) and its sequels, or his equally mediocre Hong Kong fare of the new millennium.

But look to the period between 1983 and 1994, and one discovers the apex of action cinema and some of the most remarkable physical comedy since Buster Keaton and Harold Lloyd. After a failed initial attempt to reach the U.S. market in the early 1980s, Chan took control of his career, often directing himself in a series of outrageously risky action comedies with some of the most memorable stunt set pieces in movie history. Hong Kong's post-New Wave golden age will always be linked with Chan classics such as the first two *Ging chaat goo si* films (1985, 1988) (*Police Force*); the two *'A' gai waak* (1983, 1987) (*Project A*) adventures; and the all-star team-up *Fei lung maang jeung* (1988) (*Dragons Forever*). His last best effort was the long-awaited sequel *Jui kuen II* (1994) (*Legend of the Drunken Master*). Since that, Chan's revived international career has combined with the obvious need to tone down his dangerous escapades as he pushes past middle age, making for an uncertain future career. Chan is an affable performer but a mediocre actor, and with the extreme action fading into the past, one hopes he will be able to find a comfortable twilight career for his inherent likability. **TC**

KATHLEEN TURNER

Born: Mary Kathleen Turner, June 19, 1954 (Springfield, Missouri, U.S.).

Star qualities: Beautiful leading lady; one blue eye, one hazel; voluptuous; sexy; intelligent screen siren; athletic in her youth; husky voice; civic-minded; stagecraft; director; producer.

Kathleen Turner's parents were diplomats, and she lived in Canada, Cuba, Venezuela, and England while growing up. While attending high school in London she became interested in acting, and went on to take classes at the city's Central School of Speech and Drama. Turner was first showcased in Lawrence Kasdan's *Body Heat* (1981), where she is given the 1940s glamour treatment appropriate to a film noir pastiche, but also swears and has explicit nude scenes.

She followed this stellar performance with a sublimely funny, hard woman in *The Man with Two Brains* (1983), a daffy spinster writer heroine in *Romancing the Stone* (1984), and another daringly frank role as a bipolar streetwalker in *Crimes of Passion* (1984). Rangy, deep-voiced, and obviously intelligent enough to inherit Katharine Hepburn's old roles as well as Barbara Stanwyck's, she was the speaking voice of Jessica Rabbit in *Who Framed Roger Rabbit* (1988), the hit woman in *Prizzi's Honor* (1985), the neglected wife in *The Accidental Tourist* (1988), and ran the gamut from blushing bride to murderous shrew in *The War of the Roses* (1989).

In the 1990s she was diagnosed with rheumatoid arthritis. Her illness combined with her aging years meant she found fewer worthy opportunities. She was funny in the private eye film *V.I. Warshawski* (1991), but it was a weak vehicle for her. Thereafter she tended to marginal parts such as *House of Cards* (1993), *Undercover Blues* (1994), and *Baby Geniuses* (1999), though she played interesting mad mothers, for John Waters in *Serial Mom* (1994) and for Sofia Coppola in *The Virgin Suicides* (1999). In 2005, she received critical acclaim on Broadway and in London's West End as Martha in *Who's Afraid of Virginia Woolf?* **KN**

Top Takes…

The Virgin Suicides 1999
Baby Geniuses 1999
Serial Mom 1994
House of Cards 1993
V.I. Warshawski 1991
The War of the Roses 1989
The Accidental Tourist 1988
Who Framed Roger Rabbit 1988
Peggy Sue Got Married 1986 ☆
The Jewel of the Nile 1985
Prizzi's Honor 1985
Crimes of Passion 1984
Romancing the Stone 1984
The Man with Two Brains 1983
Body Heat 1981

"I feel I get recognized for my voice more than for my face."

1950s

DENZEL WASHINGTON

Born: Denzel Washington Jr., December 28, 1954 (Mount Vernon, New York, U.S.).

Star qualities: Powerful cinematic presence; extremely handsome leading man with enviable masculinity and sex appeal; meticulous and considered in his profession; first African-American actor to receive two Academy Awards.

Top Takes...

Inside Man 2006
The Manchurian Candidate 2004
Man on Fire 2004
Antwone Fisher 2002
John Q 2002
Training Day 2001 ★
Remember the Titans 2000
The Hurricane 1999 ☆
The Bone Collector 1999
The Siege 1998
He Got Game 1998
Fallen 1998
Courage Under Fire 1996
Devil in a Blue Dress 1995
Crimson Tide 1995
Philadelphia 1993
The Pelican Brief 1993
Much Ado About Nothing 1993
Malcolm X 1992 ☆
Mississippi Masala 1991
Mo' Better Blues 1990
Glory 1989 ★
Cry Freedom 1987 ☆
A Soldier's Story 1984
Carbon Copy 1981

RIGHT: Washington as the anti-apartheid campaigner Steve Biko, in *Cry Freedom*.

Every generation has performers who seem incapable of failure in their chosen craft, so great is their talent and so forgiving is their audience for even the slightest hint of mediocrity in any role. Denzel Washington is one such performer.

Born in 1954, he was educated at Fordham University and then trained at the American Conservatory Theater in San Francisco. He broke into TV in the 1977 movie *Wilma*, then established himself as an appealing lead in his recurrent role as Dr. Philip Chandler on *St. Elsewhere* (1982–1988). Washington first made waves on the big screen in *Carbon Copy* (1981), which was followed by his memorable part in the ensemble of *A Soldier's Story* (1984). Critically recognized as a powerful actor for his portrayal of Steve Biko in *Cry Freedom* (1987), his first Oscar nomination, Washington closed the decade with his flinty, sensitive, and ultimately tragic portrayal of Private Trip in *Glory* (1989), his first Oscar win.

In 1990 he teamed up with filmmaker Spike Lee, appearing in *Mo' Better Blues* and eventually starring in *Malcolm X* (1992), *He Got Game* (1998), and *Inside Man* (2006). Throughout this period, he managed to carve a place for himself as a sexually

alive and thoughtful black everyman (*Mississippi Masala*, 1991), a tough guy (*Man on Fire*, 2004), a Shakespearean noble (*Much Ado About Nothing*, 1993), the center of several mystery thrillers (*The Pelican Brief*, 1993; *Fallen*, 1998), and the guide for divisive topical issues (*Philadelphia*, 1993; *The Manchurian Candidate*, 2004)—as well as in one biography (*The Hurricane*, 1999) and in the gripping *Training Day* (2001), his second Oscar win. In 2002 he also made his debut as director, with *Antwone Fisher*.

For years we have thrilled to Washington's work, and he's never been less than convincing. In fact, it is his winning charm, intelligence, and careful choice of roles that have made him Sidney Poitier's heir apparent in the cultural minefield of today. He has transcended the strict racial polarities of his cinematic forebears to become one of our most treasured actors. It is sobering to consider that, had he been born a decade earlier, his race would have marginalized him in the extreme. **GCQ**

ABOVE: Washington was convincing as the title character in the biopic *Malcolm X*.

Reality Check

Denzel Washington is a serious actor—he has acted in only four comedies in his film career—who chooses his roles carefully. He does not wish to be typecast, but he has been critically lauded for his studied portrayals of real-life historical figures:

- Washington trained in boxing for a year before playing Rubin "Hurricane" Carter.
- He excelled as black activist Malcolm X, but later turned down the chance to portray Martin Luther King Jr. onscreen.
- One of Washington's personal favorite performances was as Steve Biko in *Cry Freedom*, the film that made him a star.

KEVIN COSTNER

Born: Kevin Michael Costner, January 18, 1955 (Lynwood, California, U.S.).

Star qualities: Handsome; tall; sexy; charming; versatile leading man of a range of genres; solid performer; refuses to act in movie sequels; Academy Award-winning director; producer.

Top Takes...

Rumor Has It . . . 2005
The Upside of Anger 2005
Road to Graceland 2001
For Love of the Game 1999
A Perfect World 1993
The Bodyguard 1992
JFK 1991
Robin Hood: Prince of Thieves 1991
Dances with Wolves 1990 ☆
Field of Dreams 1989
Bull Durham 1988
The Untouchables 1987
Silverado 1985
Fandango 1985
The Gunrunner 1984

Kevin Costner became interested in acting while still in college, and started to take acting lessons. He later worked briefly with a California marketing firm. During a chance encounter with film veteran Richard Burton, Burton advised Costner that if he wanted to be an actor, he should give everything up completely to pursue his dreams. Famously seeing his movie debut cut from *The Big Chill* (1983), Costner nonetheless turned into the favorite guy next door after a few little-seen youth movies, *The Gunrunner* (1984) and *Fandango* (1985), among others. His sparky optimism then earned due attention in *Silverado* (1985), enough to land the starring role as Eliot Ness in *The Untouchables* (1987), which helped him conclude the 1980s as both a romantic comic lead in *Bull Durham* (1988) and a vulnerable Midwestern everyman in *Field of Dreams* (1989).

Dances With Wolves (1990) proved Costner to be a double threat, as actor and director. The movie was nominated for 12 Academy Awards and won seven, including two for him personally: Best Picture and Best Director. What followed was a quick rise to box-office and critical prominence in such work as *Robin Hood: Prince of Thieves* (1991), *JFK* (1991), *The Bodyguard* (1992), and *A Perfect World* (1993); a fall from grace perceived as overstepping (*Waterworld*, 1995; *The Postman*, 1997); a purgatory of ordinary work (*3000 Miles to Graceland*, 2001); and a resurgence based on his return to romantic comic form in *The Upside of Anger* (2005) and *Rumor Has It . . .* (2005). Costner isn't the most compelling actor. Nor is he a wholly sympathetic person, given rumors of his occasionally divalike behavior. But he is undeniably appealing, mixing boy-next-door good looks with enough charm and worldliness to suggest real pathos. **GCQ**

"Being a celebrity is probably the closest to being a beautiful woman as you can get."

RIGHT: Costner won critical acclaim as lead actor in and director of *Dances with Wolves*.

BRUCE WILLIS

Born: Walter Bruce Willis, March 19, 1955 (Idar-Oberstein, West Germany).

Star qualities: A tall, imposing figure; known for his "save the day" roles; all-American, tough action man; musically talented; successful in theater, on TV, but most prolifically in Hollywood movies; politically outspoken.

Top Takes...

One-time stutterer turned movie star, the ex-husband of Demi Moore is also father to three daughters, a political lightning rod, and a recording artist ("Respect Yourself"). Bruce Willis was born on a U.S. military base in Germany. Upon his father's discharge, the Willis clan, eventually numbering four children, settled in New Jersey, where the young Willis discovered the joy of stage performance in high school.

Following graduation, he worked in a factory before discovering music. He played harmonica for a time and returned to acting, never graduating college, and finally ended up in New York where he tended bar to make ends meet. He enjoyed a breakout role on TV as David Addison in *Moonlighting* (1985–1988). Although on set disputes with costar Cybill Shepherd were legion, he emerged an Emmy and Golden Globe Award winner with a few big-screen credits (*Blind Date*, 1987; *The Return of Bruno*, 1988) and one largely unexpected hit. *Die Hard* (1988) dropped on unsuspecting audiences and transformed the small-screen wiseguy into a true icon of the silver screen: his working-class hero cop John McClane delighted audiences with a return to old-fashioned adventure.

RIGHT: With costar Haley Joel Osment in *The Sixth Sense*, a turning point in Willis's career.

ABOVE: Memorably playing the aging cop Hartigan in the dark and violent *Sin City*.

For a while Willis was box-office gold (*Look Who's Talking*, 1989), and even a self-consciously serious actor (*In Country*, 1989). Yet two flops, *The Bonfire of the Vanities* (1990) and *Hudson Hawk* (1991), proved how mercurial audiences can be, despite having earlier lavished great love on a star. In 1994, Willis had his second of three star turns when he eschewed the normal Hollywood trappings to appear in *Pulp Fiction*. The risk proved magical and led to his resurgent appeal in *Twelve Monkeys* (1995), *The Siege* (1998), and *Armageddon* (1998). In 1999, he had his third star turn with a critically acclaimed role in M. Night Shyamalan's *The Sixth Sense*. Having settled into postdivorce bachelorhood with a return to the stage (*True West*, 2002), an Emmy Award-winning TV role (*Friends*), and more voice-over work (*Over the Hedge*, 2006), Willis seems back on top in his middle years, making some unusual choices (*Sin City*, 2005) mixed in with the mainstream fare. **GCQ**

Reluctant Hero

Although Bruce Willis appears to be the archetypal all-American hero, he is said to dislike his action image. The *Die Hard* producers apparently first cast him in the lead role because they thought he would bring warmth and humor to an otherwise cold character. Their choice was famously vindicated, and Willis ad-libbed many of the movie's one-liners. Despite saying in 2001 that he would no longer do "save-the-world" action movies, he is due to return in 2007 as John McClane in *Live Free, Die Hard*. For this outing he has chosen to forgo his usual hairpiece, to show how his character has aged.

1950s

JUDY DAVIS

Born: Judy Davis, April 23, 1955 (Perth, Western Australia, Australia).

Star qualities: Versatile actress who is often typecast as an edgy, neurotic woman; convincing in real-life roles; blue eyes and pale complexion; strong self-critic who refuses to be seduced by Hollywood; moral and artistic integrity; singer.

Top Takes...

Marie Antoinette 2006
Absolute Power 1997
Husbands and Wives 1992 ☆
Naked Lunch 1991
Where Angels Fear to Tread 1991
Barton Fink 1991
Alice 1990
High Tide 1987
A Passage to India 1984 ☆
A Woman Called Golda 1982
Heatwave 1982
Winter of Our Dreams 1981
My Brilliant Career 1979

The twice Oscar-nominated actress Judy Davis has stayed true to her Australian roots despite the lure of Hollywood. An intense and highly intuitive performer, she has been described by Woody Allen as "one of the most exciting actresses in the world." From her attention-grabbing debut as Sybylla Melvyn in Gillian Armstrong's *My Brilliant Career* (1979) to her acclaimed portrayal of Nancy Reagan in the TV movie *The Reagans* (2003) almost a quarter of a century later, she has demonstrated an awesome command of unconventional characters.

Born in Perth in 1955, Davis broke away from her strict Catholic upbringing (she was apparently forbidden to see movies as a child) while in her teens and quit convent school to go on the road with a rock band. She enrolled at Sydney's National Institute of Dramatic Art, where she played Juliet to Mel Gibson's Romeo, and graduated in 1977.

A stalwart of the Australian New Wave, Davis went on to make her mark with *Winter of Our Dreams* (1981) and *Heatwave* (1982). She landed an Oscar nomination as cultural adventuress Adela Quested in David Lean's 1984 adaptation of E. M. Forster's *A Passage To India*, although she clashed repeatedly with the director during filming. After a sublime turn as a footloose singer in *High Tide* (1987) she went on to enjoy a fruitful working relationship with Woody Allen, beginning with a small role in his romantic fantasy *Alice* (1990). Davis garnered her second Oscar nomination as the overbearing Sally in Allen's *Husbands and Wives* (1992) and won a Golden Globe for her portrayal of Judy Garland in TV's *Life with Judy Garland: Me and My Shadows* (2001). Despite her refusal to leave Australia, she manages to find regular work in Hollywood, such as in Sofia Coppola's *Marie Antoinette* (2006). **TE**

"Judy Garland was just so delicious in every way and just so honest and generous."

ISABELLE ADJANI

Born: Isabelle Yasmine Adjani, June 27, 1955 (Paris, France).

Star qualities: Dark-haired pale beauty; heart-shaped face; petite, leading lady of European cinema; stagecraft; intense screen presence; multilingual performer in English, French, and German; producer.

If Isabelle Adjani had no performance immortalized on film other than her César Award-winning, hysterically Kabuki-esque role as manic wife turned tentacled monster sex partner Anna in Andrezj Zulawski's brilliant *Possession* (1981), her status as one of cinema's boldest, bravest actresses would be assured. But *Possession* is indicative of a fascinating pattern that runs throughout Adjani's career, namely her fearless application of her fragile classical beauty to roles that utilize her exquisiteness in subversive, untraditional, and even confrontational ways.

Adjani was brought up in France to a Kabyle Algerian father and a German mother. Drawn to acting at a young age, she was playing in amateur theater by the age of twelve. She appeared in her first motion picture, *Le Petit Bougnat* (1970), just three years later. One of European cinema's great beauties, she has sporadically adopted roles that have allowed her to subsequently coast; in addition to Luc Besson's *Subway* (1985), she has also served decorative duties in a few ill-advised projects (*The Driver*, 1978; *Ishtar*, 1987; *Diabolique*, 1996).

When simply required to be attractive, Adjani looks like a frozen wild animal in a cage, waiting to pounce. But when given roles of power and strength—often of the psychologically unhinged variety—Adjani is like a one-woman cinematic inferno: from her breakout role as the love-mad heroine of François Truffaut's *L'Histoire d'Adèle H.* (1975) (*Story of Adele H.*) to the seductress in the potboiler *L'Été meurtrier* (1983) (*One Deadly Summer*), Adjani's career of fiery figures reached its peak with *La Reine Margot* (1994) (*Queen Margot*) and *Camille Claudel* (1988). The latter three films gave her more César Awards. She has worked infrequently since, preferring to focus on her family. Her intensity is missed. **TC**

Top Takes...

Monsieur Ibrahim et les fleurs du Coran 2003
  (*Monsieur Ibrahim*)
Adolphe 2002
La Repentie 2002 (*The Repentant*)
La Reine Margot 1994 (*Queen Margot*)
Camille Claudel 1988 ☆
Subway 1985
L'Été meurtrier 1983 (*One Deadly Summer*)
Antonieta 1982
L'année prochaine ... si tout va bien 1981
  (*Next Year If All Goes Well*)
Quartet 1981
Possession 1981
Nosferatu: Phantom der Nacht 1979
  (*Nosferatu the Vampyre*)
L'Histoire d'Adèle H. 1975 ☆
  (**The Story of Adele H.**)

"It's rare to find a director who likes and knows how to look at a woman through the camera."

WILLEM DAFOE

Born: William Dafoe Jr., July 22, 1955 (Appleton, Wisconsin, U.S.).

Star qualities: Versatile character actor; model; slim, pale, gaunt features; stagecraft; revolutionary of contemporary experimental theater; often plays villains; writer; producer.

Top Takes...

"Weirdness is not my game. I'm just a square boy from Wisconsin."

Some of cinema's greatest actors first made an impact onstage, and then brought their qualities to the screen. In the case of Willem Dafoe, that is an understatement. He studied drama at the University of Wisconsin-Milwaukee, but dropped out to join Milwaukee's avant-garde Theater X troupe. He toured with the group for four years in the United States and Europe. He then moved to New York in 1977, where he became a founding member of The Wooster Group. He continues to work on the stage, and his first star turn for the company was as the laborer Yank in Eugene O'Neill's *The Hairy Ape* (1996). He has helped revolutionize contemporary experimental theater, especially in the questioning of presence, charisma, and villainy. And nowhere is this better demonstrated than in Dafoe's guest villain performances onscreen, in which the brevity of screen time is turned into an advantage.

His first appearances as a baddie, as a leather-clad biker gang leader in *The Loveless* (1982) and *Streets of Fire* (1984), show a balance of maniacal charisma and melancholy that Dafoe would hone to perfection in the most outré camouflages: as Bobby Peru in *Wild At Heart* (1990), a closet gay gas attendant in *eXistenZ* (1999), a vampire with acting ambitions in *Shadow of the Vampire* (2000), the Green Goblin in *Spider-Man* (2002), and a veteran tank fish in *Finding Nemo* (2003). Even when he plays God, literally in *The Last Temptation of Christ* (1988) and symbolically in *Platoon* (1986), his characters inhabit a dark side that makes them more human and Dafoe one of the most accomplished character actors ever. It's a talent that has brought him recognition from his peers, winning two Oscar nominations, for his roles in *Platoon* and *Shadow of the Vampire*. **EM**

1950s

WHOOPI GOLDBERG

Born: Caryn Elaine Johnson, November 13, 1955 (New York City, New York, U.S.).

Star qualities: No eyebrows; dreadlock long hair; stand-up comedienne; outrageous humorist; mimic; leading lady of comedies; versatile actress; writer; director; producer.

An influential comedienne with supporters and detractors in equal measure, Whoopi Goldberg has long fascinated audiences with her vulgarity, detailed impressions, and observational humor. She began with jobs in a funeral parlor and as a bricklayer while taking small parts on New York's Broadway. She then moved to California to work with improv groups, including Spontaneous Combustion. First celebrated for stand-up comedy, her pivotal movie performance was *The Color Purple* (1985), in which she brought to life Alice Walker's Celie, and won an Oscar nomination for Best Actress. Follow-up roles were comic, and then there was *Ghost* (1990), which won her an Oscar for Best Supporting Actress.

Since then she's worked almost constantly on TV and the big screen, in smashes such as *The Lion King* (1994), flashes of brilliance such as *Boys on the Side* (1995), bombs such as *Eddie* (1996), forgettable fare such as *An Alan Smithee Film: Burn Hollywood Burn* (1998), and all levels of mediocrity in between. She has been a spokeswoman for the "Got milk?" campaign, producer of a TV game show *Hollywood Squares* (1998–2002), frequent subject of the celebrity-gossip magazines for various love affairs, and an Oscar ceremony hostess. She is also one of only a handful of elite women who have won Oscar, Tony, Emmy, and Grammy awards. Perhaps unbelievably in this age of obvious onscreen beauties, Goldberg remains popular not for her physical beauty, but because she remains rooted in a unique personality, body type, and attitude that's influenced by hard work, dyslexia, three divorces, grandmotherhood, recovery from heroin addiction, and continuous good work in the Comic Relief charity organization's series of fund-raisers. **GCQ**

Top Takes…

The Magic Roundabout 2005
Star Trek: Nemesis 2002
Rat Race 2001
Girl, Interrupted 1999
How Stella Got Her Groove Back 1998
Boys on the Side 1995
Star Trek: Generations 1994
The Lion King 1994
Sister Act 2: Back in the Habit 1993
Sister Act 1992
The Player 1992
Soapdish 1991
Ghost 1990 ★
The Telephone 1988
Jumpin' Jack Flash 1986
The Color Purple 1985 ☆

1950s

"I don't look like Halle Berry. But chances are, she's going to end up looking like me."

MEL GIBSON

Born: Mel Columcille Gerard Gibson, January 3, 1956 (Peekskill, New York, U.S.).

Star qualities: Ruggedly handsome; blue-eyed; sexy; leading man of action movies; controversial figure because of his religious beliefs; writer; award-winning director; producer.

Top Takes…

Signs 2002
What Women Want 2000
The Patriot 2000
Ransom 1996
Braveheart 1995
Forever Young 1992
Hamlet 1990
Lethal Weapon 1987, 1989, 1992, 1998
Mad Max Beyond Thunderdome 1985
Mrs. Soffel 1984
The River 1984
The Bounty 1984
The Year of Living Dangerously 1982
Mad Max 2 1981
Gallipoli 1981
Mad Max 1979

"It's a wonderful feeling, but I'm not gonna kill myself trying to win another [Oscar]."

Recognizing the controversies that surround his religious dogmatism and his struggle with alcoholism, Mel Gibson is nonetheless one of contemporary cinema's great actors, action stars, and directors. Born in the United States in 1956, he was raised in Australia and trained at the University of New South Wales in Sydney. He performed at Australia's National Institute of Dramatic Arts, and his early career was spent on the stage and TV. He first stood out on the big screen in the late 1970s and early 1980s for his work in *Tim* (1979) and *Gallipoli* (1981). Worldwide audiences first embraced him in the futuristic action movie *Mad Max* (1979) and its sequels, *Mad Max 2* (1981) and *Mad Max Beyond Thunderdome* (1985).

A host of popular roles followed: as Martin Riggs in *Lethal Weapon* (1987) and its numerous sequels, *The Patriot* (2000), and *Signs* (2002), making him a bankable star and one of *People* magazine's "sexiest men on earth." But he also offered performances that showcased his depth beyond the shoot-'em-up and romance-'em template he'd helped popularize, including the lead in Franco Zeffirelli's *Hamlet* (1980).

Approaching middle age, now wealthy, and looking to strike new ground, Gibson became a filmmaker with *The Man Without a Face* (1993). He followed this with *Braveheart* (1995), which he produced, directed, and starred in, as Scottish hero William Wallace. The epic won him two Oscars for Best Picture and Best Director. Enter faith, cue detractors, ring cash registers, and watch one of the world's great male stars transformed into a spiritual leader and experimental artist, with *The Passion of the Christ* (2004). He followed this by writing and directing an action tale of the Mayan kingdom in decline, *Apocalypto* (2006). **GCQ**

ANDY GARCIA

Born: Andrés Arturo García Menéndez, April 12, 1956 (Havana, Cuba).

Star qualities: Hispanic dark good looks; capable leading man and support player; charismatic; principled; solid screen presence; singer; composer; writer; producer; director.

Born in Havana, Cuba in 1956, Andy Garcia came with his family to the United States in the early 1960s after the Bay of Pigs invasion of Cuba. Growing up in Miami while his family prospered in the perfume business, he began acting at Florida International University and in regional theater before moving to Hollywood. He first attracted notice with roles in TV shows such as *Hill Street Blues* (1981–1984), and movies such as *8 Million Ways to Die* (1986), but it was a costarring role in Brian De Palma's *The Untouchables* (1987) that made him a major star. Since then, he has starred in many films and recently made the move to writing and directing with *The Lost City* (2005), starring himself, Bill Murray, and Dustin Hoffman.

After *The Untouchables* Garcia starred in such films as *Black Rain* (1989) and *Internal Affairs* (1990). He next landed the part of Vincent "Vinnie" Mancini, the illegitimate son of Sonny Corleone, in Francis Ford Coppola's *The Godfather: Part III* (1990). The character of Vincent, whose temper and ruthlessness matched that of his father, allowed Garcia to display his wide acting range and earned him an Oscar nomination for Best Supporting Actor. The part cemented his status as a solid, if not spectacular, Hollywood star, capable of both lead and support roles in a slate of films as diverse as *When a Man Loves a Woman* (1994) to *Modigliani* (2004). Garcia recently renewed his public profile by starring in the successful remake *Ocean's Eleven* (2001) and its sequel *Ocean's Twelve* (2004). He also garnered critical respect for his helming of *The Lost City*, in which he also stars as nightclub owner Fico Fellove in the time frame of the collapse of President Fulgencio Batista's regime in Cuba, and Fidel Castro's revolutionary takeover of the country. **PS**

Top Takes...

The Lost City 2005
Ocean's Twelve 2004
Modigliani 2004
Confidence 2003
Ocean's Eleven 2001
The Disappearance of Garcia Lorca 1997
Night Falls on Manhattan 1997
Dangerous Minds 1995
Things to Do in Denver When You're Dead 1995
When a Man Loves a Woman 1994
Jennifer Eight 1992
Dead Again 1991
The Godfather: Part III 1990 ☆
Internal Affairs 1990
Black Rain 1989
The Untouchables 1987

"You are defined by who you are, by your choices in life ... not just in doing movies."

TOM HANKS

Born: Thomas Jeffrey Hanks, July 9, 1956 (Concord, California, U.S.).

Star qualities: "The modern James Stewart"; handsome, clean-cut, leading man; superb comic timing; often plays the confused but affable good guy; box-office gold; producer; writer; director.

Top Takes...

The Da Vinci Code 2006
The Terminal 2004
The Ladykillers 2004
Catch Me If You Can 2002
Road to Perdition 2002
Cast Away 2000 ☆
The Green Mile 1999
Saving Private Ryan 1998 ☆
Toy Story/Toy Story II 1995, 1999
Apollo 13 1995
Forrest Gump 1994 ★
Philadelphia 1993 ★
Sleepless in Seattle 1993
A League of Their Own 1992
Big 1988 ☆
Splash 1984

"If you have to have a job in this world, a high-priced movie star is a pretty good gig."

RIGHT: While waiting for a bus, Hanks reflects on his fascinating life story as Forrest Gump.

Born and raised in California, after the early divorce of his parents, Tom Hanks spent much of his youth traveling the state with his itinerant cook father. After majoring in acting at college, his first big success came with the comedy Splash (1984), whose box-office take assured Hanks of instant stardom. Roles playing on his goofy but lovable, boy-next-door persona soon followed, with work on lightweight but popular comedies such as Bachelor Party (1984), The Man With One Red Shoe (1985), and The Money Pit (1986), all serving to sharpen his considerable comic talent and culminating in an Academy Award nomination for Best Actor for his role as the boy in an adult body in Big (1988).

By the late 1980s, after a run of failures, Hanks's star looked to be in freefall. But it was his Best Actor Oscar-winning turn in Philadelphia (1993), playing a homosexual lawyer dying of AIDS, that saw Hanks's career shift gear, and transform both his fortunes and place in movie history. Success came in both sweet comedies, such as Sleepless in Seattle (1993), and meatier roles that allowed him to explore the full range of his acting talents. He exploited his more mature presence in hits such as Forrest Gump (1994), which won him another Best Actor Oscar, Apollo 13 (1995), and The Green Mile (1999). He was catapulted to the position of the de facto leading man and Hollywood box-office gold, collecting another couple of Oscar nods along the way. The twenty-first century has seen him continue to put in sterling performances, and also crop up as the voice in a number of animations, including Cars (2006). His Playtone production company also had a hand in the animated feature The Ant Bully (2006), and he is becoming involved with producing as much as acting. **RH**

CHRISTOPHER LAMBERT

Born: Christophe Guy Denis Lambert, March 29, 1957 (Long Island, New York, U.S.).

Star qualities: Ruggedly handsome; crumpled face; large lips; intense, blue-eyed gaze; sexy; athletic; lithe; leading man of action movies and dramas, but also good in comic roles; writer; producer.

Top Takes...

1950s

"The beauty of [acting] is that by changing characters, it never gets boring."

Although he was born in the United States, Christopher Lambert's family left the country when he was two years old. His father was a United Nations diplomat in Switzerland, and as a result, Lambert was educated at boarding schools in Geneva. Inspired by his appearance in a school play at the age of twelve, Lambert wanted to be an actor. However, his parents saw acting as a precarious career, so to please them he went to work at the London Stock Exchange. But he left after six months and went to study theater at the Paris Conservatoire.

Lambert played a few roles in French films such as *Le Bar du téléphone* (1980) (*The Telephone Bar*) and *Asphalte* (1981) (*Asphalt*) before being cast in the demanding lead role of John Clayton/Lord Greystoke/Tarzan in *Greystoke: The Legend of Tarzan, Lord of the Apes* (1984). Lambert's Tarzan was as much Kaspar Hauser-like foundling as action hero, but he was a lithe, physical presence in the jungle scenes. He was funny as the bleached blond, tuxedo-clad runaway in Luc Besson's *Subway* (1985), then mostly left French films for international leads.

Lambert founded a franchise to which he returned several times on film and TV as the immortal head-lopping Scot in *Highlander* (1986), but was a dreary Salvatore Giuliano in Michael Cimino's would-be epic *The Sicilian* (1987). After the comedy caper *Why Me?* (1990) and the psycho-thriller *Knight Movies* (1992), Lambert slid to lower-case action and direct-to-video pictures, many directed by Albert Pyun, competing with Rutger Hauer or David Carradine for credits such as *Fortress* (1993), *Gunmen* (1994), *Mortal Kombat* (1995), *Adrenalin: Fear the Rush* (1996), *Mean Guns* (1997), *Beowulf* (1999), *Resurrection* (1999), *Absolon* (2003) and Richard Kelly's folly *Southland Tales* (2006). **KN**

DANIEL DAY-LEWIS

Born: Daniel Michael Blake Day-Lewis, April 29, 1957 (London, England).

Star qualities: Handsome; tall; stagecraft; Method actor; judicious role choice; truly credible screen presence; capable of playing an incredibly wide range of roles; renowned for submerging into roles.

Daniel Day-Lewis is the son of the late British poet laureate Cecil Day-Lewis and actress Jill Balcon, daughter of Sir Michael Balcon, former head of Ealing Studios. He is renowned for submerging into roles; enough so that his handsome features are often radically altered to play heroes or villains. Also notoriously picky with parts, focused on technical perfection, publicity shy, and based in Europe, Day-Lewis's body of movie work is relatively small.

He studied acting at the Bristol Old Vic Theatre School, and went on to work on the stage. Having made his debut young, playing a vandal in *Sunday Bloody Sunday* (1971), he had a small part in *Gandhi* (1982), and then earned wide recognition in the Merchant-Ivory film *A Room with a View* (1985). With a sensual detour through *The Unbearable Lightness of Being* (1988), his name and work ethic were dramatically put on display in his Best Actor Oscar-winning role as the severely disabled Christy Brown in *My Left Foot* (1989). Such was his devotion to staying in character that offscreen Day-Lewis had to be wheeled around the set in his wheelchair.

Since that time he has appeared in one broadly commercial title, *The Last of the Mohicans* (1992); Irish dramas such as *In the Name of the Father*, (1993); prestige productions such as *The Age of Innocence* (1993); the melodrama *The Ballad of Jack and Rose* (2005); and done a turn as a bloodthirsty monster in *Gangs of New York* (2002). In each part he is believable, canny, true, and magnificent. So much so that he garnered another two Academy Award Best Actor nominations for *In the Name of the Father* and *Gangs of New York*.

Day-Lewis is married to actress and director Rebecca Miller, daughter of the late U.S. playwright Arthur Miller. **GCQ**

Top Takes...

The Ballad of Jack and Rose 2005
***Gangs of New York* 2002** ☆
The Boxer 1997
The Crucible 1996
***In the Name of the Father* 1993** ☆
The Age of Innocence 1993
The Last of the Mohicans 1992
***My Left Foot* 1989** ★
Stars and Bars 1988
The Unbearable Lightness of Being 1988
Nanou 1986
A Room with a View 1985
My Beautiful Laundrette 1985
The Bounty 1984
Gandhi 1982
Sunday Bloody Sunday 1971

"If I weren't allowed this outlet, there wouldn't be a place for me in society."—On acting

STEVE BUSCEMI

Born: Steve Buscemi, December 13, 1957 (Brooklyn, New York, U.S.).

Star qualities: Bug-eyed; baby-faced; highly respected character actor; frequently plays strange crazy villain roles; fast talking; prolific output; producer; writer; director.

"Kinda funny-lookin'"—this was the assessment of witnesses asked to describe the kidnapper played by Steve Buscemi in *Fargo* (1996). It probably echoes the response of many moviegoers to a talented character actor famous for making a mark in the tiniest of roles.

Buscemi became interested in acting during his last year of high school. After graduating, he studied acting at New York's famed Lee Strasberg Institute. He then began acting in and writing original plays for the theater. While doing so he also worked as a New York City fireman from 1980 to 1984, a vocation returned to after the 9/11 World Trade Center terrorist attack in 2001. He went to his old firehouse the day after the tragedy to volunteer, and spent a week digging through rubble with his old comrades looking for missing firefighters.

He has been likened to the legendary actor Peter Lorre; certainly Buscemi's faintly bug-eyed, never-quite-young baby face can seem at once sinister and vulnerable, as volatile and amoral as a spoilt child. The crime world has therefore figured heavily in his resume, notably *Miller's Crossing* (1990), *Reservoir Dogs* (1992), *Pulp Fiction* (1994), and *Desperado* (1995). Yet he's equally at home in serious dramas such as *Parting Glances* (1986) and *Kansas City* (1996), and comedies such as *Mystery Train* (1989) and *Romance & Cigarettes* (2005). Indeed, his very affecting performances in *The Big Lebowski* (1998) and *Ghost World* (2001) suggest he is at his best in movies that combine both. That is true of two of the films he's so far directed: *Trees Lounge* (1996) and *Lonesome Jim* (2005), although the prison drama *Animal Factory* (2000) shows his ability to deal with far darker material. The understated realism of all three movies displays real directorial talent. **GA**

Top Takes...

1950s

"My favorite review described me as the cinematic equivalent of junk mail."

SHARON STONE

Born: Sharon Vonne Stone, March 10, 1958 (Meadville, Pennsylvania, U.S.).

Star qualities: Beauty queen looks; tall, blonde, slim, sexy, leading lady; civil rights activist; the woman in cinema's most famous leg-crossing scene; intelligent; producer; composer; director.

Ironically for a woman famous for her role as beautiful serial killer Catherine Trammel in the erotic thriller *Basic Instinct* (1992), Sharon Stone was extremely self-conscious about her appearance as a child. She grew up to become a beauty contest winner and fashion model in New York during the 1970s. At the beginning of the 1980s, Stone quit modeling to pursue a career in acting.

Her first role was in Woody Allen's *Stardust Memories* (1980), but her first big break came with the role of Arnold Schwarzenegger's betraying wife in sci-fi film *Total Recall* (1990). She also appeared nude in *Playboy* magazine, thus beginning her rise to prominence as a sex symbol. However, true stardom eluded her until her appearance as the central character in *Basic Instinct*, where she played a beautiful, bisexual, serial killer who dispatches her male victims with an ice pick during sexual intercourse. One of the most infamous shots in cinematic history appears in this film, where Stone crosses her legs during an interrogation scene with police detectives to reveal that she isn't wearing any underwear. The scene led to a heated and public controversy between Stone and director Paul Verhoeven. Stone maintained that Verhoeven had tricked her by not letting her know he had a camera filming between her legs.

Another erotic thriller, *Sliver* (1993), followed before she starred in Martin Scorsese's *Casino* (1995) and gained an Oscar nomination for Best Supporting Actress. Since then, Stone has worked steadily, forming her own production company, and striving to be taken seriously as an actress. She has had some disappointments, such as *Catwoman* (2004), but also some successes, such as her turn in *Broken Flowers* (2005). **PS**

Top Takes...

Bobby 2006
Basic Instinct 2 2006
Broken Flowers 2005
Catwoman 2004
Picking Up the Pieces 2000
Simpatico 1999
The Muse 1999
Gloria 1999
The Mighty 1998
***Casino* 1995** ☆
The Quick and the Dead 1995
Intersection 1994
Last Action Hero 1993
Sliver 1993
Basic Instinct 1992
Total Recall 1990

"If you have a vagina and an attitude in this town, then that's a lethal combination."

1950s

GARY OLDMAN

Born: Leonard Gary Oldman, March 21, 1958 (New Cross, London, England).

Star qualities: Chameleonlike leading man and character actor; famous for playing the rebel or villain; wide range of roles; stagecraft; intense screen presence; writer; producer; director.

Top Takes…

1950s

"To be able to do this job in the first place you've got to have a bit of an ego."

The son of a welder, Gary Oldman was born in London. He won a scholarship to the city's Rose Bruford Drama College, where he graduated in theater arts. He then studied with the Greenwich Young People's Theatre, and went on to appear onstage throughout the early 1980s.

His film debut was in *Remembrance* (1982), but he first attracted attention on the big screen as punk rocker Sid Vicious in the biopic *Sid and Nancy* (1986). This was the start of a trend; Oldman has enthusiastically played more pariahs, hate figures, troublemakers, rebels, and monsters than any other contemporary actor. Among them are roles as Joe Orton in *Prick Up Your Ears* (1987), a football hooligan and estate agent in *The Firm* (1988), assassin Lee Harvey Oswald in *JFK* (1991), Count Dracula in *Dracula* (1992), a terrorist hijacker in *Air Force One* (1997), and a disfigured child molester dreaming of feeding his enemy to pigs in *Hannibal* (2001).

However, he does not exclusively play the villain, and has turned to more amiable roles in recent years. In *Harry Potter and the Prisoner of Azkaban* (2004) and its sequels, he was the Animagus Sirius Black, who turns out to be not that bad, and as Jim Gordon in *Batman Begins* (2005) he played against type as the only decent man in Gotham City. Oldman's one foray so far into directing was the gritty working-class drama *Nil by Mouth* (1997), which he also wrote and produced and was partially based on his life. The movie was critically acclaimed and won numerous awards in Britain, including the British Academy Award for Best Screenplay. He has never, however, been nominated for an Oscar as an actor.

Oldman has been married and divorced three times, his second wife being actress Uma Thurman. **KN**

MICHELLE PFEIFFER

Born: Michelle Marie Pfeiffer, April 29, 1958 (Santa Ana, California, U.S.).

Star qualities: Radiantly beautiful blonde; blue eyes; petite; beauty pageant winner; versatile leading lady of dramas and romantic comedies; screen siren; singer; producer.

Michelle Pfeiffer started out training to be a journalist before she switched to study acting at The Beverly Hills Playhouse. A beauty pageant winner, she assembled the typical early resume of a stunning, thin, blonde actress: *Fantasy Island* (1978–1981) guest shots; a Goldie Hawn imitation in *Charlie Chan and the Curse of the Dragon Queen* (1981); and the lead in an unfortunate sequel, *Grease 2* (1982).

She became a star in the mid-1980s, but still tended to be used largely as a beautiful object in *Scarface* (1983), *The Witches of Eastwick* (1987), and *Tequila Sunrise* (1988). Yet Pfeiffer sparkled in *Into the Night* (1985), and surprised audiences with less icy characters. She was brassy in *Married to the Mob* (1988), and naive as Madame Marie de Tourvel in *Dangerous Liaisons* (1988), which won her an Oscar nomination for Best Actress. Her role as a torch singer in *The Fabulous Baker Boys* (1989) won her another Oscar nomination, this time for Best Supporting Actress. She also sang all her own songs.

The 1990s saw her playing a dowdy waitress in *Frankie and Johnny* (1991). She went on to show astonishing range by segueing from the demented, hypersexual Catwoman in *Batman Returns* (1992), to the Jackie Kennedy-struck Dallas housewife of *Love Field* (1992), to the primly scandalous Ellen Olenska in *The Age of Innocence* (1993). Sadly, as a major star, she is too rarely stretched. For example, *Dangerous Minds* (1995) and *What Lies Beneath* (2000) were expert but conventional. Still one of the most oft-cited most beautiful people on such lists, Pfeiffer's age has not diminished her screen siren status. What roles lie ahead that both capitalize on her looks and use her significant acting muscle to its full extent remains to be seen. **KN**

Top Takes...

White Oleander 2002
What Lies Beneath 2000
A Thousand Acres 1997
One Fine Day 1996
Up Close & Personal 1996
Dangerous Minds 1995
The Age of Innocence 1993
Love Field 1992 ☆
Batman Returns 1992
Frankie and Johnny 1991
The Fabulous Baker Boys 1989 ☆
Dangerous Liaisons 1988 ☆
Married to the Mob 1988
The Witches of Eastwick 1987
Into the Night 1985
Scarface 1983

1950s

"I still think people will find out that I'm really not very talented. I'm really not very good."

TIM ROBBINS

Born: Timothy Francis Robbins, October 16, 1958 (West Covina, California, U.S.).

Star qualities: Tall; stagecraft; founding member of the Actors' Gang theater group; versatile leading man and support player; one half of a Hollywood celebrity partnership; political liberal; musician; writer; producer; director.

Top Takes...

Catch a Fire 2006
The Secret Life of Words 2005
War of the Worlds 2005
Mystic River 2003 ★
Human Nature 2001
High Fidelity 2000
Cradle Will Rock 1999
Arlington Road 1999
Prêt-à-Porter 1994
The Shawshank Redemption 1994
The Hudsucker Proxy 1994
Short Cuts 1993
Bob Roberts 1992
The Player 1992
Jacob's Ladder 1990
Bull Durham 1988

Tim Robbins has long walked in the shadow of his notable partner, actress Susan Sarandon, although recent work has helped define him as an individual artist on his own terms and for his own efforts. This credit was hard won through studying drama at the University of California, Los Angeles, and a long commitment to theatrical experimentation. After graduation, Robbins founded the Actors' Gang, an experimental theater group, in Los Angeles with actor friends from college. He also put in time in supporting roles in such notable 1980s movies as *Top Gun* (1986) and *Howard the Duck* (1986).

His career breakthrough was opposite Sarandon as an up-and-coming baseball pitcher in *Bull Durham* (1988), followed by a challenging lead role in *Jacob's Ladder* (1990), a mind trip about post-traumatic stress in a Vietnam veteran. He made his directorial debut in *Bob Roberts* (1992), a political fable that also indicated his type of offscreen activism, which has continued through to the present with echoes in his other two movies at the helm, *Dead Man Walking* (1995) and *Cradle Will Rock* (1999). The former won him an Oscar nomination for directing. He went on to reach his acting career high for his performance in *Mystic River* (2003), which won him an Oscar for Best Supporting Actor. Tall and graying, Robbins has become a niche player in films such as *High Fidelity* (2000) and *War of the Worlds* (2005), after earlier sampling the view from the pole position in movies, including *The Player* (1992), *The Hudsucker Proxy* (1994), and *The Shawshank Redemption* (1994). Although he has tended to revert to support acting roles, perhaps focusing more on his writer/director interests, there is certainly plenty to look forward to from this versatile and significant performer. **GCQ**

"I'm fairly competent as a director and actor, but I am Mr. Neurotic as a writer."

KEVIN SPACEY

Born: Kevin Spacey Fowler, July 26, 1959 (South Orange, New Jersey, U.S.).

Star qualities: Handsome; clean-cut; stylish; well dressed; master of stagecraft; versatile leading actor of dramas; Oscar winner; theater artistic director; writer; director; producer.

In high school, Kevin Spacey used to cut class and watch revivals at the NuArt Theater in Santa Monica, California. He also became an able impressionist, and tried doing stand-up comedy. After two years at New York's Juilliard School studying theater, he performed on the Broadway stage throughout the 1980s, and gradually emerged in bit parts on TV in shows such as *Crime Story* (1987) and *Wiseguy* (1988), and in movies such as *Heartburn* (1986) and *Working Girl* (1988).

After a turn in the ensemble cast of *Glengarry Glen Ross* (1992), Spacey enjoyed one of those magic periods all artists dream about, in which he went from oddball support to leading man. There was *Swimming with Sharks* (1994), followed by *The Usual Suspects* (1995), his first Academy Award winner for Best Supporting Actor, *Se7en* (1995), and then *L.A. Confidential* (1997). These four roles proved pivotal to his career, making him ideal for roles as a well-spoken, emotionally controlled, sinister, and calculated personality. He went on to win a second Oscar for the suburban family drama *American Beauty* (1999), this time for Best Actor. He then tried his hand as film director with *Albino Alligator* (1996) and *Beyond the Sea* (2004), and became a popular actor with a grasshopper voice-over in *A Bug's Life* (1998), a possible alien mental patient in *K-PAX* (2001), and as Superman's nemesis in *Superman Returns* (2006). He has continued to do well-respected work onstage, and in 2003 became artistic director of the Old Vic Theatre Company in London. Offscreen, Spacey is guarded about his private life, saying, "The less you know about me, the easier it is to convince you that I am that character onscreen. It allows an audience to come into a movie theater and believe I am that person." **GCQ**

Top Takes...

Superman Returns 2006
Beyond the Sea 2004
The Life of David Gale 2003
The Shipping News 2001
K-PAX 2001
American Beauty 1999 ★
A Bug's Life 1998
The Negotiator 1998
Midnight in the Garden of Good and Evil 1997
L.A. Confidential 1997
A Time to Kill 1996
Se7en 1995
Outbreak 1995
The Usual Suspects 1995 ★
Swimming with Sharks 1994
Glengarry Glen Ross 1992

1950s

"If you're lucky enough to do well, it's your responsibility to send the elevator back down."

ANTONIO BANDERAS

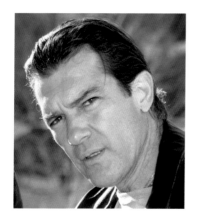

Born: José Antonio Domínguez Banderas, August 10, 1960 (Málaga, Andalucía, Spain).

Star qualities: Handsome Spanish heartthrob; sexy; dark hair and dark eyes; stylish; leading actor of dramas and swashbuckling roles; one half of a Hollywood couple; composer; writer; director; producer.

Top Takes…

Shrek 2 2004
Imagining Argentina 2003
Frida 2002
The Mask of Zorro 1998
Evita 1996
Assassins 1995
Desperado 1995
Philadelphia 1993
The House of the Spirits 1993
The Mambo Kings 1992
¡Átame! 1990 (*Tie Me Up! Tie Me Down!*)
Mujeres al borde de un ataque de nervios 1988
   (*Women on the Verge of a Nervous Breakdown*)
La ley del deseo 1987
Matador 1986

"I hate that cat. Ever since he appeared in my life he's more important than me."—On *Shrek 2*

Born in Málaga, Spain, the young Antonio Banderas wanted to play professional soccer. However, he broke his foot as a teenager, and turned to acting instead. He studied at Málaga's School of Dramatic Art before starting a five-year stint with the prestigious National Theater of Spain in Madrid. He was spotted there by up-and-coming director Pedro Almodóvar, and his movie career took off with a role in Almodóvar's *Laberinto de pasiones* (1982) (*Labyrinth of Passion*).

The actor and director made a good team, and both rose to prominence on the heels of *Matador* (1986), the sexually provocative *La ley del deseo* (1987) (*Law of Desire*), *Mujeres al borde de un ataque de nervios* (1988) (*Women on the Verge of a Nervous Breakdown*), and *¡Átame!* (1990) (*Tie Me Up! Tie Me Down!*). Banderas then headed for Hollywood, and quickly became one of Spain's most popular exports.

Having cut his teeth with a phonetically performed part in *The Mambo Kings* (1992), after earlier being ogled by Madonna in her expose *Madonna: Truth or Dare* (1991), Banderas had a few showy roles in films such as *The House of the Spirits* (1993), *Philadelphia* (1993), and *Interview with a Vampire: The Vampire Chronicles* (1994) before establishing a creative partnership with Robert Rodriguez on *Desperado* (1995). Since then he has played a singing freedom fighter in *Evita* (1996), Zorro in *The Mask of Zorro* (1998) and its sequel, an Arab in *The 13th Warrior* (1999), Pancho Villa in TV's *And Starring Pancho Villa as Himself* (2003), and a hilarious animated Puss in Boots in *Shrek 2* (2004). He has also married for the second time, to Hollywood movie actress Melanie Griffith, starred in several Broadway shows, and is now generally considered one of the world's great male beauties. **GCQ**

SEAN PENN

Born: Sean Justin Penn, August 17, 1960 (Santa Monica, California, U.S.).

Star qualities: Ruggedly handsome; smoldering screen presence; leading man of dramas; intense; controversial; dynamic performer; outspoken political liberal; writer; producer; director.

The son of actress Eileen Ryan and director Leo Penn, Sean Penn's early life featured access to the dream factory, support for his creativity, and bit parts in television series such as *Little House on the Prairie* (1974) and movies such as *Taps* (1981), before *Fast Times at Ridgemont High* (1982) put him on the map, making his character Jeff Spicoli the byword for a generation then coming of age.

Interesting roles followed in movies such as *The Falcon and the Snowman* (1985) and *At Close Range* (1986), when his marriage to pop diva Madonna drew headlines and attention away from his budding career. The media attention on the couple caused Penn to have some violent outbursts, including one incident for which he was arrested for beating a photographer. Then *Colors* (1988) was released to wide appreciation, before divorce from the songstress and his role as a psychotic commanding officer in the Vietnam War in *Casualties of War* (1989) established him as a serious actor.

The ensuing years have added to his persona as a muscled, alternately vulnerable and profane actor of untold emotional depth. Here, one thinks of *Dead Man Walking* (1995), *Sweet and Lowdown* (1999), and *I Am Sam* (2001), which all won him Oscar nominations for Best Actor before he finally won as the vengeful father in Clint Eastwood's whodunit, *Mystic River* (2003).

In later years he has learned to control his temper with the paparazzi, he has remarried to actress Robin Wright, and he has become a director with well-received films such as *The Indian Runner* (1991) and *The Pledge* (2001). Despite all this growth, the smoldering rage is what lingers on after every performance, with an intense screen presence that almost threatens to cause the audience bodily injury. **GCQ**

Top Takes...

All the King's Men 2006
The Interpreter 2005
The Assassination of Richard Nixon 2004
***Mystic River* 2003** ★
***I Am Sam* 2001** ☆
***Sweet and Lowdown* 1999** ☆
The Thin Red Line 1998
The Game 1997
***Dead Man Walking* 1995** ☆
Carlito's Way 1993
State of Grace 1990
Casualties of War 1989
Colors 1988
At Close Range 1986
The Falcon and the Snowman 1985
Fast Times at Ridgemont High 1982

"The horror of the Academy Awards is what the press does leading up to it."

1960s

HUGH GRANT

Born: Hugh John Mungo Grant, September 9, 1960 (London, England).

Star qualities: Foppish, gentlemanly good looks; very English; suave heartthrob; well dressed; leading man and character actor of light comedies and romances; intelligent and witty; comic timing.

Top Takes...

Music and Lyrics 2007
Bridget Jones: The Edge of Reason 2004
Love Actually 2003
About a Boy 2002
Bridget Jones's Diary 2001
Small Time Crooks 2000
Notting Hill 1999
Extreme Measures 1996
Restoration 1995
Sense and Sensibility 1995
An Awfully Big Adventure 1995
Four Weddings and a Funeral 1994
Sirens 1994
The Remains of the Day 1993
Bitter Moon 1992
The Lair of the White Worm 1988

> "I could do with more mobbing, particularly from women."

Born in London and a graduate in English from Oxford University, one of Hugh Grant's earliest films was the Merchant Ivory production *Maurice* (1987), instantly making him one of the most recognizable names in British independent films. He subsequently starred in movies as quirky and diverse as Ken Russell's *The Lair of the White Worm* (1988) and Roman Polanski's *Bitter Moon* (1992), and reunited with the Merchant Ivory team in *The Remains of the Day* (1993) before Mike Newell's smash-hit comedy *Four Weddings and a Funeral* (1994) made him an international household name. A memorable turn in Ang Lee's Jane Austen adaptation *Sense and Sensibility* (1995) bolstered his reputation as the thinking man's romantic lead, until an embarrassing arrest while engaged with a prostitute in 1995 threatened to bury his career in controversy.

Taking the high road, Grant charmed his way back into the public's good graces, as well as those of the studios, starring in such hits as *Notting Hill* (1999) before underscoring his instinct for playing the cad in *Bridget Jones's Diary* (2001) and *About a Boy* (2002). He reunited with *Four Weddings* and *Notting Hill* director Richard Curtis for *Love Actually* (2003) where his performance as a boogying British prime minister who falls in love with the tea girl confirmed him as a master of comedy and endeared him forever to international movie audiences. His recent performances in *Two Weeks Notice* (2002); a sequel to *Bridget Jones*, *Bridget Jones: The Edge of Reason* (2004); a role parodying snide TV's *American Idol* host Simon Cowell in *American Dreamz* (2006); and a singing part in *Music and Lyrics* (2007) were uninspired, but it will take more than that to knock Grant off his throne as the modern-day Cary Grant, and it could be that his best is yet to come. **JK**

HIROYUKI SANADA

Born: Hiroyuki Shimosawa, October 12, 1960 (Tokyo, Japan).

Star qualities: Handsome leading man and character actor of Japanese action movies and dramas; mentored by martial arts legend Sonny Chiba; stagecraft; athletic; martial arts master; swordsmanship; singer; composer.

One of Japan's most celebrated actors, Hiroyuki Sanada is known for his versatility on the screen, stage, and TV. A child model at the age of five, Sanada made his film debut in the Shinichi "Sonny" Chiba action film *Rokyoku komori-uta* (1965) (*Game of Chance*). Sanada joined Chiba's Japanese Action Club as a teenager, where he learned horseback riding, the martial arts, jazz, and traditional Japanese dance. This training, combined with Chiba's mentoring, resulted in a long-running stint as an action star in samurai and ninja movies in the 1970s and 1980s. In 1982, he graduated from the Nihon University of Art, majoring in film, and was awarded the Newcomer of the Year honor by the Japanese Academy.

Sanada's mainstream breakthrough came with *Mahjong hôrôki* (1984) for which he received his first Best Actor nomination in Japan's equivalent of the Oscars. The film started a fruitful collaboration with director Makoto Wada, and Sanada has since acted in all of Wada's movies. During this period he also maintained a successful singing career, touring Japan to play rock concerts. Sanada made his Shakespeare stage debut in *Romeo and Juliet* (1986). He then joined the British Royal Shakespeare Company to play The Fool in *King Lear* (1999–2000), earning the group's first Japanese actor a Member of the British Empire award. Sanada also starred in the horror series *Ringu* (1998–1999) (*Ring*), and won a Japanese Best Actor award for *Tasogare Seibei* (2002) (*The Twilight Samurai*). Sanada broadened his international appeal and won new fans with his role opposite Tom Cruise in *The Last Samurai* (2003). He capitalized on this to go on to play in *The White Countess* (2005), *Wu ji* (2005) (*The Promise*), and *Rush Hour 3* (2007). **WW**

Top Takes...

Rush Hour 3 2007
Wu ji 2005 (*The Promise*)
The White Countess 2005
The Last Samurai 2003
Tasogare Seibei 2002 (*The Twilight Samurai*)
Minna no ie 2001 (*All About Our House*)
Mayonaka made 1999 (*Round About Midnight*)
Ringu 2 1999 (*Ring 2*)
Ringu 1998 (*Ring*)
Hero Interview 1994
Bokura wa minna ikiteiru 1993 (*Made in Japan*)
Tugumi 1990 (*Tsugumi*)
Kaitô Ruby 1988
Kyabare 1986 (*Cabaret*)
Mahjong hôrôki 1984
Yagyû ichizoku no inbô 1978

"My orders are to kill you. I can't let you escape."
—Seibei Iguchi, *The Twilight Samurai*

1960s

EDDIE MURPHY

Born: Edward Regan Murphy, April 3, 1961 (Brooklyn, New York, U.S.).

Star qualities: Outrageous comedian; impersonator; gag artist; facial expressions; leading man and character actor of comedies; cackling laugh; stand-up comic; writer; director; producer.

Top Takes...

"Every bad decision I've made has been based on money. I grew up in the projects."

Eddie Murphy began as a stand-up comic at Manhattan's showcase, the Comic Strip Live, before he played on TV's *Saturday Night Live*. There he soon established himself as a comic talent in the mold of his idol, Richard Pryor, and went on to become a feature player on the show from 1980 to 1984. Offering observational humor, amplified through a uniquely irritating laugh, the resulting sketches, impersonations, jokes, and overall attitude mainstreamed him as one of the most sought-after performers of the 1980s and early 1990s.

The signal of things to come was *Eddie Murphy Delirious* (1983), his concert movie, but it was his role as Detroit policeman Detective Axel Foley in the box-office gold *Beverly Hills Cop* (1984) that connected him with the popular pulse. Following that success with another, *Coming to America* (1988), he commanded a high salary for his work. With this recognition, he branched out into film production as writer, director, and producer of *Harlem Nights* (1989), but the film garnered little favor from the critics and public alike.

After another hit, *Boomerang* (1992), a few commercial flops such as *The Distinguished Gentlemen* (1992) and *Beverly Hills Cop III* (1994), some real-life indiscretions, the complications of fatherhood, and eventual divorce, Murphy faces midlife with a sanitized version of his youthful self, along with a series of family-friendly performances. His leading role in the remake of Jerry Lewis's *The Nutty Professor* (1996) is the new signature, later followed by *Doctor Dolittle* (1998), and the voice of the irritating but loyal Donkey in *Shrek* (2001), and its sequels. Although this new chapter is a far cry from the strikingly funny man from 20 years earlier, it does represent a way forward, minus the anger and profanity. **GCQ**

1960s

GEORGE CLOONEY

Born: George Timothy Clooney, May 6, 1961 (Lexington, Kentucky, U.S.).

Star qualities: Handsome; sexy; clean-cut; intelligent; well dressed; charismatic; versatile leading actor of dramas; outspoken political liberal; humanitarian; writer; director; producer.

George Clooney's status in Hollywood is remarkable. One of its most charming celebrities (he's twice been voted "sexiest man alive"), he also has a well-respected outspoken political engagement. Aesthetically, Clooney is a classically sculpted star, with clear features and a quiet charisma, and not a single feminine feature in his body. But it took him a while to make it to the top. Many stars' first movies are flops, but Clooney's involvement in *The Return of the Killer Tomatoes!* (1988) proved particularly detrimental. After achieving TV stardom with the TV hospital series *ER* (1994–2000) as the dreamy Dr. Doug Ross, however, Clooney's renewed efforts proved more successful. He gained credibility through sexy, tough-guy roles in *From Dusk till Dawn* (1996) and *Out of Sight* (1998). Roles in liberal war films *The Thin Red Line* (1998) and *Three Kings* (1999) also proved that his huggable macho types had a heart.

Gradually, Clooney took up producing and directing, and he has accomplished a tremendously successful double career since. He was an activist behind (as well as in front of) the camera with *Good Night, and Good Luck.* (2005) and *Syriana,* (2005). The former won him Oscar nominations for Directing and Writing (Original Screenplay); the latter won him an Oscar for Best Supporting Actor. His win saw him follow in his family tradition, because his uncle, the late actor José Ferrer, won a Best Actor Oscar for *Cyrano de Bergerac* (1950). Clooney has portrayed less honorable characters in front of the camera, especially in *Intolerable Cruelty* (2003), and in his buddy Steven Soderbergh's franchise *Ocean's Eleven* (2001) and *Ocean's Twelve* (2004)—they're hedonistic parts for a man who obviously enjoys the freedoms stardom offers. Offscreen, Clooney is a noted political liberal. **EM**

Top Takes...

Syriana 2005 ★
Good Night, and Good Luck. 2005
Ocean's Twelve 2004
Intolerable Cruelty 2003
Confessions of a Dangerous Mind 2002
Solaris 2002
Welcome to Collinwood 2002
Ocean's Eleven 2001
The Perfect Storm 2000
O Brother, Where Art Thou? 2000
Three Kings 1999
The Thin Red Line 1998
Out of Sight 1998
Batman & Robin 1997
One Fine Day 1996
From Dusk Till Dawn 1996

"Directing is really exciting. In the end, it's more fun to be the painter than the paint."

1960s

FOREST WHITAKER

Born: Forest Steven Whitaker, July 15, 1961 (Longview, Texas, U.S.).

Star qualities: Gentle giant appeal; droopy features; tall and heavy set; ability to play complex characters and the outsiders of society with aplomb; fully immerses himself in his roles; producer; director.

Top Takes...

The Last King of Scotland 2006 ★
American Gun 2005
Phone Booth 2002
Panic Room 2002
Green Dragon 2001
Ghost Dog: The Way of the Samurai 1999
Body Count 1998
Blown Away 1994
Body Snatchers 1993
The Crying Game 1992
Bird 1988
Bloodsport 1988
Good Morning, Vietnam 1987
Platoon 1986
The Color of Money 1986
Fast Times at Ridgemont High 1982

"... 24 hours a day, even in my dreams, I was totally consumed by the character of Idi Amin."

Not born with the conventional celebrity good looks of fellow African-American Will Smith that lead to castings in romantic roles, Forest Whitaker's crumpled face and large frame have made him the director's choice for playing complex outsider characters along the lines of the sympathetic hangdog, down at heel, offbeat genius, or even crazed lunatic.

His hulking athleticism made him a convincing footballer in *Fast Times at Ridgemont High* (1982), but it was his incarnation as jazz legend Charlie "Bird" Parker in Clint Eastwood's biopic *Bird* (1988) that first showcased Whitaker's considerable acting clout, and won him a Best Actor award at Cannes Film Festival.

After this success Whitaker never looked back, and was guaranteed meaty roles in such films as Neil Jordan's *The Crying Game* (1992), where he played a British soldier kidnapped by the Irish Republican Army in a tale of unusual friendships and forbidden love. His skills at playing the contradictory character were also shown off in Jim Jarmusch's *Ghost Dog: The Way of the Samurai* (1999). Whitaker's penchant for taking on multifaceted characters reached its apex with his powerhouse turn as former Ugandan dictator Idi Amin in *The Last King of Scotland* (2006). Playing a murderous despot is hard to do without falling into trope characterizations of evil, especially when that person is such a familiar figure of recent history. Undeterred, Whitaker piled on weight and immersed himself in research in order to play the quixotic tyrant, and the onscreen result revealed a humanized Amin, making his capacity for atrocity even more frightening, and justly won him a Best Actor Oscar for his efforts. Such a magnificent perfomance should guarantee Whitaker equally demanding roles in the years to come. **CK**

ANTHONY WONG

Born: Anthony Wong Chau-Sang, September 2, 1961 (Hong Kong, China).

Star qualities: Leading man of Hong Kong action cinema; renowned for chilling psycho roles; strong character actor with an intense screen presence; rock band member; writer; director.

Throughout the 1990s, inexhaustible Hong Kong actor Anthony Wong became known for portraying intense characters on the edge such as villains, psychopaths, mass murderers, and social degenerates. Wong cultivated this onscreen persona in numerous "Category III," or adults-only, shockers and sexploitation titles such as *Mie men can an zhi nie sha* (1993) (*Daughter of Darkness*), but also simultaneously in several more ambitious, prestigious films such as John Woo's *Laat sau sen taan* (1992) (*Hard-Boiled*), and the *Xian dai hao xia zhuan* (1993) (*Heroic Trio*) films. Wong's willingness to unflinchingly incarnate the vilest of characters even paid off with a Best Actor award in Hong Kong for his work in *Baat sin faan dim ji yan yuk cha siu baau* (1993) (*Human Pork Chop*).

Wong also fronted a punk band during this era, and his music and extreme characterizations were apparently a therapeutic method of dealing with a difficult childhood; the son of a Chinese mother and British father, Wong was bullied for his mixed-race heritage. One would have expected such youthful fury to burn out after time, but an unforeseen development occurred: everyone in Hong Kong realized that Wong had become one of the most gifted actors in the world.

Although a more balanced maturity was evident even in mid-period Wong performances in police thrillers (*Sang gong yatho tungchap fan* (*Rock n' Roll Cop*), 1994), the actor has really started to shine in recent years, becoming a strong character actor whose strength and range has been compared to everyone from Humphrey Bogart to Kevin Spacey. His latest career highlights have been his work with director Johnnie To (*Fong juk* (*Exiled*), 2006), and most preeminently, his roles in the *Mou gaan dou* (2002–2003) (*Infernal Affairs*) trilogy. **TC**

Top Takes…

Fong juk 2006 (*Exiled*)
Tsoi suet yuk chi ngo oi nei 2005 (*All About Love*)
Mou gaan dou III: Jung gik mou gaan 2003 (*Infernal Affairs III*)
Mou gaan dou II 2003 (*Infernal Affairs II*)
Mou gaan dou 2002 (*Infernal Affairs*)
Miu meng ji tiu 2000 (*Ransom Express*)
Yi bo la beng duk 1996 (*Ebola Syndrome*)
Sang gong yatho tungchap fan 1994 (*Rock n' Roll Cop*)
Xian dai hao xia zhuan 1993 (*Heroic Trio 2: Executioners*)
Baat sin faan dim ji yan yuk cha siu baau 1993 (*Human Pork Chop*)
Dung fong saam hap 1993 (*The Heroic Trio*)
Laat sau sen taan 1992 (*Hard-Boiled*)

"Two men need an organ transplant, but there's only one organ."—SP Wong, *Infernal Affairs*

1960s

JIM CARREY

Born: James Eugene Carrey, January 17, 1962 (Newmarket, Ontario, Canada).

Star qualities: Rubber-featured face; tall; elastic body; wild laugh; extremely versatile comedian; stand-up comic; breakneck verbal delivery; slapstick style; writer; producer.

Top Takes...

Fun with Dick and Jane 2005
Lemony Snicket's A Series of Unfortunate Events 2004
Eternal Sunshine of the Spotless Mind 2004
Bruce Almighty 2003
How the Grinch Stole Christmas 2000
Me, Myself & Irene 2000
Man on the Moon 1999
The Truman Show 1998
Liar Liar 1997
The Cable Guy 1996
Batman Forever 1995
Dumb & Dumber 1994
The Mask 1994
Ace Ventura: Pet Detective 1994
Earth Girls Are Easy 1988

Whenever Canada claims a sense of humor, it does well to refer to Jim Carrey: tall, elastic, with a face like Silly Putty, and a vivacious verbal velocity matching that of his compatriot Dan Aykroyd. Carrey dropped out of high school at the age of sixteen to work to help support his family, doing low-skilled jobs and performing as a stand-up comedian on Canada's comedy-club circuit. At the age of nineteen, he moved to Los Angeles and started working in The Comedy Store before going on to small roles in television and film.

He appeared as comic relief in *Earth Girls Are Easy* (1988) and as a small-time villain in his hero Clint Eastwood's last Dirty Harry film, *The Dead Pool* (1988), before three box-office successes promoted him to become Hollywood's funniest man. *Ace Ventura: Pet Detective* (1994), *The Mask* (1994), and *Dumb & Dumber* (1994) all capitalized on Carrey's flexible facial features and acrobatic antics and, even though critics dismissed the movies, they made Carrey a bona fide star.

The uneasy relationship between Carrey and the critics lasted until the late 1990s, when *The Truman Show* (1998) and *Man on the Moon* (1999)—two films in which he put playing funny in a social framework—received wide acclaim. Since then Carrey has excelled in outrageous disguises in movies such as *How the Grinch Stole Christmas* (2000) and *Lemony Snicket's A Series of Unfortunate Events* (2004); sharp screwball-style comedies chronicling contemporary anxieties such as *Bruce Almighty* (2003) and *Fun with Dick and Jane* (2005); and restrained existential wonders such as *Eternal Sunshine of the Spotless Mind* (2004). All of these have made him one of the world's most versatile comedians, popular with moviegoers of all ages and tastes. **EM**

> "I'm charming, but I dip into the Prozac now and then."

JENNIFER JASON LEIGH

Born: Jennifer Lee Morrow, February 5, 1962 (Hollywood, California, U.S.).

Star qualities: Elfin beauty; leading lady and character actress of dramas; mesmerizing screen presence; stagecraft; often plays vulnerable characters; writer; producer; director.

Jennifer Jason Leigh was born with acting in her genes: she is the daughter of the late actor Vic Morrow and actress/screenwriter Barbara Turner. At the age of fourteen she attended summer acting workshops given by the famed drama coach, Lee Strasberg, which helped her on her way to land a part while still only a teenager in the Disney TV movie *The Young Runaways* (1978). She went on to drop out of high school to take a standout bit part in an ordinary film as an imperiled blind girl in *Eyes of a Stranger* (1982). After being cast as the female lead, a pregnant teenager, in the high school comedy *Fast Times at Ridgemont High* (1982), she began an adventurous screen career. It is one that has often found her playing a great many suffering characters: a rape victim in *Flesh+Blood* (1985), *Heart of Midnight* (1988), and *Last Exit to Brooklyn* (1989); a drug user in *Rush* (1991) and *Georgia* (1995); and ripped apart in *The Hitcher* (1986) and *In the Cut* (2003).

Although she has taken a few token-girl roles in movies such as *Backdraft* (1991), Leigh has tended to concentrate on interesting parts that she researches extensively according to Method acting principles. Among many memorable performances she has played a pretentious film student in *The Big Picture* (1989); a hooker in *Miami Blues*, (1990); a deranged obsessive roommate in the thriller *Single White Female* (1992); a cynical phone-sex worker in *Short Cuts* (1993); a chattering newshound who finds a heart in *The Hudsucker Proxy* (1994); a sarcastic and troubled writer and poet in the biopic *Mrs. Parker and the Vicious Circle* (1994); a moll ruthlessly out to free her hoodlum husband in *Kansas City* (1996); a Victorian spinster in *Washington Square* (1997); and a games designer in *eXistenZ* (1999). **KN**

Top Takes...

In the Cut 2003
eXistenZ 1999
Washington Square 1997
Kansas City 1996
Georgia 1995
Dolores Claiborne 1995
Mrs. Parker and the Vicious Circle 1994
The Hudsucker Proxy 1994
Short Cuts 1993
Single White Female 1992
Rush 1991
Miami Blues 1990
Last Exit to Brooklyn 1989
The Big Picture 1989
Heart of Midnight 1988
Flesh+Blood 1985

"I could never play the ingénue, the girl-next-door . . . . That would be a bore."

1960s

TOM CRUISE

Born: Thomas Cruise Mapother IV, July 3, 1962 (Syracuse, New York, U.S.).

Star qualities: Clean-cut good looks; one of the most sought-after actors in movie history; adored by women worldwide for his boyish charm and manly sex appeal; among Hollywood's highest-paid stars and top-grossing box-office attractions.

Top Takes...

Mission: Impossible III 2006
War of the Worlds 2005
Collateral 2004
The Last Samurai 2003
Minority Report 2002
Vanilla Sky 2001
Mission: Impossible II 2000
Magnolia 1999 ☆
Eyes Wide Shut 1999
Jerry Maguire 1996 ☆
Mission: Impossible 1996
*Interview with the Vampire:
   The Vampire Chronicles* 1994
The Firm 1993
A Few Good Men 1992
Far and Away 1992
Days of Thunder 1990
Born on the Fourth of July 1989 ☆
Rain Man 1988
Young Guns 1988
Cocktail 1988
The Color of Money 1986
Top Gun 1986
Legend 1985
Risky Business 1983

RIGHT: Ethan Hunt saves the day, and gets the girl, once more in *Mission: Impossible III*.

Recent interest in the mysteries of Scientology set to one side, Tom Cruise is undeniably one of the world's top leading men. That is no small accomplishment for a one-time high school athlete with a flair for stage performance but who was also saddled with difficulty reading and has suffered the embarrassment of two very public divorces (from actresses Mimi Rogers and Nicole Kidman).

Raised in a home divided by parental conflict, his ascent to superstardom was anything but inevitable. There was no process of selection of the aspiring thespian from among the ranks of the well-trained by an experienced actor with a sharp eye for skill. Nor was there a contest Cruise won, inasmuch as he toiled through the apprenticeship of all screen actors and emerged to become the personification of stardom. The early years of his career, though, weren't particularly notable, aside from supporting performances to other emerging stars in *Endless Love* (1981), *Taps* (1981), and *The Outsiders* (1983). But then came the lead in the comedy crime caper *Risky Business* (1983), a part in which Cruise combined small-town naivete with a hustler's worldly wiles.

Top Gun (1986) cemented his beefcake style and affirmed his position at the center of a consolidating movie market. In this way, Cruise has been something of a global phenomenon, having anchored such works as *The Firm* (1993), *Interview with the Vampire: The Vampire Chronicles* (1994), the *Mission: Impossible* trilogy (1996, 2000, 2006), *Jerry Maguire* (1996), *Minority Report* (2002), and *War of the Worlds* (2005). For some, though, the real attraction lay beneath his good looks—*Cocktail* (1988), *Days of Thunder* (1990)—with personality traits and vulnerabilities he would probably not consider part of his mainstream appeal. And, with *Born on the Fourth of July* (1989), the Oliver Stone-directed story of paraplegic Vietnam veteran Ron Kovic, he showed his real acting skills. That he's continued to affirm his commercial appeal above artistry, save for *Magnolia* (1999), is a convention of our times. But it is a comfort to know that our leading, leading man has masks we have yet to uncover. **GCQ**

ABOVE: Cruise and Val Kilmer as hot pilots Maverick and Ice in the smash-hit *Top Gun*.

Breaking Out of Type

Moviegoers expect to see Tom Cruise play the good guy or the hero. Although some of his characters have been flawed, they have not been fatally so. His role in *Magnolia* hinted at darker depths, but the part that has taken him furthest away from type was his portrayal of the ruthless hit man in *Collateral*. His performance also won favor with critics. Cruise said of the part: "Vincent interested me because he is such an antisocial personality, bringing destruction and chaos with him wherever he goes." Perhaps audiences can look forward to more "surprising" roles from the star in his middle years.

1960s

MICHELLE YEOH

Born: Yeoh Chu-Kheng, August 6, 1962 (Ipoh, Perak, Malaysia).

Star qualities: Beauty queen looks; leading lady of Hong Kong action movies; martial arts mistress; undertakes risky stunt work; acrobatic moves; graceful; dancer; producer.

In many ways, the career of actress Michelle Yeoh mirrors the trajectory followed by her *Jing cha gu shi III: Chao ji jing cha* (1992) (*Supercop*) costar Jackie Chan, or even, to a slightly different extent, her *Wo hu cang long* (2000) (*Crouching Tiger, Hidden Dragon*) costar Chow Yun-Fat. Through her work in Hong Kong action films of the 1980s, Yeoh became a superstar with a widespread fan following, in what was essentially a male-dominated genre. But as the 1990s ended, Yeoh, nearing middle age alongside Chan and Yun-Fat, attempted to move into international prestige cinema with mixed results.

Like Chan, Yeoh is an attractive, likable screen presence but a limited actor, and as she moves away from her trademark ballet of martial arts and risky stunt work, one worries if she has the dramatic skill to carry off the transition. Yeoh was a former Malaysian beauty queen who reached film stardom in the mid-1980s with action hits such as *Huang gu shi jie* (1985) (*Yes, Madam*) and *Zhong hua zhan shi* (1987) (*Dynamite Fighters*). Her fame was short-lived, because she married her producer Dickson Poon and left the industry for several years.

She later divorced Poon, making a huge comeback opposite Chan in *Supercop*, and went on to star in several Hong Kong genre favorites of the 1990s such as *Wing Chun* (1994). Yet few truly worthwhile pictures came out of this comeback period, and her attempts to both produce her own projects such as *The Touch* (2002), and appear in more serious dramatic fare such as *Memoirs of a Geisha* (2005) have not been very successful when compared with her more visceral early work. *Crouching Tiger* was an obvious recent highlight, but there have been few others. One hopes she can come back once again with a vengeance. **TC**

Top Takes…

"This [martial arts] genre deserves more respect and dignity than it's ever been given."

1960s

JODIE FOSTER

Born: Alicia Christian Foster, November 19, 1962 (Los Angeles, California, U.S.).

Star qualities: Child star; petite beauty; leading lady and character actress of dramas; convincing screen presence; won two Oscars before she was thirty; intelligent; publicity shy; producer; director.

An actress since she was a toddler, Jodie Foster would be forgiven for peaking early, comparatively speaking, but she's also one of the few child actors who managed a hugely successful transition to adult roles. Foster began her career through the typical episodic TV and kiddie movie route before making a significant impact as the underage prostitute in Martin Scorsese's *Taxi Driver* (1976), which won her an Oscar nomination for Best Supporting Actress. She had previously worked for Scorsese in *Alice Doesn't Live Here Anymore* (1974), in which she already seemed more mature than many of the adults in the movie. Other kids fare awaited, as well as more ambitious projects, although much of Foster's career throughout the first half of the 1980s was sidelined by her commitment to studies in English literature at Yale University.

Foster truly emerged as a major adult star with her two Best Actress Oscar-winning performances in *The Accused* (1988) and *The Silence of the Lambs* (1991), and she also made an auspicious directing debut with *Little Man Tate* (1991). But then what happened? She has spoken of a desire to focus more on her family, but nonetheless, her stardom of the late 1980s and early 1990s seems diminished when one examines the film roles that she selected during this period, excepting *Nell* (1994), perhaps. Working rather sporadically during this era anyway, Foster would largely coast through movies such as *Maverick* (1994), *Contact* (1997), and *Flightplan* (2005), roles she previously could have tackled in her sleep. Undeniably brilliant and extraordinarily talented, Foster may have lost interest in the craft after hitting the high notes while so young. She has at least continued directing with the legal drama *Sugarland* (2008), starring herself and Robert De Niro. **TC**

Top Takes...

Sugarland 2008
Inside Man 2006
Panic Room 2002
Anna and the King 1999
Contact 1997
Nell 1994 ☆
Maverick 1994
Sommersby 1993
Shadows and Fog 1992
Little Man Tate 1991
The Silence of the Lambs 1991 ★
The Accused 1988 ★
The Hotel New Hampshire 1984
Bugsy Malone 1976
Taxi Driver 1976 ☆
Alice Doesn't Live Here Anymore 1974

"Acting, for me, is exhausting. I'm always more energized by directing."

1960s

RALPH FIENNES

Born: Ralph Nathaniel Fiennes, December 22, 1962 (Suffolk, England).

Star qualities: Handsome; tall; deep voice; piercing eyes; clean-cut; suave; sexy; versatile leading man of dramas; equally convincing as a hero or a villain; Shakespearean stagecraft; powerful, intense screen presence; producer.

Top Takes...

Ralph Fiennes is a handsome Brit with impeccable breeding. He is the eldest of six children born to photographer Mark Fiennes and his wife, Jini, a novelist. Among his siblings are director Martha Fiennes and actor Joseph Fiennes. His cousin is British explorer Sir Ranulph Fiennes. He studied at London's Royal Academy of Dramatic Art, and went on to join Britain's Royal National Theatre in 1987 and the Royal Shakespeare Company in 1988. He has had a solid stage career that has seen him win a Tony Award for his lead role in *Hamlet* (1995) on Broadway. But he has rarely appeared on film as a gentlemanly charmer, which makes sense, considering how strained he is when cast in roles tailored to Patrick Macnee as in *The Avengers* (1998), or Cary Grant as in *Maid in Manhattan* (2002).

After turning in an acceptable Heathcliff in *Wuthering Heights* (1992), Fiennes established himself with a remarkable, repulsive performance as the deeply evil SS officer in *Schindler's List* (1993), which won him an Academy Award nomination for Best Actor. Since, he has sought out a succession of inwardly or outwardly freakish roles: the privileged TV cheat of *Quiz Show* (1994); the futuristic hustler of *Strange Days* (1995); a count under scars in *The English Patient* (1996); the discharged mental patient of *Spider* (2002); buffed, tattooed, and with horror dentures as the serial killer of *Red Dragon* (2002); and nastily scary as Harry Potter's archenemy, Lord Voldemort, in *Harry Potter and the Goblet of Fire* (2005) and its sequels. Fiennes occasionally reverts to type, and delivered nuanced, quality upper-middle-class repression in *Oscar and Lucinda* (1997), *The End of the Affair* (1999), and *The Constant Gardener* (2005). He also amusingly voiced the villain in *Wallace & Gromit in The Curse of the Were-Rabbit* (2005). **KN**

> "Awards are like applause, and every actor likes to hear applause."

JET LI

Born: Li Lianjie, April 26, 1963 (Beijing, China).

Star qualities: Hugely popular male lead of Hong Kong action movies; muscular maestro of Chinese martial arts and several times world champion; athletic swordsman; stuntman; writer; producer; director.

The successor to onscreen martial artists Bruce Lee and Jackie Chan, Jet Li began formally studying *wushu*—a form of Chinese martial arts—at the tender age of eight. He excelled in this field as a teenager, won medals, and performed worldwide, including in front of dignitaries such as former U.S. president Richard Nixon in 1974 on a tour to Washington, D.C., sponsored by the Chinese government.

His movie career started when he was nineteen years old with the *Shao Lin tzu* (1982–1986) (*Shaolin Temple*) series. Li relocated from his native China to San Francisco in the United States in 1988, filming *Long xing tian xia* (1989) (*The Master*) for director Hark Tsui while there. This duo teamed up again in Hong Kong on the *Wong Fei Hung* (1991–1997) (*Once Upon a Time in China*) series. From 1991 to 1998, Li starred in 18 movies in Hong Kong, including *Xiao ao jiang hu zhi dong fang bu bai* (1992) (*Swordsman II*), *Fong Sai-Yuk* (1993) (*The Legend*), and *Jing wu ying xiong* (1994) (*Fist of Legend*), a remake of Bruce Lee's *Jing wu men* (1972) (*Fist of Fury*).

Hollywood beckoned, and Li first debuted as a villain in *Lethal Weapon 4* (1998). He then headlined in *Romeo Must Die* (2000), *The One* (2001), and *Cradle 2 the Grave* (2003), with mixed results. He returned to China to star in *Ying xiong* (2002) (*Hero*)—the artistic apex of his career—and *Huo Yuan Jia* (2006) (*Fearless*). Li also collaborated with French producer Luc Besson on *Kiss of the Dragon* (2001) and *Danny the Dog* (2005). The latter has been Jet Li's strongest dramatic performance to date. Although there is an element of martial arts in the movie, Li's acting skills were demonstrated in his portrayal of an adult with the mentality of a child who has been brought up like an animal. **WW**

Top Takes...

Huo Yuan Jia 2006 (*Fearless*)
Danny the Dog 2005
Cradle 2 the Grave 2003
Ying xiong 2002 (*Hero*)
The One 2001
Kiss of the Dragon 2001
Romeo Must Die 2000
Lethal Weapon 4 1998
Jing wu ying xiong 1994 (*Fist of Legend*)
Fong Sai-Yuk 1993 (*The Legend*)
Xiao ao jiang hu zhi dong fang bu bai 1992
   (*Swordsman II*)
Wong Fei Hung 1991
   (*Once Upon a Time in China*)
Long xing tian xia 1989 (*The Master*)
Shao Lin tzu 1982 (*The Shaolin Temple*)

"You can beat me up, but don't touch my hair, I will kill you!"

1960s

MIKE MYERS

Born: Michael Myers, May 25, 1963 (Scarborough, Ontario, Canada).

Star qualities: Comic genius; leading man of comedies; expressive face; multifaceted performer who frequently plays multiple characters in one movie; master of catchphrases; writer; producer.

Top Takes...

Shrek the Third 2007

Shrek 2 2004

The Cat in the Hat 2003

Austin Powers in Goldmember 2002

Shrek 2001

Austin Powers: The Spy Who Shagged Me 1999

54 1998

Austin Powers: International Man of Mystery 1997

Wayne's World 2 1993

Wayne's World 1992

What began as a comic sketch about a man-boy unable to leave his parents' basement turned into a commercial phenomenon that placed Mike Myers firmly in the center of Hollywood. Canadian-born of British parents, Myers was groomed for comedy through performing in Toronto's comedy club circuit before he moved to New York to start a stint as a featured performer and writer on TV's variety show *Saturday Night Live* (1989–1997).

But *Wayne's World* (1992) made Myers a star. Its success allowed him considerable freedom to try out other comic ideas; some of them were not too successful, such as *So I Married an Axe Murderer* (1993), but others most certainly were such as the *Austin Powers* (1997, 1999, 2002) trilogy. Along the way, he gave a dramatic turn as New York Studio 54 nightclub owner Steve Rubell in *54* (1998), enlivened Dr. Seuss in *The Cat in the Hat* (2003), and has been the central vocal talent of the *Shrek* (2001, 2004, 2007) franchise.

Interestingly, Myers has achieved this extraordinary popularity through a series of characters, sometimes even multiple characters in the same movie, that typically appear with colorful costumes, thick accents, or other characteristics that have no resemblance to the man beneath the mask. As one example, *Austin Powers: The Spy Who Shagged Me* (1999) offers Myers as Austin Powers, a James Bond-spoof character with 1960s style, an English accent, and bad teeth; Dr. Evil, a bald, bad guy with mid-European intonation, and effete gestures; and henchman Fat Bastard, who is 400 pounds of Scottish grotesquery. Each part is masterfully rendered, and so broadly comic as to appeal to the widest possible audience. It is, and he is, pure genius. **GCQ**

> "I still believe that at any time the no-talent police will come and arrest me."

JOHNNY DEPP

Born: John Christopher Depp II, June 9, 1963 (Owensboro, Kentucky, U.S.).

Star qualities: Handsome; sexy; versatile leading man of dramas and comedies; cool screen persona; daring role choices; often plays eccentric outcasts; ability to change drastically from role to role; writer; producer; director; composer.

Johnny Depp is the ultimate cool loser, the outsider who effortlessly combines sex appeal and box-office success with critical esteem and street credibility. He dropped out of school when he was fifteen years old, and joined a series of garage bands with the aim of making a name in rock music. But it was a visit to Los Angeles in the early 1980s that was to change his career path. By chance, he met actor Nicolas Cage, who advised him to turn to acting. Depp went on to make his movie debut in *A Nightmare on Elm Street* (1984).

Keen on making (to put it mildly) risky choices that have shown him to be one of Hollywood's most versatile actors, Depp shed an earlier cute image and linked himself in the 1990s with rogue auteurs such as John Waters in *Cry-Baby* (1990), Jim Jarmusch in *Dead Man* (1995), Terry Gilliam in *Fear and Loathing in Las Vegas* (1998), Roman Polanski in *The Ninth Gate* (1999), and soul mate Tim Burton in *Edward Scissorhands* (1990), *Ed Wood* (1994), *Sleepy Hollow* (1999), and *Charlie and the Chocolate Factory* (2005). These affiliations gave him a rebel status, and both his public life, filled with supermodels and rock singers, and his work seemed consistent with that image. Depp specializes in playing relentlessly existential, occasionally ironic, aloof romantics whose surface bohemian amorality is underpinned by a deep sense of commitment and melancholy.

This has culminated in Depp's most successful role to date, as Captain Jack Sparrow in the *Pirates of the Caribbean* (2003, 2006, 2007) trilogy, a part that has launched him into celebrity status without compromising his artistic integrity. Based on Rolling Stone Keith Richards, Sparrow symbolizes a combination of populism and rebellion—the kind of pirate attitude that also defines Depp himself. **EM**

Top Takes...

Pirates of the Caribbean: At World's End 2007
Pirates of the Caribbean: Dead Man's Chest 2006
Charlie and the Chocolate Factory 2005
Finding Neverland 2004 ☆
Once Upon a Time in Mexico 2003
Pirates of the Caribbean: The Curse of the Black Pearl 2003 ☆
Blow 2001
Sleepy Hollow 1999
Fear and Loathing in Las Vegas 1998
Donnie Brasco 1997
Dead Man 1995
Ed Wood 1994
What's Eating Gilbert Grape 1993
Edward Scissorhands 1990
A Nightmare on Elm Street 1984

"Captain Jack Sparrow is like a cross between Keith Richards and Pepe Le Pew."

1960s

EMMANUELLE BÉART

Born: Emmanuelle Béart, August 14, 1963 (Saint Tropez, Var, Provence-Alpes-Côte d'Azur, France).

Star qualities: Gamine; ethereal beauty; heart-shaped face; big blue eyes; sexy leading lady of French dramas; careful role choice; stagecraft; singer; humanitarian.

Emmanuelle Béart, a critic once remarked, was "so beautiful it made my teeth hurt." Luckily, unlike so many very beautiful actresses, Béart has talent to match her looks. Her international career has never really taken off—*Mission: Impossible* (1996), her highest profile English-language movie to date, made scant use of her abilities—but a stack of César Awards testify to the high regard she enjoys in her native France.

The daughter of pop star and poet Guy Béart and actress Geneviève Galéa, she started acting at the age of nine and later went to drama school in Paris, studying under notable French drama teacher Jean-Laurent Cochet. She found stardom as the avenging angel of Claude Berri's rustic melodrama *Manon des sources* (1986) (*Manon of the Spring*). Since then, her ethereal beauty and her capacity for conveying veiled but intense emotions have been put to good use by some of France's most interesting directors. Her characters often have cultural connections: for Jacques Rivette she played artist Michel Piccoli's tantalizing model in *La belle noiseuse* (1991) (*The Beautiful Troublemaker*), and she was a classical violinist in Claude Sautet's *Un coeur en hiver* (1992) (*A Heart in Winter*). She has twice starred in a film called *L'Enfer* (*Hell*): once for Claude Chabrol (1994), and again for Danis Tanovic (2005). She also made an exquisite Gilberte in Raoul Ruiz's Proust adaptation *Le Temps retrouvé* (1999) (*Time Regained*). Offscreen, she married French actor Daniel Auteuil in 1993, and the now divorced couple have a daughter. She later went on to have a son with French composer and music producer David Moreau. Béart has been active in campaigning for the rights of immigrants in France, and also as an ambassador for the United Nations Children's Fund. **PK**

Top Takes...

A Crime 2006
L'Enfer 2005 (*Hell*)
Nathalie... 2003
8 femmes 2002 (*8 Women*)
Elephant Juice 1999
Le Temps retrouvé 1999 (*Time Regained*)
Don Juan 1998
Mission: Impossible 1996
Nelly & Monsieur Arnaud 1995
  (*Nelly and Mr. Arnaud*)
L'Enfer 1994 (*Hell*)
Un coeur en hiver 1992 (*A Heart in Winter*)
La belle noiseuse 1991
  (*The Beautiful Troublemaker*)
Date with an Angel 1987
Manon des sources 1986 (*Manon of the Spring*)

"I give everything I have to give on the screen. I feel I don't owe the public anything else."

BRAD PITT

Born: William Bradley Pitt, December 18, 1963 (Shawnee, Oklahoma, U.S.).

Star qualities: Handsome heartthrob; blue eyes; blond hair; winning smile; leading man of dramas; half of a Hollywood celebrity couple; intelligent; humanitarian; producer.

Brad Pitt attended the University of Missouri, majoring in journalism, but dropped out to move to Hollywood and pursue an acting career, studying under drama coach Roy London. A small but memorable role as a charming seducer and thief in *Thelma & Louise* (1991) brought Pitt to the attention of a wider audience and put him on the map as a male sex symbol. He made do with TV work before Ridley Scott's aforementioned fugitive film made him famous, and has since starred in mainstream work and riskier material. He juggled flops with higher-profile films such as *A River Runs Through It* (1992), *Interview with the Vampire: The Vampire Chronicles* (1994), *Legends of the Fall* (1994), *Se7en* (1995), and the film that won him an Oscar nomination for Best Actor, *Twelve Monkeys* (1995), all of which revealed his range and enduring popularity.

All the same, Pitt's box-office track record has been erratic. Films such as *Fight Club* (1999) were greater artistic successes than financial ones, and occasional hits such as *Ocean's Eleven* (2001) and its sequel have been offset by failures such as the overblown epic *Troy* (2004). Although an earlier relationship with actress Gwyneth Paltrow primed Pitt for the invasiveness of the tabloid newspapers, it was in 2000 with his marriage to Jennifer Aniston, actress and star of the hit TV show *Friends* (1994–2004), that saw Pitt firmly become grist for the rumor mill. This status was sealed after their divorce and his subsequent romance with actress Angelina Jolie. The romance helped boost the middling *Mr. & Mrs. Smith* (2005), in which they both starred, into a blockbuster. Indeed, no matter the fate of his films, Pitt remains one of Hollywood's biggest stars, and he continues to use that fame as leverage to get less commercial projects such as *Babel* (2006) produced. **JK**

Top Takes...

Babel 2006
Mr. and Mrs. Smith 2005
Ocean's Twelve 2004
Ocean's Eleven 2001
Spy Game 2001
Snatch. 2000
Fight Club 1999
Sleepers 1996
Twelve Monkeys 1995 ☆
Se7en 1995
Legends of the Fall 1994
*Interview with the Vampire:
The Vampire Chronicles* 1994
Kalifornia 1993
A River Runs Through It 1992
Thelma & Louise 1991

"I'm one of those people you hate because of genetics. It's the truth."

1960s

NICOLAS CAGE

Born: Nicholas Kim Coppola, January 7, 1964 (Long Beach, California, U.S.).

Star qualities: Swarthy, Mediterranean looks; gangly; deep voice; leading man of dramas and action movies; quirky screen persona; member of a Hollywood dynasty but keen to avoid nepotism; producer; director.

Top Takes...

Ghost Rider 2007
World Trade Center 2006
The Ant Bully 2006
Lord of War 2005
Matchstick Men 2003
Adaptation. 2002 ☆
Bringing Out the Dead 1999
Face/Off 1997
Con Air 1997
The Rock 1996
Leaving Las Vegas 1995 ★
Wild at Heart 1990
Vampire's Kiss 1989
Raising Arizona 1987
Birdy 1984
The Cotton Club 1984

"There's a fine line between the Method actor and the schizophrenic."

Nicolas Cage took his stage name from Marvel Comics's Luke Cage, since he didn't want to trade off his Coppola birth name, given his uncle is the director Francis Ford Coppola. He often essays human cartoons, but is capable of considerable subtlety. He began in early 1980s teen movies and was goonish in *Fast Times at Ridgemont High* (1982), *Valley Girl* (1983), and for his uncle in *Rumble Fish* (1983) and *Peggy Sue Got Married* (1986). His air of ratty desperation, often with strangled accents, worked well in *Raising Arizona* (1987), *Vampire's Kiss* (1989)—in which he ate a cockroach—and *Wild at Heart* (1990), but seemed jarring in blander romances such as *Moonstruck* (1987) and *Captain Corelli's Mandolin* (2000).

Cage first showed that he could turn himself down with some sensitivity as a psychologically scarred Vietnam veteran, Sergeant Al Columbato, in Alan Parker's *Birdy* (1984). He then went on to win a Best Actor Oscar as the suicidal drunk in the gritty drama *Leaving Las Vegas* (1995). He gave a committed performance as the hollowed-out paramedic in *Bringing Out the Dead* (1999), and managed a tour de force playing contrasting twin brothers in *Adaptation.* (2002). Meanwhile, he worked up a more mainstream career as an action hero in box-office successes such as *The Rock* (1996) and *Con Air* (1997), and insane super-villains such as in *Face/Off* (1997). After the remake of *The Wicker Man* (2006), he finally got to play a Marvel Comics hero as the lead in *Ghost Rider* (2007). Off camera Cage has been the subject of considerable media attention because of his marriages (three, including to Elvis Presley's daughter, Lisa Marie Presley), divorces (two), and romances with actresses Jenny Wright and Uma Thurman, and model Christina Fulton. **KN**

MATT DILLON

Born: Matthew Raymond Dillon, February 18, 1964 (New Rochelle, New York, U.S.).

Star qualities: Handsome; tall; clean-cut; high cheekbones; sexy; one-time teen idol; versatile leading man of dramas and comedies; played teenage rebels in his youth; writer; director.

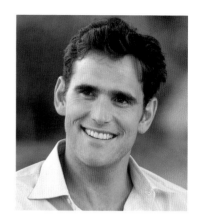

A photogenic former teen star, Matt Dillon manages to maintain his fluctuating career with a series of distinct roles. He is the son of a stockbroker and a homemaker. Dillon began acting in elementary school, and was spotted at age fourteen by Warner Brothers talent scouts. He went on to personify the 1980s teenage rebel in movies such as *Little Darlings* (1980) and *My Bodyguard* (1980), which led to him becoming a teen pinup. This image was further cemented with a trilogy of Susan Hinton adaptations: *Tex* (1982), *The Outsiders* (1983), and *Rumble Fish* (1983). Fans and critics were enthusiastic about Dillon's talent, but he struggled with this typecasting.

Dillon rebounded with a surprising turn as a junkie in Gus Van Sant's *Drugstore Cowboy* (1989), which affirmed he could make the leap from adolescent idol to mature actor. The first half of the 1990s saw Dillon shift effortlessly from dramas such as *A Kiss Before Dying* (1991) and *The Saint of Fort Washington* (1993), to comedies such as *Singles* (1992) and *To Die For* (1995), and to romances such as *Mr. Wonderful* (1993) and *Beautiful Girls* (1996). In 1998, he had a career boost with roles in the neo-noir *Wild Things* (1998) and the slapstick hit *There's Something About Mary* (1998), costarring with then-girlfriend Cameron Diaz.

Dillon later showcased his other talents by writing, directing, and starring in the crime thriller *City of Ghosts* (2002), which received a mixed response from the critics but was a nevertheless impressive and promising directorial debut. Then 2005 saw Dillon's highest industry recognition to date with an Oscar nomination for Best Supporting Actor for his portrayal of a racist cop who humiliates an African-American couple in *Crash* (2004). He flexed his comic muscles once more in *You, Me and Dupree* (2006). **WW**

Top Takes...

You, Me and Dupree 2006
***Crash* 2004** ☆
City of Ghosts 2002
One Night at McCool's 2001
There's Something About Mary 1998
Wild Things 1998
Beautiful Girls 1996
To Die For 1995
The Saint of Fort Washington 1993
Singles 1992
A Kiss Before Dying 1991
Drugstore Cowboy 1989
Target 1985
The Flamingo Kid 1984
Rumble Fish 1983
The Outsiders 1983

"I think more in terms of the work. I don't think about being a celebrity."

1960s

JULIETTE BINOCHE

Born: Juliette Binoche, March 9, 1964 (Paris, France).

Star qualities: Ethereal beauty; short dark hair; cupid-bow lips; stylish; charming; sexy leading lady of dramas; contemporary icon of French cinema; highest paid French actress to date; stagecraft; painter.

Foremost among contemporary French actresses, César Award-winning Juliette Binoche is equally at home in France, Britain, or the United States; in art theater movies or commercial prestige pictures; and in roles that call for stark minimalism, naturalism, or old-fashioned star quality.

Born to a movie director father and an actress mother, Binoche initially studied art at the Conservatoire National Supérieur d'Art Dramatique of Paris. She was first noticed in *Rendez-Vous* (1985), in a sexually provocative role that now seems fascinatingly untypical. *Mauvais sang* (1986) (*Bad Blood*) remade her as the muse of director Leos Carax, and English-language success in *The Unbearable Lightness of Being* (1988) proved her bankable internationally. Emerging personally unscathed from Carax's hugely expensive white elephant *Les amants du Pont-Neuf* (1991) (*The Lovers on the Bridge*), she was a surprise Cathy Linton in *Wuthering Heights* (1992), and an enigmatic femme fatale in Louis Malle's *Damage* (1992).

Above all, it was her young widow in Krzysztof Kieślowski's *Trois Couleurs: Bleu* (1993) (*Three Colors: Blue*) that proved Binoche's stature. It is one of the great modern screen performances, with reams of psychological and emotional information conveyed in the tiniest gestures and nuances of speech. Even as Kieślowski's camera simply stares at her blank face, she rivets attention, and all without a trace of mannerism, or forced feeling. The result was true international popularity of a kind enjoyed only occasionally by European stars, which helped her on the way to box-office success in *The English Patient* (1996), for which she won an Oscar for Best Supporting Actress, and *Chocolat* (2000), which gained her another Oscar nomination. **MC**

Top Takes…

Caché 2005 (*Hidden*)
Country of My Skull 2004
Chocolat 2000 ☆
La Veuve de Saint-Pierre 2000
   (*The Widow of Saint-Pierre*)
Les Enfants du siècle 1999
   (*The Children of the Century*)
The English Patient 1996 ★
Le hussard sur le toit 1995
   (*The Horseman on the Roof*)
Trois couleurs: Rouge 1994 (*Three Colors: Red*)
Trzy kolory: Bialy 1994 (*Three Colors: White*)
Trois couleurs: Bleu 1993 (*Three Colors: Blue*)
Damage 1992
Wuthering Heights 1992
The Unbearable Lightness of Being 1988

"Acting is like peeling an onion. You have to peel away each layer to reveal another."

RUSSELL CROWE

Born: Russell Ira Crowe, April 7, 1964 (Wellington, North Island, New Zealand).

Star qualities: Ruggedly handsome; tall; thick set; deep voice; sexy; versatile leading man of dramas; powerful screen presence; wild-man image; musician; producer; director.

Russell Crowe was born the son of movie location caterers. He got into acting as a teenager on the Australian TV soap opera *Neighbours* (1987). He then served time in Australian movies such as *Prisoners of the Sun* (1990) and *Spotswood* (1992) until a blazing performance as a neo-Nazi skinhead in *Romper Stomper* (1992) brought him to international attention.

After a shaky U.S. start as Sharon Stone's cowboy love interest in the Western *The Quick and the Dead* (1995), and a computer-generated serial killer in *Virtuosity* (1995), Crowe landed a lead role in *L.A. Confidential* (1997) as a violent but gallant cop. His remarkable streak of varied high-profile performances continued with the buttoned-down, middle-aged whistleblower Dr. Jeffrey Wiegand in *The Insider* (1999); the vengeance-seeking Maximus in *Gladiator* (2000), which won him an Oscar for Best Actor; the schizophrenic mathematics genius John Nash in *A Beautiful Mind* (2001); seafaring Captain Jack Aubrey in *Master and Commander: The Far Side of the World* (2003); and a down-at-heel boxer Jim Braddock in *Cinderella Man* (2005).

Although he sometimes takes easy acting options, especially in his Oscar-winning *Gladiator* turn and *A Beautiful Mind*, he remains capable of exceptionally fine work. *L.A. Confidential* and *The Insider* stand as his best screen work to date. A tendency to get into offscreen brawls has led to him having a wild-man image, but this has not so far detracted from his growing stardom. He plays guitar and sings in a rock band, a nod to an early desire to make a career as a rock singer. He has made his home in Australia, where he married his longtime girlfriend, Australian singer and actress, Danielle Spencer, and the couple have two children. **KN**

Top Takes...

American Gangster 2007
A Good Year 2006
Cinderella Man 2005
Master and Commander: The Far Side of the World 2003
A Beautiful Mind 2001 ☆
Proof of Life 2000
Gladiator 2000 ★
The Insider 1999 ☆
Mystery, Alaska 1999
L.A. Confidential 1997
Virtuosity 1995
The Quick and the Dead 1995
The Sum of Us 1994
Romper Stomper 1992
Proof 1991

"I want to make movies that pierce people's hearts and touch them in some way."

1960s

KEANU REEVES

Born: Keanu Charles Reeves, September 2, 1964 (Beirut, Lebanon).

Star qualities: Handsome; tall; clean-cut; sexy; athletic; leading man of dramas and action movies; cool screen persona; deadpan delivery; stagecraft; keen motorcyclist and bass player; enigmatic.

Keanu Reeves was born in Beirut, Lebanon, to U.S. and English parents, named after his Hawaiian heritage on his father's side, and then raised in Toronto, Canada. Out of these cosmopolitan origins, Reeves began working in the Canadian theater at the age of fifteen, and debuted on Canadian TV and cinema.

Reeves's first Hollywood film appearance was as an ice hockey goalie in *Youngblood* (1986). He then moved to Los Angeles, and first attracted favorable reviews for his part as a teenager suffering a crisis of conscience in *River's Edge* (1986). He achieved a certain kind of stardom as the vacuous teen icon Ted in *Bill & Ted's Excellent Adventure* (1989), a screen image that Reeves has struggled to escape ever since.

In addition to filming a Bill and Ted sequel in 1991, Reeves's 1990s career saw him expanding his range by playing Jonathan Harker in *Bram Stoker's Dracula* (1992), Don John in *Much Ado about Nothing* (1993), and pumped-up action hero Jack Traven in the blockbuster *Speed* (1994). He continued to establish a niche in the science fiction and horror genres with *Johnny Mnemonic* (1995) and *The Devil's Advocate* (1997), where he played a lawyer tempted by the devil. He capped off the decade with his portrayal of Neo, the savior of humankind against a computer takeover in *The Matrix* (1999) and its two sequels. The *Matrix* films were hits, due in no small part because Reeves personally bankrolled millions of dollars to the first film's directors, the Wachowski brothers, to complete the special effects. Since the heady days of *Matrix* fame, Reeves has worked both in genre roles such as *Constantine* (2005), and in supporting and lead romantic roles in movies like *The Lake House* (2006). Since the 1990s, Reeves has also played bass for the bands Dogstar and Becky. **PS**

Top Takes...

"I'm Mickey Mouse. They don't know who's inside the suit."

MAGGIE CHEUNG

Born: Maggie Cheung, September 20, 1964 (Hong Kong, China).

Star qualities: Radiant beauty queen looks; slim, sexy; glamorous icon of contemporary Asian cinema; elegant screen siren; multilingual; exuberant screen presence; comic timing.

Anyone who observed the nascent years in Maggie Cheung's career—a runner-up in the Miss Hong Kong beauty pageant whose early work consisted of little more than pouting in silly comedies and appearing as Jackie Chan's long-suffering girlfriend in his *Police Story* action movies—would be forgiven for not predicting her evolution into one of today's most accomplished actresses. Luckily, a series of auteur filmmakers—most notably Kar Wai Wong, but also Stanley Kwan and French director Olivier Assayas (Cheung's former husband)—recognized a quality in Cheung beyond her beauty, and she was rescued from the obscurity of 1980s Hong Kong starlets.

Cheung ranks among international cinema's preeminent actresses, her radiant appearance matched by a grace and intimate expressiveness as she nears middle age. Director Wong used her strengths best in *Wong gok ka moon* (1988) (*As Tears Go By*), *A Fei jing juen* (1991) (*Days of Being Wild*), *Dung che sai duk* (1994) (*Ashes of Time*), and, especially, the contemporary classic *Fa yeung nin wa* (2000) (*In the Mood for Love*)—Cheung also appeared briefly in its sequel *2046* (2004). But she was equally radiant in Kwan's *Yuen ling-yuk* (1992) (*The Actress*), a biopic on the tragic life of 1930s Chinese actress Ruan Ling-yu, and Assayas's *Clean* (2004), wherein Cheung delivered an extraordinary performance as a recovering drug addict building bridges with her son.

Her less serious Hong Kong fare is not to be dismissed following her more serious triumphs. Cheung's work in genre films such as *Xin long men ke zhan* (1992) (*Dragon Inn*) and *Ching Se* (1993) (*Green Snake*) was exuberant, gutsy, and enjoyable. One just wishes she worked more frequently, but she has become very selective with her projects in recent years. **TC**

Top Takes...

2046 2004

Clean 2004

Ying xiong 2002 (*Hero*)

Fa yeung nin wa 2000 (*In the Mood for Love*)

Chinese Box 1997

Song jia huang chao 1997 (*The Soong Sisters*)

Tian mi mi 1996
   (*Comrades: Almost a Love Story*)

Dung che sai duk 1994 (*Ashes of Time*)

Ching Se 1993 (*Green Snake*)

Yuen ling-yuk 1992 (*The Actress*)

Jing cha gu shi III: Chao ji jing cha 1992
   (*Supercop*)

Xin long men ke zhan 1992 (*Dragon Inn*)

A Fei jing juen 1991 (*Days of Being Wild*)

Wong gok ka moon 1988 (*As Tears Go By*)

"I've done so many different roles . . . . It's getting harder to find something interesting."

1960s

AAMIR KHAN

Born: Aamir Khan, March 14, 1965 (Mumbai, India).

Star qualities: Bollywood idol; handsome leading man and character actor; publicity shy; athletic; Method acting style; diverse role choices; perfectionist; writer; producer.

Top Takes...

Rang De Basanti 2006

The Rising: Ballad of Mangal Pandey 2005

Dil Chahta Hai 2001 (Do Your Thing)

Lagaan: Once Upon a Time in India 2001

Sarfarosh 1999

Earth 1998

Ghulam 1998

Ishq 1997 (Romance)

Raja Hindustani 1996

Rangeela 1995 (Full of Color)

Andaz Apna Apna 1994

Hum Hain Rahi Pyar Ke 1993
  (We Are Travellers on the Path of Love)

Dil 1990

Qayamat Se Qayamat Tak 1988

As a handsome leading man in contemporary Bollywood cinema, Aamir Khan occupies a unique position within today's Indian popular film industry. Although one is reluctant to generalize, there remains a tendency among young Bollywood megastars to play variations on a limited, established persona (in this way, they can be similar to young Hollywood stars as well), and many careers are constrained by the image demands of the industry. Khan is different, and fascinatingly so—although he certainly possesses the looks and allure of a top star, he's also an unusually Method-driven and committed character actor at heart, and one who has taken control of his own career path. When compared with some other top Bollywood leading men such as Salman Khan or Hrithik Roshan, Khan's versatility becomes even more notable (think of the difference between, say, Johnny Depp and Ashton Kutcher).

Khan appeared in a few films as a child (his father is producer Tahir Hussain) but became a notable Bollywood presence with the romance *Qayamat Se Qayamat Tak* (1988), followed by several other major movies throughout the 1990s: *Dil* (1990), *Hum Hain Rahi Pyar Ke* (1993) (*We Are Travellers on the Path of Love*), *Akele Hum Akele Tum* (1995), *Raja Hindustani* (1996), *Ghulam* (1998), the excellent *Dil Chahta Hai* (2001) (*Do Your Thing*), and others. But Khan's crowning achievement in recent years is the internationally successful ambitious period piece *Lagaan: Once Upon a Time in India* (2001), which he both starred in and produced. Khan shuns publicity, refusing to attend many awards presentations, and he commits himself to only one project at a time (even then, only after reading a completed screenplay), uncommonly media-shy behavior for a Bollywood idol. **TC**

"I think the talent [in India and Pakistan] should come together and entertain the world."

ROBERT DOWNEY Jʀ.

Born: Robert John Downey Jr., April 4, 1965 (New York City, New York, U.S.).

Star qualities: Handsome; the comeback kid; versatile leading man and supporting actor; compelling screen presence; intelligent; composer; singer; producer; writer.

Notorious for various addictions, Robert Downey Jr. has been supported through multiple rehabs and career kick-starts because he is a wonderful performer. Combining brown, puppy-dog eyes with a handsome face, a physique that's muscled with age, a fast-talking demeanor, and an acidic attitude tending to melancholy, he is a perfect combination of madness, vulnerability, and intelligence. In short, he is typical of 1960s children, born from postwar boom times, reared through the 1970s, only to emerge in the 1980s overwhelmed and sad at how complicated the world has become.

The son of an independent filmmaker, Robert Downey Sr., Downey cut his teeth in a spate of teen comedies such as *Weird Science* (1985) and *The Pick-up Artist* (1987). He followed this up playing a drug-addled Los Angeleno in *Less Than Zero* (1987), and later earned critical plaudits, including an Oscar nomination for Best Actor for his lead role as the silent film star in the biopic *Chaplin* (1992). After this followed a series of arrests, supporting parts, a brief smell of success in the TV comedy series *Ally McBeal* (2000–2002), and continual struggles to remain clean.

Through it all, Downey has been nothing short of brilliant. Never involved with a blockbuster, he is typically overlooked in a roll call of his generation's best leads. But there are gems to bolster his reputation, among them *Short Cuts* (1993), *Natural Born Killers* (1994), and *Kiss Kiss Bang Bang* (2005), all leading to future work, ideally without so much personal drama.

Downey also has a second career in music. He performed in a duet with Sting on The Police's "Every Breath You Take" (1983), appeared in the Elton John video for "I Want Love" (2001), and has released his debut musical album *The Futurist* (2004). **GCQ**

Top Takes...

A Scanner Darkly 2006
Good Night, and Good Luck. 2005
Kiss Kiss Bang Bang 2005
Gothika 2003
The Singing Detective 2003
Wonder Boys 2000
U.S. Marshals 1998
The Gingerbread Man 1998
Restoration 1995
Richard III 1995
Natural Born Killers 1994
Short Cuts 1993
Chaplin 1992 ☆
Soapdish 1991
Air America 1990
Less Than Zero 1987

"It's like I have a loaded gun in my mouth, and I like the taste of metal."—On his drug addiction

1960s

SHARUKH KHAN

Born: Shahrukh Khan, November 2, 1965 (New Delhi, India).

Star qualities: Bollywood screen idol; handsome leading man; "The King" of Hindi movies; often plays the romantic hero; enigmatic; easy charm; singer; dancer; producer.

Referring to Bollywood superstar Sharukh Khan as Indian cinema's preeminent everyman romantic actor isn't quite accurate; Khan is more like a super-everyman, a sweet, witty, down-to-earth leading man who is about a thousand times sweeter and wittier than mere mortals could hope to be.

Reportedly contemporary Bollywood's highest-paid actor, Khan has certainly earned that honor: his seemingly casual, effortless charm has driven many of the biggest Indian film hits of the past decade or so. After appearing in several movies and TV series in the late 1980s and early 1990s, Khan began to develop a noteworthy career. But it was the blockbuster love story *Dilwale Dulhania Le Jayenge* (1995) (*The Big-Hearted Will Win the Bride*) that transported Khan to a whole new level of fame. The significance of *DDLJ* (as it's often labeled) is astronomical—many have claimed that it is Bollywood's longest-running theatrical release, with fans still flocking to see the film, and the success is deserved. Director Aditya Chopra (son of producer Yash Chopra) has crafted a winning romantic comedy of mismatched lovers uniting against all odds, and it served as the template for the sweeping romances that would largely define Khan's subsequent career as Bollywood's top romantic hero. In addition to reuniting with Chopra on the frothy but fun *Mohabbatein* (2000) (*Love Stories*), Khan played the love-struck nice guy in other hits like *Dil To Pagal Hai* (1997) (*The Heart Is Crazy*), and *Kuch Kuch Hota Hai* (1998) (*Something Is Happening*). One of his most complex and captivating performances is in Mani Ratnam's grim love story *Dil Se* (1998) (*From the Heart*). Although not a household name in Europe and the United States, Khan is one of the biggest stars on the planet. **TC**

Top Takes…

Don 2006
Kabhi Alvida Naa Kehna 2006
 (*Never Say Goodbye*)
Paheli 2005
Swades 2004 (*Our Country*)
Mohabbatein 2000 (*Love Stories*)
Hey Ram 2000
Baadshah 1999
Kuch Kuch Hota Hai 1998
 (*Something Is Happening*)
Dil Se 1998 (*From the Heart*)
Dil To Pagal Hai 1997 (*The Heart Is Crazy*)
Dilwale Dulhania Le Jayenge 1995
 (*The Big-Hearted Will Win the Bride*)
Anjaam 1994
Baazigar 1993
Darr 1993 (*Darr: A Violent Love Story*)

"I'd rather sink trying to be different, than stay afloat like everyone else."

BEN STILLER

Born: Benjamin Edward Stiller, November 30, 1965 (New York City, New York, U.S.).

Star qualities: Dark-haired; intelligent; goofy leading man of comedies; slapstick style; impersonator; comic timing; belongs to an acting family; "Frat Pack" member; producer; director; writer.

"The Frat Pack" member Ben Stiller was born in New York City to comedy couple Jerry Stiller and Anne Meara. The elder Stiller is best known for his performances in the comedy TV show *Seinfeld* (1993–1998) as the father of George Costanza. Despite dropping out of the University of California, Los Angeles, film program, Stiller made his way as an actor with small roles in Steven Spielberg's *Empire of the Sun* (1987), and other films. He was hired as a featured player and writer for TV variety show *Saturday Night Live*, but it was the Fox Network that enabled him to produce the critically acclaimed, yet short-lived, *The Ben Stiller Show* (1992–1993), which also launched the careers of Andy Dick and Janeane Garofalo.

Stiller went on to direct *Reality Bites* (1994), *The Cable Guy* (1996), and *Zoolander* (2001). Despite the promise Stiller lacked as a director, he more than compensated for it as an actor, and it was the phenomenal success of *There's Something About Mary* (1998), in which he plays the obsessed and clumsy Ted Stroehmann that really caused Stiller's career to skyrocket, and contributed some classic comedy moments involving semen hair gel and pants zippers to comic history. His screen persona of a well-meaning, handsome nebbish has been well established in a string of comedies such as *Meet the Parents* (2000) and its equally amusing sequel, *Meet the Fockers* (2004); *Keeping the Faith* (2000); and *Along Came Polly* (2004). This persona was animated as Alex the Lion in *Madagascar* (2005). But far from being a one-note actor, Stiller has also created a number of wacky and over-the-top characters in movies such as *Mystery Men* (1999), *The Royal Tenenbaums* (2001), *Starsky & Hutch* (2004), and *Dodgeball: A True Underdog Story* (2004). **MK**

Top Takes...

Night at the Museum 2006
Tenacious D: The Pick of Destiny 2006
Madagascar 2005
Meet the Fockers 2004
Dodgeball: A True Underdog Story 2004
Starsky & Hutch 2004
Along Came Polly 2004
Duplex 2003
The Royal Tenenbaums 2001
Zoolander 2001
Meet the Parents 2000
Keeping the Faith 2000
Mystery Men 1999
There's Something About Mary 1998
The Cable Guy 1996
Reality Bites 1994

"There's an old saying in Hollywood: it's not the length of your film, it's how you use it."

1960s

LI GONG

Born: Li Gong, December 31, 1965 (Shenyang, Liaoning Province, China).

Star qualities: Fragile beauty; petite; long dark hair; versatile leading lady of Asian cinema who has achieved international recognition; stylish; well dressed; glamorous; seductive screen presence; model; singer.

Top Takes...

Miami Vice 2006

Memoirs of a Geisha 2005

2046 2004

Jing ke ci qin wang 1999
  (*The Emperor and the Assassin*)

Feng yue 1996 (*Temptress Moon*)

Yao a yao yao dao waipo qiao 1995
  (*Shanghai Triad*)

Ba wang bie ji 1993 (*Farewell My Concubine*)

Huozhe 1994 (*To Live*)

Qiu Ju da guan si 1992 (*The Story of Qiu Ju*)

Da hong deng long gao gao gua 1991
  (*Raise the Red Lantern*)

Du xia II zhi Shang Hai tan du sheng 1991
  (*God of Gamblers III*)

Ju Dou 1990

Hong gao liang 1987 (*Red Sorghum*)

Born in China, Li Gong aspired to be an actress from a young age, and eventually won a place at the Beijing Central College of Drama. She came to international prominence in a series of films directed by Yimou Zhang. These included *Hong gao liang* (1987) (*Red Sorghum*), *Ju Dou* (1990), *Da hong deng long gao gao gua* (1991) (*Raise the Red Lantern*), *Qiu Ju da guan si* (1992) (*The Story of Qiu Ju*), *Huozhe* (1994) (*To Live*), and *Yao a yao yao dao waipo qiao* (1995) (*Shanghai Triad*). *The Story of Qui Ju*, in which she portrays a poor pregnant woman from the country who battles against bureaucracy, revealed a range that her earlier movies had perhaps not suggested.

Further work with prominent directors such as Kaige Chen in *Ba wang bie ji* (1993) (*Farwell My Concubine*), *Feng yue* (1996) (*Temptress Moon*), and *Jing ke ci qin wang* (1999) (*The Emperor and the Assassin*) made her the public face of the "Fifth Generation" of Chinese filmmakers and for many world audiences the most recognizable mainland actress of the period. However, Gong had also always worked within the commercial Hong Kong industry, appearing in popular films such as *Du xia II zhi Shang Hai tan du sheng* (1991) (*God of Gamblers III*), and *Tang Bohu dian Qiuxiang* (1993) (*Flirting Scholar*), further showing her impressive ability to play in a number of styles. More recently, she has moved into projects with a higher international profile, including Kar Wai Wong's *2046* (2004), and the Hollywood films *Memoirs of a Geisha* (2005), where, as a Chinese actress playing a Japanese geisha, she caused some controversy, and *Miami Vice* (2006). She remains an actress of great versatility, but one whose beauty has often meant her acting abilities have been critically overlooked. **AW**

"People [push] me to be the center of attention . . . . I would prefer to be on the sidelines."

JOHN CUSACK

Born: John Paul Cusack, June 28, 1966 (Evanston, Illinois, U.S.).

Star qualities: Boy-next-door good looks; former "Brat Pack" member; tall; leading man and character actor; often plays the confused good guy; offbeat; reassuring screen presence; producer; writer.

John Cusack comes from an acting family: his father, Dick Cusack, is an actor and filmmaker, and his siblings Joan Cusack, Ann Cusack, Bill Cusack, and Susie Cusack are all actors too. By the age of twelve, he had already appeared onstage and done voice-over work for TV commercials. Early appearances in teen vehicles such as *Sixteen Candles* (1984), *Better off Dead* (1985), and *The Journey of Natty Gann* (1985) paved the way toward him becoming the best loved antiromantic lead of this generation. He's also dated a host of actresses throughout his career, most notably Minnie Driver, although he's never taken a wife, which only adds to his general appeal.

His motor-mouth tendencies, boy-next-door looks, his perpetual mien of sadness, and his ability to embolden everyday slackers into feats of genuine heroism have made Cusack a beloved player in *Say Anything...* (1989), *High Fidelity* (2000), *Serendipity* (2001), and *Must Love Dogs* (2005). That he is equally armed with an expressive and artistic integrity and an experimental edge has also led to important work in *The Grifters* (1990), *Bullets Over Broadway* (1994), *The Thin Red Line* (1998), and *Max* (2002). He has also produced several movies through his company, New Crime Productions, including *Grosse Pointe Blank* (1997) and *High Fidelity* (2000).

In each of these movies, Cusack is charismatic and appealing, even when behaving badly. Ultimately, it could be that audiences are constantly drawn to him because he is so much like them in their best moments, when a person is suddenly capable of seeing things clearly and articulating them well enough to take action and improve their life.

Cusack founded Chicago's The New Criminals theater group in 1988, and he continues to produce and direct plays. **GCQ**

Top Takes...

Must Love Dogs 2005
Runaway Jury 2003
Identity 2003
Max 2002
America's Sweethearts 2001
High Fidelity 2000
Being John Malkovich 1999
Cradle Will Rock 1999
Pushing Tin 1999
The Thin Red Line 1998
Midnight in the Garden of Good and Evil 1997
Grosse Pointe Blank 1997
City Hall 1996
Bullets Over Broadway 1994
The Grifters 1990
Say Anything... 1989

> "I'm not into the celebrity culture aspect of being an artist."

1960s

HALLE BERRY

Born: Halle Maria Berry, August 14, 1966 (Cleveland, Ohio, U.S.).

Star qualities: Glowing beauty; slim; beauty queen looks; model; stylish; trailblazing; versatile leading lady of dramas and action movies; intelligent; box-office gold; producer.

Top Takes...

X-Men: The Last Stand 2006
Robots 2005
Catwoman 2004
Gothika 2003
X2 2003
Die Another Day 2002
Monster's Ball 2001 ★
Swordfish 2001
X-Men 2000
Why Do Fools Fall in Love 1998
Bulworth 1998
Losing Isaiah 1995
The Flintstones 1994
Boomerang 1992
Strictly Business 1991
Jungle Fever 1991

"I want to be the next Spike Lee. I want to help other black folks to get into Hollywood."

Of mixed race but self-identified as African-American, possessed of a vulnerability, and gifted with a face ready-made for magazine covers, Halle Berry is a truly modern star. She first entered into the public arena aged seventeen when she won the Miss Teen All-American Pageant, representing the state of Ohio in 1985. Then in 1986 she was the first runner-up in the Miss U.S.A. Pageant, after which she became a catalog model. This led to her appearance in the TV series *Living Dolls* (1989).

She is a performer with a deep emotional energy that she has mined for performances in such movies as *Boomerang* (1992), *Losing Isaiah* (1995), *Bulworth* (1998), and the *X-Men* series (2000–2006), in which she plays the sexy Storm, a mutant who has the ability to control the weather.

Her considerable acting ability has been recognized, too, with various plaudits. Her lead role in the TV biopic *Introducing Dorothy Dandridge* (1999) earned Berry both a Golden Globe Award and an Emmy Award for Best Actress, for her depiction of the late actress's struggle to succeed in the racially biased industry of 1950s Hollywood. Berry then crowned this with *Monster's Ball* (2001), which saw her become the first African-American actress to win the Academy Award for Best Actress.

That she has been so readily accepted in recent years is definitely helped by her good looks. After all, she played a stripper in the action thriller *The Last Boy Scout* (1991), and she is remembered more for her body in *Swordfish* (2001) than for her dramatic contribution. Yet she is clearly in control of her image and career, enough so that she has made the transition from being a pinup to an artist in only a few years based on challenging roles after she first emerged in *Jungle Fever* (1991) and *Strictly Business* (1991). **GCQ**

SALMA HAYEK

Born: Salma Hayek-Jimenez, September 2, 1966 (Coatzacoalcos, Veracruz, Mexico).

Star qualities: Smoldering Mexican beauty; petite; curvaceous; dark curly locks; glamorous leading lady and character actress; intelligent; fiery screen presence; producer; director.

After starring in the hugely popular *telenovela Teresa* (1989–1991), in her native Mexico, Salma Hayek's first movie role came with the multi-award-winning *El callejón de los milagros* (1995) (*Midaq Alley*). Moving to Hollywood, her lack of fluency in English saw her early parts play upon her smoldering Mexican beauty. She vented her spleen on a Spanish-language TV talk show on the injustice of such typecasting and, fortunately for her, director Robert Rodriguez was watching the show. He went on to cast her in *Desperado* (1995) playing opposite Antonio Banderas, and it was the success of that cult movie along with her appearance in his star-studded *From Dusk Till Dawn* (1996) that brought Hayek to prominence.

Now a recognizable name, Hollywood didn't quite know what to do with Hayek, and although some variation followed in movies such as *Dogma* (1999) and *Chain of Fools* (2000), she still tended to be typecast in parts that stressed her curvaceous good looks, ethnicity, and steely Mexican fortitude such as *Fools Rush In* (1997), *Hotel* (2001), and *Ask the Dust* (2006*)*.

The biopic *Frida* (2002), a movie that she also coproduced, seemed to mark a new turn in her career, earning her a Best Actress Academy Award nomination for her portrayal of her countrywoman, artist and political activist Frida Kahlo. However, roles in *Wild Wild West* (1999), *Once Upon a Time In Mexico* (2003), and *Bandidas* (2006) continue to demonstrate that Hayek remains linked to the action genre that first brought her to public notice. Greater confidence in handling English-language material and a recent move to gain greater control over her own projects offer the hope of new avenues for Hayek while she retains the mantle of the premier Latina actress working in Hollywood today. **RH**

Top Takes...

Ask the Dust 2006
Bandidas 2006
Once Upon a Time in Mexico 2003
Frida 2002 ☆
Hotel 2001
La Gran vida 2000 (*Living It Up*)
Chain of Fools 2000
Wild Wild West 1999
El coronel no tiene quien le escriba 1999
 (*No One Writes to the Colonel*)
Dogma 1999
Fools Rush In 1997
Sistole Diastole 1997
From Dusk Till Dawn 1996
Desperado 1995
El callejón de los milagros 1995 (*Midaq Alley*)

"At the beginning [my career] was hard. People were like, 'Who is this Mexican jumping bean?'"

1960s

ADAM SANDLER

Born: Adam Richard Sandler, September 9, 1966 (Brooklyn, New York, U.S.).

Star qualities: Goofy leading man of comedies; box-office gold; slapstick style; stand-up comedian; impersonator; political activist; composer; singer; guitarist; writer; producer.

Adam Sandler is one of those actors critics love to hate, dismissing his comedy as vulgar and lowbrow, yet audiences seem to love him, and the loyal fan base for his features has proved he can keep box-office cash registers full. Born in Brooklyn, New York, he grew up in New Hampshire and started out playing Boston's comedy clubs as a stand-up comedian. He was only seventeen years old when he won an amateur comedy competition. While studying fine arts at New York University, he worked on New York's comedy circuit.

After a few bit parts on TV, his career really took off on TV's *Saturday Night Live,* from 1990 to 1995. Sandler left the show to focus on his movie work, writing and starring in several crude comedies, including *Billy Madison* (1995) and *Happy Gilmore* (1996). But, in 1998, Sandler began evolving as an actor, creating a series of comic roles that made some critics rethink their initial opinion of Sandler as yet another unfunny *Saturday Night Live* alumnus: *The Wedding Singer* (1998), *Punch-Drunk Love* (2002), *50 First Dates* (2004), and *Spanglish* (2004) all indicated a maturation in his career. His performance in *Punch-Drunk Love* earned him a Golden Globe Award nomination. Through his own production company, Happy Madison Productions, Sandler wrote and produced (and supplied the lead voice for) the animated musical comedy *Eight Crazy Nights* (2002). However, despite the reference to his own hit "The Chanukah Song" (1994), it was disappointing for not following through and presenting a Jewish holiday movie. Sandler's comedy albums are immensely popular, and have all reached either gold or double platinum levels; his *Stan and Judy's Kid* (1999) debuting at Number 16 on the U.S. Billboard chart. **MK**

Top Takes…

Click 2006
Deuce Bigalow: European Gigolo 2005
The Longest Yard 2005
Spanglish 2004
50 First Dates 2004
Anger Management 2003
Eight Crazy Nights 2002
Mr. Deeds 2002
Punch-Drunk Love 2002
Big Daddy 1999
The Waterboy 1998
Dirty Work 1998
The Wedding Singer 1998
Happy Gilmore 1996
Billy Madison 1995

"I don't know who I touch and who I don't. I work hard trying to make people laugh."

SOPHIE MARCEAU

Born: Sophie Danièle Sylvie Maupu, November 17, 1966 (Paris, France).

Star qualities: Voluptuous dark-haired leading lady; contemporary icon of French cinema; award winner; former teen idol; glamorous; charismatic; singer; model; writer; director.

A voluptuous lead actress who combines artistic seriousness with old-fashioned glamour, Sophie Marceau began as a teen starlet but thereafter graduated to more challenging work. The daughter of a truck driver, she was just fourteen years old, and without any acting experience, when she successfully auditioned for the lead in French director Claude Pinoteau's teen drama *La boum* (1980) (*The Party*). It was a smash hit in France, leading to a number of awards, and a sequel in 1982 won her a César Award for Most Promising Actress.

Marceau's subsequent career has been uneven, but she proved herself a committed and capable actress in the thriller *Police* (1985), and followed it with appearances for Michelangelo Antonioni, Diane Kurys, and the Polish director Andrzej Zulawski (a frequent collaborator with whom she has a child). She is convincing in period costume, although her biggest star vehicle, Bertrand Tavernier's *La Fille de d'Artagnan* (1994) (*D'Artagnan's Daughter*) was, sadly, not the expected success.

One of a number of recent French actresses to have been courted by Hollywood, Marceau was paired ignominiously with Mel Gibson as Princess Isabelle in *Braveheart* (1995). But as the first ever combined James Bond girl and villain Elektra King in *The World Is Not Enough* (1999), she looked sensational, and provided some of the best moments of that endless saga's more recent chapters. Keeping busy behind the camera as well as in front of it, Marceau made her directorial debut with *L'aube à l'envers* (1995); she followed this up with her first feature, *Parlez-moi d'amour* (2002), which was well received by the critics. She has been an official model for the image of Marianne, a French national emblem, following in the footsteps of Brigitte Bardot and Catherine Deneuve. **MC**

Top Takes...

Les Clefs de bagnole 2003 (*The Car Keys*)
Je reste! 2003
La Fidélité 2000 (*Fidelity*)
The World Is Not Enough 1999
A Midsummer Night's Dream 1999
Lost & Found 1999
Anna Karenina 1997
Braveheart 1995
La Fille de d'Artagnan 1994
  (*D'Artagnan's Daughter*)
La note bleue 1991 (*Blue Note*)
Police 1985
Joyeuses Pâques 1984
Fort Saganne 1984
La boum 2 1982
La boum 1980 (*The Party*)

"Acting is wonderful therapy.... Instead of suffering for yourself, someone will do it for you."

1960s

BENICIO DEL TORO

Born: Benicio Monserrate Rafael Del Toro Sanchez, February 19, 1967 (Santurce, Puerto Rico).

Star qualities: Brooding good looks; tall; versatile leading man and character actor of dramas; imposing screen presence; charismatic; writer; producer; director.

Top Takes...

Sin City 2005
21 Grams 2003 ☆
The Hunted 2003
The Pledge 2001
Traffic 2000 ★
Snatch. 2000
Fear and Loathing in Las Vegas 1998
Excess Baggage 1997
The Funeral 1996
The Fan 1996
Basquiat 1996
The Usual Suspects 1995
Swimming with Sharks 1994
Fearless 1993
Christopher Columbus: The Discovery 1992
Licence to Kill 1989

"My goal as an actor has always been to reach a level where I can find a lot of interesting work."

Benicio Del Toro was born in Puerto Rico but moved with his widowed father to the United States when he was thirteen years old. Planning on following in his parents' footsteps and becoming a lawyer, Del Toro changed his mind after taking an acting class. He studied at New York's Circle in the Square Acting School and the Stella Adler Conservatory in Los Angeles. A part as Duke the Dog-Faced Boy in *Big Top Pee-wee* (1988) marked Del Toro's screen debut, and he then appeared as villains in *Licence to Kill* (1989) and *Christopher Columbus: The Discovery* (1992). He followed with supporting roles in movies such as *Fearless* (1993) and *Swimming with Sharks* (1994). His breakthrough came as mumbling criminal Fred Fenster in *The Usual Suspects* (1995).

Del Toro had hit the big time, but his parts were more eclectic as he stuck to his independent film roots. He played the roommate in Julian Schnabel's *Basquiat* (1996); a car thief in Marco Brambill's *Excess Baggage* (1997); the crazed lawyer Dr. Gonzo in Terry Gilliam's *Fear and Loathing in Las Vegas* (1998); and crooks in Christopher McQuarrie's *The Way of the Gun* (2000) and Guy Ritchie's *Snatch.* (2000). A sense of promise was fulfilled with his role as a Mexican border cop in Steven Soderbergh's *Traffic* (2000), which won him the Best Supporting Actor Academy Award. The ensuing years saw diverse roles ranging from low-budget movies such as Sean Penn's *The Pledge* (2001), to mainstream films such as William Friedkin's *The Hunted* (2003) and Robert Rodriguez's *Sin City* (2005), to Alejandro González Iñárritu's critically acclaimed *21 Grams* (2003). His role in the latter as the soul-searching ex-convict, who finds God, won him another Oscar nomination for Best Supporting Actor. **WW**

NICOLE KIDMAN

Born: Nicole Mary Kidman, June 20, 1967 (Honolulu, Hawaii, U.S.).

Star qualities: Tall, pale, blonde beauty; elegant; former wife to Tom Cruise; face of Chanel; singer; dancer; extremely versatile leading lady; interesting choice of roles; producer.

Nicole Kidman was born to Australian parents in Hawaii, but she returned to her family's native home when she was a child. She dropped out of high school to serve a busy acting apprenticeship in Australia, as a cute teen star in *BMX Bandits* (1983), *Bush Christmas* (1983), and *The Year My Voice Broke* (1987). She went international as the imperiled wife in *Dead Calm* (1989), showing a maturity that gave her a range beyond her years. Yet her first Hollywood movie roles were conventional: love interest for her first husband, Tom Cruise, in *Days of Thunder* (1990) and *Far and Away* (1992), a nude gun moll in *Billy Bathgate* (1991), and under peril in *Malice* (1993).

A committed turn as the viciously ambitious housewife turned TV personality in Gus Van Sant's *To Die For* (1995) reestablished her acting credentials. She then wavered cannily between commercial efforts such as *Batman Forever* (1995) and *The Peacemaker* (1997), and art theater movies such as *The Portrait of a Lady* (1996) and *Dogville* (2003). She and Cruise also famously joined forces to play a couple in Stanley Kubrick's last movie, the erotic thriller *Eyes Wide Shut* (1999), which had the world fascinated by what they saw as a peephole into the nature of Kidman and Cruise's relationship. Whether what audiences saw onscreen as the chemistry between the couple was a reflection of their offscreen life, no one will ever know, and the couple divorced two years later.

Once single, Kidman's career seemed to take off, making her one of the most versatile contemporary female actresses in the world. *Moulin Rouge!* (2001) showed she could sing and dance, and won her an Oscar nomination; she followed this up with an Oscar win for her role as writer Virginia Woolf in *The Hours* (2002). Kidman married country singer Keith Urban in 2006. **KN**

Top Takes...

The Interpreter 2005
Birth 2004
Cold Mountain 2003
The Human Stain 2003
Dogville 2003
The Hours 2002 ★
The Others 2001
Moulin Rouge! 2001 ☆
Eyes Wide Shut 1999
The Peacemaker 1997
The Portrait of a Lady 1996
Batman Forever 1995
To Die For 1995
Billy Bathgate 1991
Days of Thunder 1990
Dead Calm 1989

"I have a boy's body. I'd prefer to have more curves because I think that's more beautiful."

MATHIEU KASSOVITZ

Born: Mathieu Kassovitz, August 3, 1967 (Paris, France).

Star qualities: Rugged good looks; member of a acting family; versatile leading man of contemporary French cinema; innovative; provocative; director; writer; producer.

Top Takes...

Avida 2006

Munich 2005

Amen. 2002

Astérix & Obélix: Mission Cléopâtre 2002
  (Asterix & Obelix: Mission Cleopatra)

Traitement de substitution n°4 2002

Birthday Girl 2001

Le Fabuleux destin d'Amélie Poulain 2001
  (Amélie)

Jakob the Liar 1999

Le Plaisir (et ses petits tracas) 1998
  (Pleasure [And Its Little Inconveniences])

The Fifth Element 1997

Assassin(s) 1997

Un héros très discret 1996 (A Self-Made Hero)

Mon homme 1996 (My Man)

La haine 1995 (Hate)

"I'm not a politician; I'm lucky to be a filmmaker and to express myself through films."

Son of Hungarian filmmaker Peter Kassovitz and his editor wife, Mathieu Kassovitz has displayed talent both behind and in front of the camera. After a series of short films, Kassovitz made his feature-length directing debut with *Métisse* (1993) (*Café au lait*), a comedy about race relations. He followed it up with *La haine* (1995) (*Hate*), a film about police brutality in the French *banlieues*, or suburbs. The controversial movie filmed in black and white earned Kassovitz a César Award for Best Film, and the Best Director Award at the Cannes Film Festival. It also put him on the map internationally as the French equivalent of U.S. directors Spike Lee and Quentin Tarantino. He then made *Assassin(s)* (1997), a reformulation of an earlier short, the French thriller *Les Rivières pourpres* (2001) (*The Crimson Rivers*), and the U.S. studio horror movie *Gothika* (2003).

As an actor, Kassovitz has said that he acts in order to gain knowledge from his favorite filmmakers about directing and to know what it is to act. In that regard, he worked with personal heroes Costa-Gavras in *Amen.* (2002) and Steven Spielberg in *Munich* (2005). He also acted for his father on several occasions, including the remake *Jakob the Liar* (1999). Kassovitz showcases his lighter side in the World War II satire *Un héros très discret* (1996) (*A Self-Made Hero*), and as Nino Quincampoix, the object of Audrey Tautou's affection in Jean-Pierre Jeunet's comedy fantasy *Le Fabuleux destin d'Amélie Poulain* (2001) (*Amélie*), the acting role he is probably best known for. Following his appearance in Gustave de Kervern's *Avida* (2006), he has said that he wants to concentrate on directing rather than acting, joking that a role as an actor under Stanley Kubrick would bring him back as a player to the big screen. Only time will tell. **WW**

JULIA ROBERTS

Born: Julia Fiona Roberts, October 28, 1967 (Smyrna, Georgia, U.S.).

Star qualities: Quite simply the most popular actress in the United States; tall and slim with a huge smile; queen of romantic comedies; one of the most highly paid leading actresses; producer.

One of the most recognized faces worldwide, a refreshing beauty with an infectious smile and legs to die for, Julia Roberts has enjoyed huge success in serious and fantasy movies, but her audience loves her best in romantic comedies, where she has had a truly unique effect.

Since first being singled out for her performances in *Mystic Pizza* and *Satisfaction* in 1988, Julia Roberts has set an unusually high standard for U.S. actresses, as both popular artist and well-compensated performer. Earning her first Academy Award nomination and her first Golden Globe Award for *Steel Magnolias* the very next year, she immediately achieved a high level of critical support for her work, allowing her to move from being a strictly youth-driven sensation into her mature career with relative ease. After the massive success of *Pretty Woman* in 1990, which was accompanied by her second Academy Award nomination and second Golden Globe Award, Roberts also managed a rare feat for someone so young: she became the standard of quality and popularity in U.S. movies, and has been able to maintain this position every year since.

Top Takes...

Ocean's Twelve 2004
Closer 2004
Mona Lisa Smile 2003
Full Frontal 2002
Ocean's Eleven 2001
America's Sweethearts 2001
The Mexican 2001
Erin Brockovich 2000 ★
Runaway Bride 1999
Notting Hill 1999
Stepmom 1998
Conspiracy Theory 1997
My Best Friend's Wedding 1997
Everyone Says I Love You 1996
Michael Collins 1996
Mary Reilly 1996
Prêt-à-Porter 1994
The Pelican Brief 1993
Hook 1991
Dying Young 1991
Sleeping with the Enemy 1991
Flatliners 1990
Pretty Woman 1990 ☆
Steel Magnolias 1989 ☆
Mystic Pizza 1988

LEFT: Pairing up with Richard Gere in *Pretty Woman* proved a phenomenal success.

Tenacious Erin

In her critically-acclaimed role in *Erin Brockovich*, Julia Roberts truly shone as the honest, streetwise character who refuses to bow down in the face of a corporate giant. The movie was based on the real-life story of Erin Brockovich-Ellis, an unemployed single mother who became a legal assistant and almost single-handedly brought down a California power company accused of polluting a city's water supply with cancer-causing chemicals. It was a fantastic story to adapt for the big screen, and Roberts brought her own particular attributes as a performer—not least the gritty strength behind the big smile—to the successful project.

- Brockovich's exposure of Pacific Gas & Electric led to the biggest settlement on record for a civil class action lawsuit.
- The movie also received Oscar nominations for Best Supporting Actor (Albert Finney), Best Director (Steven Soderbergh), Best Picture, and Best Screenplay.
- The left-handed Roberts taught herself to write with her right hand to play the right-handed Erin Brockovich.
- When it came to accepting her Best Actress Oscar, Roberts forgot to thank the real-life Erin Brockovich-Ellis in her speech. She later confessed: "It doesn't bring out the Einstein moment that you hoped it would."

Born in Georgia, she's the sister of Eric Roberts, an actor of some early promise now regularly cast as a villain and from whom she's estranged. She has famously red-brown hair, a wide, hyperbolic, toothy smile, and a large laugh that consumes all listeners. Relatively tall, thin, and not particularly curvy, these boyish attributes have contributed to an extended state of youthfully believable roles—not the ingénue, not the matron—but it's the steely strength beneath the coltish physique that makes Roberts such a rich onscreen personality.

More than just a *Pretty Woman*

Flatliners (1990) demonstrated her ease with ensemble casts in a tale of overcoming death with unexpected results, and was her first romantic pairing with costar Kiefer Sutherland, a trend that was repeated over the years, although interrupted by her first marriage to singer Lyle Lovett. But it was *Sleeping with the Enemy* in 1991 that took her previously established central vulnerabilities—slender build, seeming meekness, trusting nature—and turned them on end, as her Sara Walters character overcomes an abusive husband. Known for being beautiful, emotionally expressive, and possessing that indefinable "something" that signifies stardom, she was now also recognized for being a rock beneath the chiffon, and a person of unusual tenacity.

Over the next few years she reaffirmed her box-office appeal in *Dying Young*, *Hook* (both 1991), and *The Pelican Brief* (1993), and suffered her first career misstep with *I Love Trouble* (1994). Quickly recovering with a return to romantic comedy in *Something to Talk About* (1995), there followed the little-seen *Mary Reilly* and *Michael Collins* (both 1996), after which Roberts became the object of Woody Allen's midlife obsession in *Everyone Says I Love You* (1996), which was a showcase for her limited, but still true, singing abilities.

Although the late 1990s may be remembered for Y2K anxiety, as evidenced by high-concept sci-fi thrillers (*The Matrix*, 1999) and weird domestic dramas (*American Beauty*, 1999), the period may also be remembered as the one of

ABOVE: Roberts in an award-winning turn as *Erin Brockovich* opposite Albert Finney.

greatest commercial dominance for Roberts, who appeared in a string of hits: *My Best Friend's Wedding* (1997, Golden Globe nomination), *Conspiracy Theory* (1997), *Stepmom* (1998), *Notting Hill* (1999, Golden Globe nomination), *Runaway Bride* (1999), and *Erin Brockovich* (2000), her first Academy Award-winning, and Golden Globe Award-winning, performance. This last movie cemented the actress's position atop the Hollywood hierarchy, and has led to a slowdown in output in favor of home life with cinematographer husband Daniel Moder, her second husband, and their twins.

Roberts continues to be top-draw talent, earning $25 million for *Mona Lisa Smile* (2003), and mixing baldly commercial fare (*Ocean's Eleven*, 2001) with more independently-minded work (*Full Frontal*, 2002; *Closer*, 2004). **GCQ**

"I'm too tall to be a girl . . . . I'd say I'm somewhere between a chick and a broad."

1960s

WILL SMITH

Born: Willard Christopher Smith Jr., September 25, 1968 (Philadelphia, Pennsylvania, U.S.).

Star qualities: "The Fresh Prince"; tall; handsome; versatile leading man of drama, action, and comedies; comic timing; intelligent; box-office gold; singer; rapper; hip-hop artist; producer; writer, composer.

Top Takes...

The Pursuit of Happyness 2006 ☆
Hitch 2005
Shark Tale 2004
I, Robot 2004
Bad Boys II 2003
Men in Black II 2002
Ali 2001 ☆
The Legend of Bagger Vance 2000
Wild Wild West 1999
Enemy of the State 1998
Men in Black 1997
Independence Day 1996
Bad Boys 1995
Six Degrees of Separation 1993
Made in America 1993
Where the Day Takes You 1992

A three-way media phenomenon in the recording industry, TV, and on film, Will Smith is beloved across the world. He is also young, ambitious, and grounded in a well-publicized celebrity marriage to his second wife, actress Jada Pinkett-Smith.

Recognizing his musical interests early on, Smith turned down a scholarship to the prestigious Massachusetts Institute of Technology for a hip-hop career as front man "The Fresh Prince" for his friend Jeff Townes, also known as D.J. Jazzy Jeff. The pair performed raps ready-made for mainstream consumption, and won a Grammy for Best Rap Performance for the song "Parents Just Don't Understand" (1988). Then Smith parlayed his fame into the six-year run of the sitcom *The Fresh Prince of Bel-Air* on TV (1990–1996), during which time he developed a solo career in music and enjoyed his earliest big-screen roles in *Where the Day Takes You* (1992), and as a homosexual con artist in *Six Degrees of Separation* (1993).

Always a popular performer, the big splash was *Bad Boys* (1995), although it was his fighter-pilot hero in *Independence Day* (1996), along with more musical successes, including a second Grammy Award for "Summertime" (1991), that firmly established his position atop the popular media. More hits followed, such as *Men in Black* (1997) and its sequel, and *Hitch* (2005); along with a few bombs such as *Wild Wild West* (1999) and *The Legend of Bagger Vance* (2000). But then Smith earned critical accolades, including an Oscar nomination for Best Actor, as the lead in Michael Mann's biopic of boxer Muhammad Ali, *Ali* (2001), suggesting new career directions he will no doubt pursue in time. His music career surges on. His album *Willennium* (1999) and the single "Will2K" (1990) sold more than two million copies each. **GCQ**

"I love being black in America, and especially being black in Hollywood."

JAVIER BARDEM

Born: Javier Ángel Encinas Bardem, March 1, 1969 (Las Palmas, Gran Canaria, Canary Islands, Spain).

Star qualities: Ruggedly handsome; dark-haired sex symbol; part of an acting family; charismatic; versatile leading man of Spanish cinema; chameleonlike; producer.

Recent years have seen Javier Bardem establish himself as one of the most high-profile Spanish actors on the international scene. To date the only Spanish actor nominated for a Best Actor Oscar, he is a member of one of Spain's most famous film families. The son of actress Pilar Bardem and the nephew of director Juan Antonio Bardem, he has displayed a wide acting range, often resisting the easy option of taking roles that would exploit his rugged good looks.

Bardem's early career included successful collaborations with director Bigas Luna. After a small but eye-catching role in Luna's *Las edades de Lulú* (1990) (*The Ages of Lulu*), Bardem gained an international profile with two further collaborations, *Jamón, jamón* (1992) (*A Tale of Ham and Passion*) and *Huevos de oro* (1993) (*Golden Balls*). Since then he has been consistently cast in lead roles by the best directors in contemporary Spanish cinema. He has worked, for example, with Pedro Almodóvar on *Carne trémula* (1997) (*Live Flesh*), Alex de la Iglesia on *Perdita Durango* (1997) (*Dance with the Devil*), and Manuel Gómez Pereira on *Boca a boca* (1995) (*Mouth to Mouth*). The latter film, a screwball comedy, demonstrated Bardem's lighter touch.

Bardem appeared as persecuted Cuban writer Reinaldo Arenas in *Before Night Falls* (2000), a film that won him greater fame and led to roles in U.S. films such as *Collateral* (2004). However, unlike his fellow Spaniard Antonio Banderas, Bardem still works in challenging Spanish films such as the social realist *Los Lunes al sol* (2002) (*Mondays in the Sun*) alongside his more international projects. Bardem won plaudits around the world for his portrayal of quadriplegic Ramón Sampedro in Alejandero Amenábar's *Mar adentro* (2004) (*The Sea Inside*). **AW**

Top Takes...

Love in the Time of Cholera 2007
Goya's Ghosts 2006
Mar adentro 2004 (The Sea Inside)
Collateral 2004
Los Lunes al sol 2002 (Mondays in the Sun)
The Dancer Upstairs 2002
Before Night Falls 2000 ☆
Perdita Durango 1997 (Dance with the Devil)
Carne trémula 1997 (Live Flesh)
Boca a boca 1995 (Mouth to Mouth)
Huevos de oro 1993 (Golden Balls)
Jamón, jamón 1992
   (A Tale of Ham and Passion)
Las edades de Lulú 1990 (The Ages of Lulu)

"I don't really care where movies come from as long as they're worth making."

1960s

CATE BLANCHETT

Born: Catherine Elise Blanchett, May 14, 1969 (Melbourne, Victoria, Australia).

Star qualities: Luminous beauty; tall, long blonde hair; prominent cheekbones; glamorous; versatile leading lady of dramas; stagecraft; chameleonlike; steely screen presence; producer.

Top Takes...

Notes on a Scandal **2006** ☆
Babel 2006
Little Fish 2005
***The Aviator* 2004 ★**
The Life Aquatic with Steve Zissou 2004
The Missing 2003
Veronica Guerin 2003
Heaven 2002
The Lord of the Rings trilogy 2001, 2002, 2003
Charlotte Gray 2001
Bandits 2001
The Gift 2000
Pushing Tin 1999
An Ideal Husband 1999
***Elizabeth* 1998** ☆
Oscar and Lucinda 1997

> "I basically did it so that I could have the [pointed] ears."
>
> — On *The Lord of the Rings*

Born, raised, and trained in Australia, Cate Blanchett studied at Australia's National Institute of Dramatic Art. After graduation she joined the Sydney Theatre Company, where her performance as Felice Bauer, the bride, in Timothy Daly's *Kafka Dances* (1993), won her the Newcomer Award from the Sydney Theatre Critics Circle. She worked on the stage and found parts in TV before making her film debut in *Paradise Road* (1997).

She was first given truly international acclaim in *Elizabeth* (1998), as England's virgin queen, and won an Oscar nomination for Best Actress. Blanchett has since played a suburban U.S. wife in *Pushing Tin* (1999), a kidnap victim in *Bandits* (2001), a French Resistance fighter in *Charlotte Gray* (2001), an Irish martyr in *Veronica Guerin* (2003), a Western heroine in *The Missing* (2003), an elf elder in *The Lord of the Rings* trilogy (2001–2003), and Hollywood queen Katharine Hepburn in the Howard Hughes biopic *The Aviator* (2004), for which she won a deserved Oscar for Best Supporting Actress.

Through all this work, and other memorable performances in *Oscar and Lucinda* (1997), *Heaven* (2002), and *Babel* (2006), Blanchett has altered the polarity of her screen performances, like Meryl Streep submerging herself—and her true physical beauty—into a series of roles that see her transformed into believable characters, portraits of real people living in conflict with circumstances. Blanchett is also a chameleon. She is tall with expressive eyebrows, a long face, and blonde hair, and she resembles a fashion plate. But then she speaks with a terrific sense of control in every word, making audiences realize just how extraordinary is her every performance, carefully tailored, as they all are, for the camera, scene by scene, moment by moment. **GCQ**

1960s

EDWARD NORTON

Born: Edward James Norton Jr., August 18, 1969 (Boston, Massachusetts, U.S.).

Star qualities: Tall, slim, and intelligent; versatile leading man; mesmerizing screen presence; singer; stagecraft; producer; director; writer; composer; social and environmental activist.

When the courtroom drama *Primal Fear* (1996) was released, twenty-seven-year-old Yale University history graduate Edward Norton was a regionally known theater actor with the Signature Players, a New York company set up to produce Edward Albee's plays; he still serves as a board director. Thus acclaimed, he blew audiences away as Aaron Stampler, an altar boy accused of killing a Catholic bishop. An Academy Award nomination for Best Supporting Actor followed, opening the door to roles as the love-struck Holden Spence opposite Drew Barrymore in Woody Allen's musical comedy *Everyone Says I Love You* (1996) and a lawyer in Milos Forman's *The People vs. Larry Flynt* (1996); but the essential Norton was already on display, charming and boyish, solicitous even, while also cold-blooded and smarter than everyone else.

A challenging actor, he electrified critics in *American History X* (1998), in which he beefed up to play a violent skinhead. The role won him his second Oscar nomination, this time for Best Actor. Now muscular and no longer bungling, he followed with David Fincher's *Fight Club* (1999), a *fin de siècle* masterstroke; made his directorial debut in the comedy *Keeping the Faith* (2000), which he also produced, cowrote, and starred in; appeared in the biopic *Frida* (2002); headlined *Red Dragon* (2002) and *25th Hour* (2002); and was a masked supporting player in *Kingdom of Heaven* (2005). He then went on to play a magician in early-1900s Vienna in *The Illusionist* (2006), showing he can turn his hand to costume drama. Norton is the type of actor who is choosy about roles, strict about preparation, and at times difficult to work with; yet it is a small price to pay for the leading talent of his generation, a chameleon with an eye for great projects. **GCQ**

Top Takes...

The Illusionist 2006
Kingdom of Heaven 2005
The Italian Job 2003
25th Hour 2002
Red Dragon 2002
Frida 2002
Death to Smoochy 2002
The Score 2001
Catch Her in the Eye 2001
Keeping the Faith 2000
Fight Club 1999
American History X 1998 ☆
Rounders 1998
Everyone Says I Love You 1996
The People vs. Larry Flynt 1996
Primal Fear 1996 ☆

"People wrestle sometimes making movies, and I think that conflict is a very essential thing."

1960s

CATHERINE ZETA-JONES

Born: Catherine Jones, September 25, 1969 (Swansea, West Glamorgan, Wales).

Star qualities: Sexy, voluptuous beauty; glamorous; long dark hair; exotic looks; leading lady of dramas and musicals; dancer; singer; married into a Hollywood acting dynasty.

Top Takes...

The Legend of Zorro 2005
Ocean's Twelve 2004
The Terminal 2004
Intolerable Cruelty 2003
Sinbad: Legend of the Seven Seas 2003
Chicago 2002 ★
America's Sweethearts 2001
Traffic 2000
High Fidelity 2000
The Haunting 1999
Entrapment 1999
The Mask of Zorro 1998
The Phantom 1996
Blue Juice 1995
Christopher Columbus: The Discovery 1992

An almost otherworldly beauty shadows her early work, but with *Chicago* (2002) Catherine Zeta-Jones demonstrated more than a two-dimensional ability to model clothes and motivate male costars. Her role as Velma Kelly also won her an Oscar as Best Supporting Actress. That it took an integrated musical, a complicated and heavily pedigreed Broadway vehicle at that, instead of an adventure or conventional drama, to showcase her versatility is a problem concerning the kinds of roles offered to women in movies—an old complaint. Yet it's interesting to note what a brilliant singer and dancer Zeta-Jones really is when remembering that her earliest fame rested on being Antonio Banderas's moll in *The Mask of Zorro* (1998) or Sean Connery's erotic charge in *Entrapment* (1999).

Zeta-Jones was interested in a stage career from an early age, and trained as a singer and dancer, going on to find parts in musicals in London's West End. She first came to public attention in the early 1990s when she starred in the British TV series *The Darling Buds of May* (1991). For gossip hounds, her marriage to actor Michael Douglas in 2000 (prenuptial agreement included) is a gold mine of speculative May-to-December fantasies writ large with globe-trotting superstars.

But Zeta-Jones has done more than just sing, dance, marry well, and procreate. She's been an ice queen in *High Fidelity* (2000), a spokesperson for cell phones and Elizabeth Arden cosmetics, a gold digger in *Intolerable Cruelty* (2003), and an Interpol officer with a soft spot for con men in *Ocean's Twelve* (2004). Perhaps most surprising, though, is her perfomance as a pregnant drug lord's wife in *Traffic* (2000). She depicts a kind of evil rarely put on screen: Mom as pragmatist, at once cold-blooded, calculating, and fertile. **GCQ**

"I wish I was born in that era: dancing with Fred Astaire and Gene Kelly."

UMA THURMAN

Born: Uma Karuna Thurman, April 29, 1970 (Boston, Massachusetts, U.S.).

Star qualities: Very tall; exquisite beauty; model; sex symbol; leading lady of dramas and comedies; one-time muse of cult director Quentin Tarantino; producer; writer.

Uma Thurman started out as a fashion model at the age of sixteen. Tall, blonde, and slim, she soon found success and was even a cover girl on *Rolling Stone* magazine in 1989. Such goddess looks helped when she stepped nude out of a half shell as Venus in *The Adventures of Baron Munchausen* (1988). She was then porcelain pretty as the innocent in *Dangerous Liaisons* (1988) and Maid Marian in *Robin Hood* (1991). Showing spirit in half-title roles in *Henry & June* (1990) and *Mad Dog and Glory* (1993), she began to appear in disasters with the big-thumbed hitchhiker of *Even Cowgirls Get the Blues* (1993), compounded by terrible impressions of Julie Newmar and Diana Rigg when cast as Poison Ivy in *Batman & Robin* (1997) and Emma Peel in *The Avengers* (1998).

This was disappointing following her cool dance moves with John Travolta—a wry nod to *Saturday Night Fever* (1977)—combined with a dramatic overdose scene that enlivened Quentin Tarantino's *Pulp Fiction* (1994). Her sexy performance and bewigged appearance had elevated her to stardom and also won her an Oscar nomination for Best Supporting Actress. She returned to Tarantino's world, with some success, as a maternal killing machine in *Kill Bill: Vol. 1* (2003) and its sequel.

Otherwise, Thurman has been as adventurous as a beautiful blonde actress can be. She was the dim bulb model of *The Truth About Cats & Dogs* (1996), the artificially perfect human of *Gattaca* (1997), a nasty woman in *Sweet and Lowdown* (1999), and the third act surprise of *Tape* (2001). With talent to spare, her recent clutch of underwhelming credits such as *Be Cool* (2005), *Prime* (2005), *The Producers* (2005), and *My Super Ex-Girlfriend* (2006) are, it is hoped, a mere blip. **KN**

Top Takes...

The Producers 2005
Prime 2005
Be Cool 2005
Kill Bill: Vol. 2 2004
Paycheck 2003
Kill Bill: Vol. 1 2003
Tape 2001
Sweet and Lowdown 1999
Gattaca 1997
Batman & Robin 1997
The Truth About Cats & Dogs 1996
Beautiful Girls 1996
Pulp Fiction 1994 ☆
Mad Dog and Glory 1993
Henry & June 1990
Dangerous Liaisons 1988

"Tall, sandy blonde, with sort of blue eyes, skinny in places, fat in others. An average gal."

1970s

RIVER PHOENIX

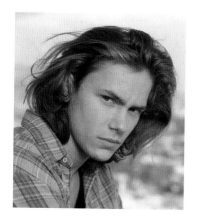

Born: River Jude Bottom, August 23, 1970 (Madras, Oregon, U.S.); died 1993 (Hollywood, California, U.S.).

Star qualities: Child actor; leading man of cult movies; often played rebellious roles; transcendent screen presence; songwriter; guitarist; environmentalist.

Top Takes…

Silent Tongue 1994
The Thing Called Love 1993
Sneakers 1992
Dogfight 1991
My Own Private Idaho 1991
I Love You to Death 1990
Indiana Jones and the Last Crusade 1989
Running on Empty 1988 ☆
Little Nikita 1988
A Night in the Life of Jimmy Reardon 1988
The Mosquito Coast 1986
Stand by Me 1986
Explorers 1985

"I would rather quit while I was ahead. There's no need in overstaying your welcome."

RIGHT: Giving a touching performance as the street hustler in *My Own Private Idaho*.

River Phoenix was born River Bottom to parents who were members of the Children of God sect. The family lived in South America when Phoenix was a child, before returning to the United States in 1977 and changing their surname to "Phoenix." His parents encouraged their children to get into movies, and by the age of ten, he was acting on TV. He became a superb child actor who showed major promise as an adult star before his premature death from a drug-induced heart attack.

After TV credits including the *ABC Afterschool Specials* episode "Backwards: The Riddle of Dyslexia" (1984), Phoenix made his movie debut in Joe Dante's *Explorers* (1985), then impressed as the doomed leader of the gang of young friends in Rob Reiner's *Stand by Me* (1986) and the teen with mixed priorities in *A Night in the Life of Jimmy Reardon* (1988).

Given his background, Phoenix brought a lot of personal energy to the rebel sons of nonconformist parents in *The Mosquito Coast* (1986) and *Running on Empty* (1988), which earned him an Academy Award nomination as Best Supporting Actor. After a lone fun role as the Young Indy in *Indiana Jones and the Last Crusade* (1989), he was exceptional as the narcoleptic hustler smitten with Keanu Reeves in *My Own Private Idaho* (1991), and the draftee who picks up Lily Taylor for a bet in *Dogfight* (1991). His last completed films were *The Thing Called Love* (1993) and *Silent Tongue* (1994); on his death 11 days before the scheduled completion date, the half-finished *Dark Blood* (1993) was abandoned. He died at the age of only twenty-three outside the Viper Room, a Los Angeles club then owned by actor Johnny Depp. He was the brother of actors Joaquin Phoenix, Summer Phoenix, Rain Phoenix, and Liberty Phoenix. **KN**

MATT DAMON

Born: Matthew Paige Damon, October 8, 1970 (Cambridge, Massachusetts, U.S.).

Star qualities: Hollywood golden boy; handsome, clean-cut, all-American looks; versatile leading man; intelligent; physically fit; ambitious; committed; varied choice of roles; producer; director.

Top Takes...

Born in Cambridge, Massachusetts, Matt Damon's film debut came in *Mystic Pizza* (1988), with a small role alongside the similarly nascent star Julia Roberts. Steady success with minor roles led him to leave Harvard University just shy of graduation, a gamble that paid off with well-received parts in movies such as *Courage Under Fire* (1996), as a heroin-addicted Gulf War veteran. Yet it was *Good Will Hunting* (1997), which he wrote and costarred in with friend and fellow actor Ben Affleck, that gave him stardom and won him an Oscar for Best Original Screenplay. He was also nominated for Best Actor.

In the wake of that movie's success, Damon and Affleck produced, with mixed results, the TV program *Project Greenlight* (2001), a documentary series that awarded inexperienced filmmakers a chance to make it big in the independent film world. Damon still worked on a number of critically praised and commercially rewarded films, including *Saving Private Ryan* (1998) and *The Talented Mr. Ripley* (1999). He also took part in smaller films for respected filmmakers such as Steven Soderbergh, Kevin Smith, Gus Van Sant, and Terry Gilliam. As Jason Bourne, the amnesiac trained killer on the run, he entered blockbuster territory with *The Bourne Identity* (2002) and its sequel *The Bourne Supremacy* (2004). He then revisited the independent realm with *Syriana* (2005), playing a conflicted business consultant and starring alongside George Clooney, with whom he worked on *Ocean's Eleven* (2001) and its sequel, and who directed him in *Confessions of a Dangerous Mind* (2002). Given that Damon often flips between good and bad-guy roles, he played his ideal role as Colin Sullivan, the undercover criminal posing as a cop in Martin Scorsese's thriller *The Departed* (2006). **JK**

"I never wanted to go that [safe] route. If I go down, I'm going down swinging."

EWAN McGREGOR

Born: Ewan Gordon McGregor, March 31, 1971 (Crieff, Perthshire, Scotland).

Star qualities: Rugged good looks; leading man of dramas and action movies; sexy Scottish voice; winning charm; light-saber swordsmanship; avid motorcyclist; singer; producer; director.

Scotsman Ewan McGregor followed in the footsteps of his uncle, actor Dennis Lawson, and studied acting at London's Guildhall School of Music and Drama. But he left before graduation to have his first taste of success at the age of twenty-two in Dennis Potter's British TV miniseries *Lipstick on Your Collar* (1993). The role won him admirers and led to Danny Boyle's *Shallow Grave* (1994), which carried him through the world art theater circuit. Then Boyle's *Trainspotting* (1996) put McGregor firmly on the map as Renton, an Edinburgh druggie trying to get straight. With that performance, at once desperate, charming, dirty, and sad, he demonstrated a vulnerability that would be useful in other circumstances.

In the United States he worked in the Jane Austen adaptation *Emma* (1996) and the comedy *Brassed Off* (1996), played an impressive guest role on TV's *ER* (1997), and finished the 1990s with two gems, *Little Voice* (1998) and *Velvet Goldmine* (1998), on the way to gargantuan exposure. For in 1999, McGregor took on Obi-Wan Kenobi, first made famous by Sir Alec Guinness, and witnessed the rejuvenation of the *Star Wars* franchise in *Star Wars: Episode I—The Phantom Menace* (1999), *Star Wars: Episode II—Attack of the Clones* (2002), and *Star Wars: Episode III—Revenge of the Sith* (2005). Along the way he proved able to sing, opposite Nicole Kidman in *Moulin Rouge!* (2001), and proved flexible inside an ensemble in the war movie *Black Hawk Down* (2001), comical in *Down with Love* (2003), and circumspect in *Big Fish* (2003).

McGregor is married with three children. He recently rode a motorcycle around the world with his actor friend Charley Boorman. The pair filmed their trip, making it into a TV documentary series, *Long Way Round* (2004). **GCQ**

Top Takes...

Miss Potter 2006
The Island 2005
Big Fish 2003
Young Adam 2003
Down with Love 2003
Black Hawk Down 2001
Moulin Rouge! 2001
Star Wars: Episodes I–III 1999, 2002, 2005
Rogue Trader 1999
Little Voice 1998
Velvet Goldmine 1998
A Life Less Ordinary 1997
Brassed Off 1996
Emma 1996
Trainspotting 1996
Shallow Grave 1994

> "I've been waiting nearly 20 years to have my own light saber. Nothing's cooler."

GWYNETH PALTROW

Born: Gwyneth Kate Paltrow, September 27, 1972 (Los Angeles, California, U.S.).

Star qualities: Svelte; tall; versatile leading lady of dramas; frequently plays geeky roles; delicate beauty; indefatigable work ethic; celebrity marriage; stagecraft; model; director; writer.

Top Takes...

Running with Scissors 2006

Proof 2005

Sky Captain and the World of Tomorrow 2004

Sylvia 2003

View from the Top 2003

Shallow Hal 2001

The Royal Tenenbaums 2001

Bounce 2000

Duets 2000

The Talented Mr. Ripley 1999

Shakespeare in Love 1998 ★

Great Expectations 1998

Sliding Doors 1998

Emma 1996

Se7en 1995

Jefferson in Paris 1995

The daughter of actress Blythe Danner and movie producer Bruce Paltrow, Gwyneth Paltrow was born in Los Angeles. After attending the Spence School in New York, she moved to California, where she went to the University of California in Santa Barbara, majoring in art history. She soon left, realizing that she wanted to follow her mother on to the stage. And she did so, literally, and began acting in the Williamstown Theatre play *Picnic*, with her mother. A few small roles led to a haunting, harrowing, supporting turn in *Se7en* (1995) alongside Brad Pitt, with whom she became romantically linked at the time. Her title role of Emma Woodhouse in the Jane Austen adaptation *Emma* (1996) and *Sliding Doors* (1998) revealed her abilities with a British accent and, along with countless independent films, her indefatigable work ethic. That hard work paid off with her being cast as Viola in *Shakespeare in Love* (1998), for which Paltrow was awarded the Best Actress Oscar.

After a quirky performance as a depressed writer in Wes Anderson's *The Royal Tenenbaums* (2001), and a sentimental comedic lead in *Shallow Hal* (2001), as well as a very public relationship and breakup with actor Ben Affleck, Paltrow's work schedule slowed considerably as she focused on other endeavors: namely, new boyfriend Chris Martin, lead singer of the British rock band Coldplay. The couple live in London, where she pursues a detoxified lifestyle and is a fan of yoga. Their romance and subsequent marriage overshadowed the release of films such as *View from the Top* (2003), *Sylvia* (2003), and *Proof* (2005), as did the birth of her two children, Apple and Moses, but ignore any threats of early retirement. An actress of Paltrow's considerable talents should never be counted out. **JK**

> "I'd rather not have a big house ... [but] a body of work that I'm proud of."

TADANOBU ASANO

Born: Tadanobu Satô, November 27, 1973 (Yokohama, Kanagawa, Japan).

Star qualities: Handsome; versatile leading man of Japanese contemporary cinema; charismatic; cool; trendy; laconic style; punk rock musician; artist; model; composer; director.

If the essence of a genuine movie star is defined by a specific mixture of natural physical beauty, acting talent, and that certain enigmatic extra ingredient of charismatic presence on camera, then Tadanobu Asano could be the perfect representative of this ideal. Asano is contemporary Japanese cinema's hottest leading man and one of today's most magnetic world film figures.

His father, an actors' agent, suggested he take on what became his first role, in the TV series *San-nen B-gumi Kinpachi sensei 3* (1988), at the age of sixteen. He went on to make his film debut in *Bataashi kingyo* (1990) (*Swimming Upstream*). Today Asano is Japan's equivalent to a Johnny Depp or Leonardo DiCaprio; he has their looks and style, but not their Method intensity. He is someone who considers himself more of a musician and artist than an actor, and is in a punk band with his frequent director Sogo Ishii. Asano has a laid-back, laconic slacker quality that is contemporary and hypnotic even in hyper-violent fare such as *Koroshiya 1* (2001) (*Ichi the Killer*) or samurai period pieces such as *Gohatto* (1999) (*Taboo*), *Zatôichi* (2003) (*The Blind Swordsman: Zatoichi*), and Ishii's *Gojo reisenki: Gojoe* (2000) (*Gojoe: Spirit War Chronicle*). Although appropriately melancholy in somber dramatic work, notably *Vital* (2004), Asano also has an understated, dry wit. This has permeated some of his most offbeat roles: surrealist comedies along the lines of the brilliant *Survive Style 5+* (2004), and the indescribable *Naisu no mori: The First Contact* (2005) (*Funky Forest: The First Contact*). Projects such as these are another defining mark of Asano's prolific career: he adopts roles that no other star of his caliber would accept, making his career all the more fascinating. **TC**

Top Takes...

Invisible Waves 2006
Rampo jigoku 2005 (*Rampo Noir*)
Naisu no mori: The First Contact 2005
    (*Funky Forest: The First Contact*)
Takeshis' 2005
Umoregi 2005 (*The Buried Forest*)
Survive Style 5+ 2004
Tori 2004
Vital 2004
Cha no aji 2004 (*The Taste of Tea*)
Zatôichi 2003 (*The Blind Swordsman: Zatoichi*)
Koroshiya 1 2001 (*Ichi the Killer*)
Gojo reisenki: Gojoe 2000
Gohatto 1999 (*Taboo*)
Maboroshi no hikari 1995
Bataashi kingyo 1990 (*Swimming Upstream*)

"If you're going to give someone pain, you've got to get into it!"

—Kakihara, *Ichi the Killer*

1970s

PENÉLOPE CRUZ

Born: Penélope Cruz Sánchez, April 28, 1974 (Madrid, Spain).

Star qualities: Pretty, dark-eyed leading lady of Spanish cinema; multilingual; jazz and ballet dancer; humanitarian; frequent collaborator with Spanish director Pedro Almodóvar.

Top Takes...

Volver 2006 (*To Return*) ☆
Bandidas 2006
Sahara 2005
Non ti muovere 2004 (*Don't Move*)
Gothika 2003
Vanilla Sky 2001
Captain Corelli's Mandolin 2001
Blow 2001
All the Pretty Horses 2000
Todo sobre mi madre 1999
  (*All About My Mother*)
Abre los ojos 1997 (*Open Your Eyes*)
Carne trémula 1997 (*Live Flesh*)
Belle epoque 1992 (*The Age of Beauty*)
Jamón, jamón 1992
  (*A Tale of Ham and Passion*)

"In Spain, actresses work until they are old. That's my plan."

The daughter of a retailer and a hairdresser, as a youngster, Madrid-born Penélope Cruz did nine years of classic ballet training at the Conservatorio Nacional in Madrid, four years of dance performance with several dance courses at the Cristina Rota School in New York, and three years of Spanish Ballet with Ángela Garrido. She also had jazz dance courses with Raúl Caballero. She then landed work in TV and music videos.

Her early movie career saw her in well-received supporting roles, such as Bigas Luna's quirky *Jamón, jamón* (1992) (*A Tale of Ham and Passion*), for which she won Spain's highly acclaimed Goya award, and Pedro Almodóvar's BAFTA-nominated *Carne trémula* (1997) (*Live Flesh*). Her star now on the rise, working again with Almodóvar, it was her more prominent role in *Todo sobre mi madre* (1999) (*All About My Mother*) that brought her wider public acclaim when it won an Academy Award for Best Foreign Language Film.

Hollywood beckoned, and her style of raw, naive characterizations combined with a gentle Latin beauty ensured a flurry of high-profile support roles in quick succession, starring opposite some of the industry's leading male stars such as Johnny Depp in *Blow* (2001), Nicolas Cage in *Captain Corelli's Mandolin* (2001), and Tom Cruise in *Vanilla Sky* (2001). Yet despite box-office success, her Hollywood roles have tended to be steady rather than spectacular, and it was her high-profile romance with Cruise that first brought her to the attention of U.S. audiences. Working again with Almodóvar in her native Spain has enabled Cruz to break out of the supporting actress mold, playing the lead in *Volver* (2006) (*To Return*), for which she won the Best Actress Award at the Cannes Film Festival. **RH**

HILARY SWANK

Born: Hilary Ann Swank, July 30, 1974 (Bellingham, Washington, U.S.).

Star qualities: Striking, dark-haired beauty; warm smile; takes on brave roles in artistic films that challenge her mentally and physically; hardworking and down to earth; clean living; athletic.

It's one of Hollywood's wonderful ironies that the story of Hilary Swank's rise to the rank of movie star would itself probably make for a good film. Born in 1974 and raised in the Pacific Northwest, Swank moved to Los Angeles while still a teenager, briefly living with her mother out of a car as her acting career progressed in fits and starts. Inevitably, that meant small television parts, followed by a starring role in *The Next Karate Kid* (1994), and a doomed casting as a single mother in the TV series *Beverly Hills, 90210* (1997–1998). But if such jobs were safe and predictable steps toward success, Swank's performance in *Boys Don't Cry* (1999) as a young woman pretending to be a young man was anything but. The actress earned near unanimous acclaim for her courageous performance, including the Best Actress Oscar, and suddenly, at the age of just twenty-five, Swank was transformed from struggling nobody to Next Big Thing.

A series of strong roles and performances followed, many outshining the movies they were in and all revealing Swank as someone who has thought quite a bit about how she would like her career to proceed. Indeed, she won a second Academy Award for her performance as doomed boxer Maggie Fitzgerald in Clint Eastwood's *Million Dollar Baby* (2004), a demanding role for which she had to undergo intensive physical training and gain substantial weight in muscle. She has since used her Oscar cachet as leverage to pursue more personal projects, including a rare performance as a femme fatale in *The Black Dahlia* (2006). If a public divorce from her husband of eight years, Chad Lowe, proved a rare setback, Swank, barely in her thirties, seems to have set herself up for a long and fruitful life in pictures. **JK**

Top Takes...

The Reaping 2007
Freedom Writers 2007
The Black Dahlia 2006
Million Dollar Baby 2004 ★
Red Dust 2004
The Affair of the Necklace 2001
The Gift 2000
The Audition 2000
Boys Don't Cry 1999 ★
The Next Karate Kid 1994

> "My most annoying question is 'Hilary, are you ever going to play a pretty girl?'"

1970s

LEONARDO DiCAPRIO

Born: Leonardo Wilhelm DiCaprio, November 11, 1974 (Hollywood, California, U.S.).

Star qualities: Tall, blond, blue-eyed, slim, handsome heartthrob; baby-faced beauty; teen pinup; versatile leading man of dramas; not afraid to take on adventurous roles; environmental campaigner; writer; producer.

Top Takes...

"Portraying emotionally ill characters gives me the chance to really act."

His starring role in the epic blockbuster *Titanic* (1997), still the highest grossing film of all time, made him an international icon, but Leonardo DiCaprio had been steadily working up to that success with a number of well-received, risky roles. Born in Los Angeles, of Italian and German descent, DiCaprio's father was a distributor of comic books and his mother a legal secretary. He was called "Leonardo" because his pregnant mother was viewing a Leonardo da Vinci painting at a museum in Italy when she felt her baby kick; she decided to name the baby "Leonardo" after the famous artist.

DiCaprio got his first big break on TV, with a recurring role as a homeless boy on *Growing Pains* (1991–1992) before appearing in a number of acclaimed independent films, including *What's Eating Gilbert Grape* (1993) alongside Johnny Depp, and *This Boy's Life* (1993) with Robert De Niro, the former earning him an Academy Award nomination for Best Supporting Actor at just nineteen years old.

The stylishly reimagined Shakespeare adaptation *Romeo + Juliet* (1996) made DiCaprio a pinup, but *Titanic* pushed his profile over the top; he half spoofed his own stardom in a small role in Woody Allen's *Celebrity* (1998) before taking some time off, focusing on environmental causes and developing various projects. DiCaprio reemerged in Danny Boyle's adaptation of Alex Garland's best seller *The Beach* (2000), which was poorly received. He has worked with some of Hollywood's biggest directors, including Steven Spielberg on *Catch Me If You Can* (2002), and most notably Martin Scorsese on a trio of films, *Gangs of New York* (2002), *The Aviator* (2004), and *The Departed* (2006). DiCaprio recently garnered his third Oscar Best Actor nomination for *Blood Diamond* (2006). **JK**

DREW BARRYMORE

Born: Drew Blyth Barrymore, February 22, 1975 (Culver City, California, U.S.).

Star qualities: Blonde beauty; child actress; member of an acting dynasty; leading lady of dramas and romantic comedies; comic timing; approachable demeanor; director; model; producer; writer.

Drew Blyth Barrymore is heiress to an acting dynasty dating back more than 150 years, and her father is the late legendary actor John Drew Barrymore. Her godfather is director Steven Spielberg, and her godmother Italian actress Sophia Loren. She made her film debut in *Altered States* (1980), but achieved prominence as the wide-eyed little sister in her godfather's *E.T. the Extra-Terrestrial* (1982). With this pedigree behind her, she became the youngest person ever to host the TV variety show *Saturday Night Live* (1982), performing a sketch where she killed the alien E.T. Barrymore also starred in the Stephen King adaptations *Firestarter* (1984) and *Cat's Eye* (1985) before her tenth birthday.

A troubled adolescence, reflected in the TV movie *15 and Getting Straight* (1989), seemed to file her with many child stars who foundered in later life. And in her autobiography, *Little Girl Lost* (1990), she reveals how she had an alcohol and drug habit while only a young teenager. But in her midteens, she took interesting roles as junior sociopaths in Katt Shea's *Poison Ivy* (1992) and Tamra Davis's *Guncrazy* (1992). Emerging as an adventurous actress, a blonde pinup, and full-grown star, she accomplished solid work in ensemble efforts such as *Bad Girls* (1994), *Boys on the Side* (1995), *Batman Forever* (1995), *Everyone Says I Love You* (1996), and memorably as the opening victim in the horror movie *Scream* (1996).

As she has matured, Barrymore has astutely alternated working on awards bids, such as *Riding in Cars with Boys* (2001), with populist romantic comedy leads, such as *The Wedding Singer* (1998) and *Music and Lyrics* (2007). She has also produced her own vehicles, including *Never Been Kissed* (1999), *Charlie's Angels* (2000), and *Donnie Darko* (2001). **KN**

Top Takes...

Music and Lyrics 2007
Fever Pitch 2005
50 First Dates 2004
Charlie's Angels: Full Throttle 2003
Confessions of a Dangerous Mind 2002
Riding in Cars with Boys 2001
Donnie Darko 2001
Charlie's Angels 2000
The Wedding Singer 1998
Scream 1996
Everyone Says I Love You 1996
Boys on the Side 1995
Bad Girls 1994
Guncrazy 1992
Cat's Eye 1985
E.T. the Extra-Terrestrial 1982

"In the end, some of your greatest pains become your greatest strengths."

1970s

ANGELINA JOLIE

Born: Angelina Jolie Voight, June 4, 1975 (Los Angeles, California, U.S.).

Star qualities: Curvaceous sex symbol; sultry beauty; big lips; controversial; love-hate relationship with the media; member of an acting family; half of a Hollywood celebrity couple; model; humanitarian.

Famous for her provocative behavior offscreen as well as her professional achievements, Angelina Jolie is the daughter of Marcheline Bertrand and actor Jon Voight, who divorced when she was just one year old. Her interest in acting began as a child when, at the age of seven, she appeared in *Lookin' to Get Out* (1982), starring Voight; she later trained at the Lee Strasberg Theater Institute.

Her earliest major film was *Hackers* (1995), at which time she met her first husband and costar, Johnny Lee Miller. Jolie's best accolade came when she won an Oscar for Best Supporting Actress for her portrayal of a psychiatric hospital inmate in *Girl, Interrupted* (1999). Her leading role as the video-game heroine in the blockbuster *Lara Croft* movies (2001, 2003) included a minor role for her father, from whom Jolie has since become estranged, blaming his infidelities for her parents' divorce.

Her second marriage, to actor Billy Bob Thornton in 2000, ended in divorce in 2003. Undeterred, Jolie went on to have a romance with another costar, Brad Pitt, with whom she filmed the comedy *Mr. and Mrs. Smith* (2005). Whether the romance began on set or after, it hit the headlines worldwide, given that Pitt was then married to actress Jennifer Aniston. The divorced Pitt now has a daughter with Jolie, born in 2006. While working in Cambodia on *Lara Croft: Tomb Raider* (2001), Jolie became an advocate for the world's underprivileged. She was named a Goodwill Ambassador by the United Nations High Commissioner for Refugees in 2001. She also has three adopted children. Although Jolie is famous for her humanitarian efforts, she has attracted attention for her troubled childhood, her feuds with her father, her attraction to men and women, and her flamboyant tattoos. **RU**

Top Takes...

The Good Shepherd 2006
Mr. & Mrs. Smith 2005
Alexander 2004
The Fever 2004
Sky Captain and the World of Tomorrow 2004
Shark Tale 2004
Taking Lives 2004
Lara Croft Tomb Raider: The Cradle of Life 2003
Life or Something Like It 2002
Original Sin 2001
Lara Croft: Tomb Raider 2001
Gone in Sixty Seconds 2000
Girl, Interrupted 1999 ★
The Bone Collector 1999
Pushing Tin 1999
Hackers 1995

"If I make a fool of myself, who cares? I'm not frightened by anyone's perception of me."

1970s

KATE WINSLET

Born: Kate Elizabeth Winslet, October 5, 1975 (Reading, Berkshire, England).

Star qualities: Child actress; glowing, natural beauty of an English rose; part of an acting family; leading lady of dramas who excels in costume roles; passionate and gutsy actress; eclectic choice of roles.

Kate Winslet comes from a family of actors: her parents, grandparents, and uncle all spent their lives on the stage. She took acting classes as a child, and became a well-spoken, bright-eyed child actress in BBC TV series such as *Dark Season* (1991) and *Casualty* (1993), before director Peter Jackson cast her as Juliet Hulme, one half of the murderous yet innocent teen duo of *Heavenly Creatures* (1994).

She then became a fixture in corset roles in literary adaptations such as Marianne Dashwood in *Sense and Sensibility* (1995), which won her an Academy Award nomination for Best Supporting Actress; Sue Bridehead in *Jude* (1996); and Ophelia in *Hamlet* (1996). Then director James Cameron gave her the full, old movie star entrance, under a fabulous hat, as the leading lady opposite the baby-faced Leonardo DiCaprio in the box-office smash hit *Titanic* (1997). It won her a second Oscar nod, this time for Best Actress.

Being in the most successful film of all time didn't derail Winslet, although she started playing louder, less victimized ladies such as the lead, Iris Murdoch, in the biopic *Iris* (2001), which won her another Oscar nomination for Best Supporting Actress. She also turned to playing an odd, irresponsible, kooky hippie in *Hideous Kinky* (1998), among more costume dramas such as *Quills* (2000).

She is at her best in a very complex role in *Eternal Sunshine of the Spotless Mind* (2004), playing a woman fascinating enough to fall for but irritating enough to need wiping from the memory. The performance won her another Oscar nomination. She received her fifth, and most recent, Oscar nomination for *Little Children* (2006). Winslet's many admirers eagerly anticipate the time when she finally takes home the well-deserved statuette. **KN**

Top Takes...

Little Children **2006** ☆
Romance & Cigarettes 2005
Finding Neverland 2004
Eternal Sunshine of the Spotless Mind **2004** ☆
The Life of David Gale 2003
Iris **2001** ☆
Enigma 2001
Quills 2000
Holy Smoke 1999
Hideous Kinky 1998
Titanic **1997** ☆
Hamlet 1996
Jude 1996
Sense and Sensibility **1995** ☆
Heavenly Creatures 1994

"After each movie, I always think, how different can I possibly be?"

REESE WITHERSPOON

Born: Laura Jeanne Reese Witherspoon, March 22, 1976 (New Orleans, Louisiana, U.S.).

Star qualities: Pretty; fresh-faced; long blonde hair; blue-eyed Southern belle; all-American appeal; leading lady of dramas and comedies; vivacious; intelligent; singer; producer.

Top Takes...

Penelope 2006
Just Like Heaven 2005
Walk the Line 2005 ★
Vanity Fair 2004
Legally Blonde 2: Red, White & Blonde 2003
Sweet Home Alabama 2002
The Importance of Being Earnest 2002
Legally Blonde 2001
The Trumpet of the Swan 2001
Little Nicky 2000
American Psycho 2000
Best Laid Plans 1999
Election 1999
Cruel Intentions 1999
Pleasantville 1998
The Man in the Moon 1991

"You're never going to win the pretty race. I just want to be the best version of myself."

With her shiny blue eyes and button nose, Reese Witherspoon has the sparkling cuteness of an escaped child automaton from a Disney theme park ride. Her looks might have spelled terminal mediocrity for the career of a less-talented actress, but Witherspoon wields her features with such confidence and precision in otherwise futile films such as *Freeway* (1996) that it allowed her to become, by 2006, both the highest-paid actress in Hollywood and one of the most acclaimed.

Witherspoon's father is a surgeon, and her mother a nurse and college professor. Young Reese spent the first four years of her life in Wiesbaden, Germany, where her father was a lieutenant colonel in the U.S. army reserves. After this, the family returned to the United States to settle in Nashville, Tennessee. Witherspoon started acting classes at a community college at the age of seven, and was educated at elite schools, followed by Stanford University as a literature major.

She first caught Hollywood's eye at the age of fourteen with her remarkable performance in *The Man in the Moon* (1991). Subsequent roles ranged widely across comedic and dramatic terrain, including *Pleasantville* (1998), *Election* (1999), and *Legally Blonde* (2001). All of which were set in restrictive regimes—a 1950s sitcom, a high school, and an Ivy League university—that she injected with bubbling vitality. Her portrayal of country music singer June Carter Cash in the musical biopic of Johnny Cash, *Walk the Line* (2005), in which she did her own singing, won her the Oscar for Best Actress. It signified how Witherspoon had entered the public imagination as an icon of independent modern womanhood. Offscreen, she has two children with her ex-husband, actor Ryan Phillippe. **EM**

AUDREY TAUTOU

Born: Audrey Tautou, August 9, 1976 (Beaumont, Puy-de-Dôme, France).

Star qualities: Petite, gamine leading lady of French cinema; natural fresh-faced beauty; dark curly hair; arched eyebrows; waiflike charm; beguiling screen presence.

Audrey Tautou is Amélie Poulain, and Amélie Poulain is Audrey Tautou. Strong identification with a single role can be a blessing or a curse, but early evidence suggests that Tautou might be one of the lucky ones, equally at home in the grimly realistic *Dirty Pretty Things* (2002) as in the stylized world of Alain Resnais's musical pastiche *Pas sur la bouche* (2003) (*Not on the Lips*). Certainly the confidence with which she tackled the female lead in her first Hollywood movie, *The Da Vinci Code* (2006), opposite Tom Hanks, is indicative of her versatility and determination, even if the movie itself was a disappointment.

Tautou studied at Paris's Cours Florent drama school. The romantic comedy *Le Fabuleux destin d'Amélie Poulain* (2001) (*Amélie*), director Jean-Pierre Jeunet's delightful, completely unexpected fable, now seems unimaginable without her. However, she was not the first choice and would never have got the part if Jeunet had not spotted her on a poster for *Vénus beauté (institut)* (1999) (*Venus Beauty Institute*), in which she gives an equally beguiling, and Best New Actress, César Award-winning performance.

A similar but more complex role in Jeunet's adaptation of a World War I novel by Sébastien Japrisot, *Un long dimanche de fiançailles* (2004) (*A Very Long Engagement*), helped underline her range, as Mathilde, a woman obsessed with finding her fiancé, Manech. He is one of five French soldiers who wound themselves to escape the fighting on the Somme and are abandoned in no-man's-land as a punishment. Her natural innocence and elfin charm were also cleverly deployed to delay realization that her character is mentally ill and extremely dangerous in *À la folie... pas du tout* (2002) (*He Loves Me... He Loves Me Not*). **MC**

Top Takes...

The Da Vinci Code 2006
Les Poupées russes 2005 (*The Russian Dolls*)
Un long dimanche de fiançailles 2004
  (*A Very Long Engagement*)
Nowhere to Go But Up 2003
Pas sur la bouche 2003 (*Not on the Lips*)
Dirty Pretty Things 2002
L'Auberge espagnole 2002
  (*The Spanish Apartment*)
À la folie... pas du tout 2002
  (*He Loves Me... He Loves Me Not*)
Dieu est grand, je suis toute petite 2001
  (*God Is Great, I'm Not*)
Le Fabuleux destin d'Amélie Poulain 2001
  (*Amélie*)
Vénus beauté (institut) 1999
  (*Venus Beauty Institute*)

"I certainly don't want to be in Thingy Blah Blah III, if you know what I mean."

1970s

ZIYI ZHANG

Born: Ziyi Zhang, February 9, 1979 (Beijing, China).

Star qualities: Petite, elegant beauty; long hair; pouting lips; sexy leading lady of Asian and international cinema; erotic screen presence; athletic grace; model; dancer; singer.

Top Takes...

The daughter of an economist father and teacher mother, Ziyi Zhang graduated from the Central Drama Academy, the top acting college in China, after a stint at Beijing Dance Academy. She has only a handful of pictures to her credit, and several of them are quite good: *Wo de fu qin mu qin* (1999) (*The Road Home*), *Wo hu cang long* (2000) (*Crouching Tiger, Hidden Dragon*), and *Ying xiong* (2002) (*Hero*). Some of them are less so, such as *Rush Hour 2* (2001) and *Memoirs of a Geisha* (2005), and some of them are noble and fascinating misfires, such as *Operetta tanuki goten* (2005) (*Princess Raccoon*) and *Shi mian mai fu* (2004) (*House of Flying Daggers*). It's still quite a career to pack in to only a few years, and Zhang is probably contemporary cinema's most internationally famous and popular Chinese actress. She is also extremely beautiful, although perhaps no more so than other Chinese actresses in recent memory.

Zhang is every bit the movie star today. But does she have the acting credentials to go with it? Her range has largely been limited so far. She has been pouting and scowling ferociously in action fare, and often little more than decorative in period piece films, but there is definite promise. Look no further than *2046* (2004). It is Kar Wai Wong's follow-up to *Fa yeung nin wa* (2000) (*In the Mood for Love*) and is not one of his stronger works, but he always brings out the best in his actresses, and Zhang is no exception. In Wong's film, Zhang finally becomes an emotionally rich, confident woman, rather than the girl-playing-woman she has so often appeared to be. Elegant and surprisingly erotic, Zhang illuminates every scene she is in, stealing the film from some of her more experienced costars. Good for her, and one hopes she continues down this character-driven path. **TC**

> "I still don't think of myself as a Hollywood actress."

NATALIE PORTMAN

Born: Natalie Hershlag, June 9, 1981 (Jerusalem, Israel).

Star qualities: Petite dark-haired beauty; child actress who successfully made the transition to adult actress; dancer; stagecraft; model; intelligent; leading lady of dramas and action movies.

Natalie Portman was born in Israel, but her family moved to the United States when she was three years old. She started taking dancing lessons at the age of four, and spent her school holidays at theater camps. She stood out in a striking debut as the twelve-year-old nymphet waif semi-adopted by an emotionally damaged hit man in Luc Besson's *Léon* (1994). Obviously a talent, Portman was featured in increasingly prominent daughter roles in *Heat* (1995), *Beautiful Girls* (1996), *Everyone Says I Love You* (1996), *Mars Attacks!* (1996), in which she was very funny as a wry presidential daughter, and *Anywhere But Here* (1999).

George Lucas cast her as Queen Padmé Amidala, eventual mother of twins Luke Skywalker and Princess Leia Organa, in *Star Wars: Episode I—The Phantom Menace* (1999). The movie and its sequel gave Portman bizarre hairstyles and costumes, and let her grow up in public before her character died in childbirth in *Star Wars: Episode III—Revenge of the Sith* (2005), but it scarcely demanded much of her as an actress. Through this period she also appeared on Broadway and studied psychology at Harvard University. However, she took challenging roles as a pregnant teen in *Where the Heart Is* (2000); a U.S. Civil War survivor with a young child in *Cold Mountain* (2003); and a pole dancer at the heart of a love quadrangle in *Closer* (2004), which won her an Academy Award nomination for Best Supporting Actress. She was recently at sea with a shaved head in the comic-book dystopia of *V for Vendetta* (2005), and returned to Israel for *Free Zone* (2005), where she caused controversy by filming a kissing scene at Jerusalem's Western Wall. So much so that the scene was not included in the final release. **KN**

Top Takes...

The Other Boleyn Girl 2007
Goya's Ghosts 2006
Paris, je t'aime 2006
V for Vendetta 2005
Free Zone 2005
Domino One 2005
***Closer* 2004** ☆
Cold Mountain 2003
Where the Heart Is 2000
Anywhere But Here 1999
Star Wars: Episodes I–III 1999, 2002, 2005
Mars Attacks! 1996
Everyone Says I Love You 1996
Beautiful Girls 1996
Heat 1995
Léon 1994

"There's a big intellectual aspect that's kind of lacking [in acting]."

1980s

CONTRIBUTORS

Geoff Andrew (GA) is Head of Film Programme at London's National Film Theatre and Contributing Editor to *Time Out London* magazine. He has written a number of books on film, including studies of Nicholas Ray and the U.S. "indie" filmmakers of the 1980s and 1990s, and monographs on Kiarostami's *10* and Kieslowski's *Three Colours* trilogy.

Aleksandar Becanovic (AB) is a Montenegrin writer and film critic.

Edward Buscombe (EB) has written several books on the American Western and is Visiting Professor of Film at the University of Sunderland.

Garrett Chaffin-Quiray (GCQ) is a writer and teacher living in San Diego County.

Matthew Coniam (MC) is a freelance writer specializing in vintage cinema, culture, philosophy, science, and other disreputable topics.

Travis Crawford (TC) has served as a programmer for the Philadelphia Film Festival, and a contributing writer to such magazines as *Film Comment, Filmmaker, MovieMaker,* and *Fangoria.*

Wheeler Winston Dixon (WWD) is the James Ryan Endowed Professor of Film Studies, Professor of English at the University of Nebraska, Lincoln, and, with Gwendolyn Audrey Foster, Editor-in-Chief of the *Quarterly Review of Film and Video.*

Tim Evans (TE) is reviews editor for Skymovies.com. Born in London, he worked as a British Rail signals technician before becoming a journalist specializing in news and latterly film.

Matt Hills (MH) is a Reader in Media & Cultural Studies at Cardiff University, Wales, and author of *The Pleasures of Horror.*

Mark Holcomb (MH) writes about movies, books, and television for *Time Out New York* and *Las Vegas Weekly.* He lives in Brooklyn.

Russ Hunter (RH) is a Doctoral candidate at the University of Wales, Aberystwyth. He is currently researching the cross-cultural reception of the films of Dario Argento.

David Kalat (DK) is a film historian, author, and DVD producer with All Day Entertainment, an independent DVD label dedicated to "movies that fell through the cracks."

Philip Kemp (PK) is a freelance reviewer and film historian, a regular contributor to *Sight & Sound, Total Film,* and *DVD Review.* He teaches Film Journalism at Leicester and Middlesex Universities.

Carol King (CK) is a freelance writer and editor living in London. She fell in love with cinema on her first trip to the movies to see Disney's *Snow White.* She is a graduate in English Literature from the University of Sussex, and also studied Fine Art at Central St. Martin's.

Joshua Klein (JK) is a regular contributor to the *Chicago Tribune, Time Out Chicago,* and *Pitchfork Media.*

Mikel J. Koven (MK) is lecturer in Film and Television Studies at Aberystwyth University. He recently published *La Dolce Morte: Vernacular Cinema and the Italian Giallo Film.*

Frank Lafond (FL), PhD, teaches Film Studies in Lille, France, and has published a book on Jacques Tourneur.

Mirek Lipinski (ML) is the webmaster of *Latarnia: Fantastique International* (www.latarnia.com) and *The Mark of Naschy* (www.naschy.com), and is currently finishing editing and writing work on *Vampiros and Monstruos: The Mexican Horror Film of the 20th Century.*

Lauri Loytokoski (LL) is a Finnish film writer and researcher with a penchant for horror.

Ernest Mathijs (EM) writes on cult cinema and its audiences. He is Assistant Professor of Film and Drama at the University of British Columbia. His most recent books are *The Cult Film Reader, The Cinema of David Cronenberg,* and *Watching The Lord of the Rings.*

Jay McRoy (JM) is Associate Professor of English and Cinema Studies at the University of Wisconsin-Parkside. He is the editor of *Japanese Horror Cinema,* coeditor of *Monstrous Adaptations: Generic and Thematic Mutations in Horror Film,* and author of *Nightmare Japan.*

Gary Needham (GN) teaches film and television at Nottingham Trent University, England.

Kim Newman (KN) is a novelist, critic, and broadcaster. He is a contributing editor to *Sight & Sound* and *Empire,* and the author of *Nightmare Movies, Wild West Movies, Apocalypse Movies,* and *BFI Classics: Cat People.*

R. Barton Palmer (BP) is Calhoun Lemon Professor of Literature and Director of Film Studies at Clemson University. He is the author or editor of more than 30 books on film and literary subjects, including *Hollywood's Dark Cinema: The American Film Noir.*

David Sanjek (DS) is the Director of the BMI Archives and will publish *Always On My Mind: Music, Memory and Money and Stories We Could Tell: Putting Words to American Popular Music* in 2008.

Philip Simpson (PS) is currently Academic Dean of Liberal Arts at Brevard Community College in Florida. He is the author of numerous published works on film, literature, and popular culture.

Rebecca A. Umland (RU) is Professor of English at the University of Nebraska at Kearney. She coauthored *Donald Cammell: A Life on the Wild Side* with Samuel J. Umland.

Samuel J. Umland (SU) is Professor of English and Film Studies at the University of Nebraska at Kearney. He is coauthor with Rebecca Umland of *Donald Cammell: A Life on the Wild Side.*

Darryl Wiggers (DW) is a BFA graduate of York University and most recently Director of Programming for the horror channel SCREAM in Canada.

Andy Willis (AW) teaches film and media studies at the University of Salford, England.

William Sean Wilson (WW) is a film writer who currently resides in Williamsburg, Virginia. He graduated from The College of William & Mary with a degree in Literary and Cultural Studies.

GLOSSARY

Avanspettacolo
Literally "curtain raiser," this is a style of Italian musical revue that predated TV. It has its roots in variety theater and comprises a short, often poorly presented performance that nevertheless thrills its audiences.

BAFTA
British equivalent of an Academy Award.

Blackface
A makeup technique used to make white actors resemble stereotypical black characters. Also refers to the genre of musical comedy in which blackface makeup is utilized.

Brat Pack
A group of actors made famous in the 1980s by regularly appearing in movies popular among teenage audiences. The group socialized off set and their activities were well documented by the media.

Burlesque
Popular in the early twentieth century, burlesque is a genre of live musical comedy entertainment with elaborate sets and titillating costumes. Novelty acts were often featured alongside well-choreographed dancing girls and slapstick comedy routines.

César
French equivalent of an Academy Award.

Commedia all'italiana
A genre of Italian comedy films popular during the 1950s, commonly threaded with an element of morality. The term was used, by some, in contempt.

Commedia dell'arte
Italian term for the improvised performances by professional traveling players popular since the fifteenth century. Characters usually wore masks, and played out a series of familiar scenarios with happy endings.

Emmy
TV equivalent of an Oscar. Daytime, primetime, and international TV production is honored in annual award ceremonies.

Florenz Ziegfeld
Staged the Ziegfeld Follies on Broadway—spectacular theatrical revue-based performances featuring lavish sets, beautiful girls, and elegant musical compositions. Inspired by the Folies Bergères of Paris.

Frat Pack
A media-imposed nickname for a group of male actors, writers, and directors who have worked together in Hollywood comedies since the mid-1990s.

Guitti
Term for the traveling actors who performed in the *commedia dell'arte* and lived a somewhat harsh existence. Initially of low regard, the status of *giutti* improved with the increased recognition of their art form.

Hays Code
Also known as the Production Code, this was a set of regulatory guidelines drawn up in the 1930s to censor the film industry. The regulations were strict and made clear that the depiction of sex, crime, violence, and other such activities was not morally acceptable onscreen. Enforcement of the Code was abandoned in the late 1960s.

House Un-American Activities Committee
A committee of the House of Representatives that, in 1947, investigated alleged incidences of communist propaganda within the film industry. Many artists were blacklisted and subsequently dropped by their respective studios, some never to resurrect their careers.

Kabuki
Traditional form of stylized Japanese theater incorporating song and dance.

Maggiorata
Italian term used in the 1950s for curvaceous actresses such as Sophia Loren and Gina Lollobrigida who were cast on the strength of their physical attributes.

Method acting
Pioneered by Konstantin Stanislavski and made popular by Lee Strasberg, Method acting is a demanding technique that requires actors to analyze the emotional motivation of their character to facilitate a more realistic performance. Performers are encouraged to draw parallels with their life experiences to inform their characterization.

Mise-en-scène
The artistic elements that contribute to the visual appearance of a scene, including the set, props, costumes, and types of camera shots used. Also used to describe a scene whose appearance conveys the mood of a character or situation without the need for dialogue and in a nonrealistic manner.

Neorealism
Italian film movement that produced low-budget, often improvised, movies using nonprofessional actors in "real" locations to depict tales of everyday life. Mostly associated with the directors Michelangelo Antonioni, Luchino Visconti, and Gianni Puccini.

Pink neorealism
Italian film genre that emerged as a reaction against the pessimistic narratives of neorealism. More upbeat in nature, it introduced such celebrity beauties as Claudia Cardinale and Sophia Loren.

Pre-Code
Movies made in the 1920s and 1930s before the Hays Code was enforced in 1934. Typically the films enjoyed risqué subject matter and a liberal attitude to moral correctness.

Rat Pack
Group of successful artists and friends formed in the 1950s. The line-up varied over the years but famously included Humphrey Bogart, Frank Sinatra, and Judy Garland.

Screen Actors Guild
Founded in 1933 in response to the exploitation of actors by studio contracts. The labor union strives to improve working conditions and represents more than 120,000 film actors in the United States.

Spaghetti Western
Originally used as a derogatory term, the genre retained many of the elements of a conventional Western. The movies were shot in Europe and became popular in the mid-1960s for their violent and unromantic depiction of the West.

Tony
An award presented to honor outstanding theatrical achievement on Broadway.

Variety
Performed in UK music halls between the 1870s and 1960s. A hugely popular form of live entertainment that included comedy turns, specialty acts, song and dance, and plenty of audience participation.

Vaudeville
Popular in the United States between the 1880s and 1920s. A live stage show that presented a variety of unrelated acts including magicians, musicians, animal acts, and comedy skits.

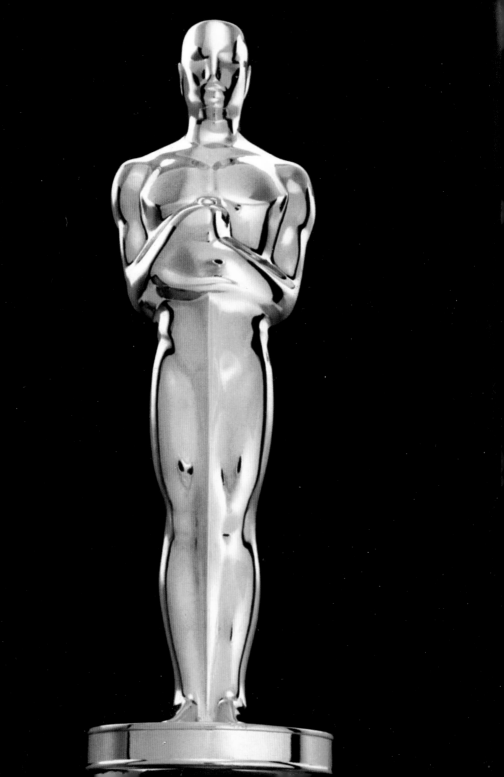

INDEX